I0894931

Increasing Supply Chain Performance in Digital Society

Ramona Diana Leon
Universitat Politècnica de València, Spain

Raul Rodriguez-Rodriguez
Universitat Politècnica de València, Spain

Juan-Jose Alfaro-Saiz
Universitat Politècnica de València, Spain

IGI Global
PUBLISHER of TIMELY KNOWLEDGE

A volume in the Advances in Logistics, Operations, and Management Science (ALOMS) Book Series

Published in the United States of America by
IGI Global
Business Science Reference (an imprint of IGI Global)
701 E. Chocolate Avenue
Hershey PA, USA 17033
Tel: 717-533-8845
Fax: 717-533-8661
E-mail: cust@igi-global.com
Web site: http://www.igi-global.com

Copyright © 2022 by IGI Global. All rights reserved. No part of this publication may be reproduced, stored or distributed in any form or by any means, electronic or mechanical, including photocopying, without written permission from the publisher. Product or company names used in this set are for identification purposes only. Inclusion of the names of the products or companies does not indicate a claim of ownership by IGI Global of the trademark or registered trademark.

Library of Congress Cataloging-in-Publication Data

Names: Leon, Ramona-Diana, 1986- editor. | Rodriguez-Rodriguez, Raul, 1976- editor. | Alfaro-Saiz, Juan-Jose, 1968- editor.
Title: Increasing supply chain performance in digital society / Ramona Diana Leon, Raul Rodriguez-Rodriguez, and Juan-Jose Alfaro-Saiz, editors.
Description: Hershey, PA : Business Science Reference, [2022] | Includes bibliographical references and index. | Summary: "This book presents innovative approaches to measure, manage and project towards the future of the digital capabilities of supply chains and the relationship these have with performance (at the operative, tactic and strategic level), not only where they are today but also where they may be in the medium/long-term and the resources they need to get there"-- Provided by publisher.
Identifiers: LCCN 2021058152 (print) | LCCN 2021058153 (ebook) | ISBN 9781799897156 (hardcover) | ISBN 9781799897163 (paperback) | ISBN 9781799897170 (ebook)
Subjects: LCSH: Business logistics--Technological innovations. | Marketing--Management. | Organizational effectiveness.
Classification: LCC HD38.5 .I473 2022 (print) | LCC HD38.5 (ebook) | DDC 658.8--dc23/eng/20220120
LC record available at https://lccn.loc.gov/2021058152
LC ebook record available at https://lccn.loc.gov/2021058153

This book is published in the IGI Global book series Advances in Logistics, Operations, and Management Science (ALOMS) (ISSN: 2327-350X; eISSN: 2327-3518)

British Cataloguing in Publication Data
A Cataloguing in Publication record for this book is available from the British Library.

All work contributed to this book is new, previously-unpublished material. The views expressed in this book are those of the authors, but not necessarily of the publisher.

For electronic access to this publication, please contact: eresources@igi-global.com.

Advances in Logistics, Operations, and Management Science (ALOMS) Book Series

John Wang
Montclair State University, USA

ISSN:2327-350X
EISSN:2327-3518

Mission

Operations research and management science continue to influence business processes, administration, and management information systems, particularly in covering the application methods for decision-making processes. New case studies and applications on management science, operations management, social sciences, and other behavioral sciences have been incorporated into business and organizations real-world objectives.

The **Advances in Logistics, Operations, and Management Science** (ALOMS) Book Series provides a collection of reference publications on the current trends, applications, theories, and practices in the management science field. Providing relevant and current research, this series and its individual publications would be useful for academics, researchers, scholars, and practitioners interested in improving decision making models and business functions.

Coverage

- Organizational Behavior
- Political Science
- Marketing engineering
- Services management
- Finance
- Risk Management
- Operations Management
- Information Management
- Computing and information technologies
- Networks

IGI Global is currently accepting manuscripts for publication within this series. To submit a proposal for a volume in this series, please contact our Acquisition Editors at Acquisitions@igi-global.com or visit: http://www.igi-global.com/publish/.

The Advances in Logistics, Operations, and Management Science (ALOMS) Book Series (ISSN 2327-350X) is published by IGI Global, 701 E. Chocolate Avenue, Hershey, PA 17033-1240, USA, www.igi-global.com. This series is composed of titles available for purchase individually; each title is edited to be contextually exclusive from any other title within the series. For pricing and ordering information please visit http://www.igi-global.com/book-series/advances-logistics-operations-management-science/37170. Postmaster: Send all address changes to above address. Copyright © 2022 IGI Global. All rights, including translation in other languages reserved by the publisher. No part of this series may be reproduced or used in any form or by any means – graphics, electronic, or mechanical, including photocopying, recording, taping, or information and retrieval systems – without written permission from the publisher, except for non commercial, educational use, including classroom teaching purposes. The views expressed in this series are those of the authors, but not necessarily of IGI Global.

Titles in this Series

For a list of additional titles in this series, please visit: http://www.igi-global.com/book-series/advances-logistics-operations-management-science/37170

Handbook of Research on Global Networking Post-COVID-19
Ana Pego (Nova University of Lisbon, Portugal)
Business Science Reference • © 2022 • 400pp • H/C (ISBN: 9781799888567) • US $295.00

Sales Management for Improved Organizational Competitiveness and Performance
José Duarte Santos (Instituto Superior Politécnico Gaya, Portugal)
Business Science Reference • © 2022 • 325pp • H/C (ISBN: 9781668434307) • US $240.00

Handbook of Research on Post-Pandemic Talent Management Models in Knowledge Organizations
Mohammad Rafiqul Islam Talukdar (American International University-Bangladesh, Bangladesh) Carmen z. Lamagna (American International University-Bangladesh, Bangladesh) Charles Carillo Villanueva (American International University-Bangladesh, Bangladesh) Rezbin Nahar (American International University-Bangladesh, Bangladesh) and Farheen Hassan (American International University-Bangladesh, Bangladesh)
Business Science Reference • © 2022 • 415pp • H/C (ISBN: 9781668438947) • US $295.00

Global Air Transport Management and Reshaping Business Models for the New Era
Kannapat Kankaew (Suan Sunandha Rajabhat University, Thailand)
Business Science Reference • © 2022 • 300pp • H/C (ISBN: 9781668446157) • US $250.00

International Perspectives on Value Creation and Sustainability Through Social Entrepreneurship
Hesham Magd (Modern College of Business and Science, Oman) Dharmendra Singh (Modern College of Business and Science, Oman) Raihan Taqui Syed (Modern College of Business and Science, Oman) and David Spicer (Bradford University, UK)
Business Science Reference • © 2022 • 300pp • H/C (ISBN: 9781668446669) • US $250.00

Examining the Vital Financial Role of SMEs in Achieving the Sustainable Development Goals
Dalila Taleb (A. Belkaid University, Algeria) Mohammed El Amine Abdelli (University Of Brest, France) Afef Khalil (University Of Tunis Carthage, Tunisia) and Asma Sghaier (University Of Sousse, Tunisia)
Business Science Reference • © 2022 • 325pp • H/C (ISBN: 9781668448342) • US $250.00

Creativity Models for Innovation in Management and Engineering
Carolina Machado (University of Minho, Portugal) and J. Paulo Davim (University of Aveiro, Portugal)
Business Science Reference • © 2022 • 300pp • H/C (ISBN: 9781668423394) • US $240.00

IGI Global
PUBLISHER of TIMELY KNOWLEDGE

701 East Chocolate Avenue, Hershey, PA 17033, USA
Tel: 717-533-8845 x100 • Fax: 717-533-8661
E-Mail: cust@igi-global.com • www.igi-global.com

Editorial Advisory Board

Ana Aleksic, *University of Zagreb, Croatia*
Carla Andrade Arteaga, *Universidad de Guayaquil, Ecuador*
Raúl Francisco Oltra Badenes, *Universitat Politècnica de València, Spain*
Marius Pislaru, *"Gheorghe Asachi" Technical University of Iasi, Romania*
Ximena Rojas-Lema, *Escuela Politécnica Nacional, Ecuador*

Table of Contents

Section 3
Back to Basics: From Robotization and Digitalization to the Current and Future Human Resource

Detailed Table of Contents

The research aims to explore the topic of supply chain performance in the Industry 4.0 context, based on knowledge mapping. Thus, qualitative and quantitative approaches are combined in a documentary study that uses 354 articles published on Web of Science as a cornerstone. Methods like co-authorship analysis, co-citation analysis, clusters density analysis, and content analysis are employed, and the results bring forward the fact that (1) almost a quarter of the scientific publications regarding supply chain performance in the Industry 4.0 context are concentrated in five high-ranked journals; (2) the most cited articles provide a systematic and content-centric review of the literature, and set the framework for the empirical analysis; (3) the theoretical background of the analyzed articles have their roots in the resource-based theory; and (4) the future research requires establishing a link between supply chain management, Industry 4.0, and sustainable development at the micro, meso, and macro levels.

The most important purpose of supply chain management is ensuring the maximum level of material and information flow within and outside the companies. However, supply chain management has gone through many changes in the 21st century. The developing IT sector, the digitalization, the appearance of smart tools are the results of Industry 4.0. Companies need to recognize the importance to adapt technical innovations and digitalize their processes. The influences of Industry 4.0 are digitalized supply chain management (SCM 4.0) and digitalized logistics (Logistics 4.0). The chapter defines the most frequently used tools of both areas. On the other hand, the chapter deals with the problems of supply chain coordination as well. The determined factors can be handled by the technical innovations, which are used by SCM 4.0 and Logistics 4.0. The chapter analyses the connection between the determined problems and smart tools as the solutions.

Geopolitical risks, business globalization, increasing complexity of transactions have required companies to adapt to changes. This chapter examines the digital transformation of supply chains and digitalization challenges in Japan. Many companies seem to realize the importance of digital transformation; however, on their way to digitalization companies face numerous challenges like a shortage of human and financial resources, a lack of awareness and understanding of digital transformation processes, etc. Moreover, Japanese culture does not easily fit digital transformation which also slows down the pace of transformation. As a result, the supply chain processes in the Japanese manufacturing companies remain old-fashioned, fragmented, siloed, with a lack of global vision and proper understanding of potential risks. To meet the needs of diverse customers, ensure global supply, and compete in uncertain environment, the SCM of Japanese companies has to be digitally upgraded and become more complex to achieve end-to-end supply chain optimization and an advanced decision-making.

Distribution companies in the Spanish agri-food sector have shown a high level of resilience during the COVID-19 crisis, as they have always guaranteed a high availability of product in stores (more than 90%) despite the changes in demand themselves from such an uncertain context. The scientific literature already identifies some specific factors that can positively influence the robustness of their logistics processes, such as proximity supply models, collaboration between value chain actors, and customer-oriented strategies. But this chapter seeks to delve into the relevance that technology can have as an element of supply chain resilience, concluding that it is an important but not yet determining factor. The companies that took part in the study, which represent more than 50% of the Spanish agri-food distribution, have shown that the technological capacity of their companies does not have a direct correlation with their current level of resilience, although in at the same time, they consider it a binomial that has a lot of potential and needs to be developed.

The COVID-19 pandemic has altered many organizations' operations management and accelerated the failure of those without resilient supply chains. It has greatly accelerated organizations' adoption of digital technologies and digital transformation. Digital technologies such as robotic process automation (RPA) play important roles in companies' operations-management activities and digital supply-chain transformation in the COVID-19 era. However, empirical research on RPA implementation in supply chains remains scarce. To fill this research gap, this case study was conducted to examine a global retail company's RPA implementation initiative to enhance its digital supply-chain capabilities. The authors examined three key project phases: pre-implementation, implementation, and post-implementation. They identified patterns of managerial practices and challenges related to digital technology implementation. The findings could help other organizations understand the most important issues to be addressed when seeking to implement RPA for operations activities and supply-chain processes.

Over the years, organizations have had to adapt to constant changes in their surroundings. To this end, they began to adopt methodologies such as lean manufacturing and Industry 4.0. Their implementation has increased the competitiveness of organizations. Sustainability is getting much attention, leading to the advent of Industry 5.0, which, unlike Industry 4.0, takes sustainable production into account. Forestry sectors are significant for the Portuguese economy, especially cork. This study examines a company in the cork sector to determine how automation and monetization of new resources could increase efficiency, quality, and safety. A qualitative approach was applied in the study through literature review and participant observation actions to analyze and propose improvements. The study fulfilled the purposes defined, identifying options to improve the production process and increase customer satisfaction and worker safety.

Fast-moving consumer goods (FMCG) are driven by threats and nascent challenges that range from logistical issues to disruptions in the environment. The chapter aimed to determine the efficacy of supply chain collaboration on resilience in the industry. Scholars have constantly highlighted the need for supply chain collaboration by building supply chain resilience, necessitated against sporadic, disruptive, and unforeseen events in the business environment. The argument for businesses to desist from working in silos within their supply chain provokes this study. There seems to be a mismatch between the supply chain members in terms of integrating or collaborating efforts and their capabilities to be resilient when faced with disruptions. Organisations need to identify the variables that exist inside and outside of their environment to ensure alignment, collaboration, and integration. Centralisation of stocks, foreign exchange fluctuation, joint business plans, and longstanding collaboration with vendors could help promote supply chain resilience.

In today's digital age, many managers need to find new ways to manage collaborations where complementary partners co-create digital solutions. Collaborations with partners are at the centre of digital projects, but managing these collaborations is challenging. The research objective is to investigate how collaborations with business partners contribute to digital transformation through a qualitative investigation of Brazilian and British large manufactures that are already on their journey towards digitalization. Interviews and questionnaires and non-participant observations were collected, followed by content analysis. The findings indicate that the companies, mainly the Brazilian cases, are at the early stage of building a digital ecosystem for a more connected supply chain. The use of digital solutions in cases brings obstacles but also opportunities and advantages for supply chains in the near future. The study discussed these implementation challenges and what digital technologies are under development and already used to make the supply chain smarter and more connected.

This research focused on the challenges experienced when executing risk management processes in information technology (IT) projects. The lack of knowledge management support for risk management processes has caused many project failures in the past and encountered unanticipated resistance and never met expectation. The purpose of this research is to study how Saudi companies consider knowledge process to support risk analysis and how they use and foster it. The present research will be based on a sample of the data collected from managers and senior managers in selected organizations which represent the manufacturing, information technology (IT), and services. The key contribution is to explore how Saudi companies are integrating knowledge management with risk management for information technology projects which provides the capability to mediate the problem of IT project failures by integrating KM and RM in a single context.

COVID-19 has shown how fragile our societies and economies are. Supply chains have particularly been affected. We all had to learn again that the basic supply of some goods is not as crisis-proof as we thought. Moreover, the strong division of labour and the concentration on a few companies in certain areas present considerable weaknesses in the case of a new external crisis such as the pandemic. Small and medium-sized enterprises (SMEs) have been affected by the current pandemic, particularly as they are highly sensitive to external threats. Using data collected between December 2020 and January 2021

In the digital world, computers have turned into objects that know more than humans. Devices are redefining the human way of living in a network that allows people to talk to each other. On the one hand, suspicion and fear about technology increased; on the other hand, it became impossible to stay away from a life without technology. In this process, the contribution of digitalization to productivity, the convenience and speed it provides to the business world has made digitalization necessary in all sectors. The role of human resources management (HRM) is very important in the realization of digital transformation in businesses. This role comes to the fore both in adapting to changing social norms and adapting to changes within the enterprise. HRM also has difficulties in this process. This chapter provides background on the challenges HRM faces in the digital society. The digitalization process, digitalization and its effects in businesses, the effects of the digitalization process on employees, working environment, and HR technologies are mentioned.

Industry 4.0 implies a reconfiguration of work organization and new approaches to human resources management (HRM). This research aims to delve deeper into the impacts of Industry 4.0 on the human resources system (HRS). A literature review identifies the potential links between these two core concepts. Finally, secondary data analysis in the form of a literature review on topical scientific researches will explore the following research question: How does Industry 4.0 impact conventional human resources systems (HRS)?

Countries are striving to opt for digital economy by adopting miscellaneous state programs and translating them into national projects. The chapter describes digital relations and the digital economy. It examines the effectiveness of the government strategies on digitalization and indulges the programs' context in terms of their priorities, objectives, and tools for implementation, based on the rigorous critique of the programs in the literature. Furthermore, it audits the chronicle of events in programs development, actors involved, and the decision-making process. Moreover, it focuses on the legal regulation of the digital economy with a specific focus on the situation in the Russian Federation. In addition, it examines governance and economics in the context of a digitally hybridized civilization. Moreover, it assesses Russia's potential and innovative performance in the context of the Global Innovation Index to better implement robust innovation policy conditions.

Preface

The highest levels of performance come to people who are centered, intuitive, creative, and reflective – people who know to see a problem as an opportunity. ~Deepak Chopra

In the past few years, the industry has witnessed a rise in disruptive innovations and a fast pace of change in customers' expectations and behaviors. On the one hand, customers started to be more and more interested in receiving personalized, differentiated and unique experiences; they wanted to be involved in goods and/or service production while having the freedom of choice. As a consequence, the companies try to become more customer-centric and to adapt every stage of customer journey, using digital technologies. They invest in developing chat-boots that can provide customers with immediate response 24h/day; make use of augmented reality in order to offer to customers a real-time perspective on their products and/or services; use social media for advertising and social listening processes; digitalize business processes so they can adapt faster to market's change; and focus on smart manufacturing (which includes cloud computing, advanced sensor technologies, robotics, digital twins, machine learning, etc.) so that they can reduce waste generation and increase operational efficiency.

On the other hand, the business models are challenged by the development of information technologies, the need to implement collaborative creation processes, and also by the fact that the competition has drifted from an individual to a supply chain basis. Thus, in order to adapt to the changes from the general macro-environment, the companies are called to perform better and to enhance their collaboration and communication with the actors from the specific external environment. Furthermore, they have to: (i) identify their current position in terms of digital capabilities; (ii) link these capabilities to supply chain performance; (iii) define their future desired competitive position and how their digital capabilities are going to help them to get there; (iv) forecast their future desired performance not only at the company level but also at the supply chain level; and (v) link together current and future digital capabilities, operations efficiency and strategic performance. Last but not least, a change of perspective is required and a switch from an individualist to a federation approach is needed at the supply chain level. Nevertheless, while the technological environment provides the tools for such a switch to be made the unique organizational aspects are the ones capable of generating real added-value. As presented in this book, the challenges and opportunities induced by the digital society could influence the performance of supply chain management at an abstract and tangible level (linked to the results of robotization, digitalized logistics and supply chain) but also at a relative and intangible level (connected to internal and external collaboration and the knowledge base ensured by human resources).

Against the backdrop, the purpose of this book is to bring forward innovative approaches for measuring, managing and projecting towards the future digital capabilities of both individual companies and supply chains and also the relationships these have with performance at the operative, tactic and strategic level. It aims to reflect not only where the companies are today in terms of the dual relationships digital capabilities and performance (AS-IS state) but also where they may be on the medium and long term and the resources they need to get there (TO-BE state).

The reminder of the book is organized around three sections that shed light on the changes that occurred at the supply chain level and also on how these changes could become a source of competitive advantage with an effective external collaboration and highly-qualified human resources. Thus, the *first section* of this book, entitled *Supply Chain Management in the Context of Industry 4.0: Challenges and Opportunities*, brings forward how the business environment has been transformed under the influence of the digital capabilities. In other words, it concentrates on emphasizing how robotization and digitalization have modified the policies and practices related to supply chain management, and also on highlighting future research avenues. The perspective adopted varies form national to international level, and from the general framework of a literature review to the particularities of specific industries like, agri-food, retail, and cork.

Chapter 1, entitled *Supply Chain Performance in Industry 4.0 Context: Knowledge Mapping and Analysis*, highlights the results of a systematic literature review regarding the influence of digitalization on supply chain management, in general, and supply chain performance, in particular. Thus, on the one hand, it shows that the resource-based theory provides the main theoretical foundation of the studies developed so far, and that lately, the topic is analyzed in the context of the circular economy. On the other hand, it exhibits the need of developing new business models and analyzing the link between supply chain management, Industry 4.0 and sustainable development at the micro-, meso-, and macro level.

Chapter 2, called *SCM 4.0: Not Just an Opportunity, It Is a Need*, goes further and, based on the resource-based theory of the firm, scrutinizes the most frequently used tools for the digitalization of supply chain management and logistics. Furthermore, it takes into consideration the problems of supply chain coordination and it shows how these could be solved by using several smart tools, like digital twinning; collaborative planning, forecasting and replenishment; enterprise resources planning systems; warehouse management systems; and transportation management systems.

Chapter 3, titled *Supply Chain and Digital Transformation in Japan*, focuses also on the digitalization of the supply chain management but it adopts a more specific approach, concentrating on the Japanese culture. Thus, it considers the cultural tension that tends to appear whenever the old-fashioned, fragmented Japanese manufacturing companies have to digitalize their processes in order to meet customers' needs and ensure global supply. It is one of the few studies that take into account the importance of cultural specificity in a context in which digitalization focuses on standardizing internal processes and customizing products, services, and experiences.

Chapter 4, entitled *Analysis of Technology as a Factor of Resilience in the Agri-Food Supply Chain*, brings out the characteristics of the Spanish agri-food sector, especially its level of resilience. Hence, it reveals the existence of a contradiction at the management level when it comes to the relationship between technology and supply chain resilience; although the managers state that companies technological capacity has a lot of potential and must be further developed, their actions show that this is not directly correlated with their current level of resilience. As a consequence, further research is required in order to determine whether there is a difference between what the managers say and what they do or the digital capabilities do not have a significant impact on supply chain resilience in the agri-food sector.

Chapter 5, called *RPA and the Digitalisation of Supply-Chain Processes: A Case Study,* maintains the attention on the resilient supply chains only this time the focus is on the retail sector. The three main phases of the implementation of robotic process automation are analyzed and the patterns of managerial practices are identified. The results point out that: (i) in the pre-implementation stage, stakeholders' collaboration represents the cornerstone since it shapes the attitudes of all the members involved; (ii) in the implementation stage, the transactional and transformational management strategies are critical for integrating robot process automation into routine supply-chain processes; and (iii) in the post-implementation stage, the use of the Plan-Do-Study-Act cycle is required in order to ensure supply chain performance on ongoing basis.

Chapter 6, titled *Lean Manufacturing and Industry 4.0/5.0: An Applied Research in Portuguese Cork Industry*, closes the first section of this book by emphasizing how automation and monetization of new resources could increase efficiency, quality and safety in the Portuguese cork industry. It takes into account the satisfaction of both internal and external stakeholders and it provides various options on how could this be increased while improving the production process.

Section 2 is entitled *Enhancing Supply Chain Performance Through Collaboration, Sophistication, and Risk Management* and it deals with the influence of tacit knowledge (such as, collaboration, trust, values, organizational culture, etc.) on supply chain digitalization. The characteristics of both small and large companies are taken into consideration, and the particularities of the firms from the manufacturing and service sectors are revealed since each and every one of them tries to develop its digital capabilities and to increase its supply chain resilience and performance.

Chapter 7, called *Efficacy of Supply Chain Collaboration on Resilience in the Fast-Moving Consumer Goods Retail Industry*, analyzes the industry of the fast-moving consumer goods and emphasizes the influence of collaboration on supply chain resilience. The latter depends on the supply chain members' capacity of centralizing stock, developing joint business plans and establishing longstanding collaboration.

Chapter 8, entitled *Digital Supply Chain Insights from Large Factories: How Can Collaborations With Customers and Suppliers Accelerate Digitalization?* remains focused on supply chain collaboration but it switches from a general perspective to a more concrete one, dwelling on the collaboration during digitalization. Brazilian and British large manufactures that have already started their digitalization are investigated and the challenges encountered on they way are discussed.

Chapter 9, titled *Place of Knowledge Management With Risk Management for Information Technology Projects in Saudi Organization*, takes a step further and integrates knowledge management and risk management in the context of manufacturing, information technology and services supply chains. The results prove that, in the information technology projects, knowledge management processes influence risk identification, analysis, planning, and monitoring.

Chapter 10, called *SMEs in the Face of Crisis: The Supply Chain Risk Management Perspective*, remains concentrated on the risk management perspective but it addresses the challenges faced by the small and medium enterprises (SMEs) from the European countries. Thus, it highlights how SMEs deal with supply chain risk management in times of an external and dynamic crisis and it offers several solutions and recommendations, such as: (i) enhancing inter-organizational trust; (ii) using tailored supply chain risk management approaches; and (iii) sharing the risk maps with the internal and external stakeholders, especially with the members of the supply chain network.

Chapter 11, titled *Supply Chains Sophistication in "Smart" Local Communities*, combines the organizational with the institutional framework and emphasizes how the development of "smart" local communities generates various changes at the supply chains level. On the one hand, it points out the main challenges that supply chain management has to overcome, namely: (i) the adoption of digital technologies among the value chain; (ii) climate changes and shortage of resources; (iii) massive migration; (iv) customers demand for customized products and services; and (v) uncertain changes of regulation. On the other hand, it presents the sophistication of supply chains as the next stage of its development, reflecting the need for communities and businesses to build sustainable partnerships, enhancing the creation of smart networks.

Section 3 is entitled *Back to Basics: From Robotization and Digitalization to the Current and Future Human Resource* and it puts forth the only organizational resource that is capable of generating added-value by transforming all the other tangible and intangible resources. Thus, the human resources represent the center of attention of this section as they are the ones that are going to use the digital technologies and foster inter-organizational trust, communication and collaboration among the supply chain members. Furthermore, since supply chain performance requires the development of a future image / desired state, the characteristics of the future human resources are taken into account through the lens of the educational system.

Chapter 12, entitled *Sustainable Supply Chain Learning and Employee Green Creativity: Implications for Disruption Management and Green Competitiveness*, combines the natural resource-based view with dynamic capabilities perspectives, and concentrates on the relationships established among supply chain disruption, green competitiveness and economic performance. The opinion of 252 managers from manufacturing SMEs is analyzed and the results show that: (i) sustainable supply chain learning is positively correlated with employees green creativity, green competitiveness, disruption management, and economic performance; (ii) employees green creativity positively influences green competitiveness, disruption management, and economic performance; and (iii) disruption management positively influences green competitiveness and economic performance.

Chapter 13, called *Human Resources Management: Challenges in the Digital Society*, brings forward the challenges that human resource management faces in the process of digitalizing the supply chain. Thus, concepts like digital employee, digital work and digital employee management are defined and the psychological pressure generated by digitalization is underlined. Against this backdrop, the companies tend to enter into a "digital fog"; they develop the required digital capabilities but neglect to invest in enhancing employees' and companies' digital skills.

Chapter 14, titled *Impact of Industry 4.0 on Human Resources Systems: The Emergence of Work 4.0*, addresses the impact of Industry 4.0 on the conventional human resource systems. Using an ethical approach and a documentary study, it reflects the evolution of the human resource practices in the context of the digital society, and it stresses out the need for: (i) analyzing the influence of the human resource system functions on Industry 4.0; and (ii) developing maturity indices.

Chapter 15, entitled *Digital Relations and Innovative Ecosystem for Sustainable Engineering Education: A Case of Russia*, changes the perspective from the current to the future human resources and examines governance and economics in the context of a digitally hybridized civilization. Thus, in light of the legal regulation of the digital economy, the sustainable education is linked to innovation performance and innovation policy conditions.

As Winston Churchill used to say, "to improve is to change; to be perfect is to change often", the current digital society requires not only a change of tools and methods but also a change of perspective. The supply chain members have to jointly develop their digital capabilities in order to succeed and they have to aim for the sophistication level, involving all the members of the community in the process and completing the systemic view of the business environment. Furthermore, they have to continuously keep an eye on the gap between AS-IS and TO-BE states so that they can effectively anticipate and manage risks and opportunities, and make sure that they have the proper tangible and intangible resources.

Ramona Diana Leon
Universitat Politècnica de València, Spain

Raúl Rodríguez-Rodríguez
Universitat Politècnica de València, Spain

Juan-Jose Alfaro-Saiz
Universitat Politècnica de València, Spain

Section 1

Supply Chain Management in the Context of Industry 4.0: Challenges and Opportunities

Chapter 1
Supply Chain Performance in the Industry 4.0 Context: Knowledge Mapping and Analysis

Ramona-Diana Leon
https://orcid.org/0000-0002-1448-0522
Universitat Politècnica de València, Spain

Raul Rodríguez-Rodríguez
Universitat Politècnica de València, Spain

Juan-José Alfaro-Saiz
Universitat Politècnica de València, Spain

ABSTRACT

The research aims to explore the topic of supply chain performance in the Industry 4.0 context, based on knowledge mapping. Thus, qualitative and quantitative approaches are combined in a documentary study that uses 354 articles published on Web of Science as a cornerstone. Methods like co-authorship analysis, co-citation analysis, clusters density analysis, and content analysis are employed, and the results bring forward the fact that (1) almost a quarter of the scientific publications regarding supply chain performance in the Industry 4.0 context are concentrated in five high-ranked journals; (2) the most cited articles provide a systematic and content-centric review of the literature, and set the framework for the empirical analysis; (3) the theoretical background of the analyzed articles have their roots in the resource-based theory; and (4) the future research requires establishing a link between supply chain management, Industry 4.0, and sustainable development at the micro, meso, and macro levels.

DOI: 10.4018/978-1-7998-9715-6.ch001

Copyright © 2022, IGI Global. Copying or distributing in print or electronic forms without written permission of IGI Global is prohibited.

INTRODUCTION

Within the digitalization framework, Industry 4.0 is capturing the attention of both practitioners and academics due to its influence on various areas like, supply chain management, operation management, sustainable development, and information technologies. It is characterized by technological innovations such as Machine to Machine communications, Internet of Things, Internet of Everything, Cyber-Physical Systems, artificial intelligence and Big Data Analytics (Brettel, Friederichsen, Keller, & Rosenberg, 2014), and it requires a change at the level of the business models and supply chains (Schmidt, Möhring, Härting, Reichstein, Neumaier, & Jozinovic, 2015).

Against the backdrop of a highly digitalized world where customers' opinions are spread among continents in a few miliseconds and the market is no longer disputed among companies but among supply chains networks, the business models focus on multi-level communication and collaboration. However, this approach brings forward several challenges since its success depends on stakeholders; alignment in terms of values, objectives, and processes.

First of all, in order for the multi-level collaborative supply chain networks to be successful, the supply chain members must share a common set of values and principles and they must trust one another. This fosters knowledge shaing among members and as emphasized by Leon, Rodriguez-Rodriguez, Gomez-Gasquet, and Mula (2020), it has a strong impact on business process improvement.

Secondly, enterprise interoperability has to be ensured in order for the Industry 4.0 to act as an opportunity and not a threat. Thus, the supply chain networks can take advantage of the technological innovations, ensuring compatibility of data exchange formats, interface architecture, and IT infrastructure among the members of the supply chain network (Khisro & Sundberg, 2020).

Last but not least, a particular attention should be given to supply chain performance since this is able to emphasize the efficiency of collaboration within the multi-level supply chain network. For more than three decades, hundreds of studies analyzed the concept of supply chain performance (Bhagwat & Sharma, 2009; Gunasekaran & Ngai, 2004; Neely, 2005), but the change of perspective required by Industry 4.0 is still open to debate. As Fatorachian and Kazemi (2021, p.64) state, "there is little insight on how performance benefits can be realised throughout the Industry 4.0 enabled supply chain". The studies developed so far either concentrate on highlighting how Industry 4.0 could foster supply chain interoperability (Cisneros-Cabrera et al., 2021; Sony & Naik, 2019) or they focus on measuring the performance at the focal firm level (Dubey et al., 2020; Hald & Mouritsen, 2018; Jha, Sharma, Kumar, & Verma, 2022). Despite the fact that both approaches provide valuable insights, they neglect that "at the supply chain level, Industry 4.0 can allow for a holistic approach towards supply chain management and lead to performance improvements through enabling extensive integration and connectivity" (Fatorachian & Kazemi, 2021, p.65).

Against this backdrop, the current chapter aims to explore the topic of supply chain performance in the Industry 4.0 context, based on knowledge mapping. Therefore, an exhaustive analysis and mapping of the existing knowledge of this topic is carried out, in such a way that it helps researchers and practitioners to understand and delve into the essential aspects that may give rise to future work.

Following this introduction, the paper consists of three more sections. The next section describes the research methodology followed in this work and sheds light on the knowledge mapping processes. Then, the perspectives from which the topic of supply chain performance in a digitalized economy is addressed are revealed. Special emphasis has been placed on descriptive statistics and knowledge mapping (content analysis and research avenues). Finally, the main findings are synthesized and further research directions are described.

RESEARCH METHODOLOGY

The research aims to explore the topic of supply chain performance in the Industry 4.0 context, based on knowledge mapping. Thus, the qualitative and quantitative approaches are combined in a documentary study which is suitable for "uncovering meaning, developing understanding, and discovering insights relevant to the research problem" (Merriam, 1988, p.118).

A four step methodology is employed which involves identifying the studies indexed in Web of Science, screening the records, knowledge mapping and content analysis.

Step 1. Identifying the Studies Indexed in Web of Science

Initially, a search is launched on Web of Science for all the articles that include the words "supply chain performance" and "Industry 4.0" in title, abstract, and keywords. Web of Science is selected as a starting point due to the fact that it is a high-quality digital database that covers a wide range of publications from different fields (Ding & Yang, 2020). On a first instance, the search generates 490 results, out of which 1 is an editorial material, 1 is a correction, 75 are proceedings papers, and 413 are journal articles.

Step 2. Screening the Records

In order to assess articles relevance for the research goal, all the titles and abstracts are analyzed and those which fall out of scope are eliminated (Adams, Jeanrenaud, Bessant, Denyer, & Overy, 2016; Pukall & Calabro, 2014). An article is considered to be relevant if it takes into account both aspects: supply chain performance and Industry 4.0. Against this backdrop, 354 articles are selected.

Step 3. Knowledge Mapping

For knowledge mapping, VOSViewer 1.6.17 and CiteSpace 5.8.R3 are used due to their capacity of facilitating co-authorship analysis, co-occurrence and cluster analysis, co-citation analysis and clusters density analysis. Furthermore, the steps indicated by van Eck and Waltman (2010) are followed. In other words:

- the similarity matrix is developed, based on the association strength. This is determined based on the co-occurrence principles and it is calculated as:

$$s_{ij} = \frac{c_{ij}}{w_i * w_j} \tag{1}$$

where s_{ij} reflects the similarity between item i and j;
c_{ij} represents the number of co-ocurrences of item i and j;

w_i and w_j denote weight or the number of occurences of item *i*, respectively *j*.

- the mapping technique is employed in order to obtain a visual representation of the similarity matrix. The objective function is defined based on:

$$V\left(x_1,\ldots,x_n\right) = \sum_{i<j} s_{ij} x_i - x_j^{\,2} \tag{2}$$

where $x_i=(x_{i1}, x_{i2})$ marks the location of item *i*;
Δ is the Euclidean norm.

- the items densities are calculated, using the following equation:

$$D\left(x\right) = \sum_{i=1}^{n} w_i K\left(\frac{x - x_i}{\left(\bar{d}h\right)}\right) \tag{3}$$

where *D(x)* is item's density at point $x=(x_1, x_2)$;
K is the Gaussian kernel function;
h represents kernel width;
$\bar{d}$ reflects the average distance between two items, and it is determined based on:

$$\bar{d} = \frac{2}{n\left(n-1\right)} \sum_{i<j} x_i - x_j \tag{4}$$

- the cluster density is determined, as follows:

$$D_p\left(x\right) = \sum_{i=1}^{n} I_P\left(i\right) w_i K\left(\frac{x - x_i}{\left(\bar{d}h\right)}\right) \tag{5}$$

where $D_p(x)$ is cluster's density;
$I_p(i)$ represents an indicator function that equals 1 when the item *i* belongs to cluster *p* and 0 otherwise.

Co-authorship analysis emphasizes the relationships established among scholars, reflecting the collaborative activity within the field. As suggested by Köseoglu, Yıldız, Putra, and Cıftcı (2018, p.202), it provides an answer to the following questions: "Do authors from different disciplinary backgrounds work together in new fields of research or do they remain within their disciplinary boundaries? Which factors determine co-authorship? What is the effect of collaboration on a study's impact? Are co-authored articles cited more frequently than articles authored by one person? Do more prolific authors collaborate more frequently? Are internationally co-authored papers cited more frequently than articles authored by one person? What is the social structure of a field?"

Co-citation analysis takes into account the structure and development of the scientific community and stresses the authors and journals that have a significant contribution to the development of the research field, by analyzing citation records. As defined by Reyes-Gonzalez, Gonzalez-Brambila, and Veloso (2016, p.1174), it is "a forward-looking assessment of the semantic similarity of documents, so that it measures the frequency with which two documents are cited together by other documents".

Clusters density analysis brings forward the evolution of a research area and sheds light on the hot topics that are drawing academics' attention. Furthermore, it points out to potential research avenues.

Step 4. Content Analysis

Content analysis is employed at the level of the identified clusters; this has analytical flexibility, it is non-intrusive and it entails the specification of category criteria for reliability and validity tests (Duriau, Reger, & Pfarrer, 2007).

SUPPLY CHAIN PERFORMANCE IN A DIGITALIZED ECONOMY

Descriptive Statistics

In the past years, 490 articles have been published on Web of Science regarding supply chain performance in Industry 4.0, and the growth rate of the academic production increased significantly in 2020-2021 (Figure 1). Among these, 75 were conference papers and 413journal articles. As previously mentioned, out of the 413 journal articles only 354 were representative for the research goal.

Figure 1. Time evolution of the articles published and cited on Web of Science, regarding supply chain performance in Industry 4.0 (Web of Science, 2022)

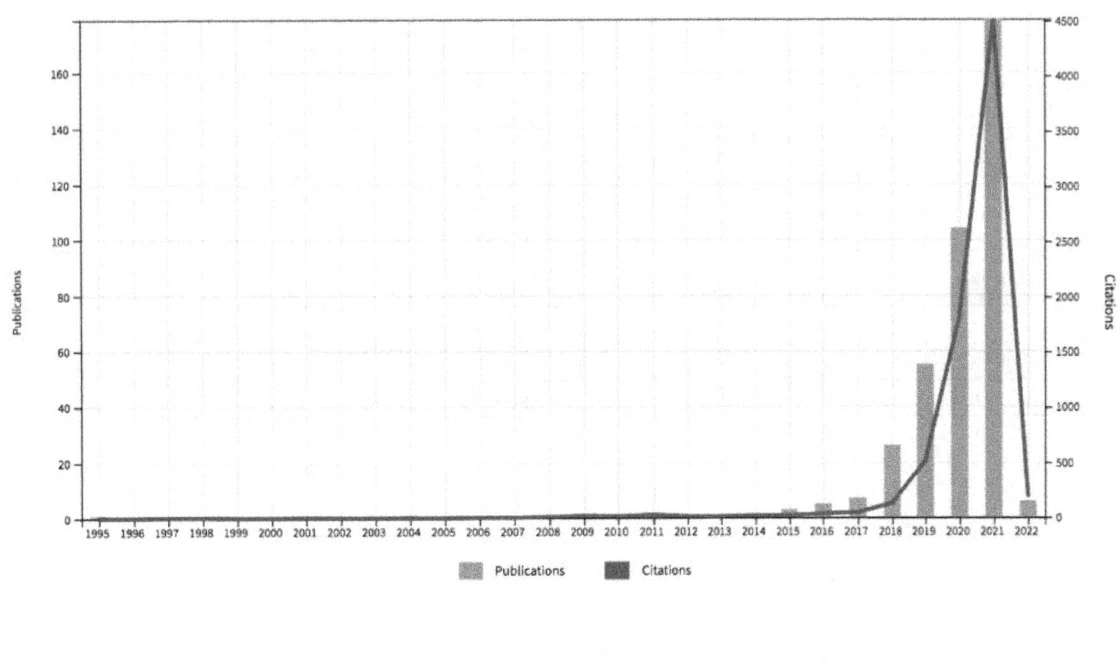

The aforementioned articles are published in 174 journals but the ones that higly supported the dissemination of the research conducted in this field are presented in Table 1. As Dzikowski (2018) states, a journal's impact on a field's development is reflected by the number of papers published and the number of citations it possesses. As reflected, almost a quarter of the scientific publications can be found in *Journal of Cleaner Production* (published 6.21% of the articles), *Production Planning & Control* (6.21%), *International Journal of Production Research* (5.37%), *Sustainability* (4.52%), and *Technological Forecasting and Social Change* (3.67%). These can be considered as the main academic outlets for promoting new research avenues on supply chain performance. Furthermore, the fact that these are top-tier journals in both science and social science areas proves that the issue is approached from both technical and human perspective, enhancing the transition towards the circular economy that is based on Industry 5.0 and Society 5.0.

Table 1. The journals that supported the mainstream

Journal	Published articles	Research Area	Citations
Journal of Cleaner Production	22	Green & Sustainable Science & Technology; Engineering, Environmental; Environmental Sciences	533
Production Planning & Control	22	Operations Research & Management Science; Engineering, Industrial; Engineering, Manufacturing	549
International Journal of Production Research	19	Operations Research & Management Science; Engineering, Industrial; Engineering, Manufacturing	448
Sustainability	16	Environmental Studies; Green & Sustainable Science & Technology; Environmental Sciences	313
Technological Forecasting and Social Change	13	Regional & Urban Planning; Business	365
Benchmarking: An International Journal	12	Management	127
Journal of Manufacturing Technology Management	11	Management; Engineering, Industrial; Engineering, Manufacturing	716
International Journal of Production Economics	8	Operations Research & Management Science; Engineering, Industrial; Engineering, Manufacturing	333
Journal of Enterprise Information Management	8	Information Science & Library Science; Management	23
Computers In Industry	7	Computer Science, Interdisciplinary Applications	305
Resources Conservation and Recycling	7	Engineering, Environmental; Environmental Sciences	363
Annals of Operations Research	6	Operations Research & Management Science	107
Business Strategy and The Environment	6	Environmental Studies; Business; Management	40
Computers & Industrial Engineering	6	Computer Science, Interdisciplinary Applications; Engineering, Industrial	309
IEEE Access	6	Telecommunications; Computer Science, Information Systems; Engineering, Electrical & Electronic	61
International Journal of Operations & Production Management	6	Management	205
International Journal of Productivity and Performance Management	6	Management	38

According to data presented in Table 2, the most cited articles were published in 2018 and provided a systematic and content-centric review of the literature, setting the framework for the empirical analysis. Thus, Ghobakhloo (2018) analyzes 178 academic and non-academic articles, published on Google, Scopus and Web of Science, and brings forward 12 key design principles and 14 technology trends of Industry 4.0; the transition towards Industry 4.0 is supposed to be enhanced by design principles like, Internet of Things, Smart Product, Smart Factory, virtualization, and horizontal integration, and technology trends such as, cloud computing, Big Data Analytics, cyber-physical systems, cyber security, and industrial robotics. Kamble, Gunasekaran, and Gawankar (2018) perform a literature review of 85 articles and conference publications, indexed on Web of Science databases, and emphasize that the deployment of Big Data Analytics and Internet of Things provide guidelines for organizational performance. Last but not least, Ivanov and Dolgui (2021) propose a computerized model of a digital supply chain twin and highlight the interrelations existing among risk data, disruption modeling, and performance assessment; hence, supply chain performance is directly and indirectly influenced by disruptions and the use of digital technologies.

Table 2. Top 10 most cited articles (Web of Science, 2022)

Articles details (Author, title, journal)	Article type	Citations	
		Average per year	Total
Ghobakhloo, M. (2018). The future of manufacturing industry: A strategic roadmap toward Industry 4.0. *Journal of Manufacturing Technology Management,* 29(6), 910-936.	Review	61.4	307
Kamble, S.S., Gunasekaran, A., & Gawankar, S.A. (2018). Sustainable Industry 4.0 framework: A systematic literature review identifying the current trends and future perspectives. *Process Safety and Environmental Protection,* 117, 408-425.	Review	58	290
Ivanov, D., & Dolgui, A. (2021). A digital supply chain twin for managing the disruption risks and resilience in the era of Industry 4.0. *Production Planning & Control,* 32(9), 775-788.	Conceptual	58.67	176
Manavalan, E., & Jayakrishna, K. (2019). A review of Internet of Things (IoT) embedded sustainable supply chain for industry 4.0 requirements. *Computers & Industrial Engineering,* 127, 925-953.	Review	43.75	175
Lockamy, A., & McCormack, K. (2004). Linking SCOR planning practices to supply chain performance - An exploratory study. *International Journal of Operations & Production Management,* 24(11-12), 1192-1218.	Empirical	9.21	175
Mattos Nascimento, D.L., Alencastro, V., Quelhas, O.L.G., Caiado, R.G.G., Garza-Reyes, J.A., Lona, L.R., & Tortorella, G. (2019). Exploring Industry 4.0 technologies to enable circular economy practices in a manufacturing context A business model proposal. *Journal of Manufacturing Technology Management,* 30(3), 607-627.	Empirical	42.25	169
Horvath, D., & Szabo, R.Z. (2019). Driving forces and barriers of Industry 4.0: Do multinational and small and medium-sized companies have equal opportunities?. *Technological Forecasting and Social Change,* 146, 119-132.	Empirical	41.75	167
Fatorachian, H., & Kazemi, H. (2018). A critical investigation of Industry 4.0 in manufacturing: theoretical operationalisation framework. *Production Planning & Control,* 29(8), 633-644.	Conceptual	31.8	159
Mansouri, S.A., Aktas, E., & Besikci, U. (2016). Green scheduling of a two-machine flowshop: Trade-off between makespan and energy consumption. *European Journal of Operational Research,* 248(3), 772-788.	Empirical	22.71	159
Dolgui, A., Ivanov, D., Sethi, S.P., & Sokolov, B. (2019). Scheduling in production, supply chain and Industry 4.0 systems by optimal control: fundamentals, state-of-the-art and applications. *International Journal of Production Research,* 57(2), 411-432.	Empirical	27	135

Despite the quantitative nature of the analyzed topic, the empirical studies that are higly cited are based on a qualitative approach. They use semi-structered interviews for data collection which brings forward on the one hand, scholars attempt to obtain meaningful insights and on the other hand, it reflects the that the field is in an embryonic stage of development, requiring for more quantitative analyses.

Figure 2. The theoretical background of the analyzed articles. References analysis

References analysis show that the theoretical background of the analyzed articles is provided by 10 articles (Figure 2) which can be grouped in 3 interdependent clusters. The first cluster sets the foundation of supply chain performance with the works of Barney (1991), Flynn, Huo, and Zhao (2010), and Frohlich and Westbrook (2001). As a consequence, the resource-based theory is defined as a cornerstone and strategic coordination becomes a must in the inter-organizational framework. Besides, the methodological approach is defined by Fornell and Larcker (1981) who demonstrate the efficiency of structural equation modeling in measuring both latent and composite variables. Additionaly, Waller and Fawcett (2013) define several research avenues, taking into account the challenges raised by the fast pace of the technological progress. Starting from these, the second and third clusters capitalize on the technic approach and deal with the characteristics of logistics-oriented Industry 4.0 (Hofmann & Rusch, 2017), digital supply chains (Buyukozkan & Gocer, 2018), blockchain technology (Saberi, Kouhizadeh, Sarkis, & Shen, 2019) and the ripple effect (Dolgui, Ivanov, & Sokolov, 2018; Ivanov, Dolgui, & Sokolov, 2019).

Table 3. The 10 most influential authors in field of supply chain performance in the Industry 4.0 context (Web of Science, 2022)

Author	Number of published articles	Research interests
Bag S.	13	Digital supply chain management; Viability; Lean; Green; Sustainability; Key Performances
Kumar A.	13	Supply Chain; Performance Measurement; Balanced Scorecard
Gupta S.	12	Supply chains; Technological innovation; Big data analytics; Healthcare Supply Chain; Responsive Supply Chain; Innovation; Resilience
Kumar V.	8	Supply Chain; Performance Measurement; Balanced Scorecard
Mangla S.K.	8	Circular economy; Industry 4.0; Smart circular supply chain; Sustainable development goals
Garza-Reyes J.A.	7	Supply Chain; Performance Measurement; Balanced Scorecard
Kazancoglu Y.	7	Supply chain relationship capital; Enterprise green management; Financial performance; Manufacturing
Luthra S.	7	Sustainable supply chain; Circular economy; Solution measures
Narkhede B.E.	7	Big data; Sustainable agriculture supply chains; Sustainability; Circular economy
Agrawal R.	6	Resilient supply chain; Process performance; Sustainability

Table 3 presents the 10 most influential authors while Figure 3 sheds light on the relationships established among them, based on co-authorship principles. Thus, given the common interests that they share, the research is concentrated in 4 interconnected clusters, lead by Bag Surajit, Kazancoglu Yigit, Luthra Sunil, and Kumar Vikas.

Figure 3. The relationships established among the most influential scholars who analize supply chain performance in the context of Industry 4.0: a co-authorship perspective

However, due to academic collaboration (Figure 4), the knowledge base owned by the most influential scholars is shared and developed with several other clusters that are lead by Gunasekaran Angappa, Raut Rakesh, Priyadarshinee Pragati, Jabbour Charbel Jose Chiappetta, and Gupta Himanshu. Furthermore, significant progress is made in 28 more clusters than currently act isolated from the main center.

Figure 4. The relationships established among the scholars who analize supply chain performance in the context of Industry 4.0: a general perspective on authorship

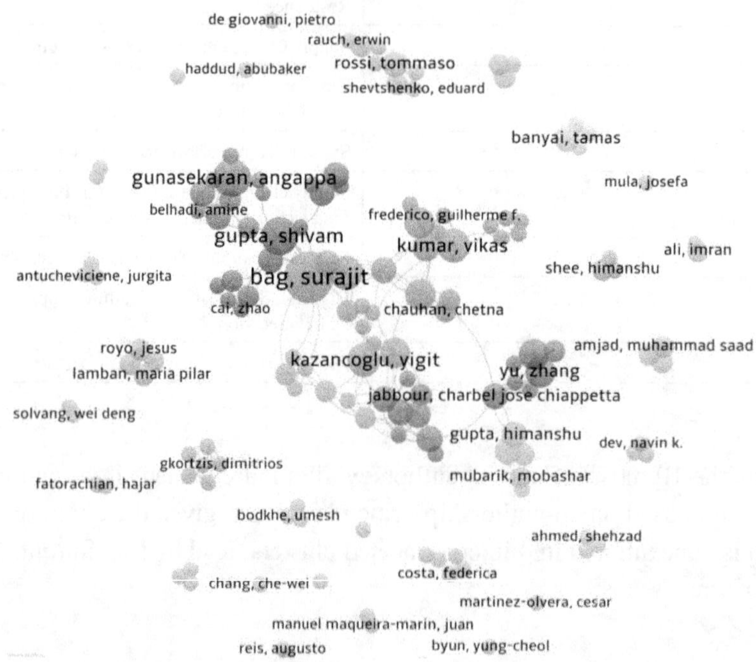

If authors' geographic distribution (Table 4) is taken into consideration, then more than 70% of the research regarding supply chain performance in the Industry 4.0 context is concentrated 5 countries (namely, India, England, China, France, and USA) and 3 continents (Asia, North America and Europe).

Table 4. Authors' geographic distribution (Web of Science, 2022)

Country	Number of published articles	Share (%)
India	75	21.19
England	61	17.23
China	51	14.41
France	39	11.02
USA	39	11.02
Italy	35	9.89
Brazil	26	7.34
Germany	24	6.78
Malaysia	24	6.78
Spain	22	6.21
Australia	19	5.37
UK	19	5.37
Turkey	18	5.08
South Africa	17	4.80
Pakistan	15	4.24
Taiwan	13	3.67
Canada	11	3.12
Denmark	10	2.82
United Arab Emirate	10	2.82

Knowledge Mapping: Content Analysis and Research Avenues

If articles' content is considered (Figure 5), it can be noticed that the scholars focus mainly on the manufacturing industry and bring forward topics like digital technologies (data, Internet of Things – IoT, cloud, networks, systems) and sustainability (environmental, green, energy, waste). Given the high frequency of using the words "model", "circular", "economy", "barriers" and "factors", it can be assumed that the topic of supply chain performance in Industry 4.0 is analyzed in the context of the circular economy and that the academic community concentrates on developing new business models that could support firms' transition to the new economic reality.

Figure 5. General perspective on the analyzed topics

As reflected in Figure 6, the knowledge developed so far is organized around 7 clusters, namely: supply chain management, industry 4.0, sustainable development, decision-making, economic and social effects, decision support systems, and data analytics. The characteristics of each and every one of these is presented further.

Cluster 1: Supply Chain Management (Red Cluster)

The articles included in this cluster use the Balanced Scorecard as a reference model and reflect the influence of digital technologies on financial, customers, business processes, and innovation and learning level. Some scholars (Eslami, Jafari, Achtenhagen, Carlback, & Wong, 2021; Kimseng, Javed, Jeenanunta, & Kohda, 2020; Sawangwong & Chaopaisarn, 2021; Thekkoote, 2021) analyze each dimension at a time while others adopt a global perspective on the matter (Frederico, Garza-Reyes, Kumar, & Kumar, 2021; Sundram, Bahrin, Munir, & Zolait, 2018). Thus, Eslami et al. (2021) investigate 274 Swedish manufacturing companies and demonstrate that digital technologies strengthen the effect of supply chain agility on financial performance while Sawangwong and Chaopaisarn (2021) analyze the impact of digitalization on the supply chain performance of Thai small and medium-sized enterprises and demonstrate that human, automation, real-time and security have a positive influence on processes performance, especialy on delivery reliability, resource efficiency, and delivery time. Kimseng et al. (2020) focus on the innovation and learning dimension and prove that global supply chain networks have highest product and process innovations. On the other hand, Sundram et al. (2018) indicate that supply chain integration mediates the relationship between supply chain information management and supply chain information system infrastructure toward business performance while Frederico et al. (2021) go further and propose a Supply Chain 4.0 Scorecard that includes the same four dimensions of Balanced scorecard with the difference that the classical "business processes" dimension refers to supply chain processes, and the "innovation and learning" dimension concentrates on technologies, interoperability and capabilities.

Figure 6. The main research avenues that have been explored so far

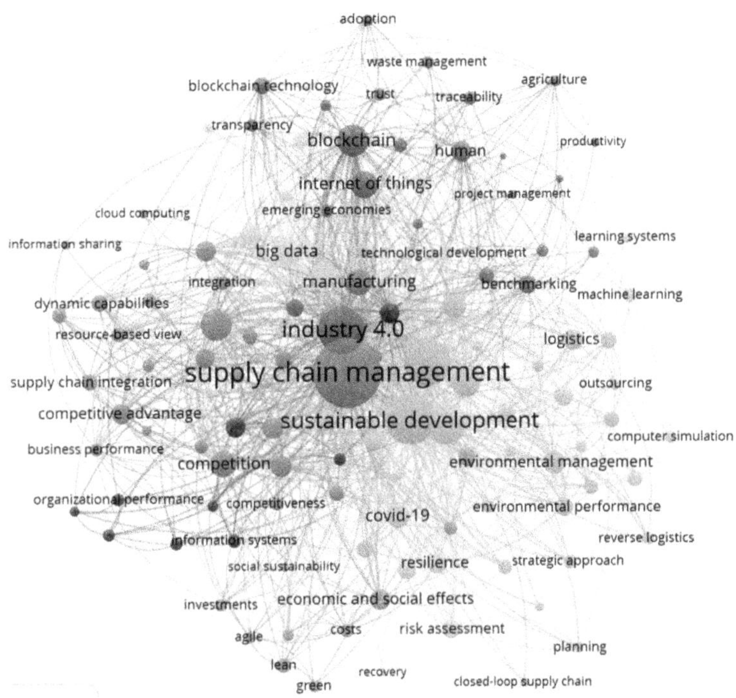

Cluster 2: Industry 4.0 (Blue Cluster)

The articles included in this cluster have a pure technical approach and bring forward issues like blockchain technology, additive manufacturing, lean production and Internet of Things. The aim is to develop algorithms, systems, and platforms that could shorten the supply chain procedures, increase tracebility, facilitate collaborative product design and enhance waste management. As Zhang et al. (2021) state "the most fundamental causal drivers [...] are overcoming operational challenges, recovering value, speeding up operations, saving cost and improving profit". Hence, the resource-view theory is combined with the organization information processing theory in order to explore the impact of Industry 4.0 technologies on supply chain performance. Nevertheless, the approaches vary from conceptual to empirical. For example, Wang, Wu, Chen, and Evans (2021) present the attributes of blockchain while Longo, Nicoletti, Padovano, d'Atri, and Forte (2019) use simulations to highlight how blockchain technology could increase the supply chain overall performance, fostering collaboration and communication among the supply chain members.

The empirical analysis developed at this level present the characteristics of the construction (Meng, 2019), pharma (Bamakan, Moghaddam, Manshadi, & Klemes, 2021), manufacturing (Dzhuguryan & Deja, 2021), healthcare (Dau, Scavarda, Scavarda, & Portugal, 2019).

Cluster 3: Sustainable Development (Green Cluster)

Within this group, the concept of circular economy is brought forward and the importance of the United Nations Sustainable Development Goals is emphasized. As a consequence, supply chain performance and digitalization are approached from an environmental perspective, and concepts like "green supply chains", and "reverse logistics" are promoted.

Chang (2021) adopts a simplistic perspective and defines the green supply chains as the traditional supply chains that incorporated environmental indicators. In other words, technology is used at the supply chain level in order to reduce chemical emissions and pollutions, eliminate waste and increase resource utilization efficiency. Umar, Khan, Yusoff Yusliza, Ali, and Yu (2021) adopt a more systematic approach, focusing on specific green supply chain practices, and prove that adopting green purchasing, green manufacturing, and green design can increase significantly the environmental performance of the supply chain.

Reverse logistics is among the fastest-growing supply chain management research (Swanson, Goel, Francisco, & Stock, 2018), and it is considered a vital component of the circular economy (Bernon, Tjahjono, & Ripanti, 2018) due to its a restorative or regenerative view by intention and design. Previous studies emphasize that reverse logistics helps companies achieve environmental and economic goals, such as: efficient resource use, savings from the reuse of low-cost inputs, recovery of the value still incorporated in the used products, revenues generated by the sale of salvaged materials, and increased customer satisfaction Cricelli, Greco, and Grimaldi (2021) analyze the effect of inter-organizational collaboration on reverse logistics and they point out that stakeholders' collaboration and willingness to improve performance represent the drivers of reverse logistics. On the other hand, Darkow, Foerster, and von der Gracht (2015) state that the success of reverse logistics depends on customers' awareness of sustainable and ethical practices.

Cluster 4: Decision-Making (Orange Cluster)

At this level, the scholars shed light on how specific technologies, like big data analytics (Bag, Gupta, Choi, & Kumar, 2021; Patrucco, Moretto, Trabucchi, & Golini, 2021), machine learning (Shahbazi & Byun, 2021; Wang & Zhang, 2020), and digital twins (Wang, Wang, Tao, & Liu, 2021) could be used for increasing the operational performance of supply chain networks. Hence, Bag et al. (2021) show that big data analytics have a crucial role in bulding responsive and innovative supply chains while Patrucco et al (2021) show that big data analytics improve supply chain performance by fostering buyer-supplier collaboration. Besides, Shahbazi and Byun (2021) use machine learning to foster products' tracebility and optimize warehouse transactions while Wang and Zhang (2020) evaluate its impact on organizational performance through power optimization. Ocampo et al. (2021) complement these findings by proposing a list of 62 indicators that could support decision-making among the supply chain members.

Lately, researchers' attention is drawn by the development and use of digital twins which are defined as "a virtual representation of their real-world counterparts, which contain all essential elements, such as all geometrical components and material properties; simulate accurately and realistically all relevant processes and their kinetics throughout the product's life-cycle; and are connected to the real-world product and processes by sensor data, which is preferably continuously updated in real-time" (Marmolejo-Saucedo, 2021). Due to their capacity to facilitate process optimization and faults prediction based on physical and digital data, they proved to be capable of making the processes more flexible, adaptable, and predictable (Wang et al., 2021).

Cluster 5: Economic and Social Effects (Purple Cluster)

The articles that belong to this cluster address the economic and social impact of the supply chain, transgressing the organizational boundaries. Adopting an inside perspective, Benzidia, Makaoui, and Subramanian (2021) take into consideration the human aspects of the relational social capital and state that shared values and the ability to maintain social connections with the stakeholders foster innovation. Furthermore, "manufacturing companies must create a relational environment to understand the social issue from the sustainability perspective with suppliers to meet Industry 4.0 requirements including environmental perspective from the sustainability dimensions and innovative product development (privacy, security, etc.)." (Benzidia et al., 2021, p.8). On the other hand, Esmaeilian, Sarkis, Lewis, and Behdad (2020) adopt an inside-out perspective and argue that in order to increase supply chain performance, the policy-makers must: (i) design incentive mechanisms to promote consumer green behavior; (ii) enhance visibility across the entire product lifecycle; and (iii) monitoring and reporting performance across supply chain members.

Cluster 6: Decision Support Systems (Black Cluster)

Under this umbrella are reunited the articles that point out which tools and methods could be used for increasing supply chain performance. These mainly belong to knowledge management and quality management areas and the empirical studies developed so far reflect how the situation goes in the agriculture and service industry. For example, Fernandes, Vilhena, Oliveira, Sampaio, and Carvalho (2021) argue that continuous improvement, innovation and product/service quality have a significant impact on organizational performance, especialy at the financial and customer satisfaction levels while Karia (2018) proves that knowledge resources (such as, skills, experience, leadership, organizational culture) mediate the relationship between supply chain digitalization and economic performance.

Cluster 7: Data Analytics (Turquoise Cluster)

The articles reunited under the "data analytics" panacea accentuate the influence of technology adoption on supply chain performance, stressing out the impact of automation and industrial revolution. Fatorachian and Kazemi (2021) argue that automation allow for significant performance improvements at the level of all supply chain processes, namely: procurement, production, inventory management and retailing while Yu, Khan, and Uman (2021) analyze the automotive sector and provide evidence on the positive impact that supply chai automation has on operational performance; at the same time, they underline the insignificant association that exists between automation and economic performance.

The results of the co-occurrence analysis present the hot topics and the future research avenues (Figure 7). Currently, the hot topics are represented by supply chain digitalization (adapting the supply chain management to the challenges raised by Industry 4.0) and the influence of sustainable development on supply chain resilience. On the other hand, the topics that are starting to gain interest connect variables like: (i) blockchain technologies and Internet of Things, (ii) supply chain performance and digital technologies; (iii) big data analytics and operational performance; (iv) performance assessment and supply chain network; (v) environmental performance and digital twins; (vi) competitive advantage and collaboration; and (vii) agility and competition.

Figure 7. Hot topics and future research avenues

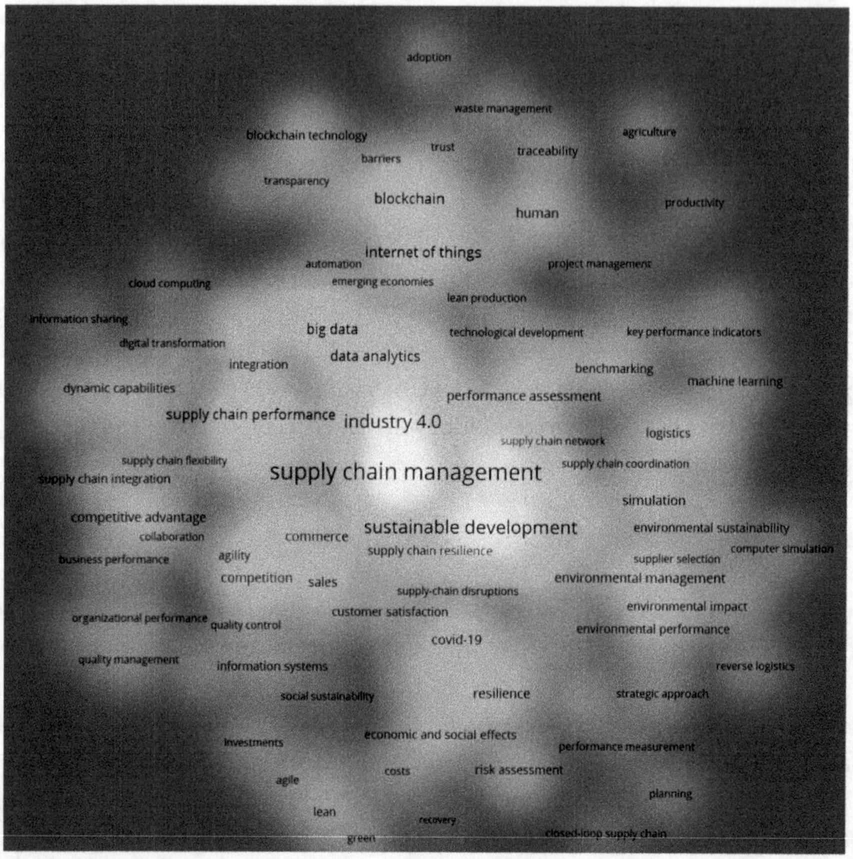

Synthesizing, a nexus among the first three clusters (namely, supply chain management, industry 4.0, and sustainable development) is required in order facilitate companies transition to circular economy which is defined as "an economic system that represents a change of paradigm in the way that human society is interrelated with nature and aims to prevent the depletion of resources, close energy and materials loops, and facilitate sustainable development through its implementation at the micro (enterprises and consumers), meso (economic agents integrated in symbiosis) and macro (city, regions and governments) levels. Attaining this circular model requires cyclical and regenerative environmental innovations in the way society legislates, produces and consumes" (Prieto-Sandoval, Jaca, & Ormazabal, 2018, p.610). This transition will involve not only digitalizing the supply chain processes but also redefining supply chain performance from a sustainable perspective. Although the competitive advantage, costs, and investments remain impartant, the focus is switched towards a more social and environmental approach; environmental performance, customer satisfaction and social effects are starting to capture the attention of academics and practitioners.

CONCLUSION AND FURTHER RESEARCH DIRECTIONS

The current chapter focused on exploring the topic of supply chain performance in the Industry 4.0 context, based on knowledge mapping and content analysis. Based on the results provided by the carried out analysis, several theoretical and practical implications are identified.

First of all, given the type of scientific publications in which almost a quarter of the most relevant papers are published, it can be argued that the issue is approached from both technical and human perspectives; this enhances the transition towards the circular economy that is based on Industry 5.0 and Society 5.0. On the other hand, the empirical studies that are highly cited are based on a qualitative approach; thus, it proves that the field is in an embryonic stage of development, requiring more quantitative analyses.

Secondly, references analysis is summarized in three interdependent clusters: the first one sets the foundation of supply chain performance while the second and the third ones capitalize on the technic approach and deal with the characteristics of logistics-oriented Industry 4.0, digital supply chains, blockchain technology, and the ripple effect.

In third place, the most influential authors are: Bag Surajit, Kazancoglu Yigit, Luthra Sunil, and Kumar Vikas, and more than 70% of the research regarding supply chain performance in the Industry 4.0 context is concentrated in 5 countries (namely, India, England, China, France, and the USA).

Fourth, related to the knowledge mapping (content analysis and research avenues), it is important to remark that the main focus is on the manufacturing industry, and it brings forward topics like digital technologies and sustainability. Linked to these, the topic of supply chain performance in Industry 4.0 is analyzed by the academic community in the context of the circular economy, paying attention to developing new business models, able to facilitate the transition to the new economic reality.

Last but not least, under the perspective of the analyzed topics, the knowledge developed so far is organized around 7 clusters, namely: supply chain management, Industry 4.0, sustainable development, decision-making, economic and social effects, decision support systems, and data analytics. Somehow they are treated as independent topics although their interconnection could provide valuable tools and methods for the policy-makers. Further research is required at this point.

The Industry 4.0 concept is quite broad, and as stated in the introduction, it is characterized by complex technological innovations. This circumstance makes it difficult to compare the degree of performance of one supply chain in relation to another. Furthermore, it is a challenging task to establish the relative importance that each individual partner has in the supply chain network, as a whole. Starting from these, the following research avenues can be pursued: (i) measuring the performance at the level of both supply chain members and supply chain network; (ii) analyzing the relationship between the maturity degree of supply chain and the digital capabilities of the supply chain members; (iii) increasing the awareness of the supply chain members to the benefits of circular economy and reverse logistic; (iv) developing tools and methods for measuring the performance of sustainable supply chains; (v) forecasting the desired performance not only at the individual company but also at the supply chain level; and (vi) identifying the tolls and methods that link together digital capabilities, operations efficiency and strategic performance.

ACKNOWLEDGMENT

The research reported in this paper is supported by the Spanish Agencia Estatal de Investigación for the project "Cadenas de suministro innovadoras y eficientes para productos-servicios altamente personalizados" (INNOPROS), Ref.: PID2019-109894GB-I00.

REFERENCES

Adams, R., Jeanrenaud, S., Bessant, J., Denyer, D., & Overy, P. (2016). Sustainability-oriented innovation: A systematic review. *International Journal of Management Reviews, 18*(2), 180–205. doi:10.1111/ijmr.12068

Bag, S., Gupta, S., Choi, T. M., & Kumar, A. (2021). Roles of Innovation Leadership on Using Big Data Analytics to Establish Resilient Healthcare Supply Chains to Combat the COVID-19 Pandemic: A Multimethodological Study. *IEEE Transactions on Engineering Management*, 1–14. Advance online publication. doi:10.1109/TEM.2021.3101590

Bamakan, S. M. H., Moghaddam, S. G., Manshadi, S. D., & Klemes, J. J. (2021). Blockchain-enabled pharmaceutical cold chain: Applications, key challenges, and future trends. *Journal of Cleaner Production, 302*, 127021. doi:10.1016/j.jclepro.2021.127021

Barney, J. (1991). Firm resources and sustained competitive advantage. *Journal of Management, 17*(1), 99–120. doi:10.1177/014920639101700108

Benzidia, S., Makaoui, N., & Subramanian, N. (2021). Impact of ambidexterity of blockchain technology and social factors on new product development: A supply chain and Industry 4.0 perspective. *Technological Forecasting and Social Change, 169*, 120819. doi:10.1016/j.techfore.2021.120819

Bernon, M., Tjahjono, B., & Ripanti, E. F. (2018). Aligning retail reverse logistics practice with circular economy values: An exploratory framework. *Production Planning and Control, 29*(6), 483–497. doi:10.1080/09537287.2018.1449266

Bhagwat, R., & Sharma, M. K. (2009). An Application of the Integrated AHP-PGP Model for Performance Measurement of Supply Chain Management. *Production Planning and Control, 20*(8), 678–690. doi:10.1080/09537280903069897

Brettel, M., Friederichsen, N., Keller, M., & Rosenberg, M. (2014). How Virtualization, Decentralization and Network Building Change the Manufacturing Landscape: An Industry 4.0 Perspective. *International Journal of Science. Engineering and Technology, 8*(1), 37–44.

Buyukozkan, G., & Gocer, F. (2018). Digital supply chain: Literature review and a proposed framework for future research. *Computers in Industry, 97*, 157–177. doi:10.1016/j.compind.2018.02.010

Chang, C. W. (2021). Constructing an intelligent shoe production plant using a green supply chain and knowledge management. *Knowledge Management Research and Practice*. Advance online publication. doi:10.1080/14778238.2021.1970488

Cisneros-Cabrera, S., Pishchulov, G., Sampaio, P., Mehandjiev, N., Liu, Z. X., & Kununka, S. (2021). An approach and decision support tool for forming industry 4.0 supply chain collaborations. *Computers in Industry, 125*, 103391. doi:10.1016/j.compind.2020.103391

Cricelli, L., Greco, M., & Grimaldi, M. (2021). An investigation on the effect of inter-organizational collaboration on reverse logistics. *International Journal of Production Economics, 240*, 108216. doi:10.1016/j.ijpe.2021.108216

Darkow, I. L., Foerster, B., & von der Gracht, H. A. (2015). Sustainability in food service supply chain: Future expectations from European industry experts toward the environmental perspective. *Supply Chain Management, 20*(2), 163–178. doi:10.1108/SCM-03-2014-0087

Dau, G., Scavarda, A., Scavarda, L. F., & Portugal, V. J. T. (2019). The Healthcare Sustainable Supply Chain 4.0: The Circular Economy Transition Conceptual Framework with the Corporate Social Responsibility Mirror. *Sustainability, 11*(12), 3259. doi:10.3390u11123259

Ding, X., & Yang, Z. (2020). Knowledge mapping of platform research: A visual analysis using VOSviewer and CiteSpace. *Electronic Commerce Research.* Advance online publication. doi:10.100710660-020-09410-7

Dolgui, A., Ivanov, D., & Sokolov, B. (2018). Ripple effect in the supply chain: An analysis and recent literature. *International Journal of Production Research, 56*(1-2), 414–430. doi:10.1080/00207543.2017.1387680

Dubey, R., Gunasekaran, A., Childe, S. J., Papadopoulos, T., Luo, Z. W., & Roubaudl, D. (2020). Upstream supply chain visibility and complexity effect on focal company's sustainable performance: Indian manufacturers' perspective. *Annals of Operations Research, 290*(1-2), 343–367. doi:10.100710479-017-2544-x

Duriau, V. J., Reger, R. K., & Pfarrer, M. D. (2007). A Content Analysis of the Content Analysis Literature in Organization Studies: Research Themes, Data Sources and Methodological Refinements. *Organizational Research Methods, 10*(1), 5–34. doi:10.1177/1094428106289252

Dzhuguryan, T., & Deja, A. (2021). Sustainable waste management for a city multifloor manufacturing cluster: A framework for designing a smart supply chain. *Sustainability, 13*(3), 1540. doi:10.3390u13031540

Dzikowski, P. (2018). A bibliometric analysis of born global rms. *Journal of Business Research, 85*, 281–294. doi:10.1016/j.jbusres.2017.12.054

Eslami, M. H., Jafari, H., Achtenhagen, L., Carlback, J., & Wong, A. (2021). Financial performance and supply chain dynamic capabilities: The Moderating Role of Industry 4.0 technologies. *International Journal of Production Research*, 1–18. Advance online publication. doi:10.1080/00207543.2021.1966850

Esmaeilian, B., Sarkis, J., Lewis, K., & Behdad, S. (2020). Blockchain for the future of sustainable supply chain management in Industry 4.0. *Resources, Conservation and Recycling, 163*, 105064. doi:10.1016/j.resconrec.2020.105064

Fatorachian, H., & Kazemi, H. (2021). Impact of Industry 4.0 on supply chain performance. *Production Planning and Control, 32*(1), 63–81. doi:10.1080/09537287.2020.1712487

Fernandes, A. C., Vilhena, E., Oliveira, R., Sampaio, P., & Carvalho, M. S. (2021). Supply chain quality management impact on organization performance: Results from an international survey. *International Journal of Quality & Reliability Management*. Advance online publication. doi:10.1108/IJQRM-05-2020-0159

Flynn, B. B., Huo, B., & Zhao, X. (2010). The impact of supply chain integration on performance: A contingency and configuration approach. *Journal of Operations Management*, *28*(1), 58–71. doi:10.1016/j.jom.2009.06.001

Fornell, C., & Larcker, D. F. (1981). Evaluating structural equation models with unobserved variables and measurement error. *JMR, Journal of Marketing Research*, *11*(1), 39–50. doi:10.1177/002224378101800104

Frederico, G. F., Garza-Reyes, J. A., Kumar, A., & Kumar, V. (2021). Performance measurement for supply chains in the Industry 4.0 era: A balanced scorecard approach. *International Journal of Productivity and Performance Management*, *70*(4), 789–807. doi:10.1108/IJPPM-08-2019-0400

Frohlich, M. T., & Westbrook, R. (2001). Arcs of integration: An international study of supply chain strategies. *Journal of Operations Management*, *19*(2), 185–200. doi:10.1016/S0272-6963(00)00055-3

Ghobakhloo, M. (2018). The future of manufacturing industry: A strategic roadmap toward Industry 4.0. *Journal of Manufacturing Technology Management*, *29*(6), 910–936. doi:10.1108/JMTM-02-2018-0057

Gunasekaran, A., & Ngai, E. W. (2004). Information Systems in Supply Chain Integration and Management. *European Journal of Operational Research*, *159*(2), 269–295. doi:10.1016/j.ejor.2003.08.016

Hald, K. S., & Mouritsen, J. (2018). The evolution of performance measurement systems in a supply chain: A longitudinal case study on the role of interorganisational factors. *International Journal of Production Economics*, *205*, 256–271. doi:10.1016/j.ijpe.2018.09.021

Hofmann, E., & Rusch, M. (2017). Industry 4.0 and the current status as well as future prospects on logistics. *Computers in Industry*, *89*, 23–34. doi:10.1016/j.compind.2017.04.002

Ivanov, D., & Dolgui, A. (2021). A digital supply chain twin for managing the disruption risks and resilience in the era of Industry 4.0. *Production Planning and Control*, *32*(9), 775–788. doi:10.1080/09537287.2020.1768450

Ivanov, D., Dolgui, A., & Sokolov, B. (2019). The impact of digital technology and industry 4.0 on the ripple effect and supply chain risk analytics. *International Journal of Production Research*, *57*(3), 829–846. doi:10.1080/00207543.2018.1488086

Jha, A., Sharma, R. R. K., Kumar, V., & Verma, P. (2022). Designing supply chain performance system: A strategic study on Indian manufacturing sector. *Supply Chain Management*, *27*(1), 66–88. doi:10.1108/SCM-05-2020-0198

Kamble, S. S., Gunasekaran, A., & Gawankar, S. A. (2018). Sustainable Industry 4.0 framework: A systematic literature review identifying the current trends and future perspectives. *Process Safety and Environmental Protection*, *117*, 408–425. doi:10.1016/j.psep.2018.05.009

Karia, N. (2018). Knowledge resources, technology resources and competitive advantage of logistics service providers. *Knowledge Management Research and Practice*, *16*(4), 451–463. doi:10.1080/14778238.2018.1521541

Khisro, J., & Sundberg, H. (2020). Enterprise interoperability development in multi relation collaborations: Success factors from the Danish electricity market. *Enterprise Information Systems*, *14*(8), 1172–1193. doi:10.1080/17517575.2018.1528633

Kimseng, T., Javed, A., Jeenanunta, C., & Kohda, Y. (2020). Sustaining Innovation through Joining Global Supply Chain Networks: The Case of Manufacturing Firms in Thailand. *Sustainability*, *12*(13), 5259. doi:10.3390u12135259

Köseoglu, M. A., Yıldız, M., Putra, E. D., & Cıftcı, T. (2018). Co-Authorship Networks in Business Ethics: A Longitudinal Study. *Journal of Scientometric Research*, *7*(3), 201–209. doi:10.5530/jscires.7.3.32

Leon, R. D., Rodriguez-Rodriguez, R., Gomez-Gasquet, P., & Mula, J. (2020). Business process improvement and the knowledge flows that cross a private online social network: An insurance supply chain case. *Information Processing & Management*, *57*(4), 102237. doi:10.1016/j.ipm.2020.102237

Longo, F., Nicoletti, L., Padovano, A., d'Atri, G., & Forte, M. (2019). Blockchain-enabled supply chain: An experimental study. *Computers & Industrial Engineering*, *136*, 57–69. doi:10.1016/j.cie.2019.07.026

Marmolejo-Saucedo, J. A. (2021). Digital Twin Framework for Large-Scale Optimization Problems in Supply Chains: A Case of Packing Problem. *Mobile Networks and Applications*. Advance online publication. doi:10.100711036-021-01856-9

Meng, X. H. (2019). Lean management in the context of construction supply chains. *International Journal of Production Research*, *57*(11), 3784–3798. doi:10.1080/00207543.2019.1566659

Merriam, S. B. (1988). *Case study research in education: A qualitative approach*. Jossey-Bass.

Neely, A. (2005). The Evolution of Performance Measurement Research: Developments in the Last Decade and a Research Agenda for the Next. *International Journal of Operations & Production Management*, *25*(12), 1264–1277. doi:10.1108/01443570510633648

Ocampo, L., Himang, C., Obiso, J. J., Bongo, M., Caballes, S. A., Abellana, D. P., Jabilles, E. M., Deocaris, C., & Ancheta, R. Jr. (2021). Industry 4.0 Indicators and Their Roles in Strategy Formulation. *Journal of Advanced Manufacturing Systems*, *20*(3), 631–662. doi:10.1142/S0219686721500311

Patrucco, A., Moretto, A., Trabucchi, D., & Golini, R. (2021). How Do Industry 4.0 Technologies Boost Collaborations in Buyer-Supplier Relationships? In assessing Industry 4.0 technologies, this study found that buyer-supplier visibility and buyer-supplier integration matters more than the digital technologies used. *Research Technology Management*, *65*(1), 48–58. doi:10.1080/08956308.2021.1999131

Prieto-Sandoval, V., Jaca, C., & Ormazabal, M. (2018). Towards a consensus on the circular economy. *Journal of Cleaner Production*, *179*, 605–615. doi:10.1016/j.jclepro.2017.12.224

Pukall, T. J., & Calabro, A. (2014). The internationalization of family firms: A critical review and integrative model. *Family Business Review*, *27*(2), 103–125. doi:10.1177/0894486513491423

Reyes-Gonzalez, L., Gonzalez-Brambila, C. N., & Veloso, F. (2016). Using co-authorship and citation analysis to identify research groups: A new way to assess performance. *Scientometrics*, *108*(3), 1171–1191. doi:10.100711192-016-2029-8

Saberi, S., Kouhizadeh, M., Sarkis, J., & Shen, L. (2019). Blockchain technology and its relationships to sustainable supply chain management. *International Journal of Production Research*, *57*(7), 2117–2135. doi:10.1080/00207543.2018.1533261

Sawangwong, A., & Chaopaisarn, P. (2021). The impact of applying knowledge in the technological pillars of Industry 4.0 on supply chain performance. *Kybernetes*. Advance online publication. doi:10.1108/K-07-2021-0555

Schmidt, R., Möhring, M., Härting, R., Reichstein, C., Neumaier, P., & Jozinovic, P. (2015). Industry 4.0- potentials for creating smart products: empirical research results. In W. Abramowicz (Ed.), *Proceedings of International Conference on Business Information Systems* (pp.16-27). Springer. 10.1007/978-3-319-19027-3_2

Shahbazi, Z., & Byun, Y. C. (2021). A procedure for tracing supply chains for perishable food based on Blockchain, Machine Learning and Fuzzy Logic. *Electronics (Basel)*, *10*(1), 41. doi:10.3390/electronics10010041

Sony, M., & Naik, S. (2020). Critical factors for the successful implementation of Industry 4.0: A review and future research direction. *Production Planning and Control*, *31*(10), 799–815. doi:10.1080/09537287.2019.1691278

Sundram, V. P. K., Bahrin, A. S., Munir, Z. B. A., & Zolait, A. H. (2018). The effect of supply chain information management and information system infrastructure The mediating role of supply chain integration towards manufacturing performance in Malaysia. *Journal of Enterprise Information Management*, *31*(5), 751–770. doi:10.1108/JEIM-06-2017-0084

Sutduean, J., Harakan, A., & Jermsittiparsert, K. (2019). Exploring the Relationship between Supply Chain Integration, Product Innovation, Supply Chain Performance and Firm Performance: Does Supply Chain Information Strategy Matter? *International Journal of Innovation, Creativity and Change*, *5*(2), 175–192.

Swanson, D., Goel, L., Francisco, K., & Stock, J. (2018). An analysis of supply chain management research by topic. *Supply Chain Management*, *23*(2), 100–116. doi:10.1108/SCM-05-2017-0166

Tarafdar, M., & Qrunfleh, S. (2017). Agile supply chain strategy and supply chain performance: Complementary roles of supply chain practices and information systems capability for agility. *International Journal of Production Research*, *55*(4), 925–938. doi:10.1080/00207543.2016.1203079

Thekkoote, R. (2021). Understanding big data-driven supply chain and performance measures for customer satisfaction. *Benchmarking*. Advance online publication. doi:10.1108/BIJ-01-2021-0034

Umar, M., Khan, S. A. R., Yusoff Yusliza, M., Ali, S., & Yu, Z. (2021). Industry 4.0 and green supply chain practices: An empirical study. *International Journal of Productivity and Performance Management*. Advance online publication. doi:10.1108/IJPPM-12-2020-0633

van Eck, N. J., & Waltman, L. (2010). Software survey: VOSviewer, a computer program for bibliometric mapping. *Scientometrics*, *84*(2), 523–538. doi:10.100711192-009-0146-3 PMID:20585380

Waller, M. A., & Fawcett, S. E. (2013). Data science, predictive analytics, and big data: A revolution that will transform supply chain design and management. *Journal of Business Logistics*, *34*(2), 77–84. doi:10.1111/jbl.12010

Wang, D., & Zhang, Y. M. (2020). Implications for sustainability in supply chain management and the circular economy using machine learning model. *Information Systems and e-Business Management.* Advance online publication. doi:10.100710257-020-00477-1

Wang, M., Wu, Y., Chen, B., & Evans, M. (2021). Blockchain and Supply Chain Management: A New Paradigm for Supply Chain Integration and Collaboration. Operations and Supply Chain Management - An International Journal, 14(1), 111-122. doi:10.31387/oscm0440290. doi:10.31387/oscm0440290

Wang, X., Wang, Y., Tao, F., & Liu, A. (2021). New paradigm of data-driven smart customization through digital twin. *Journal of Manufacturing Systems, 58*(B), 270-280. doi:10.1016/j.jmsy.2020.07.023

Web of Science. (2022). *Citation Report.* Retrived from https://www.webofscience.com/wos/alldb/citation-report/cc37d966-17de-4043-a551-621e0fac4f2b-1fb2265a

Yu, Z., Khan, S. A. R., & Uman, M. (2021). Circular economy practices and industry 4.0 technologies: A strategic move of automobile industry. *Business Strategy and the Environment.* Advance online publication. doi:10.1002/bse.2918

Zhang, A., Venkatesh, V. G., Wang, J. X., Mani, V., Wan, M., & Qu, T. (2021). Drivers of industry 4.0-enabled smart waste management in supply chain operations: A circular economy perspective in China. *Production Planning and Control*, 1–17. Advance online publication. doi:10.1080/09537287.2021.1980909

KEY TERMS AND DEFINITIONS

Data Analytics: The science of collecting, transforming and organizing data in order to have a meaning for the user.

Decision Support System: Technological tools that can be used by the policy-makers in order to analyze the environment, estimate probabilities, forecast future trends and evaluate courses of action.

Decision-Making: The process of chosing a solution for a given problem, after analyzing the pros and cons of the available alternatives.

Economic Effects: Results generated at the micro, meso and macro level that can be financially quantified.

Industry 4.0: Technological trend that aims to foster processes automation, increasing productivity and reducing carbon footprint and waste generation.

Performance: An organization's or alliance's capacity of achieving its goals by overcoming potential barriers and taking advantage of the opportunities.

Social Effects: Results generated at the micro, meso and macro level that are reflected by stakeholders' quality of life and values.

Supply Chain: The interconnected activities that have to be efficiently performed in order to deliver the products and/or services to the customers.

Sustainable Development: An organizing principle that brings together the economic, social and environmental needs and capacities of the current and future generations of individuals, companies and societies.

Chapter 2
SCM 4.0:
Not Just an Opportunity; It Is a Need

Tamás Faludi
University of Miskolc, Hungary

ABSTRACT

The most important purpose of supply chain management is ensuring the maximum level of material and information flow within and outside the companies. However, supply chain management has gone through many changes in the 21st century. The developing IT sector, the digitalization, the appearance of smart tools are the results of Industry 4.0. Companies need to recognize the importance to adapt technical innovations and digitalize their processes. The influences of Industry 4.0 are digitalized supply chain management (SCM 4.0) and digitalized logistics (Logistics 4.0). The chapter defines the most frequently used tools of both areas. On the other hand, the chapter deals with the problems of supply chain coordination as well. The determined factors can be handled by the technical innovations, which are used by SCM 4.0 and Logistics 4.0. The chapter analyses the connection between the determined problems and smart tools as the solutions.

INTRODUCTION

In this world, where the environment around the companies is changing constantly, every company needs to have the tools, which help them to survive. In this context, survival means to keep the competitive advantages. These tools help the companies to stay in the game and motivate them to develop. But what are the characteristics of this era which is called digitalization? The chapter will answer this question.

First of all, the author will introduce the phenomena of the appearance of smart technologies, which are derived from the process of digitalization. The literature calls it industry 4.0, which name is already unavoidable in the everyday life as well. A brief historical introduction of the industrial revolution is needed to understand the importance of the adaption to this new, industry 4.0.

Industry 4.0 seeks into every area both in the industry and in the business life. That is the reason why smart logistics and smart supply chain solutions are used more and more frequently. These tools belong the logistics 4.0 and supply chain management 4.0. The chapter will focus on the topic of supply chain

DOI: 10.4018/978-1-7998-9715-6.ch002

Copyright © 2022, IGI Global. Copying or distributing in print or electronic forms without written permission of IGI Global is prohibited.

4.0, but logistics 4.0 will be also introduced because they complement each other. Logistics 4.0 is a very important tool to manage, coordinate and optimize the internal processes, and the tasks of supply chain management 4.0 are concentrating on the whole supply chain, so manage, coordinate and optimize the external processes, which are between the partners, and the key processes for the high-level cooperation of the chain members. These tools can help to coordinate the supply chain very well (Frazzon, Rodriguez, Pereira, Pires, & Uhlmann 2019; Szymczak, 2019).

Because supply chains are getting to be global and it means they are so extended, they count many members, so the cooperation between the partners is a little bit difficult. Thus, the typical problems and factors need to be determined. If the problems are known, it is easier to recommend the solutions for them (Chandak, Chandak, & Sharma, 2014; Vidrová, 2020).

Thus, the research will highlight the importance of using these smart tools. In the digital era, companies need to handle more and more problems, because there are more and more partners. To keep in touch with these partners needs a system, because without these systems, information will be lost, and there will be barriers in the information- and the material-flow, which will lead to unforeseeable consequences. It means, if there is a gap or gaps in the information flow because of a supply chain member, the efficiency of the whole chain will decrease. The gap can derive for example from an un-digitalized member.

Thus, first of all, companies need to recognize that digitalization is not a chance or opportunity – it is a need. Second, the new situation causes new problems, especially in the coordination between the members. The many members result in the big data, that need to be handled. Besides that, the contact, the delivery, the warehousing, the purchasing, and the scheduling all are crying out for new solutions. That is the reason why the research is aiming to discover the potential digital solution for various problems. After the determination of the coordination problems, which are caused by the digital era, different IT solutions – especially focused on the digital tools of Supply Chain Management 4.0 and Logistics 4.0 – will be paired to the right problems.

BACKGROUND

In 2018, in Roland Berger: Focus, there was a research of Bock (2018), which is focused on the digitalization of companies. The main question of this research was are the companies are ready to digitalize themselves. The result of this research has very surprising: based on the answers more than half of the surveyed companies – exactly 56% – are not ready for digitalization. 56% of the analyzed companies do not have the suitable, the right IT infrastructure to manage more complex software or robots. Furthermore, these companies are not able to integrate new, even a virtual process into their own operations. Thus, the main problem of these companies is that they do not have a digital vision referring to their future (Bock, 2018). However, if there is no vision, they will not be able to digitalize, which could be a significant disadvantage for the companies in terms of the market competition. And if the companies have disadvantages, it affects the whole supply chain, as well. The results are cooperation problems, efficiency problems, etc. which lead to the fall of the supply chain. The research also determined the problem of forecasting, which is based on the lack of digitalization. Companies can not eliminate the inventory surpluses, which hinder the existence of a supply chain that dynamically adapts to environmental and customer needs (Bock, 2018). But the biggest advantages derived from this: because of the 'customer-is-the-king' theory, if companies can adapt the customer's needs and they strive to satisfy these needs as soon as possible, the company could earn a high level of customer service. The results are a competitive advantage and a higher profit.

According to the author's own internet-based research, which is focused on the biggest, market-leader companies in different industries, the author tries to emphasize the importance of the digitalization. this brief research proves, that the biggest companies are in the game, and their purpose is to stay in the game, with the help of their competitiveness. Figure 1 summarizes the different kinds of smart or digital solutions, which is used by the biggest global companies.

Figure 1. Digital solutions of various industries (own edited based on internet based research)

NAME	INDUSTRY	USED DIGITAL SOLUTION
	Automotive Industry	
AUDI		*e-Ink Displays*
VOLVO TRUCKS and DFDS		*Vera – an intelligent and self-driven vehicle*
SCANIA		*self-driven trucks (under testing)*
MERCEDES-BENZ		*smart manufacturing with automatic robots*
	Manufacturing	
HELL ENERGY		*automated high bay warehouse*
BOSCH		*online monitoring and service of production equipment*
LEGO		*smart warehousing*
JOYSON SAFETY SYSTEMS		*automatic inventory*
	Commercial and Logistics Services	
IKEA		*exoskeleton (under testing)*
BHS Trans		*Android based shippng app*
Amazon		*Prime Air – parcel delivery drone*
Waberer's		*Tracking system*

Figure 1 shows that the biggest companies are not just using some kind of digital or smart solution, but they are making many innovations, which are actually under testing. On the other hand, the author analyzes the importance of the topic of digital solutions. Various platforms are chosen, which include the most viewed internet websites, and the high appreciated databases (Figure 2).

Figure 2. Development of scientific interest in SCM 4.0 (own edited based on the data of Emerald and ScienceDirect)

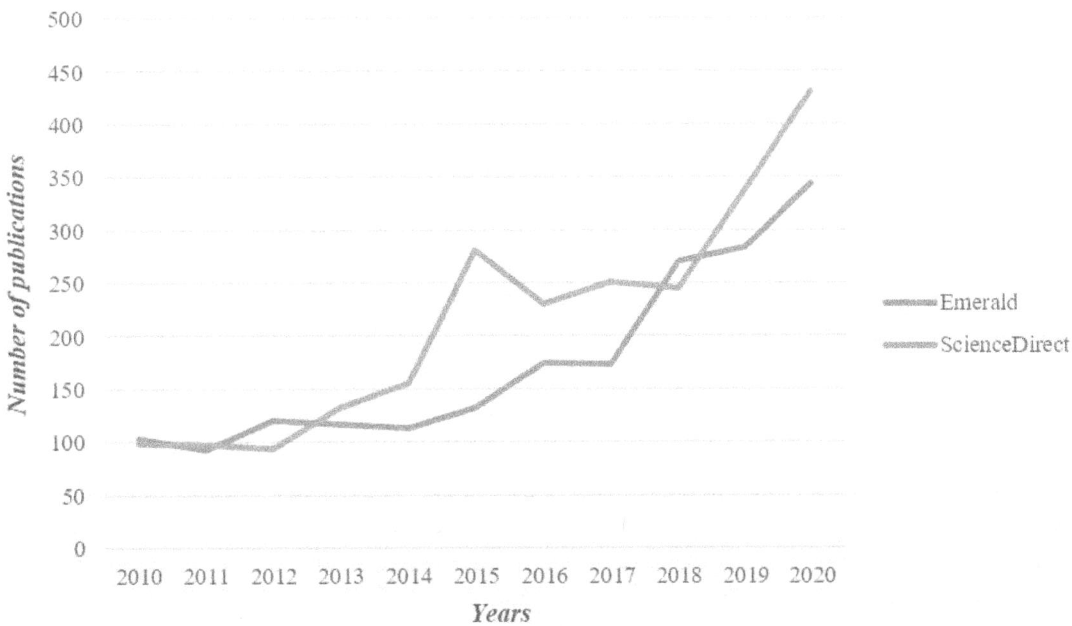

The keyword was SCM 4.0. Author analyses the last 10 years, from 2010 to 2020 the number of publications in terms of the keyword. Figure 2 shows an increasing trend in both databases. Until 2015 and 2017, there is a low-growth trend, but from 2017 the number of publications suddenly and abruptly increases. It means, that there has always been a constant interest in the subject that the field has a constantly interesting in the digitalization of supply chain management, but when digitalization became a reality, there was an increasing interest in the field. Based on these researches, digitalization presents itself in business life, and companies would not like to be disadvantaged, because of the missing of adapting themselves to this changing environment.

As Bock (2018) and the author's brief research show the digitalization could be the key to a successful operation. Digitalization, the smart tools, the digital solutions help the companies to cooperate and to be virtually interconnected. This connection helps the information flow, so real-time information could be available. This information is the basis of an accurate forecast. In fact, the digitalization and the smart tools help companies to cooperate, and in this era, when there are so many members in a supply chain, this is the most important thing. This could help to coordinate the whole chain.

THE IMPORTANCE OF SUPPLY CHAIN COORDINATION IN THE 21ST CENTURY

According to the researchers of the 21st century, the supply chain management is not a supporting process of the logistics field, now it was the other way about: the logistics are a very important part of the supply chain management. Back in time, in the second half of the 20th century, neither the literature nor the business sphere does not identify supply chain management as a conscious management field. In this era, every task, process, or tool belongs to the logistics.

But the proof of the increasing importance of supply chain management has appeared in 2005. In the same year, the Council of Logistics Management (CLM) has changed its name, and the new name represents that its research topics are expanded. From 2005 the Council of Supply Chain Management Professionals (CSCMP) is founded.

Many definitions are adopted from the Council of Logistics Management, according to the latest bylaws of CSCMP the purpose of supply chain management is to "integrate supply and demand management within and across companies" (CSCMP, 2017, p.3). It means supply chain includes planning and management processes of all internal – logistics –, and all external – especially focused on the collaboration – processes.

The definition of logistics management is also adopted by the CSCMP, which emphasizes that logistics is the part of the supply chain management and includes every process of the information and the material flow, forward and reverse from the point of origin and the point of consumption (CSCMP, 2017).

However, the importance of planning and coordinating the supply chain management was getting to be clear at the beginning of the 2000s (Christopher, 2005; Gelei, 2003; Nagy 2006). The main reason for this is the globalization. Borders were no longer an impenetrable barrier to trade. There were free-trade agreements, which opened the way to being multinational. Companies have founded more and more subsidiaries in different countries or on different continents. The goal is to reduce cost – because some factors, for example, the human resources, or some materials could be cheaper than in the origin country – and at the same time to be more profitable. These subsidiaries had to create their own supply chain or supply network or they had to apply in the existing chain. But if the corporate group has some strategic partners – for example, suppliers – subsidiaries have to stay in touch with these members. It is a kind of limit. Because they have to satisfy the demand of the local market, but they also have to work with the strategic partners, who are in a different country, the cooperation could be difficult. It means that the growing networks and supply chains were embraced by more and more companies, so the supply chain network is constantly getting to be extended. At the management level, it is required to organize, plan, and coordinate the supply chains.

Another reason for the increasing number of members in a supply chain is the outsourcing. Companies outsource the processes, for which they do not have the expertise, skills, competencies, or resources. But there is a case when they use the outsourcing simply for the reason of cost-efficiency. As a result of such outsourcing processes, several service industries have emerged; the logistics service companies were also emerged and spread. They offer warehousing, distribution, shipping, and more complex services. However, from the point of view of supply chains, this generated additional problems, as it only increased the number of chain members. Within the chain, the communication, the cooperation, the material- and the information flow have become difficult. The key to the successful operation of the supply chain is a high level of cooperation. From the year of 2010, researchers focus on supply chain coordination.

According to the publications of Gupta and Weerawat (2006) and Kaipia (2007), the success of coordination requires the chain members to adapt the activities that can be used to optimize the operation of the whole chain. Thus, it is necessary to define a collective goal that can be placed above individual goals, and in order to achieve that goal, mechanisms that unify and manage the various interactions are essential. This is the purpose of supply chain coordination.

Of course, many problems influences the quality of coordination. Urgent challenges of the new era are forcing supply chain management – and so the coordination – to develop and keep up with the development. The short lead time, the need for fast delivery, the strict safety and security standards, the product lifecycle management required from the point of view of chain members the highest possible level of cooperation (Corallo, Latino, Menegoli, & Pontradolfo, 2020; Dai, Tseng, & Zipkin, 2005; Marucheck, Greis, Mena, & Cai, 2011). Besides that many supply chain suffers from the negative effect of the bullwhip-effect (Constantino, Di Gravio, Shaban, & Tronci, 2013; Yin, 2021).

Arshinder and Deshmukh (2008) have determined the major factors which influence coordination. Common findings are the different product life cycle and delivery times mismatch could be an obstructive factor, but besides that, the researchers found that the different organizational cultures, the non-coherent goals, and many mismatches in terms of the information flow, the ordered quantities, or replenishment times.

Figure 3. summarizes the influencing factors of supply chain coordination.

Figure 3. Influencing factors of supply chain coordination (own edited based on Arshinder & Deshmukh, 2008; Constantino et al., 2013; Corallo et al., 2020; Dai et al., 2005; Marucheck et al., 2011; Yin, 2021)

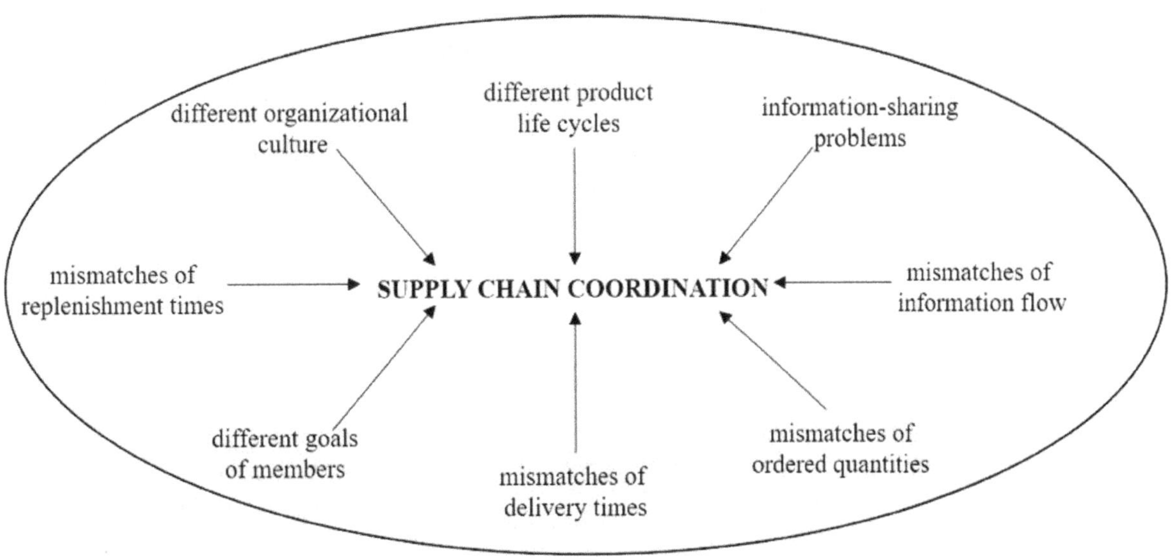

The defined factors are getting to be more important in the 21st century. The increasing number of members makes coordination more difficult, and these factors get a stronger influencing level.

The new IT solutions, called smart technologies could help to keep companies their competitive advantages and minimize the previously presented negative factors. In fact, these tools are necessary to survive and keep the advantages.

EVOLUTION OF SUPPLY CHAIN MANAGEMENT 4.0

The SCM 4.0 Concept

First of all, it is needed to talk about the industrial revolutions, which lead us to the digital age. The digital evolution can be linked to the steps of technology development (Figure 4).

Figure 4. The digital evolution of SCM (own edited based on Frazzon et al. 2019)

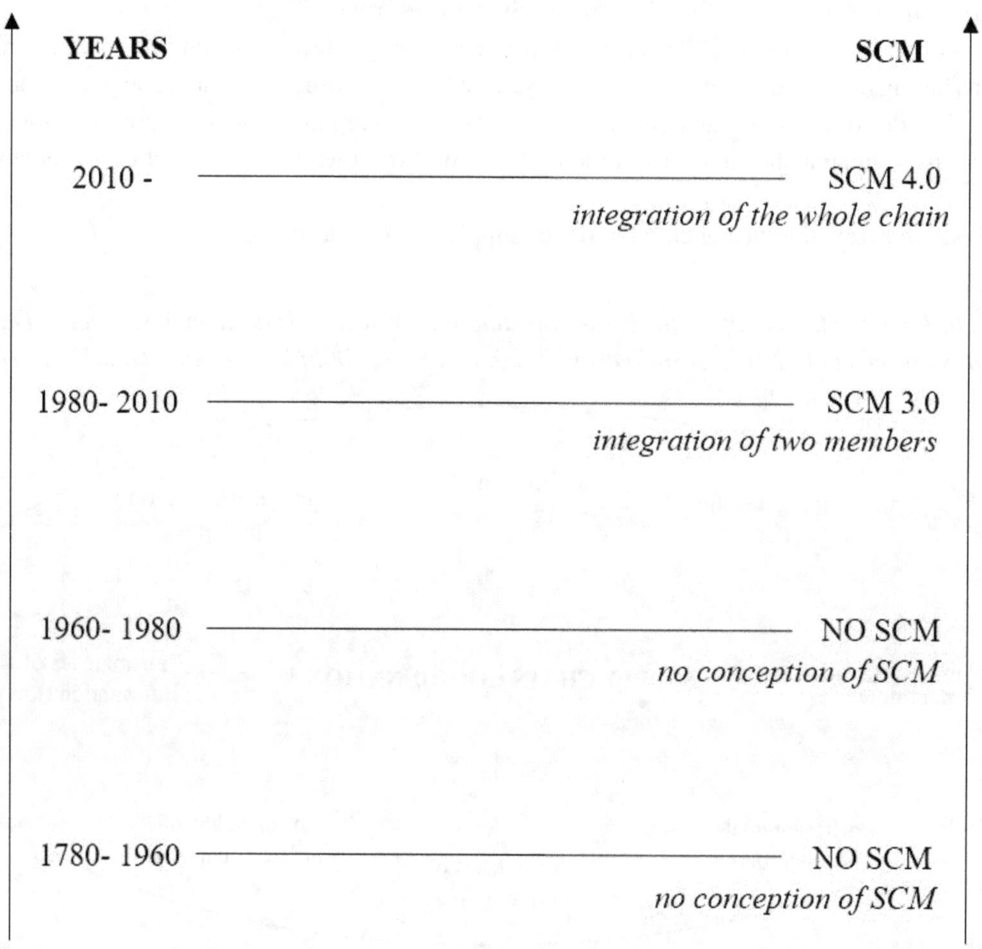

In terms of supply chain management, the beginning of the development is the 1980's. This is the time when the IT sector was beginning to develop rapidly. This development allowed to integrate the processes – mainly the value-creating ones – between two supply chain members. But the development was not stopped. The supply chains were extending, the number of members was increasing and the IT has evolved even faster, which allowed handling the coordination between more than two members of the supply chains. Supply chain management has arrived in the fourth industry evolution (Frazzon et al., 2019).

The fourth industrial revolution is usually called Industry 4.0. The two definitions are not focused exactly on the same. The fourth industrial revolution is a bigger thing, and Industry 4.0 is the part of it. The fourth industrial revolution takes effect both on the business sphere, on the industry, and the society, as well (Brettel, Friederichsen, Keller, & Rosenberg, 2014; Heynitz, Bremicker, Amadori, & Reschke, 2016; Wang, Wan, Li, & Zhang, 2015). Industry 4.0 concentrates only on the business sphere. An interesting fact: several years ago there is no common name of Industry 4.0. "Industrie 4.0" from the German government, China called it "Internet +", and the American version is the "Industrial Internet" (Wang et al., 2015). After the years, from 2020 the Industry 4.0 includes almost all of these approaches.

However, the different approaches have a common finding: Industry 4.0 influences the cooperation of companies. The concept of supply chain management is to coordinate and manage the internal and external processes, which includes business relations. That is the reason why Industry 4.0 has a strong effect on supply chain management, as well. Industry 4.0 needs the horizontal and the vertical integration of the value-creating processes within the company and between the companies, so exactly it needs the whole supply chain to be integrated. It means that the change of certain attitudes is needed. This change leads the business sphere to the smart supply chain management, or the SCM 4.0.

The 21st century's supply chain model is based on an integrative and automatic approach. Companies must integrate the value-creating processes with each other to get real-time data because, with the help of these movements, every member can adjust to the dynamically changing needs of customers. It means that the ERP systems are also needed to connect with the processes of supply chain management. A case study, based on the manufacturing industry proves that the integration of ERP and SCM systems could increase the efficiency of the partners. Cost reduction, lead-time reduction, and the improvement of the visibility of the partners can appear as results (Koh, Saad, & Arunachalam, 2006).

Customer expectations along with the wide range of services which thanks to the IT development are also changed. The customers focus on the perfect order fulfillment and the lowest possible delivery time. From the point of the supply chain members, relationship management is one of the most important factors in the supply chain management business processes. These factors lead to the maximum satisfaction of the customers or the supply chain partners (Hintsa, Ayyash, Hameri, Myers, Coulibaly, & Gutierrez, 2007).

The changing needs and high expectations of customers are not the only influencing factors of the supply chain management. To be an almost constant competitive company, it is needed to be sustainable. It is true in the case of the supply chain, as well. So it means the companies have to create a sustainable supply chain. In the UK, there is a program, called SC21 or 'Supply Chains for the twenty-first century'. It focuses on the aerospace industry and its purpose is to define standards, performance goals to the members that are more sustainable (Manville, Papadopoulos, & Garengo, 2019). An other research proves that sustainability is extremely important in the automotive industry, as well. This industry is one of the most complex systems, with many suppliers, many technology processes (Ramirez-Peña, Mayuet, Vazquez-Martinez, & Batista, 2020).

The previously presented factors, such as integration, real-time data, changing customers' expectations and needs, and the topic of sustainability are getting to be more important in the era of the Industry 4.0. It is true, that it is a long process, derived from the past, exactly from the second half of the '90s when the globalization caused the multinational companies, which resulted in bigger supply chains and networks. Now, it is unbelievable that these global chains can operate in a traditional way. Because of the distance, the quantity of information it is impossible to connect the members without an online, internet-based platform. When the Industry 4.0 has appeared, the IT solution potential approach to these main problems, which tools could be used in the supply chain management. It is called supply chain management 4.0.

The purpose of supply chain management 4.0 (SCM 4.0) is to integrate the whole supply chain. To reach this point, it allows using of real-time data in the information flow with the help of various online platforms and digital solutions. Thus, the members are able to respond to the changing customer needs, the fluctuating demand, and the different environmental conditions.

To adapt the SCM 4.0 into the company, it is necessary to have a strong IT infrastructure and support. Because without this technology, companies can not connect and integrate virtually.

Connection with the Logistics 4.0

It has been discussed that logistics and supply chain management have many connections points. The official definitions clearly formulate that the logistics are the part of the supply chain management that is the reason why one can not exist without the other. It means that logistics have to integrate into the supply chain management. Thus, the logistics were also developing in parallel with the industrial revolutions and todays' logistics is called Logistics 4.0 (Figure 5).

Figure 5. The digital evolution of logistics (own edited based on Frazzon et al., 2019)

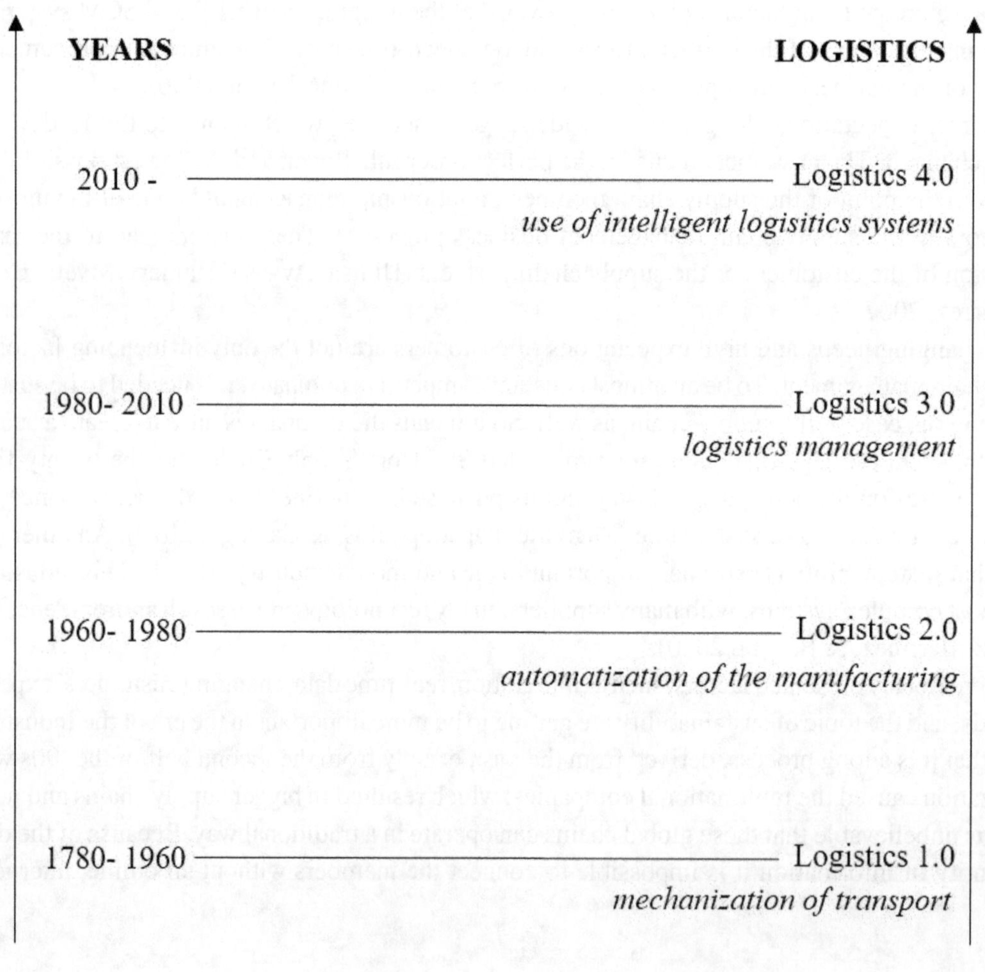

As the supply chain strives for virtual integration between chain members, logistics seeks to automate the internal processes in the company and optimize them with the use of digital solutions. These digital solutions are mainly able to share the resources and plan the use of the resources.

Thus, Logistics 4.0 coordinates the resource-sharing mechanisms, minimizes the problems of companies' internal processes, and optimizes the communication within the companies, between the different departments, as well. Resource-sharing planning is the keystone of the digitalization of logistics. Besides that, the planning includes the controlling and monitoring processes, which support the different strategical decisions.

Starting from the official definitions, it can be seen that logistics will actually be the core of supply chain management, making logistics 4.0 a major contributor to the efficient operation of supply chain management 4.0. Therefore, it is worth adopting tools from both areas to increase efficiency even more.

Smart Solutions of SCM 4.0 and Logistics 4.0

The different IT solutions of Supply Chain Management 4.0 and Logistics 4.0 strengthen the system approaches, the process-oriented approaches. The use of them supports the integration within the companies, and between the companies or the supply chain members. They allow real-time data flow, which is the reason why the information flow could be more efficient. On the other hand, the real-time data contributes to the evolving of the corporate strategy and the planning of financial and investments or the constant monitoring of the partners, suppliers.

Let's see, what are the exact tools, smart solutions of the SCM 4.0 and the Logistics 4.0. The common thing is information security. The threat of digital ages is to steal the data from online storage. That is the reason why that information security is one of the most important factors. If companies step onto the online sphere, it is needed to make an adequate protection. There are many IT company, which offers a different kind of protection. Full online protection, data protection, own protected platforms, and storage.

Supply Chain Management 4.0 is specifically focusing on electronic, online communication. The real-time data in the information flow is the most significant expectation. To companies be digital, first of all, they need a very hard IT background with the right software, and a good IT infrastructure. If it is given, it is needed to fill with some cloud-based information-sharing platforms. With the help of this, the supply chain members are able to know the real market demand and even the changes of that. Thus, the whole chain can be much more prepared to accept the changes. But because of the number of chain members, and the relatively fast-changing needs, the result is the big amount of data, which is called big data in the era of Industry 4.0.

The Internet of Things, shortly the IoT is able to handle and manage the big data and allows to stay in touch on the internet, in real-time. For the realization of the IoT system, it is needed to create another system, which is called Cyber-Physical System, or shortly the CPS. This system allows communication between the humans and machines. Thus, the key to implementing CPS is the IoT system, which includes tools, that enable humans to communicate with humans, and enable machines to communicate with machines, and also enable humans to communicate machines with the sharing of significant data.

According to a research, which is led by Szymczak (2019), cloud-based collaborative platforms, digital twinning, and automation are the best tools for creating the digital supply chains. The main advantage of the cloud-based collaborative platforms is the opportunity for real-time cooperation with real-time information-sharing. There are no wasted times, the information appears immediately on the platforms, every member of the chain sees the data and every member can work with this data without delays. The digital twin is a virtual model that simulates a physical process, service, or system. This concept uses artificial intelligence (AI), machine learning (for example, with the use of autonomous robots or cobots, which can be adapted to the environmental changes and can connect to other robots or humans), and software analytics to simulate how a device works in a given situation and later in its entire lifecycle. With the help of digital twinning, the current and the future performance of systems from design to operation can be more effectively assessed and predicted. Automation helps to eliminate human mistakes because certain processes are managed by software and some workflows are done by robots.

A very good tool for Supply Chain Management 4.0. This tool is the IT-supported CPFR, or Collaborative Planning, Forecasting, and Replenishment. This tool makes it possible for all members of the supply chain to know the selling plans, which are created by the customer needs. The information is also available on an online platform and it is editable, as well. Thus, it becomes available to be able to continuously monitor the change of demand for all supply chain members. Thereby, this tool reduces information losses and maintains a high level of customer service (Hill, Zhang, & Miller, 2018).

These tools, such as cloud-based platforms, IoT platforms are also suitable for Logistics 4.0. Logistics 4.0 offers to automate the warehousing and transportation processes. The main components of Logistics 4.0 are the resource-planning, the Warehouse Management System (WMS), the Transportation Management System (TMS) (O'Donnell, 2021).

The online resource planning allows decentralized decision-making processes. This planning software is the ERP system. With the help of a mobile application, which connects to an online ERP system, decision-makers could solve real-time problems in terms of the resource planning. It means this is the top of the smart logistics system.

WMS, the Warehouse Management System is a software, which deals with stocks. WMS manages the operations and processes, which connects to the warehousing. Within the warehouse automatizes the receiving processes, it makes it easier the positioning of the items and the conveyance of materials. Thereby, WMS can support the warehouse staff in real-time data and make the warehousing processes more efficient. To assist inventory management, WMS can integrate into the ERP system (O'Donnell, 2021).

There is another online logistics platform, which plans, executes, and optimizes the physical movements of incoming and outgoing goods. This tool is the TMS, the Transportation Management System. The tasks of the TMS are to standardize the processes, which connect to the transportation – such as it chooses the appropriate vehicles for transportation, ensuring that the necessary documents for delivery are available. Additionally, the TMS automatizes the data collection and cost tracking. TMS also tries to reduce the redundancy within the big data. It supports the WMS and is also able to integrate with the ERP system. In Hungary, from the 1st of March in the year 2021, there is a standard TMS tool, which is preferred to use in the building industry. This tool is the digital, intelligent bill of delivery. The intelligent bill of delivery is a QR code-based document, which can be used by smartphones. The QR code includes every information, which connects to the delivery, such as the name and the quantity of the delivered goods, the handling rules of the delivered goods, the destination, the time of receipt of the goods, and the customer's information. This type of bill of delivery is compatible with a digital inventory management system. This system is based on a standard goods-identification system, which includes the unified codes of the items of the building industry. Thus, this is a kind of a Warehouse Management System, which is supported by a Transportation Management System, actually, it is called the intelligent bill of delivery.

One of the most commonly used ERP systems is the SAP. SAP offers a complete system, including many modules, such as WMS, TMS, etc.

The previously presented tools show that the integration of internal processes is necessary to implement the digitalization and to be competitive. In terms of Logistics 4.0, an ERP system is needed, which could be supported with a Warehouse Management System, and a Transportation Management System.

From the point of logistics, these are the two basic processes. But it must be not forgotten, that any kind of online system is used, adequate information protection must be ensured.

To summarize the presented smart tools, Figure 6 shows the frequent types of solutions, which are offered by the Supply Chain Management 4.0 and the Logistics 4.0.

Figure 6. The frequent types of Supply Chain Management 4.0 and Logistics 4.0 tools (own edited)

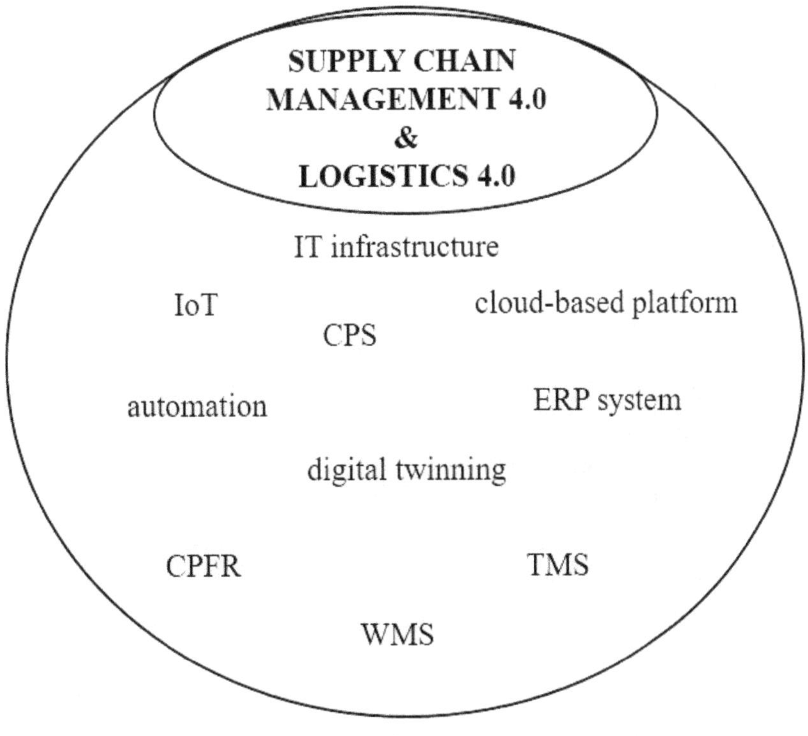

It is sure, that these solutions could help to be more competitive and more profitable. In the next chapter, the author tries to create a decision framework, which could help to identify the best fitting smart tools to the defined factors, which are reducing the performance of the supply chain coordination.

METHODOLOGY

The research is focused on solving the coordination problems, which are directly or indirectly caused by the digital era. The first purpose of the research is to define the frequent coordination problems. After it, it is necessary to get an inside view of the new IT solution, which are the effects of Industry 4.0, especially the Supply Chain Management and the Logistics 4.0. The goal is to create a decision-support system to help coordinate and define the exact IT tools for each problem.

The research is based on the literature review of supply chain coordination and the effects of Industry 4.0. Besides that, the researcher made internet-based empirical research, to get to know other practical problems and other IT solutions.

The second section of the methodology is the pairing. It means that the cognition of coordination problems and the operation mechanisms of the various IT solutions could make it possible to pair them. The researcher will define the IT solutions for the different kinds of coordination problems, as a part of a decision-support system. Managers, owners, and leaders could face with living problems of their companies, which could cause inefficient operation. On the other hand, with the help of this system, the decision-makers could calculate the investments, which are needed to implement the new IT solutions to increase the efficiency of their operations.

SOLUTIONS AND RECOMMENDATIONS

The purpose of the paper is to define one or more Supply Chain Management 4.0 or Logistics 4.0 tools to the specific problems of supply chain coordination.

First, it is needed to list the exact negative factors to be able to fit them into the possible solutions. According to the research, these factors are:

- different organizational culture;
- different product life cycle;
- problems of information-sharing;
- non-coherent goals of the members;
- delivery times mismatches;
- information flow mismatches;
- mismatches in the ordered quantities;
- replenishment times mismatches.

It is needed to complement the list with a typical digitalization-caused problem. Because the Industry 4.0 has a result, which also influences the supply chain coordination. This result is the big data. The consequence of the digital age is the increasing quantity of data. And it is hard to handle it. It is inconceivable that this data should be stored on paper, as a traditional form. Thus, big data needs an online storage. But it is not enough to store the data, it is important to be able to see the data, to be able to select the information according to the logistics principles. Because omitting this can cause errors in the information flow. Therefore, the list has plus one factor: the big data – handling problems.

As a next step, it is needed to the possible smart solutions are listed. Including but not limited to the most important and most frequently used tools are listed:

- modern IT infrastructure;
- cloud-based collaborative online platform;
- Internet of Things platform (IoT);
- Cyber-Physical System (CPS);
- information security;
- automation;

- digital twinning;
- Collaborative Planning, Forecasting and Replenishment (CPFR);
- Enterprise Resource Planning systems (ERP);
- Warehouse Management System (WMS);
- Transportation Management System (TMS).

To visualize the problem, the house of digital supply chain management and logistics are represented in Figure 7.

Figure 7. The possible structure of the SCM 4.0 and Logistics 4.0 (own edited)

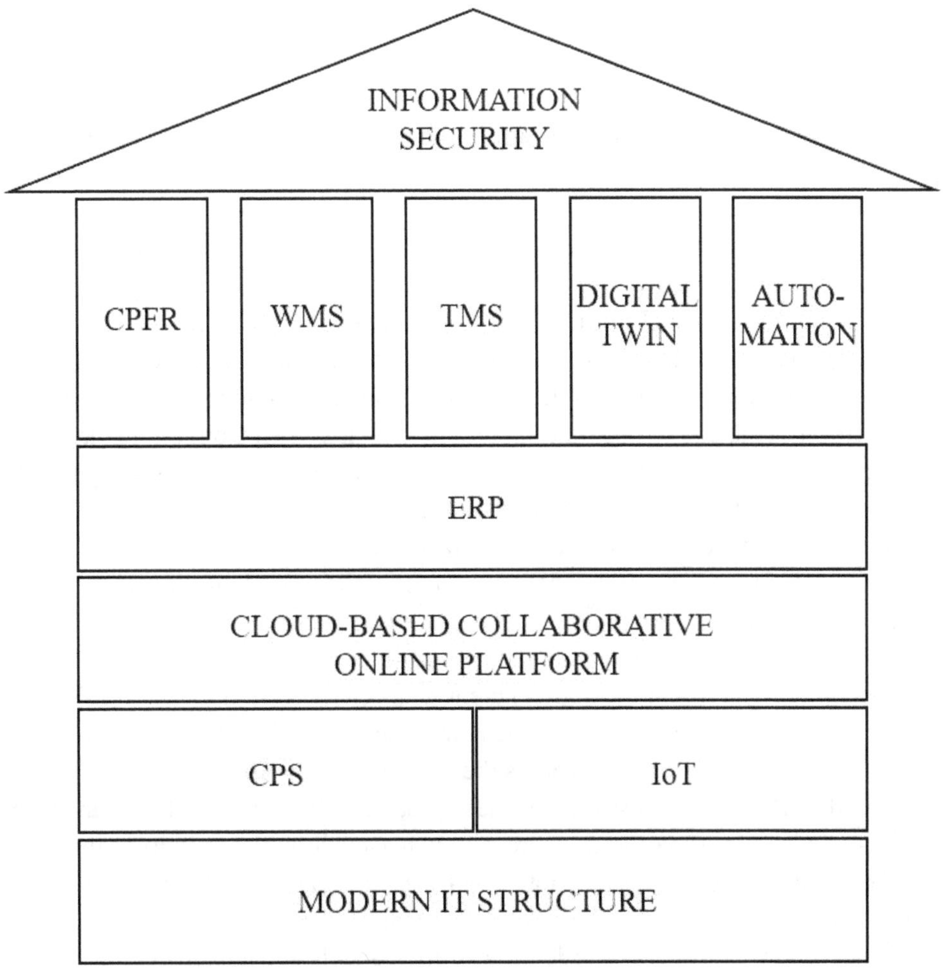

According to the research, the most important and essential thing is to companies have a modern IT structure. This is the root of the structure, the fundament of the house. Without this, companies can not be digitalized. The modern IT structure allows to make a Cyber-Physical System (CPS) and use the Internet of Things (IoT). If companies have these systems, they can step into the digital world – cloud-based platforms for the internal and external processes. In the case of internal processes, the information flow and the information-sharing mechanisms between the departments can be efficient. The digitalized external processes can make the communication and also information-sharing more easier. The ERP system concentrates on the external processes, but it allows the management of the relationships (for example in the case of vendor-managed inventory). There are many tools, which can integrate into the ERP systems, the house represents the most frequently used ones, such as the Collaborative Planning, Forecasting, and Replenishment (CPFR), the Warehouse Management System (WMS), the Transportation Management System (TMS), the digital twinning or the automation, which is extending to the automatic information processing or the automatic manufacturing or the topic of using robots. In the digital age, and for the companies, which are using the digital solutions, the most important thing is to secure their data. That is the reason why the information security is the rooftop of the house.

If these elements are ready, companies can make their own house. It is sure, that these elements help to make the supply chain coordination more efficient, but the purpose of the paper is to fit the determined obstructive factors of supply chain coordination to the various tools of Supply Chain Management 4.0 and Logistics 4.0.

Different organizational culture includes some soft factors. It means, that the culture is based on behaviors, habits, etc., which can not make it exact. The culture can determine the company's attitudes, which can influence the information-sharing mechanisms. But, if there is a system, which connects these companies, it can help to standardize the processes. In other words, the culture will not influence the information flow anymore, because it will be led by a system, without feelings. The system is programmed to select significant information, make orders, etc. Thus, automation can be the solution. It is also a good opportunity if companies integrate their ERP systems. Thus, cultural differences can be eliminated.

To handle the different product life cycles, companies of the whole supply chain need to be integrated. Every member needs to be prepared if a product is withdrawn from the market and a new one has appeared. The Collaborative Planning, Forecasting and Replenishment, or shortly the CPFR is able to monitor the products lifecycle and allows to get real-time information about the selling. And from the selling information, the product life cycles become traceable.

Non-coherent goals of members are the root of the coordination problems. It excludes the satisfactory level of cooperation and it causes other problems. For example, because companies have no common goals, they will compete with each other. To maintain their competitive advantage, they will not share certain kinds of information. It means, that the non-coherent goals can lead to information-sharing problems, as well. These problems can be solved with the help of integrated ERP systems or a collaborative online platform, but it is a more complex thing. That is the reason why, the ERP systems or the collaborative online, cloud-based platforms only just support these problems, but do not solve them absolutely.

The mismatches of the information flow are also manageable with the help of the previously discussed tools. The cloud-based platforms allow real-time information exchange, which is resulting in lower response times.

The mismatches of delivery times, the ordered quantities, and the replenishment times can be managed together in terms of digital solutions. These factors are typically the responsibility of the logistics. Thus, the tools of logistics 4.0 are compatible to help to eliminate these factors. It means, that an integrated ERP system, which includes the Warehouse Management System and the Transportation Management System can manage the whole internal logistics processes. Another good solution can be the Collaborative Planning, Forecasting and Replenishment, or the CPFR. The delivery times and the replenishment times may belong to the distribution logistics, as well. Thus, the final products' delivery times can be adjusted to the customers' needs. And the replenishment times of the distribution centers, or the warehouses of distribution centers can be also adjusted to demand. That is the reason why the CPFR can be useful for the companies if they have problems with the delivery of the replenishment times.

Figure 8 represents the suggestions, which include the determined problems of supply chain coordination and the recommended tools of Supply Chain Management 4.0 and Logistics 4.0 to solve the problems.

Figure 8. A possible solution to increasing the efficiency of the supply chain coordination with the help of the digital solutions (own edited)

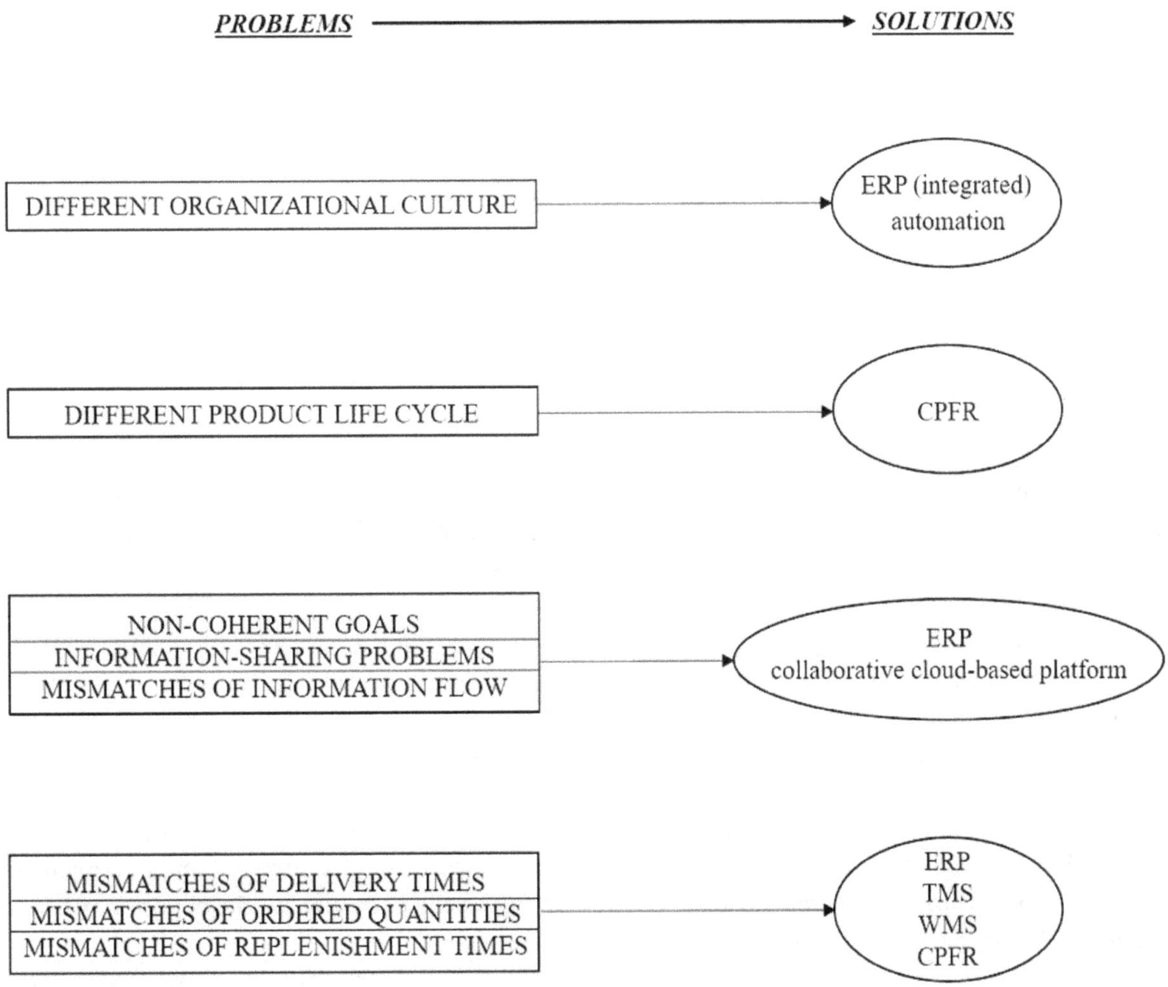

The model has limitations, of course, which limitations determine the future research directions.

FUTURE RESEARCH DIRECTIONS

The main limitation of the decision-support system is the simple pairing. It can be worth it if companies could rank their coordination problems. With the help of this ranking, researchers could define weights, and a more complex model (for example, an AHP) could be created. Because it is not sure, that only one problem appears in the life of a company. The problem could be complicated. There are IT tools, which handle more problems than only one, but the company can be disposed to make more investments, to buy the appropriate software or IT background. That is the reason why an AHP can define the most important factors, and it can simplify the decision. An investment-cost analysis could help to realize, which solution or solutions can be reachable for the company. Thus, as a supplement of the decision-support system, a cost-analysis can be also needed.

On the other hand, a more up-to-date empirical background should be useful to define new coordination problems. It may be worth making an empirical analysis, which will be focused on what can be the new kind of problems, which are caused by the new digital age. It is probable, that the determined influencing factors of supply chain coordination are still existing, but new problems may also have emerged. The first step of future research is to determine these new problems if they exist at all.

The development of the IT sector is always resulting in new and newer solutions. That is the reason why technological changes must be constantly monitored, because another solution may make the operation of the company even more efficient. Thus, the paper presented the frequent types of the smart solutions but not all. An extended review may be also useful for the companies.

The lifting of these limitations can be the basis of future research.

CONCLUSION

Time is changing and with these changes, the business sphere, the environment of companies are also changing. Some sectors, such as IT is developing rapidly, which includes many opportunities. The opportunities are not limited to the new technologies of manufacturing, robotics, or process automation; the chances to use the online space, cloud-based platforms, or some new software, which help to be virtual and digitalized is also contained by the development, which development is called the Industry 4.0.

This model, which is presented by the paper emphasizes the importance of using the smart tools, focusing on the digital solution and tools of Supply Chain Management 4.0 and the Logistics 4.0. Digitalization is an unavoidable thing. There are many other tools, for example, the various management tools to handle the problems of supply chain coordination. But the digitalization supports all of these tools and offers others. It means, they can complement each other and digital tools can provide a basis for the application of individual management tools. Thus, if the company has the infrastructure to implement the digital tools, it can have competitive advantages. However, the company has the opportunity to use a smart solution for the problems they have.

Figure 1 shows market-leader multinational companies, which use some interesting smart tools. There must be a connection between the fact, that these companies are both successful and all of them use some smart technology. Because all of these technologies make the operation easier with decrease some of the obstructive factors of supply chain coordination. The obstructive factors or the frequent problems of supply chain coordination are also determined by the paper. These factors degrade the performance not only in the case of the individual members, but the whole supply chain's performance will fall, as well. That is exactly why an important topic the supply chain coordination.

On the other hand, companies are physically far away from each other. The different types of supply chain members, such as the suppliers, the manufacturers, the distribution centers, the wholesalers, the retailers, and sometimes the final customers themselves are on another continent, or at least in another country. The best solution is to stay in touch in the online space. But for this, it is needed to have the IT structure to run the right software and programs. With the help of this, real-time exchange of data is available, which improves the quality of the information flow. This is the essential condition for proper cooperation.

Digitalization seeks into the supply chain management, as well. It influences and tries to digitalize the internal processes, from which the tools of Logistics 4.0 have evolved. These tools focus on the companies' logistics system, which means, that an ERP system is suggested to integrate the different departments of the companies. But Logistics 4.0 went beyond that. It automates manufacturing, creates robots and cobots, automates the processes of warehousing, transporting. Thereby also minimizing the mistakes made by man. Supply Chain Management 4.0 offers various types of online communication forms, whose purpose is to members are able to react to the changes in each other's needs as quickly as possible. Cloud-based online platforms allow real-time communication and help the Collaborative Planning, Forecasting, and Replenishment, or the CPFR. Digital twinning, as a new design tool, allows simulating the existing and the new processes in virtual reality. This tool can help to recognize the problems in the processes sooner than they appeared.

But it is all based on a modern IT structure that allows the communication between people and machines, which is called Cyber-Physical System, in shortly CPS. Only in the presence of this can allow the use of the Internet of Things or the IoT tools. If these tools are available in the company's toolbox, and they are ready to be built, the house of digital supply chain management and logistics can be founded.

Thus, the decision-support model, which is created by the paper can help companies to face the coordination problems of their relationships and recommend some new Supply Chain Management and Logistics 4.0 tools to make their operation more efficient. Two advantages are realized in the paper for the managers: it contains the structured summarization of the frequency coordination problems; it also totalizes the new IT tools, especially focused on the Supply Chain Management and Logistics 4.0, which can directly influence the coordination positively; and it shows how do the different tools help to solve the coordination problems. This decision-support system can be the base of the investments-decision, managers can decide that is it worth investing in new software or machine.

But one thing is a fix: in the 21st century, companies have to step into the digital world. If they do not do that, they can suffer from the disadvantages, because they will be out of the development, and they can be fallback from the other chain members. But it can decrease the efficient operation of the whole chain, and that is the reason why it is an important topic in terms of supply chain management and supply chain coordination.

Therefore, supply chain members and all companies have to recognize, that the digitalization and the use of the tools of Supply Chain Management 4.0 is not just an opportunity, it is a need.

REFERENCES

Arshinder, A. K., & Deshmukh, S. G. (2008). Supply chain coordination: Perpectives, empirical studies and research directions. *International Journal of Production Economics, 115*(2), 316–335. doi:10.1016/j.ijpe.2008.05.011

Bock, C. (2018). *Supply Chain Planning 4.0.* Retrieved on October 20, 2021 from https://www.rolandberger.com/publications/publication_pdf/roland_berger_supply_chain_planning.pdf

Brettel, M., Friederichsen, N., Keller, M., & Rosenberg, M. (2014). How virtualization, decentralization and network building change the manufacturing landscape: An Industry 4.0 Perspective. *International Journal of Mechanical. Industrial Science and Engineering*, *8*(1), 37–44. doi:10.5281/zenodo.1336426

Chandak, S., Chandak, A., & Sharma, A. (2014). Globalisation of Supply Chain Management for an Automotive Industry-future Perspective. *International Review of Applied Engineering Research*, *4*(2), 155–164.

Christopher, M. (2005). *Logistics and supply chain management: Creating value-adding networks*. Prentice Hall.

Constantino, F., Di Gravio, G., Shaban, A., & Tronci, M. (2013). Exploring the Bullwhip Effect and Inventory Stability in a Seasonal Supply Chain. *International Journal of Engineering Business Management*, *5*, 23. Advance online publication. doi:10.5772/56833

Corallo, A., Latino, M. E., Menegoli, M., & Pontradolfo, P. (2020). A systematic literature review to explore traceability and lifecycle relationship. *International Journal of Production Research*, *58*(15), 4789–4807. doi:10.1080/00207543.2020.1771455

CSCMP. (2017). *Bylaws*. Retreived on October 25, 2021 from https://cscmp.org/CSCMP/Connect/Form_a_Roundtable_.aspx?WebsiteKey=0b3f453d-bd90-4121-83cf-172a90b226a9

Dai, H., Tseng, M. M., & Zipkin, P. H. (2015). Design of traceability systems for product recall. *International Journal of Production Research*, *53*(2), 511–531. doi:10.1080/00207543.2014.955922

Frazzon, E. M., Rodriguez, C. M. T., Pereira, M. M., Pires, M. C., & Uhlmann, I. (2019). Towards Supply Chain Management 4.0. *Brazilian Journal of Operations & Production Management*, *16*(2), 180–191. doi:10.14488/BJOPM.2019.v16.n2.a2

Gelei, A. (2003). Az ellátási lánc típusai és menedzsment kérdései. *Vezetéstudomány*, *34*, 24–34.

Gupta, D., & Weerawat, W. (2006). Supplier-manufacturer coordination in capacitated two-stage supply chains. *European Journal of Operational Research*, *175*(1), 67–89. doi:10.1016/j.ejor.2005.04.021

Heynitz, H. V., Bremicker, M., Amadori, D. M., & Reschke, K. (2016). *The factory of future*. KMPG AG. Retrieved on October 29, 2021 from https://assets.kpmg/content/dam/kpmg/es/pdf/2017/06/the-factory-of-the-future.pdf

Hill, C. A., Zhang, G. P., & Miller, K. E. (2018). Collaborative planning, forecasting, and replenishment & firm performance: An empirical evaluation. *International Journal of Production Economics*, *196*, 12–23. doi:10.1016/j.ijpe.2017.11.012

Hintsa, J., Ayyash, F. A., Hameri, A.-P., Myers, P., Coulibaly, N., & Gutierrez, X. (2007). *The 21st Century Supply Chain Model*. Technical Report, WCO Council Meeting.

Kaipia, R. (2007). *Supply Chain Coordination – Studies on planning and information sharing mechanisms*. Helsinki University of Technology Laboratory of Industrial Management Doctoral dissertation series 2007 / 2.

Koh, S. C. L., Saad, S., & Arunachalam, S. (2006). Competing in the 21st century supply chain through supply chain management and enterprise resource planning integration. *International Journal of Physical Distribution & Logistics Management*, *36*(6), 455–465. doi:10.1108/09600030610677401

Manville, G., Papadopoulos, T., & Garengo, P. (2019). Twenty-first century supply chain management: A multiple case study analysis within the UK aerospace industry. *Total Quality Management & Business Excellence*, *32*(7-8), 869–885. doi:10.1080/14783363.2019.1642101

Marucheck, A., Greis, N., Mena, C., & Cai, L. (2011). Product safety and security in the global supply chain: Issues, challenges and research opportunities. *Journal of Operations Management*, *29*(7-8), 707–720. doi:10.1016/j.jom.2011.06.007

Nagy, J. (2006). *The attitude of Hungarian companies to the concept of supply chain management. 15th Annual IPSERA Conference*, San Diego, CA.

O'Donnell, J. (2021). *Definition – How supply chain systems process orders*. Retrieved on February 15, 2021 from https://searcherp.techtarget.com/definition/warehouse-management-system-WMS

Ramirez-Peña, M., Mayuet, P. F., Vazquez-Martinez, J., & Batista, M. (2020). Sustainability in the Aerospace, Naval, and Automotive Supply Chain 4.0: Descriptive Review. *Materials (Basel)*, *13*(24), 5625–5649. doi:10.3390/ma13245625 PMID:33321743

Szymczak, M. (2019). Digital Smart Logistics. Managing Supply Chain 4.0: Concepts, Components and Strategic Perspective. In Z. Bekirogullari (Ed.), *The European Proceedings of Social & Behavioural Sciences* (pp. 357–368). Future Academy. doi:10.15405/epsbs.2019.10.02.33

Vidorvá, Z. (2020). Supply chain management in the aspect of globalization. In *SHS Web of Conferences. Globalization and its Socio-Economic Consequences 2019* (vol. 74, pp. 1-10). 10.1051hsconf/20207404031

Wang, S., Wan, J., Li, D., & Zhang, C. (2016). Implementing smart factory factory of industrie 4.0: An outlook. *International Journal of Distributed Sensor Networks*, *12*(1), 3159805. doi:10.1155/2016/3159805

Yin, X. (2021). Measuring the bullwhip effect with market competition among retailers: A simulation study. *Computers & Operations Research*, *132*(2), 105341. doi:10.1016/j.cor.2021.105341

Chapter 3
Supply Chain and Digital Transformation in Japan

Sergei Shaposhnikov
Higher School of Economics, National Research University, Russia

Anna Veselova
https://orcid.org/0000-0002-8538-4757
Higher School of Economics, National Research University, Russia

ABSTRACT

Geopolitical risks, business globalization, increasing complexity of transactions have required companies to adapt to changes. This chapter examines the digital transformation of supply chains and digitalization challenges in Japan. Many companies seem to realize the importance of digital transformation; however, on their way to digitalization companies face numerous challenges like a shortage of human and financial resources, a lack of awareness and understanding of digital transformation processes, etc. Moreover, Japanese culture does not easily fit digital transformation which also slows down the pace of transformation. As a result, the supply chain processes in the Japanese manufacturing companies remain old-fashioned, fragmented, siloed, with a lack of global vision and proper understanding of potential risks. To meet the needs of diverse customers, ensure global supply, and compete in uncertain environment, the SCM of Japanese companies has to be digitally upgraded and become more complex to achieve end-to-end supply chain optimization and an advanced decision-making.

INTRODUCTION

Geopolitical risks, business globalization, increasing complexity of transactions have required companies to adapt to changes. In addition, the future is less predictable and in a rapidly changing business environment it is important to become more reactive to changes in supply chain, global procurement, and purchasing operations to maintain competitive advantage. It is essential to build resilient processes that can respond to crises. As companies are operating not in isolation but in interaction with their external environment, the way how they approach the new calls originated both in the external and internal

DOI: 10.4018/978-1-7998-9715-6.ch003

Copyright © 2022, IGI Global. Copying or distributing in print or electronic forms without written permission of IGI Global is prohibited.

environments determines their success. The importance of the context of operations and the specificity of inherent organizational culture is crucial; hence, unique context provides valuable insights for both theory and practice of digital transformation. This chapter examines the digital transformation of supply chain management in Japanese companies. Japanese context is interesting and worthy studying as Japan is used to be a motherland for the most advanced and efficient companies which nowadays feel threatened due to their inability to quickly adapt to changing environment. Moreover, Japan has unique cultural traditions that impact organizational routines and processes, as well as relationships with partners within supply chains. After clarifying the need for a digital transformation in Japan, the chapter discusses the main challenges of supply chain management digitalization and provides illustrative cases of Japanese companies that respond to these challenges through the introduction of digital solutions.

BACKGROUND

The new reality is characterized by a complex, dynamic environment, highly competitive business conditions and digitalization. Digital transformation as the highest level of digitalization is an emerging phenomenon that affects many aspects of life. Today, more and more attention is paid to supply chain management (SCM) to enhance the competitive advantage of enterprises, effectively control costs, and achieve customer satisfaction. SCM is essential for manufacturing companies to gain a competitive advantage through maximizing customer value (Christopher, 2016; Kamath, 2016). SCM has emerged as a cornerstone of manufacturing and has become one of the most important means for manufacturing companies to gain a competitive advantage (Rusli, Rahman, Ho, & Abdullah, 2013).

Supply chain processes are heavily influenced by digitalization. Digital transformation is pushing companies to become agile to quickly identify, respond and adapt to changing expectations and demands of consumers, employees, and other elements of business environment. It became obvious that the shift from a traditional supply chain to a digital supply chain appears as a competitive advantage creating sustainable value for organizations (Ageron, Bentahar, & Gunasekaran, 2020). Supply chain digital transformation is proven to drive growth, mitigate risk, and optimize costs (Gartner, 2020). Several industrial reports have introduced a digital transformation as an important trend for supply chain management in the next five years.

Traditionally, in supply chain raw materials are sourced and products are manufactured in one or more factories, shipped to warehouses for storage, and then delivered to retailers or end customers. Therefore, an effective supply chain strategy considers interactions at different levels of a supply chain and requires reducing costs and improving service levels. Consumers' expectations are growing, and their loyalty and support are volatile and difficult to secure, hence, companies must encourage innovations and embrace new realities imposed by digitalization. In addition, challenges related to natural disasters also affect supply chains and should be considered in the context of Japanese business.

Japan is currently ranked as the world's third-largest economy, but it has seen negative growth in total factor productivity in recent years. Moreover, Japan is ranked 28th in the Global Digital Competitiveness Index in 2021 which is five positions lower than in 2015 (IMD, 2021). Among Asian countries, Japan is ranked 7th in digital competitiveness, behind Hong Kong, Singapore, Taiwan, South Korea, China, and Malaysia. The effect of relatively low digital competitiveness is evident in industries such as e-commerce, telemedicine, mobile banking, and advanced digital manufacturing. In the past, Japanese manufacturing and high-tech industries were extremely competitive due to high quality as a differentiating factor, that was possible due to the concentration of know-hows through vertically integrated production systems, a typical characteristic of Japanese companies, and the industriousness of the Japanese people. Since 2000, however, almost zero growth has been witnessed. The main reason is that they have failed to abandon their faith in quality and have been slow to respond to the changes in the business environment brought about by digitalization. The result is that Japanese companies have lagged behind in digital transformation. The current momentum will not allow Japan to remain in the third place in the ranking of economies, as Japan's digital competitiveness regresses. As digital competitiveness and productivity are inextricably linked, digital transformation in Japan is no longer a choice but an imperative. Amidst a shrinking population, digital transformation is providing the way for renewed productivity growth in Japan, as well as a national perception of global leadership and competitiveness.

To implement digital transformation is not just about digitalization, but also about realizing digital processes that match business processes and improve efficiency and productivity. For Japanese companies' internationalization on the global markets and digital transformation could help to achieve flexibly and higher speed of respond to various changes, such as changes in social conditions, amendments to legal systems, and expansion and diversification of business partners. Digital transformation is a foundation and a challenge for companies aiming for sustainable management these days. This is especially true in the supply chain management of Japanese companies, where old-fashioned instruments of management, accounting, and control are still widely in use. Despite these challenges, Japanese companies are showing some complacency and not willing to change their approach to quality assurance, hence, digital transformation is delayed.

FROM DIGITIZATION TO DIGITAL TRANSFORMATION

The world is in the transition to the "fourth industrial revolution" driven by disruptive innovations such as the IoT, big data and artificial intelligence. The notion of "digital transformation" (DX) is frequently used as the ability of companies to use digital technologies to transform their organizations and business models, and to radically change the way they deliver value. Despite the growing interest in innovative digital technologies and the recognition of their competitive necessity, the extent of their integration into the supply chains of companies differ. Some of them are quite digitally advanced and have significantly restructured their processes to benefit from digital solutions, while others are yet on the very initial stages of digital technologies integration. Thus, the traditional path involves three consequent stages that varies in terms of the extent of digitalization.

- *Digitization* that can be defined as a technical process of converting analog signals into a digital form, and ultimately into binary digits (Tilson, Lyytinen, & Sorensen, 2010) and refers to the changes in processes resulted from increased use of digital equipment.
- *Digitalization* that enables positive shifts in a company's innovation, efficacy, sustainability, pricing strategy and directly affects the global value chains (Loebbecke & Picot, 2015; Yang, Fu, & Zhang, 2021). It has a direct effect on the competitiveness of the business and its prominent development (Leao & da Silva, 2021). Digital innovations could stimulate new forms of cooperation between companies and more intensified and integrated relationships with customers and employees (Rachinger, Rauter, Müller, Vorraber, & Schirgi, 2018). The digitalization involves implementing advanced digital technologies like online trading, blockchain, internet of things (IoT),

5G, digital currencies, cloud computing, artificial intelligence (AI), serverless computing, 3D printing, quantum computing, machine learning, natural language processing, lager data analysis, robotics, virtual and augmented reality (Lee & Trim, 2020). In essence, digitalization helps to facilitate a real-time sharing of information within a supply chain that strives for further data-based decision-making. The relevance of digital technologies for a company's supply chains is growing due to the increased dispersion of manufacturing facilities, higher customer engagement, higher expectations for agility and responsiveness as top priorities (Deepu & Ravi, 2021).

- *Digital transformation* that stimulates additional value generation in supply chains through higher process efficiency (e.g., costs reduction, shorter cycle time, higher productivity). Among other effects, it is observed to encourage collaborative arrangements for value creation and decrease resource constraints for entrepreneurial activities (Nambisan, 2017; Oliveira, Fleury, & Fleury, 2021). Stolterman and Fors (2004) present "digital transformation" as an idea of ever-evolving technology that will enrich people's lives; in other words, it transforms people's lives for the better by infusing them with advanced digital technologies. However, DX is not just about transformation, it is about digital disruption - a revolutionary innovation that upends existing values and frameworks. DX is an organizational change that uses digital technologies to materially improve performance (Marchand & Wade, 2014), restructure economies, institutions and society on a system level (Brennen & Kreiss, 2016; Unruh & Kiron, 2017).

Since the positive impact of digital transformation on supply chains' efficiency, innovation and sustainability is hardly questioned, a supply chain structure might be threatened by dramatic changes. The integration of advanced digital technologies may require transformation and significant restructuring when companies must rethink their operational processes, controlling rules, and coordination of functions. It is just a beginning of an inevitable process of transition from digitalization to digital transformation of Japanese businesses and their supply chains. On this way of transformation there are numerous challenges which do not allow digital transformation to take roots on a large scale in Japan.

The Evolution of Supply Chain Management in Japan

Since the late 1980s, Japan has become heavily dependent on overseas production, so called, *kudoka* (hollow-out due to offshoring). In the last decades, more than 50% of Japanese manufacturing has been located abroad, mainly in China, ASEAN countries, the United States and Europe (Dharish, 2020). This experience of Japan's integration into the global production network allowed Japanese companies to expand their supply chains to meet and serve new domestic markets. In this pre-COVID era, a global division of labor (global value chain) was formed, and the activities of Japanese companies were based on the premise of supply chains that were constructed across national borders. During that period, China's rapid rise in the global market caused a wide range of conflicts (decoupling) with the United States, including trade, technology, economic security, and personnel exchanges, that resulted in the fragmentation of supply chains on the global scale. All of those had a major impact on the activities of Japanese companies closely connected to China.

In 2011, Japanese domestic production was severely damaged by the impact of natural disasters when the supply chains of Japanese car and electronics manufacturers were destroyed by the massive flooding in Thailand which occurred only several months after the Great East Japan Earthquake. During that time, assembly plants in Thailand were closed which led to significant components shortages and a fall in the Japanese companies' share prices. The supply of petrochemical complexes, mainly used in the manufacturing of semiconductors, was also disrupted. The disruptions in supply chains also damaged local transportation systems and reduced Japanese manufacturing exports around the world.

The global outbreak of the COVID in 2020 led to the restrictions on the transfers of people and goods between countries. The inactivity in the flows of people and distribution of goods increased the disruption of supply chains on a global scale. In response to this fragmentation, Japanese companies began to relocate production bases that were previously established in China to third countries or return them to Japan. According to a survey by the Development Bank of Japan (DBJ, 2020), companies took steps to review their supply chains, including diversification of suppliers, standardization of products and parts, and strengthening mutual assistance systems with other companies.

The latest "White Paper on Manufacturing Industries" prepared annually by the METI of Japan reports the vision of the current situation by the government and states the importance of digital transformation and data utilization in the manufacturing industry (METI, 2020). In 2018, METI published a report on digital transformation that pointed out significant challenges on the long way of Japanese business towards real DX (METI, 2018) which can bring Japan to, so-called, "The 2025 Digital Cliff". The 2025 Digital Cliff can cause a large economic loss after 2025 due to the low competitiveness of Japanese business. The report predicts that a decline in competitiveness will result in the annual economic loss of around 12 trillion yen per year (about USD 105 billion) after 2025. DX has the potential to improve productivity in supply chains, and many companies seem to realize its importance, however, on the way of digital transformation Japanese business faces numerous challenges that slows down its pace.

There is an increasing focus on the digital transformation of supply chains which is at the heart of the manufacturing industry. Some of the most advanced companies in the world have clearly defined DX of their supply chains as a tool to increase their competitiveness. On the other hand, in the Japanese manufacturing industry the pace of implementation has not been fast enough, and many companies, even recognizing the need, have not yet implemented extensive initiatives. In essence, SCM is the control of the gap between supply and demand, though the term "supply chain" tends to make us think of the supply side, but the demand is the starting point of the process. Demand is not constant; changes create a gap between supply and demand and SCM aims to control a series of processes to respond to changes and eliminate that gap. Therefore, it is important to communicate the "data" from both sides quickly and reliably to make the right decisions.

Until now, most of the SCM initiatives in the Japanese manufacturing industry have focused on improving the efficiency of each department on the shop floor, prioritizing the operational efficiency of their organizations and areas of execution. Although there is a cost reduction effect by maintaining stable quality and improving efficiency, the result is individual optimization rather that the total one. Within such approach each supply chain member has its own strategy to achieve efficiency. However, what is the best for one supply chain member, may not work at all for another member. The more interconnected the partners are, the more serious consequences could be caused by one member's inefficiency for another member's operations or even for the whole supply chain (Liang, Yang, Cook, & Zhu, 2006).
The digitalization of SCM in Japan went through several stages:

- **From the 1980s to early 2000s**, Japanese companies tended to reduce fixed costs by making operations more efficient, reducing the number of people, automating processes, and reducing wasted inventory. As a starting point, demand forecasting was done automatically and without human contribution, IT systems were often used to provide the engine for automatic calculations. In practice, however, it was difficult to adjust supply and demand as IT was used fragmentedly. As a result, it was difficult to cope with changes and it did not lead to the automation that was initially aimed.

- **From the mid-2000s to the mid-2010s**, Japanese companies began to place greater emphasis on human decision-making, rather than rely completely on logic-based automation. It was also the period when the decision-making process, previously based on quantity alone, began to consider profitability or value. The advancement in IT systems made it possible to quickly simulate human decision-making and evaluate the results in monetary terms rather than just in terms of quantity (SCP[1]/S&OP[2] tools). However, many Japanese companies didn't introduce such SCP/S&OP tools and continued to use spreadsheets. As a result, the data required for decision-making was siloed and not fully utilized, keeping the SCM process quite inefficient. As a result, SCM in the Japanese manufacturing industry stayed old-fashioned, fragmented, a shop flow efficiency-oriented with a lack of global vision and potential risk assessment (Shishido, 2021).
- **From mid-2010 to nowadays**, Japanese companies started to look at IoT, cloud computing, AI, machine learning, natural language processing, larger data analysis, virtual and augmented reality, etc. to transform their supply chains and achieve higher competitiveness and flexibility.

However, it should be admitted that the digital transformation in Japan is delayed and "lagging behind" in comparison to Europe and the United States. The digitalization of many Japanese companies is still limited to basic IT solutions for improving operational efficiency, in contrast to Western companies where digital transformation is a transformation of business models (IPA, 2020). This backlog in introducing and scaling of digital solutions within Japanese companies is related to low awareness of top management about DX and a deficit of communication between business units. Considering that in Japanese companies, 80% of IT-related costs are used for the maintenance of the complicated existing systems, if a company postpones the introduction of a new system and continues to use the existing system, it will become extremely costly in a long-run perspective (METI, 2019).

Cultural Specificity of Japanese Business

Business culture in Japan tends to be a high-context one, when a preference is given to subtle communication, prioritizing interpersonal relationships, group harmony and consensus, rather than making quick decisions and changes that can disrupt the work environment and potentially separate parties. The diligence, perfectionism and uncertainty avoidance are also in the national character of Japanese managers.

Moreover, because of the high importance of trust, which is often prioritized in decision making, there is an internal resistance to taking risks that could potentially break trust; for example, a failed attempt to implement a new technology that could break the trust of a company's stakeholders, or a data breach that could break a customer' trust. Additionally, strong relations are based on trust and loyalty between business entities and people stimulate companies to rely on vendors to deploy and operate digital transformation. As a vendor provides digital tools as requested, it is often the case that the know-hows related to data utilization are not transferred to a client. For the digital transformation to be successful, employees must adopt and master the IT solutions that suit the purpose of each company. However, if a company relies on vendors, employees will not have the opportunity to learn about IT solutions, and it is difficult to develop human resources able to handle digital transformation (KDDI, 2021).

These contextual constrains on digital transformation make Japanese companies reluctant to introduce new technologies if there are any concerns about immediate difficulties in accepting new technologies and contribute to a system that inherently cannot adopt the type of management system needed for digital transformation, a system that requires for empowered teams, agile execution, test-and-learn thinking, a risk-taking with the prospect of leadership in the new space, and an acceptance of failures as an investment in innovation to accelerate long-term growth.

Traditional Japanese companies are gradually diversifying, but there are still relatively few outsiders to join the workforce, and the seniority system tends to persist. Since many employees have never changed jobs their thinking is homogeneous, creating a culture in which the company's past successes and standardized processes are shared as a common language. In this environment changes are hardly possible. The average age of executives in Japan has steadily increased since 1990 having reached 59.9 years by 2020 (McKinsey, 2021). Influential senior executives are unprepared or unable to change business models, organizational structures, and processes in response to technological change and transformations in consumer demand.

In some companies digital literacy tends to be low due to limited in-house digital talent. In such an environment it is very difficult for externally hired digital experts to make changes. Without a strong commitment from the top of the organization, it is almost impossible for externally recruited experts to drive the organization and transform the core processes of the existing business model. As a result, such experts often end up promoting digitization on a very limited scope.

Japanese companies typically lack digital talents because they have traditionally outsourced their IT operations (IPA, 2020). Engineers and designers are not the only ones needed to achieve digital transformation; those who play the role of "producer" and can create and run actual business processes based on technology are also indispensable. Another problem is that specialists who can manage existing systems are aging.

Internal curbs appear when a company employs a digital leader to initiate digital transformation and not able to obtain buy-in from the heads of business units. The importance of digital transformation can be accepted but there is no willingness to change their approach or pay much attention to steps to be taken to initiate this transformation. In addition, young leaders do not understand the dynamics required to mobilize a Japanese organization (McKinsey, 2021).

Some Steps for More Efficient and Digitalized Supply Chains in Japan

Globalization and the Need for Higher Visibility

Globalization and digitalization are changing various elements of supply chains: suppliers, sub-contractors, consumers, as well as the ways they are linked with each other. Globalization increases competitive pressure in supply chains and requires solutions that can provide strategic benefits for a focal company and the whole supply chain. To get an access to global production networks and build stable relationships with foreign partners, companies must co-align their practices with the ones shared in the network. In this regard, digitalization stimulates integration and visibility in the global supply chains that help to interconnect geographically dispersed members of the supply chain (Koberg & Longoni, 2019; Prater, Frazier, & Reyes, 2005; Ryan, Buciuni, Giblin, & Andersson, 2022; Van der Zee & Van der Vorst, 2005; Wang, Pan, Wang, & Zhou, 2020).

Many Japanese companies are finding it increasingly difficult to build their supply chains solely with Japanese companies. Japan is facing many challenges, including a shortage of labor due to a low birth rate, an aging population, and the rise of emerging economies. Therefore, it is important to build an optimal supply chain on a global level to maintain competitiveness. However, to be able to manage a global supply chain effectively, there is a need to have an understanding of a real time status of key process which makes a call for higher visibility of the entire supply chain.

Until recently the concept of visibility of supply chains has been under-investigated and used interchangeably with information sharing (Swaminathan & Tayur, 2003). However, they are not the same: information sharing is an activity, while visibility is a potential outcome of such activity. Supply chain visibility is "the extent to which actors within a supply chain have access to or share information which they consider key or useful to their operations and which they consider will be of mutual benefit" (Barratt & Oke, 2007). Supply chain visibility improves supply chain responsiveness (Berry, Towill, & Wadsley, 1994), improves planning and replenishment capabilities (Mentzer, Min, & Bobbitt, 2004), decision-making (Kent & Mentzer, 2003), quality of products (Armistead & Mapes, 1993). The most apparent areas that usually require higher visibility include 'real' demand control (Barratt & Oliveira, 2001), a customer's inventory control (Petersen, Ragatz, & Monczka, 2005), process visibility (Van der Zee & Van der Vorst, 2005), and products movement along the supply chain (Prater et al., 2005). To optimize the supply chain, there is a need to visualize the status of each process.

A typical Japanese sales company collects data on actual performance and external conditions via email and telephone and compiles them into a spreadsheet file which is used to plan sales, inventory and purchasing. As the data required for planning is collected via email and telephone, the time to collect and compile the data into a spreadsheet is significant and does not allow the other, more important tasks of planning, to be adequately performed. On the other hand, the factory receives purchase requests from the sales company, but does not know actual results, sales plans, and inventory plans behind the requests. Therefore, a factory optimizes the gap between sales, purchase requirements and production constraints only from the factory's point of view but does not know how the results will affect the sales and inventory plans of a sales company. The case of Porite Corporation illustrates how visibility and integration within the supply chain helps to increase efficiency of the business that operates globally.

Porite Corporation

Porite Corporation is a manufacturer of powder metallurgy products for automotive parts, industrial machinery, information equipment and household appliances. The company had been expanding globally from the very beginning, with overseas sales accounting for more than 80% of the total sales.

The company's overseas sales account for more than 80% of its total sales and each base has its core system, and there is no control within the company. In Japan alone, there are separate systems for accounting, sales, purchasing and production management, so orders, inventory and production planning could not be linked. Sales staff used to forecast and adjust the number of orders manually, but because the sales system and the production management system were able to exchange data only several times a day (not in a real-time mode), the timing of reflecting the basic inventory quantity was slow, and the forecasting accuracy was not high.

The direct linkage between systems has automated manual work, significantly reducing time and errors while improving data accuracy and control levels. The system automatically calculates the optimum number of products to be produced from orders, demand forecasts, stock and purchase order backlogs, optimizing stock levels. The company has adopted a completely made-to-order production system to produce according to customer orders to reduce stock. By sharing the same accounting, sales and purchasing platforms, the company can reduce waste and increase the turnover of inventory and funds within supply chain. The company can share the management infrastructure on a global basis that might provide more opportunities to grow the company. Even in case of disasters groupware on the cloud can help the company to be connected. Also, the system can help to expand overseas easily for companies with limited staff by taking advantage of the cloud technologies.

Customer-Focused and Open Supply Chains

Traditionally, research on the relevance of a customer focus for the competitiveness of a company was conducted at a firm-level; however, more and more companies realized that recent changes in external environment and shifts in the models and forms of value generation require collaborative solutions with supply-chain partners at the inter-organizational level (e.g., Defee & Fugate, 2010; Gulati, Nohria, & Zaheer, 2000; Pu, Wang, & Chan, 2020; Rahmanzadeh, Pishvaee, & Govindan, 2022; Solaimani & van der Veen, 2021) to gain and sustain strategic advantage. Customer focus may enable supply chain partners to achieve competitive advantage by fostering supply chain relational capabilities (Lado, Paulraj, & Chen, 2011). Sousa (2003) identified several groups of customer-focused practices that contribute to higher supply chain performance. Establishing strong relationships with customers through partnership arrangements, direct customer contacts (face to face meetings, plant visits), integration of the operations with customers (logistics co-operation, mutual technical assistance, etc.), involvement of customers in new product design/introduction, collection of information on customer needs, dissemination of this information within the company and along a supply chain and responsiveness to it are expected to have a positive affect supply chain performance. In this regard, technological advancements in digitalization of supply chains make these practices more available for companies and stimulate their implementation along the supply chain.

Japanese companies aim to build trust with their customers. To achieve this, companies aim to build an optimal supply chain, purchasing quality components and materials at low prices and promptly on time. However, in practice, after many years of doing business, the Japanese suppliers can become so closely tied to the company that there are delays in understanding customer needs in terms of product development and demand planning. This is due to a closed supply chain which stifles the circulation of information and makes it less customer-oriented. Thus, there is an urgent need for companies to build supply chains that are flexible, open and customer-focused. The case of Suzuki Motor Corporation provides an illustration of the digital solution that makes supply chains more open and customer-focused through the integration of the information on real-time customer needs and supplier production capacities, as well as the possibility for the redirection of the supply flows.

Suzuki Motor Corporation

Suzuki Motor Corporation, a manufacturer of automobiles, motorcycles and outboard motors, procures parts and manufactures its products from a large number of suppliers, with over 300 primary suppliers alone, and a huge number of secondary and tertiary suppliers. Natural disasters pose a threat to this efficient production cycle. When delays occur, it is important to identify the priority of production lines to supply parts to meet delivery deadlines. In case of natural disasters, it takes time to identify suppliers affected by the disaster and to assess the impact on production at their factories. To visualize the situation of suppliers Suzuki Motor Corporation uses a map-based information system. By visualizing suppliers in the affected area on a map, a company reduces the time to assess the situation on the production line, investigate the impact and report back to the customer. When a disaster strikes, several things are needed to be checked: what are the suppliers in the affected area, which parts are due to be delivered to which factories, whether there will be delays, how many units the company can produce with the parts in stock at the factories, and what are the deadlines for delivery.

The company introduces a map information system with no running costs. The system has a layered structure and is scalable to include disasters, weather, and traffic information, and it can be linked to existing systems of the company. The system takes into consideration the framework of production and logistics. The aim is to quickly identify shortages on the production line. A geospatial information solution allows company to build a system with minimum configurations that allows free expansion in the future.

With the introduction of this crisis management system the company can act immediately. The system is currently in place at the company's four-wheeler plants in Japan and at knockdown plants that manufacture parts for overseas markets. Once the system is complete, it can be used in other countries such as India, Thailand, and Indonesia. The company wants to cover all plants with a system that is easy to operate so that everyone can decide which plant and which production line is suited to the parts of one supplier.

Complex IT Legacy Systems

IT systems built over many years of shop-floor improvements have become so complex that no one has an accurate understanding of what is inside them after so many years. IT systems are often designed to improve the efficiency of existing operations to support improvements in the workplace. The current digital environment is a so-called "combinatorial" value proposition, where value is created by connecting various digital services and technologies. However, despite the use of the latest technologies such as artificial intelligence (AI) and robotic process automation (RPA), the current approach to digital transformation in Japan's manufacturing industry has not changed significantly in terms of short-term thinking, prioritizing individual areas, and creating a "fit and match" approach. The case of Kyocera Corporations illustrates the benefits of a complex IT platform that serves multiple functions for the improvement of process efficiency and productivity.

Kyocera Corporation

Kyocera Corporation is a maker of fine ceramics that is diversified into information and communications, automotive, environmental energy, and medical healthcare spheres. It aims to make production lines unmanned and autonomous. Kyocera has been manufacturing fine ceramics for nearly 40 years and has accumulated a high level of know-how, however, defects are still inevitable. By introduction of a system that eliminates defects the company aimed to lower manufacturing costs and achieve cost leadership in the global market. By reforming the manufacturing site through implementation of the optimal monthly procurement plan utilizing the automatically collected data, the company doubled its productivity. At the same time, by shifting human's work to more creative tasks and transferring a routine work to a complex IT system, the company managed to add value and increase profits.

The company uses a digital platform that integrates production planning, manufacturing execution and data utilization. Kyocera launched a series of model lines at its plants to demonstrate how unmanned production, combining AI and robots, can improve production efficiency. The key principle of the platform is "autonomy". To create an autonomous production line that never stops, the system monitors and manages not only manufacturing equipment, but also the AGVs (automated guided vehicles) that transport materials and work in progress between processes.

The digital platform is used for production planning to optimize monthly input and procurement, and as to schedule optimal daily resources. The platform issues instructions of operators and control equipment. It also collects IoT data from the production floor and analyses it in the real time. In addition, the company introduced a data cloud to link, store, process, analyze, and manage data not only in the factory but throughout the company. By using an AI, the company can identify the causes of defects that even were not evident even for the most experienced workers. In just a few months with the use of a new IT system the company managed to decrease the rate of defects that had not been reduced for decades.

The system not only helps operators to change their tasks, but also provides a digital platform that goes beyond simple data storage to a communication tool between humans and humans, and between humans and machines. The digital platform accelerates Kyocera's overall digital transformation to achieve further competitiveness and business growth through additional value creation. The company aims to evolve the system to inspire the workplace for the future of young people.

CONCLUSIONS

Japanese companies have maintained a high level of process efficiency at separate sites and operational units through the years of "SCM reform" and *"kaizen"* activities, but they remained less efficient in terms of interconnectivity, relying heavily on humans and spreadsheets to deal with complex tasks. As a result, they have been unable to achieve end-to-end supply chain optimization or advanced global decision-making. Even now, IT systems in many Japanese companies are often designed to improve the efficiency of existing operations and support improvements in the workplace, rather than radically transform the processes to maintain competitive advantage on the global scale. Even among the most advanced Japanese manufacturing companies with global operations, there are just a few examples of companies that have performed essential transformations in their supply chains to benefit from digital advancements.

The reasons of a slow and fragmented integration of digital solutions in business processes and supply chains of Japanese companies are diverse and range from deeply rooted cultural traditions to obvious deficit of financial and well-qualified human resources. As more and more Japanese companies start to realize the necessity of significant restructuring of their operational processes and the role of digitalization in the potential increased productivity, they are looking for the way to overcome these challenges.

REFERENCES

Ageron, B., Bentahar, O., & Gunasekaran, A. (2020). Digital supply chain: challenges and future directions. *Supply Chain Forum: An International Journal, 21*(3), 133-138. 10.1080/16258312.2020.1816361

Armistead, C. G., & Mapes, J. (1993). The impact of supply chain integration on operating performance. *Logistics Information Management, 6*(4), 9–14. doi:10.1108/09576059310045907

Barratt, M., & Oke, A. (2007). Antecedents of supply chain visibility in retail supply chains: A resource-based theory perspective. *Journal of Operations Management, 25*(6), 1217–1233. doi:10.1016/j.jom.2007.01.003

Barratt, M. A., & Oliveira, A. (2001). Exploring the experiences of collaborative planning initiatives. *International Journal of Physical Distribution & Logistics Management, 31*(4), 266–289. doi:10.1108/09600030110394932

Berry, D., Towill, D. R., & Wadsley, N. (1994). Supply chain management in the electronics products industry. *International Journal of Physical Distribution & Logistics Management, 24*(10), 20–32. doi:10.1108/09600039410074773

Brennen, J. S., & Kreiss, D. (2016). Digitalization. In K. B. Jensen, E. W. Rothenbuhler, J. D. Pooley, & R. T. Craig (Eds.), *The International Encyclopedia of Communication Theory and Philosophy* (pp. 556–566). Wiley-Blackwell. doi:10.1002/9781118766804.wbiect111

Christopher, M. (2016). *Logistics & Supply Chain Management* (5th ed.). Pearson.

Deepu, T. S., & Ravi, V. (2021). A conceptual framework for supply chain digitalization using integrated systems model approach and DIKW hierarchy. *Intelligent Systems with Applications, 10–11*, 200048. doi:10.1016/j.iswa.2021.200048

Defee, C. C., & Fugate, B. S. (2010). Changing perspectives of capabilities in the dynamic supply chain era. *International Journal of Logistics Management, 21*(2), 180–206. doi:10.1108/09574091011071915

Dharish, D. (2020). Japan's experience in reducing its supply chain insecurity. *Asia Power Watch*. Retrieved on December 01, 2021, from https://asiapowerwatch.com/japans-experience-in-reducing-its-supply-chain-insecurity/

Gartner. (2020). *Supply Chain Digital Transformation*. Retrieved on November 27, 2021, from https://www.gartner.com/en/supply-chain/insights/supply-chain-digital-transformation

Gulati, R., Nohria, N., & Zaheer, A. (2000). Strategic networks. *Strategic Management Journal, 21*(3), 203–214. doi:10.1002/(SICI)1097-0266(200003)21:3<203::AID-SMJ102>3.0.CO;2-K

IMD. (2021). *World Digital Competitiveness Ranking*. Retrieved on February 12, 2022, from https://www.imd.org/centers/world-competitiveness-center/rankings/world-digital-competitiveness/

IPA. (2020). *Dejitarutoransufume-shon suishin jinzai no kinō to yakuwari no arikata nikansuru chōsa* [Survey on the functions and roles of human resources for digital transformation]. Retrieved on December 15, 2021, from https://www.ipa.go.jp/files/000073700.pdf

Kamath, N. (2016). *Handbook of research on strategic supply chain management in the retail industry*. IGI Global. doi:10.4018/978-1-4666-9894-9

KDDI. (2021). *Dejitarutoransufu-me-shon wa naze DX to ryakusareru? DX no igi ya gutaiteki jirei made shōkai* [Why is digital transformation abbreviated as DX, and what does it mean?]. Retrieved on December 01, 2021, from https://www.kddimatomete.com/magazine/210201134321

Kent, J. L., & Mentzer, J. T. (2003). The effect of investment in inter-organizational information technology in a retail supply chain. *Journal of Business Logistics*, *24*(2), 155–176. doi:10.1002/j.2158-1592.2003.tb00050.x

Koberg, E., & Longoni, A. (2019). A systematic review of sustainable supply chain management in global supply chains. *Journal of Cleaner Production*, *207*, 1084–1098. doi:10.1016/j.jclepro.2018.10.033

Lado, A. A., Paulraj, A., & Chen, I. J. (2011). Customer focus, supply-chain relational capabilities and performance: Evidence from US manufacturing industries. *International Journal of Logistics Management*, *22*(2), 202–221. doi:10.1108/09574091111156550

Leao, P., & da Silva, M. M. (2021). Impacts of digital transformation on firms' competitive advantages: A systematic literature review. *Strategic Change*, *30*(5), 421–441. doi:10.1002/jsc.2459

Lee, S. M., & Trimi, S. (2020). Convergence innovation in the digital age and in the COVID-19 pandemic crisis. *Journal of Business Research*, *123*, 14–22. doi:10.1016/j.jbusres.2020.09.041 PMID:33012897

Liang, L., Yang, F., Cook, W. D., & Zhu, J. (2006). DEA models for supply chain efficiency evaluation. *Annals of Operations Research*, *145*(1), 35–49. doi:10.100710479-006-0026-7

Loebbecke, C., & Picot, A. (2015). Reflections on societal and business model transformation arising from digitization and big data analytics: A research agenda. *The Journal of Strategic Information Systems*, *24*(3), 149–157. doi:10.1016/j.jsis.2015.08.002

Marchand, D., & Wade, M. (2014). *Digital business transformation: where is your company on the journey.* Retrieved on November 28, 2021, from https://www.imd.org/contentassets/9be2125354424aa5afd52f5b03f639a0/digital-business-transformation-pfm-final.pdf

McKinsey. (2021). *Using digital transformation to thrive in Japan's new normal: An urgent imperative.* Retrieved on November 28, 2021, from https://www.mckinsey.com/~/media/mckinsey/locations/asia/japan/our%20work/digital/using%20digital%20transformation%20to%20thrive%20in%20japans%20new%20normal_an%20urgent%20imperative_upd201223.pdf

Mentzer, J. T., Min, S., & Bobbitt, L. M. (2004). Toward a unified theory of logistics. *International Journal of Physical Distribution & Logistics Management*, *34*(7/8), 606–627. doi:10.1108/09600030410557758

METI. (2018). *IT Shisutemu 2025 nen no gake no kokufuku to DX no honkakuteki na tenkai* [Overcoming the "2025 Cliff" in IT systems and full-scale development of DX]. Retrieved on December 02, 2021, from https://www.meti.go.jp/shingikai/mono_info_service/digital_transformation/pdf/20180907_03.pdf

METI. (2019). *DX suishin shihyō to sono gaidansu* [DX Promotion Index and its Guidance]. DX. Retrieved on December 02, 2021, from https://www.meti.go.jp/press/2019/07/20190731003/20190731003-1.pdf

Nambisan, S. (2017). Digital entrepreneurship: Toward a digital technology perspective of entrepreneurship. *Entrepreneurship Theory and Practice*, *41*(6), 1029–1055. doi:10.1111/etap.12254

Oliveira, L., Fleury, A., & Fleury, M. T. (2021). Digital power: Value chain upgrading in an age of digitization. *International Business Review*, *30*(6), 101850. doi:10.1016/j.ibusrev.2021.101850

Petersen, K. J., Ragatz, G. L., & Monczka, R. M. (2005). An examination of collaborative planning effectiveness and supply chain performance. *The Journal of Supply Chain Management*, *41*(2), 14–25. doi:10.1111/j.1055-6001.2005.04102002.x

Prater, E., Frazier, G. V., & Reyes, P. M. (2005). Future impacts of RFID on e-supply chains in grocery retailing. *Supply Chain Management*, *10*(2), 134–142. doi:10.1108/13598540510589205

Pu, X., Wang, Z. X., & Chan, F. T. S. (2020). Leveraging Open E-Logistic Standards to Achieve Ambidexterity in Supply Chain. *Journal of Computer Information Systems*, *60*(4), 347–358. doi:10.1080/08874417.2018.1488543

Rachinger, M., Rauter, R., Müller, C., Vorraber, W., & Schirgi, E. (2018). Digitalization and its influence on business model innovation. *Journal of Manufacturing Technology Management*, *30*(8), 1143–1160. doi:10.1108/JMTM-01-2018-0020

Rahmanzadeh, S., Pishvaee, M. S., & Govindan, K. (2022). Emergence of open supply chain management: The role of open innovation in the future smart industry using digital twin network. *Annals of Operations Research*. Advance online publication. doi:10.100710479-021-04254-2

Rusli, K. A., Rahman, A. A., Ho, J. A., & Abdullah, R. (2013). How green is your supply chain? Evidence from ISO 14001 certified manufacturers in Malaysia. *Pertanika Journal of Social Science & Humanities*, *21*, 213–230.

Ryan, P., Buciuni, G., Giblin, M., & Andersson, U. (2022). Global Value Chain Governance in the MNE: A Dynamic Hierarchy Perspective. *California Management Review*, *64*(2), 97–118. Advance online publication. doi:10.1177/00081256211068544

Shishido, T. (2021). *Nippon kigyō niokeru dejitaru SCM no hōkōsei ishi kettei no shitsu to supi-do o kōjōsaseru dejitaru tekunoroji- no katsuyōhō to wa* [The Direction of digital SCM in Japanese companies- how to use digital technology to improve the quality and speed of decision-making]. Qunie Corp. Retrieved on December 05, 2021, from https://www.qunie.com/quriosity/210304_00

Solaimani, S., & van der Veen, J. (2021). Open supply chain innovation: An extended view on supply chain collaboration. *Supply Chain Management*. Advance online publication. doi:10.1108/SCM-09-2020-0433

Sousa, R. (2003). Linking quality management to manufacturing strategy: An empirical investigation of customer focus practices. *Journal of Operations Management*, *21*(1), 1–18. doi:10.1016/S0272-6963(02)00055-4

Stolterman, E., & Fors, A. C. (2004). *Information Technology and the Good Life*. Retrieved on December 08, 2021, from https://www8.informatik.umu.se/~acroon/Publikationer%20Anna/Stolterman.pdf

Swaminathan, J. M., & Tayur, S. R. (2003). Models for supply chains in e-business. *Management Science*, *49*(10), 1387–1406. doi:10.1287/mnsc.49.10.1387.17309

Tilson, D., Lyytinen, K., & Sorensen, C. (2010). Digital infrastructures: The missing IS research agenda. *Information Systems Research*, *21*(4), 748–759. doi:10.1287/isre.1100.0318

Unruh, G., & Kiron, D. (2017). Digital transformation on purpose. *MIT Sloan Management Review, 6*. Retrieved December 08, 2021, from https://sloanreview.mit.edu/article/digital-transformation-on-purpose/

Van der Zee, D. J., & Van der Vorst, J. G. A. J. (2005). A modeling framework for supply chain simulation: Opportunities for improved decision making. *Decision Sciences, 36*(1), 65–95. doi:10.1111/j.1540-5915.2005.00066.x

Wang, H., Pan, C., Wang, Q. W., & Zhou, P. (2020). Assessing sustainability performance of global supply chains: An input-output modeling approach. *European Journal of Operational Research, 285*(1), 393–404. doi:10.1016/j.ejor.2020.01.057

Yang, M., Fu, M., & Zhang, Z. (2021). The adoption of digital technologies in supply chains: Drivers, process and impact. *Technological Forecasting and Social Change, 169*, 120795. doi:10.1016/j.techfore.2021.120795

ENDNOTES

1 Supply Chain Planning.
2 Sales and Operations Planning.

Chapter 4
Analysis of Technology as a Factor of Resilience in the Agri-Food Supply Chain

Oriol Montanyà Vilalta
https://orcid.org/0000-0002-9092-2820
School of Management, UPF Barcelona, Spain

Núria Arimany Serrat
University of Vic-Central University of Catalonia, Spain

ABSTRACT

Distribution companies in the Spanish agri-food sector have shown a high level of resilience during the COVID-19 crisis, as they have always guaranteed a high availability of product in stores (more than 90%) despite the changes in demand themselves from such an uncertain context. The scientific literature already identifies some specific factors that can positively influence the robustness of their logistics processes, such as proximity supply models, collaboration between value chain actors, and customer-oriented strategies. But this chapter seeks to delve into the relevance that technology can have as an element of supply chain resilience, concluding that it is an important but not yet determining factor. The companies that took part in the study, which represent more than 50% of the Spanish agri-food distribution, have shown that the technological capacity of their companies does not have a direct correlation with their current level of resilience, although in at the same time, they consider it a binomial that has a lot of potential and needs to be developed.

INTRODUCTION

As businessman Warren Buffet puts it: "Only when the tide goes down can you see who was swimming naked" (Edwards, 2016). A phrase that could be perfectly applied to Spanish supply chains, as the crisis of Covid-19 has exposed its true resilience, demonstrating the fragility of some logistics structures and the strength of others (Mena, Karatzas, & Hansen, 2022). For example, it is well known that at the begin-

DOI: 10.4018/978-1-7998-9715-6.ch004

Copyright © 2022, IGI Global. Copying or distributing in print or electronic forms without written permission of IGI Global is prohibited.

ning of the pandemic the medical equipment suffered a collapse in its supply system, caused by a sudden and sharp increase in demand, which depleted the stocks of items as necessary as masks, hydroalcoholic gel, or respirators (Derqui, Filimonau, & Matute, 2021). In addition, the reaction time was not fast, but it took several weeks to restore an optimal level of service, able to respond to the needs of the population.

On the other hand, the agri-food chains always showed a remarkable degree of resilience, as, although they also suffered significant changes in demand, they were able to withstand the onslaught and overcome the difficulties, managing not to interrupt supply. of products (Matthews, 2020). In fact, according to the databases of Nielsen and AECOC (the largest Spanish association of company's manufacturers, distributors and logistics of consumer goods) that collect daily information on the behavior of sales of 40,000 references in 1,800 supermarkets throughout Spain (Brugarolas, Martínez-Carrasco, Rabadán, & Bernabéu, 2020), agri-food distribution maintained a level of product availability in stores above 90% during 2020. Even in March, when demand varied the most due to the unexpected confinement of the entire population, the lack of product at points of sale did not exceed 8%. Figure 1 shows the evolution of this barometer, called OSA (AECOC, 2021), which collects information on the most essential categories: packaged food, refrigerated food, frozen food, beverages, drugs, and perfumery.

Figure 1. Percentage of product availability at the points of sale of the large Spanish agri-food distribution during the year 2020 (AECOC, 2021)

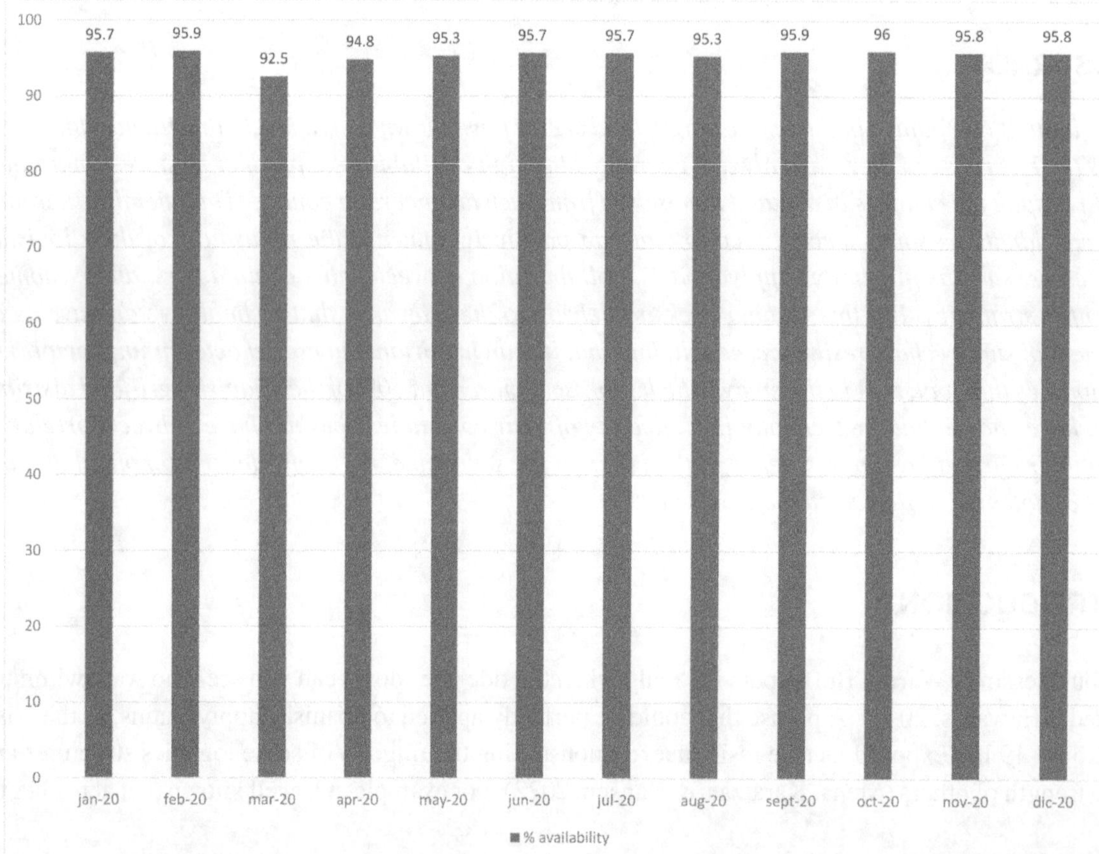

Considering the importance of the strength of agri-food supply chains for the social welfare of any country (Kerr, 2020), and more in an international context highly exposed to political, environmental or health crises (Boyacı-Gündüz, Ibrahim, Wei, & Galanakis, 2021), this chapter aims to analyze the factors that may have favored the resilience of commodity supply processes in Spain.

To do this, we will first conduct a literature review to identify the most classic factors that have already been widely debated by the scientific community. And then we will present the research work to provide new knowledge on one of the issues that still does not find a clear answer in the academic literature, which is the relationship between resilience and technology. In fact, the specific question that motivates the present study is this: **Is the technological capacity of companies a factor that has a positive impact on the degree of resilience of agri-food supply chains?**

REVIEW OF LITERATURE

In order to analyze this resilience of the agri-food supply chain, it is first convenient to narrow the conceptual framework, as did Stone and Rahimifard (2018), who conducted a strict systematic review of 137 academic articles to conclude defining resilience as "the collective capacity of stakeholders in agri-food supply chains to ensure acceptable, sufficient and stable food supply at the required times and places, by accurately anticipating disruptions and the use of strategies that delay the impact, help the rapid recovery and allow the cumulative learning after the interruption".

Having delineated the scope of the main concept, the scientific literature also allows us to identify some relevant factors that have a positive impact on the degree of resilience of companies in the agri-food sector (Jabbarzadeh, Fahimnia, Sheu, & Moghadam, 2016). It has been shown that there are at least three strategic elements that increase the strength of logistics processes and supply guarantees, especially in contexts of high demand volatility. These are:

1. **Customer-oriented strategy**: Companies with a business model based on customer satisfaction build more resilient value chains, as they provide them with sourcing techniques very focused on maximizing service, such as maintaining a good level of stocks or high replacement frequencies (Perona, 2002; Verdouw, Beulens, & Trienekens, 2010).
2. **Geographical proximity**: Distribution models that do not accumulate long distances are less exposed to disruption risks from global trade and international transportation. In fact, during the Covid-19 pandemic, the so-called "short supply chains", which are designed to minimize the miles between production and distribution, have shown a much higher responsiveness (Cappelli & Cini, 2020; Todorovic, Maslaric, Bojic, Jokic, Mircetic, & Nikolicic, 2018).
3. **Collaboration between actors**: Resilience is also higher in those supply chains that have strong and stable relationships between the components that make it up. Companies with a tendency to share information and integrate processes, either horizontally or vertically, have a competitive advantage when it comes to anticipating and coping with difficult times (Eksoz, Mansouri, Bourlakis, & Önkal, 2019; Leat & Revoredo-Giha, 2013; Xu & Dong, 2004).

It should be noted that companies in the agri-food sector are more likely to incorporate these three management paradigms, both because of the characteristics of the market in which they operate, which is highly competitive, and the particularities of the products they supply, which usually have a cycle of short life (Zhao, Liu, & Lopez, 2017).

But one of the limitations of reviewing the literature on this topic is to delve deeper into the role that technology and digitalization can play in the resilience of agri-food supply chains (Amentae & Gebresenbet, 2021). In fact, if we search the Scopus database with the keywords "resilience", "technology", "supply chain" and "agri-food", we find only 39 articles indexed during the last decade. As shown in Figure 2, the scientific interest in this area is very recent, as most publications (up to 27) are from 2021.

Figure 2. Academic articles over the last 10 years on resilience and technology in agri-food supply chains

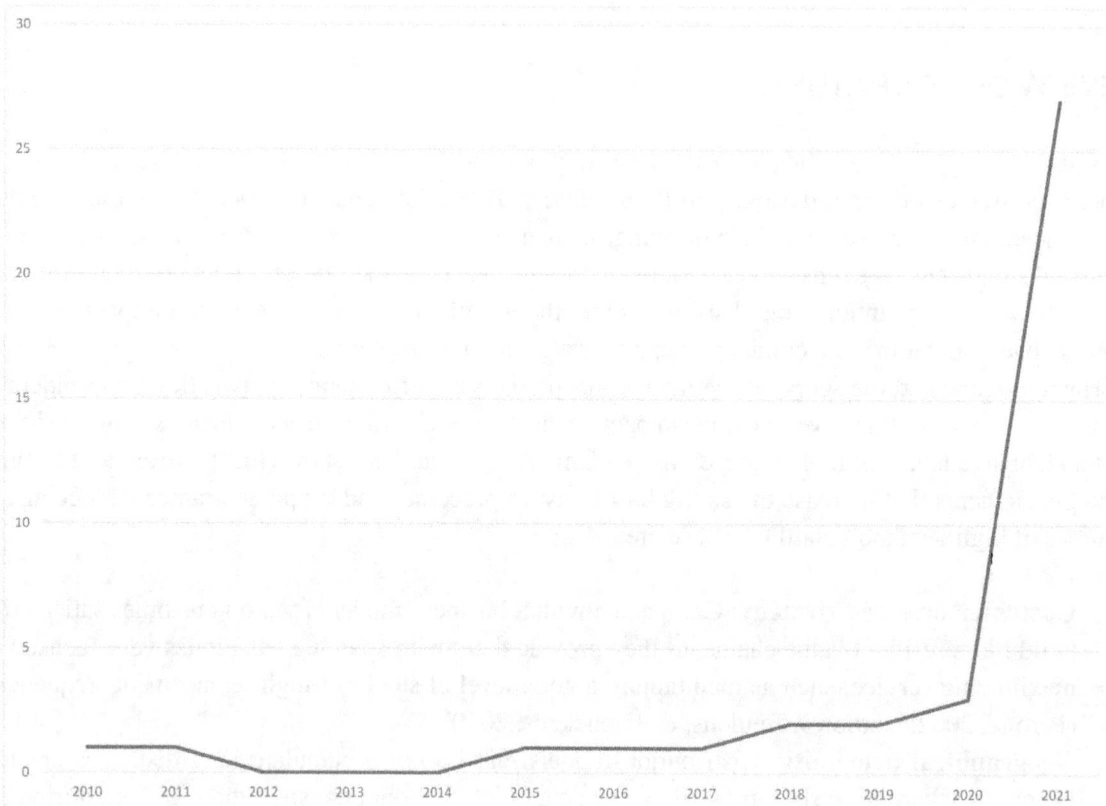

In another reference database, Web of Science, the number of publications on the subject is even more limited. Using the same search parameters, only 13 articles appear, of which 11 were published between 2020 and 2022.

The fact that we have a limited number of publications with little time perspective means that we find unequal results and certain points of contradiction, as some research gives technology an important and positive specific weight when it comes to set up resilient supply chains (Joshi & Sharma, 2021), while other work does not find sufficient evidence to identify technology as a determining factor in the resilience of agribusinesses (Trabucco & Giovanni, 2021).

Some relevant articles have done very careful (and very recent) literature reviews to try to draw the knowledge map of digitization in agri-food supply chains (Abideen et al., 2021; Rejeb, Rejeb, Abdollahi, Zailani, Iranmanesh, & Ghobakhloo, 2021) but they can't establish an irrefutable link between the technological capacity and the degree of resilience of companies.

There are other scientific studies that analyze how some more specific technologies can increase the resilience of procurement processes, such as Blockchain (Motta, Tekinerdogan, & Athanasiadis, 2020), Big Data (Miller, 2021) or Digital Twins (Ivanov & Dolgui, 2019). But in all of them the future potential stands out more than the contrasted reality. In fact, they identify the barriers that currently prevent these technologies from being deployed and effective. Barriers that can be of legal, organizational, or technical nature.

In any case, the review of the literature on the role of technology in the resilience of agri-food supply chains is a real invitation to continue research to shed light on a field full of shadows.

METHODOLOGY

In order to answer the question that motivates the chapter, a methodology has been chosen that combines qualitative techniques to prepare the questionnaire (Annex 1) and select a relevant sample (Annex 2), with quantitative tools to analyze the resulting data and make the corresponding contrasts.

The questionnaire was developed based on five variables that have already been validated in academic articles published in scientific journals, as can be seen in Table 1. The first two variables are used to assess the degree of resilience of companies and ask -they consider the most important factors when designing resilient processes. The following two variables focus on the technological issue and have been selected to assess the digital competence of companies, as well as to know what benefits they perceive from their integration. Finally, the last variable must be used to state that resilience is perceived as an attribute that ends up translating into better supply chain performance.

Table 1. Variables and indicators used in the research, with the corresponding sources (Balakrishnan & Ramanathan, 2021; Gu, Yang, & Huo, 2021; Neboh & Mbhele, 2021)

VARIABLES	INDICATORS	REFERENCE
1. DEGREE OF RESILIENCE	1.1. Predictive level	Gu et al. (2021)
	1.2. Reaction level	
2. RESILIENCE FACTORS	2.1. Business model	Neboh and Mbhele (2021)
	2.2. Financial reserve	
	2.3. Proximity	
	2.4. Technology	
3. TECHNOLOGICAL COMPETENCE	3.1. Investment	Balakrishnan and Ramanathan (2021)
	3.2. Utility	
	3.3. Simplicity	
	3.4. Frequency	
4. TECHNOLOGICAL INTEGRATION	4.1. Improve information	
	4.2. Facilitate tasks	
	4.3. Improve processes	
	4.4. Optimize resources	
	4.5. Encourage collaboration	
	4.6. Increase resilience	
5. RESILIENCE PERFORMANCE	5.1. Improve costs	
	5.2. Reduce delivery time	
	5.3. Service guarantees	
	5.4. Increase sustainability	

It should be noted that the three sources chosen for the questionnaire are articles dealing with resilience and technology in supply chains. However, due to the lack of existing literature on the subject, only one publication refers specifically to agri-food chains, while the second covers the subject more generally and the third focuses on studying the relationship between resilience and technology in the automotive sector.

As for the sample, the study was aimed at large agri-food distribution companies in Spain, as they are the part of the value chain with the highest degree of concentration (Langreo & Germán, 2018) and, at the same time, the one at the end of any procurement process, which is where the degree of resilience can be most effectively measured (Alikhani, Torabi, & Altay, 2021). Therefore, the SABI database was used to define this sample using the following filters:

- Status: Active
- Location: Spain
- Sector of activity: Agri-food retail trade. Using CENAE codes 4711, 4721, 4722, 4723, 4724, 4725, 4729.
- Dimension: Large company. According to the criteria of the European Union (Bylok & Cichobłaziński, 2020) +250 workers, +50 million turnover and +43 million total assets.

With these criteria, a sample of 57 companies was obtained, which were contacted through the professional network LinkedIn, sending a direct message to the top managers of their supply chains, of which they ended up answering the questionnaire a total of 35.

Therefore, although the finite population is very small from a statistical point of view, it should be noted that information was collected from 61.4% of the total sample, and that these data come from people with a very high knowledge of the subject being researched. It is also important to note that the 35 companies that have confirmed their participation in this study represent more than 50% of the share of retail distribution in the Spanish market (Kantar, 2020).

Regarding the treatment of the data, first a descriptive analysis of each of the indicators that make up variables 2, 4 and 5 has been carried out. For all of them we have calculated the mean, the standard deviation, the median, the minimum and maximum.

On the other hand, to ensure the internal validity and reliability of the variables "degree of resilience" and "technological competence" we have calculated the Cronbach's Alpha for each of them. For the variable "degree of resilience" the Cronbach's Alpha is 0.65, while for the "technological competence" it is 0.84. However, since the indicators that make up both variables are ordinal, it is more appropriate to study the internal consistency of the two variables over a matrix of polyconic correlations (Oliden & Zumbo, 2008). Thus, the ordinal alpha for the variable "degree of resilience" is 0.70 and the ordinal alpha for the variable "technological competence" is 0.90. Therefore, we can conclude that according to the statistical tests performed, the consistency of both variables would be at least acceptable (> 0.7) and therefore both scales would be reliable to be used in subsequent analyzes.

Once the validity of the two variables had been verified, we proceeded to perform a Spearman correlation analysis (an appropriate method for calculating the correlation between indicators or ordinal variables) to measure the statistical association between the two variables. Finally, we also analyzed by Spearman's correlation test the degree of association between the variable "degree of resilience" and the different individual indicators that make up the variable "technological competence".

RESULTS

First, it should be noted that resilience is an attribute that large Spanish distribution companies consider positive for improving the performance of their supply chains. The questionnaire asked managers to assess whether having more resilient processes could lead to advantages in at least four specific areas: improving customer service guarantees, reducing product delivery time, lowering transaction costs, and increase business sustainability. The result, as can be seen in Table 2, is that all the indicators used obtain an average score higher than 3 (on an ordinal scale of 1 to 5) evidencing the benefits associated with resilience.

Table 2. Mean and median of indicators that refer to supply chain performance

Variable	Mean	Std. Dev	Min	Median	Max	N.Valid	Pct.Valid
Service guarantees	4,34	0,64	3	4	5	35	100,0%
Increase Sustainability	3,20	0,90	1	3	5	35	100,0%
Improve costs	3,88	1,09	2	4	5	34	97,1%
Reduce delivery time	4,06	0,74	2	4	5	34	97,1%

But it is worth mentioning the performance associated with service guarantees and the reduction of delivery times, as they are the indicators that have received a higher average score (higher than 4) and which have also generated more consensus among respondents (with a standard deviation of less than 0.8). Therefore, it can be argued that distribution companies associate resilience with a substantial improvement in product sourcing processes, both in terms of reliability and speed.

The other two performance indicators, which refer to improved sustainability and costs, also received a positive assessment, although with averages below 4 and higher standard deviations. So, we need to be more careful about linking supply chain resilience with improving economic efficiency or the ecological footprint. In such cases, further research should be conducted to draw more conclusive conclusions.

Fully entering the analysis of the factors that may determine the degree of resilience of a supply chain, the study asked respondents to rate the four factors that, according to the literature review, may determine the degree of resilience of a supply chain. The results of the questionnaire indicate that the "business model" is the most relevant aspect. As other studies at the international level (Chen, Huang, Su, Štreimikienė, & Baležentis, 2021) point out, management paradigms are the ones that determine strategic priorities and, consequently, also the methods that strengthen or weaken supply chain structures. In fact, this is where some strategies that were already identified in the literature review could be included, such as collaboration between actors or customer orientation.

The other three major factors that Spanish distributors had to link to resilience are the economic strength of the company, the proximity of its distribution model and the level of technological innovation. In all three cases, factors can be considered to be taken into account, as they received an average score higher than 3.5 (out of 5) and a median score of 4, although the standard deviation in the answers is equal to or greater than 1, which indicates a possible degree of divergence. In fact, Table 3 clearly shows the distance between the factor that companies consider most decisive ("business model") and the other three factors, which are also valued positively but with less force.

Table 3. Mean and median of the indicators that refer to the factors that determine the resilience of supply chains

Variable	Mean	Std. Dev	Min	Median	Max	N. Valid	Pct. Valid
Business model	4,51	0,74	2	5	5	35	100,0%
Proximity	3,71	1,07	2	4	5	35	100,0%
Financial Reserve	3,54	0,98	1	4	5	35	100,0%
Technology	3,77	1,09	2	4	5	35	100,0%

Therefore, to answer the question that motivates the chapter and delve into how technology can affect the resilience of supply chains, it is necessary to go one step further and analyze the association between the two variables. For this reason, the questionnaire included specific questions to measure the technological competence of companies (such as investment in new technologies or the simplicity and frequency of their use) and, on the other hand, questions that assessed their degree of resilience (such as the ability to anticipate and respond to the unforeseen).

The result of this exercise can be seen in Figure 3, which shows that there is no clear correlation between the technological competition and the degree of resilience of the companies surveyed, as the Spearman correlation coefficient is 0.31 and does not reach the required statistical significance ($p > 0.05$).

Figure 3. Spearman correlation between the degree of resilience and the technological competence of firms

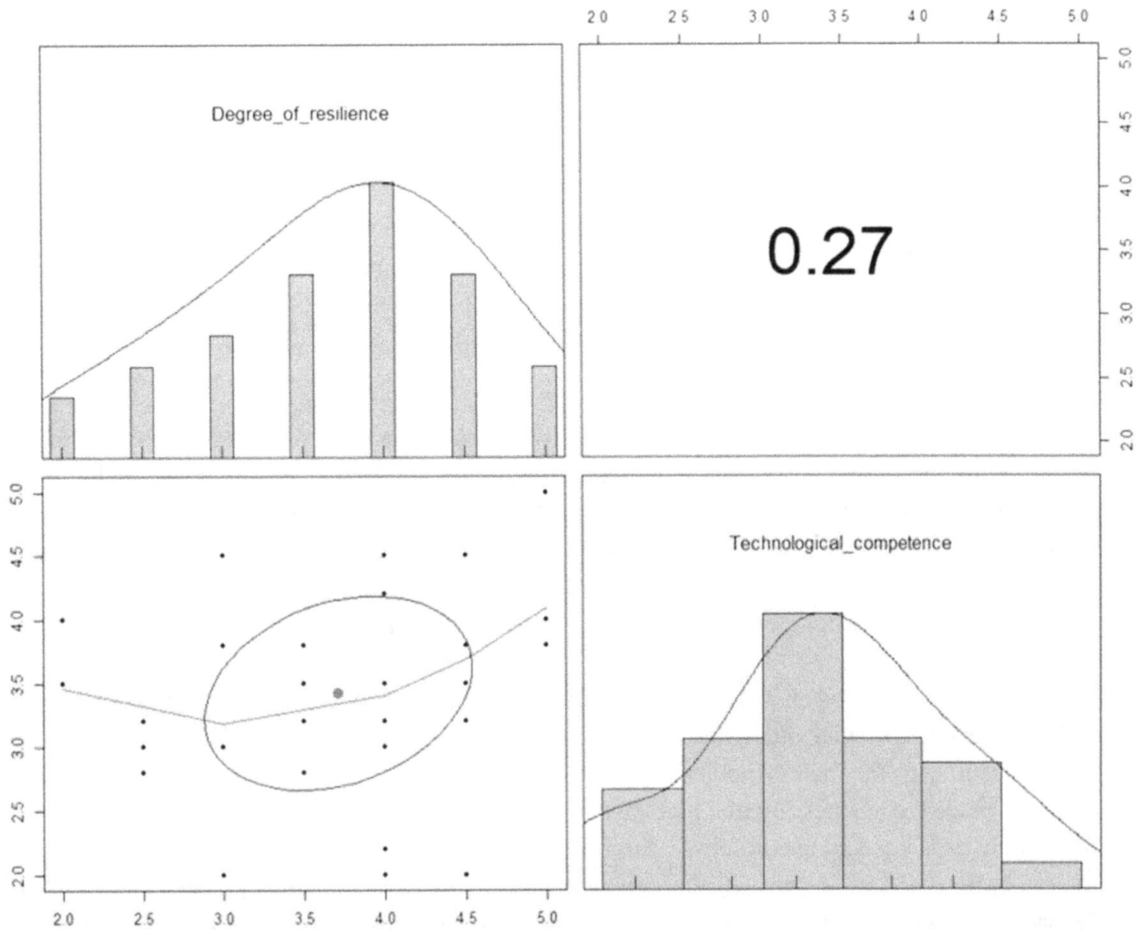

To deepen the analysis, the association between the "degree of resilience" and each of the indicators that make up the variable "technological competence" was also measured (see Figure 2). But the results are in line with the fact that none of the four technology indicators are associated with the degree of resilience of the companies included in the study ($p > 0.05$). The only thing that stands out is that the correlation between the "degree of resilience" and the indicator "investment in technology" shows a slight positive association (0.37) with a statistical significance of $p < 0.05$, which would invite continue to investigate whether it can really be said that the companies that invest the most in technology are also the most resilient.

Despite not finding a correlation between technology and resilience, this article has sought to add another element to complete the analysis of the issue, which is to ask companies about the main benefits that technology integration can bring to the agri-food supply chains. In this sense, as can be seen in Table 4, technology is considered a component that can significantly promote aspects such as collaboration between actors, process improvement, resource optimization, quality of information and the facilitation of some tasks. All these technology-related advantages receive an average of more than 4.5 (out of 5), a median of 5 (out of 5), and standard deviations always less than 1.

Table 4. Mean and median of the indicators that refer to the benefits of technology integration

Variable	Mean	Std. Dev	Min	Median	Max	N. Valid	Pct. Valid
Encourage collaboration	4,66	0,48	4	5	5	35	100,0%
Increase resilience	4,23	0,69	3	4	5	35	100,0%
Facilitate tasks	4,57	0,65	3	5	5	35	100,0%
Improve information	4,71	0,46	4	5	5	35	100,0%
Improve processes	4,86	0,36	4	5	5	35	100,0%
Optimize resources	4,63	0,55	3	5	5	35	100,0%

In terms of resilience, the companies surveyed also see this as a potential advantage of technology integration, with an average score of 4.23 (out of 5). In other words, they consider that technological advances can favor the resilience of supply chains, although it should be noted that, on a comparative level, it is the benefit with the least support of the six collected, both in terms of average and median, as in the standard deviation.

Therefore, at least four lessons can be learned from this analytical process:

1. Resilience is considered an important factor in improving the performance of supply chains, especially in terms of service guarantees and delivery times.
2. When identifying the factors that improve the resilience of supply chains, companies emphasize in the first place the business model, placing at a lower-level variable such as proximity distribution, economic capacity, and technology.
3. There is no correlation between the degree of resilience of companies and their technological capacity, showing that now no direct association can be established between the two variables.
4. Distribution companies believe that technology can bring a variety of operating benefits to supply chains, including improved resilience (although this is the least valued advantage).

CONCLUSIONS

Resilience is the attribute of supply chains that allows them to anticipate possible disruptions in their operation and respond firmly to restore normal business in an agile manner. This is a quality that improves the performance of companies, as resilient processes offer greater guarantees of service to customers and reduce delivery times. Companies also associate resilience with other potential benefits, such as increased sustainability or reduced costs, although in these cases they do so in a less conclusive and consensual way.

To study the factors that determine the degree of resilience of supply chains, it is very relevant to analyze the large agri-food distribution companies operating in Spain, as throughout the Covid-19 pandemic they have guaranteed a very high level of service, more than 90%, despite the context of uncertainty and the constant alterations in demand. In addition, they are companies with a very high impact, as the 35 companies that have participated in this chapter supply the basic products of food, drugstore, and perfumery to more than 50% of the country's population.

The study of these large distribution companies reveals that the factor they consider most relevant to the degree of resilience of supply chains is the business model that underpins them. And it is that the business model ends up conditioning much of the corporate strategies that can provide greater or lesser resilience to supply processes. In fact, the scientific literature on the subject already identifies some of these key strategies, such as customer orientation or collaboration between actors.

When companies are asked to specifically value the weight that technology can have on the degree of resilience of supply chains, they give it a positive value, at the same level as other important factors, such as the company's financial muscle or proximity in their distribution process. However, these factors are always at a significant distance from what is valued in the first place: the business model.

Therefore, as the aim of the chapter is to be able to analyze the impact that technological capacity can have on the resilience of logistics processes, it has been measured whether the large Spanish agri-food distribution companies, which have demonstrated a great capacity for dealing with supply chain disruptions, they currently show a direct correlation between their technological capability and their degree of resilience. This statistical contrast exercise gives us the result that there is no association between the two variables, so it cannot be linked to the fact that these companies have been able to guarantee the supply of commodities during the pandemic with their current level of technological endowment.

However, the companies themselves consider that one of the main benefits that the integration of technology can bring them is the increase in their resilience, as the binomial receives very high support in the results of the questionnaire (4.23 about 5).

Thus, the research allows us to conclude that technology is not yet a factor that directly and significantly affects the degree of resilience of agri-food supply chains, although it has a potential that should be further developed, as companies they argue that digitization can play an important role in dealing with process disruptions, both in its prediction and in reacting quickly (Hobbs, 2021). In contrast, poorly integrated technology can create a highly vulnerable digital dependency, which may even become a factor in the resilience of process resilience (Klumpp & Loske, 2021).

As limitations of this research work, it is possible to indicate the size of the analyzed population (the great Spanish distribution companies), since according to the used criteria it is reduced to 57 companies. As a result, despite having a high response rate (61.4%), the absolute number of companies that participated in the study is 35, which implies limitations from the point of view of statistical significance.

On the other hand, it is also important to note that the study was conducted in a very limited time frame (between October and December 2021) and in a truly exceptional historical period (global coronavirus pandemic). As a result, extrapolation of results should be done with caution.

Finally, it should be noted that the study speaks at all times of technology as a unique and homogeneous concept, without going into shelling out and assessing the different technological solutions and their possible impact on the resilience of supply chains. Therefore, this limitation indicates the path of future research, which could delve into which digital tools are the most important in the strength of logistics processes.

Similarly, one of the most suggestive lines that emerge from the article is the possibility of doing research work with the same logic but studying the relationship between resilience and sustainability (Khan, Ponce, Tanveer, Aguirre-Padilla, Mahmood, & Shah, 2021). That is, to observe the extent to which they can be compatible variables and, therefore, induce companies to work with them in a coordinated manner.

ACKNOWLEDGMENT

The authors of the article sincerely thank the collaboration of Oriol Amat, Professor of Financial Economics and Accounting at Pompeu Fabra University, and Joan Llosada, PhD in Sociology from the University of Girona, because their suggestions have improved the content of the research.

REFERENCES

Abideen, A. Z., Pandiyan, V., Sundram, K., Pyeman, J., Othman, A. K., Sorooshian, S., Thomé, M., Bourlakis, M., Guarnieri, P., & My, A. K. O. (2021). Food Supply Chain Transformation through Technology and Future Research Directions—A Systematic Review. *Logistics*, *5*(4), 83. doi:10.3390/logistics5040083

AECOC. (n.d.). *AECOC BARÓMETRO OSA*. Retrieved on December 27, 2021, from https://www.aecoc.es/servicios/estudios/barometro-osa/

Alikhani, R., Torabi, S. A., & Altay, N. (2021). Retail supply chain network design with concurrent resilience capabilities. *International Journal of Production Economics*, *234*, 108042. doi:10.1016/j.ijpe.2021.108042

Amentae, T. K., & Gebresenbet, G. (2021). Digitalization and Future Agro-Food Supply Chain Management: A Literature-Based Implications. *Sustainability*, *13*(21), 12181. doi:10.3390u132112181

Balakrishnan, A. S., & Ramanathan, U. (2021). The role of digital technologies in supply chain resilience for emerging markets' automotive sector. *Supply Chain Management*, *26*(6), 654–671. doi:10.1108/SCM-07-2020-0342

Boyacı-Gündüz, C. P., Ibrahim, S. A., Wei, O. C., & Galanakis, C. M. (2021). Transformation of the Food Sector: Security and Resilience during the COVID-19 Pandemic. *Foods*, *10*(3), 497. doi:10.3390/foods10030497 PMID:33669146

Brugarolas, M., Martínez-Carrasco, L., Rabadán, A., & Bernabéu, R. (2020). Innovation Strategies of the Spanish Agri-Food Sector in Response to the Black Swan COVID-19 Pandemic. *Foods*, *9*(12), 1821. doi:10.3390/foods9121821 PMID:33302384

Bylok, F., & Cichobłaziński, L. (2020). Social determinants of development of inter-group social capital in enterprises. In *Proceedings of the 15th European Conference on Management, Leadership and Governance* (pp. 83–90). ACPI. 10.34190/MLG.19.102

Cappelli, A., & Cini, E. (2020). Will the COVID-19 pandemic make us reconsider the relevance of short food supply chains and local productions? *Trends in Food Science & Technology*, *99*, 566–567. doi:10.1016/j.tifs.2020.03.041 PMID:32288230

Chen, J., Huang, J., Su, W., Štreimikienė, D., & Baležentis, T. (2021). The challenges of COVID-19 control policies for sustainable development of business: Evidence from service industries. *Technology in Society*, *66*, 101643. doi:10.1016/j.techsoc.2021.101643 PMID:34898758

Derqui, B., Filimonau, V., & Matute, J. (2021). Assessing the scale of adoption of sustainability practices by community pharmacies in Spain in the time of COVID-19. *Sustainable Production and Consumption*, *27*, 1626–1636. doi:10.1016/j.spc.2021.03.034

Edwards, T. (2016). Of Truth, Pragmatism, and Sour Grapes: The Second Circuit's Decision in SEC v. Citigroup Global Markets. *Duke Law Journal*, *65*(6), 1241–1280.

Eksoz, C., Mansouri, S. A., Bourlakis, M., & Önkal, D. (2019). Judgmental adjustments through supply integration for strategic partnerships in food chains. *Omega*, *87*, 20–33. doi:10.1016/j.omega.2018.11.007

Gu, M., Yang, L., & Huo, B. (2021). The impact of information technology usage on supply chain resilience and performance: An ambidexterous view. *International Journal of Production Economics*, *232*, 107956. doi:10.1016/j.ijpe.2020.107956 PMID:33071462

Hobbs, J. E. (2021). Food supply chain resilience and the COVID-19 pandemic: What have we learned? *Canadian Journal of Agricultural Economics/Revue Canadienne d'agroeconomie, 69*(2), 189-196. doi:10.1111/cjag.12279

Ivanov, D., & Dolgui, A. (2019). New disruption risk management perspectives in supply chains: Digital twins, the ripple effect, and resileanness. *IFAC-PapersOnLine*, *52*(13), 337–342. doi:10.1016/j.ifacol.2019.11.138

Jabbarzadeh, A., Fahimnia, B., Sheu, J. B., & Moghadam, H. S. (2016). Designing a supply chain resilient to major disruptions and supply/demand interruptions. *Transportation Research Part B: Methodological*, *94*, 121–149. doi:10.1016/j.trb.2016.09.004

Joshi, S., & Sharma, M. (2021). Digital technologies (DT) adoption in agri-food supply chains amidst COVID-19: An approach towards food security concerns in developing countries. *Journal of Global Operations and Strategic Sourcing*. doi:10.1108/JGOSS-02-2021-0014

Kantar. (n.d.). *Cuotas de mercado de la distribución*. Retrieved on December 17, 2021, from https://www.kantarworldpanel.com/es/grocery-market-share/spain

Kerr, W. A. (2020). The COVID-19 pandemic and agriculture: Short- and long-run implications for international trade relations. *Canadian Journal of Agricultural Economics/Revue Canadienne d'agroeconomie*, *68*(2), 225–229. doi:10.1111/cjag.12230

Khan, S. A. R., Ponce, P., Tanveer, M., Aguirre-Padilla, N., Mahmood, H., & Shah, S. A. A. (2021). Technological Innovation and Circular Economy Practices: Business Strategies to Mitigate the Effects of COVID-19. *Sustainability*, *13*(15), 8479. doi:10.3390u13158479

Klumpp, M., & Loske, D. (2021). Sustainability and resilience revisited: Impact of information technology disruptions on empirical retail logistics efficiency. *Sustainability*, *13*(10), 5650. doi:10.3390u13105650

Langreo, A., & Germán, L. (2018). Transformations in the food system and the role of industrial and food distribution changes in the Spanish diet during the twentieth century. *Historia Agraria*, *74*, 167–200. doi:10.26882/histagrar.074e06l

Leat, P., & Revoredo-Giha, C. (2013). Risk and resilience in agri-food supply chains: The case of the ASDA PorkLink supply chain in Scotland. *Supply Chain Management*, *18*(2), 219–231. doi:10.1108/13598541311318845

Matthews, A. (2020). EU Food System Strengths and Vulnerabilities during Covid-19. *EuroChoices (Uckfield)*, *19*(3), 4–12. doi:10.1111/1746-692X.12300

Mena, C., Karatzas, A., & Hansen, C. (2022). International trade resilience and the Covid-19 pandemic. *Journal of Business Research*, *138*, 77–91. doi:10.1016/j.jbusres.2021.08.064 PMID:34538982

Miller, M. (2021). Big data, information asymmetry, and food supply chain management for resilience. *Journal of Agriculture, Food Systems, and Community Development*, *11*(1), 171–182. doi:10.5304/jafscd.2021.111.017

Motta, G. A., Tekinerdogan, B., & Athanasiadis, I. N. (2020). Blockchain Applications in the Agri-Food Domain: The First Wave. *Frontiers in Blockchain*. doi:10.3389/fbloc.2020.00006

Neboh, N. D., & Mbhele, T. P. (2021). Supply chain design dimensions for supply chain resilience in the South African fast-moving consumer goods retail industry. *Africa Journal of Management*, *7*(sup1, S1), 58–81. doi:10.1080/23322373.2021.1930742

Oliden, P. E., & Zumbo, B. D. (2008). Coeficientes de fiabilidad para escalas de respuesta categórica ordenada. *Psicothema*, *20*(4), 896–901. PMID:18940100

Perona, M. (2002). A New Customer-Oriented Methodology to Evaluate Supply Chain Lost Sales Costs Due to Stockout in Consumer Goods Sectors. In S. Seuring & M. Goldbach (Eds.), *Cost Management in Supply Chains* (pp. 289–307). Springer. doi:10.1007/978-3-662-11377-6_17

Rejeb, A., Rejeb, K., Abdollahi, A., Zailani, S., Iranmanesh, M., & Ghobakhloo, M. (2021). Digitalization in Food Supply Chains: A Bibliometric Review and Key-Route Main Path Analysis. *Sustainability*, *14*(1), 83. doi:10.3390u14010083

Stone, J., & Rahimifard, S. (2018). Resilience in agri-food supply chains: A critical analysis of the literature and synthesis of a novel framework. *Supply Chain Management*, *23*(3), 207–238. doi:10.1108/SCM-06-2017-0201

Todorovic, V., Maslaric, M., Bojic, S., Jokic, M., Mircetic, D., & Nikolicic, S. (2018). Solutions for More Sustainable Distribution in the Short Food Supply Chains. *Sustainability*, *10*(10), 3481. doi:10.3390u10103481

Trabucco, M., & de Giovanni, P. (2021). Achieving Resilience and Business Sustainability during COVID-19: The Role of Lean Supply Chain Practices and Digitalization. *Sustainability*, *13*(22), 12369. doi:10.3390u132212369

Verdouw, C., Beulens, A., & Trienekens, J. (2010). Reference process modelling in demand-driven agri-food supply chains: a configuration-based framework. In J. Trienekens, J. Top, J. Van Der Vorst, & A. Beulens (Eds.), *Towards effective food chains: Models and applications*. Wageningen Academic Publishers.

Xu, K., & Dong, Y. (2004). Information gaming in demand collaboration and supply chain performance. *Journal of Business Logistics*, *25*(1), 121–144. doi:10.1002/j.2158-1592.2004.tb00172.x

Zhao, G., Liu, S., & Lopez, C. (2017). A Literature Review on Risk Sources and Resilience Factors in Agri-Food Supply Chains. *IFIP Advances in Information and Communication Technology*, *506*, 739–752. doi:10.1007/978-3-319-65151-4_66

ADDITIONAL READING

Arora, C., Kamat, A., Shanker, S., & Barve, A. (2022). Integrating agriculture and industry 4.0 under "agri-food 4.0" to analyze suitable technologies to overcome agronomical barriers. *British Food Journal*. Advance online publication. doi:10.1108/BFJ-08-2021-0934

Belaud, J. P., Prioux, N., Vialle, C., & Sablayrolles, C. (2019). Big data for agri-food 4.0: Application to sustainability management for by-products supply chain. *Computers in Industry*, *111*, 41–50. doi:10.1016/j.compind.2019.06.006

Dadi, V., Nikla, S. R., Moe, R. S., Agarwal, T., & Arora, S. (2021). Agri-Food 4.0 and Innovations: Revamping the Supply Chain Operations. *Production Engineering Archives*, *27*(2), 75–89. doi:10.30657/pea.2021.27.10

Fu, H., Zhao, C. P., Cheng, C. X., & Ma, H. Y. (2020). Blockchain-based agri-food supply chain management: Case study in China. *The International Food and Agribusiness Management Review*, *23*(5), 667–679. doi:10.22434/IFAMR2019.0152

Lezoche, M., Hernandez, J. E., Alemany Diaz, M. D. E., Panetto, H., & Kacprzyk, J. (2020). Agri-food 4.0: A survey of the supply chains and technologies for the future agriculture. *Computers in Industry*, *117*, 103187. doi:10.1016/j.compind.2020.103187

Menon, S., & Jain, K. (2021). Blockchain Technology for Transparency in Agri-Food Supply Chain: Use Cases, Limitations, and Future Directions. *IEEE Transactions on Engineering Management*, 1–15. Advance online publication. doi:10.1109/TEM.2021.3110903

Morella, P., Lamban, M. P., Royo, J., & Sanchez, J. C. (2021). Study and Analysis of the Implementation of 4.0 Technologies in the Agri-Food Supply Chain: A State of the Art. *Agronomy (Basel)*, *11*(12), 2526. doi:10.3390/agronomy11122526

APPENDIX 1. QUESTIONNAIRE

Degree of Resilience

1. In our supply chain ...

    1.1. We have a high level of knowledge at all times of the conditions that may affect its operation (prevention).
    1.2. We are able to give a quick response to interruptions (recovery).

Resilience Factors

2. Supply Chain Resilience depends on...

    2.1. The business model and its ability to adapt to a changing environment.
    2.2. The financial reserve of the company to face moments of crisis.
    2.3. The geographical proximity between suppliers, warehouses and points of sale.
    2.4. The digitization and technological investment of the company.

Technological Competence

3. In our supply chain, technology...

    3.1. He has the investment support of senior management.
    3.2. It is considered useful
    3.3. It is perceived as easy to use.
    3.4. Employees use it frequently.

Technological Integration

4. The technology in the supply chain allows ...

    4.1. Have more information to improve decision making.
    4.2. Facilitate the tasks of the workers.
    4.3. Improve the quality of operational processes.

4.4. Optimize resources.
4.5. Improve coordination between value chain agents.
4.6. Improve the company's response to adverse events.

Supply Chain Performance

5. A highly resilient supply chain ...

   5.1. Improves costs.
   5.2. Reduce delivery times.
   5.3. Increases service reliability and minimizes distribution risks.
   5.4. It offers more sustainability of operations.

APPENDIX 2. SAMPLE

Table 5. Characteristics of the research sample

	Company name	NIF code	Country	Turnover (in 1000 €)
1.	MERCADONA SA	A46103834	SPAIN	24.649.629
2.	CENTROS COMERCIALES CARREFOUR SA	A28425270	SPAIN	8.491.008
3.	LIDL SUPERMERCADOS SAU	A60195278	SPAIN	4.443.165
4.	DIA RETAIL ESPAÑA SA.	A80782519	SPAIN	3.871.844
5.	ALCAMPO SAU	A28581882	SPAIN	3.349.271
6.	CONSUM S COOP V	F46078986	SPAIN	3.090.362
7.	EROSKI, S. COOP.	F20033361	SPAIN	2.021.617
8.	AHORRAMAS, SA	A28600278	SPAIN	1.805.559
9.	BON PREU SA	A08665838	SPAIN	1.788.199
10.	DINOSOL SUPERMERCADOS SL	B61742565	SPAIN	1.186.970
11.	VEGO SUPERMERCADOS SA	A36651313	SPAIN	1.014.980
12.	CAPRABO SA	A08115032	SPAIN	838.209
13.	GRUP SUPECO MAXOR SL	B60981057	SPAIN	832.257
14.	GRUPO EL ARBOL DISTRIBUCION Y SUPERMERCADOS, SA	A80223258	SPAIN	782.171
15.	DISTRIBUCIONES FROIZ SAU	A36036739	SPAIN	735.491
16.	SUPERCOR SA	A78476397	SPAIN	720.933
17.	ALIMERKA, SA	A33093097	SPAIN	716.288
18.	SEMARK AC GROUP SA	A39050349	SPAIN	678.700
19.	DISTRIBUCION SUPERMERCADOS SL	B20099586	SPAIN	541.972
20.	SUPERMERCADOS CHAMPION SA	A28090108	SPAIN	511.451
21.	SUPERSOL SPAIN SL	B86310521	SPAIN	497.289
22.	CECOSA SUPERMERCADOS SOCIEDAD LIMITADA UNIPERSONAL	B95390761	SPAIN	478.937
23.	HIPER USERA SL	B85139855	SPAIN	374.649
24.	ALDI MASQUEFA SUPERMERCADOS S.L.U.	B63667109	SPAIN	359.454
25.	FRAGADIS SL	B43396985	SPAIN	321.821
26.	SUPERMERCADOS ERCORECA SOCIEDAD ANONIMA	A48092985	SPAIN	311.857
27.	CASH LEPE SL	B21053848	SPAIN	311.582
28.	JUAN FORNES FORNES SA	A03140456	SPAIN	308.815
29.	ALDI PINTO SUPERMERCADOS S.L.U.	B84160233	SPAIN	296.013
30.	ECO MORA SA	A45038809	SPAIN	254.648
31.	HIJOS DE LUIS RODRIGUEZ SA	A33026105	SPAIN	250.394
32.	ALDI SAN ISIDRO SUPERMERCADOS S.L.U.	B53948204	SPAIN	248.712
33.	SUPERFICIES DE ALIMENTACION SA	A08586539	SPAIN	242.343
34.	ALDI DOS HERMANAS SUPERMERCADOS S.L.U.	B91405142	SPAIN	233.841

Continued on following page

Table 5. Continued

	Company name	NIF code	Country	Turnover (in 1000 €)
35.	SUPSA SUPERMERCATS PUJOL SL	B25008632	SPAIN	214.655
36.	WORLD DUTY FREE GROUP SOCIEDAD ANONIMA UNIPERSONAL.	A84205863	SPAIN	206.050
37.	LUIS PIÑA SA	A23060288	SPAIN	196.678
38.	FAMILYCASH SL	B98565906	SPAIN	180.727
39.	LIDER ALIMENT, SA	A06335582	SPAIN	172.155
40.	LA SIRENA ALIMENTACION CONGELADA SA	A63935555	SPAIN	163.528
41.	CASA AMETLLER SL	B62591359	SPAIN	162.977
42.	NAGARMUR SL	B30374540	SPAIN	156.292
43.	HIPER MANACOR SA	A07169287	SPAIN	154.736
44.	COSTASOL DE HIPERMERCADOS SL	B29866019	SPAIN	147.113
45.	HIPERBER DISTRIBUCION Y LOGISTICA SA	A53747929	SPAIN	142.590
46.	KUUPS DESIGN INTERNATIONAL SL	B54401930	SPAIN	137.547
47.	DEZA CALIDAD SA	A14051585	SPAIN	124.477
48.	SUPERMERCADOS HIBER SA	A28571750	SPAIN	123.449
49.	MASKOMO SL	B29539210	SPAIN	112.352
50.	ILITURGITANA DE HIPERMERCADOS SOCIEDAD LIMITADA	B23357700	SPAIN	94.263
51.	JOSE PADILLA FRANCES SOCIEDAD LIMITADA	B35325422	SPAIN	92.463
52.	SUPERMERCADOS MARCIAL SL	B35637792	SPAIN	91.858
53.	PRIMAPRIX SL.	B86977014	SPAIN	91.669
54.	DISTRIBUCIONES FRIONORTE SL	B38054003	SPAIN	73.399
55.	VALVI ALIMENTACIO I SERVEIS SL	B17205410	SPAIN	65.143
56.	SOCIEDAD DE DISTRIBUCION COMERCIAL AEROPORTUARIA DE CANARIAS SL	B82165440	SPAIN	52.638
57.	SUPERMERCADOS MOGAN SOCIEDAD LIMITADA	B35291798	SPAIN	36.086

Chapter 5
RPA Implementation and the Digitalization of Logistics Operations in the COVID-19 Era: A Case Study

Eric Gaston Lambourdiere
University of French West Indies, Martinique

Elsa Laurence Corbin
University of French West Indies, Martinique

Hervé Ledru
Afrobio, France

ABSTRACT

The COVID-19 pandemic has altered many organizations' operations management and accelerated the failure of those without resilient supply chains. It has greatly accelerated organizations' adoption of digital technologies and digital transformation. Digital technologies such as robotic process automation (RPA) play important roles in companies' operations-management activities and digital supply-chain transformation in the COVID-19 era. However, empirical research on RPA implementation in supply chains remains scarce. To fill this research gap, this case study was conducted to examine a global retail company's RPA implementation initiative to enhance its digital supply-chain capabilities. The authors examined three key project phases: pre-implementation, implementation, and post-implementation. They identified patterns of managerial practices and challenges related to digital technology implementation. The findings could help other organizations understand the most important issues to be addressed when seeking to implement RPA for operations activities and supply-chain processes.

DOI: 10.4018/978-1-7998-9715-6.ch005

Copyright © 2022, IGI Global. Copying or distributing in print or electronic forms without written permission of IGI Global is prohibited.

INTRODUCTION

The COVID-19 pandemic has contributed to huge uncertainties in demand and the disruption of global supply chains (Ye, Liu, Li, Lai, Zhan, & Kumar, 2022) and, overall, organizations' operations management; key challenges include delivery delays and goods shortages (Tietze, Vimalnath, Aristodemou, & Molloy, 2020). Disaster recovery programs have been activated to stabilize organizations' processes and operations (Siderska, 2021), for instance by shifting to online business operations (Atilgan, 2020). Business continuity capability – the ability to ensure essential functions during and after a crisis, collapse, catastrophe, disaster, or pandemic – is the most important priority for organizations in the COVID-19 era (Siderska, 2021). Organizations must mitigate the negative impact of the pandemic on their operations; many have optimized their supply chains to ensure a certain amount of safety stock and the on-time delivery of goods to customers (Choi, 2021).

To build resilient supply chains, organizations strive to improve their operations efficiency by redesigning and managing their business processes. Automation is an invaluable asset in this respect. Digital technologies can support organizations' achievement of end-to-end transparency, replace employees who are absent because of COVID-19, predict potential risks across supply chains, and reduce demand uncertainties (Ivanov, Dolgui, & Sokolov, 2019). They play key roles in supporting organizations' implementation of resilient supply-chain strategies, and supply-chain digitalization is a major investment priority for numerous organizations. The most frequently cited disruptive digital technologies deployed throughout supply chains, which can enhance business operations resilience and continuity, include artificial intelligence, robotics, big data, cloud computing, virtual reality, and digital information technologies (Mbunge, Akinnuwesi, Fashoto, Metfula, & Mashwama, 2021; Nah & Siau, 2020). Automation strategies play key roles in firms' digital supply-chain transformations (Attaran, 2020), enhancing supply-chain processes and sustainability, and thereby resilience (Frederico, 2021; Paul, Moktadir, & Ahsan, 2021). Robotic process automation (RPA), an advanced digital technology, is increasingly used in the redesign, optimization, and automation of supply-chain processes (Doğuç, 2021). Supply-chain managers are leveraging technologies such as RPA to improve operations and create value for customers and resilience and sustainability in the COVID-19 environment (Doğuç, 2021; Viale & Zouari, 2020). RPA considerably reduces costs and saves time, increasing organizations' competitiveness (e.g., Viale & Zouarie, 2020). The automation of logistics processes and supply-chain management is advancing rapidly, and most operational logistics functions could be handled with nearly full autonomy by 2029 (Junge, Verhoeven, Reipert, & Mansfeld, 2019; Nitsche, 2021). Practitioner articles and consultancy white papers have documented the potential benefits of RPA in terms of opportunities for digital supply-chain and operations management and supply-chain resilience (Doğuç, 2021; Syed et al., 2020). However, few guidelines and best practices for the realization of these benefits have been established (Syed et al., 2020). Strategic issues related to RPA implementation have been discussed (Viale & Zouari, 2020), and recent publications provide examples of the requirements for and challenges stemming from the shift toward digital supply-chain management (e.g., Hennelly, Srai, Graham, & Fosso Wamba, 2019). Academic studies of the impacts of RPA adoption on organizations' processes, capabilities, and professionals remain scarce (Flechsig, Anslinger, & Lasch, 2021).

The establishment of guidelines for successful RPA implementation across organizations is important. According to Zangiacomi, Pessot, Fornasiero, Bertetti, and Sacco (2020), the successful adoption of digital technologies and practices entails disruptive changes and far-reaching opportunities. Digitalization strategy development requires the consideration of elements such as advances at the managerial, organizational, and strategic levels (Schumacher, Erol, & Sihn, 2016). Digital technology implementation through operations-management processes is not well understood, and many companies are still investigating its benefits (Buer, Strandhagen, & Chan, 2018; Yin, Stecke, & Li, 2018). This case study was conducted to investigate managerial practices following RPA adoption in a global retail company (company A) for which the COVID-19 crisis accelerated the digitalization of its supply chains and thereby its supply-chain processes. It contributes to ongoing debate on the implications of digitalization and industry 4.0 evolution in operations and supply-chain management (e.g., Frederico, Garza-Reyes, Anosike, & Kumar, 2020) and the use of disruptive technologies in supply-chain strategies during and after the COVID-19 crisis (Modgil, Singh, & Hannibal, 2021; Paul et al., 2021). The purpose of this article is to create a better picture of digital transformation in the RPA deployment context by examining issues that company managers can influence directly (Schneider, 2018). Two research questions (RQs) are addressed:

RQ1: From a managerial perspective, what phases did company A consider when elaborating its RPA implementation?

RQ2: What challenges related to RPA implementation did company A face, and what practices did it use to address those challenges?

BACKGROUND

RPA and Digital Transformation Acceleration in the COVID-19 Pandemic Era

RPA is an "emerging form of business process automation technology based on the notion of software robots or artificial intelligence (AI) workers" (Madakam, Holmukhe, & Jaiswal, 2019, p.4). It is a powerful intangible asset that allows a computer to complete human tasks (Arias, Beltrán, & Bedoya, 2020). According to van der Aalst, Bichler, and Heinzl (2018, p.269), "RPA is an umbrella term for tools that operate on the user interface of other computer systems in the way a human would do". It can be implemented for human resources, finance, accounting, customer service, and supply-chain management processes, and has been used in the telecommunications, utilities, mining, travel, retail, and healthcare industries (IBM, 2019). Practitioners and scholars consider RPA to be an advanced, cutting-edge core solution for digital transformation (Karumsi, Prokopets, Clements, & Parva, 2020; Viale & Zouari, 2020). This technology encompasses a wide range of administrative tasks through specific software that interacts with multiple applications and computer-centric processes. It can be used to execute transactional processes at the user interface level.

The strengths of RPA outweigh its weaknesses (Hindel, Cabrera, & Stierle, 2020). RPA implementation can increase cost effectiveness and the quality of transactional processes, such as the transfer of data from multiple input sources (e.g., emails and spreadsheets) to systems of record for enterprise resource planning and customer relationship management (Lacity & Willcoks, 2016). It cuts the costs of human resources–related spending by 20–50% (e.g., Rae, 2016; Slaby, 2012) and transaction processing by 30–60% (Lacity & Willcoks, 2016), and reduces process-cycle, task-handling, and waiting times by 30–70% (Chakroborty, 2017). With RPA, workers do not manipulate existing application software as they did previously for transaction processing or process completion. Sullivan, Simpson, and Li (2021) found empirical support for RPA implementation among Konica Minolta employees reflecting the efficiency and effectiveness of operations management; the deployment of 55 RPA bots with similar work pipelines in 2018 has saved the company about 19,000 work hours. RPA is very efficient for rule-based, predictable, and replicable processes that require the handling of high volumes of structured data (IBM, 2019). It provides many opportunities when applied to processes falling in the "white space" between those managed by other technologies. RPA can help companies achieve competitive advantage, create value by enabling the re-appropriation of high-value skills for innovation, improve accuracy and reduce downstream errors, reduce risks, and deliver measurable outcomes with visible impact (IBM, 2019). Hence, it can improve productivity and allow employees to participate in more value-added activities involving more personal interaction, problem solving, and decision making (Kroll, Bujak, Darius, Enders, & Esser, 2016). It can bring immediate value to firms' core businesses. RPA can be deployed quickly without major upfront investment, unlike previously introduced automation technologies and digital transformation strategies (e.g., Hofmann, Samp, & Urbach, 2020).

Firms interested in RPA deployment for their business operations focus on rule-based robotic automation solutions. Currently, this approach is applied to uncomplex back-office processes, such as invoicing; as the technology evolves and develops new capabilities (i.e., becomes more knowledge based), it can be used to manage more-unstructured patterned tasks (e.g., in customer service). Eventually, RPA will become cognitively based (i.e., "think" for itself) and will be able to execute unstructured, free-form processes, working alongside humans on value-adding initiatives. Hence, RPA deployment has a variety of benefits and can be a valuable component of companies' digitalization strategies (Siderska, 2020; Viale & Zouari, 2020).

Globally, the COVID-19 pandemic has accelerated business process transformation, optimization, and automation, thereby reinforcing RPA use (Doguç, 2021; Lacity & Willcocks, 2021; McKinsey, 2020). Organizations who had adopted RPA before the pandemic have fared better than have those that had not (Lacity & Willcocks, 2021). Huge numbers of consumers have moved toward online channels, contributing to the acceleration of customer interaction digitalization, during the pandemic (McKinsey, 2020). The pandemic also augmented the need for logistics and supply-chain management automation. At its outbreak, for instance, logistics and supply-chain managers could not perform business tasks (Siderska, 2021); they recognized that increasing supply-chain responsiveness and the gaining of partial independence from personnel were the most important pandemic-related challenges (Nitsche, 2021; Straube & Nitsche, 2020). Connectivity and security, which can restrict access to important information and organization systems when they are at stake, were threatening business continuity (Siderska, 2021). RPA has been used to redesign supply chains to enhance their responsiveness and resilience and the continuity of business operations (Belhadi, Kamble, Jabbour, Gunasekaran, Ndubisi, & Venkatesh, 2021; Hobbs, 2021; Nah & Siau, 2020; Wuest, Kusiak, Dai, & Tayur, 2020), and to support organizations' sustainable maintenance of business processes while ensuring employee safety (Siderska, 2021). For instance, the use of software robots, which are not vulnerable to organic pathogens, has allowed organizations to address issues such as lost worker days, gaps due to sick employees, and the pausing of production lines (Bloom & Pretter, 2020). At the height of the COVID-19 crisis, RPA enabled the continuation of service provision to customers (Doguç, 2021). Although generally considered to be easy, initial RPA implementation fails in about 30–50% of cases (Ravn, Halberg, Gustafsson, & Groes, 2016) and the realization of benefits from RPA adoption cannot be taken for granted (Syed et al., 2020). Many issues may arise (Gotthardt, Koivulaakso, Paksoy, Saramo, Martikainen, & Lehner, 2020; Herm et al., 2020), and they become important factors for organizations that ignore them (Santos, Pereira, & Vasconcelos, 2019). Moreover, many uncertainties related to successful RPA implementation remain (Syed et al., 2020). Given the challenges faced (Gotthardt et al., 2020; Ivančić, Vugec, & Vukšić, 2019), more in-depth study of RPA and its implementation is needed (Herm et al., 2020); this empirical case study seeks to address this need.

RPA Implementation in Three Phases

Framework

As theoretical guidance is in high demand among practitioners, the availability of systematic approaches to successful RPA implementation remains very important (Herm et al., 2020). Practitioners seek solutions to avoid implementation pitfalls and cope with numerous challenges while undertaking digital transformation. Despite the scarcity of RPA implementation, some recent publications address this need. Santos et al. (2019) provide a conceptual model for successful RPA implementation in three steps: strategic goal setting, process assessment, and tactical evolution. Herm et al. (2020) presented a model for RPA implementation where guidelines are suggested at each stage. This framework is also divided into three phases: initialization, implementation, and scaling. Literature on non-RPA system implementation and business technologies [e.g., enterprise resource planning (ERP)] can also inform the development of a theoretical framework for the successful implementation of digital technologies such as RPA, given the existence of common issues and methodologies. In this study, the ERP lifecycle framework introduced by Esteves and Bohórquez (2007) and further discussed by Ali and Miller (2017) was adopted. This simple logistical framework focuses on three essential phases: pre-implementation, implementation, and post-implementation (Figure 1). It is a means, not an end, and was selected to accommodate as many different organizations as possible. Our study adopts the lens of implementation science theory as well (Goodrich, Miake-Lye, Braganza, Wawrin, Kilbourne, & Initiative, 2020; Bauer, Damschroder, Hagedorn, Smith, & Kilbourne, 2015; Fixsen, Naoom, Blase, Friedman, & Wallace, 2005).

Figure 1.

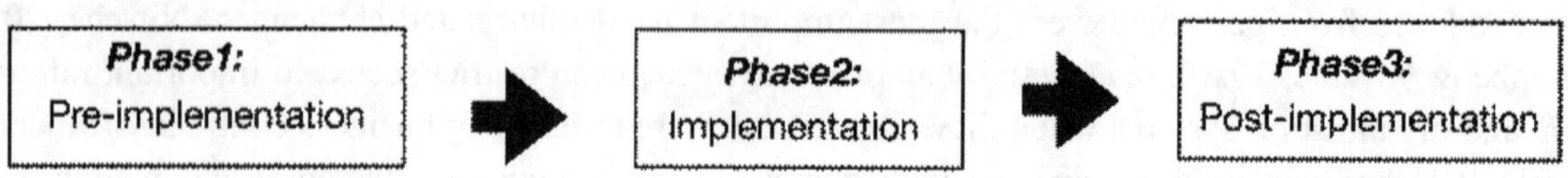

Pre-Implementation Phase

The pre-implementation phase is critical; it has direct impacts on implementation and its outcome (Ali & Miller, 2017). It is the origin of attitudes and processes such as resistance, involvement, and feedback among those charged with implementation, which shape future phases (Herold, Farmer, & Mobley, 1995). Understanding the nature and origin of certain attitudes is among the most important pre-implementation factors (Herold et al., 1995). Before beginning digital transformation, companies must have a clear understanding of the technological opportunities available (Heavin & Power, 2018). As digital-solutions design and implementation are very diverse (Gölzer & Fritzsche, 2017), proper formulation of the problem that a company wishes to solve with digital technology is crucial for digitalization path development (Zangiacomi et al., 2020). Companies should be able to prioritize and invest in such technologies (Baur & Wee, 2015). In this phase, managers usually engage in activities such as technology introduction planning, determining the roles of vendors and in-house resources, providing primary training to employees, planning the logistics of change, and deciding whether to conduct a pilot study. They make decisions about the rate of change (i.e., all at once or gradual phase-in) (Abdinnour-Helm, Lengnick-Hall, & Lengnick-Hall, 2003). Initial practical experiences with digital technology in operations management often involve prototypes and pilot projects (Gölzer & Fritzche, 2017); managers must decide which such projects should be prioritized (Heavin & Power, 2018). In addition, digital technologies have large impacts on organizations' business models (Müller, Buliga, & Voigt, 2018), and the definition of a roadmap and long-term investment are required (Khan & Turowski, 2016b). In developing digital transformation strategies, managers should address the challenge of governing an innovative ecosystem and supporting performance monitoring (Jardim-Goncalves, Romero, & Grilo, 2017) by relying on better collaboration between their organizations and digital-technology service providers.

Implementation Phase

Digital technology implementation for operations-management processes can effectively strengthen companies' digital strategies (Schiavone & Sprenger, 2017); it, and digital transformation overall, can be seen as opportunities to improve and change current company processes (Moeuf, Pellerin, Lamouri, Tamayo-Giraldo, & Barbaray, 2018). Managers of companies involved in operations-process digitalization must be aware of the changes and challenges that they may encounter when they promote digital technology initiatives (Moeuf et al., 2018). The long-term success of transformation paths requires the integration of infrastructural capabilities and connectivity, and the use of a stepwise approach (Khan & Turowski, 2016a; Srai et al., 2016). Uncertainty, and ambiguity regarding the impact of digital transformation on the organizational structure, are parts of any digital technology implementation effort (Srai et al., 2016). The implementation phase includes several activities that are essential for success, and thus can last a long time. Its termination can be difficult to identify (Abdinnour-Helm et al., 2003). Hence, top management must be proactively involved during this phase (Aladwani, 2001).

Organizations create centers of excellence (CoEs) during this phase. With RPA implementation for supply-chain processes, they are introducing new risks to their business environments. For instance, managers may find the range of RPA technologies on the market confusing, and want to know the categories and best applications of these technologies. CoE teams can help to address the introduced risks. CoEs are psychologically safe environments where individuals, including those of lower organizational status, are willing to contribute ideas, questions, and concerns without fearing retaliation. They play a key role in the implementation phase because they help organizations to maximize logistics activities for RPA use, thereby creating competitive advantage. Successful implementation requires the establishment of CoEs with overall visions and directions for RPA programs. CoEs also aid strategizing regarding the use of automation in a way that ensures a return on investment (Davenport & Shaefer, 2021). They help managers to focus on cost-reduction strategies and the scaling of automation as rapidly as possible. After managers have decided which strategy to pursue and production has begun, CoEs must oversee robotic workers. Some managers believe deeply that RPA deployment marks the end of a project, and that oversight from the organization is not required. In fact, RPA implementation necessitates a digital workforce maintenance program to ensure that automation systems are optimized to deliver the best performance. Monitoring and reporting on the measurable value delivered and the holistic benefits to operations processes occur through CoEs (Davenport & Shaefer, 2021). Managers must collaborate with executives to understand the implications of automation for workforce organization. Human resources should also be connected to CoEs for the design of employee retraining programs, enabling determination of which activities employees should undertake following RPA installation. Discussions between managers and others about the circumstances under which automation leads to downsizing and the types of training and reskilling required with RPA adoption also occur in CoEs (Davenport & Shaefer, 2021).

Post-Implementation Phase

The post-implementation phase is an important part of implementation (Ali & Miller, 2017). The ERP implementation literature (e.g., Davenport, 1998) indicates that the consideration of digital technology implementation as a project with a termination date is erroneous; rather, ERP projects have "go-live" dates (Willis & Willis-Brown, 2002) and do not end once the systems become operational (Nah, Lau, & Kuang, 2001). Real challenges emerge in the post-implementation phase. This phase involves the reviewing of the overall project scope; evaluation of organizational learning; continuous monitoring, maintenance, and adoption of internal know-how and capabilities; and internal promotion (Nicolaou, 2004). Companies' systems networking in digital ecosystems relies on interconnectivity and interoperability among intelligent components, and thus knowledge of intelligent vertical and horizontal networking, on which actions and decisions can be based (Capestro & Kinkel, 2020; Tao, Qi, Liu, & Kusiak, 2018). The huge amounts of data produced by digital systems require human processing for the creation and management of useful new knowledge (e.g., about products or processes) (Bogers, Hadar, & Bilberg, 2016; Ramzi, Ahmad, & Zakaria, 2019). For instance, employees and managers must acquire new knowledge about data management (e.g., acquisition, conversion, and application) and processes (Dragicevic, Ullrich, Tsui, & Gronau, 2020) in a digital environment. Moreover, to be able to manage their companies' processes in a new way, employees must obtain knowledge that contributes to the creation of digital thinking in the organization (Schniederjans, Curado, & Khalajhedayati, 2020). Thus, managers must consider proper sharing and skills when thinking about operations-management digitalization (Fatorachian & Kazemi, 2018); they must build digital capabilities for the proper handling of changes along the digitalization transformation path (Schneider, 2018). Successful digital technology implementation and use require the acquisition of new skills and competences (Schwab, 2017).

METHODS

Research Design and Case Selection

As the variables contributing to the RQs were largely unknown, this work was conducted using an exploratory case-study design. The case-study approach is recommended for research in an emerging area, in the stages of understanding, discovery, and description (Bandara, Indulska, Chong, & Sadiq, 2007; Stuart, McCutcheon, Handfield, McLachlin, & Samson, 2002), and is most appropriate for the qualitative exploration of "why," "what," and "how" questions (Yin, 2012). Case studies enable the in-situ examination of contemporary organizational phenomena (Ketokivi & Choi, 2014). By utilizing current and past data from "real-life" situations, they create new knowledge and insight that might not be captured with the use of other research methods (Baxter & Jack, 2008; Yin, 2012). Such research can make useful contributions to management practices and theory development in a new field.

The examination of a single case, as here, is most appropriate to gain insight on a unique firm with the researchers placed in the context of the phenomena being examined (Andrew, Pedersen, & McEvoy, 2019). The authors selected company A, an international firm specializing in the trade of consumer goods, due to its reputation as an early adopter of emerging digital technologies, considering the company's approach to RPA adoption and the degree of its implementation. As proposed by Zangiacomi et al. (2020), they focused on the company's strategy, goals, and key performance indicators (KPIs). They have agreed to protect the company's identity, withholding or slightly modifying several details (Adelman, Jenkins, & Kemmis, 1976). Observations were made for 1 year after RPA introduction at company A.

Case Context

Supply-chain operations processes are corrupted by many monotonous document-oriented tasks. For example, the searching of business paperwork content and scanning and uploading of documents are time consuming. Such activities diminish the productivity of company A's sales department employees, who otherwise could contribute to value creation for the organization. The failure to collect business-critical information and lack of customer service may occur in this context. Hence, company A's employees face various problems with back-office administration. They have issues with the collection of information and simultaneously keeping in touch with customers by telephone or email; they are not able to devote their full time to company A's customers. Company A is under immense pressure to provide the highest-quality service at a low cost, leading to the decision to enhance its existing supply-chain operations through digitalization to improve its competitive advantage. With the COVID-19 pandemic, company A has decided to continue to bring life to its customers' dreams through a unique digital experience. RPA deployment enables the introduction of innovative digitalized logistics activities that help employees overwhelmed with the extra workload resulting from the pandemic, increasing their online interaction with customers. The company had already begun the digital transformation of their supply-chain processes, and accelerated RPA adoption for logistics activities with the pandemic.

Data Collection and Analysis

This study was based primarily on historical data analysis (covering 2018–2021) and semi-structured interviews with three senior executives (the CEO, project manager, and operations manager) who were responsible for company A's RPA implementation for supply-chain processes. Because they were routinely involved in the organization's high-level strategic digital decision making, these individuals were the richest sources of information about this process. They had operations and supply-chain management backgrounds, and several years of experience with supply-chain management at company A. Their technical knowledge was ensured by their close contact with the consulting company responsible for the design of company A's complete RPA solution; additional clarification was obtained from this company as needed. The use of convenience sampling and key-informant interviews was appropriate, given the managerial perspective of the research. Access to these executives was gained via a combination of personal networks and snowball sampling.

Data collection and analysis were performed manually in interaction, with review and refinement of the emerging findings as needed. The interviews (average, 3 hours) began with broad questions, which allowed the informants to present the material in their own terms. The interviewees were then asked open-ended questions related to the RQs and the researchers took notes. Each participant was given a transcript of his or her interview for cross-referencing and to ensure consistency between the recorded data and intended meaning. The data were classified into two orders: first-order data corresponding to informants' views and second-order data emerging from concept coding. The pattern-matching technique was used to identify practices related to company A's digitalization (Voss, Tsikriktsis, & Frohlich, 2002; Yin, 2012). Theme coding was performed in three steps (recording of raw data and preliminary and final coding) as described by Saldaña (2015). It was guided by the research objective, with special attention given to the company's investment in digital technology, ability to perceive the path toward digital transformation and knowledge sharing, and design and management of supply-chain processes underpinned by RPA (Zangiacomi et al., 2020). Similarities and differences between data and code groups were identified (Eisenhardt, 1989; Yin, 2012). Then, RPA implementation challenges, possible mistakes, and benefits for company A's supply-chain processes were examined. To ensure the integrity of the research, sampling, reliability, and validity were addressed. The interviewees were chosen based on their ability to provide reliable contributions; interview transcription, coding, and data collection were performed directly; and interview data and written records were analyzed together. To avoid researcher bias to the greatest possible extent, the research was designed and performed with special attention to contextual aspects (Nagappan, 2001).

The secondary data reflected a broad search of materials such as published documents, press reports, company websites, and business press articles. Insights gained from them supported the interpretation of the terms emerging from the interview data analysis. The use of multiple sources contributes to the reliability and validity of the data, reducing the risk of common method bias (Jakobsen & Jensen, 2015).

RESULTS

Pre-Implementation Phase

Identification of "Problems" with Current Supply-Chain Process Practices

RPA uptake for supply-chain processes at company A had been slow, but was accelerated due to the COVID-19 pandemic and the development of new digital technology capabilities. During the COVID-19 crisis, the company experienced increased sales volumes for items such as fashion leather and goods. Before the pandemic, shipment status communication was entirely manual; company A's employees received emails from clients, logged into the ERP system to find shipment records, sent status updates to customers, and closed each case. The company's logistics and transportation department regularly receives customer inquiries about shipment status, which increased with the pandemic. Thus, it deployed RPA, enabling customers to inquire with a chatbot or live agent. In addition, company A enabled several of its employees to work from home. As one manager said:

In the beginning phases of RPA technology in our logistics activities, the robot solution we settled on was not flexible enough to handle complex operations. Accordingly, RPA technology implementation across our organization has been very slow, since we have started to implement the technology. COVID-19 did accelerate the digital transformation of our logistics activities. Hence, we have able to eliminate 40–50% of the manual effort required to answer customer status queries. (Informant 3)

Stakeholder Engagement

Before investing in RPA, company A' managers sought the support of experts and intermediaries, who helped the company make investment and strategic decisions. One executive stated:

RPA technology experts did help us to invest efficiently in the technology and guide us in our strategy choices based on our specific priorities. (Informant 1)

Another enabling practice identified in the analysis was the use of small pilot projects for RPA adoption to understand, for instance, governance issues. Company A's managers used a modular approach, applying RPA to operations-management activities before applying it to the company's overall supply-chain processes. One executive stated:

RPA was deployed in the company's transport and customer-service units, and was set for implementation in other units, such as procurement. [...] We did not exploit technical demonstrators to test and highlight related opportunities because they considered RPA technology to be a mature digital technology. (Informant 3)

All three managers recognized the need to invest in digital technology training for successful RPA adoption. One executive stated:

To be successful in our digital transformation strategy through the RPA advanced technology implementation, we needed to stimulate all of our human resources and this at any level of our organization. New skills and attitudes and culture related to digital technology have to emerge inside all over our company. (Informant 1)

Regarding the adoption of lean management approaches before investing in RPA, the three interviewees considered that their company had a lean structure, an important capability, and was already flexible and ready for new technology adoption. They were convinced that their experience and knowledge of lean management was an enabler of RPA implementation for supply-chain processes. At this stage, they re-ensured that people capable of redesigning the organization's business processes were present. The operations manager stated:

We had this great project to implement RPA technology in our organization. Nevertheless, I don't think it would be possible to successfully deploy this technology without clear knowledge of the company's supply-chain processes. I always think with a lean approach we will have a quick and efficient rollout of the RPA technology across our organization's supply-chain processes. (Informant 2)

Acquisition of Performance Data

The three managers monitored performance metrics such as KPIs and the number of hours gained by implementing RPA for supply-chain processes over time to reveal differences between manual and automated logistics activities. One manager stated:

Knowing your performance at the start of the project not only provides you with baseline data against which you can measure your progress. Those results will also guide our decision making about how high to set our initial goals to improve our logistics operations once we implement our RPA technology. (Informant 3)

Implementation Phase

RPA Implementation

All three interviewees emphasized that the RPA rollout went beyond the addressing of IT infrastructure issues. One manager stated:

It was important for us to improve the transversal communication among our business units. We did then everything to extend the vision of our supply-chain processes to underpin RPA advanced technology to our overall organization. The aim here is to avoid that people from the operations department are the only employees concerned with the new technology. (Informant 3)

The three informants had a pioneer mindset that enabled them to motivate decision making, speed up RPA implementation, and overcome reactive or negative attitudes toward it. They stated:

We try to develop competence through our employees to allow them to understand the RPA advanced technology, the advantages that this technology can bring to our logistics operations. For this goal we have not hesitated to include "technology enthusiasts" in the project. (Informant 1)

We did identify and prepare champions and obtain formal commitments from some of our best employees. Developing employee interrelationships has been practiced at the center of our implementation strategies. (Informant 2)

Training and educating our associates in RPA technology has been also another pillar of our implementation strategy. Accordingly, we offer ongoing and dynamic training. (Informant 3)

The managers were able to achieve scaling by first introducing RPA to a small number of employees with greater capabilities and readiness to accept digital technologies (i.e., innovators and early adopters). One interviewee stated:

Recruiting early adopters to attend stakeholder meetings to present their experiences was very important to me. Indeed, I think, they have been a good pool to learn from their experiences with the effective practice of the RPA technology and its benefits for the tested logistics operations. Their attitude toward the technology influences the messages they disseminate through word of mouth. They have been so useful that because of them we could improve our organizational implementation process by integrating the information and knowledge acquired from users. (Informant 2)

Company A's managers avoided the targeting of barriers that could not be overcome feasibly or had little impact on outcomes. One executive stated:

We did prioritize strategies that were feasible. We did not want to waste time on challenges we know that we would not be able to overcome. Indeed, what we did was to prioritize barriers that we did know have a high probability of making a positive impact on digitalized processes. (Informant 1)

All participants described the creation of a CoE in company A with the participation of managers with various competences in all of the company's functions, RPA experts, and process administrators to supervise RPA introduction. The CoE is responsible for RPA governance, license management, integration into the IT landscape, and maintenance, as well as management changes. It is where ideas are shared and organizational skills are improved. Personnel and programming are devoted to supporting the scaling up of logistics operations digitalization with RPA. The intraorganizational promotion of RPA also occurs through the CoE. One executive explained:

The CoE is a place where all managers of our company can gather and share ideas, results, etc. It is another essential resource center dedicated to supporting the implementation of effective logistics operations practices by using various communication strategies such as publications and conferences. (Informant 1)

The three interviewees emphasized that successfully implementation strategies created a learning climate and psychologically safe environment. They integrated RPA implementation activities into their organization by prioritizing efforts, setting goals, and fostering accountability while empowering concerned stakeholders. Additionally, stakeholders can provide feedback on the logistics-operations processes during RPA implementation. The interviewees stated:

Our implementation strategies are not just rollout to build capacity to implement the RPA technology, but building a broad capacity across our organization to implement future digital technology such as AI as skills are developed as well. (Informant 3)

I do think that the staff that participate in the RPA technology project should feel comfortable while they are either sharing successful strategies to address implementation challenges or expressing their hard time during the whole RPA technology project. I do seriously believe it is the only way for learning to occur. If we did ignore that, the employees would have probably not been willing to speak up. (Informant 1)

All three interviewees emphasized the importance of reporting progress to stakeholders, as they needed timely feedback about their current performance relative to goals and evidence-based benchmarks. Feedback loops among stakeholders revealed what was (not) working with RPA implementation in targeted supply-chain processes. The informants emphasized the importance of thoughtful engagement in performance feedback. They periodically shared the results of formative evaluations with employees, reinforcing the participation of the team involved in the RPA project across company A. Barriers and successes encountered with RPA deployment in the company's supply-chain processes were quickly reported to the managers involved in the digital transformation project. The reporting of progress to stakeholders was facilitated by the availability of accessible and transparent data at all organizational levels. One interviewee stated:

Data was shared and discussed during recurring meetings between managers, senior leaders, and operational stakeholders. The data were digestible and relevant to allow managers of our organization to make changes in their implementation efforts. Additionally, we used improvement methods like Plan-Do-Study-Act when failure to achieve performance goals was reported by stakeholders. (Informant 3)

Post-Implementation Phase

RPA Sustainment

Company A built internal RPA knowledge and capabilities to take full advantage of this digital technology over the long term. The CoE has conducted training to build general capacity across the company. Experts from the company delivering the RPA have provided technical assistance and facilitation of RPA implementation processes. Tools to support implementation have been provided to company A's employees. To facilitate RPA acceptance throughout the organization, some employees were promoted. The interviewees discussed the importance of sustained RPA use to enhance the effectiveness of the organization's logistics operations, and presented several cost analyses showing the return on investment in RPA implementation. One interviewee stated:

Thinking of setting performance benchmarks to determine the RPA technology practice effectiveness and demonstrate the value of the digital technology did help us indeed to develop our business plan to continue the use of RPA technology with logistics operations as henceforth innovated digitalized logistics activities. (Informant 2)

DISCUSSION

This case study of RPA implementation revealed key activities that occurred during the pre-implementation, implementation, and post-implementation phases. Objectives were defined at each stage. During pre-implementation, the key activities were a series of collaborative steps taken by Company A's senior managers. They worked with employees to identify logistics operations whose effectiveness would be improved by RPA. They engaged employees at all organizational levels to contribute to the planning of RPA implementation for supply-chain processes. They also assessed barriers to RPA implementation across the organization and developed strategies to overcome them. They agreed on a plan for evaluation with meaningful measures, which enabled them to keep stakeholders informed about achievements in RPA implementation for key supply-chain processes. The phase-specific focus and this pre-implementation approach were critical; the strategies that the managers adopted directly impacted the implementation and post-implementation phases, and thus the overall outcome of digital transformation with RPA. The pre-implementation phase should be considered the starting point of attitudes that shape the other implementation phases (Ali & Miller, 2017).

During the implementation phase, the managers finalized the selection and deployment of their RPA implementation strategies with the aim of enhancing the uptake of this digital technology. The managers helped stakeholders successfully integrate RPA into routine supply-chain processes using transactional and transformational management strategies. They implemented strategies and plans to address barriers and resource constraints in the COVID-19 context. They accessed employees' technical, adoptive, and relational skills to spread RPA use throughout the company. The interviewees used transformative leadership approaches to empower their organization's employees to own the implementation process. They also reported progress and performance information, which allowed them to receive timely feedback on the organization's RPA implementation process. Company A's employees have been engaged in iterative problem solving for the adjustment of implementation plans and strategies. Additionally, reporting helped employees to find ways to improve supply-chain process performance and spread RPA adoption to all functions of the organization. The dedicated CoE team set standards, provided consulting and development assistance, and monitored the role of RPA at this stage of the company's digital transformation. During the implementation phase, top management support, good project teams, and good communication are very important to increase the odds of successful RPA implementation (Ali & Miller, 2017). Focusing on these factors helped the senior executives reduce implementation-associated risks. The managers' transactional and transformational leadership styles contributed to RPA uptake, influencing organizational climate, culture, and environment factors, which are enablers of innovation, learning, and improvement (Kilbourne, Goodrich, Miake-Lye, Braganza, & Bowersox, 2019). Transactional leadership practices were used to make incremental changes, and transformational leadership practices are used to support collaborative work (Kilbourne et al., 2019).

The post-implementation phase includes activities such as the testing of system effectiveness, assessment of reliability, system utilization, and evaluation of the benefits of system implementation (Huang, Chang, Li, & Lin, 2004; Nah et al., 2001). Company A created a business plan to support ongoing effective digitalized logistics activities across the organization, as RPA implementation did not end once the technology became operational. Real challenges emerge in the post-implementation phase (Ali & Miller, 2017). Accordingly, the three managers assessed RPA effectiveness and performance on an ongoing basis in this phase. They used the Plan-Do-Study-Act cycle (Deming, 1991; Taylor, McNicholas, Nicolay, Darzi, Bell, & Reed, 2014), an iterative problem-solving approach, to help them address gaps between current performance and benchmarked goals. They supported systematic experimentation for RPA improvement and adoption. In these ways, the employees involved learned from small failures inherent to particular supply-chain processes and made adjustments. Company A has adopted effective digitalized logistics operations with RPA over time to maintain or improve the effectiveness of new supply-chain processes. Its senior executives periodically review these processes to inform decisions about whether to sustain digitalized logistics activities with RPA.

Limitations

Expanding on other research, this paper provides a more comprehensive view of digital technology (RPA) implementation for supply-chain processes. However, some limitations of the work should be addressed. First, the authors examined a single case of successful RPA implementation in a single organization. Case studies are not representative or generalizable. Thus, the authors recommend that managers use the RPA implementation framework presented here cautiously. The investigation of additional cases would improve the robustness and external validity of the results. Second, although the case study approach is suitable for the generation of insights and development of new theories when previous research is scarce, subsequent quantitative research is needed to test the generalizability of the findings. Third, the RPA implementation project was analyzed using data collected only from managers who assumed that RPA adoption would benefit their company's supply-chain processes. Employees were not asked about their views on or satisfaction with RPA adoption in this context. In addition, organizational factors that may have influenced the project and the interorganizational exchange of project members were not examined. Future research could focus more on organizational issues, details of operational processes, and project management structures to determine how RPA implementation project teams work together successfully. Although the company A managers were asked about the challenges they encountered while implementing RPA, this research focused largely on the positive impacts of the digital technology on supply-chain processes. The introduction of some negative results would help to balance the findings.

CONCLUSION

To remain competitive, organizations strive to improve their operations efficiency, often focusing on business process redesign and management via digital technologies. Successful RPA adoption and efficient business processes can have positive impacts on organizations' strategic goals, staff productivity, and customer service (Lacity & Willcoks, 2016). The COVID-19 pandemic increased the adoption of automation technologies, thereby reinforcing automation solutions. RPA has helped oragnizations to overcome unforeseen changes in their business operations in this context (Doguç, 2021).

Many RPA vendors and products are in the market. Companies seeking guidance in preparing for RPA adoption and selecting and implementing an RPA system can seek advice from vendors or consultancy organizations (Syed et al., 2020), but such actors can be hyperbolic about the contributions of digital technology, and their guidelines and frameworks for RPA solution selection and implementation may be biased. Guidelines and best practices for successful RPA deployment are scarce, and academic research in this area has only begun (Syed et al., 2020). Supporting practices and benefits of digital technology use for operations management remain to be investigated (Buer et al., 2018).

In this study, ERP implementation theory and the implementation science approach were used to investigate RPA implementation in a global retailer. The chronology of events and key activities that took place during company A's RPA implementation (in the pre-implementation, implementation, and post-implementation phases) were described. This case study can provide guidance for organizations' existing and potential RPA implementation projects. Practitioners can gain insight enabling them to increase the odds of successful RPA deployment from the study findings, presented in terms of managerial challenges and good practices. This approach allows practitioners to identify and focus on issues related to RPA implementation in their organizations. In addition, researchers can use the insight provided by this study to inform the development of future empirical studies.

Senior managers who consider RPA to be a central component of their next level of digital transformation should develop a targeted road map for the process. The authors conclude from the case presented here that managers in charge of RPA implementation projects must consider opportunities and challenges at the centers of their organizations' digital transformation through RPA. In the case described here, the managers conducted a pilot project that provided good knowledge about RPA, such as its functionality, prerequisites, and drawbacks. This capability enabled assessment of the appropriateness of the digital technology in the given technological, organizational, and business environments. Managers should consider common process understanding, alignment, and digitalization (Kurpjuweit, Schmidt, Klöckner, & Wagner, 2021) in the RPA pre-implementation phase. RPA implementation has been addressed in the operations and supply-chain management literature, but a holistic perspective remains lacking. The holistic approach taken with the framework used in this study enables the prioritization of and focus on relevant issues, facilitating organization-wide RPA adoption for managers involved in digital transformation. The implementation procedure, stages, and practices presented here can help managers to improve the odds that digital strategies underpinned by RPA will succeed. In this case study, the managers applied RPA to intraorganizational supply-chain processes. The authors recommend that managers begin with small RPA projects, as in the case presented here, to gain experience with the technology together with consultants. The theoretical framework presented here can also aid practitioners who would like to use RPA to improve interorganizational supply-chain processes. Moreover, this study revealed that managers must take the time needed to address issues that arise in RPA projects. The authors recommend that managers continuously involve stakeholders such as the organization's employees from the initiation of such projects to reduce the risk of user resistance and thereby increase the success of RPA implementation. Managers should create a personnel development plan for each employee involved, and clearly explain the goal of digital technology adoption and the steps and outcomes of RPA implementation. Responsibilities, monitoring, maintenance, know-how building, and upscaling – in other words, internal RPA development and governance – are important managerial activities during RPA implementation in an organization, and CoE establishment can be very beneficial to address the challenges associated with such efforts.

REFERENCES

Abdinnour-Helm, S., Lengnick-Hall, M. L., & Lengnick-Hall, C. A. (2003). Pre-implementation attitudes and organizational readiness for implementing an enterprise resource planning system. *European Journal of Operational Research*, *146*(2), 258–273. doi:10.1016/S0377-2217(02)00548-9

Adelman, C., Jenkins, D., & Kemmis, S. (1976). Re-thinking case study: Notes from the second Cambridge Conference. *Cambridge Journal of Education*, *6*(3), 139–150. doi:10.1080/0305764760060306

Aladwani, A. M. (2001). Change management strategies for successful ERP implementation. *Business Process Management Journal*, *7*(3), 266–275. doi:10.1108/14637150110392764

Ali, M., & Miller, L. (2017). ERP system implementation in large enterprises – a systematic literature review. *Journal of Enterprise Information Management*, *30*(4), 666–692. doi:10.1108/JEIM-07-2014-0071

Andrew, D. P., Pedersen, P. M., & McEvoy, C. D. (2019). *Research methods and design in sport management*. Human Kinetics.

Arias, J. A. E., Beltrán, J. A. B., & Bedoya, S. (2020). *RPA implementation for automation of management process of personal in Compañía nacional de empaques SA*. Paper presented at the 15th Iberian Conference on Information Systems and Technologies (CISTI), Sevilla, Spain. 10.23919/CISTI49556.2020.9140994

Atılgan, Ö. (2020). Covid-19 and crisis management. In COVID-19 and new business ecosystem (pp. 141-153). Gazi Publishing.

Attaran, M. (2020). Digital technology enablers and their implications for supply chain management. *Supply Chain Forum: An International Journal*, *21*(3), 158-172. 10.1080/16258312.2020.1751568

Bandara, W., Indulska, M., Chong, S., & Sadiq, S. (2007). *Major issues in business process management: en expert perspective*. Paper presented at the 15th European Conference on Information Systems (ECIS), University of St Gallen.

Bauer, M., Damschroder, L., Hagedorn, H., Smith, J., & Kilbourne, A. (2015). An introduction to implementation science for the non-specialist. *BMC Psychology, 3*(1), 32. doi:10.118640359-015-0089-9 PMID:26376626

Baur, C., & Wee, D. (2015). *Manufacturing's next act: Industry 4.0 is more than just a flashy catchphrase.* Retrieved on November 25, 2021 from https://www.mckinsey.com/business-functions/operations/our-insights/manufacturings-next-act

Baxter, P., & Jack, S. (2008). Qualitative Case Study Methodology: Study Design and Implementation for Novice Researchers. *Qualitative Report, 13*(4), 544–559. doi:10.46743/2160-3715/2008.1573

Belhadi, A., Kamble, S., Jabbour, C. J. C., Gunasekaran, A., Ndubisi, N. O., & Venkatesh, M. (2021). Manufacturing and service supply chain resilience to the COVID-19 outbreak: Lessons learned from the automobile and airline industries. *Technological Forecasting and Social Change, 163*, 120447. doi:10.1016/j.techfore.2020.120447 PMID:33518818

Bloom, D., & Prettner, K. (2020). *The macroeconomic effects of automation and the role of COVID-19 in reinforcing their dynamics.* Retrieved on September 15, 2021 from https://voxeu.org/article/covid-19-and-macroeconomic-effects-automation

Bogers, M., Hadar, R., & Bilberg, A. (2016). Additive manufacturing for consumer-centric business models: Implications for supply chains in consumer goods manufacturing. *Technological Forecasting and Social Change, 102*, 225–239. doi:10.1016/j.techfore.2015.07.024

Buer, S.-V., Strandhagen, J. O., & Chan, F. T. (2018). The link between Industry 4.0 and lean manufacturing: Mapping current research and establishing a research agenda. *International Journal of Production Research, 56*(8), 2924–2940. doi:10.1080/00207543.2018.1442945

Capestro, M., & Kinkel, S. (2020). Industry 4.0 and knowledge management: a review of empirical studies. In M. Bettiol, E. Di Maria, & S. Micelli (Eds.), *Knowledge management and industry 4.0: new paradigms for value creation* (pp. 19–52). Springer. doi:10.1007/978-3-030-43589-9_2

Chakroborty, A. (2017). Robotic process automation for transforming financial KPO industry. *Imperial Journal of Interdisciplinary Research, 3*(3). Retrieved on November 1, 2020, from http://imperialjournals.com/index.php/ijir/article/view/4013

Choi, T.-M. (2021). Risk analysis in logistics systems: A research agenda during and after the COVID-19 pandemic. *Transportation Research Part E, Logistics and Transportation Review, 145*, 102190. doi:10.1016/j.tre.2020.102190

Davenport, T. H. (1998). Putting the enterprise into the enterprise system. *Harvard Business Review, 76*(4), 121–131. PMID:10181586

Davenport, T. H., & Schaefer, G. (2021). *How to establish an automation.* Center of Excellence. Retrieved on November 2, 2021 from https://sloanreview.mit.edu/article/how-to-establish-an-automation-center-of-excellence

Deming, W. E. (1991). *Out of the crisis, 1986.* Massachusetts Institute of Technology Center for Advanced Engineering Study.

Doğuç, Ö. (2021). Robotic Process Automation (RPA) Applications in COVID-19. In H. Dincer & S. Yüksel (Eds.), *Management Strategies to Survive in a Competitive Environment: How to Improve Company Performance* (pp. 233–247). Springer International Publishing. doi:10.1007/978-3-030-72288-3_16

Dragicevic, N., Ullrich, A., Tsui, E., & Gronau, N. (2020). A conceptual model of knowledge dynamics in the Industry 4.0 smart grid scenario. *Knowledge Management Research and Practice*, *18*(2), 199–213. doi:10.1080/14778238.2019.1633893

Eisenhardt, K. M. (1989). Building theories from case study research. *Academy of Management Review*, *14*(4), 532–550. doi:10.2307/258557

Erdem, H., & Özçelik, T. Ö. (2022). An Example of Merit Analysis for Digital Transformation and Robotic Process Automation (RPA). In N. M. Durakbasa & M. G. Gençyılmaz (Eds.), *Digitizing Production Systems* (pp. 233–242). Springer International Publishing. doi:10.1007/978-3-030-90421-0_20

Esteves, J., & Bohorquez, V. (2007). An updated ERP systems annotated bibliography: 2001-2005. *Communications of the Association for Information Systems*, *19*(1), 18. doi:10.17705/1CAIS.01918

Fatorachian, H., & Kazemi, H. (2018). A critical investigation of Industry 4.0 in manufacturing: Theoretical operationalisation framework. *Production Planning and Control*, *29*(8), 633–644. doi:10.1080/09537287.2018.1424960

Fixsen, D. L., Naoom, S. F., Blase, K. A., Friedman, R. M., & Wallace, F. (2005). Implementation research: a synthesis of the literature. Tampa, FL: University of South Florida, Louis de la Parte Florida Mental Health Institute, The National Implementation Research Network: William T. Grant Foundation.

Flechsig, C., Anslinger, F., & Lasch, R. (2021). Robotic Process Automation in purchasing and supply management: A multiple case study on potentials, barriers, and implementation. *Journal of Purchasing and Supply Management*. Advance online publication. doi:10.1016/j.pursup.2021.100718

Frederico, G. F. (2021). Towards a Supply Chain 4.0 on the post-COVID-19 pandemic: A conceptual and strategic discussion for more resilient supply chains. *Rajagiri Management Journal*, *15*(2), 94–104. doi:10.1108/RAMJ-08-2020-0047

Frederico, G. F., Garza-Reyes, J. A., Anosike, A., & Kumar, V. (2020). Supply Chain 4.0: Concepts, maturity and research agenda. *Supply Chain Management*, *25*(2), 262–282. doi:10.1108/SCM-09-2018-0339

Gölzer, P., & Fritzsche, A. (2017). Data-driven operations management: Organisational implications of the digital transformation in industrial practice. *Production Planning and Control*, *28*(16), 1332–1343. doi:10.1080/09537287.2017.1375148

Goodrich, D., Miake-Lye, I., Braganza, M., Wawrin, N., Kilbourne, A. M., & Initiative, Q. E. R. (2020). *QUERI Roadmap for implementation and quality improvement*. Retrieved on September 27, 2021 from https://www.queri.research.va.gov/tools/roadmap

Gotthardt, M., Koivulaakso, D., Paksoy, O., Saramo, C., Martikainen, M., & Lehner, O. (2020). Current state and challenges in the implementation of smart robotic process automation in accounting and auditing. *ACRN Journal of Finance and Risk Perspectives*, *9*(1), 90–102. doi:10.35944/jofrp.2020.9.1.007

Heavin, C., & Power, D. J. (2018). Challenges for digital transformation–towards a conceptual decision support guide for managers. *Journal of Decision Systems, 27*(1), 38–45. doi:10.1080/12460125.2018.1468697

Hennelly, P., Srai, J., Graham, G., & Fosso Wamba, S. (2019). Rethinking supply chains in the age of digitalization. *Production Planning and Control, 31*(2-3), 1–3. doi:10.1080/09537287.2019.1631469

Herm, L.-V., Janiesch, C., Helm, A., Imgrund, F., Fuchs, K., Hofmann, A., & Winkelmann, A. (2020). A Consolidated Framework for Implementing Robotic Process Automation Projects. In D. Fahland, C. Ghidini, J. Becker, & M. Dumas (Eds.), *Business Process Management* (pp. 471–488). Springer International Publishing. doi:10.1007/978-3-030-58666-9_27

Herold, D. M., Farmer, S. M., & Mobley, M. I. (1995). Pre-implementation attitudes toward the introduction of robots in a unionized environment. *Journal of Engineering and Technology Management, 12*(3), 155–173. doi:10.1016/0923-4748(95)00008-7

Hindel, J., Cabrera, L., & Stierle, M. (2020). *Robotic Process Automation: Hype or Hope?* Paper presented at the 15th International Conference on Wirtschaftsinformatik, Potsdam, Germany.

Hobbs, J. E. (2021). Food supply chain resilience and the COVID-19 pandemic: What have we learned? *Canadian Journal of Agricultural Economics/Revue canadienne d'agroeconomie, 69*(2), 189-196.

Hofmann, P., Samp, C., & Urbach, N. (2020). Robotic process automation. *Electronic Markets, 30*(1), 99–106. doi:10.100712525-019-00365-8

Huang, S. M., Chang, I. C., Li, S. H., & Lin, M. T. (2004). Assessing risk in ERP projects: Identify and prioritize the factors. *Industrial Management & Data Systems, 104*(8), 681–688. doi:10.1108/02635570410561672

IBM. (2019). *IBM robotic process automation anywhere*. Retrieved on November 3, 2021 from https://www.ibm.com/products/robotic-process-automation

Ivančić, L., Vugec, D. S., & Vukšić, V. B. (2019). *Robotic process automation: systematic literature review.* Paper presented at the International Conference on Business Process Management.

Ivanov, D., Dolgui, A., & Sokolov, B. (2019). The impact of digital technology and Industry 4.0 on the ripple effect and supply chain risk analytics. *International Journal of Production Research, 57*(3), 829–846. doi:10.1080/00207543.2018.1488086

Jakobsen, M., & Jensen, R. (2015). Common method bias in public management studies. *International Public Management Journal, 18*(1), 3–30. doi:10.1080/10967494.2014.997906

Jardim-Goncalves, R., Romero, D., & Grilo, A. (2017). Factories of the future: Challenges and leading innovations in intelligent manufacturing. *International Journal of Computer Integrated Manufacturing, 30*(1), 4–14. doi:10.1080/0951192X.2016.1258120

Junge, A. L., Verhoeven, P., Reipert, J., & Mansfeld, M. (2019). Pathway of digital transformation in logistics: best practice concepts and future developments. In S. Franck (Ed.), *Scientific Series Logistics at the Berlin Institute of Technology* (Vol. 8). Universitätsverlag der TU Berlin.

Karumsi, D., Prokopets, L., Clements, C., & Parva, N. (2020). *Automation in Procurement: Your New Workforce Is Here*. Retrieved on November 11, 2021 from https://assets.kpmg/content/dam/kpmg/xx/pdf/2019/11/automation-in-procurement.pdf

Ketokivi, M., & Choi, T. (2014). Renaissance of case research as a scientific method. *Journal of Operations Management, 32*(5), 232–240. doi:10.1016/j.jom.2014.03.004

Khan, A., & Turowski, K. (2016a). A Perspective on Industry 4.0: from challenges to opportunities in production systems. In *Proceedings of the International Conference of Internet of Things and Big Data* (Vol. 2, pp. 441-448). Setúbal, Portugal: SCITEPRESS. 10.5220/0005929704410448

Khan, A., & Turowski, K. (2016b). A survey of current challenges in manufacturing industry and preparation for industry 4.0. In *Proceedings of the First International Scientific Conference "Intelligent Information Technologies for Industry"(IITI'16)* (pp. 15-26). London, UK: Springer. 10.1007/978-3-319-33609-1_2

Kilbourne, A. M., Goodrich, D. E., Miake-Lye, I., Braganza, M. Z., & Bowersox, N. W. (2019). Quality Enhancement Research Initiative Implementation Roadmap: Toward Sustainability of Evidence-based Practices in a Learning Health System. *Medical Care, 57*(10, Suppl 3), S286–S293. doi:10.1097/MLR.0000000000001144 PMID:31517801

Kroll, C., Bujak, A., Darius, V., Enders, W., & Esser, M. (2016). *Robotic process automation: robots conquer business processes in back offices*. Retrieved on November 27, 2021 from https://www.capgemini.com/consulting-de/wp-content/uploads/sites/32/2017/08/robotic-process-automation-study.pdf

Kurpjuweit, S., Schmidt, C. G., Klöckner, M., & Wagner, S. M. (2021). Blockchain in additive manufacturing and its impact on supply chains. *Journal of Business Logistics, 42*(1), 46–70. doi:10.1111/jbl.12231

Lacity, M., & Willcocks, L. P. (2021). Becoming strategic with intelligent automation. *MIS Quarterly Executive, 20*(2), 169–182. doi:10.17705/2msqe.00047

Lacity, M. C., & Willcocks, L. P. (2016). New Approach to Automating Services. *MIT Sloan Management Review, 58*(1), 41–49.

Madakam, S., Holmukhe, R. M., & Jaiswal, D. K. (2019). The future digital work force: Robotic process automation (RPA). *JISTEM-Journal of Information Systems and Technology Management, 16*, 1–17. Advance online publication. doi:10.4301/S1807-1775201916001

Mbunge, E., Akinnuwesi, B., Fashoto, S. G., Metfula, A. S., & Mashwama, P. (2021). A critical review of emerging technologies for tackling COVID-19 pandemic. *Human Behavior and Emerging Technologies, 3*(1), 25–39. doi:10.1002/hbe2.237 PMID:33363278

McKinsey. (2020). *How COVID-19 has pushed companies over the technology tipping point-and transformed business forever*. Retrieved on December 5, 2021 from https://www.mckinsey.com/business-functions/strategy-and-corporate-finance/our-insights/how-covid-19-has-pushed-companies-over-the-technology-tipping-point-and-transformed-business-forever

Modgil, S., Singh, R. K., & Hannibal, C. (2021). Artificial intelligence for supply chain resilience: Learning from Covid-19. *International Journal of Logistics Management*. Advance online publication. doi:10.1108/IJLM-02-2021-0094

Moeuf, A., Pellerin, R., Lamouri, S., Tamayo-Giraldo, S., & Barbaray, R. (2018). The industrial management of SMEs in the era of Industry 4.0. *International Journal of Production Research, 56*(3), 1118-1136. doi:10.1080/00207543.2017.1372647

Müller, J. M., Buliga, O., & Voigt, K.-I. (2018). Fortune favors the prepared: How SMEs approach business model innovations in Industry 4.0. *Technological Forecasting and Social Change, 132*, 2–17. doi:10.1016/j.techfore.2017.12.019

Nagappan, R. (2001). *Dealing with biases in qualitative research: a balancing act for researchers*. Paper presented at the Qualitative research convention, Kuala Lumpur, Malaysia. Retrieved on November 7, 2021 from http://merr.utm.my/id/eprint/4087

Nah, F. F.-H., Lau, J. L. S., & Kuang, J. (2001). Critical factors for successful implementation of enterprise systems. *Business Process Management Journal, 7*(3), 285–296. doi:10.1108/14637150110392782

Nah, F. F.-H., & Siau, K. (2020). COVID-19 pandemic – Role of technology in transforming business to the new normal. In C. Stephanidis, G. Salvendy, J. Wei, S. Yamamoto, H. Mori, G. Meiselwitz, F. F.-H. Nah, & K. Siau (Eds.), *HCI International 2020 – Late Breaking Papers: Interaction, Knowledge and Social Media* (Vol. 12427, pp. 585–600). Springer International Publishing. doi:10.1007/978-3-030-60152-2_43

Nicolaou, A. I. (2004). Quality of postimplementation review for enterprise resource planning systems. *International Journal of Accounting Information Systems, 5*(1), 25–49. doi:10.1016/j.accinf.2004.02.002

Nitsche, B. (2021). Exploring the Potentials of Automation in Logistics and Supply Chain Management: Paving the Way for Autonomous Supply Chains. *Logistics, 5*(3), 51. Retrieved on November 5, 2021 from https://www.mdpi.com/2305-6290/5/3/51

Paul, S. K., Moktadir, M. A., & Ahsan, K. (2021). Key supply chain strategies for the post-COVID-19 era: Implications for resilience and sustainability. *International Journal of Logistics Management*. Advance online publication. doi:10.1108/IJLM-04-2021-0238

Rae, S. (2016). *Bots in the back office, the coming wave of digital workers*. Retrieved on November 5, 2021 from https://assets.kpmg/content/dam/kpmg/pdf/2016/02/bots-in-the-back-office.pdf

Ramzi, N., Ahmad, H., & Zakaria, N. (2019). A conceptual model on people approach and smart manufacturing. *International Journal of Supply Chain Management, 8*(4), 1102–1107.

Ravn, R., Halberg, P., Gustafsson, J., & Groes, J. (2016). *Get ready for robots: Why planning makes the difference between success and disappointment*. Retrieved on November 3, 2021 from https://eyfinancialservicesthoughtgallery.ie/wp-content/uploads/2016/11/ey-get-ready-for-robots.pdf

Saldana, J. (2015). *The coding manual for qualitative researchers*. Sage Publications Ltd.

Santos, F., Pereira, R., & Vasconcelos, J. B. (2019). Toward robotic process automation implementation: An end-to-end perspective. *Business Process Management Journal, 26*(2), 405–420. doi:10.1108/BPMJ-12-2018-0380

Schiavone, F., & Sprenger, S. (2017). Operations management and digital technologies. *Production Planning and Control, 28*(16), 1281–1283. doi:10.1080/09537287.2017.1375151

Schneider, P. (2018). Managerial challenges of Industry 4.0: An empirically backed research agenda for a nascent field. *Review of Managerial Science, 12*(3), 803–848. doi:10.100711846-018-0283-2

Schniederjans, D. G., Curado, C., & Khalajhedayati, M. (2020). Supply chain digitisation trends: An integration of knowledge management. *International Journal of Production Economics, 220*, 107439. doi:10.1016/j.ijpe.2019.07.012

Schumacher, A., Erol, S., & Sihn, W. (2016). A maturity model for assessing Industry 4.0 readiness and maturity of manufacturing enterprises. *Procedia CIRP, 52*, 161–166. doi:10.1016/j.procir.2016.07.040

Schwab, K. (2017). *The fourth industrial revolution*. Geneva: World Economic Forum.

Siderska, J. (2020). Robotic Process Automation — A driver of digital transformation? *Engineering Management in Production and Services, 12*(2), 21-31. doi:10.2478/emj-2020-0009

Siderska, J. (2021). The adoption of robotic process automation technology to ensure business process during the Covid-19 pandemic. *Sustainability, 13*(14), 8020. doi:10.3390u13148020

Slaby, J. R. (2012). *Robotic automation emeges as a threat to traditional low-cost outsourcing*. Retrieved on September 30, 2021 from www.hfsresearch.com

Srai, J. S., Kumar, M., Graham, G., Phillips, W., Tooze, J., Ford, S., Beecher, P., Raj, B., Gregory, M., Tiwari, M. K., Ravi, B., Neely, A., Shankar, R., Charnley, F., & Tiwari, M. K. (2016). Distributed manufacturing: Scope, challenges and opportunities. *International Journal of Production Research, 54*(23), 6917–6935. doi:10.1080/00207543.2016.1192302

Straube, F., & Nitsche, B. (2020). Heading into "The New Normal". *Internationales Verkehrswesen, 72*(3), 31.

Stuart, I., McCutcheon, D., Handfield, R., McLachlin, R., & Samson, D. (2002). Effective case research in operations management: A process perspective. *Journal of Operations Management, 20*(5), 419–433. doi:10.1016/S0272-6963(02)00022-0

Sullivan, M., Simpson, W., & Li, W. (2021). The Role of Robotic Process Automation (RPA) in Logistics. In M. Sullivan & J. Kern (Eds.), *The Digital Transformation of Logistics* (pp. 61–78). Wiley. doi:10.1002/9781119646495.ch5

Syed, R., Suriadi, S., Adams, M., Bandara, W., Leemans, S. J. J., Ouyang, C., ter Hofstede, A. H. M., van de Weerd, I., Wynn, M. T., & Reijers, H. A. (2020). Robotic Process Automation: Contemporary themes and challenges. *Computers in Industry, 115*, 103162. doi:10.1016/j.compind.2019.103162

Tao, F., Qi, Q., Liu, A., & Kusiak, A. (2018). Data-driven smart manufacturing. *Journal of Manufacturing Systems, 48*, 157–169. doi:10.1016/j.jmsy.2018.01.006

Taylor, M. J., McNicholas, C., Nicolay, C., Darzi, A., Bell, D., & Reed, J. E. (2014). Systematic review of the application of the plan–do–study–act method to improve quality in healthcare. *BMJ Quality & Safety, 23*(4), 290–298. doi:10.1136/bmjqs-2013-001862 PMID:24025320

Tietze, F., Vimalnath, P., Aristodemou, L., & Molloy, J. (2020). Crisis-critical intellectual property: Findings from the COVID-19 pandemic. *IEEE Transactions on Engineering Management*. Advance online publication. doi:10.1109/TEM.2020.2996982

van der Aalst, W. M. P., Bichler, M., & Heinzl, A. (2018). Robotic Process Automation. *Business & Information Systems Engineering*, *60*(4), 269–272. doi:10.100712599-018-0542-4

Viale, L., & Zouari, D. (2020). Impact of digitalization on procurement: the case of robotic process automation. *Supply Chain Forum: An International Journal, 21*(3), 185-195. 10.1080/16258312.2020.1776089

Voss, C., Tsikriktsis, N., & Frohlich, M. (2002). Case research in operations management. *International Journal of Operations & Production Management*, *22*(2), 195–219. doi:10.1108/01443570210414329

Willis, T. H., & Willis-Brown, A. H. (2002). Extending the value of ERP. *Industrial Management & Data Systems*, *102*(1), 35–38. doi:10.1108/02635570210414640

Wuest, T., Kusiak, A., Dai, T., & Tayur, S. R. (2020). *Impact of COVID-19 on manufacturing and supply networks—The case for AI-inspired digital transformation*. Retrieved on November 5, 2021 from https://papers.ssrn.com/sol3/papers.cfm?abstract_id=3593540

Ye, F., Liu, K., Li, L., Lai, K.-H., Zhan, Y., & Kumar, A. (2022). Digital supply chain management in the COVID-19 crisis: An asset orchestration perspective. *International Journal of Production Economics*, *245*, 108396. doi:10.1016/j.ijpe.2021.108396 PMID:34931109

Yin, R. K. (2012). *Applications of case study research*. Sage.

Yin, Y., Stecke, K. E., & Li, D. (2018). The evolution of production systems from Industry 2.0 through Industry 4.0. *International Journal of Production Research*, *56*(1-2), 848–861. doi:10.1080/00207543.2017.1403664

Zangiacomi, A., Pessot, E., Fornasiero, R., Bertetti, M., & Sacco, M. (2020). Moving towards digitalization: A multiple case study in manufacturing. *Production Planning and Control*, *31*(2-3), 143–157. doi:10.1080/09537287.2019.1631468

Chapter 6
Lean Manufacturing and Industry 4.0/5.0:
Applied Research in the Portuguese Cork Industry

Joao P. C. Fernandes Thomaz
https://orcid.org/0000-0002-8007-8558
Institute of Management and Administration of Santarém, Portugal

Helena I. N. Bispo
Institute of Management and Administration of Santarém, Portugal

ABSTRACT

Over the years, organizations have had to adapt to constant changes in their surroundings. To this end, they began to adopt methodologies such as lean manufacturing and Industry 4.0. Their implementation has increased the competitiveness of organizations. Sustainability is getting much attention, leading to the advent of Industry 5.0, which, unlike Industry 4.0, takes sustainable production into account. Forestry sectors are significant for the Portuguese economy, especially cork. This study examines a company in the cork sector to determine how automation and monetization of new resources could increase efficiency, quality, and safety. A qualitative approach was applied in the study through literature review and participant observation actions to analyze and propose improvements. The study fulfilled the purposes defined, identifying options to improve the production process and increase customer satisfaction and worker safety.

INTRODUCTION

The current market is constantly evolving, open to universal competition, and recognized for new technologies and knowledge. Given this fact, administrators are encouraged to optimize all processes in their company, eliminating or reducing waste (Jastia & Kodali, 2015). Several philosophies have emerged

DOI: 10.4018/978-1-7998-9715-6.ch006

Copyright © 2022, IGI Global. Copying or distributing in print or electronic forms without written permission of IGI Global is prohibited.

to accomplish this, including lean manufacturing (LM) or operational optimization, based on Toyota's success; Industry 4.0 (I 4.0), from the internet of things (IoT); big data, 3D printing; cloud computing; artificial intelligence (AI); and cyber-physical systems (Liker, 2004).

Actually, the fifth industrial revolution (I 5.0) is characterized by human-robot cooperation in everyday life and bioeconomy. I 5.0 will increase productivity and operability, reduce workplace accidents, and shorten production processes in a sustainable and environmentally friendly way. It will create jobs, most of them in programming, artificial intelligence, maintenance, training, reuse, and the design of new robots (Demir, Döven, & Sezen, 2019; Nahavandi, 2019).

The present study highlights the interaction between LM and I 4.0/5.0 through a case study in a company in the agroforestry sector, specifically in an industrial cork unit (ICorkU). The forestry and agroforestry sectors are very significant for the Portuguese economy, in which cork exploitation plays a fundamental role. Portugal is the world's largest cork producer and exporter. The Portuguese cork industry is an example of profitable production, with the advantage that the raw material comes from a traditional, environmentally sustainable cultivation system that is well-adapted to the local climate conditions, exemplifying a circular economy (APCOR, 2020).

BACKGROUND

Lean Manufacturing (LM)

According to Drew, McCallum, and Roggenhofer (2004, p.15), lean manufacturing is

a combination of principles, practices, tools, and techniques designed to address the causes of poor operational performance. It is a systematic approach to eliminating losses along a company's value chain to bring current performance closer to customer needs.

The LM production was featured in the book "The machine that changed the world" by Womack et. al. (1990), where they contrasted the difference between the Toyota Production System (TPS) and other automotive companies and concluded that this system made Toyota the most competent organization worldwide in its sector. Figure 1 represents a simplified Toyota Production System (TPS) where there is independence between the concepts, components, people, and practices that apply to the industry and commerce and services.

Figure 1. Toyota Production System (TPS) scheme
Source: Liker, 2004

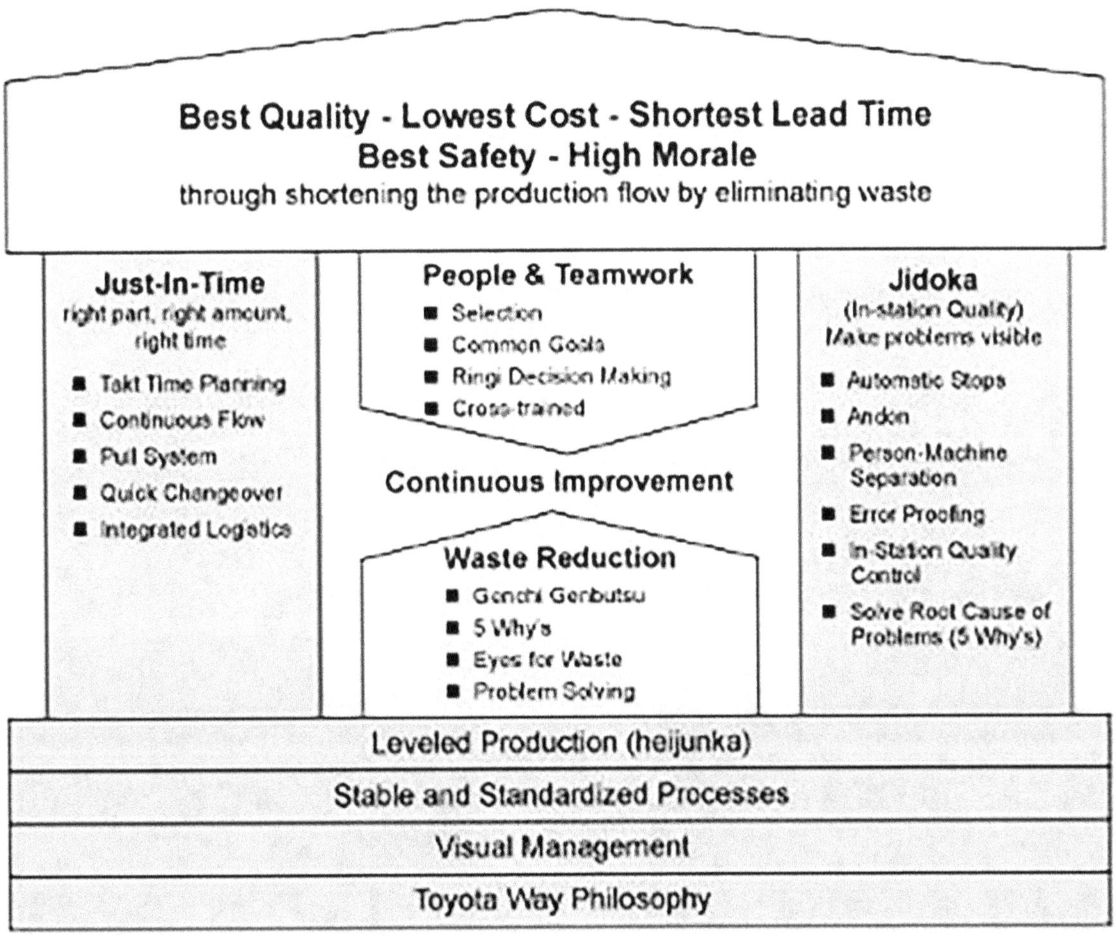

To achieve LM is necessary to understand the manufacturing process and its ultimate goals to rationalize the process and the people involved without creating more unnecessary costs (Womack & Jones, 2004). Markovitz (2011) showed that Toyota is permanently looking to improve its processes, in tune with the LM concept and philosophy directly linked to the development of awareness and learning to eliminate problems, the ability to self-correct, and opportunities for everyone involved to improve, from factory floor people to the top management.

The LM philosophy is a matter of continuity of organizations by the rectification of processes both to minimize costs and to implement best practices, based on getting quality first, continuous process improvement, and problem-solving, is supported by five principles: (i) create value (particularities that a product or service must have and how much the customer is willing to deliver to meet their needs and requirements); (ii) identify the value stream (production process composed only of activities that add value and eliminate non-value-adding activities); (iii) continuous flow (organize all activities to take place continuously and fluidly, without waste); (iv) pull production (start a product or service only when the customer requests, in quantity, and when asked [just-in-time], eliminating exaggerated stocks, increasing productivity and adding value to the product); and (v) pursuing perfection (create opportunities for improvement as new waste and new obstacles arise, with transparent processes in which everyone involved in the value chain has deep knowledge, being able to dialogue and improve the processes) (Davis, 2009; Pinto, 2014; Womack & Jones, 2004).

Pinto (2014) proposed the inclusion of two more principles (Figure 2): Know the stakeholders (know in detail the stakeholders in the process and then eliminate possible existing waste through continuous improvement) and constantly innovate (be based on the constant analysis of stakeholders, constantly evolving, thus achieving a better vision and definition of future goals for companies).

Figure 2. Seven Lean Manufacturing principles
Source: Pinto, 2014

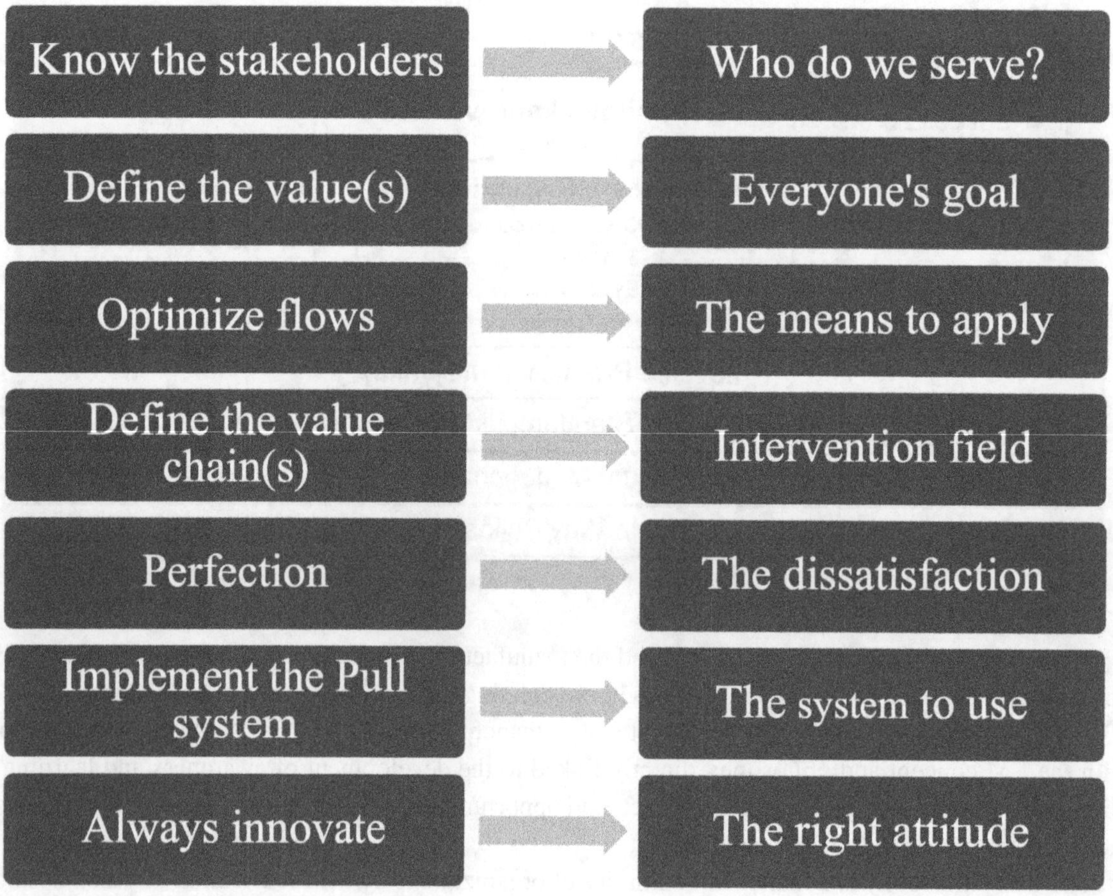

Successful LM implementation is mainly due to its efficiency in reducing the complexity of processes and suppressing process steps that do not create value (Jastia & Kodali, 2015).

LM Tools

LM seeks to create a period of continuous improvement with the help of a wide range of tools which, when well implemented, allows improving the general performance of companies at the operational, financial, human, market, and environmental levels (Gaziero & Cecconello, 2019), as presented in Table 1.

Table 1. LM tools

Tool	Objectives	Authors
SMED (single-minute exchange of die)	It reduces production preparation time and seeks to reduce costs, change, and continuous improvement	Ribeiro et al. (2019); Shingo (1985)
5S (*seiri, seiton, seiso, seiketsu, shitsuke*)	It organizes the workplace as its primary function by reducing activities that do not add value to the process 5S five steps: *seiri* (identify and separate tools that are useful or not), *seiton* (organization of valuable tools), *seiso* (maintenance and cleaning of the workplace to simplify the process), *seiketsu* (patterns must be able to maintain the three previous steps), and *shitsuke* (keep the previous steps as a routine, on change the existing behavior	Mayr et al. (2018); Omogbai and Salonitis (2017); Osada (1991)
JIT (just-in-time)	It focuses on producing the necessary quantity for the customer, thus allowing the complete elimination of waste during the process	Ante, Facchini, Mossa, and Digiesi (2018); Hirano (2009); Monden (1993)
Kaizen	It allows the identification and implementation of continuous improvements in the organization, with the help of everyone involved, which aims to constantly improve productivity and quality	Arai and Sekine (1992); Lima, de França Alcantara, Santos, Silva, and Da Silva (2016)
Kanban	It helps identify the location of the material and the order of entry into production. Types of *Kanban*: (i) production – work as authorizations to produce a product, and (ii) transportation – demonstrate the need to transport the product to the production line or warehouse	Buer, Fragapane, and Strandhagen (2018); Hammarberg and Sunden (2014); Strandhagen (2018)
VSM (value stream mapping)	It allows one to visualize and understand all process flows, identify waste, and proceed with its elimination	Duggan and Healey (2016); Gaziero and Cecconello (2019)
Jidoka	"never letting a defect pass to the next stage of the process, but freeing people from the machines" (p. 209)	Liker (2004); Ohno (1988)
Heijunka	It achieves balance and synchronize all operations at a productive level to precisely and flexibly match customer demand	Jones (2006); Liker (2004)
PDCA (plan, do, check, act)	It works as a cycle and represent the path to be followed and the goals achieved at each stage. Set goals and define the methods to achieve them (plan), carry out the planned tasks and collect data for verification in the next step (do), verify and compare data with the intended goals (check), and act in the process based on the data obtained (act)	Shewhart (1931/1980); Werkema (2013)

Industry 4.0 (I 4.0)

The fourth industrial revolution (I 4.0) is characterized by significant convergence and technological advancement. It is already possible to intelligently explore the integration of the physical, biological, and digital worlds (Silva, Scoton, Dias, & Pereira, 2018). The fundamental objective of I 4.0 is to provide the factory floor with more information about consumers and help with real-time production planning, which allows for increased flexibility, productivity, and quality, reducing the production costs and time delivery (Gaziero & Cecconello, 2019).

Fourth Revolution Technologies

Bahrin, Othman, Azli, and Talib et al. (2016) say that the fourth revolution is based on nine technologies (Figure 3). The market is considered "smart" because it allows consumers to participate in the individual personalization of products. The use of new technologies, such as IoT, big data, cyber-physical systems (CPS), sensors and actuators, augmented reality, cybersecurity, electric vehicles, 3D printing, cloud computing, and artificial intelligence (AI), allows the interaction between real-time and virtual and physical worlds, referred to as cyber-physical systems (Nahavandi, 2019).

The main pillars of I 4.0, according to Bahrin et al. (2016), are: internet of things (IoT; physical and virtual objects connected to the internet and the application of sensors to boost wireless communication, permitting the monitoring of performance and making possible decisions at the right time to the correct problems, optimizing available resources); big data (the large amount of data stored at any given moment, originating in information generated by computers, sensors, and other equipment through various formats); and cyber-physical systems (CPS; "intelligent" machines, products, or devices that exchange information autonomously, working in cooperation with the physical world around them).

Figure 3. I 4.0 Technologies
Source: Bahrin et al., 2016

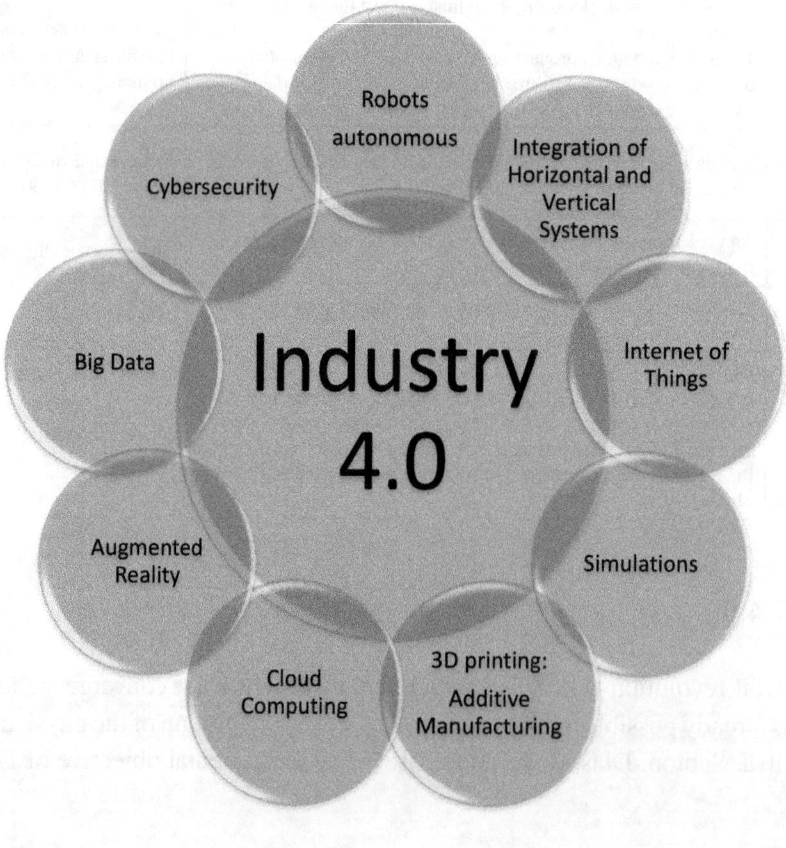

From now on, simulations will be based on real-time data to replicate the physical world in a virtual model, including machines, products, and human beings. In this way, it is possible to test product configurations and machines in a virtual line before moving on to production, that is, to the physical world. It makes it possible to reduce setup times and increase product quality (Bahrin et al., 2016; Gunal, 2019; Luściński & Ivanov, 2020; Xu, Huang, Hsieh, Lee, Jia, & Chen, 2017).

Hozdić (2015) states that I 4.0 is characterized by three dimensions: Vertical integration (connections of people, objects, and systems to create dynamic value networks); horizontal integration (the interaction of different agents through value networks); and end-to-end digital integration (interaction between vertical and horizontal integration, as the collection of product lifecycle information adds value, from its production to the final logistics).

According to Deloitte (2014), I 4.0 can bring numerous benefits, including specific solutions for unique areas, individualized customization, unit batch production, and profit-making; increased competitiveness and flexibility, ability to adapt to value chain changes; obtaining real-time optimization; increased productivity and increased efficiency (more production with the same resources); new employment opportunities and innovative services, among others; more professional balance, flexibility, motivation, and career development; and the possibility of reducing energy and labor costs.

Mixed (Augmented and Virtual) Reality and Artificial Intelligence

Augmented reality (AR) could be defined as (i) enrichment between the real environment with virtual objects, using some technological devices that work in real-time; (ii) improvement of the real world with text, images, and virtual objects with the aid of a computer; (iii) integration of the real and virtual worlds at some points of continuous reality/virtuality, where real environments and virtual environments are linked; and (iv) a system that completes the real world with computer-generated objects, appearing to integrate the same space and combining real and virtual objects in the real environment, interacting in real-time with all the user's senses (Kirner & Siscoutto, 2007).

AR is one of the most used technologies to help professionals in different areas that cannot be present on-site. However, in the future, it can be widely used in real-time, helping in decision-making, and optimizing work procedures (Ikeziri, Melo, Campos, Okimura, & Gobbo Jr., 2020).

Virtual reality (VR) is an advanced user interface to access applications running on a computer, offering the user visualization, movement, and interaction, in real-time, in three-dimensional environments created and managed by a computer. Vision is usually the basis of VR; however, other senses such as touch and hearing can enrich this experience (Kirner & Siscoutto, 2007).

Simulation is fundamental in I 4.0, as it facilitates the assessment of improvements and mirrors the real world through the virtual world. It can help update and improve equipment, layouts, products, and even the positioning of people before approving projects. In this way, it is possible to reduce setup times and increase the quality of processes (Ikeziri et al., 2020).

Industrial applications of artificial intelligence (AI) can be defined as the simulation of intelligence like the human brain, capable of autonomously controlling and making decisions about industrial processes, physical operations, or systems. Industrial AI includes product manufacturing, supply chains, and warehouse management, among many others (Bécue, Praça, & Gama, 2021).

The Interaction of Lean Manufacturing With Industry 4.0

Kolberg and Zühlke (2015) identified some flaws in the interaction of LM with I4.0, which highlights the lack of a framework to help integrate manual and automated workstations. Standardization, organization, and transparency of work are LM concepts highlighted as support for implementing I4.0 solutions.

Sanders, Elangeswaran, and Wulfsberg (2016) concluded that I4.0 is, in fact, efficient to help implement the concept of LM in companies. They analyzed existing barriers to its implementation and alternative conceptual proposals for solving these problems, verifying that I4.0 allows the company to increase its productivity and reduce waste, a LM principle.

Interoperability between LM and I4.0 occurs at the operational and sociotechnical levels. At the operational level, it is possible to observe vertical and horizontal integration existing in the production process through the integration of LM and I4.0 tools and principles. Sociotechnical factors are based on the complex interaction between people, machines, and environmental aspects of organizational strategies. The most significant complexity happens with the increase of this interaction and the way people accept the changes at each corporate level (Davies et al., 2017).

The application of I4.0 technologies to LM methods generates lean automation, a concept that points to the inclusion of the best practices of both models. An example of this harmony is the addition of modern information and communications technologies (ICTs) in the *kanban* method, improving efficiency (Ikeziri et al., 2020).

Several authors have described the dimensions of LM management and how the concepts and technologies of I4.0 manage to simplify its application. Table 2 presents the possible scenarios of results.

Table 2. Possible interactions between LM and I4.0 (Sanders et al., 2016)

LM Objectives	LM Implementation Challenge for I4.0	Solutions obtained through I4.0
Suppliers' opinion	Limited knowledge and staff	Collaborative manufacturing
	Different types of businesses, operations, and maintenance	Data synchronization
		Better communication mechanisms
JIT deliveries made by suppliers	Delays during transport	Smart order reallocation
	Poor quality of transported items	Wireless tracking of goods
Supplier developments	Inadequate resources and knowledge	Standardized interfaces
	Equipment compatibility between companies	Virtual organizations synergistic cooperation
Customer involvement	Low flexibility for product change	Extended freezing period
	Relationship between function and need	Implementation of the quality function deployment (QFD) in large volumes
	Get exact quantities from customers	Usage analysis
Pulled production	Improper quantity of material supplied	Material tracking monitoring
	Changing the production schedule	Tracking and updating the production schedule, and *kanban*
Continuous flow	Errors in stock counts	Real-time stock tracking
	Lack of capacity	Subcontracting
	Centralized control systems	Decentralized decision making

Continued on following page

Table 2. Continued

LM Objectives	LM Implementation Challenge for I4.0	Solutions obtained through I4.0
Setup time reduction	System adaptation based on human experience	Communication between parts and machines
		Self-optimization and machine tuning
Preventive maintenance / Total productive	No control over machine breakdowns	Machine worker communication
	"New" problem-solving time	Automated maintenance assessment
		Predictive maintenance control systems
Statistical process control	Lack of knowledge of operators	Communication between machines and people
	Inability to track process variations	Better human-machine communication
		Tracking in the integral of processes
Worker involvement	Incorrect communication mechanisms	Smart communication devices
	Performance appraisal practices	Employee support systems
	Work monotony	Better human-machine communication

Prinz, Kreggenfeld, and Kuhlenkötter (2018) studied a factory to prepare workers for the new reality resulting from I4.0. Various production line operations and failures already had the LM tools implemented and simulated to solve problems and improve the current system. Thus, they had to use digitization as a resource to obtain real-time information and assistance, using elements such as CPS and IoT, that is, tools from I4.0. The main objective was to make clear the benefits of LM and I4.0.

However, for a successful implementation of digitization, the production process must be optimized and organized based on LM principles. In this way, companies ensure more effective use of resources, achieving the processes and production flow standardization transparently, increasing productivity. They proved that organizations with a solid LM system benefit from implementing I4.0 through more extraordinary operational performance, as shown in Figure 4.

Figure 4. Productivity curve between LM and I4.0
Source: Prinz et al. (2018)

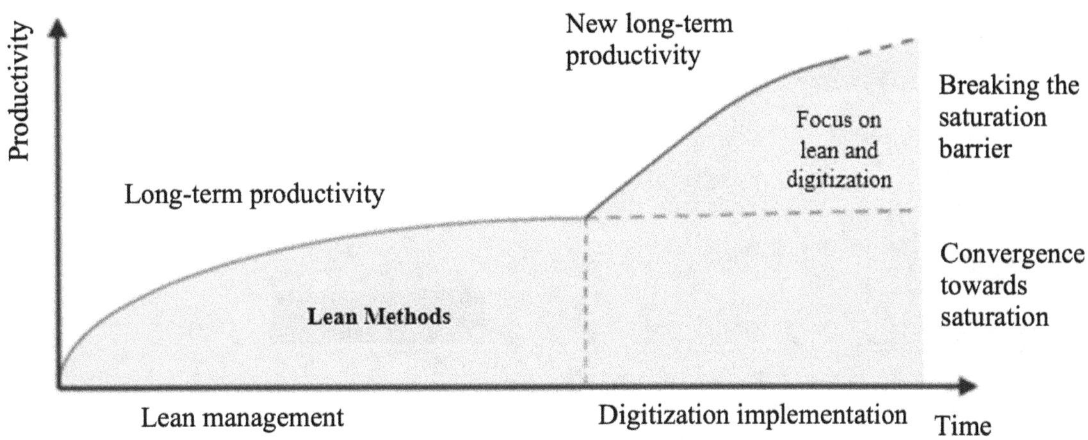

Based on the available literature, LM thinking simplifies the implementation of I4.0, but it is recognized that it is necessary to make a high investment in digitizing the production process. However, this investment will not pay off if it cannot improve the existing process and has much waste. LM thinking helps implement I4.0, as it streamlines operations, permanently eliminates waste, and clarifies processes and work planning (Bittencourt, Alves, & Leão, 2019).

Rosin, Forget, Lamouri, and Pellerin (2019) found excellent support of I4.0 in just-in-time and *jidoka* concepts and substantial help from IoT and simulation in LM technologies. However, several authors found that I4.0 technologies cannot fully integrate LM principles, but they strengthen its efficiency. Thus, there is a clear need to progress in the implementation of LM management and, at the same time, improve its principles, using technologies that are in line with the possibilities. I4.0, IoT, and CPS demonstrate more harmony with LM practices and more financial return in a short period. So, these technologies are suggested for starting the transition instead of an advanced robotization, as they present less complexity (Pagliosa, Tortorella, & Ferreira, 2019). Digitization processes in companies can be costly and challenging at an early stage, but they lead to improved competitiveness in the long term. Developments in digitalization have proven to be a feasible commercial strategy for the continuity of companies in different sectors (Ghobakhloo & Fathi, 2020).

Lean Manufacturing & Industry 4.0 tools

The LM related to I4.0 tools are, among others, *kanban, heijunka, kaizen,* just-in-time (JIT), standardized work, and *jidoka* (Ikeziri et al., 2020). Several researchers are analyzing the benefits of technologies for (i) the visual management of production and logistics flows; (ii) production leveling; (iii) continuous improvement; (iv) acquisition of materials only in the quantities needed and when necessary (JIT); (v) reduction in production instability; (vi) simplification of the training process for employees; (vii) reinforcement of operational security; (viii) documentation simplicity; and (ix) synergy between automation and technologies that monitor product quality without the help of employees (Ejsmont, Gladysz, Corti, Castaño, Mohammed, & Martinez Lastra, 2020). Table 3 presents the LM tools and their interaction with I4.0 technologies.

Table 3. LM tools and their direct interaction with I4.0 technologies (Ejsmont et al., 2020; Pagliosa et al., 2019)

LM tools	I4.0 technologies
Kanban	Horizontal integration; cloud computing; simulation
Heijunka	Horizontal integration; simulation; vertical integration; big data; sensors and actuators; cloud computing
Kaizen	Horizontal integration; simulation; vertical integration; big data; sensors and actuators; cloud computing; augmented reality (AR); virtual reality (VR)
Just-in-time	Horizontal integration; simulation; vertical integration; big data; AR; sensors and actuators; cloud computing; RFID
Standardized work	Horizontal Integration; simulation; vertical integration; big data; sensors and actuators; cloud computing; AR; VR
Jidoka	Horizontal integration; simulation; vertical integration; big data; cloud computing
Waste reduction	Horizontal integration; simulation; vertical integration; big data; IoT
People management and teamwork	Simulation; big data; AR; VR
Pulled production (pull)	Horizontal integration; vertical integration; sensors and actuators; IoT
Suppliers and customers management (stakeholders)	Horizontal integration; big data; cloud computing; IoT
VSM	Horizontal integration; big data; simulation; RFID
Visual management	IoT; big data; simulation; AR; RFID
SMED	Additive manufacturing (3D printing); AR
5S	AR; VR
Continuous flow	RFID; IoT; simulation
TPM	Simulation; big data; AR; VR
SMED, *Kaizen*, *Heijunka*	Simulation
VSM, Standardized work	Horizontal integration; vertical integration
5S, Standardized work	Sensors and actuators

I4.0 technologies that stand out in the LM tools interaction are (i) horizontal integration (helps manage the entire production chain with the aim of allow everyone to achieve the company's goals); (ii) vertical integration (make it possible to visualize the efficiency of all LM elements in the company's production process); (iii) big data (aggregates all historical and current data, allowing for its analysis and demonstrating its value in the daily lives of companies); (iv) augmented & virtual reality (certifies I4.0 with the productive processes implemented in companies); (v) sensors and actuators (data collection sources to be archived in big data and examined in simulations, such as leveling production); (vi) cloud computing (closely related to all LM concepts, confirming its widespread use, given its capabilities are increasing in systems and infrastructure); and (vii) simulation (linked to training activities and the use of test scenarios without interfering with the current reality, thus managing to avoid unnecessary expenses and helping to predict future situations (Bahrin et al., 2016; Hozdić, 2015; Ikeziri et al., 2020; Nahavandi, 2019; Pinto, 2020). Table 4 presents the I4.0 technologies and their interaction with LM tools.

Table 4. I4.0 technologies and their direct interaction with LM tools (Ejsmont et al., 2020; Pagliosa et al., 2019)

I 4.0 technologies	LM tools
Horizontal integration	*Kanban; heijunka; kaizen; just-in-time;* standardized work*; jidoka;* waste reduction, pull production*;* suppliers and customers management (stakeholders)
Vertical integration	*Heijunka; kaizen;* just-in-time; standardized work*; jidoka;* waste reduction*;* pulled production
Big data	*Heijunka; kaizen;* just-in-time; standardized work; *jidoka;* waste reduction;
Augmented reality	*Kaizen;* just-in-time; standardized work; people management & teamwork; 5S
Virtual reality	*Heijunka; kaizen;* standardized work; people management & teamwork; 5S
Sensors and actuators	*Heijunka;* just-in-time; standardized work, pulled production; 5S
Cloud computing	*Kanban; heijunka; kaizen;* just-in-time; standardized work; *jidoka*
Simulation	*Heijunka; kaizen;* just-in-time; standardized work*; jidoka;* waste reduction; people management & teamwork; 5S
IoT	Waste reduction, pull production; visual management on the workstation
Big data + simulation	People management & teamwork; management of suppliers and customers (stakeholders); visual management
Horizontal integration + vertical integration	VSM + standardized work
Simulation + IoT	Continuous flow
Cloud computing + IoT	*Jidoka*

The integrated implementation of LM and I4.0 can improve company results (Tortorella, Narayanamurthy, & Thurer, 2021).

Industry 5.0 (I5.0)

While the most recent advances reduced human intervention in the production process, I5.0 translates into a human-machine symbiosis aiming to improve the production process in real-time, called customizable autonomous production. The focus of I4.0 does not include sustainability, so I 5.0 will also consider protecting the environment, promoting sustainable production (Nahavandi, 2019). Currently, there are two visions for the I5.0. One highlights the human-robot symbiosis, where both will work together whenever possible, with humans assigned to the most complex creativity activities and robots the remaining tasks. The other vision highlights the bioeconomy, where biological resources for industrial purposes will balance the environment, industry, and economy.

According to the European Commission, the bioeconomy is the production using renewable biological materials and the conversion of waste into products that add value, for example, food, feed, bio-based products, and bioenergy. These resources highlight agriculture, forestry, fishing, food, and the production of pulp and paper and parts of the chemical, biotechnology, and energy industries. In combination, these factors can participate in or be the lever for the next industrial revolution (Demir et al. 2019). Table 5 presents the comparison of the vision of I4.0 and I5.0.

Table 5. I4.0 and I5.0 vision comparison (Demir et al., 2019)

	I4.0	I5.0 (v. 1)	I5.0 (v. 2)
Concept	Smart production	Human-robot symbiosis	Bioeconomy
Motivation	Mass production	Smart society	Sustainability
Power supply	Electricity Fossil-based fuels Renewable energy sources	Renewable energy sources electricity	Electricity Renewable energy sources
Technologies	Cloud computing using IoT Big data Robotics and AI	Human-robot collaboration Renewable resources	Agriculture and sustainable production Renewable resources
Involved areas	Process improvement and innovation Business administration	Smart environments Process improvement and innovation Business administration	Agriculture Biology Waste Business administration Economy

I5.0 will be a significant change for organizations, whether the work is done in conjunction with humans and robots or not. Probably the most significant change is the involvement of robots in everyday life, as their progress meets human characteristics. This evolution and cooperation raise legal, psychological, social, ethical, and regulatory issues. Issues of collaboration or competition between humans and robots will emerge, with possible negative attitudes on cooperation and acceptance (Demir et al., 2019).

It is necessary to reduce the costs of robots without reducing their capacity, efficiency, and safety. I5.0 will increase productivity and operability, reduce workplace accidents, and shorten production processes in a sustainable and environmentally friendly way. Contrary to expectations, I5.0 will create jobs, mainly in programming, artificial intelligence, maintenance, training, reuse, and the design of new robots (Nahavandi, 2019).

Several studies demonstrate that the main difference from I4.0 to I5.0 is the shift from intelligent production to intelligent consumption. While I4.0 focuses on production, I5.0 focuses on time and experiences while consuming the product (Rosemann et al., 2021). I5.0 has been based on 6R methodology and logistics efficiency design (LED) principles, leading to occasional comparisons with the circular economy.

The 6R methodology comprises: (i) reduce (identify the origin of the waste and that one with more significance in process, and seek to reduce it); (ii) reuse (find alternatives for the residues of the production process); (iii) recycle (look for a destination for the waste produced; (iv) rethink (identify the waste sources and the method to safely dispose of it, taking into account best environmental practices); (v) recover (recover the waste and send it to another industry that can recycle it); and (vi) refuse (refuse to produce waste and try to find alternatives (Mekkunnel, 2019).

The primary objective of LED is to improve the supply chain's efficiency by eliminating waste generated in the current process (Peraković, Periša, Cvitić, & Zorić, 2020). One of the technologies supported by I5.0 is robotic process automation (RPA), which consists of robotic software that allows users to collect and analyze user interactions and verify the actions of devices in the various production processes (Mekkunnel, 2019).

Companies can improve the production area through adaptability (automation allows organizations to direct personnel to different departments, removing them from unsafe areas, increasing the organization's competitiveness); security and protection (reduction of concern about problems due to interruptions in the production process with the improvement of cybernetic resources); control and clarity (precise, reliable, and current [real-time] production processes and their availability in a short period); customer satisfaction (helps the factory interact with the customer, optimizing time and creating collaborative production opportunities between manufacturers and industries globally); and customization (reaching new markets with 3D printers helps quickly produce specific products and with smaller-scale productions) (Mekkunnel, 2019).

The synergy between humans and the technology in I5.0 will affect the economy, the ecology, and the social world, being accompanied by an aspect of waste prevention applied in industrial recycling, which can be physical waste (produced by the production and logistics lines; also includes general common waste); urban waste (unnecessary spaces, empty spaces, inadequate infrastructure); process residues (overproductions, empty trucks in circulation, excess stock); and social waste (people who want to work but do not have the opportunity; this also includes people who do not want to work). These four types of waste significantly impact the economy and the environment in reducing wasted materials and resources since manufacturers are focused on reducing material costs and reducing the social impact on their production processes (Paschek, Mocan, & Draghici, 2019).

One of the biggest challenges will be human-machine interaction, where robots will no longer be independent in the automation process but will become partners. In I5.0, the new generation of robots will be called Cobots. Their main functionality of quick understanding and memory will also deal with safety criteria and processes related to the risks inherent in the work. Cobots will also oversee repetitive and heavy work. Meanwhile, people will adapt the product or service to the end consumer's needs (Peraković et al., 2020).

Figure 5. I5.0 factory example (Peraković et al., 2020)

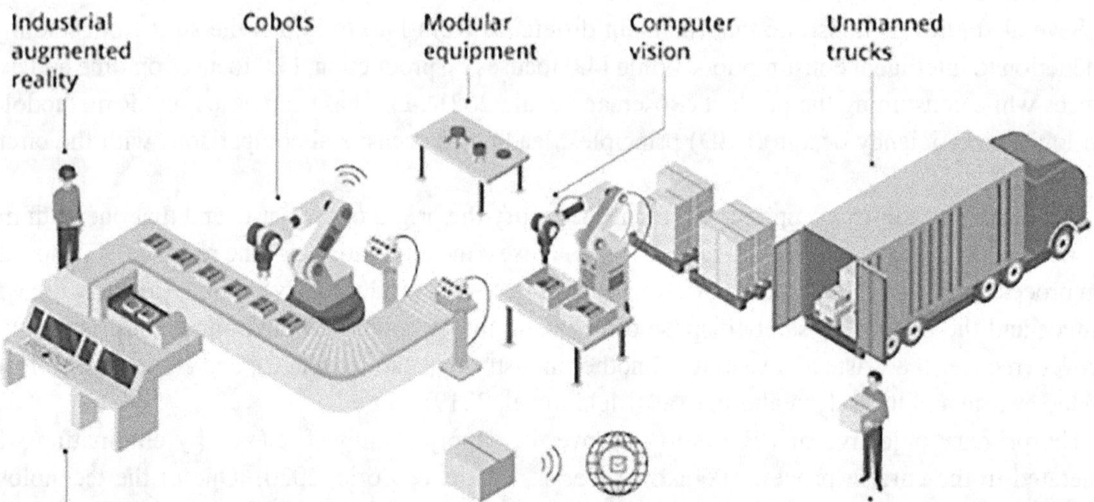

In I5.0, a large amount of information collected through sensors in manufacturing facilities (in physical space) accumulates in cyberspace, where artificial intelligence (AI) analyzes it. The results of that analysis are returned to users in the field in various ways. This process adds new value to the production process in the value chain of delivering the final product or service that allows the provision of products or services tailored to the different individual needs of users. In the industry, big data analysis includes various types of information, including supplier stocks, delivery times for the final product or service, demand for products, or final service (Peraković et al., 2020).

Rosemann et al. (2021, p.123) state that I5.0 would impact another macro-organization, the city, defined as "a livable city that is (re)modeled to eliminate restrictions to its citizens, using digitization to supply goods and public services". An unrestricted city would be an ideal state that can never be reached. The City 5.0 context provides a vital goal expected to drive innovation and improve quality of life. This notion facilitates the transition of the city's environments, focusing on facilitating unrestricted free access to public goods and services.

METHODOLOGY

The general objective of the present study is to: Study the interaction between LM and I4.0/5.0 in an ICorkU and demonstrate that technological investment can result in lower labor dependence and higher production efficiency and quality.

The specific objectives are: (i) analyze the advantages of the interaction between LM and I4.0; (ii) understand the tools' evolution and interactions; (iii) explore the LM and I4.0 tools to be applied in the case study; and (iv) identify I5.0 concepts and tools to be applied in the case study.

The literature review made possible to obtain the necessary conceptual framework to be complemented with research / field work in the company, thus developing an empirical investigation in a cork sector organization.

The methodology was adapted to the company's processes and operations specificity, object of the study, focusing on the use of direct and participant observation. So, this research study follows an applied nature, with descriptive and explanatory objectives, in a qualitative approach using technical procedures: bibliographic, document analysis, and survey, through participant observation to collect and analyze data and propose improvements, in a participatory and cooperative way, characteristic of the action-research technique (Campenhoudt, Marquet, & Quivy, 2019).

Industrial Cork Unit

The industrial cork unit (ICorkU), the case study object, is dedicated to the reception and processing of raw materials and is divided into four sections, as shown in Figure 6.

Figure 6. Diagram of the ICorkU sections

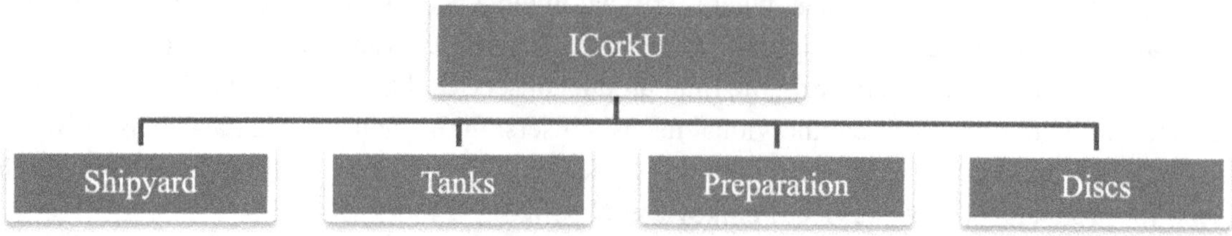

The shipyard section receives and stores the raw material, in this case, cork. It also gets the by-products inherent to its extraction, subsequently selling it to natural by-product processing units (customers). The cork storage and stabilization period are at least six months so that the cork can lose its "greenness", i.e., the excess water. Stabilization can reach a maximum of two years since sensory problems may arise in the raw material after this period. After this stabilization period, the first qualitative sorting process is carried out for two alternatives: *refugo* (low utilization cork) and *amadia* (*delgado* and *cheio* cork) (Note: *refugo*, *delgado*, *cheio* and *amadia* are Portuguese terms for cork selection).

In this selection process, main by-products are removed, such as the wedges found in the part of the corkboard directly in contact with the earth. These by-products remain at the shipyard until they are sold in bulk to various natural by-product processing customers. Figure 7 schematically illustrates the shipyard section processes.

Figure 7. Shipyard section processes diagram

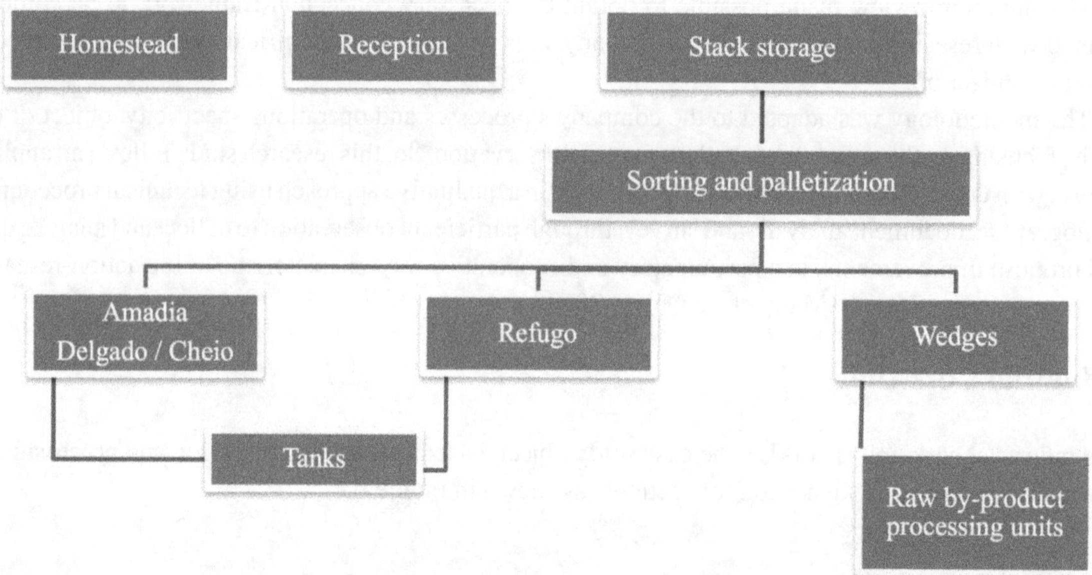

From this process, cork leaves pallets and goes to the tanks section. The cork pallets resulting from the shipyard's first sorting process are cooked in tanks for one hour at 98°C to make the cork malleable for the subsequent manufacturing processes. That cleans the cork of dust and dirt, TCA (trichloroanisole), and other sensory problems such as mold, restoring the natural cork's moisture water renewed each time it is cooked. The *refugo* is boiled and sent to customers (processing units for cooked by-products).

The preparation section is where the *amadia* pallets, coming from the tanks section are subject to a corkboard sorting process between *delgado* (low thickness) and *cheio* (high thickness). Figure 8 presents the preparation section processes.

Figure 8. Preparation section processes diagram

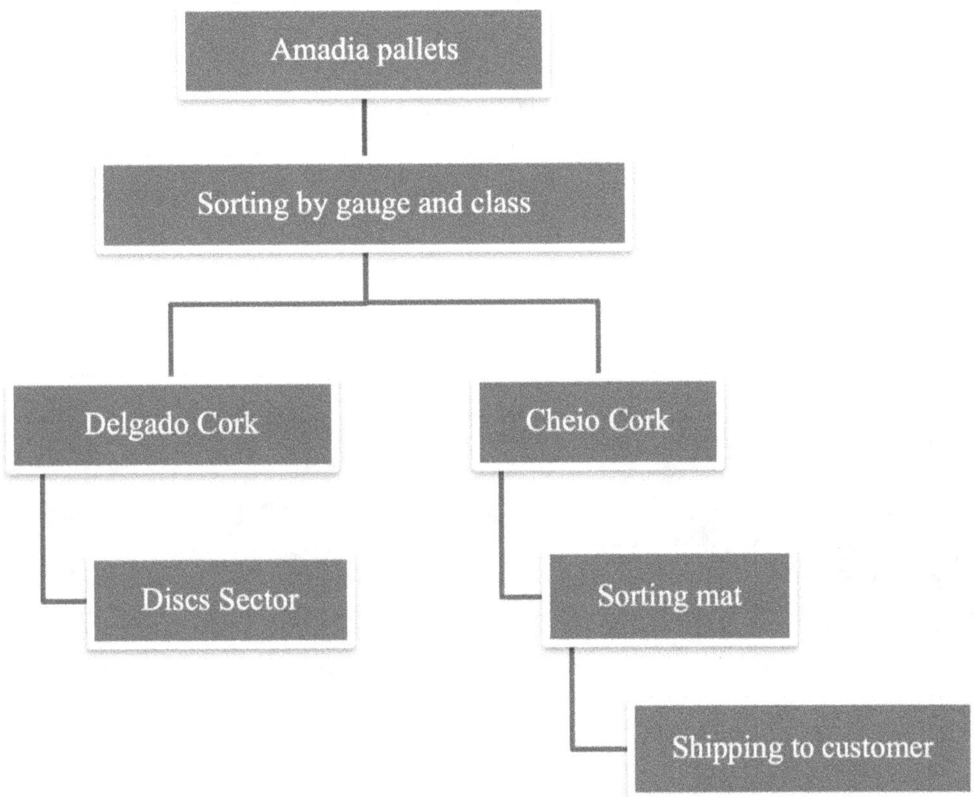

Cheio corkboards are subject to a process of selection by gauge and class, in a very traditional way where the sorting is made with the aid of a "line foot" for the selection of gauge. The sorting by class is performed with the naked eye based on workers' knowledge and later palletized to be sent to an industrial cork stopper unit, where it will be transformed into natural cork stoppers.

The *delgado* corkboards are also processed and subjected to a traditional process of sorting in gauge and class where the worker is the key person; these are also palletized and later sent to the discs section, where they undergo a cork disc manufacturing process, resulting in thousands of discs and by-products.

The discs undergo a process of rectification and an electronic selection by classes to be applied in champagne or wine stoppers. Figure 9 shows 34.5mm discs and Champagne stoppers.

Figure 9. 34.5mm discs and Champagne stoppers
Source: Industrial cork unit

Discs that fail to reach the dimensions or characteristics required for Champagne stoppers are disqualified and sent to the cork disc customer to be used as wine stoppers. Figure 10 shows wine stoppers and 26.5 mm natural cork discs.

Figure 10. 26.5mm discs and wine stoppers
Source: Industrial cork unit

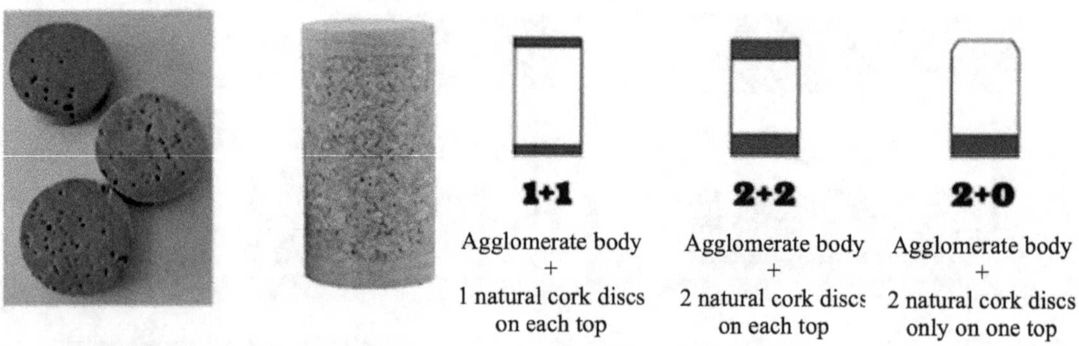

The by-products are sent to customers in the granulate area to be applied to other cork products.

CASE STUDY

Cork Selection Processes

Shipyard Section—Previous & Actual Situations, Comparison of the Two Realities

As shown in Figure 7 before, the previous first sorting process carried out at the shipyard section identifies three alternatives: *refugo* (low-use cork), *delgado* (thin cork), and *cheio* (thick cork). During this process, by-products called wedges are identified and removed. Three workers are needed for the first sorting: two for sorting, and one for palletizing the corkboards. The wedges are loaded into storage bins and transported to the raw by-products storage location, where they will later be loaded in bulk to by-product processing units (customer).

In the selection process, workers remove the corkboards from stacks and evaluate them, cutting the corkboard's end to remove the wedges. Corkboards are then separated by *delgado* and *cheio* and placed in a line-up on each pallet. The *delgado* and *cheio* pallets go on to the cooking process in the tanks section.

The entire first sorting process carried out at the shipyard section must be quantified and registered in the computer system. Given the section's size, it is impossible to make this record directly in the system, so manual records are kept. These records contain information on the number of kilograms worked and how many pallets were made by each team. It is thus possible to know how many people are needed to achieve the section's objectives. For example, around 25 people are needed to work 60,000 kg of cork, handling an average of 2,400 kg per day for the sorting and palletizing processes. In the actual first sorting process, teams are made up of two workers to sort and palletize simultaneously instead of the previous three. The process starts with the worker removing the corkboard from a pile, identifying the by-products, cutting them with the help of a cutting machine, and placing them in a cage and palletizing the remaining corkboard. *Refugo* and *amadia* (*delgado* and *cheio*) are now on pallets for the cooking process, carried out in the tanks section. After the cooking process the *amadia* go to the preparation section to be submitted to a second sorting. *Refugo* remains in a routing circuit to units for the processing of cooked by-products.

With this new type of sorting, there is greater profitability, and it is possible to reduce the number of workers. For example, for the same 60,000 kg of cork, it takes about 15 people (10 fewer) to make an average of 2,500 kg per day (plus 100 kg).

Daily meetings are held with the staff at the beginning of each working day. The lack of information/knowledge observed about the importance of the process led to a weekly meeting to disseminate each team's daily planning, production data, the section's total, and the objectives and goals to be achieved. This action led to greater involvement of all stakeholders, with greater focus and significant intervention, helping to make a more detailed survey of all actions/activities developed in the processes, especially those that did not add value.

All the improvements obtained, currently or in the future, aim to continuously improve productivity and quality for all interested parties in these processes. Several solutions were developed in response to the detected problems to increase the flexibility of the selection and palletizing processes and make the system more efficient.

From the perspective of LM principles, the survey of existing processes allowed the identification of existing waste, for example, excessive processing or actions/activities developed that did not add value to the product.

The *kaizen* tool helps in exchanging information between all parties, which allows identifying and carrying out a detailed value flow mapping to detect and eliminate unnecessary processes and implement continuous improvement actions in the quality area and productivity.

The PDCA proves to be an asset in this process by setting goals and analyzing processes to be achieved. In carrying out the tasks, it is necessary to involve the workers, and for this, the necessary information was provided, and their training developed. Finally, the verification of results and actions is carried out given the established goals. Table 6 presents the shipyard section comparison of the two realities (previous and actual) and the improvements (obtained and future).

Table 6. Comparison of the two realities (previous and actual) and improvements in the shipyard section

Shipyard Section—*Cork first sorting*				
#	Previous reality	Actual reality with LM & I 4.0/5.0	Obtained improvements	Future improvements
1	3 Alternatives (*refugo, delgado,* and *cheio*)	2 Alternatives (*refugo* and *amadia*)	Fewer classes, less complexity, minor specialization	
2	3 workers (2 on sorting and 1 on palletization)	2 workers who carry out sorting, and palletizing	Reduction of 1 worker	
3	Repetitive movements (pick up corkboards from the floor)	Workers sort and palletize (placement of the board logo on the pallet)	Minor discomfort for workers, less absenteeism	
4	Ignorance of the intended planning, objectives, and goals	Planning information, objectives, and goals to be achieved	More information, involvement of all employees in the processes	
5	Weighing, production, and team registration carried out on paper	Weighing, production, and registration of the team carried out on paper		Tablet implementation on machines for computerized registration, reducing repetitive work, and margin of error
6	Fixed scale weighing	Fixed scale weighing		Implementation of scales on machines directly connected to the tablet, real-time information, and no margin for error

Preparation Section—Previous and Actual Situations, Comparison of the Two Realities

There is a worker per bench in the preparation section second selection process, surrounded by cages to sort the corkboards by gauge and class. In this process, the worker must also sort the corkboards by defects. The *delgado* pallets are divided into 6/8 gauges (which go to the discs production line with one blade; the cork is thin, so you can only get a strip of the board to produce the cork discs), and 8/12 (which go to the discs production line with two or three blades; the greater thickness of the cork makes it possible to obtain more strips from the initial board and, thus, be more profitable by producing more discs).

In the second sorting process, the *cheio* cork pallets arrive at the worker's bench, and the worker has to trace one of the ends, which helps him decide on the cork gauge, having to look/observe three aspects: belly, the inner part of the corkboard (which is in contact with the tree trunk); back, the outer part of the corkboard (which is in contact with the environment, dark part of the cork); and mass of the board, cells that, when developing, give thickness to the corkboard. The gauge standards are shown in Figure 11 (a). The *cheio* part is divided into 12/14, 13/15, 15/20, and 18/24 gauges. For example, the 12/14 gauge has a thickness between 27 and 32 mm, and its division varies the size and length of the cork stopper that customers produce. In addition, it is necessary to analyze each corkboard's class, as shown in Figure 11 (b), as these are the two processes with the highest degree of complexity in this phase.

Figure 11. Cheio gauge and class pattern
Source: Industrial cork unit

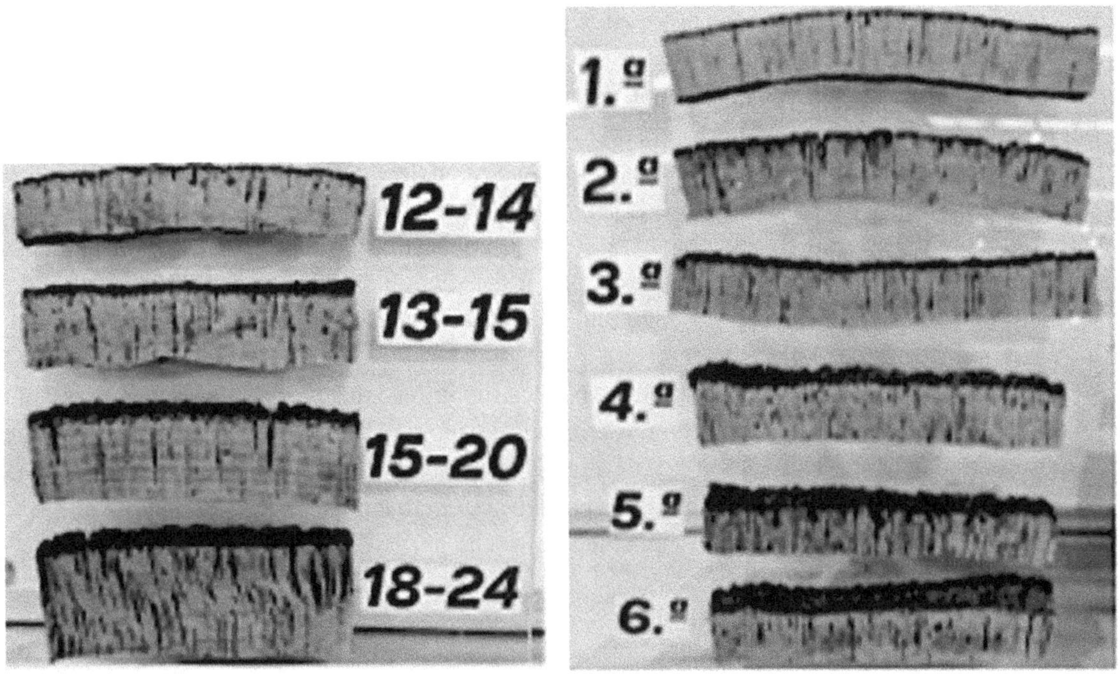

Figure 12 (a) shows the cork sorting bench, where the corkboard cut form and the cages (storage box with wheels) around the worker can be seen. After the entire selection process, the worker places the boards in the corresponding cage, identified by gauge and class, as shown in Figure 12 (b).

Figure 12. Cork sorting bench and cages
Source: Industrial cork unit

The entire selection process must be registered and quantified, which is done by the forklift operator through a tablet available on the equipment and with the TrakSYS platform, which collects and stores, in real-time, all the information of the production process, from the entry of raw material to the output of the finished product. The input data are the weight of each pallet placed on the bench, batch (source of raw material – Company lands), and identification of the worker who will carry out the work.

Suppose there are unfinished pallets and cages at the end of the workday. In that case, the cages are all weighed to obtain production indicators, in real-time, based on the number of kilograms worked during the day and the quantity for each worker. It is essential to know if all workers have similar productivity and are following the general section objective. If not verified, it becomes necessary to understand the worker's needs or existing difficulties. For example, if the section aims to work 50,208 kg of cork, to achieve this goal, it needs 24 people to trace (cut the end of the corkboard) and sort the cork; that is, each worker must be able to work an average of 2,092 kg.

Actually, the *amadia* pallets are placed on the pallet structures so that workers at the beginning of the sorting line can again make a second sorting, where the *delgado* will be removed and separated by gauge but not by class; that is, it goes as 6/8 and 8/12 directly to the discs section. Then, the workers place the corkboards entirely on the mat to pass through a portico system that makes the laser reading of the cork gauge (12/14, 13/15, 15/20, and 18/24). Figure 13 shows the portico's system circuit.

Figure 13. Circuit of the portico system
Source: Industrial cork unit

At the end of each mat, there is a worker to sort and classify each corkboard by class, initially analyzing its coast, belly, and mass and, later, the class, in a similar way to the previous process, where the sorting is made mainly based on the worker's knowledge. According to the customer's needs, there are open classes groups, such as 1st/4th or fifth/sixth, to guarantee the stoppers production with the wanted customer's diameter and length. For example, in gauge 18/24 [see Figure 11 (a)], the 1st/6th class [see Figure 11 (b)] is used, as this is a very peculiar cork in terms of thickness and density, being specific for a particular type of stopper.

In this selection process, the worker will trace each corkboard (cut off the end of the corkboard, to check the quality, that is, the grade) and place it on the pallet with the help of a metal structure that helps the alignment of the corkboard to be shipped to the customer, as shown in Figure 14.

Figure 14. Metal structure to finish the cork pallet
Source: Industrial cork unit

All pallets entering the beginning of the line are weighed, and all pallets and cages resulting from the class selection process are registered on the TrakSYS platform. In addition, a laser sorting machine provides information on the number of kilograms per gauge that passes through the portico. This information is manually registered later on the TrakSYS platform.

The need to understand whether all workers have homogeneous productivity and are following the general objective of the section remains, as in the previous process. For example, if the section aims to work 50,540 kg of cork, to achieve this goal, it will need 20 people to trace and sort, now only per class; that is, each worker should be able to work an average of 2,527 kg.

In the preparation section, the second sorting process requires workers with knowledge about the raw material obtained during their stay in the shipyard section to acquire sufficient experience to make an appropriate gauge cork sorting. Due to the complex raw material sorting, the acquisition of the automatic sorting portico system helped simplify all processes. It proved to be an asset in the recruitment and ergonomics of workers in the class sorting phase because the boards are left on the met, which requires less effort.

One of the essential factors is the significant reliability of the automatic sorting, compared to the worker's non-automatic sorting if the machine is well programmed and aligned with the defined standards. However, there is still no evidence of time savings in this process, given that the machine is still in a testing and tuning phase.

One problem is automatic sorting software that does not migrate data to TrakSYS platform. That does not allow real-time visualization of global data, with that data being placed manually on the TrakSYS Platform, repetitively and with a more significant margin for error (greater human intervention).

I 4.0 can help the entire production process through vertical and horizontal integration (integrate all movements from raw material purchase, production, inventories, and shipment in real time), cloud computing (store data and queries), simulation (test various process improvement scenarios from raw material to final product shipment), sensors and actuators (integrate systems installed along the portico and mats with information transmission and help in optimizing the use of the machine and the reduction of production times), and IoT (integration of all hardware connected via wireless).

These tools provide real-time information, helping production management acquire only the necessary raw materials, reducing product waste and human actions. Another critical point is documentation simplification, which makes it possible to increase product monitoring, in terms of quality, without resorting to many workers.

I5.0 highlights sustainability through the 6Rs. In this process, it is possible to make the most of the raw material without waste, achieved through adaptability (exchange of jobs, removing employees from the task of cutting cork and relocating them to other functions or departments), safety and protection (reduce the number of workers in more insecure functions and improve technological resources), control and clarity (making data available in real-time, through existing software), customer satisfaction (making the process automated and meeting the customers' needs, through a common definition of the desired quality standards) and personalization (enabling the customer to sort a product, quantities, quality, and characteristics). Table 7 compares the two realities (previous and actual) in the Preparation Section and improvements.

Table 7. Preparation section—Comparison of the previous and actual realities and improvements

Preparation Section—*Second sorting of cork*				
#	**Previous reality**	**Actual reality with LM & I 4.0/5.0**	**Obtained improvements**	**Future improvements**
1	Sorting of *delgado* by gauge (2 options) and class (6 options)	Sorting of *delgado* by gauge (2 options)	No sorting by classes, less complexity, minor specialization, placement of a mat where the sorting of gauge and cut was also made	Place a mat where the sorting of the *delgado* gauge was also made
2	Sorting of *cheio* by gauge (4 options) and class (6 options)	Sorting of *cheio* by class (6 options)	Less complexity, minor specialization	Place a portico for *cheio* sorting by class
3	Sorting manual calibration	Automated sorting	Greater reliability of sorting; greater customer satisfaction, and customization possibility per customer (standards tailored to your needs)	
4	Manually remove the cork from the pallet (greater effort)	Loose corkboards along the mat for sorting	Reduction of physical effort	
5	TrakSYS platform registration	Sort on the machine without connection to TrakSYS platform, manual records		Passing (migration) of information automatically to the TrakSYS platform (increasing the system reach)
6	Cutting the end of the board manually	Cutting the end of the corkboard manually		Placement of a met cutting automatism that reduces accidents with more safety

Process Improvement Proposals

Process improvement proposals were obtained by participant observation and comparison of previous and actual situations. Through informal conversations with workers and the observation carried out, it was possible to see that sorting classes still requires some observation time and experience in the area. The proposal is to place one more portico or a set of sensors along the met to determine the corkboards' classes. Figure 15 presents a prototype of a reading portico.

Figure 15. Reading portico prototype
Source: Industrial cork unit

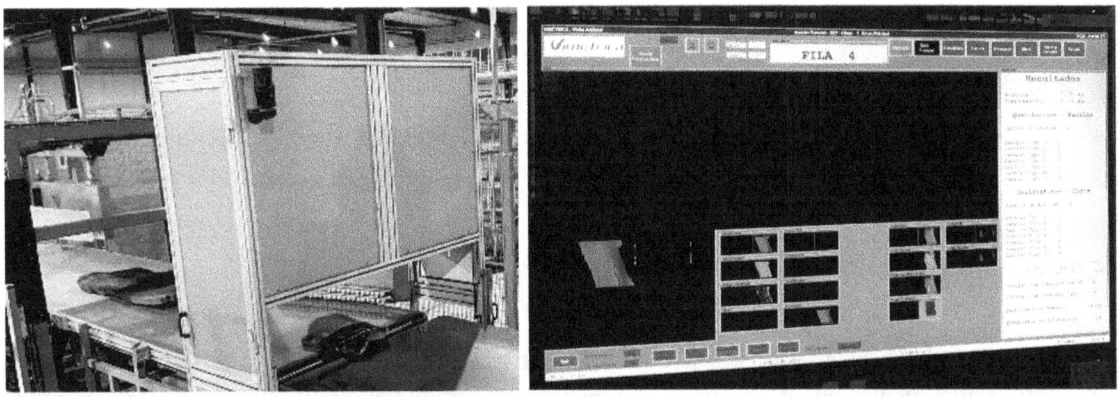

Actually, *cheio* sorting process automation is taking place. It is essential to integrate the *delgado* sorting gauges, including a mat and the programming of the frame, for this purpose. This improvement would make it possible to reduce the number of workers from four to two at the beginning of the mat. It was found a more significant human effort in the process at the beginning of the mat. In this area, the worker must remove the corkboards from the pallet and reach the entire area, making him move to the surrounding areas. This phase requires special attention, so a robotic arm is proposed to remove the corkboards from the pallet and place them on the mat [Figure 16 (a)]. It is also important the inclusion of a lifting platform with a swivel top to put the pallet at the worker's height, so he did not have to bend to remove the corkboards, reaching them at the other end in a more comfortable work position (Figure 16 (b)).

Figure 16. Example of an Industrial robotic arm and a lift platform with swivel cover
Source: DF Robotics and Saxlift

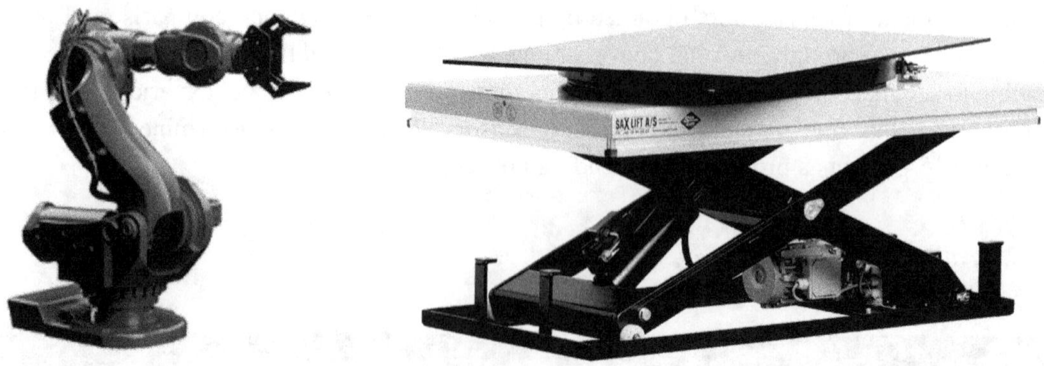

These improvement proposals aim at a better and more efficient sorting process and workers' ergonomics and work safety so that the workers' skills can be used for tasks of greater intellectual complexity.

CONCLUSION

This case study concludes that it is possible to further reduce product waste and human actions, simplify existing documentation, and increase product quality monitoring without using a large number of employees.

To optimize and make the best use of the new resources available, the sorting mats and portico implementation reduce the people's physical effort and simplify the selection process. However, the software used by the automatic sorting machine is not integrated into the TrakSYS platform.

Improvement: The company could optimize and monetize existing resources with an extension of the TrakSYS platform with automatic data migration from the new portico, making it possible to obtain data in real-time and compile all the information in a single software, simplifying the entire analysis of the production process without human intervention and with access to information anywhere. As there is less complexity at the beginning of the human part of the process, it is possible to reduce the number of workers in this job

To increase efficiency and improve quality, the portico turns the process of sorting more automated and straightforward, as it is carried out according to the standards defined by the customer. This evolution, using I 4.0, already includes some principles of I 5.0, such as reduction of repetitive tasks by human actions, clarity, and control of the process, increase in customer satisfaction, reduction, and elimination of waste from the material raw material to the final product, and reduction of the complexity of the production process.

Improvement: The company could install a portico for the cork grade sorting and extend this automated sorting of gauge and grade to the cork that produces cork discs, which would increase the sorting reliability and increase customer satisfaction while also customizing patterns with the customers' needs.

To increase workers' safety, the process automation focuses on the cork sorting, but throughout the process, it becomes necessary to place the board on the mats and carry out a manual cut of the end of the corkboard.

Improvement: The company could install a robot to place the boards on the mats, a portico with a cutting system, and a lifting platform to increase worker safety and protection, thus reducing accidents and absenteeism.

As future research it is intention to carry out a study after the implementation of all the automation equipment, focused on time and resource indicators to analyze and restructure the Company's KPIs.

REFERENCES

Ante, G., Facchini, F., Mossa, G., & Digiesi, S. (2018). Developing a key performance indicators tree for lean and smart production systems. *IFAC-PapersOnLine*, *51*(11), 13–18. doi:10.1016/j.ifacol.2018.08.227

APCOR (Associação Portuguesa da Cortiça/Portuguese Cork Association). (2020). *Noticias*. Retrieved on November 17, 2021 from https://www.apcor.pt/

Arai, K., & Sekine, K. (1992). *Kaizen for Quick Changeover: Going Beyond SMED*. Productivity Press.

Bahrin, M. A. K., Othman, M. F., Azli, N. H. N., & Talib, M. F. (2016). Industry 4.0: A review on industrial automation and robotic. *Journal Teknologi, 78*(6-13), 137-143. doi:10.11113/jt.v78.9285

Bécue, A., Praça, I., & Gama, J. (2021). Artificial intelligence, cyber-threats and Industry 4.0: Challenges and opportunities. *Artificial Intelligence Review*, *54*(5), 3849–3886. doi:10.100710462-020-09942-2

Bittencourt, V. L., Alves, A. C., & Leão, C. P. (2019). Lean Thinking contributions for Industry 4.0: A systematic literature review. *IFAC-PapersOnLine*, *52*(13), 904–909. doi:10.1016/j.ifacol.2019.11.310

Buer, S. V., Fragapane, G. I., & Strandhagen, J. O. (2018). The data-driven process improvement cycle: Using digitalization for continuous improvement. *IFAC-PapersOnLine*, *51*(11), 1035–1040. doi:10.1016/j.ifacol.2018.08.471

Campenhoudt, L. V., Marquet, J., & Quivy, R. (2019). Manual de Investigação em Ciências Sociais. Gradiva.

Davies, R., Coole, T., & Smith, A. (2017). Review of socio-technical considerations to ensure successful implementation of Industry 4.0. *Procedia Manufacturing*, *11*, 1288–1295. doi:10.1016/j.promfg.2017.07.256

Davis, J. W. (2009). *Lean Manufacturing: Implementation Strategies that Work: A Roadmap to Quick and Lasting Success*. Industrial Press Inc.

Deloitte. (2014). *Industry 4.0: Challenges and solutions for the digital transformation and use of exponential technologies*. Retrieved on November 17, 2022 from https://www2.deloitte.com/content/dam/Deloitte/ch/Documents/manufacturing/ch-en-manufacturing-industry-4-0-24102014.pdf

Demir, K. A., Döven, G., & Sezen, B. (2019). Industry 5.0 and human-robot coworking. *Procedia Computer Science*, *158*, 688–695. doi:10.1016/j.procs.2019.09.104

Drew, J., McCallum, B., & Roggenhofer, S. (2004). *Journey to lean: Making operational change stick*. Palgrave Macmillan. doi:10.1057/9781403948410

Duggan, K. J., & Healey, T. (2016). *Operational Excellence in Your Office: A Guide to Achieving Autonomous Value Stream Flow with Lean Techniques*. Productivity Press.

Ejsmont, K., Gladysz, B., Corti, D., Castaño, F., Mohammed, W. M., & Martinez Lastra, J. L. (2020). Towards 'Lean Industry 4.0': Current trends and future perspectives. *Cogent Business and Management*, *7*(1), 1781995. doi:10.1080/23311975.2020.1781995

Gaziero, C., & Cecconello, I. (2019). Simulação computacional do fluxo de valor: Uma proposta de integração da Indústria 4.0 e lean production. *Scientia Cum Industria*, *7*(2), 52–67. doi:10.18226/23185279.v7iss2p52

Ghobakhloo, M., & Fathi, M. (2020). Corporate survival in Industry 4.0 era: The enabling role of lean-digitized manufacturing. *Journal of Manufacturing Technology Management*, *31*(1), 1–30. doi:10.1108/JMTM-11-2018-0417

Gunal, M. M. (2019). *Simulation for Industry 4.0: Past, Present, and Future*. Springer. doi:10.1007/978-3-030-04137-3

Hammarberg, M., & Sunden, J. (2014). *Kanban in Action*. Manning Publications Co.

Hirano, H. (2009). JIT Implementation Manual: The Complete Guide to Just-in-Time Manufacturing (2nd ed.). New York, NY: Productivity Press.

Hozdić, E. (2015). Smart Factory for Industry 4.0: A review. *International Journal of Modern Manufacturing Technologies*, *VII*(1), 28–35. doi:10.1016/j.promfg.2018.02.034

Ikeziri, L. M., Melo, J. C., Campos, R. T., Okimura, L. I., & Gobbo, J. A. Jr. (2020). A perspectiva da indústria 4.0 sobre a filosofia de gestão lean manufacturing. *Brazilian Journal of Development*, *6*(1), 1274–1289. doi:10.34117/bjdv6n1-089

Jastia, N. V. K., & Kodali, R. (2015). Lean production: Literature review and trends. *International Journal of Production Research*, *53*(3), 867–885. doi:10.1080/00207543.2014.937508

Jones, D. T. (2006). Heijunka: Leveling production. *Manufacturing Engineering*, *137*(2), 29–36.

Kirner, C., & Siscoutto, R. (Eds.). (2007). *Realidade virtual e aumentada: Conceitos, projeto e aplicações*. SBC.

Kolberg, D., & Zühlke, D. (2015). Lean automation enabled by Industry 4.0 technologies. *IFAC-PapersOnLine*, *28*(3), 1870–1875. doi:10.1016/j.ifacol.2015.06.359

Liker, J. (2004). *The Toyota Way: 14 management principles the world's greatest manufacturer*. McGraw-Hill.

Lima, D. F. S., de França Alcantara, P. G., Santos, L. C., Silva, L. M. F., & Da Silva, R. M. (2016). Mapeamento do fluxo de valor e simulação para implementação de práticas lean em uma empresa calçadista. *Produção Online*, *16*(1), 366–392.

Luściński, S., & Ivanov, V. (2020). A simulation study of Industry 4.0 factories based on the ontology on flexibility with using FlexSim® software. *Management and Production Engineering Review*, *11*, 74–83. doi:10.24425/mper.2020.134934

Markovitz, D. (2011). *A factory of one: Applying lean principles to banish waste and improve your personal performance*. CRC Press.

Mayr, A., Weigelt, M., Kühl, A., Grimm, S., Erll, A., Potzel, M., & Franke, J. (2018). Lean 4.0: A conceptual conjunction of lean management and Industry 4.0. *Procedia CIRP, 72*, 622-628. doi:10.1016/j.procir.2018.03.292

Monden, Y. (1993). *Toyota Production System: An integrated approach to Just-In Time* (2nd ed.). Industrial Engineering and Management Press. doi:10.1007/978-1-4615-9714-8

Nahavandi, S. (2019). Industry 5.0: A human-centric solution. *Sustainability, 11*(16), 1–13. doi:10.3390u11164371

Ohno, T. (1988). *Toyota Production System: Beyond large-scale production*. Productivity Press.

Omogbai, O., & Salonitis, K. (2017). The implementation of 5S lean tool using system dynamics approach. *Procedia CIRP, 60*, 380–385. doi:10.1016/j.procir.2017.01.057

Osada, T. (1991). *The 5S's: Five Keys to a Total Quality Environment*. Asian Productivity Organization.

Pagliosa, M., Tortorella, G., & Ferreira, J. C. E. (2019). Industry 4.0 and lean manufacturing: A systematic literature review and future research directions. *Journal of Manufacturing Technology Management, 32*(3), 543–569. doi:10.1108/JMTM-12-2018-0446

Paschek, D., Mocan, A., & Draghici, A. (2019). Industry 5.0: The expected impact of next industrial revolution. In *Proceedings of the MakeLearn and TIIM International Conference* (pp.15–17). Bangkok: ToKnowPress.

Peraković, D., Periša, M., Cvitić, I., & Zorić, P. (2020). Information and communication technologies for the Society 5.0 environment. In *Proceedings of the XXXVIII Simpozijum o Novim Tehnologijama u Poštanskom i Telekomunikacionom Saobraćaju* (pp. 203-212). Belgrade: University of Belgrade. 10.37528/FTTE/9788673954318/POSTEL.2020.020

Pinto, J. (2014). *Introdução ao pensamento Lean: A filosofia das organizações vencedoras*. Lidel.

Pinto, J. P. (2020). *A relação entre Lean Manufacturing e Indústria 4.0: Uma revisão sistemática da literatura*. Tese de Doutoramento, Instituto Superior de Economia e Gestão.

Prinz, C., Kreggenfeld, N., & Kuhlenkötter, B. (2018). Lean meets Industry 4.0: A practical approach to interlink the method world and cyber-physical world. *Procedia Manufacturing, 23*, 21–26. doi:10.1016/j.promfg.2018.03.155

Ribeiro, R. B., De Souza, J., Beluco, A., Biehl, L. V., Medeiros, J. L. B., Sporket, F., Rossini, E. G., & Amaral, F. A. D. (2019). Application of the single-minute exchange of die system to the CNC sector of a shoe mold company. *Cogent Engineering, 6*(1), 1606376. doi:10.1080/23311916.2019.1606376

Rosemann, M., Becker, J., & Chasin, F. (2021). City 5.0. *Business & Information Systems Engineering, 63*(1), 71–77. doi:10.100712599-020-00674-9

Rosin, F., Forget, P., Lamouri, S., & Pellerin, R. (2019). Impacts of Industry 4.0 technologies on Lean principles. *International Journal of Production Research, 58*(6), 1644–1661. doi:10.1080/00207543.2019.1672902

Sanders, A., Elangeswaran, C., & Wulfsberg, J. P. (2016). Industry 4.0 implies lean manufacturing: Research activities in industry 4.0 function as enablers for lean manufacturing. *Journal of Industrial Engineering and Management, 9*(3), 811–833. doi:10.3926/jiem.1940

Shewhart, W. A. (1931/1980). *Economic control of quality of manufactured product*. American Society for Quality.

Shingo, S. (1985). *A revolution in manufacturing: The SMED system*. Productivity Press.

Silva, E. B., Scoton, M. L. R. P. D., Dias, E. M., & Pereira, S. L. (2018). *Automação & Sociedade: Quarta Revolução Industrial, um olhar para o Brasil*. Brasport.

Tortorella, G. L., Narayanamurthy, G., & Thurer, M. (2021). Identifying pathways to a high-performing lean automation implementation: An empirical study in the manufacturing industry. *International Journal of Production Economics, 231*, 1–13. doi:10.1016/j.ijpe.2020.107918

Womack, J. P., & Jones, D. T. (2004). Lean thinking: Banish waste and create wealth in your corporation. *The Journal of the Operational Research Society, 48*(11), 1148–1148. doi:10.1057/palgrave.jors.2600967

Xu, J., Huang, E., Hsieh, L., Lee, L. H., Jia, Q.-S., & Chen, C.-H. (2017). Simulation optimization in the era of Industrial 4.0 and the Industrial Internet. *Journal of Simulation, 10*(4), 310–320. doi:10.105741273-016-0037-6

Section 2

Enhancing Supply Chain Performance Through Collaboration, Sophistication, and Risk Management

Chapter 7
Efficacy of Supply Chain Collaboration on Resilience in the Fast-Moving Consumer Goods Retail Industry

Nkechi Dorothy Neboh
Nelson Mandela University, Port Elizabeth, South Africa

Thokozani Patmond Mbhele
University of KwaZulu-Natal, Westville, South Africa

Winston Shakantu
Nelson Mandela University, Port Elizabeth, South Africa

ABSTRACT

Fast-moving consumer goods (FMCG) are driven by threats and nascent challenges that range from logistical issues to disruptions in the environment. The chapter aimed to determine the efficacy of supply chain collaboration on resilience in the industry. Scholars have constantly highlighted the need for supply chain collaboration by building supply chain resilience, necessitated against sporadic, disruptive, and unforeseen events in the business environment. The argument for businesses to desist from working in silos within their supply chain provokes this study. There seems to be a mismatch between the supply chain members in terms of integrating or collaborating efforts and their capabilities to be resilient when faced with disruptions. Organisations need to identify the variables that exist inside and outside of their environment to ensure alignment, collaboration, and integration. Centralisation of stocks, foreign exchange fluctuation, joint business plans, and longstanding collaboration with vendors could help promote supply chain resilience.

DOI: 10.4018/978-1-7998-9715-6.ch007

Copyright © 2022, IGI Global. Copying or distributing in print or electronic forms without written permission of IGI Global is prohibited.

INTRODUCTION

Retailing provides most essentials and daily necessities of life, such as groceries and stable food products. However, the retail industry has faced tough economic times stimulated by unprecedented and environmental issues. These issues may arise from natural disasters to consumer reduction on purchasing of products due to a rise in inflation. Furthermore, these challenges are further compounded by labour unrest, insufficient service delivery provision for the communities, corruption with the high unemployment rate, and currently, the pandemic (Covid-19) that is raging havoc in the world today. The emerging pandemic has shown structural problems that existed in global supply chains (Lakovou & White 2020), hence a reset in the retail supply chain design to improve resilience is needed. These challenges are associated with a rate of increase in crimes and as well, expose the modern supply chain fragility. These setbacks affect the entire network of retail supply chain members. These disruptions are changing industries and impeding the survival ability of businesses. Despite all these, customers still demand better product pricing and positive service offerings from retailers. Hence, maximising profits through creating and delivering value for customers through quality product availability is the objective of retailers at every point. But the flow of goods into retail stores is comparatively distorted, as these supply chain issues persist, hence disrupting defined set performance objectives and strategies and sending the business on a downward trajectory. The retail supply chain is characterised by the constant influx of goods across the supply chain and the short shelf life of the products. The extension of this industry goes beyond the borders of a country, when trying to find a cheap source of supply, a strategic distribution centre, and a high volume of the consumer market hence exposing it to many supply chain interruptions. These challenges are mostly noticed at the downstream side of the supply chain, as it is difficult to be resilient in those precarious times when disruption strikes. Moreover, a global call has been made for businesses to build resilience as a strategy to mitigate shocks in their business environment through supply chain collaboration. Resilience aims at restoring a distorted activity to normal or to a better position after being affected by a negative occurrence (Neboh, Mbhele, & Phiri 2019). In other words, the focus of resilience is to bounce back or conserve its stance from disruptions that may arise from external turbulences. Hence, organisations or businesses aimed at achieving supply chain resilience must be able to collaborate with supply chain partners to mitigate risk. This chapter aimed to determine the value of supply chain collaboration on supply chain resilience in the fast-moving consumer goods industry (FMCGs). At a macro level, this paper aims to understand the usefulness of retail supply chain collaboration on supply chain resilience.

BACKGROUND

The retail industry in many African Countries operates in a complex, ever-changing, and challenging business environment. For instance, notwithstanding its flamboyant dispositions and maturity, the South African fast-moving consumer goods (FMCG) industry is confronted with dire business threats (Stoltz 2018) such as the increase in the theft of goods delivery trucks, especially en route to destinations of demand across South Africa (SA). Even the recent mayhem of looting of shops and arson coupled with the cyberattack on their infrastructure. have negatively influenced and disrupted the supply chain operations system of the retail industry (Writer 2021). These concerns increase as the bottom line of the entire retail industry is directly affected by the losses incurred from such incidences, and ultimately impacts the consumer (Appalsamy 2017). Even more disheartening is the sporadic distortion of energy supply in Nigeria, which has also hampered economic activities, business service offering performances in industries such as FMCG, and growth in the economy. The expanse of disruptions on supply chains is not limited to only SA, as beyond the borders of this country, places such as Uganda were besieged with Foot and Mouth Disease in the retail industry (Kerfia, Shirma, Kusiluka, Ayebazibwe, Mwebe, Cleaveland & Haydon 2018). Shortage of goods in the global world indicates that the coronavirus pandemic disruption persistence and the extent of its effect on businesses, is huge because deliveries are not timely, price and cost also increased (Ellyatt 2021). With globalisation, FMCG businesses are expanding past the borders of the African and European continent, however, supply chain disruptions impact its operational efficiency. As supply chains expand globally, companies are exposed to a plethora of supply chain risks that shrunk GDP from 61% to 58%. Hence, leading businesses such as retail are gradually aware that it is critical to managing these risks for sustained competitiveness (Lakavou & White 2020). Businesses need to collaborate and display their resilience capabilities to reduce disruptions. The argument for businesses to desist from working in silos within their supply chain provokes the need to examine the extent of collaboration on resilience in a complex industry such as retail.

This chapter acknowledges the contingency theory framework because the retail industry operates its businesses in an environment amassed with turbulence and uncertain conditions. Supply chain disruptions affect the internal and external structures of any organisation. When the supply chain structure is radically transformed by unanticipated man-made and natural occurrences that shift its entire network, many companies are affected, hence this chapter investigated the use of supply chain collaboration for resilience in the retail context. There seems to be a mismatch between the supply chain members in terms of integrating or collaborating efforts and their capabilities to be resilient when faced with disruptions. Contingency theory encompasses three collaborative aspects: a) the environment - where the organisation thrives and operates; b) the organisation's capabilities - such as resources, policies, and cultures; and c) the strategies – which an organisation uses to benchmark the environmental capabilities (Haavisto 2014). Therefore, organisations need to identify the variables that exist inside and outside of their environment to ensure alignment, collaboration, and integration between the two factors. This would enable interrelationship between the open system (organisation) and its external environment. Hence, contingency factors were presented as a standard of use: the environment, the organisation's capabilities (resources, mission, organisational culture, structure, policies, practices, product line, and employees) and plans to match capabilities with the external environment. Hence, to grow and expand geographically, firms must consider their environment in terms of advancement in innovations and improvement in performance. These advocates for using strategies that best suit an organisation's policies, boundaries, and objectives and matching it with the business external environment. Contingency approach analyses the organisation's internal and external factors that are anticipated to affect investments (Lamminen, Forsvik, Voipio & Lehtonen 2015). Thus, firms are forced to implement plans that can handle environmental variations.

FAST-MOVING CONSUMER GOODS

FMCGs are referred to as goods that are disposed of regularly (Mustapha 2010; Vaishnani 2011) and are low-value items regularly sold by retailers (Kotler and Armstrong 2011) at a relatively low-cost (Mustapha 2010; Selvakumar, Jansirani & Jegatheesan 2013). Fouladivanda, Pashandi, Hooman & Khanmohammadi (2013) view FMCGs as retail goods used up fully or replaced generally over a minimum period of days, weeks, or in one year. FMCGs have a short shelf life and are non-durable (KPMG 2016). The most common products in FMCG meant for frequent consumption are toothpaste, shoe polish, household accessories, detergents, shampoos, and shaving products. Procuring of these products occurs at supermarkets, hypermarkets, and grocery stores (Singh, 2014). Extensive decision-making or financial investment is not required for FMCGs, and the products deteriorate rapidly (Ittmann, Meyer, Havenga & Marais 2014) as they operate within the characteristics of quick, fast, and agile features. It is a known industry that has its supply chains benchmarked by others through innovative ideas, high flow of its product with close interaction with its customers (Bala & Kumar 2011). For example, in India, the FMCG sector is claimed to be the fourth largest sector that creates employment in the economy for more than three million people (Srinivasu 2014). From a retailer perspective, FMCGs are referred to as a low-margin high volume industry (KPMG, 2016:2; Singh & Acharya 2014) due to high demand in the market and have a quick turnover and relatively low cost (Mohan & Sequeira 2015). FMCGs principally involve the manufacturing, distribution of packaged goods for consumers (Quasim & Agarwal 2015) and are also known as consumer-packaged-goods (Mohan & Sequeira 2012). Selvakumar *et al.* (2013) indicate that the volume of money in circulation in an economy is very high due to the number of consumers that buy the products. The FMCG retail outlet is a simple store that offers one an opportunity to select from a variety of household and food items, according to their needs. Each retail item is laid out in departments at a low price. Most of the FMCGs are located near residential areas, central business district areas, or shopping malls. These allow and give consumers the choice of location to visit and purchase the goods within a limited time. The layout of the product mix is part of the FMCGs marketing strategy that entices the consumers to select and buy the product of their choice. According to Mbhele (2014), customers obtain value from FMCG retail stores. Against this background, the strength of the FMCG industry lies in the strong presence of low operating costs, distribution networks, and multinational firms.

SUPPLY CHAIN

A supply chain is regarded as "an open and economic system that is based on resource communication and integration in an enterprise or external environment" (Geng, Xiao & Xu 2014:2) with a network integration of facilities and transportation modes of supply, storage, products, and materials distribution (Garcia & You 2015) where the sizes, industrial scales, and complexity differ from one industry to the other (Chopra & Meindl 2012). Jacobs, Chase & Lummus (2011) refer to the supply chain as the processes that are used to convey information and material to and from any firm's manufacturing and service processes. Information flow, product flow, and finance flow are identified as the three primary supply chain flow (Nel & Badenhorst-weiss 2010), and this perspective was supported by Day (2014) by citing the importance of the flows, which must be synchronised. A supply chain could be defined as a complex network that starts from the suppliers to customers and involves technology, activities, and information transformed from raw materials to finished goods and eventually distributed to end customers (Lambiase, Mastrocinque, Miranda & Lambiase 2013). Mari, Lee, Memon, Park & Kim (2015:102) defined a supply chain "as a complex network with interdependencies and an overwhelming number of connections among the varied resources, processes, and entities". Although there are extant investments, study and research in the supply chain, critics are generally unconvinced about its efficiency. For instance, Geng *et al.* (2014) assert that the globalisation of the economy, which has improved efficiency in supply chains, still makes it a risky activity. This may be because, the business environment is dynamic and changes like 'the speed of light', hence the supply chain strategy that worked today may be obsolete tomorrow. Likewise, Artsiomcyk & Zhivitskaya (2013) affirm that contemporary supply chains face several challenges that are caused by uncertainty. For example, customer ever-changing demands on service and product qualities are increasing and any failure in a supply chain may cause a ripple effect in an organisation's ability to operate (Soni & Jain 2011) with potential disruptions to the upstream, downstream, and associating firms (Azadeh., Atrchin, Salehi & Shojaei 2013). It, therefore, follows that supply chains may need to use strategies that can respond cost-effectively and rapidly to the unpredictable and increasing turbulence in the environment. Communication amongst the different entities in the supply chain needs to be effectively channeled to meet up with the demand of the consumers, at the right time, at the right place, and with the actual quantity of goods requested. The supply chains must have the complete visualisation of the entire supply chain in terms of visibility and understand the flow of materials, information and money and keep pace to sorting bottlenecks if any, to ensure optimal performance. In a supply chain, firms are often privileged to see end to end of their business, build a unique relationship with partners and create the best value in services provided to the end customer. Different organisations are interconnected with partners in the business, for the sole aim of getting the right products to consumers through better communication. For a supply chain to succeed, all the entities' top management should support and commit to establishing and achieving set objectives, targets, and missions, even if it means directly involved in operational activities. By doing this, it would become easier to share information in the supply chain.

RETAIL SUPPLY CHAIN

It cannot be denied that supply chains are complex (Janamanchi & Burns 2014) and brittle (Pettit, Croxton & Fiksel 2019); hence, it is important to understand how it works to manage them well. The retail supply chain is complex with structures that depend on one another for business growth, stability, and survival. Retail trade depicts the last member in the supply chain link with a direct connection to the end/final consumer. It includes service providers, distributors, suppliers, retailers, manufacturers, and customers, that participate in this dependency toward competitive growth. A retail supply chain links all these stakeholders so that products and services are always available when needed. The supply chain of any retail primarily consists of the suppliers that source the raw materials and then supply this to the manufacturer who transforms them into finished products. These products are supplied to the retailers either directly or using intermediaries. The retailers display the product to the visible eye of the customers. The end consumers access and procure the products from the retailers' stores. According to Srivastava, Chaudhuri & Srivastava (2015), complexity in relationships increases due to the interactions amongst all the stakeholders.

The key to developing a successful supply chain lies in achieving seamless information flow between the links in the chain, using information technology as a strategy in integrating the steps in the supply chain. However, Inman & Blumenfeld (2014), argued that the more the lead time, number of stakeholders, and number of steps in the supply chain, the higher the risk of disruption that can alter an industry's financial prospect or affect its operational performances. Therefore, information technology plays a pivotal role in a business. However, careful considerations can be adopted to strategise and reduce the number of steps or processes taken to deliver products or services to a consumer. The retail supply chain is an industry that is complex with structures that depends on one another for business growth and survival.

Dependence on the supply chain members occurs since retailers sell some of their members' products to consumers for their consumption (Dos Santos 2010). Retail supply is all about how fast products can be made and delivered to customers quicker than ever through the interactions of the supply chain members. It is all about gaining a market position earlier than competitors. Customers are becoming savvier with a high ordering habit and expectations of service rendered. Therefore, retailers need to evolve and improve their operations to meet the changing desires of the customer seamlessly.

SUPPLY CHAIN COLLABORATION

Collaboration has been cited amongst resilient supply chain elements (Christopher & Peck 2004; Scholten & Schilder 2015:471). These elements include supply chain agility, supply chain collaboration, supply chain reengineering, and risk management culture. The extent of relationship and collaboration developed in the retail supply chain becomes imperative as sourcing of goods can be improved as well as risk reduction, hence enabling the supply chain to be more resilient. This implies that before an impending disruption occurs, all supply chain members become aware earlier, hence allowing for a coordinated effort towards risk reduction thereof. This belief is the core of resilience. An entire retail supply chain can strengthen its supply chain through responsiveness, agility, and inventory reduction due to collaborative initiatives (American Production and Inventory Control Society (APICS) 2013). In as much as businesses thrive to exist and to trade individually, it is critical to bear in mind that no single firm in a modern market context, can compete successfully on its own (Janvier-James 2012) but between supply chains (Christopher 2011). Retailers' swift rise to collaborate will advance the network and lead a continuous stream of product availability that satisfies end consumers. By collaborating, supply chains can picture its vulnerability at a network level and will properly examine, mitigate, and manage the risk that may occur (Kamalahmadi & Mellat-Parast 2016). These risks and benefits that may accrue can be shared between supply chain partners (Soosay & Hyland 2015). Collaboration with suppliers and partners to reinforce supply chain resilience includes mutual agreement on risk-sharing, collaborative continuity plans, and risk hedging within the supply chain partners (Scholten & Schilder 2015). As a key thought, many industries are making a concerted effort to collaborate with supply chain members (Boyce, Mano & Kent 2016).

Furthermore, supply chain collaboration is seen as applying shared knowledge and exchange of information to increase customer service level, efficiency, and effectiveness, the entire supply chain visibility, and to reduce risks (Scholten, Sharkey & Fyne 2014). The lack thereof may lead to inefficiencies in production, process waste, cost inflation, and redundant inventory stock; hence supply chain collaboration is referred to as core competence in a worldwide market (Li 2012). Simatupang and Sridharan (2002) claimed that collaborative practice can be evaluated using three scopes: Information sharing, decision synchronisation, and incentive alignment. Information sharing has been acknowledged to significantly affect supply chain collaboration through cost-saving; it is evidenced to increase visibility and integrate supply chain plan, which further reduces the bullwhip effect (Hudnurkar, Jakhar & Rathod 2014:197). Information sharing is valuable for all supply chain partners (Anand & Grover 2015:150). When information is shared, retailers get first-hand notice of what transpires at the lower end of the supply chain especially from the consumer perspective (downstream side of the retail supply chain). This implies that speed in performance is thus critical in supply chains as it measures the effectiveness in satisfying customer needs.

Overall real-time visibility is suggested, to improve a supply chain. However, Tan, Zhang & Cai (2019), highlighted that it is unfortunate that many firms still do not have a visible view of their supply chains such as information concerning suppliers' transportation routes or supplier sources. In synchronising decisions, supply chain partners transform issues about operations and customers to achieve a streamlined optimal solution. Actions such as these promote clear visibility of the end-to-end supply chain (Hudnukar *et al.* 2014). If decisions are not coordinated between partners, it may cause ambiguity and non-transparency, hence distorting information on customer demand patterns throughout the entire supply chain network.

The mutual perspective on which independent supply chain partners act to achieve the overall objective ensures an equal contribution to the chain. Since the success of a partnership involves the equitable share of gains and losses (Cao, Vonderembse, Zhang & Ragu-Nathan 2010)., incentive alignment may include every resource and the risk which leverages business and can be shared amongst its supply chain partners. Every member that contributes towards achieving the objective of the supply chain expects to be rewarded equitably. Even though there is huge complexity in retailing, the supply chain partners align and achieve set outcomes in the business. Hence, it can be argued that incentive alignment, information sharing, and visibility all contribute to supply chain collaboration which bolsters resilience capabilities. There are also many benefits of collaboration such as cost reduction, reduced inventory, and shortened lead-time. Collaboration is a risk mitigation strategy and is fundamental in addressing resilient supply chains (Banomyong 2018). Through collaboration emanating from synergies created amongst supply chain members, resources and capabilities are combined, and this increases customer services and the value of goods.

SUPPLY CHAIN RESILIENCE

Originating from material science, resilience refers to the system's ability to recover to an initial state after an elastic manipulation without a change in its nature (Ponomarov & Holcomb 2009). Resilience is more than the recovery ability (Barroso, Machado & Machado 2011); it is also the ability to be better placed than competitors in managing risks and market positioning. The authors suggest that resilience infers that a certain flexibility level and the capability to adapt to environmental impact, is critical to sustainable economic development. The first study conducted on supply chain resilience was in the United Kingdom after a transport disruption facilitated by fuel protests in the year 2000 (Christopher & Peck 2004). It is argued that resilience may offer businesses the capability to adapt to modification and succeed in the long term. For instance, the trade-off for retailers to display their products on shelves comes with the cost of warehouse stock of inventory. However, the efficiency and responsiveness in ensuring product availability increase profit gained in the long term for the business. Meanwhile, it is demonstrated that from the negative experiences of crises, organisations learn to be resilient. Thus, supply chains tend to become resilient when all companies engage amicably to overcome disruptive situations than working alone (Rha 2020) and sharing valuable information (Pettit, Croxton & Fiksel 2013). It is evidenced that resilience may be a source of competitive advantage when it can respond quickly faster than its rivals (Banemyong 2018). In the era of uncertainty, businesses put in their best to achieve a competitive advantage to succeed, however, a test of resilience is needed to stay afloat and perform optimally. Supply chain collaboration presents a tighter and connected global economy, however, the usual management practices are confronted by foreign, turbulent disturbances and alterations that are unavoidable. Reducing these risks and their effects becomes a huge management challenge as the risks are evolving constantly and daily. In dealing with risk mitigation, supply chain risk management practitioners suggested the resilient ability (Ouabouch 2015). For instance, amid COVID-19, supply chains regular activity almost stopped such as delays in goods delivery, short supply of materials worldwide, and labour shortages. Supply chain management as well as business owners need more extensive planning that focuses on balancing efficiency and cost with resilience to predict supply disruptions (Ferreira, Cardoso, Travassos, Paiva, Pestana, Lopes & Oliverira 2021). Few works of literature have been studied on supply chain resilience in terms of structures, determinants, conceptual in nature, and definitions (Rice & Caniato 2003; Christopher & Peck 2004; Juttner & Maklan 2011; Barroso, Machado & Machado 2011; Ponis & Koronis 2012; Jabbarzadeh, Fahimnia, & Sabouhi 2018; Pettit *et al.* 2019). Despite the interest in the context thus far, there is limited research on the contribution of supply chain collaboration on supply chain resilience. It is evidenced that investing in a resilient supply chain will place companies in a good position to withstand any obstruction on the flow of goods in the future, as those that invested in the concept, reduced product development cycles from 40% to 60% (Schatteman, Woodhouse & Terino 2020). Essentially, supply chain resilience may be seen as a lifeline for survival both for businesses and organisations alike since it is needed to mitigate risk as noted in the literature. It is noteworthy to appraise the 80% of global companies that support supply chain resilience due to increased globalization and market volatility (Aigbogun, Ghazali & Razali 2018). The results of a resilient supply chain include cycle time reduction, visibility in transactional activities, cost reductions in operations, and increased service level (Ochieng 2018). Therefore, in a competitive environment, supply chain resilience can be a critical strategic weapon to weather every disruption and improve any business's market share. The integration and coherence amongst supply chain partners prompt the need to be continually resilient especially in the retail industry which is characterised by its complexity. Hence, resilience is a fundamental attribute needed to be adopted by all supply chains (Shen & Sun 2021) and a desirable trait to possess especially in dealing with disruptions.

Relationship between Supply Chain Collaboration and Supply Chain Resilience

In literature, collaboration has been treated as a resource (Chen, Tian, Ellinge & Daugherty, 2010). It has been emphasised that supply chain collaboration (SCC) is usually regarded by scholars as an essential part of dealing with enterprise risks in relation to supply disruptions which can occur in either the downstream or upstream supply chain side (Chen, Sohal & Prajogo, 2013; Leat & Revoredo-Giha, 2013; Li, Fan, Lee & Cheng, 2015). The objective of supply chain collaboration in improving operational flexibility that comes from facilitating cooperation amongst supply chain members to manage supply and demand uncertainty (Botes, Niemann & Kotze 2017) and to improve demand forecasts and inventory management and accuracy of information (Li, 2012). Literature has highlighted the essentials of collaboration to developing a resilient supply chain (Petit, Croxton & Fiskel 2013; Juttner and Maklan 2011) since during crisis, it holds the supply chains together (Richey, Roath, Whipple & Fawcett 2010). Wilding (2013) and Christopher, Mena, Khan & Yurt (2011) have indicated the essence of firms investing in collaborative relationships as an enabler of supply chain resilience, but this has often been ignored. Collaboration enables information and knowledge sharing through joint efforts (Juttner and Maklan, 2011; Petit *et al.,* 2013). For instance, Wal-Mart and Procter and Gamble were able to stimulate agility through collaboration and are more resilient in dealing with risks associated with changing market demands (Mensah, Merkuryev & Longo 2015). The extent of relationship and collaboration developed in the retail supply chain becomes imperative as sourcing of goods can be improved as well as risk reduction, hence enabling the supply chain to be more resilient. This implies that prior to an impending disruption occurrence, all members of a supply chain become aware earlier, allowing for coordinated reduction thereof. This is the core of resilience.

Research Methods and Data Analysis

Cooper & Schindler (2014) assert that research design involves a step-by-step guideline of the research, summarizing approaches to explain the research problems. The liaison staff were informed of the anonymity of the respondents, that it was voluntary to be part of the study. The unit of analysis is the individual selected supermarkets in Durban, South Africa. For the qualitative data, a semi-structured interview was conducted by selecting supermarkets' managers and supervisors that formed the participants of the study. The data collections were carried out concurrently, analysed, and reported separately but reported simultaneously. An ethical clearance letter was issued by the academic institution for the study. This study used the non-probability sampling design known as the purposive sampling type known as judgment sampling. This is because when selecting individuals with the same ideology, they provide the actual information required (Etikan & Bala 2017). NVivo software was used to analyse the qualitative data and emerging themes were noted.

Conceptual Model on the Qualitative Data Analysis Result

The themes emerging from the qualitative data include centralisation of stocks, foreign exchange fluctuation, joint business plans, and longstanding collaboration with vendors. Figure 1illustrates the themes.

Figure 1. Conceptual representation of the relationship between supply chain collaboration and other variables

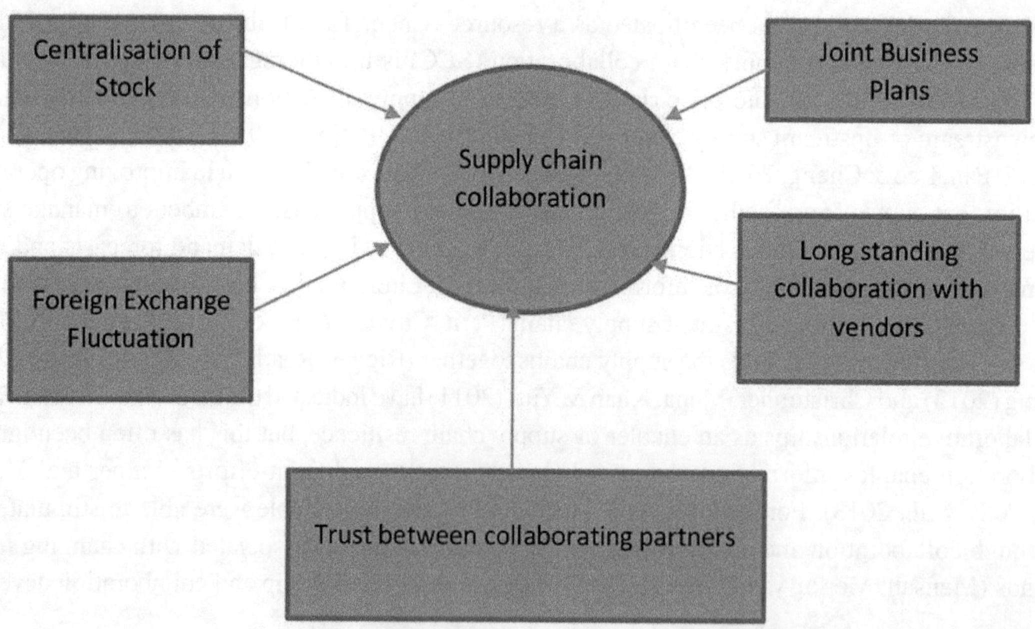

Centralisation of stocks: The participants believed centralisation of stocks could add immense value to their organisation. The comment below captures most of the study participants' views.

Participant 2:

"In this company now, we are in a process of centralising all our stock, so this means that all our vendors deliver at our DC, then we deliver to the stores. Now, we are in a good space with our vendors, which are our suppliers. We are getting close to that 100% centralisation, and we are using our trucks to get some of the stocks from our suppliers for us to reduce the price and cost. A higher cost is incurred when a vendor delivers to the businesses, but when the products are picked by the business itself, the cost is saved and trucks that are used in picking up the stocks may be used for backhauling. With this, the supplier relationship is improved daily".

Foreign exchange fluctuation: The fluctuation in the foreign exchange market may influence the supply chain. If a supply chain imports some of its products, foreign exchange earnings are higher, and the prices of local commodities increases. Below are the views of two of the interview participants, which captures the aggregate views of all the participants surveyed.

Participant 7:

"For the local SA business, we don't take the risk of exchange rate because that risk is for suppliers who may import products or materials internationally. We usually buy in massive stock and hold stock in case of Rand fluctuations. We can hold a certain price for the benefit of the customers, as the old stock price stays the same".

Participant 3:

"Exchange rate will constantly affect prices and increases the price-fixing of products. The pricing of our products is not affected much when the exchange rate is steady, but when it is fluctuating, the product, manufacturing, and our imported product prices will be affected too. We are not the only retailers affected too. Specialised products come with a higher price range when imported".

Joint business plans: As mentioned by the participants, joint business collaboration refers to the collaboration between local and national level industries within a country. The comment below captures the main response that emerged from the qualitative data gathered.

Participant 7:

"We have joint business plans where we meet regularly with the national suppliers, and then we analyse the end-to-end food supply chain and based on trust, the suppliers will then disclose their cost in the supply chain and vice versa." Thereafter, both parties examine their organisational processes to improve efficiencies. This can be done through either increasing order quantities from layers to full pallets, then reduce the cost in the supply chain, get the best deals, and translate these saving to the consumers".

In other words, all parties in a supply chain must be involved in the process of designing an optimal business (Nguegan & Mafini 2017) to embrace competitiveness and better opportunity for operational excellence.

Longstanding collaboration with vendors: The study participants are of the view that collaboration with vendors is important for the smooth operation of the supply chain. For instance, participant 3 affirms that:

"We have a good understanding and relationship with our vendors as they understand what the requirements for the business entail."

The qualitative data output proposed that centralising stocks, joint business planning, and longstanding collaboration with partners enhance supply chain collaboration. Businesses have the option of decentralising or centralising their operations. However, selecting the best way to embark on, is a decision for the retail managers, and this is based on joint decisions from the supply chain partners.

With centralisation of stocks, participants agreed that when products are collected in a place, it becomes cheaper to distribute to different stores. Furthermore, foreign exchange fluctuation affects retail businesses when there are economic factors in place. It is noted also that joint business plans and long-standing relationship with partners enhance collaboration amongst supply chain partners. Existing literature supports this notion and concurs with the important role of trust in sharing of information and joint planning (Kumar, Banerjee, Meena & Ganguly, 2017:46).

Results Discussions

Mapping processes and closer associations with suppliers will mean organisations are in a better position to handle future global disruptions (Business Continuity Institute (BCI), 2021). Shen & Sun (2021) suggested that firms need to enhance their operational flexibility ability by collaborating with the entire society. Collaboration allows a reduction of uncertainty on the state of the supply chain. For instance, sharing and exchanging information, a supply chain collaboration leads to supply chain resilience and awareness of disruptions threats, and opportunities. Serving as a form of environmental scanning, supply chain collaboration enables organsiations to spot threats (Banomyong 2018). Furthermore, Scholten & Schilder (2015) suggested that certain collaborative activities increase supply chain resilience such as visibility, velocity, and flexibility. For instance, Neboh *et al.* (2019) suggest some values of supply chain collaboration on resilience in FMCG:

- **Centralisation of stocks:** Centralisation stock or otherwise known as risk pooling is employed by businesses to manage, allocate and store a limited amount of inventory hence integrating all factors into one result (Milewski 2020). Centralisation of stock contributes to logistics service improvement measured by available inventory when required. The consequences of centralisation strategy create greater benefits as inventories are stored in warehouses such that even in disruptive events (natural disasters), businesses can still operate (Corts, Herbert-Hansen, Larsen & Khalid 2019). This supports resilience as well as collaboration resulting in higher cost-effective strategies, as transport cost, risk, and lean operations. Centralising supply chain stocks with information technology can help increase resilience. It can also be used to reduce costs, economies of scale, reduce risk by increasing the inventory buffer such that any sudden disruptive shock can be handled appropriately.
- **Foreign exchange fluctuation:** The fluctuation in the foreign exchange market may influence the supply chain. If a supply chain imports some of its products and foreign exchange earnings are

higher, then, the prices of local commodities increase. According to Kandil, Berument & Dincer (2007), exchange rate fluctuations are liable to determine economic performance. Therefore, collaboration in supply chain entities allows partners to work and procure goods together, thereby taking advantage of the exchange rate cost and boosting its resilience ability.

- **Joint business plans:** Joint business plans refer to the collaboration between local and national level industries within a country to achieve an objective. It is important to facilitate collaboration to build resilience especially in businesses such as FMCGs that are characherised by uncertainty. In a report presented by Smith in 2016, collaboration in businesses is seen as a key to adjusting to turbulent and unforeseen situations. Qrunfleh & Tarafdar (2013) acknowledged this notion by stating that improved information sharing amongst supply chain partners increases the ability to anticipate changes early in the system. How people work together, invest, and manage businesses are structurally embedded in resilience through diversity, access to knowledge and information
- **Longstanding collaboration with vendors**: Collaboration with vendors is important for the smooth operation of the supply chain. Lack of collaboration affects the relationship between partners in a supply chain (Mandal, Sarathy, Korasiga, Dastidar & Bhattacharya 2016). In addition, closer associations amongst suppliers may create an important value and further assists supply chains to become more resilient (Gutierrez, Kothari, Mazuera, &Schoenherr 2020).
- **Trust between collaborating partners:** Trust is the basis for a business venture to succeed. Trust creates a good opportunity to share relevant business information to collaborating partners as well as the risk associated with the business. It is important to build trust among strategic partners to mitigate risk and build resilience (Gutierrez *et al.* 2020). When trust is present, chances for successful supply chain collaboration improve and it also facilitates interaction to solve problems and make decisions amongst members (Sridharan & Simatupang 2013). Trust is believed to be a defining trait of the presence of supply chain collaboration (Kaibara de Almeida, Marins, Salgado, Santos & Silva 2017).

RECOMMENDATIONS

As supply chain resilience gradually seeps into the core of businesses and draws attention to scholars and policymakers, there is the need for FMCGs to embrace the culture of collaborative practices in response to unforeseen disruptive challenges from the environment as well as within their businesses. The heightened demand for businesses, government entities as well private dealerships, to build resilience at its best, for optimal performance and advantage, is an indication of the shift in disruptive impacts of events such as the recent pandemic in the world today (coronavirus), which will culminate into a higher preference for businesses that can survive and remain competitive in the future. Therefore, a business should acknowledge and adopt collaborative strategies to ensure supply chain resilience. Retailers and their business management need to understand that technology has reshaped consumer expectations, which are now unique and higher than before. The business must acquire and align processes that can streamline customer demands to the business objectives.

AREAS FOR FUTURE STUDIES

This chapter has contributed to the body of literature on supply chain management. The uncertainty and dynamism in the retail environment have made it possible to supply chain partners and businesses to consider building resilience through collaborative initiatives. There is a need to conduct an empirical study on the relationship between supply chain collaboration and supply chain resilience using a quantitative and mixed-methods research design. Future researchers should adopt a longitudinal approach to test these elements of supply chain resilience from other sector perspectives.

The chapter outlined provides evidence information on the definitions as well as the dimensions of collaboration. It is one discussion on the understanding of supply chain collaboration, but it is better to seek understanding and application in a practical environment as public and private entities. Through this scholarly work, firms and professionals are to use this avenue to understand their position, as well as means of employing collaboration as a business strategy and benchmark to other businesses in the supply chains. It will be of practical use, especially for academics, to gain a better understanding of the collaboration stance. It is also important to pay special attention to the value of building supply chain resilience in practice. Future research needs to support supply chain managers to identify the need and weaknesses when supply chains avoid collaboration, but it is interesting to note that businesses always encounter resilience bottlenecks as disruptions never fade away but evolve increasingly. For instance, it is necessary to adjust operations to address disruptive issues and achieve supply chain performance. In addition, further studies can test the relationship between supply chain collaboration and other elements of supply chain resilience to determine its importance and contribution in other areas, contexts or industries other than retail.

CONCLUSION

Most retail businesses depend on suppliers to ensure product availability, and as such, the relationship needs to be seamless for business continuity. Moreover, these suppliers may be supplying a retailer's competitors; hence, it becomes a daunting task for the retailers to decide on the type of information that must be shared with the suppliers. But eventually, the benefit of sharing information is significant, in as much as the risk is there, as any exposure to risks or disruptions may impede or cripple a retail supply chain's probability to gain market share and meet customers' demands, because when information is shared, it incredibly facilitates a reduction of a variety of risks in the retail supply chain, hence allowing it to return to an enhanced state. Besides, the decisions taken by the supply chain partners need to be synchronised and tightly integrated, as the benefit of collaboration removes discrepancies and rather enables visibility, agility, and flexibility of services in the entire supply chain. Supply chain resilience is a characteristic equally shared by every business sector. Therefore, retail partners must work together to understand the elements that underlie the business, to position it better to manage disruptions. These collaborative efforts stimulate redesigning of the supply chain for resilience through collaboration. The tenacity of the retail supply chain to continually scan its environment enables it to monitor disruption propensity and create measures to mitigate such by building resilience. An alert business prepares for uncertainties and disruptions of unforeseen events and can even become better. Through collaboration amongst supply chain partners, information on a product level can be accessed and related to the suppliers, hence ensuring product availability and order fulfillment. Great importance should be an imperative of supply chain partners, to serve customers better through logistics performance by linking all the logistic service providers in the chain. The illusion times of working in silos are over, as competitions in businesses occur in chains nowadays. The personality of any sector plays a pivotal role in determining the level or degree of collaboration amongst supply chain partners. Embracing supply chain collaboration enhances supply chain resilience and contributes to healthy work operations.

Funding Information

This chapter received no specific grant from any funding agency in the public, commercial, or not-for-profit sectors.

REFERENCES

Aigbogun, O., Ghazali, Z., & Razali, R. (2018). Supply chain resilience and measurement dimensions: The case of halal pharmaceuticals in Malaysia. *SHS Web of Conferences, 56*. doi: 10.1051hscpnf/20185605001

American Production and Inventory Control Society (APICS). (2013). *The essential supply chain reference, APICS Dictionary*. APICS.

Anand, N., & Grover, N. (2015). Measuring retail supply chain performance; Theoretical model using key performance indicators (KPIs). *Benchmarking, 22*(1), 135–166. doi:10.1108/BIJ-05-2012-0034

Appalsamy, N. (2017). *Freight looting a growing concern*. Retrieved on 8/11/2021 from http://www.truckandbus.co.za/freight-looting-a-growing-concern/

Artsiomchyk, Y., & Zhivitskaya, H. (2013). Designing Supply Chain with Robustness Analysis. *7th IFAC Conference on Manufacturing Modelling, Management, and Control International Federation of Automatic Control*.

Azadeh, A., Atrchin, N., Salehi, V., & Shojaei, H. (2013). Modeling and improvement of supply chain with imprecise transportation delays and resilience factors. *International Journal of Logistics Research and Applications, 17*(4), 269–282. doi:10.1080/13675567.2013.846308

Bala, M., & Kumar, D. (2011). *Supply Chain Performance Attributes for the Fast-Moving Consumer Goods Industry*. Department of Management. doi:10.4102/jtscm.v5i1.19

Banomyong, R. (2018). *Collaboration in Supply Chain Management: A Resilience Perspective: Discussion Paper*. Retrieved on 5/11/2021 from https://www.researchgate.net/publication/328581572_Collaboration_in_Supply_Chain_Management_A_Resilience_Perspective_Discussion_Paper

Barroso, A. P., Machado, V. H., & Machado, V. C. (2011). *Supply Chain Resilience Using the Mapping Approach, Supply Chain Management*. Retrieved on October 14, 2021 from https://www.intechopen.com/books/supply-chain-management/supply-chain-resilience-using-themapping-approach

Botes, A., Niemann, W., & Kotze, T. (2017). Buyer-Supplier Collaboration and Supply Chain Resilience: A case study in the Petrochemical Industry. *South African Journal of Industrial Engineering, 24*(4), 183–199. doi:10.7166/28-4-1736

Boyce, W. S., Mano, H., & Kent, J. L. (2016). The influence of Collaboration in Procurement Relationships. *International Journal of Managing Value and Supply Chains, 7*(3), 1–18. doi:10.5121/ijmvsc.2016.7301

Business Continuity Institute. (2021). *Supply chain resilience report 2021*. Retrieved on November 7 from https://www.thebci.org/static/e02a3e5f-82e5-4ff1-b8bc61de9657e9c8/BCI-0007h-Supply-Chain-Resilience-ReportLow-Singles.pdf

Cao, M., Vonderembse, M. A., Zhang, Q., & Ragu-Nathan, T. S. (2010). Supply chain collaboration: Conceptualization and instrument development. *International Journal of Production Research, 48*(22), 6613–6635. doi:10.1080/00207540903349039

Chen, H., Tian, Y., Ellinger, A. E., & Daugherty, P. J. (2010). Managing Logistics Outsourcing Relationships: An Empirical Investigation in China. *Journal of Business Logistics, 31*(2), 279–299. doi:10.1002/j.2158-1592.2010.tb00152.x

Chen, J., Sohal, A. S., & Prajogo, D. I. (2013). Supply chain operational risk mitigation: An agency and collaboration perspective. *International Journal of Production Research, 51*(7), 2186–2199. doi:10.10 80/00207543.2012.727490

Chopra, S., & Meindl, P. (2012). *Supply Chain Management: Strategy, Planning and Operation* (5th ed.). Prentice-Hall.

Christopher, M. (2011). *Logistics & supply chain management*. Financial Times.

Christopher, M., Mena, C., Khan, O., & Yurt, O. (2011). Approaches to managing global sourcing risk. *Supply Chain Management, 16*(2), 67–81. doi:10.1108/13598541111115338

Christopher, M., & Peck, H. (2004). Building the Resilient Supply Chain. *International Journal of Logistics Management, 15*(2), 1–13. doi:10.1108/09574090410700275

Cooper, D. R., & Schindler, P. S. (2014). *Business Research Methods* (12th ed.). McGraw-Hill.

Corts, N. F., Herbert-Hansen, Z. N. L., Laersen, S. B., & Khalid, W. (2019). The degree of inventory centralisation for food manufacturers. *Production Engineering, 13*(1), 21–32. doi:10.100711740-018-00872-1

Day, J. M. (2014). Fostering emergent resilience: The complex adaptive supply network of disaster relief. *International Journal of Production Research, 52*(7), 1970–1988. doi:10.1080/00207543.2013.787496

Dos Santos, M. A. O. (2010). *Benefits derived by a major South African retailer through collaboration and innovation within its supply chain*. Department of Marketing Management, University of Johannesburg. doi:10.4102/jtscm.v4i1.14

Ellyatt, H. (2021). *Supply chain chaos is already hitting global growth. And it's about to get worse*. Retrieved on November 5, 2021 from https://www.cnbc.com/2021/10/18/supply-chain-chaos-is-hitting-global-growth-and-could-get-worse.html

Etikan, I., & Bala, K. (2017). Sampling and Sampling Methods. *Biometrics and Biostatistics International Journal, 5*(6), 1–3. doi:10.15406/bbij.2017.05.00149 PMID:28111614

Ferreira, C., Cardoso, C., Travassos, M., Paiva, M., Pestana, M., Lopes, J. M., & Oliveira, M. (2021). Disorders, Vulnerabilities and Resilience in the Supply Chain in Pandemic Times. *Logistics*, *5*(3), 1–16. doi:10.3390/logistics5030048

Fouladivanda, F., Pashandi, M. A., Hooman, A., & Khanmohammadi, Z. (2013). The Effect of Brand Equity on Consumer behavior in term of FMCG in Iran. *Interdisciplinary Journal of Contemporary Research in Business*, *4*(9), 945–957.

Garcia, D. J., & You, F. (2015). Supply chain design and optimization: Challenges and opportunities. *Computers & Chemical Engineering*, *8*, 153–170. doi:10.1016/j.compchemeng.2015.03.015

Geng, L., Xiao, R., & Xu, X. (2014). Research on MAS-Based Supply Chain Resilience and Its Self-Organized Criticality. *Hindawi Publishing Corporation Discrete Dynamics in Nature and Society*, *621341*, 1–14. Advance online publication. doi:10.1155/2014/621341

Gutierrez, A., Kothari, A., Mazuera, C., & Schoenherr, T. (2020). *Taking supplier collaboration to the next level*. Retrieved on November 5, 2021 from https://www.mckinsey.com/business-functions/operations/our-insights/taking-supplier-collaboration-to-the-next-level

Haavisto, I. (2014). *Performance in Humanitarian Supply Chains*. Hanken School of Economics.

Hudnurkar, M., Khar, S., & Rathod, U. (2014). Factors affecting collaboration in the supply chain: A literature Review. *Procedia: Social and Behavioral Sciences*, *133*, 189–202. doi:10.1016/j.sbspro.2014.04.184

Inman, R. R., & Blumenfeld, D. E. (2014). Product complexity and supply chain design. *International Journal of Production Research*, *52*(7), 1956–1969. doi:10.1080/00207543.2013.787495

Ittmann, H., Meyer, I., Havenga, J., & Marais, M. (2014). *Implementing logistics strategies in a developing economy*. Retrieved on November 5, 2021 from https://researchspace.csir.co.za/dspace/handle/10204/1139

Jabbarzadeh, A., Fahimnia, B., & Sabouhi, F. (2018). Resilient and sustainable supply chain design: Sustainability analysis under disruption risks. *International Journal of Production Research*, *56*(17), 5945–5968. doi:10.1080/00207543.2018.1461950

Jacobs, F. R., Chase, R. B., & Lummus, R. R. (2011). *Operations and Supply Chain Management* (Global Edition). McGraw-Hill.

Janamanchi, B., & Burns, J. R. (2014). Control Theory Concepts Applied to Retail Supply Chain: A System Dynamics Modeling Environment Study. *Hindawi Publishing Corporation*, *201*, 1–14.

Janvier-James, A. M. (2012). A New Introduction to Supply Chains and Supply Chain Management: Definitions and Theories Perspective. *International Business Research*, *5*(1), 194–206. doi:10.5539/ibr.v5n1p194

Juttner, U., & Maklan, S. (2011). Supply Chain Resilience in the Global Financial Crisis: An Empirical Study. *Supply Chain Management*, *16*(4), 246–259. doi:10.1108/13598541111139062

Kaibara de Almeida, M. M., Marins, F. A. S., Salgado, A. M. P., Santos, F. C. A., & Silva, S. L. (2017). The importance of trust and collaboration between companies to mitigate the bullwhip effect in supply chain management. *Acta Scientiarum, 39*(2), 201. Advance online publication. doi:10.4025/actascitechnol.v39i2.29648

Kamalahmadi, M., & Mellat-Parast, M. (2016). A review of the literature on the principles of enterprise and supply chain resilience: Major findings and directions for future research. *International Journal of Production Economics, 171*, 116–133. doi:10.1016/j.ijpe.2015.10.023

Kandil, M., Berument, M. H., & Dincer, N. (2007). The effects of exchange rate fluctuations on economic activity in Turkey. *Journal of Asian Economics, 18*(3), 466–489. doi:10.1016/j.asieco.2006.12.015

Kerfia, S. D., Shirma, G., Kusiluka, L., Ayebazibwe, C., Mwebe, R., Cleaveland, S., & Haydon, D. (2018). Spatial and Temporal Distribution of Foot and Mouth Disease in Four Districts, Situated Along the Uganda – Tanzania Border: Implications for Cross-border Efforts in Disease Control. *The Onderstepoort Journal of Veterinary Research, 85*(1). Advance online publication. 10.4102%2Fojvr.v85i1.1528

Kotler, P., & Armstrong, G. (2011). *Principles of Marketing*. Pearson Education South Africa (Pty) Ltd Prentice Hall.

KPMG. (2016). *Fast Moving Consumer Goods Sector Report*. Retrieved on November 8, 2021 from https://assets.kpmg.com/content/dam/kpmg/br/pdf/2016/09/fast-moving-consumer-goods.pdf

Kumar, G., Banerjee, R. N., Meena, P. L., & Ganguly, K. K. (2017). Joint Planning and Problem-Solving Roles in Supply Chain Collaboration. *IIMB Management Review, 29*(1), 45–57. doi:10.1016/j.iimb.2017.03.001

Lakovou, E., & White, C. C. (2020). *How to build more secure, resilient, next-gen U. S. supply chains*. Retrieved from November 6, 2021 from https://www.brookings.edu/techstream/how-to-build-more-secure-resilient-next-gen-u-s-supply-chains/

Lambiase, A., Mastrocinque, E., Miranda, S., & Lambiase, A. (2013). Strategic Planning and Design of Supply Chains: A Literature Review. *International Journal of Engineering Business Management, 5*, 1–11. doi:10.5772/56858

Lamminen, J., Forsvik, H., Voipio, V., & Lehtonen, L. (2015). Decision-making process for clinical investments in a public health care organization – contingency approach to support the investment decision process. *Finnish Journal of eHealth and eWelfare, 7*(2-3), 122-134.

Leat, P., & Revoredo-Giha, C. (2013). Risk and resilience in agri-food supply chains: The case of the ASDA Porklink supply chain in Scotland. *Supply Chain Management, 18*(2), 219–231. doi:10.1108/13598541311318845

Li, G., Fan, H., Lee, P. K. C., & Cheng, T. C. E. (2015). Joint supply chain risk management: An agency and collaboration perspective. *International Journal of Production Economics, 164*, 83–94. doi:10.1016/j.ijpe.2015.02.021

Mandal, S., Sarathy, R., Korasiga, V. R., Dastidar, S. G., & Bhattacharya, S. (2016). Achieving supply chain resilience: The contribution of logistics and supply chain capabilities. *International Journal of Disaster Resilience in the Built Environment*, *7*(5), 544–562. doi:10.1108/IJDRBE-04-2016-0010

Mari, S. I., Lee, Y. H., Memon, M. S., Park, Y. S., & Kim, M. (2015). Adaptivity of Complex Network Topologies for Designing Resilient Supply Chain Networks. *International Journal of Industrial Engineering*, *22*(1), 102–116. doi:10.23055/ijietap.2015.22.1.1326

Mbhele, T. P. (2014). *Electronic supply chain management systems in managing the bullwhip effect on selected Fast-Moving Consumer Goods* (PhD dissertation). University of KwaZulu-Natal, South Africa.

Mensah, P., Merkuryev, Y., & Longo, F. (2015). Using ICT in Developing a Resilient Supply Chain Strategy. *Procedia Computer Science*, *43*, 101–108. doi:10.1016/j.procs.2014.12.014

Milewski, D. (2020). Total Costs of Centralized and Decentalized Inventory Strategies – Including External Costs. *Sustainability*, *12*(22), 9346. doi:10.3390u12229346

Mohan, B. C., & Sequeira, A. H. (2012). Customer-Based Brand Equity in the Fast-Moving Consumer Goods Industry in India. *International Journal of Management*, *1*(4), 1–19.

Mohan, B. C., & Sequeira, A. H. (2015). The impact of customer-based brand equity on the operational performance of FMCG companies in India. *IIMB Management Review*, *28*(1), 13–19. doi:10.1016/j.iimb.2015.11.002

Mustapha, U. M. (2010). *The Role of Product Design, Manufacturing Systems and Environmental Uncertainty in Nigeria Manufacturing Organizations*. Engineering Doctorate. Retrieved on November 8 2021 from https://eprints.usq.edu.au/19606/1/Mustapha_2010_front.pdf

Neboh, N. D., Mbhele, T. P., & Phiri, M. (2019). *Retail supply chain design for resilience: selected Durban Supermarkets* (PhD dissertation).

Nel, J. D., & Badenhorst-weiss, J. A. (2010). *Supply chain Design: Some Critical Questions*. Department of Business Management University of South Africa (Unisa) South Africa.

Nguegan, C. A., & Mafini, C. (2017). Supply Chain Management Problems in the Food Processing Industry: Implications for Business Performance. *Acta Commercii*, *17*(1). Advance online publication. doi:10.4102/ac.v17i1.485

Ochieng, A. O. (2018). *Supply chain resilience and organizational performance of pharmaceutical manufacturing companies in Nairobi* (Master's thesis). School of Business University of Nairobi.

Ouabouch, L. (2015). Supply chain resilience. *Materials Management Review*, 16 – 18.

Pettit, T., Croxton, K. L., & Fiskel, J. (2019). The Evolution of Resilience in Supply Chain Management: A Retrospective on Ensuring Supply Chain Resilience. *Journal of Business Logistics*, *40*(1), 56–65. doi:10.1111/jbl.12202

Pettit, T. J., Croxton, K. L., & Fiksel, J. (2013). Ensuring Supply Chain Resilience: Development and Implementation of an Assessment Tool. *Journal of Business Logistics*, *34*(1), 46–76. doi:10.1111/jbl.12009

Ponis, S. T., & Koronis, E. (2012). Supply Chain Resilience: Definition of Concept and Its Formative Elements. *Journal of Applied Business Research*, *28*(5), 921–930. doi:10.19030/jabr.v28i5.7234

Ponomarov, S. Y., & Holcomb, M. C. (2009). Understanding the concept of supply chain resilience. *International Journal of Logistics Management*, *20*(1), 124–143. doi:10.1108/09574090910954873

PWC. (2016). *So much in store: prospects in the retail and consumer goods sector in ten sub-Saharan countries*. Retrieved on November 8, 2021 from https://www.pwc.co.za/en/assets/pdf/retail-in-africa.pdf

Qrunfleh, S., & Tarafdar, M. (2013). Lean and agile supply chain strategies and supply chain responsiveness: The role of strategic supplier partnership and postponement. *Supply Chain Management*, *18*(6), 571–582. doi:10.1108/SCM-01-2013-0015

Quasim, S., & Agarwal, S. (2015). Consumer Behaviour towards selected FMCG (Fast Moving Consumer Goods in Delhi NCR. *International Journal of Informative and Futuristic Research*, *2*(7), 2041–2048.

Rha, J. S. (2020). Trends of Research on Supply Chain Resilience: A Systematic Review Using Network Analysis. *Sustainability*, *12*(4343), 1–27. doi:10.3390u12114343

Rice, J., & Caniato, F. (2003). Building a secure and resilient supply chain network. *Supply Chain Management Review*, *7*(5), 22–30.

Richey, R. G. Jr, Roath, A. S., Whipple, J. M., & Fawcett, S. E. (2010). Exploring Governance Theory of Supply Chain Integration: Barriers and Facilitators to Integration. *Journal of Business Logistics*, *31*(1), 237–256. doi:10.1002/j.2158-1592.2010.tb00137.x

Schatteman, O., Woodhouse, D., & Terino, J. (2020). *Supply chain lessons from COVID-19: Time to refocus on resilience*. Retrieved on November 7, 2021 from https://www.bain.com/contentassets/d6b7a373b2b242d2be114cb46345fce2/bain-brief-supply-chain-lessons-from-covid-19.pdf

Scholten, K., & Schilder, S. (2015). The role of Collaboration in supply chain resilience. *Supply Chain Management*, *20*(4), 471–484. doi:10.1108/SCM-11-2014-0386

Scholten, K., Sharkey, P., & Fynes, S. F. (2014). Mitigation Processes – antecedents for building supply chain resilience. *Supply Chain Management*, *19*(2), 211–228. doi:10.1108/SCM-06-2013-0191

Selvakumar, M., Jansirani, M. M., & Jegatheesan, K. (2013). *Fast-Moving Consumer Goods: A Bright Future in India*. Retrieved on November 7, 2021 from http://ffymag.com/admin/issuepdf/FMCG_FFY-Feb13.pdf

Shen, Z. M., & Sun, Y. (2021). Strengthening supply chain resilience during COVID-19: A case study of JD. Com. *Journal of Operations Management*, joom.1161. Advance online publication. doi:10.1002/joom.1161

Simatupang, T. M., & Sridharan, R. (2002). The collaborative supply chain. *International Journal of Logistics Management*, *13*(1), 15–30. doi:10.1108/09574090210806333

Singh, J. (2014). FMCG (Fast Moving Consumer Goods) An Overview. *International Journal of Enhanced Research in Management and Computer Applications*, *3*(6), 14–16.

Singh, R. K., & Acharya, P. (2014). Identification and Evaluation of Supply Chain Flexibilities in Indian FMCG Sector Using DEMATEL. *Global Journal of Flexible Systems Managment, 15*(2), 91–100. doi:10.100740171-013-0050-9

Smith, M. (2016). *Collaboration for Resilience*. Retrieved on November 5, 2021 from https://portals.iucn.org/library/sites/library/files/documents/2016-047.pdf

Soni, U., & Jain, V. (2011). *Minimising the vulnerabilities of supply chain: A new framework for enhancing the resilience*. Paper presented at Industrial Engineering and Engineering Management (IEEM), 2011 IEEE International Conference, Singapore.

Soosay, C. A., & Hyland, P. (2015). A decade of supply chain collaboration and directions for future research. *Supply Chain Management, 20*(6), 613–630. doi:10.1108/SCM-06-2015-0217

Sridharan, R., & Simatupang, T. M. (2013). Power and trust in supply chain collaboration. *International Journal of Value Chain Management, 7*(1), 76–96. doi:10.1504/IJVCM.2013.057344

Srinivasu, R. (2014). Fast Moving Consumer Goods Retail Market, Growth Prospect, Market Overview and Food Inflation in Indian Market – An Overview. *International Journal of Innovative Research in Science, Engineering and Technology, 3*(1), 8422–8430.

Srivastava, S. K., Chaudhuri, A., & Srivastava, R. K. (2015). Propagation of risks and their impact on performance in fresh food retail. *International Journal of Logistics Management, 26*(3), 568–602. doi:10.1108/IJLM-02-2014-0032

Stoltz, M. (2018). *Theft on the move: how to safeguard goods and personnel in transit*. Retrieved on August 27, 2020 from https://www.bizcommunity.com/SendToFriend.aspx?l=196&c=746&ct=1&ci=176872

Tan, W. J., Zhang, A. N., & Cai, W. (2019). A graph-based model to measure structural redundancy for supply chain resilience. *International Journal of Production Research, 57*(20), 6385–6404. doi:10.1080/00207543.2019.1566666

Vaishnani, H. B. (2011). *Effects of Sales Promotions on Consumer Preferences and Brand Equity Perception* (PhD thesis). Saurashtra University. Retrieved on November 8, 2021 from https://etheses.saurashtrauniversity.edu/63/

Wilding, R. (2013). Supply chain temple of resilience. *Logistics & Transport Focus, 15*(11), 54–59.

Writer, S. (2021). *Economic impacts of riots and looting in South Africa and wider emereging problems*. Retrieved on November 5, 2021 from https://businesstech.co.za/news/government/506136/economic-impact-of-riots-and-looting-in-south-africa-and-wider-emerging-problems/

KEY TERMS AND DEFINITIONS

Agility: Being able to act as fast as possible and it has to do with speed, especially on information one has received.

Chanel: A lead or guide to a destination or point one to a direction.

Emerging: To start afresh or newly.

Fast Moving Consumer Goods Outlet: The Fast-Moving Consumer Goods retail outlet is a simple store that offers one an opportunity to select from a variety of household and food items, according to their needs.

Resilience: An ability to overcome challenges, issues or disruptions and come out better than before.

Strategy: A plan set up for a future action.

Unemployment: The lack of Job or work towards earning an income.

Chapter 8
Digital Supply Chain Insights From Large Factories:
How Intercollaborations Accelerate Digitalization

Clarissa Figueredo Rocha
Pontifical Catholic University of Paraná, Brazil

Carlos Olavo Quandt
Pontifical Catholic University of Paraná, Brazil

Fernando Deschamps
https://orcid.org/0000-0002-5269-3721
Pontifical Catholic University of Paraná, Brazil

ABSTRACT

In today's digital age, many managers need to find new ways to manage collaborations where complementary partners co-create digital solutions. Collaborations with partners are at the centre of digital projects, but managing these collaborations is challenging. The research objective is to investigate how collaborations with business partners contribute to digital transformation through a qualitative investigation of Brazilian and British large manufactures that are already on their journey towards digitalization. Interviews and questionnaires and non-participant observations were collected, followed by content analysis. The findings indicate that the companies, mainly the Brazilian cases, are at the early stage of building a digital ecosystem for a more connected supply chain. The use of digital solutions in cases brings obstacles but also opportunities and advantages for supply chains in the near future. The study discussed these implementation challenges and what digital technologies are under development and already used to make the supply chain smarter and more connected.

DOI: 10.4018/978-1-7998-9715-6.ch008

Copyright © 2022, IGI Global. Copying or distributing in print or electronic forms without written permission of IGI Global is prohibited.

INTRODUCTION

The dynamic and competitive business environment in which most organizations operate requires the development of capabilities to support technological and organizational transformations. The rapidly increasing adoption of digital technologies requires collaborative R&D efforts (Rocha et al., 2021; Benitez et al., 2020; Kahle et al., 2020; Rong et al., 2015), and consequently the need to manage collaborations with complementary partners to co-create digital solutions. Collaborative partnerships are at the center of digital projects (Camarinha Matos et al., 2019), but they pose significant challenges.

The need to improve supply chain management drives companies to collaborate with suppliers, customers and other business partners, seeking gains in distribution and efficiency, expansion of product diversification, and increased manufacturing flexibility and agility (Abdalla & Nakagawa, 2021). A company's innovative capability can be advanced by such collaborations (Rocha et al., 2021), particularly due to the sharing of market intelligence that results in the expansion of its knowledge base.

The adoption of digital solutions such as IoT, Cloud Computing, Big Data & Analytics, Artificial Intelligence, and Blockchain is widely acknowledged as a powerful drive of increased efficiency and adaptability of firms. By taking advantage of digital technologies, organizations can collect data on the status of their internal and external environments, analyze and transform such data into relevant information, and disseminate it in real time, allowing better decision making. The use of these technologies allows tracking information about product origin, placing of orders, and performing transactions in a digital trust environment (Silkina, 2019). However, the mere implementation of digital technologies is not sufficient (Abdalla & Nakagawa, 2021). In a world where talent and valuable know-how are widely distributed, organizations cannot pursue innovation independently, no matter how large or capable they are (Burchardt & Maisch, 2019). Disruptive digital technologies cannot be used in isolation, demanding organizational changes that encompass not only the technological architecture, but also the strategic, managerial, and social domains (Rocha et al., 2021; Bogers et al., 2019a; Schwab, 2017), a perspective that is encompassed by the Digital Transformation (DT) concept (Nambisan et al., 2019).

The change introduced by digital technologies brings opportunities, as well as obstacles, for most enterprises. The advantages of using digital technologies to manage a supply chain are limited without including inter-collaborative innovation activities that transcend organizational borders (Rocha et al., 2022; 2021). This issue is significant as open innovation practices (Chesbrough and Bogers, 2014) are increasingly facilitating organizational digitalization. The process of supply chain digitalization allows firms to seize opportunities in unstable and agile markets, bringing potential benefits such as improved customer service, more integration with suppliers, increased sales, and greater agility and quality in deliveries (Agrawal et al., 2019).

A renewed focus on customer-centric orientation has also led to the need to engage in closer collaborations and integration in supply chains, improving efficiency, increasing transparency, adaptability, and trust. However, traditional mechanisms of supply chain management are unable to quickly identify and meet the expectations of customization of increasingly demanding end-users. A smarter and more integrated supply chain requires technological infrastructure for advanced logistics. The supply chain of the digital age needs to incorporate digital solutions to shift from traditional, simple, and linear economic relationships to adaptable and harmonized partner networks (Shcherbakov & Silkina, 2021).

Recent literature on DT has explored the application of disruptive technologies in supply chain management (Wamba et al., 2020; Frederico et al., 2019; Büyüközkan & Göçer, 2018). The extant literature has investigated the impact of disruptive technologies on supply chains, such as for IoT (Gunasekaran et al., 2016; Mishra et al., 2016; Ben-Daya et al., 2019), Artificial Intelligence (Min, 2010), Cloud Computing (Jede & Teuteberg, 2015), Big Data Analytics (Queiroz & Telles, 2018; Gunasekaran et al., 2017; Hazen et al., 2016), Blockchain (Gurtu & Johny, 2019; Durach et al., 2020) and Additive Manufacturing (Durach, et al., 2017; Luomaranta & Martinsuo, 2019). Additionally, Ghadge et al. (2020) stress that companies need to adopt digital technologies in their business processes and manage the increasing data flow between partners for effective management of next generation digital supply chains. However, understanding the benefits and possible limits of collaborative innovation to make supply chains more integrated, agile, transparent, and reliable is still a challenge for practitioners and academia (Shcherbakov & Silkina, 2021; Bogers et al., 2019).

In a context of evolving business ecosystems, DT has pushed operating structures and management strategies to adapt to new challenges (Ghadge et al., 2020). Collaboration between supply chain actors is paramount to overcome the challenges of DT (Benitez et al., 2020; Kahle et al., 2020; Rong et al., 2015). The need for more empirical studies and a better understanding of the relation between inter-organizational collaborations and the digital journey of firms is emphasized by Rocha et al. (2021), Bogers et al. (2019a, b), Burchardt and Maisch (2019) and Camarinha-Matos et al. (2019). Therefore, an inter-collaboration-centered approach seems appropriate to investigate the complexity of the supply chain digitalization process under socio-managerial lenses.

In addition to the significant changes in organizations and society brought about by digitalization, the Covid-19 pandemic that started in 2020 has accelerated the need to digitalize, and more broadly, the way people work and relate – perhaps forever. Even before that, companies started to use digital technologies for a more connected, agile, smart, and sustainable SC (Belhadi et al., 2021). However, for many organizations, the urgency of the pandemic has forced them to a level of digitalization that would not have happened otherwise.

Given this contextualization, the research objective of this study is to investigate how collaborations with suppliers and customers contribute to the digital supply chain of large factories that have initiated their digitalization process. This paper analyzes three British and three Brazilian cases to answer 1) whether and how the use of digital solutions affects the integration with customers and suppliers regarding information flows; 2) which solutions the firms have been developing or using to build strong connections with their business partners. The qualitative analysis is focused on understanding how digital innovation in processes or products can strengthen connectivity with customers and/or suppliers in these cases. This study is one of the first to examine the relation between digital technologies use and inter-collaborations with business partners for smarter supply chains, comparing factories in a developing country with counterparts in an industrialized economy.

This research is organized as follows: in the literature review, a theoretical framework is developed based on supply chain management, DT, and inter-collaboration concepts. A multiple case study method is adopted and is explained in the methodology chapter. The findings from the case studies are discussed in a subsequent section, and the main highlights of each case are compared with the literature in the discussion section. Lastly, theoretical contributions, practical implications and directions for future studies are presented in the concluding section.

LITERATURE REVIEW

To address the research question, this study explores the literature related to the implications of DT for industrial management (Kagermann et al., 2013; Bücker et al., 2016; Bunse et al., 2014), as well as the literature on the use of digital solutions to build more connected, integrated, and smarter supply chains. A conceptual framework is then synthesized upon the main theoretical concepts and findings from the literature review.

Digital Transformation Conceptualization

DT has become an increasingly popular topic for researchers and practitioners. Vial et al. (2019: 118) define it as "a process that aims to improve an entity – defined as an organization, a system or a supply chain – by triggering significant changes to its properties through combinations of information, computing, communication, and connectivity technologies". DT aims to improve a firm's operational performance by impacting its products, processes, supply chains (Frederico et al., 2019), and even business models. For Rogers (2016: 308) DT "is fundamentally not about technology, but about strategy". Similarly, for Verhoef et al. (2019: 2) "digital transformation is multidisciplinary by nature, as it involves changes in strategy, organization, information technology, supply chains and marketing". Hence, in addition to the technological challenge, digital technologies pose several socio-managerial and strategic implications for organizations (Rocha et al., 2021). They create opportunities to develop more flexible, agile, and innovative business models, building and strengthening networks with diverse partners, including customers and suppliers (Bogers et al., 2019a; Chesbrough & Bogers, 2014). Collaborative networks enable the development and dissemination of disruptive technologies among the partners.

DT is particularly challenging for incumbent firms. In their search for digital business model innovation, they are often forced to deal with tradeoffs between existing and new ways of working (Rocha et al., 2021). Incumbents may start with minor changes, such as isolated digitization efforts, to gradually transform their traditional business into a digital one. Often, the move to digital may often require a marked departure from the *status quo* and may lead to the obsolescence of existing business models (Teece, 2018). Therefore, DT requires the company to rethink its managerial practices. The firm's redefinition of how it creates and delivers value to customers often requires it to access, acquire or develop new digital capabilities (Benitez et al., 2020; Queiroz et al., 2019).

The adoption of Cyber-Physical System (CPS), a central aspect of DT in manufacturing, triggers a paradigm shift in how organizations create value (Benitez et al., 2020). This can be achieved by the orchestrated use of digital solutions, to collect, transfer, analyze, and make sense of data from internal manufacturing operations as well as relevant external data (Frank et al., 2019). This supports the development of Smart Factories (Bunse et al., 2014) which facilitate integration with customers and suppliers (Camarinha-Matos et al., 2019; 2017) and increase agility and responsiveness to market demands for high-quality, customized products and services.

As noted, a customer-oriented approach is often a key element of DT. This has led to cooperation and integration in supply chains, improving their efficiency and increasing transparency, awareness, and trust. However, conventional supply chain management procedures are unable to pinpoint potential value proposals for particular users. Businesses need to build integrated supply chains, which require well-developed infrastructure and easily available complementary services, relying on logistics as a networking technology (Shcherbakov & Silkina, 2021).

Digital Technology as an Enabler for Greater Horizontal Integration

Digital technologies bring about innovations that involve diverse actors with different goals and capabilities, creating a new generation of innovation processes. The importance of DT in supply chains is emphasized in recent studies (Büyüközkan & Göçer, 2018; Queiroz et al. 2019; Frederico et al., 2019; Garay-Rondero et al., 2019; Ghadge et al., 2020), which point out some aspirational goals or potential benefits of DT to optimize supply chains. For example, DT aims to facilitate seamless supply chain collaborations with input suppliers and/or clients to reduce cost and to improve performance (Camarinha-Matos et al., 2019).

In practice, several large software companies have developed applications in analytics, demand planning, warehouse, inventory management, transportation, and distribution operations, whereas big retailers are tracing the flow of food from farmers to retailers using blockchain technology (Gurtu & Johny, 2019). When using Big Data analytics capabilities, firms can develop solutions that perform real-time supply chain management, in the form of proactive, customized data-based solutions (Xiao et al., 2020). The use of additive manufacturing (3D printing) may support supply chain quality management through a reduction of mass manufacturing variability (Luomaranta & Martinsuo, 2019). Supply Chain agility may also be improved by applying 3D printing for rapid prototyping and decentralized, flexible integration of customers and manufacturers (Durach et al., 2017).

The Internet of Things (IoT) allows the connection and interaction of a variety of objects around a company, through unique addressing schemes and standard communication protocols (Mishra et al., 2016). IoT and other digital solutions enable connections within a specific industrial system, a supply chain, and other stakeholders. This could lead to more complex supply chains with many players and complex, but rich interactions (Rong et al., 2015). Moreover, IoT offers a wealth of new opportunities for the development of products and services based on greater insight into individual customer needs and preferences (Brody & Pureswaran, 2015; Porter & Heppelmann, 2014). Also, it can be used to improve both process efficiency and human productivity (Balakrishna, 2012). With a connected product, a supplier can maintain regular contact with the customer without relying on extra time-consuming manual work, and the enhanced information may ultimately lead the manufacturing firm to sell its product as a customized service or function rather than a physical good or a piece of hardware (Saarikko et al., 2020). In sum, there is great potential in the application of digital solutions for rebuilding and reconfiguring supply chains.

Digital platforms enable companies to collect customer information and acquire user-generated content from digital channels, which coordinate customer data production, search, and delivery (De Reuver et al., 2018; Karimi & Walter, 2015). There are two types of platforms (Xiao et al., 2020): one connecting to customers to collect customer experience, opinion, and derived knowledge, and another connecting to businesses to obtain information from institutions around customers and conducting marketing activities directly to targeted customer groups (Karimi & Walter, 2015). Digital platform capabilities offer opportunities for new services, technology development, and increased processing capability with low cost (Sedera et al., 2016). A digital platform for logistics includes special organizational structures that coordinate the processes of physical distribution, including internal and external flows and forms of association of economically and legally independent participants in the supply chain. This enables them to achieve common strategic and tactical goals for optimizing the physical distribution process with the lowest labor, material, and financial costs (Shcherbakov & Silkina, 2021).

Digital technologies allow interconnectivity between manufacturing assets and actors, increasing the volume and diversity of business data in real time. Decision-making is made easier and faster by extracting large volumes of data, exporting the data to cloud computing and analyzing it to produce relevant information. Many industries have already taken steps toward DT by linking their business processes from supply to aftermarket with digital technologies, aiming to create a fully integrated digital value chain (Frederico et al., 2019).

In addition to the adoption of digital technologies, internal, cross-functional collaborations within a firm are crucial for successful DT (Rocha et al., 2021; Kahle et al., 2020; Frank et al. 2019). For Chesbrough and Bogers (2014), firms can also benefit from harvesting ideas from external parties, and from sharing their ideas. Thus, for DT to succeed in creating and sustaining competitive advantage, firms need to establish agile and collaborative organizational structures (Abdalla & Nakagawa, 2021; Benitez et al., 2020; Bogers et al., 2019a, b). The relation of digitalization and collaborative innovation facilitates access to big data and rapid processing using digital tools such as artificial intelligence (Burchardt & Maisch, 2019).

Today, interaction arrangements are provided by digital means of communication, such as: social networks, digital platforms and collaboration services. In particular, the development of cloud technologies has led to the emergence of concepts such as Production on Demand and Everything-as-a-Service, which have become the foundation of many business models and a basis for economic interactions in the digital environment (Shcherbakov & Silkina; 2021; Pustovrh et al., 2020). By using digital technologies, organizations modify their value creation processes and discover new ways to create value in response to changes in the environment (Huang et al., 2017). That is, the adoption of digital technologies must be associated with changes in strategy, culture and organizational structure that emphasize the use of internal and external knowledge sources to sustain competitive advantages (Rocha et al., 2022; 2021).

Business Partnerships as Inputs for Digital Innovation

As business environments become increasingly dominated by digital technologies, firms realize the need to adopt a network-centric view and co-create value with a set of digitally connected firms (Koch & Windsperger, 2017). A survey indicates that 75% of executives think that their competitive advantage is not determined internally, but by the strength of partners and ecosystems they choose to work with (Accenture, 2018). Relational competencies or collaborative capabilities are required to achieve greater connectivity with their customers. A digital networking capability refers to the firm's ability to bring together and match distinct users to address their mutual needs via digital means. This capability becomes essential to compete in a digital setting.

The interaction between Big Data Analytics (BDA) and digital platforms may trigger digital innovation. For instance, firms can perform real-time perception of customer sentiment and then provide demand-oriented services with the efficient utilization of BDA resources and third-party digital social media platforms (Xiao et al., 2020). Furthermore, a firm may allow customers to co-create value on its digital platforms by generating their own content, customizing their products, and becoming brand ambassadors via social media, so that customers become a strategic asset to support competitive advantage (Dong & Wu, 2015). The capability of firms to select, attract, and engage a heterogeneous set of network stakeholders strongly stimulates the value creation and growth of platforms that involve suppliers and customers (McIntyre & Srinivasan, 2017).

The use of digital technologies can be interpreted as an enabling factor for collaborations, fostering richer and greater data integration with partners of a manufacturing supply chain (Bogers et al., 2019a; Camarinha-Matos, et al., 2019). The continuous data flows that result from improved connectivity can be valuable inputs for the manufacturing R&D sector to develop new products and services and customize them to the needs and preferences of customers.

While the development of collaborative arrangements to tap external sources of information and knowledge to incorporate effective digital practices is seen as a key to competitive advantage, it is not yet clear how it should be done. Collaborations with business actors in the manufacturing supply chain are arguably a facilitator of digital manufacturing innovation. However, research on digital supply chains is at an early stage. Many manufacturing companies are still trying to understand DT and its impacts. More specifically, there are uncertainties regarding DT strategy, maturity of digital technologies, management of collaborative arrangements with different actors, management of digital competences, and implementation of digital projects. In addition, firms express concerns about reluctance to change, and about how to achieve greater operational performance, competitiveness, and sustainability using digital practices (Rocha et al., 2021).

Based on the contextualization above, a theoretical framework (Fig. 1) was proposed to be tested on the cases under study. The objective is to better understand how digital technologies, whether in the operational processes or products, can strengthen integrations or connectivity with customers and suppliers of those factories. Additionally, richer connectivity can enable companies to obtain real-time customer feedback, integration with supplier information systems, and new ideas for creating more customized and digitalized products or services (Arnold et al, 2016; PWC, 2016; Prause, 2015. In the context of DT, Bogers et al. (2019a) and Trantopoulos et al. (2017) point out that companies need to coordinate strategies to extract external knowledge and information from customers and suppliers, using digital technologies, to improve their innovation performance.

Figure 1. Digital Supply Chain from an Ecosystem Perspective

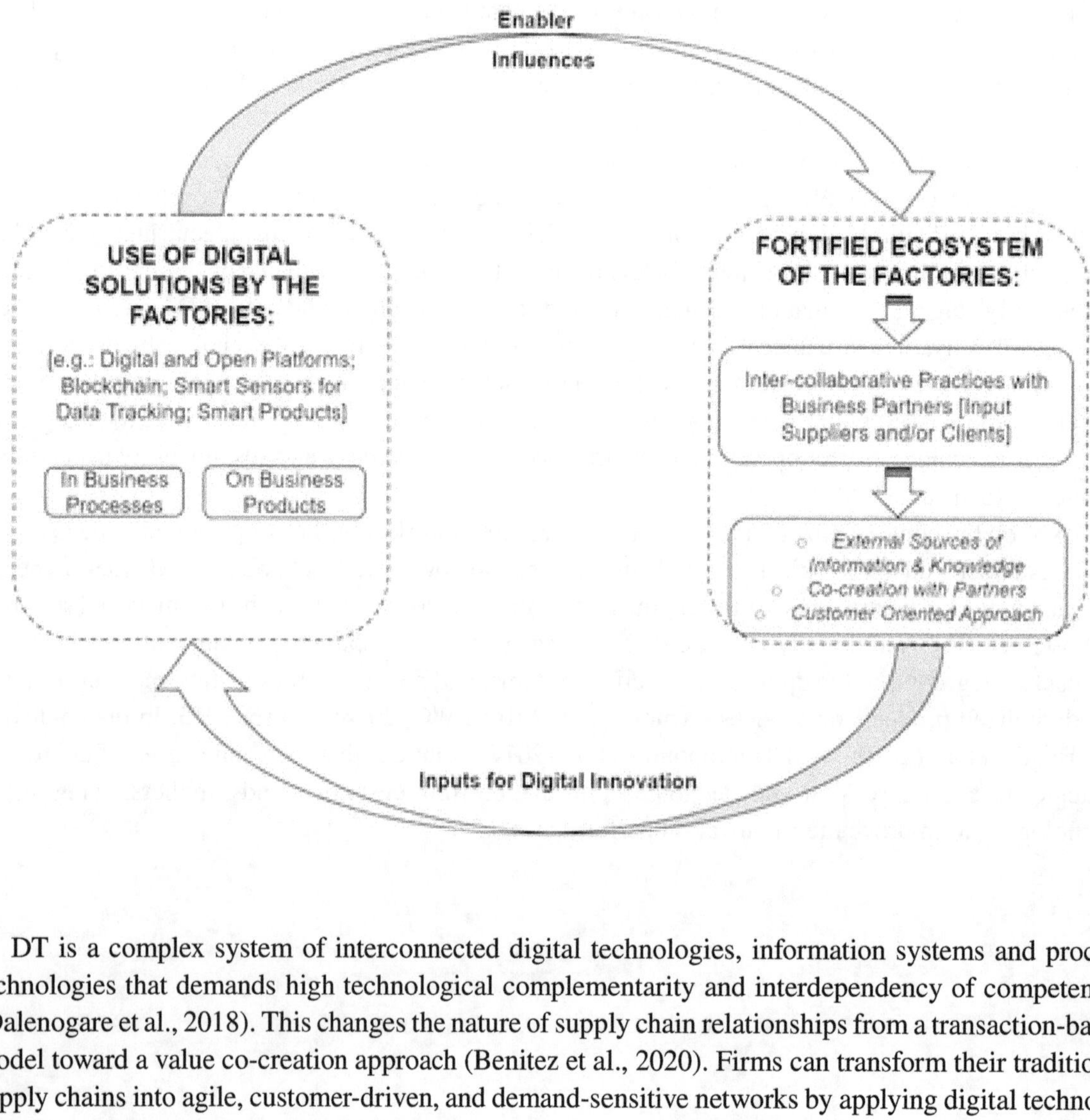

DT is a complex system of interconnected digital technologies, information systems and process technologies that demands high technological complementarity and interdependency of competences (Dalenogare et al., 2018). This changes the nature of supply chain relationships from a transaction-based model toward a value co-creation approach (Benitez et al., 2020). Firms can transform their traditional supply chains into agile, customer-driven, and demand-sensitive networks by applying digital technologies (Büyüközkan & Göçer, 2018). Thus, firms can improve the visibility of their operations, leading to reduced costs and delivery times, and leveraged efficiency (Abdalla & Nakagawa, 2021; Büyüközkan & Göçer, 2018). The use of digital technologies assists firms in this pursuit by sensing and responding rapidly to the shifts in the external environments, since they increase customer proximity and enhance scanning for new consumer trends (Hansen & Sia, 2015).

Supply chains are shifting from individual, desynchronized economic relations – that is, linear models with some feedback and simple network configurations – to adaptable, harmonized partner networks (Shcherbakov & Silkina, 2021). Digital innovation ecosystems, which involve interdependency and value co-creation, have emerged as a more suitable configuration for technology development and provision than the linear supply chain (Benitez et al., 2020; Rong et al., 2015). The complexity of ecosystems of digital solutions in the context of large manufacturing supply chains raises the need for further understanding of their main mechanisms and how the stakeholders can co-evolve with each other (Rong et al., 2015).

METHODOLOGICAL PROCEDURES

The main objective of this study is to investigate how collaborations with suppliers and clients contribute to the development of a digital supply chain in large incumbent factories. To address this objective with a focus on the strategic, social-managerial aspects of the DT process, six cases were conducted. The case selection focused on large manufacturing firms from the automotive, electro-electronic and telecommunication industries from Brazil and the UK. The case selection was also based on the innovation literature, which states that large firms are more prone to invest in process and product innovation, and on the adoption of digital technologies (Frank et al. 2019). Moreover, the companies chosen as cases are those whose factories are developing or already implementing digital solutions with the support of partnerships with their suppliers and/or customers. The choice of cases also allowed a comparison of digital supply chain efforts and practices identified in factories located in a developing country, represented by Brazil, and an industrialized country, represented by the UK. In addition, the selection took into account their economic relevance, since the manufacturing sectors accounts for 10% of the total economy in the UK, 44% of exports and 70% of R&D, as well as their maturity in terms of digital technology adoption (Innovate UK, 2019).

While open innovation approaches have been increasingly adopted in developed countries (West & Bogers, 2014), firms from emerging markets such as Brazil have lagged. De Paulo et al. (2017) revealed a large discrepancy between the G7 group of developed countries and the BRICS group of emerging countries, with the latter lagging significantly, both in terms of quantity and impact of scientific production in the field. The choice of cases was aided by information from DT scholars and practitioners, who indicated that the manufacturers under analysis are on the way to digitalization. The terms for data collection precluded the disclosure of company names. Hence, the names are represented fictionally by Greek letters. For each case, participants were chosen from both the tactical and strategic levels who work directly with digital innovation projects and are experts in the R&D activities of innovation projects in their respective factories. An outline of the cases and interviewees is shown in Table 1.

Table 1. Profile of case studies and interviewees

Case	Sector	Product	Headquarters	Employees (Worldwide)	Number of interviews		
					Strategic	Tactical	Total
Alpha BR	Automotive	Cars	France/Japan	+450,000	4	2	6
Gamma BR	Industrial	Diesel injection systems	Germany	400,000	5	2	7
Delta BR	Automotive	Trucks	Sweden	100,000	1	4	5
Sigma UK	Automotive	Luxury cars	UK	+4,000	4	0	4
Kappa UK	Industrial	Aircraft engines	UK	50,000	5	0	5
Iota UK	Automotive	Cars	Japan	140,000	4	0	4

The theoretical framework guided the development of a questionnaire and an interview script, as well as non-participant observations regarding the technological infrastructure. The constructs and their relationships led to the definition of the preliminary qualitative variables. The interview script was evaluated previously by manufacturing DT experts. After external validation, the interviews were conducted with participants from the case studies. Each interview lasted an average of 70 minutes. The Brazilian interviews were carried out in person. The British ones were applied in person with some remote exceptions. Brazilian data collection took place from October 2018 to March 2019, the same period of visits for non-participating observations. British data collection started in August 2019 and ended in March 2020.

Data collection was followed by content analysis (Bardin 2000; Saldaña 2013). For these analyses, *ATLAS.ti 8.4* software was used to support the search for convergences, assisting in data triangulation, comparative analysis, and providing elements to cross-check the information. The content analysis technique by codification followed the three phases proposed by Bardin (2000) – pre-analysis; material exploration, or coding, and categorization of the written texts; treatment of results, inferences, and interpretations – complemented by the coding cycles proposed by Saldaña (2013). The content coding process addresses subjectivity without losing reliability when treating the data produced in the field (Vosgerau et al., 2016). The methodology was also reviewed by an expert in *ATLAS.ti* content analysis. The results were then compared with the contents of Fig. 1, allowing the framework to be adjusted according to the specific contexts under analysis. The process was then reviewed by other researchers involved in the project to verify and discuss possible differences on the analyses. Lastly, the research results were reviewed by one interviewee of each case, to check for divergences related to interpretation.

MAIN RESULTS OF THE CASE STUDIES

The Use of Digital Technologies for Greater Integration with Business Partners

Sigma UK has used artificial intelligence to improve *My Sigma*, a customized mobility service for drivers. Through the app, drivers can view the vehicle status, including fuel range, mileage, predictive maintenance information, and other alerts directly on the dashboard. The app exemplifies Sigma's initial dedication to having clients more involved and satisfied with the brand, not only because of the product, but also because of the customized services made possible by the use of sensors connected to the car. By using this remote service, drivers have greater interaction with their vehicles.

Sigma UK a factory that is highly dependent on suppliers. However, it faces resistance from some suppliers to access and monitor their data, and consequently to identify component quality and delivery dates. There is a digital solution that identifies and quantifies failures of a certain component produced by one of the suppliers. Sigma explains that this supplier was reluctant to know about this technology, as it claimed it would only focus on how many problems it would have, rather than thinking that the identification of problems could help it to make long-term improvements, benefiting itself and its customers – automakers such as Sigma. Due to the lack of awareness and education in digitalization, some suppliers do not realize the benefits of new technologies that inform not only how they are performing in real time, but also allow them to improve.

Kappa UK is a pioneer in the field of technologies in sensing and data analytics in its products – "*for obtaining real-time, clean and good quality data stream*" (K-03). IoT and other digital solutions are focused on solving problems or meeting customer needs. They are seen as more basic technologies that prepare Kappa to use more complex solutions such as AI. Since 2005, Kappa UK's way of doing business and monetizing has been renewed. The new business model, in which advanced data analysis is done by Kappa for customers, is that customers only pay the cost of using aircraft engines for the hour they fly, instead of purchasing the engines at high prices. Thus, the customer no longer pays for spare parts, maintenance, and overhaul costs, but only for the use of the engine. As customers use and benefit from such solutions, Kappa services and improves its smart engines. When Kappa manages data on the way aircraft pilots are flying and therefore using the engine, Kappa, with its domain in data analysis and AI, offers pilots customized services in real time about their performance and aircraft performance, assisting airline crews to provide more efficient and safer flights for passengers.

While pioneering many applications of digital technologies in products, Kappa recognizes that it has not mastered all digital technologies due to their changeable nature. Kappa is globally recognized for its commitment to technological R&D, and most of its digital solutions, whether in use or under development, explore different ways to provide information to customers – what is called digital servitization. Kappa focuses more on developing a smart product rather than on the adoption of digital solutions in its manufacturing process. Due to this, the factory has achieved greater maturity in the use of digital solutions that can offer customized services related to engine performance to clients such as airline companies.

The use of digital solutions also facilitates greater integration with suppliers to manufacture the engines. Kappa has suppliers for materials such as aluminum, which is hygroscopic, absorbing large quantities of water. When the engine operates under rapidly changing humidity conditions, Kappa, using applications with supplier connectivity, transmits warnings about the wet engine status and asking this supplier to do something different, for example, manufacture an aluminum alloy for the engine that is not affected by high humidity in flight. Thus, Kappa offers an opportunity for its suppliers to offer a better material. This exemplifies how the use of digital solutions used by Kappa can help suppliers deliver customized materials to develop better engines. This finding clarifies the need to extend digitalization from manufacturers to other supply chain actors.

In addition to offering products to the general market, Delta BR has been developing customized solution packages to customers. Through the intermediation of telemetry technology, Delta's R&D professionals can provide guidance to truck drivers regarding the best route information when they need to carry out preventive maintenance. However, who will decide whether or not to do what Delta signals is the truck driver. Delta only brings the information to them. The use of digital telemetry solutions strengthens relationships between Delta and its end users, generating greater and better-quality integrations with customers.

Alpha BR and Iota UK aim in to create the future a direct integration with clients through a B2C platform for car sales. However, this project to create online sales to enable mass customizations is in the ideation phase, without budget approval (Table 2). Iota has not developed a process yet to collect customer data regarding car design preferences. When choosing and finalizing a purchase, Iota also wants its customers to be able to follow up on their purchase order. When using Data Analytics, these cases will have a large amount and diversity of data on purchasing profiles and customer preferences. This data can serve as input for factories to have new car designs. These cases believe that, by having greater engagement with clients, they can help co-create new product designs, in addition to creating greater connection and customer satisfaction for the car and the brand. The digital solutions per case and their status focused on a smarter supply chain are presented in Table 2.

Table 2. Status of digital technologies for smart supply chain

Case	Digital solutions used	Solutions in Development	Solutions in Ideation / No Budget
Alpha	[None]	Chatbot still in early development stage: digital assistant designed to communicate with users, often using AI to get an experience that is closer to reality	Unspecified AI solutions to be used to assist in Alpha business renewal - DT
		Data Lakes & Advanced Analytics: single storage of all corporate data (structured, semi or unstructured) to be transformed into reports, or to be visualized using advanced analytics or machine learning, helping decision makers. Although "no one knows exactly what it is" (A-01), there is a group of people in Alpha dedicated to exploring and better understanding the Data Lakes	
Gamma	[None]	[None]	Cloud computing: according to the company's privacy policy, Gamma does not use it and still doesn't see the need at the factory. There are restrictions to work with public cloud
			Unspecified AI projects - there is interest in obtaining large gains, but nothing effective; no benefit for the plant has yet been found.
Delta	Advanced Analytics using Telemetry: multiple sensors on trucks to track how drivers are using them. This traceability, real-time and remote monitoring makes Delta bring customized information to final users	[None]	Cloud Computing - for reasons of data security and privacy, Delta still uses a private server
	AGT [Automated Guided Transport] – applied to Agribusiness trucks to bring intelligence in sugarcane harvesting, minimizing losses. The vehicle follows the harvesting equipment, keeping at a standard speed, which helps to reduce the possibility of trampling on the sugarcane		
Iota	Virtual Reality - to be applied in an environment where customers can try out their custom vehicle and see what it can look like, literally, on the road	[None]	Advanced Analytics and AI solutions to be used to help renew Iota's business on car customizations. By making use of these technologies for this purpose, Iota seeks to better manage and integrate the Supply Chain
			Blockchain – 1) to be used for better supply chain on integration; connectivity with input suppliers' data and how they sequence their products in the Iota production process via the use of this technology; 2) to connect Iota production systems with external systems such as those of customers and some parts suppliers
			Preventive maintenance on cars in use: use the same preventive maintenance system already applied in the production process to be replicated on used cars - project still in the initial stage of development
			5G Connectivity - bringing shorter response time, greater security, and stability, making room for a much more complete connection from the factory

Continued on following page

Table 2. Continued

Case	Digital solutions used	Solutions in Development	Solutions in Ideation / No Budget
Sigma	Smart Sensors – there is the cockpit /dashboard room in which different KPIs are displayed that measure and monitor, in real time, the factory conditions of each stage of the production process, monitoring not only machinery, but also components, and cars	Big Data & Advanced Analytics for the company to appropriate data on how customers are using the cars - "*vehicles have been producing terabytes, a huge amount of data. We haven't done a good job of taking advantage of it yet.*" *[S-01]*	Blockchain – its real benefit for manufacturers is yet to be explored. Sigma already foresees the future possibility of implementing it to have a smarter Supply Chain, more securely connecting the data of the involved actors
	AI in the GT car model launched in 2019 to celebrate the company's 100th anniversary. This model represents smart mobility for the luxury segment: the car offers autonomous, fully connected driving and a new driving experience for customers/drivers		AI – other applicability [not detailed by respondents] to have greater connectivity with customers to obtain data that will serve as inputs for adaptive innovations in cars
			Intelligent information systems, not detailed by the factory, to be used by all Sigma suppliers so that the factory is fully connected to these systems and has more integrated logistics and suppliers - horizontal integration
			Cloud Computing – due to strict data privacy policy and a history of hacker intrusion into its systems, Sigma still uses an internal server
Kappa	AI - for preventive and predictive maintenance on the product, optimizing decision making; AI also used to improve decisions about when to order components from suppliers - automation of the raw material purchasing process	AI – for improvements in production processes and to improve integrations with Supply Chain partners [downstream of the chain such as suppliers]: "*focus more on these technologies to be used in our backstage of the chain*" *(K-01)*	Blockchain - Kappa already sees the future possibility of implementing it to have a smarter Supply Chain, and connecting more securely the data of the actors involved
	IoT architecture: sensing, Big Data & Advanced Analytics in the product [Kappa as a pioneer in the field of these solutions] – "*to obtain real-time, clean and good quality data flow*" *(K-02)*		Cloud Computing – not yet allowed by the company due to IT policy restrictions

Open Innovation with Business Partners for Digital Innovation

The cases reveal that inter-collaborations are important in building joint technological knowledge. Table 3 outlines the inter-collaborative projects status for manufacturing digital innovation. Most projects are under development, some still progressing modestly, and few projects have already been completed. This general status may be because the applications of digital technologies are recent, and due to the diversity of challenges that the organizations face and need to manage in order to digitalize themselves. There is a predisposition of each factory to engage in new external business partnerships. Alpha is the most mature Brazilian case regarding building and working for a digital innovation ecosystem (Table 3).

The Brazilian case Gamma is at the beginning of an effort to build a digital ecosystem that encompasses business partners, since the factory recognizes that DT has the potential to create a fully integrated and smart value chain. However, Gamma BR is far from connecting customers, suppliers, machines, and information systems via the intermediation of digital solutions.

At Delta BR, customers (fleet owners or end users) are considered business partners for being an input for a possible development of new, more customized trucks to meet their real needs. This customization is only possible using digital technology in telemetry, which monitors how customers are using the trucks using smart sensors, which collect data in real time, and then this data is combined to generate relevant information to customers. From the applicability of this solution, Delta aims to make use of one of the aspects of DT: digital servitization. Delta not only offers ready-made products, but also has been offering customized solution packages, including services that can support drivers' decision-making processes.

Alpha BR and Iota UK have started researching ways in which the use of digital technologies can improve interactions with customers. When they implement web based B2C sales of their cars, the factories will be able, through Data Analytics, to analyze the purchase profile of customers. Thus, there would be no need for intermediation by dealers. These cases would use their production lines according to customer purchase orders, reducing inventory costs and implementing just-in-time processes. Direct contact with customers would enable Iota UK and Alpha BR to build a database on the consumption preferences of potential car buyers. The data would then be used to adapt and develop new cars. When finalizing the purchase, customers would be able, by using a collaborative platform, to track their purchase order from the manufacturer, following each stage of production and stages of quality testing of their vehicle until delivery. Online sales to customers can lead to future business disruption in these cases. However, the B2C sales project is in the ideation phase. These cases are expected to be able to work with digital servitization and mass customization.

The use of digital solutions platforms on which AI is used has strengthened connections regarding the exchange of information between Kappa UK and its customers, exemplifying horizontal integration. However, it was not clear, in the participants' perceptions, whether this integration with customers could generate insights that would be used as inputs for Kappa to develop new and better products.

All factories consider integration with buyers and suppliers as factors that "*will take us to the next level of digital*" (I-03), even in those cases that do not yet use business partnerships. Innovation is more than a combination of processes, tools, and people; it involves the entire digital ecosystem and new ways of working. This creates challenges, but also opportunities, because connectivity and access to information to a global knowledge base across corporate boundaries has been expanded and makes manufacturers able to gain a much wider spectrum of resources and knowledge to innovate: "*Innovation is no longer a kind of ivory tower or isolated vacuum; it is part of an ecosystem and that is what I find different now. Manufacturers must take advantage of this to benefit from their digital journey* "(K-02)

Table 3. Inter-collaborations with business partners for digital innovation

Case	Partnerships in progress	Digital solutions in progress	Solution applicability
Alpha BR	Customers	Smart sensors in cars via the Advanced Driver Assist System, also known as Safety Design Software [system still expanding]	Advanced electronic systems that assist the driver while driving, increasing vehicle safety. This is made possible by the secure human-machine interface
	Prospected partnerships	**Prospected digital solutions**	**Solution applicability**
	Input suppliers	Smart sensors in logistics to monitor the delivery and conditions of inputs to the factory in real time	Optimization of logistics - Significant improvements to Just-in-time process
		Supplier system integration via web	Online integration platform for validation of parts; better monitoring and information exchange
	Customers	Big data & advanced analytics	B2C sales
		Telemetry - remote tracking sensors; monitoring the use of cars by only fleet owners (currently). Desirable expansion for consumers	M2M communication
Gamma BR	**Completed partnerships**	**Completed digital solutions**	**Solution applicability**
	Input supplier	RFID sensors in Gamma components; Integration between different systems: information system of Gamma and supplier, sharing data in real time	Obtain information flow for the physical chain: tracking of materials and their quality condition in real time until their arrival at the factory
Delta BR	**Partnerships in progress**	**Digital solutions in progress**	**Solution applicability**
	Customers (fleet owners and/ or truck drivers)	Advanced analytics in telemetry data when using the AGTs (Automated Guided Transport): Delta's trucks for agribusiness	Performance monitoring. Through telemetry, Delta can monitor the way customers are using the trucks. With this data, it is possible to generate predictive information for customers (predictive maintenance, analyze how customers are actually using their trucks, remote monitoring of fuel consumption). This can be used to customize future production of Delta trucks
Kapa UK	**Completed partnerships**	**Completed digital solutions**	**Solution applicability**
	Input supplier (Aluminum for making engines)	Data Analytics	Kappa, using applications with supplier connectivity, can inform the supplier to implement changes - make aluminum alloy for the engine that is not affected by conditions of high humidity in flight
	Customers (Airlines)	AI and creation of an App with friendly digital interface with customers – customer centric design.	Kappa gets real-time data on customer engine usage and data on customer experience. This data feeds the design stage of engine production
Iota UK	**Prospected partnerships**	**Prospected digital solutions**	**Solution applicability**
	Customers	Data Analytics	B2C sales
	Input supplier	Blockchain	Connectivity with supplier data and how they sequence their products in the Iota production process via the use of this technology

Continued on following page

Table 3. Continued

Case	Partnerships in progress	Digital solutions in progress	Solution applicability
	Partnerships in progress	**Digital solutions in progress**	**Solution applicability**
Sigma UK	Customers (Drivers)	AI and Data Analytics	Tracking and real-time monitoring of car usage by customers. This focus on the customer can bring product (car) adaptations and greater profitability per vehicle
	Prospected partnerships	**Prospected digital solutions**	**Solution applicability**
	Input supplier	Smart Sensors and AI to be used by suppliers, whose data would also be made available in real time for Sigma to monitor	More connected and smarter supply chain by sharing part condition data before arriving in Sigma (horizontal integration)

DISCUSSION

This section compares the Literature Review (Section 2) with evidence from the case studies (Section 4). to understand the relationship between the use of digital technologies in the cases and the collaborations with customers and suppliers as a factor that supports a smarter supply chain. From this discussion, theoretical-empirical propositions were created (see P1 and P2 in Table 4). Despite the current dearth of partnerships with customers and/or suppliers (Table 3), all cases recognize that inter-collaborations need to play a strategic role for factory digitalization, as it is a potential source of creation, modification and expansion of new knowledge and technological resources. As such, this will enable them to adapt and even transform the business so that it becomes able to compete in an uncertain and competitive environment. These findings are in line with previous research results (North et al., 2020; Vial, 2019; Teece, 2018).

Findings indicate that organizations are at the beginning of their digital ecosystem development. However, these companies have already seen the first results in the form of an improved competitive advantage in their factories, through the relationship between the use of digital solutions and integration with business partners. The positive impacts on the supply chain from this relationship are perceived in some cases. This shows how the adoption of digital technologies can enrich connections with customers and/or suppliers, which helps in the development of a digital supply chain. For all cases, inter-collaborations play a crucial role towards a digital supply chain.

Regarding P1 – *Digital technologies are enablers that assist collaborations of large manufacturers with business partners* – it was not supported in Gamma BR, and partially supported in Alpha BR, and Delta BR. Although all Brazilian cases were aware of the relevance of business partnerships, they are still in an initial stage of developing such type of integration through the mediation of digital technologies. For Alpha BR and Delta BR, business partnerships are still being developed, and digital technologies are enablers of collaboration and integration between manufactures and their clients or suppliers, therefore, changing the relationships in their value chain. This confirms the findings of Obal and Lancionini (2013) and Alicke et al. (2017).

Regarding P2 – *Business partners in the ecosystem are sources for digital innovation in manufacturers* – benefits such as those found in Kagemann, et al., (2013); Arnold et al., (2016); and Ryynänen and Hyyryläinen, (2018) were not identified in the Brazilian context. The cases emphasize that much has to be done to achieve the benefits of a complete digital supply chain, in which business partners can actively contribute to the process of digital innovation through co-creation practices.

Although a dearth of business partners was identified, all cases considered not only customers and input suppliers, but also other key actors that drive the digital manufacturing journey, including research, science, and technology institutions; universities; startups that develop digital solutions; government incentives; and providers of technologies for industrial automation. Therefore, it can be inferred that outside-in practices of open innovation (Bogers et al., 2019a; Chesbrough & Bogers, 2014) are seen as drivers or accelerators to operationalize digital projects in the factories under study.

It is inferred that those cases that blended a greater use of digital solutions with more intense collaboration with their business partners tended to increase the adaptability and agility of their supply chains. This finding is in line with recent research such as that of Abdalla and Nakagawa (2021), who observed that open innovation with suppliers and customers can increase the positive impacts of DT on supply chain adaptability. Also, in the current digital context, manufactures realize the crucial necessity of exploring external sources of technology and ideas to develop in-house R&D. Thus, creating business value requires firms to open up their innovation processes and develop capabilities to combine internally developed technologies. Such findings are consistent with previous research (Chesbrough & Bogers, 2014).

In sum, the case studies indicate that collaboration is gaining momentum in digitalized environments, corroborating previous research (Rocha et al., 2021). An important aspect of inter-collaborations in the digitalization process of supply chains is to determine which raw material suppliers, customers and other channels are useful sources of knowledge on digital technologies. The findings indicate that digital supply chains need to solve obstacles regarding the applicability of digital solutions, how to integrate digital technologies with existing ones, how to stimulate the experimentation of different technologies, and how to align the use of digital solutions from manufacturing with its different supply chain members. This finding corroborates results of recent research (Wessel et al., 2020). Additionally, it is noted that the literature on the digital supply chain and its capabilities are in the early stages (Queiroz et al., 2019). A systematic literature review by Frederico et al. (2019) showed that there is limited research linking digitalization to supply chains. That study pointed out that maturity propositions for digitalization are still in early stages and entirely missing in the context of supply chains.

Table 4. Results by cases for each proposition

Proposition	Results	Highlights from the cases
P1: Digital technologies are enablers that assist collaborations of large manufacturers with business partners		**General aspects: 1**. The companies display an incipient stage of development; **2.** Companies could not determine whether technologies were enabling factors to collaborate with business partners, as they rely mainly on scientific partners (e.g.: startups, government, universities, science and technology institutions); **3**. Business partnerships for digital innovation received less emphasis in Brazilian cases than in the UK cases**; 4.** Brazilian employees still have to increase their knowledge on DT in order to successfully assess the importance of business partners and other external collaborations for digital innovation; **5.** For UK cases, the collection and analysis of customer data promotes greater connectivity with the information systems of suppliers in the manufacturing supply chain, and "*allows greater interaction and communication with us more efficiently with customers. This is where the advantages of digital technologies lie*" [I-01];; **6.** Digitalization is already in place, even if it is still at an early stage, except for Kappa, which is in an advanced stage, transforming the value chain relationships of these companies; **7.** Much still needs to be done to reach the potential of the promised benefits of a Digital Supply Chain in which business partners can actively contribute to the digital innovation process with manufacturing via co-creation practices.
	BR Cases Partially supported in Gamma [supplier only]; Partially supported in Alpha, Delta [only with customers at an initial phase or prospects]	**Alpha**: It is in an initial phase of understanding how the use of digital technologies can strengthen interactions with customers; the establishment of a B2C platform for car sales is seen as a prerequisite for such kind of partnership and customer behavioral analyses. However, the B2C sales project is still in the ideation stage, without budget approval for its feasibility**; Gamma**: It is still distant from connecting customers, internal users, machines, and information systems via the intermediation of digital solutions. However, Gamma already has its input suppliers as partners, with real-time data exchange, which contributes to a more efficient and agile supply chain; **Delta:** Uses digital platforms to track data from customers and suppliers in real time but recognizes that it is at an early stage.
	UK Cases Partially supported in Sigma and Iota [only with customers at an initial phase or prospects] Supported in Kappa	**Kappa:** is the most advanced case regarding the use of digital solutions (AI and Data Analytics) to have greater integration with customer data; **Sigma:** Mediated by a platform on which AI and Data Analytics technologies are embedded, Sigma offers a car linked to a personalized mobility service package for clients. Sigma is still far from reaching the full potential that these technologies can offer in terms of digital servitization; **Iota**: The use of digital technologies has initially been promoting greater interaction with customers and suppliers, although these connections have many possibilities for improvement.
P2: Business partners in the ecosystem are sources for digital innovation in manufacturers	**Brazilian Results** Not supported in Alpha, Gamma; Partially supported in Delta	**Alpha 1.a)** Regarding business partners, Alpha is still in an ideation phase, and the establishment of a B2C platform is a prerequisite for such partnership; **1.b)** Alpha, in the future, aims to improve its capabilities to collect and monitor consumer data on how they are using their cars; therefore, smart and digital products would be a way for Alpha to interact with costumers in real time; **Gamma:** It is at the beginning of an effort to build a digital ecosystem that encompasses business partners; **Delta:** Although at an initial stage, customers are considered as business partners for being an input for a possible development of new solutions, enabled by the use of digital technologies in telemetry.
	British Results Not supported in Iota; Supported in Kappa and Sigma	**Iota:** In the future, aims to improve its capabilities to collect and monitor consumer data on how they are using their cars; therefore, smart, and digital products would be a way for Iota to interact with costumers in real time; **Sigma and Kappa:** the main purpose of using digital solutions is to promote greater integration and connectivity with customer data: *"digitalization is about Supply Chain, it is about customers; you need to think of an end to end environment" [S-02]; "This is probably the fastest route in the Supply Chain; the better the communication and collaboration we have with our supply chain, the better we can operate as a business. Our business is to deliver" [K-02]*

FINAL CONSIDERATIONS

New digital technologies have brought about global challenges and opportunities that affect developed and developing nations. Such a context gives rise to the need for more collaborative solutions to complex problems. The findings of the present study highlighted that collaborative networks have never been more important. Interorganizational collaborations gain strength in digitalized environments. In order to stimulate digital R&D and innovation, to accelerate technological learning, to balance relationships and obtain competitive advantages from the results of these collaborations, solid relationships with external partners are crucial. However, the use of digital solutions to make supply chains more connected, integrated, and smarter, is neither easy nor without challenges. The possibility of total supply chain integration using digital technologies is still far from happening in most of these cases.

The impacts of DT are so significant that they change the way companies operate. Changes can yield new possibilities to do things more effectively or affordably, but they can also very disruptive to current operations. Digital solutions are key enablers for providing efficiency and agility, and for providing external opportunities such as new and tailored offerings to customers through digital servitization. The cases make clear that DT is a multi-dimensional concept and a customized process. Each company's needs are different. Thus, there is no "one size fits all" model for tackling DT.

The results of this study indicate that factories, mainly the Brazilian ones, are at an early stage in the construction of a digital ecosystem and supply chain. Results also show that business success depends more on how digital technologies are developed and used by engaged people to add value to the enterprise rather than simply buying new technologies from third party companies. The path towards DT is gradual and complex and involves organizational change, as companies need to prepare people to understand its value and impact. Top managers and employees, as well as external partners, must be prepared to play important roles as agents that drive transformation.

Practical Implications

This research contributes to organizational practice by helping supply chain managers to understand the relevance of closer integration with suppliers and customers who, in the current digital age, are increasingly becoming co-creators for digital solutions. By comparing the theoretical framework with the findings of each case, this study provides an examination of R&D and implementation of digital innovation projects in terms of their impacts on manufacturing supply chains in two different socio-economic contexts, Brazil, and the UK.

Research findings of this work offer contributions for managers, drawing particular attention to the relevance of an ecosystem rather than to a linear and traditional supply-chain perspective when dealing with digital solutions. Therefore, managers should consider this perspective if they want to achieve complex solutions for the current digital market. Regarding the practical implications for policy makers, the results of this study can be useful to prompt larger business associations and government agencies to create mechanisms for the development of digital innovation ecosystems. Different national and regional digital initiatives have been recently launched around the world, following the movements of leading countries. Furthermore, the perspective of collaborative innovation networks of this study highlights the importance of establishing strong relationships among ecosystem players.

Theoretical Implications

This study presents a reciprocal relationship between the use of digital technologies and inter-collaborations for innovation. Using an inter-collaborative approach facilitates digital innovation practices. Maintaining relationships with external partners is paramount to stimulate R&D&I on digital technologies, and to accelerate technological learning. Simultaneously, the enhanced connectivity provided by digital technologies makes it easier to collaborate with actors outside the firm for joint innovation. As the current digital context raises the need to seek and engage with external partners, the identification of practices that foster the success of digital projects sheds light on the role of interorganizational relations for business innovation. Therefore, DT can be a shared purpose facilitated by inter-collaborative practices, as well as an enabler of those practices.

An inter-collaborative perspective can strengthen the business environment in a context of market instability by supporting an agile combination of capabilities and by facilitating the sharing of data, information, ideas, and resources. The literature and the research findings highlight the role of collaboration for the identification of business opportunities and threats in highly volatile and competitive environments. The development of collaborative relationships can increase resilience and facilitate risk sharing among partners.

This work also contributes to the literature by providing qualitative empirical evidence of the role of inter-collaborations, mediated by the use of digital technologies, in the agility and adaptability of supply chains. The interaction of DT, external collaborations and knowledge search can positively influence the adaptability of supply chains.

Suggestions for Future Research

As digital supply chains are still in their infancy, there is a range of research questions for researchers to further develop this area of study (Frederico et al., 2019). Qualitative research results may be consolidated to analyze inter-collaborations for digital innovation between manufacturing companies and other organizational actors that may influence the journey towards digital supply chains, such as startups, universities, government agencies, and R&D centers. The perceptions of other ecosystem actors can also be investigated to expand the understanding of this research field. An even broader perspective that can provide further insights could be obtained by comparative case studies of digital innovation ecosystems for smart supply chains between manufacturing companies in Brazil and in countries that have a mature digital industrial policy, such as Germany, Japan, and the USA.

Furthermore, the pandemic reinforced the use of digital technologies as an enabler for greater flexibility, agility, connectiveness, and faster growth. The COVID-19 health emergency forced organizations to make unprecedented efforts to manage supply chains (Belhadi et al., 2021). It would be interesting to better understand how the impacts of the pandemic accelerated the need for large manufacturers to digitalize their supply chains.

REFERENCES

Abdalla, S., & Nakagawa, K. (2021). The interplay of digital transformation and collaborative innovation on supply chain ambidexterity. *Technology Innovation Management Review*, *11*(3), 45–56. doi:10.22215/timreview/1428

Accenture. (2018). *Accenture Technology Vision*. Available on: https://www.accenture.com/t20180227T215953Z__w__/us-en/_acnmedia/Accenture/next-gen-7/tech-vision-2018/pdf/Accenture-TechVision-2018-Tech-Trends-Report.pdf

Agrawal, P., Narain, R., & Ullah, I. (2019). Analysis Of Barriers in Implementation of Digital Transformation of Supply Chain Using Interpretive Structural Modelling Approach. *Journal of Modelling in Management*, *15*(1), 297–317. doi:10.1108/JM2-03-2019-0066

Arnold, C., Kiel, D., & Voigt, K. (2016). How the Industrial Internet of Things Changes Business Models in Different Manufacturing Industries. *International Journal of Innovation Management*, *20*(8), 1–25. doi:10.1142/S1363919616400156

Balakrishna, C. (2012). Enabling technologies for smart city services and applications. *Proceedings of the 6th International Conference on Next Generation Mobile Applications, Services, and Technologies*, 223-227.

Bardin, L. (2000). *Análise de Conteúdo*. Lisboa: Edições 70.

BEIS. (2020). *Business Population Estimates for the UK and Regions*. Available at: https://www.gov.uk/government/uploads/system/uploads/attachment_data/file/254552/13-92-business-population-estimates-2013-stats-release-4.pdf

Belhadi, A., Kamble, S., Chiappetta, C., Gunasekaran, J., Ndubisi, N., & Venkatesh, M. (2021). Manufacturing and service supply chain resilience to the COVID-19 outbreak: Lessons learned from the automobile and airline industries. *Technological Forecasting and Social Change*, *163*, 120447. doi:10.1016/j.techfore.2020.120447 PMID:33518818

Ben-Dayaa, M., Hassinib, E., & Bahroun, Z. (2019). Internet of Things and Supply Chain Management: A Literature Review. *International Journal of Production Research*, *57*(15), 4719–4742. doi:10.1080/00207543.2017.1402140

Benitez, G., Ayala, N., & Frank, A. (2020). Industry 4.0 innovation ecosystems: An evolutionary perspective on value cocreation. *International Journal of Production Economics*, *228*, 107735. doi:10.1016/j.ijpe.2020.107735

Bogers, B., Chesbrough, H., & Moedas, C. (2019a). Open Innovation: Research, Practices, and Policies. *California Management Review*, *60*(2), 5–16. doi:10.1177/0008125617745086

Bogers, M., Chesbrough, H., Heaton, S., & Teece, D. (2019b). Strategic Management of Open Innovation: A Dynamic Capabilities Perspective. *California Management Review*, *62*(1), 77–94. doi:10.1177/0008125619885150

Brody, P., & Pureswaran, V. (2015). The next digital gold rush: How the Internet of Things will create liquid, transparent markets. *Strategy and Leadership*, *43*(1), 36–41. doi:10.1108/SL-11-2014-0094

Bücker, I., Hermann, M., Pentek, T., & Otto, B. (2016). Towards a Methodology for Industrie 4.0 Transformation. In *Business Information Systems* (pp. 209–221). Springer. doi:10.1007/978-3-319-39426-8_17

Bunse, B., Kagermann, H., & Wahlster, W. (2014). Foreword. In *Industrie 4.0: Smart manufacturing for the future* (pp. 1–40). Ed. GTAI - Germany Trade and Invest.

Burchardt, C., & Maisch, B. (2019). Digitalization needs a cultural change – examples of applying Agility and Open Innovation to drive the digital transformation. *Procedia CIRP*, *84*, 112–117. doi:10.1016/j.procir.2019.05.009

Büyüközkan, G., & Göçer, F. (2018). Digital Supply Chain: Literature review and a proposed framework for future research. *Computers in Industry*, *97*, 157–177. doi:10.1016/j.compind.2018.02.010

Camarinha-Matos, L., Fornasiero, R., & Afsarmanesh, H. (2017). Collaborative Networks as a Core Enabler of Industry 4.0. In Collaboration in a Data-Rich World. PRO-VE 2017. Springer.

Camarinha-Matos, L., Fornasiero, R., Ramezani, J., & Ferrada, F. (2019). Collaborative Networks: A Pillar of Digital Transformation. *Applied Sciences (Basel, Switzerland)*, *9*(24), 1–33. doi:10.3390/app9245431

Chesbrough, H., & Bogers, M. (2014). Explicating Open Innovation: Clarifying an Emerging Paradigm for Understanding Innovation. *Political Science*.

CNI. (2016). *Challenges for Industry 4.0 in Brazil*. Available at: https://www.portaldaindustria.com.br/media/filer_public/49/e5/49e5c28d-5bdc-4ea2-ba3c-a11481e1b4a1/challenges_for_industry_40_in_brazil.pdf

Dalenogare, L., Benitez, G., Ayala, N., & Frank, A. (2018). The expected contribution of Industry 4.0 technologies for industrial performance. *International Journal of Production Economics*, *204*, 383–394. doi:10.1016/j.ijpe.2018.08.019

De Paulo, A., Carvalho, L., Costa, M., Lopes, J., & Galina, S. (2017). Mapping Open Innovation: A Bibliometric Review to Compare Developed and Emerging Countries. *Global Business Review*, *18*(2), 291–307. doi:10.1177/0972150916668600

De Reuver, M., Sørensen, C., & Basole, R. (2018). The digital platform: A research agenda. *Journal of Information Technology*, *33*(2), 124–135. doi:10.105741265-016-0033-3

Dong, J., & Wu, W. (2015). Business value of social media technologies: Evidence from online user innovation communities. *The Journal of Strategic Information Systems*, *24*(2), 113–127. doi:10.1016/j.jsis.2015.04.003

Durach, C., Blesik, T., von Düring, M., & Bick, M. (2020). Blockchain Applications in Supply Chain Transactions. *Journal of Business Logistics*, *42*(1), 7–24. doi:10.1111/jbl.12238

Durach, C., Kurpjuweit, S., & Wagner, S. (2017). The impact of additive manufacturing on supply chains. *International Journal of Physical Distribution & Logistics Management*, *47*(10), 954–971. doi:10.1108/IJPDLM-11-2016-0332

Frank, A., Dalenogare, L., & Ayala, N. (2019). Industry 4.0 technologies: Implementation patterns in manufacturing companies. *International Journal of Production Economics*, *210*, 15–26. doi:10.1016/j.ijpe.2019.01.004

Frederico, G., Garza-Reyes, J., Anosike, A., & Kumar, V. (2019). Supply Chain 4.0: Concepts, Maturity and Research Agenda, Supply Chain Management. *International Journal (Toronto, Ont.)*, *25*(2), 262–282.

Garay-Rondero, C., Martinez-Flores, J., Smith, N., Caballero Morales, S., & Aldrette-Malacara, A. (2019). Digital supply chain model in Industry 4.0. *Journal of Manufacturing Technology Management*, *31*(5), 887–933. doi:10.1108/JMTM-08-2018-0280

Ghadge, A., Kara, M., Moradlou, H., & Goswami, M. (2020). The impact of Industry 4.0 implementation on supply chains. *Journal of Manufacturing Technology Management*, *31*(4), 669–686. doi:10.1108/JMTM-10-2019-0368

Gunasekaran, A., Papadopoulos, T., Dubey, R., Wamba, S., Childe, S., Hazen, B., & Akter, S. (2017). Big data and predictive analytics for supply chain and Organizational Performance. *Journal of Business Research*, *70*, 308–317. doi:10.1016/j.jbusres.2016.08.004

Gunasekaran, A., Subramanian, N., & Tiwari, M. (2016). Information technology governance in Internet of Things supply chain networks. *Industrial Management & Data Systems*, *116*(7). doi:10.1108/IMDS-06-2016-0244

Gurtu, A., & Johny, J. (2019). Potential of blockchain technology in supply chain management: A literature review. *International Journal of Physical Distribution & Logistics Management*, *49*(9), 881–900. doi:10.1108/IJPDLM-11-2018-0371

Hansen, R., & Sia, S. (2015). Hummel's Digital Transformation Toward Omnichannel Retailing: Key Lessons Learned. *MIS Quarterly Executive*, *14*(2), 51–66.

Hazen, B., Skipper, J., Ezell, J., & Boone, C. (2016). Big data and predictive analytics for supply chain sustainability: A theory-driven research agenda. *Journal of Computers & Industrial Engineering*, *101*, 592–598. doi:10.1016/j.cie.2016.06.030

Huang, J., Henfridsson, O., Liu, M., & Newell, S. (2017). Growing On Steroids: Rapidly scaling the user base of digital ventures through digital innovation. *Management Information Systems Quarterly*, *41*(1), 301–314. doi:10.25300/MISQ/2017/41.1.16

IBGE. (2020). *Demografia das Empresas e Estatísticas de Empreendedorismo*. IBGE.

Innovate UK. (2019). *Innovate UK Delivery Plan*. Author.

Jede, A., & Teuteberg, F. (2015). Integrating cloud computing in supply chain processes: A comprehensive literature review. *Journal of Enterprise Information Management*, *28*(6), 872–904. doi:10.1108/JEIM-08-2014-0085

Kagerman, H., Wahlster, W., & Helbig, J. (2013). Recommendations for implementing the strategic initiative Industry 4.0. Academic Press.

Kahle, J., Marcon, É., Ghezzi, A., & Frank, A. (2020). Smart Products value creation in SMEs innovation ecosystems. *Technological Forecasting and Social Change*, *156*, 120024. doi:10.1016/j.techfore.2020.120024

Karimi, J., & Walter, Z. (2015). The Role of Dynamic Capabilities in Responding to Digital Disruption: A Factor-Based Study of the Newspaper Industry. *Journal of Management Information Systems*, *32*(1), 39–81. doi:10.1080/07421222.2015.1029380

Koch, T., & Windsperger, J. (2017). Seeing through the network: Competitive advantage in the digital economy. *Journal of Organization Design*, *6*(1), 6. doi:10.118641469-017-0016-z

Luomaranta, T., & Martinsuo, M. (2019). Supply chain innovations for additive manufacturing. *International Journal of Physical Distribution & Logistics Management*, *50*(1), 54–79. doi:10.1108/IJPDLM-10-2018-0337

McIntyre, D., & Srinivasan, A. (2017). Networks, platforms, and strategy: Emerging views and next steps. *Strategic Management Journal*, *38*(1), 141–160. doi:10.1002mj.2596

Min, H. (2010). Artificial intelligence in supply chain management: Theory and applications. *International Journal of Logistics Research and Applications*, *13*(1), 13–39. doi:10.1080/13675560902736537

Mishra, D., Gunasekaran, A., Childe, S., Papadopoulos, T., Dubey, R., & Wamba, S. (2016). Vision, applications, and future challenges of Internet of Things: A bibliometric study of the recent literature. *Industrial Management & Data Systems*, *116*(7), 1331–1355. doi:10.1108/IMDS-11-2015-0478

Nambisan, S., Wright, M., & Feldman, M. (2019). The digital transformation of innovation and entrepreneurship: Progress, challenges, and key themes. *Research Policy*, *48*(8), 103773. doi:10.1016/j.respol.2019.03.018

North, K., Aramburu, N., & Lorenzo, O. (2020). Promoting digitally enabled growth in SMEs: A framework proposal. *Journal of Enterprise Information Management*, *33*(1), 238–262. doi:10.1108/JEIM-04-2019-0103

Porter, M., & Heppelmann, J. (2014). How smart, connected products are transforming competition. *Harvard Business Review*, *92*(11), 64–88.

Prause, G. (2015). Sustainable business models and structures for industry 4.0. *Journal of Security and Sustainability Issues*, *5*(2), 159–169. doi:10.9770/jssi.2015.5.2(3)

PriceWaterhouse Coopers Report. (2016). *Indústria 4.0: Digitalização como vantagem competitiva no Brasil*. PWC.

Pustovrh, A., Rangus, K., & Drnovšek, M. (2020). The role of open innovation in developing an entrepreneurial support ecosystem. *Technological Forecasting and Social Change*, *152*, 119892. doi:10.1016/j.techfore.2019.119892

Queiroz, M., Pereira, S., Telles, R., & Machado, M. (2019). Industry 4.0 and digital supply chain capabilities: A framework for understanding digitalization challenges and opportunities, Benchmarking. *International Journal (Toronto, Ont.)*, *28*(5), 1761–1782.

Queiroz, M., & Telles, R. (2018). Big data analytics in supply chain and logistics: An empirical approach. *International Journal of Logistics Management*, *29*(2), 767–783. doi:10.1108/IJLM-05-2017-0116

Rocha, C., Quandt, C., Deschamps, F., & Philbin, S. (2022). R&D Collaboration Strategies for industry 4.0 implementation: A case study in Brazil. *Journal of Engineering and Technology Management*, *63*, 101675. doi:10.1016/j.jengtecman.2022.101675

Rocha, C., Quandt, C., Deschamps, F., Philbin, S., & Cruzara, G. (2021). Collaborations for Digital Transformation: Case Studies of Industry 4.0 in Brazil. *IEEE-TEM*, 1-15.

Rogers, D. (2016). *The Digital Transformation Playbook: Rethink Your Business for the Digital Age*. Columbia Business School Publishing. doi:10.7312/roge17544

Rong, K., Guangyu, H., Lin, Y., Shi, Y., & Guo, L. (2015). Understanding business ecosystem using a 6C framework in Internet-of-Things-based sectors. *International Journal of Production Economics*, *159*, 41–55. doi:10.1016/j.ijpe.2014.09.003

Saarikko, T., Westergren, U., & Blomquist, T. (2020). Digital transformation: Five recommendations for the digitally conscious firm. *Business Horizons*, *63*(6), 825–839. doi:10.1016/j.bushor.2020.07.005

Saldaña, J. (2013). *The Coding Manual for Qualitative Researchers*. Sage.

Schwab, K. (2017). *The Fourth Industrial Revolution*. Crown Publishing Group.

Sedera, D., Lokuge, S., Grover, V., Sarker, S., & Sarker, S. (2016). Innovating with enterprise systems and digital platforms: A contingent resource-based theory view. *Information & Management*, *53*(3), 366–379. doi:10.1016/j.im.2016.01.001

Seuring, S. (2008). Assessing the rigor of case study research in supply chain management. *Supply Chain Management*, *13*(2), 128–137. doi:10.1108/13598540810860967

Shcherbakov, V., & Silkina, G. (2021). Supply Chain Management Open Innovation: Virtual Integration in the Network Logistics System. *Journal of Open Innovation*, *7*(1), 54. doi:10.3390/joitmc7010054

Silkina, G. (2019). From analogue to digital tools of business control: Succession and transformation. *IOP Conf. Ser. Mater. Sci. Eng.*, *497*, 012018.

Teece, D. (2018). Profiting from innovation in the digital economy: Standards, complementary assets, and business models in the wireless world. *Research Policy*. Advance online publication. doi:10.1016/j.respol.2017.01.015

Trantopoulos, K., Von Krogh, G., Wallin, M., & Woerter, M. (2017). External knowledge and information technology: Implications for process innovation performance. *MIS Q. Manag. Inf. Syst.*, *41*(1), 287–300. doi:10.25300/MISQ/2017/41.1.15

Verhoef, P., Broekhuizena, T., Bartb, Y., Bhattacharyaa, A., Qi Donga, J., Fabiana, N., & Haenlein, M. (2021). Digital transformation: A multidisciplinary reflection and research agenda. *Journal of Business Research*, *122*, 889–901. doi:10.1016/j.jbusres.2019.09.022

Vial, G. (2019). Understanding Digital Transformation: A Review and a Research Agenda. *The Journal of Strategic Information Systems*, *28*(2), 118–144. doi:10.1016/j.jsis.2019.01.003

Vosgerau, D., Pocrifka, D., & Simonian, M. (2016). Associação Entre a Técnica de Análise de Conteúdo e Os Ciclos de Codificação: Possibilidades a Partir Do Software ATLAS.Ti. *RISTI - Revista Ibérica de Sistemas e Tecnologias de Informação, 19*(September), 93–106.

Wamba, S., Queiroz, M., & Trinchera, L. (2020). Dynamics between blockchain adoption determinants and supply chain performance: An empirical investigation. *International Journal of Production Economics, 229*(C).

Wessel, L., Baiyere, A., Ologeanu-Taddei, R., Cha, J., & Jensen, T. (2020). Unpacking the difference between digital transformation and IT-enabled organizational transformation. *Journal of the Association for Information Systems, 22*(1), 102–129. doi:10.17705/1jais.00655

West, J., & Bogers, M. (2014). Leveraging External Sources of Innovation: A Review of Research on Open Innovation. *Journal of Product Innovation Management, 31*(4), 814–831. doi:10.1111/jpim.12125

Xiao, X., Tian, Q., & Mao, H. (2020). How the Interaction of Big Data Analytics Capabilities and Digital Platform Capabilities Affects Service Innovation: A Dynamic Capabilities View. *IEEE Access: Practical Innovations, Open Solutions, 8*, 1–1. doi:10.1109/ACCESS.2020.2968734

Yin, R. (2013). Estudo de caso: Estudo de caso planejamento e métodos (3rd ed.). Academic Press.

Chapter 9
Place of Knowledge Management With Risk Management for Information Technology Projects in the Organization

Amine Nehari-Talet
https://orcid.org/0000-0003-3242-8610
King Fahd University of Petroleum and Minerals, Saudi Arabia

ABSTRACT

This research focused on the challenges experienced when executing risk management processes in information technology (IT) projects. The lack of knowledge management support for risk management processes has caused many project failures in the past and encountered unanticipated resistance and never met expectation. The purpose of this research is to study how Saudi companies consider knowledge process to support risk analysis and how they use and foster it. The present research will be based on a sample of the data collected from managers and senior managers in selected organizations which represent the manufacturing, information technology (IT), and services. The key contribution is to explore how Saudi companies are integrating knowledge management with risk management for information technology projects which provides the capability to mediate the problem of IT project failures by integrating KM and RM in a single context.

INTRODUCTION

The world witnessed major turbulence in the global economy. These environmental changes may introduce new risks and organizations must arm themselves with comprehensive knowledge to address the risks introduced by this unstable environment promptly. COVID-19 could be the black swan event that finally forces many companies, and entire industries, to rethink and transform their investment in

DOI: 10.4018/978-1-7998-9715-6.ch009

Copyright © 2022, IGI Global. Copying or distributing in print or electronic forms without written permission of IGI Global is prohibited.

digital technology, all right, but in many cases, they're merely bolting them on to business-as-usual practices and processes, rather than using them to make fundamental changes in how employees work together and share knowledge and information. It's those deep changes that allow the digital workplace to drive greater productivity and, ultimately, profitability for the business. Moreover, in today's business environment, strong forces of competition and globalization have created an urgency to focus on how organizations control and care for their intellectual capital (Perrott, 2007). They depend on their own resources or external resources to meet their objectives and be better prepared for changes in their surrounding environment. By considering that, organizations can create accessible improved knowledge content in the development and provision of products and services to managers and to all levels of the firm, achieve shorter new product development cycles, facilitate, and manage organizational innovation and learning (Lancioni & Chandran, 2009).

On the other hand, many companies restructured themselves, some merged with others, filed for bankruptcy, acquired another company, and some implemented drastic layoffs. This resulted in a decrease in the resources available to all departments and a subsequent increase in business risks. One of the enormous costs of this economic downturn is the loss of 6 million payroll jobs over the past 15 months (Bernanke, 2009). Another issue facing companies is globalization. The need to change is forcing corporations to organize their projects and their systems. Many companies depend on their own resources or external resources to meet their objectives and be better prepared for changes in their surrounding environment.

For companies to be competitive, they turn to IT for innovative solutions. There are clear advantages to IT in regards to the speed in which our environment is changing both organisationally and privately (Tohidinia & Mosakhani, 2010). The purpose is to streamline the business and reduce costs. Business turned to IT to enable the integration of operational, transactional, and financial information to be active in identifying business risks and resolve risk-related issues. Therefore, IT is faced with many challenges and risks in conducting new projects with fewer resources available than before. A report by CHAOS dated in 2009 stated that there is a decrease in success rate in projects due to many reasons (Johnson, 2009). As a result, managing risks properly in projects is extremely critical for success and risk management (RM) might need renovation to perform more effectively.

The resaerch is structured as follows. Firstly, a discussion of the theoretical background; the next section examines the development on the research model and hypothesis, and introduces the research methodology (i.e., the design of the questionnaire, sample, and data collection). Centered on the research's result, the discussion and analysis unit present a conclusion, limitations of the study, and areas for additional research.

LITERATURE REVIEW

Knowledge and Knowledge Management

As a growing focus of concern within management, knowledge management is an area of research and practice that is still searching for a stable set of core concepts and practical applications. The increase flow of articles on and consulting approaches KM practice today reveals a wide range of recommended processes and techniques. In order to have a new knowledge economy and business, organizations are now facing major challenges due to external pressures as well as the nature of the workplace. The term knowledge management is often problematic as there is little consensus regarding its definition (Neef,

1997). Many authors avoid the term completely, rather preferring to focus on specific aspects of the topic such as knowledge, innovation, or learning (Costello, 1996) . Furthermore, others argue that knowledge management is closely related to concepts such as organizational learning, organizational memory, information sharing, and collaborative work (Schultze, 1998).

Knowledge is as a mix of framed experience, values, contextual information, and expert insight that provides a structure for evaluating and integrating new experiences and information. It originates and is applied in the minds of the knowledge workers. It can be viewed as the result of merging information with practice, perspective, and expression, resulting in insinuation and presents approaches and plans on which decision is based on (Kahn & Adams, 2000). Also, Michael, Zhdanova, and Fensel (2005) define knowledge as information used for resolving a precise dilemma, which presents the realistic stage. KM is an art of transforming information and intellectual assets to a permanent value for the organization, its partners, and clients (Marin-Garcia & Zarate Martínez, 2007). KM as the systemic and organizationally a specified process for acquiring, organizing, and communicating knowledge of employees so that other employees may make use of it to be more effective and productive in their work (Alavi & Leidner, 2001). Moreover, KM as an entity's systematic and deliberate efforts to expand, cultivate, and apply available knowledge in ways that add value to the entity, in the sense of positive outcome in achievement its objectives or fulfilling its purpose (Holsapple & Joshi, 2004). It represents the significant issues of organizational procedures, through the exercise of suitable technologies to connect dissimilar kinds of knowledge assets.

This provides rises to the necessity of improvement of a strategic, comprehensive, holistic and adoption Knowledge Management (KM) to enhance the process and get the competitive advantage (Nehari-Talet, Alhawari, & Alryalat, 2010).

Many researchers and industrialists' postulate that knowledge management centers on the creation or generation of knowledge (Nonaka, 1994). Others believe that knowledge management should focus less on knowledge creation and more its capture and integration (Martin, DeHayes, Hoffer, & Perkins, 1991). However, most agree that knowledge management encompasses all of these activities, that is, the creation or generation, codification, storage, dissemination, and implementation of knowledge in the organization. Thus, systems designed to support knowledge in organizations may not appear radically different from other forms of information systems but will be geared toward enabling users to assign meaning to information and to capture some of their knowledge in information and or in data. Knowledge core contains both tangible and intangible assets in values and culture, people, technology, and business capabilities (Halawi, Aronson, & McCarthy, 2005).

Knowledge management in a support entity can be defined as any process or practice of creating, acquiring, capturing, sharing, and using knowledge, wherever it resides, to enhance learning and performance in organizations (Scarbrough, Swan, & Preston, 1999).

The business becoming ever more information intensive, the successful organization are information intensive and trying to get competitive advantage from implementation Knowledge and determine the way for managing it (De la Vega & Stankosky, 2006). Therefore, to compete and become successful in their own market, organizations must now discover how to manage their intangible asset, that is knowledge, and this practice is generally known as KM or sometimes is referred to as business intelligence (Ali & Ahmad, 2006). Table 1 summarizes all the definitions above, and presents the taxonomy of definitions KM.

KM has progressed from an emergent concept to an increasingly common function in business organizations. As evidence of its maturity as an area of academic study, a host of journals have been devoted to KM and intellectual capital management have been created (McKeen, D., Zack, H., & Singh,

S., 2006). However, KM it is an emerging field that has demanded attention and support from the industrial community.

Table 1. Taxonomy of definitions of KM

Dimensions (KM Definitions)	Description	References
Role of IT	Systemic and organizationally specified process for acquiring, organizing, and communicating knowledge of employees so that other employees may make use of it to be more effective	(Alavi, M., & Leidner, D, 2001)
Business Process	Human activity that is part of the KM Process of an agent or collective.	(Firestone, 2001)
Research and Development/IT company	Requires viewing all organizational activities as knowledge generating, thus transforming the firm into a LO.	(Parikh, 2001).
KM Technology in Law Firms	A method to simplify and improve the process of sharing, distributing, creating, capturing, and understanding knowledge in the company.	(Gottschalk, 2002) (Intezari, A., Taskin, N., & Pauleen, D. J., 2017)
KM Learning	A framework that builds on past experiences and creates new mechanisms for exchanging and creating knowledge with the express purpose of improving the organization's effectiveness.	(Miltiadis, L., Pouloudi, A., & Poulymenakou, A., 2002) (Jennex, 2005)
Innovation Process	Deals with the creation, acquisition, integration, distribution, and application of knowledge to improve the operation effectiveness and competitive advantage of an organization.	(Albers, 2003) (Wang, Z., & Wang N., 2012)
Knowledge Architecture	Systematic way of managing this precious resource. KM promotes an integrated approach to identifying, capturing, structuring, organizing, retrieving, sharing, and evaluating an enterprise's knowledge assets.	(Kim, K., Lim, S., & Mitchell, B. , 2004)
Successful Implementation of KM	Broad subject with many facets ranging from databases to patents, from the Intranet to the mentor, from coldly technical to warmly personal concepts.	(Choy, S., & Suk, Y., 2005)

The Importance of Knowledge Management Process

KM process is essential in modern and successful organizations which look at knowledge as major factor in competitiveness. KM can be seen as a fast response to weakness and threats that affect the way of organization business. KM process is viewed as a kind of business process in the existing corporate business processes (Deng & Yu, 2006).

Additionally, KM system is considered as being vital in both theory and practice, Lasting advantage comes from using KM systems to support what we do well and to add value to resources we possess that are not readily available to competitors (Halawi, Aronson, & McCarthy, 2005).

KM in organizations can help grow such a stage to enhance and expand innovation process (Parikh, 2001). Therefore, the successful KM is the creation of management processes and infrastructure to get together knowledge and communities in a common ecology that will sustain the creation, utilization and retention of knowledge, KM also help to keep good relationships with clients by growing customer knowledge, expediting response to customer queries, suggestions, and complaints. It also ensures improved consistency and quality when serving customers (Sun & Gang, 2006). KM has been investigated in the context of decision support and expert systems for over a decade, interest in and attention to this topic have exploded (Nissen, Kamel, & Sengupta, 2000). Also, the realization of KM is complete through a series of knowledge activities or knowledge processes that specify consequently life cycles (Miltiadis, Pouloudi, & Poulymenakou, 2002).

A prerequisite of implementation of KM is to understand and develop the infrastructure elements required to support the acquisition, management, and transfer of tacit and explicit organizational knowledge. Three areas of importance form the literature on organizational knowledge infrastructure; these are the emphasis on people, process, and technology (Halawi, Aronson, & McCarthy, 2005). KM processes as well have turned out to become a strategic resource for the organizations. KM can have a great influence on reducing organizations' risks (Karadsheh, Mansour, AlHawari, Azar, & El-Bathy, 2009). However, using KM processes to improve the application of RM processes is a recent and significant research area. In spite of its importance, this area of research has not been addressed intensively up to now. Table 2 summarizes Taxonomy of KM process.

Table 2. Taxonomy of KM process

Main Dimension/ KM Process	Sub Dimension/ Description of Process							References
	1	2	3	4	5	6	7	
Practical development KM/ highly Knowledge intensive industry	Initiation	Generate	Modeling	Repository	Distributing and transfer	Use	Retrospect	(Lai, 2000)
Research and development/ IT company	Acquisition	Organize	Disseminate	Application				(Parikh, 2001) (Tohidinia & Mosakhani, 2010).
Role of IT	Creation	Storage and Retrieval	Transfer	Applications				(Alavi & Leidner, 2001)
Potential differences with Information Management	Discovery	Acquire	Creation	Storage and organization	Sharing	Use and Application		(Bouthillier & Shearer, 2002)
KM implementation strategy/ OL	Create New Knowledge	Verify	Capture & Organize	Disseminate	Use	Create Knowledge. Initially		(Sunassee and Sewry, 2002).
KM Learning	Relate value	Acquire	Organize	Enable	Reuse	Transfer and Use		(Miltiadis et al., 2002).
KM platform/ development in high tech sight project	Identify	Acquire	Preparation	Allocation	Disseminate	Usage	Retention	(Stollberg, Zhdanova, and Fensel, 2004).
Experience Management	Understand	Discover	Acquisition	Classify	Storage structure	Ontology Design	Generation /Creation	(Sun, 2004).
	8	9	10	11	12			
	Measure/ evaluation	Visualize	Distribution	Sharing / Utilization	Retention			
Spiral model KM/ OL	Selection	Creation	Sharing	Preservation and Retention	Updated			(Sun & Gang, 2006).
Collaboration in organization	Acquiring	Store	Disseminate	Use				(Abdullah, Selamat, Sahibudin, & Alias,. 2005)
Product development	Identify Knowledge	Capture	Select	Stored	Knowledge Service			(Deng & Yu, 2006)

Risk and Risk Management

Risks in an organization can span the gamut of natural disasters, security breaches, failings of human resource, third-part vendors, financial turmoil, unstable business environments and project failures. Risk is an uncertain event or condition that, if it occurs, has a positive or a negative effect on at least one project objective, such as time, cost, scope, or quality (where the project time objective is to deliver in accordance with the agreed-upon schedule; where the project cost objective is to deliver within the agreed-upon cost) (Project Management Institute, 2004). A risk may have one or more causes and, if it occurs, one or more impacts. Also, risk conditions could include aspects of the projects or organization's environment that may contribute to project risk, such as poor project management practices, lack of integrated management systems, concurrent multiple projects, or dependency on external participants who cannot be controlled (Project Management Institute, 2004). Furthermore, risk refers to all events, occurrences and actions that may prevent you or your organization from realizing its ambitions, plans and goals. Risk surrounds us in our personal and professional lives and is a potential problem that might happen. Regardless of the outcome, it is a good idea to identify risk, assess its probability of occurrence and estimate its impact.

In general, risk can have two-dimensional meaning, namely negative and positive events. It is defined as the probability of loss or gain occurrence multiplied by its respective magnitude (Olsson, 2008). A Guide to the Project Management Body of Knowledge-PMBOK (Project Management Institute, 2004) defines risk as an uncertain event that has a positive or negative impact on the project's objectives. Other researchers argue that risk is mostly related to project barriers and threats. For example, Miles (1998) defines risk as a barrier to success.

Risk Management has developed rapidly over the recent decades as an integral part of project management (Del Cano & Cruz, 2002). It includes the processes concerned with RM planning, identification, analysis, responses, and monitoring and control on a project" (Project Management Institute, 2004). RM is a distinct discipline, which integrates knowledge from a variety of other business fields. It is the discipline where wide varieties of methodologies are brought to bear on a specific problem. RM is a distinct discipline, which integrates knowledge and methodologies from a variety of other business fields to bear on a specific problem. The RM objective is to identify all applicable risks in a project, business, or product. It involves ranking the above elements based on their importance, frequency of occurrence, level of impact and then establishes the actions needed to control the identified risks. It is possible for every individual risk aspect to be documented in further details (Cule, Schmidt, Lyyttnen, & Keil, 2000). Since no one can predict what losses will occur, the objective of RM is to ensure that no risk will occur during the execution of a project in order to minimize losses to an acceptable level. If a loss occurs, then the objective of RM has failed to achieve the objectives intended, which prevent the organization from pursing their goals.

The purpose of RM is to develop a detailed analysis of the organization and project domains to develop a complete set of risk factors and to ensure they are appropriately organized to reflect all the stakeholders and the various risk perspectives that are required (Roy, 2004).

According to project management theory (Pinto, 2007) project risk management has a positive effect on project success in terms of "on time, within budget" delivery of a pre-defined result. Project management handbooks and methodologies. Therefore, stress the importance of the use of risk management techniques and provide project managers with guidelines on how to apply risk management within their projects. However, despite the recommendation to employ risk management, there are indications in literature that risk management used in Information Systems/Information Technology (IS/IT) projects only occasionally contributes to project success (Bakker, Boonstra, & Wortmann, 2010). Nevertheless, project managers often choose to execute various risk management activities in their projects (Bannerman, 2008), in order to manage their risks and uncertainties (Knight, 1921).

Risk management is considered to be a tool that limits the impact of the unexpected events or prevents the events from happening. Accordingly, it is generally assumed that risk management contributes to the success of the project (Olsson, 2008). The empirical evidence is often based on assumptions about how risk management is supposed to work, assumptions that emerge as incorrect for most IS/IT projects (de Bakker, 2010). The failure of IT systems development projects has been well documented (Tesch, Kloppenborg, & Frolick, 2007). While there are many reasons for these failures, they can typically be categorized as cost, time and performance or quality issues. The result is a Project Risk Management approach involves the systematic process of identifying, analyzing, and responding to project risk. According to Tesch et al. (2007) project risk involves understanding the probability for problems as they might hinder project success. Finally, the RM project's objectives are to minimize the probability and impact of potential risks while maximizing the probability and impact of potential opportunities.

The Role of Knowledge Management Process in Project Risk Management

The project risk management process, as described in project management handbooks, is an example of a rational problem-solving method (Kutsch & Hall, 2005) based on an instrumental view. For this process to be effective, it is necessary to follow all prescribed steps. For example, it has been have shown that the prescribed sequence of risk identification, risk analysis, planning actions, and executing actions is rarely followed (Bannerman, 2008). The sequence of activities that characterizes project risk management consists of identifying risks, analyzing risks, defining action, implementing action, and monitoring the situation. However, despite the recommendation to employ risk management, there are indications in literature that risk management used in (IS/IT) projects only occasionally contribute to project success (Bakker et al., 2010). Nevertheless, project managers often choose to execute various risk management activities in their projects (Bannerman, 2008).

Currently, KM and its Risk require significant attention within the majority of organizations. Nowadays, organizations are surrounded by turbulent environment, which might change and initiate new risks. Therefore, organizations must arm themselves with comprehensive knowledge to be able to face the risks introduced by the unstable environment. Additionally, Knowledge risk management (KRM) is an emerging field which suggests a solution to the problems connected with conventional risk management methods (Massingham, 2010). The problem of environmental complexity is manifested by individuals not knowing enough about the risk to anticipate its likelihood and consequences. To improve RM processes, the researchers will examine the relation between KM processes and RM processes. The objective is to introduce the Knowledge-Based Risk Management (KBRM) process to improve RM process efficiency by employing some of KM process. It can be generally characterized as including of knowledge creation activities and knowledge transfer activities (Hurley & Green, 2005).

Based on research conducted by Rodriguez and Edwards (2008) an effective RM process model can't be achieved without the assistant of a well-established KM process model. Therefore, a well-defined and designed integrated KM and RM framework is essential to improve decision-making in IT projects. In another study, KM as a discipline can add positively to RM implementation in reference to data and information management, risk-knowledge sharing and analysis consolidation and reporting (Shaw, 2005)

Risk Management is becoming a key factor within organizations since it can minimize the probability and impact of IT project threats and capture the opportunities that could occur during the IT project life cycle. A number of business and academic gurus that in order for organizations to have a lasting competitive advantage they will have to be knowledge driven (Holsapple, C. and Joshi, K., 2002).

According to Neef (2005), a company cannot manage its risks effectively if it cannot manage its knowledge. Many projects failed due to lack of knowledge among the project team or lack of knowledge sharing during project progress. A project failure can be the result of capturing the appropriate knowledge at an inappropriate time of the project (Fuller, Valacich, & George, 2008). In fact, without KM as a tool to communicate risks among members of a project team, RM might suffer from ineffectiveness and inefficiencies (Schwalbe, 2007).

Furthermore, the application of KM processes to support RM processes has the potential of iteratively mitigating the probability of risks, thereby raising the probability of successful project execution (Fuller et al., 2008). It is important that the organization prioritizes knowledge infusion of RM which, would require the creation, capturing and sharing of knowledge related to potential risks to key assets of stakeholders (Neef, 2005).

Three KM principles can be applied to information RM in order to generate risk intelligence and to maximize the return on value from information RM (investments. Business focus includes five steps: 1) Start with key business risks, 2) Prioritize the business risks based on their importance to the business strategy, 3) Identify information sources for the high-business risk areas, 4) Identify at-risk information sources through establishing what information is critical to the business process, and 5) Establish risk-mitigation strategies. Furthermore, KM accountability requires domain experts to be assigned to work with knowledge managers to maintain various information sources (Caldwell, 2008).

As shown in Figure 1, they claimed that in three key components of ERM (Enterprise Risk Management) there are relations between data, search of problem solutions, policies, and organization of outcomes such as risk (Rodriguez & Edwards, 2008).

Figure 1. Knowledge Management Acts through Risk Modeling in Different Components of Enterprise Risk Management Processes (Rodriguez & Edwards, 2008)

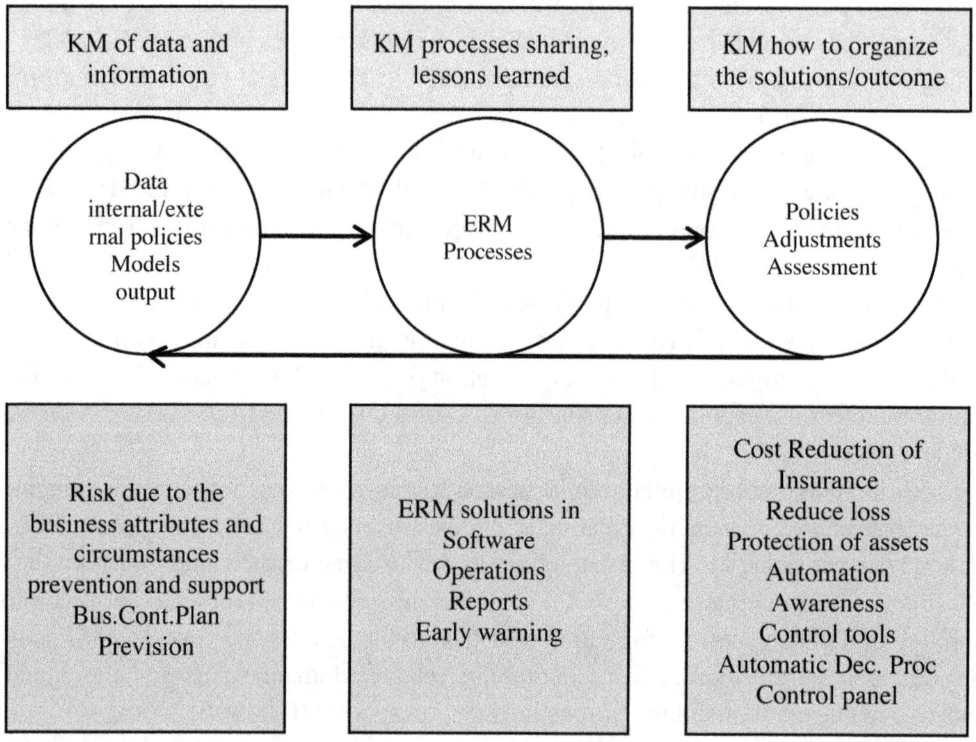

As a result, their proposed methodology used the context and experience to improve the risk modeling process and it's composed of the following steps: 1) Answering questions related to the strategy and strategic planning. 2) Determining the enablers to transfer risk knowledge from tacit to explicit knowledge and vice versa. 3) Producing knowledge by understanding the information flows. 4) Understanding risk knowledge organization. 5) Finding out KM technologies and techniques. 6) Designing the Enterprise Risk KM System to support risk modeling. 7) Finally, connecting organizational performance metrics and risk modeling.

DATA COLLECTION AND RESEARCH METHODOLOGY

Research philosophy refers to the way the researcher thinks about the development of knowledge (Saunders, lewis, & Thornhill, 2012). In order to assure the quality of the data collected, the researcher targeted three categories: the first one is small size companies the second one medium size and the third one to big size companies investing in IS/IT systems. The questionnaires were distributed to the respondents in three different job positions working in small, medium, and large sized companies: (1) Top management, (2) Middle management (3) Operational management.

Sample Size

The sample of the survey was distributed to three sized companies (small, medium, and large companies) that are investing in IS /IT systems. Table 3 shows a summary of the sample size. The internal consistency reliabilities .905 for Cronbach's alpha as shown in Table 4.

Table 3. Summary of the sample size

Category	Number of Questionnaire Distributed	Number of Completed Questionnaires Returned (Usable)	Number of Uncompleted Questionnaires Returned	Number of Questionnaires Unreturned
Small Size companies	100	28	25	47
Medium Size companies	200	132	28	40
Big Size Companies	500	190	180	130
Total Rate		**43,75%**	**29.125%**	**27.125%**

Table 4. Reliability statistics

Cronbach's Alpha	N of Items
.905	93

Research Hypotheses

H0: The integration of KM principles in support of RM processes, when applied to IT projects, may improve the organization's ability to manage risks response planning by enhancing risk identification, analysis, and mitigation. The sub- research hypotheses are stated in Table 5.

Table 5. Research hypotheses

Hypotheses	Description
H1	There is direct positive relationship between KM process and Risk Identification.
H2	There is direct positive relationship between KM process and Risk Analysis
H3	There is direct positive relationship between KM process and Risk Planning
H4	There is direct positive relationship between KM process and Risk Monitoring

Survey Results and Findings

The study used Statistical Package for the Social Sciences (SPSS) version 27.0 software for data analysis. The study used descriptive statistical tools to describe the variables of interest. This study consists of 310 males with a percentage of 88.6%and 40 females with a percentage of 11.4%. The reported figure is almost exactly the same as (Igbaria & Toraskar, 1994). The aim is to expose gender distinctions, not to explain or theorize why these distinctions have arisen and continue to exist. Examples of this include investigations of women's vs. men's use (adoption, acceptance, etc.) of IT (Gefen & Straub, 1997) and women's participation rate in the IS profession (Truman & Baroudi, 1994). The reason for the substantial percentage difference of respondents' gender is due to the male dominance of managerial and executive positions generally found throughout organizations in Saudi Arabia,

The largest group of respondents (184 or 52.6%) indicates that their area of specialization was Information Technology (IT). Additionally, the largest group of respondents (128 or 36.6%) indicates that their years of experience are more than 10 years). The rest of demographic information about the sample is detailed in Table 6.

Table 6. Demographic data - Project (N=350)

Measure	Categories	#	%	Measure	Categories	#	%
Gender	Male	310	88.6	**Company Size**	Small	28	8.0
	Female	40	11.4		Medium	132	37.7
					large	190	54.3
Educational Background	Postgraduate (Masters & Doctoral)	132	37.7	**Company Activity**	Production	37	10.6
	Undergraduate (Bachelor)	157	44.9		Services	286	81.7
	High school	16	4.6		Trading	15	4.3
	Other	45	12.9		Retailing	12	3.4
Area of specialization	Information Technology	184	52.6	**Department**	Human Resource	62	17.7
	Business	74	21.1		IT	163	46.6
	Engineering	48	13.7		Accounting & Finance	76	21,7
	Other	40	11.4		Marketing	36	10,3
					Production	13	3,7
Working Experience (year)	Less than 1 year	32	9.1	**Position**	Top Management level	28	8
	Between 1-5 years	95	27.1		Middle Management level	132	37.7
	Between 5-10 years	95	27.1		Operation Management level	190	54.3
	More than 10	128	36.6				

To measure the homogeneity of variance, Analysis of Variance (ANOVA) analysis was used to test the significance of differences among the groups of respondents.

H0: The integration of KM principles in support of RM processes, when applied to IT projects, may improve the organization's ability to manage risks response planning by enhancing risk identification, analysis, and mitigation. The test of hypotheses by using analysis of variance (ANOVA), the following rule is used to choose the Null or alternative hypothesis and to judge SPSS statistical output. The value of R Square represents the percentage with which the independent variables explain the variation in the dependent variable (George & Mallery, 2011).

First Hypothesis

There is direct positive relationship between KM process and Risk Identification. The first hypothesis includes five parts illustrate as follows:

H1.1: There is direct positive relationship between Knowledge-Based Risk Identify Source and Risk Identification.

H1.2: There is direct positive relationship between Knowledge-Based Risk Verify Source and Risk Identification.

H1.3: There is direct positive relationship between Knowledge-Based Risk Capture and Risk Identification.

H1.4: There is direct positive relationship between Knowledge-Based Risk Discovery and Risk Identification

H1.5: There is direct positive relationship between Knowledge-Based Risk Education and Risk Identification.

In order to have a deeper understanding of this theoretical framework, all the above five factors were combined into a single one named ***Knowledge Based Risk*** then the aggregated data were analyzed using ANOVA. This approach helps us to identify how these factors all together will be significantly more important compared to each factor independently.

This paper examined the effects of (Knowledge-Based Risk Identify Source, Knowledge-Based Risk Verify Source, Knowledge-Based Risk Capture, Knowledge-Based Risk Discovery, and Knowledge-Based Risk Education) on risk identification, the findings and insights of the constructs that proposed in the conceptual model are presented as follows in Table 3. ANOVA was used to analyze the data represent the test of the hypotheses based on the significant level of 0.05.

Table 7. ANOVA test for Knowledge processes-based Risk and Risk identification

Dependent variable	Independent Variable	R	R Square	Adjusted R Square	F	Sig
Risk Identification	**Knowledge-Based Risk Identify Source**	0.211	0.044	0.042	15.765	0.00
Risk Identification	**Knowledge-Based Risk Verify Source**	0.291	00.85	0.082	31.819	0.00
Risk Identification	**Knowledge-Based Risk Capture**	0.241	0.058	0.056	21.242	0.00
Risk Identification	**Knowledge-Based Risk Discovery**	0.295	0.087	0.084	32.583	0.00
Risk Identification	**Knowledge-Based Risk Education**	0.397	0.0157	0.0154	64.264	0.00

Referring to Table 7, 4.4% of the variance in Risk Identification accounted by Knowledge-Based Risk Identify Source, the F value is 15.765 with a significance equal 0.00, which is less than 0.05. In this case, we accept the hypothesis, which indicates that there is a Knowledge-Based Risk Identify Source on Risk Identification used to identify project, product, and business risks. (Sommerville, 2006)

Additionally, 8.5% of the variance in Risk Identification accounted by Knowledge-Based Risk Verify Source, the F value is 31.819 with significance equal 0.000, which is less than 0.05. In this case, we accept the hypothesis, which indicates that there is an effect of Knowledge-Based Risk Verify Source on Risk Identification which results in a variety of technological content, environmental communications, the execution and operation approaches, programmatic constraints, and the mission duration (Cornford, 1998).

Also, 5.8% of the variance in Risk Identification accounted by Knowledge-Based Risk Capture the F value is 21.242 with significance equal 0.00, which is less than 0.05. In this case, we accept the hypothesis, which indicates that there is an effect of Knowledge-Based Risk Capture on Risk Identification. The access to such a knowledge means that the tool is capable of enabling the use of past successes and failures captured to minimize risks in project management (Kayis, Zhou, Savci, Khoo, Ahmed, & Kusumo, 2007).

Moreover, 8.7% of the variance in Risk Identification accounted by Knowledge-Based Risk Discovery the F value is 32.583 with significance equal 0.03, which is less than 0.05. In this case, we accept the hypothesis, which indicates that there is an effect of Knowledge-Based Risk Discovery on Risk Identification. Given the profile of a new project, it is possible to collect information about any other project that has similarities with the current one, be aware of people that are interested in the same subject, or identify documents that talk about the same argument (Agostini et al., 2003).

Finally, 1.54% of the variance in Risk Identification accounted by Knowledge-Based Risk Education the F value is 64.264 with significance equal 0.00, which is greater than 0.05. In this case, we accept the hypothesis, which indicates that there is an effect of Knowledge-Based Risk Education on Risk Identification. The lack of knowledge access can create failures. (Rodriguez-Montes & Edwards, 2008), and the stored knowledge of risk in the repository can serve as a training, education, and awareness tool (Malhotra, 2005)

Based on previous analysis, the results from the study offered empirical support for the existence of a positive and statistically significant influence of KM process on Risk Identification. Our study of Saudi companies presents support for the hypothesized positive effects of KM process on Risk Analysis. The findings validate the research questions by answering them as follows:

1. Knowledge-Based Risk (KBR) Identify Source has a positive impact on scope establishment and the Risk Identification Therefore, the integration of KM and RM processes can form a valid KBR Identification
2. Knowledge Capture has a positive impact on scope establishment and risk identification. Therefore, the integration of KM and RM processes can form a valid KBR Capture.
3. Knowledge Discovery has positive impact on scope establishment and risk identification. Therefore, the integration of KM and RM processes can form a valid KBR Discovery.
4. Knowledge Education has a positive impact on RM processes and employees. The integration of KM and RM repository provides better training, education, and awareness. Therefore, the integration of KM and RM can form a valid KBR Education.

ANOVA analysis was run to test hypothesis H6 resulted for this study from the five previous hypotheses. In Table 8 the data clearly indicated that the aggregate factors have a high positive impact on the Risk identification and are highly significant. Thus, Hypothesis 6 cannot be rejected. Having live and dynamic integrated knowledge is essential to the organization to perform RM. Therefore, the combination of KM and RM processes can form a valid Knowledge-Based Risk Management. The integration of all the factors will give a higher coefficient of correlation 44.8% than correlation for each factor related independently with risk identification from 21.11% to 39.7. This means that all factors need to be together in order identify any risks arising from the IT project to generate a comprehensive list of risks that could impact on the objectives.

Table 8. ANOVA test for Knowledge based Risk and Risk identification

Dependent variable	Independent variable	R	R Square	Adjusted R Square	F	Sig
Risk Identification	Knowledge-Based Risk Identify Source + Knowledge-Based Risk Verify Source + Knowledge-Based Risk Capture + Knowledge-Based Risk Discovery + Knowledge-Based Risk Education	0.448	0.201	0.198	82.579	0.00

The results are supported by the previous studies for instance (Neef, 2005) claimed that the key to proactive RM processes lies in the company's ability to mobilize the knowledge and expertise of its employees regarding risk mitigation so the key decision makers in the organization can receive accurate and timely information about potential harmful incidents, as an example. The rationale for applying KM techniques to risk programs is stated in the following:

- Sensing and responding to risks in an organization is directly dependent on the knowledge and judgment of employees at all levels.
- Key decision makers need to mobilize this employee knowledge and the large amount of information available concerning potentially threatening situations in a way that will allow them to respond quickly and appropriately to threatening risks.
- Utilizing KM techniques through opening communication channels to provide a system of incentives for managers and to encourage employees to uncover potentially dangerous issues could be beneficial to the organization.
- Finally, capture lessons learned, apply proven RM techniques, and create decision support systems to assist in developing preventive RM policies and avoid costly repetition of errors.

Second Hypothesis

There is direct positive relationship between KM process and Risk Analysis. The Second hypothesis includes two parts illustrate as follows:

Four hypotheses address the associations between Knowledge processes and Risk Analysis

H2.1: There is direct positive relationship between Knowledge-Based Risk Rationalization and Risk Analysis.
H2.2: There is direct positive relationship between Knowledge-Based Risk Comprehension and Risk Analysis.
H2.3: There is direct positive relationship between Knowledge-Based Risk Examination and Risk Analysis.
H2.4: There is direct positive relationship between Knowledge-Based Risk Validation and Risk Analysis.
H2.5: There is direct positive relationship between Knowledge-Based Risk and Risk Analysis

Table 9. ANOVA test for knowledge processes-based risk and risk analysis

Dependent variable	Independent variable	R	R Square	Adjusted R Square	F	Sig
Risk Analysis	Knowledge-Based Risk Rationalization	0.474	0.225	0.222	100.803	0.00
Risk Analysis	Knowledge-Based Risk Comprehension	0.333	0.111	0.108	43.472	0.00
Risk Analysis	Knowledge-Based Risk Examination	0.436	0.190	0.188	81.894	0.00
Risk Analysis	Knowledge-Based Validation Risk	0.495	0.245	0.243	112.988	0.00

Referring to Table 9, 22.5% of the variance in Risk Analysis accounted by Knowledge-Based Risk Rationalization, the F value is 100.803 with a significance equal 0.00, which is less than 0.05. In this case, we accept the hypothesis, which indicates that there is a Knowledge-Based Risk Rationalization on Risk Analysis. Additionally, 11.11% of the variance in Risk Analysis accounted by Knowledge-Based Risk Comprehension, the F value is 43.472 with significance equal 0.000, which is less than (0.05). In this case, we accept the hypothesis, which indicates that there is an effect of Knowledge-Based Risk Comprehension on Risk Analysis. Also, 19.0% of the variance in Risk Analysis accounted by Knowledge-Based Risk Examination the F value is 21.242 with significance equal 0.00, which is less than 0.05. In this case, we accept the hypothesis, which indicates that there is an effect of Knowledge-Based Risk Examination on Risk Analysis. Finally, 24.5% of the variance in Risk Analysis accounted by Knowledge-Based Risk Validation the F value is 112.988 with significance equal 0.00, which is greater than 0.05. In this case, we accept the hypothesis, which indicates that there is an effect of Knowledge-Based Risk Validation on Risk Analysis.
The findings validate the research questions by answering them as follows:

1. Knowledge-Based Risk (KBR) Rationalization has a positive impact on scope establishment and the Risk Analysis Therefore, the integration of KM and RM processes can form a valid KBR Rationalization
2. Knowledge-Based Risk (KBR) Comprehension has a positive impact on scope establishment and risk Analysis. Therefore, the integration of KM and RM processes can form a valid KBR Comprehension.
3. Knowledge-Based Risk (KBR) Examination has positive impact on scope establishment and risk Analysis. Therefore, the integration of KM and RM processes can form a valid KBR Examination.

4. Knowledge-Based Risk (KBR) Validation has a positive impact on RM processes Analysis. Therefore, the integration of KM and RM can form a valid KBR Validation.

ANOVA analysis was run to test hypothesis five H25 resulted for this study from the four previous hypotheses. In Table 10 the data clearly indicated that the aggregate factors have a high positive impact on the Risk Analysis and are highly significant. Thus, Hypothesis 6 cannot be rejected. Having live and dynamic integrated knowledge is essential to the organization to perform RM. Therefore, the combination of KM and RM processes can form a valid Knowledge-Based Risk Management. The integration of all the factors will give a higher coefficient of correlation 60.8% than correlation for each factor related independently with risk Analysis from 33.3% to 49.5%.

Table 10. ANOVA test for Knowledge based Risk and Risk Analysis

Dependent Variable	Independent Variable	R	R Square	Adjusted R Square	F	Sig
Risk Analysis	Knowledge-Based Risk Rationalization + Knowledge-Based Risk Comprehension + Knowledge-Based Risk Examination + Knowledge-Based Risk Validation	0.608	0.369	0.367	203.636	0.00

Third Hypothesis

There is direct positive relationship between KM process and Risk Planning. The Third hypothesis includes three parts illustrate as follows:

H3.1: There is direct positive relationship between Knowledge-Based Risk action development and Risk Planning.
H3.2: There is direct positive relationship between Knowledge-Based Risk Prioritization and Risk Planning.
H3.3: There is direct positive relationship between Knowledge-Based Risk Integration and Risk Planning.
H3.4: There is direct positive relationship between Knowledge-Based Risk and Risk Planning

Table 11. ANOVA test for knowledge processes-based risk and risk planning

Dependent variable	Independent Variable	R	R Square	Adjusted R Square	F	Sig
Risk Planning	**Knowledge-Based Risk** action development	0.649	0.419	0.418	251.323	0.00
Risk Planning	**Knowledge-Based Risk** Prioritization	0.535	0.286	0.284	139.494	0.00
Risk Planning	**Knowledge-Based Risk** Integration	0.494	0.244	0.241	112.046	0.00

Referring to Table 11, 41.9% of the variance in Risk Planning accounted by Knowledge-Based Risk Action development, the F value is 251.323 with a significance equal 0.00, which is less than 0.05. In this case, we accept the hypothesis, which indicates that there is a Knowledge-Based Risk action development on Planning. Additionally, 28.60% of the variance in Risk Planning accounted by Knowledge-Based Risk Prioritization, the F value is 139.494 with significance equal 0.000, which is less than 0.05. In this case, we accept the hypothesis, which indicates that there is an effect of Knowledge-Based Risk Prioritization on Risk Planning. Finally, 24.4% of the variance in Risk Planning accounted by Knowledge-Based Risk Integration the F value is 112.046 with significance equal 0.00, which is Greater than (0.05). In this case, we accept the hypothesis, which indicates that there is an effect of Knowledge-Based Risk Integration on Risk Planning.
The findings validate the research questions by answering them as follows:

1. Knowledge-Based Risk (KBR) Action development has a positive impact on scope establishment and the Risk Planning Therefore, the integration of KM and RM processes can form a valid KBR action development.
2. Knowledge-Based Risk (KBR) Comprehension has a positive impact on scope establishment and risk Planning. Therefore, the integration of KM and RM processes can form a valid KBR Prioritization.
3. Knowledge-Based Risk (KBR) Validation has a positive impact on RM processes planning. Therefore, the integration of KM and RM can form a valid KBR Integration.

ANOVA analysis was run to test hypothesis four **H34** resulted for this study from the three previous hypotheses. In Table 12 the data clearly indicated that the aggregate factors have a high positive impact on the Risk Planning and are highly significant. Thus, Hypothesis 4 cannot be rejected. Having live and dynamic integrated knowledge is essential to the organization to perform RM. Therefore, the combination of KM and RM processes can form a valid Knowledge-Based Risk Management. The integration of all the factors will give a higher coefficient of correlation 69.6% than correlation for each factor related independently with risk Analysis from 49.40% to 64.9%.

Table 12. ANOVA test for knowledge based risk and risk planning

Dependent Variable	Independent Variable	R	R Square	Adjusted R Square	F	Sig
Risk planning	**Knowledge-Based Risk action development** + **Knowledge-Based Risk** Prioritization + **Knowledge-Based Risk** Integration	0.696	0.484	0.479	108.119	0.00

Fourth Hypothesis

There is direct positive relationship between KM process and Risk Monitoring. The Fourth hypothesis includes three parts illustrate as follows:

H4.1: There is direct positive relationship between Knowledge-Based Risk update and Risk Monitoring.

H4.2: There is direct positive relationship between Knowledge-Based Risk evaluation and Risk Monitoring.
H4.3: There is direct positive relationship between Knowledge-Based Risk Modification and Risk Monitoring.
H4.4: There is direct positive relationship between Knowledge-Based Risk and Risk Monitoring.

Table 13. ANOVA test for knowledge processes-based risk and risk monitoring

Dependent Variable	Independent Variable	R	R Square	Adjusted R Square	F	Sig
Risk Monitoring	Knowledge-Based Risk Update	0.121	0.015	0.012	5.197	0.23
	Knowledge-Based Risk Evaluation	0.156	0.24	0.22	8.705	0.03
	Knowledge-Based Risk Modification	0.689	0.463	0.461	299.815	0.00

Referring to Table 13, 1.5% of the variance in Risk Monitoring accounted by Knowledge-Based Risk Update, the F value is 5.197 with a significance equal 0.23, which is less than 0.05. In this case, we reject the hypothesis, which indicates that there is a Knowledge-Based Risk update on Monitoring. Additionally, 24.00% of the variance in Risk Monitoring accounted by Knowledge-Based Risk Evaluation, the F value is 8.705 with significance equal 0.03, which is less than 0.05. In this case, we accept the hypothesis, which indicates that there is an effect of Knowledge-Based Risk Evaluation on Risk Monitoring. Finally, 46.3% of the variance in Risk Monitoring accounted by Knowledge-Based Risk Modification the F value is 299.815 with significance equal 0.00, which is greater than 0.05. In this case, we accept the hypothesis, which indicates that there is an effect of Knowledge-Based Risk Modification on Risk Monitoring.

The findings validate the research questions by answering them as follows:

1. Knowledge-Based Risk (KBR) update has a positive impact on scope establishment and the Risk Monitoring Therefore, the integration of KM and RM processes can form a valid KBR Update.
2. Knowledge-Based Risk (KBR) Evaluation has not a positive impact on scope establishment and risk Monitoring. Therefore, the integration of KM and RM processes can form a valid KBR Evaluation.
3. Knowledge-Based Risk (KBR) Modification has a positive impact on RM processes monitoring. Therefore, the integration of KM and RM can form a valid KBR Monitoring.

ANOVA analysis was run to test hypothesis four **H3.4** resulted for this study from the three previous hypotheses. In Table 14 the data clearly indicated that the aggregate factors have a high positive impact on the Risk Monitoring and are highly significant. Thus, Hypothesis 4 cannot be rejected. Having live and dynamic integrated knowledge is essential to the organization to perform RM. Therefore, the combination of KM and RM processes can form a valid Knowledge-Based Risk Management. The integration of all the factors will give a higher coefficient of correlation 69.8% than correlation for each factor related independently with risk Analysis from 1.50% to 46.3%.

Table 14. ANOVA test for knowledge based risk and risk monitoring

Dependent Variable	Independent variable	R	R Square	Adjusted R Square	F	Sig
Risk Monitoring	Knowledge-Based Risk Update + Knowledge-Based Risk Evaluation + Knowledge-Based Risk Modification	0.698	0.487	0.482	109.372	0.00

Testing of Main Hypothesis

In order to have a deeper understanding of this theoretical framework and to answer the main research question is the integration of KM principles in support of RM processes, when applied to IT projects, may improve the organization's ability to manage risks response planning by enhancing risk identification, analysis, and mitigation. All the above factors were combined into a single one named ***Knowledge Based Risk*** then the aggregated data were analyzed using ANOVA. This approach helps us to identify how these factors all together will be significantly more important compared to each factor independently.

Referring to Table 15, 50% of the variance in Risk Monitoring accounted by Knowledge-Based Risk Update, the F value is 384.674 with a significance equal 0.00, which is less than 0.05. In this case, we reject the hypothesis, which indicates that there a positive impact to improve the organization's ability to manage the mitigate risks in IT projects.

Table 15. ANOVA test for knowledge management and risk management applied to IT projects

Dependent Variable	Independent variable	R	R Square	Adjusted R Square	F	Sig
Risk Management	Knowledge-Based Risk Identification + Knowledge-Based Risk Analysis + Knowledge-Based Risk Planning + Knowledge-Based Risk Monitoring	0.707	0.500	0.499	384.674	0.00

CONCLUSIONS AND RECOMMENDATIONS

This research has addressed the challenges facing organizations in the area of RM in IT projects. The findings validate the research questions by answering them as follows:

1. Knowledge-Based Risk Identify Source has a positive impact on scope establishment and risk identification. Therefore, the integration of KM and RM processes can form a valid KBRI.
2. Knowledge-Based Risk Verify Source has a positive impact on scope establishment and risk identification. Therefore, the integration of KM and RM processes can form a valid KBRV.

3. Knowledge-Based Risk Capture Source has a positive impact on scope establishment and risk identification. Therefore, the integration of KM and RM processes can form a valid KBRC.
4. Knowledge-Based Risk Discovery Source has a positive impact on scope establishment and risk identification. Therefore, the integration of KM and RM processes can form a valid KBRD.
5. Knowledge-Based Risk Education Source has a positive impact on scope establishment and risk identification. Therefore, the integration of KM and RM processes can form a valid KBRE.
6. Knowledge-Based Risk Rationalization has a positive impact on Risk Analysis. Therefore, the integration of KM and RM process can form a valid KBRR.
7. Knowledge-Based Risk Comprehension has a positive impact on Risk Analysis. Therefore, the integration of KM and RM process can form a valid KBRC.
8. Knowledge-Based Risk Examination has a positive impact on Risk Analysis. Therefore, the integration of KM and RM process can form a valid KBREx.
9. Knowledge-Based Risk Validation has a positive impact on Risk Analysis. Therefore, the integration of KM and RM process can form a valid KBRV.
10. Knowledge Sharing has a positive impact on risk analysis and planning. Therefore, the integration of KM and RM processes can form a valid KBRS.
11. Knowledge Evaluation has a positive impact on risk execution and risk monitoring. Therefore, the integration of KM and RM processes can form a valid KBRE.
12. Having live and dynamic integrated knowledge and risk repository is essential to the organization to execute RM. Therefore, the integration of KM and RM processes can form a valid KBRR.
13. The integration of KM and RM on IT projects has a positive impact to improve the organization's ability to manage the mitigate risks in IT projects.

In support of the hypothesis, the research validates the integration of KM in support of RM processes, when applied to IT projects, which improves the organization's ability to manage risk response planning by enhancing risk identification, analysis, and mitigation.

Although the findings are encouraging and useful, the present study has certain limitations. First, although we believe that risk Management is a universal fact and most countering approaches have common effects the results cannot be generalized because it considered only one developing country. Data from multiple areas are still recommended to exclude potential biases caused by cultural issues. Therefore, future studies would be geared towards reproducing this study across several other countries for comparative purposes.

Second, the variables used show that the correlation between knowledge-based Risk and risk identification is not higher, which leads to consider other variables for future studies such as the organization's ability to manage KM tools, techniques, technologies, and the culture of risks in IT projects.

Finally, interview has not been considered as research instrument, future research could be included to attain robust findings.

The findings of this research will suggest an adequate level of interest from both the KM and RM communities in the field of IT and encourage further investigation to address RM using KM tools and techniques. Implications will certainly help both academia researchers and practitioners to get a better understanding about the knowledge processes on Risk identification.

This study identified several determinants the challenges facing organizations in the area of RM in IT projects. Its t is important for managers to (1) create formal mechanisms that allow the integration of KM in support of RM processes, when applied to IT projects, which improves the organization's ability to manage risk response planning by enhancing risk identification. (2), Develop Knowledge-Based Risk Management System.

REFERENCES

Abdullah, R., Selamat, H., Sahibudin, S., & Alias, A. (2005, March). A Framework For Knowledge Management System Implementation In Collaborative Environment For Higher Learning Institution. *Journal of Knowledge Management Practice.* http://www.tlainc.com/articl83.htm

Agostini, A., Albolino, S., Boselli, R., De Michelis, G., De Pauli, F., & Dondi, R. (2003). Stimulating Knowledge Discovery and Sharing. In *International ACM SIGGROUP Conference on Supporting Group Work* (pp. 248–257). ACM Press.

Alavi, M., & Leidner, D. (2001). Review: Knowledge Management and Knowledge Management System: Conceptual Foundations and Research Issues. *Management Information Systems Quarterly*, *25*(1), 107–136.

Albers, A. (2003). Knowledge Management and the Innovation Process The Eco Innovation Model. *Journal of Knowledge Management Practice*.

Ali, M., & Ahmad, H. (2006). Knowledge Management in Malaysian Banks: A new Paradigm. *Journal of Knowledge Management Practice*, *7*(3).

Bakker, K., Boonstra, A., & Wortmann, H. (2010). Risk Management Affecting IS/IT Project SuccessThrough Communicative Action. *Project Management Journal*, *42*(3), 75–90.

Bannerman, L. (2008). Risk and risk management in software projects: A reassessment. *Journal of Systems and Software*, *81*(12), 2118–2133.

Bernanke, B. (2009, November 16). *The economic outlook.* Retrieved September 13, 2011, from Board of Governors of the Federal Reserve System (U.S.): https://www.federalreserve.gov/newsevents/speech/bernanke20091116a.htm

Bouthillier, F., & Shearer, K. (2002). Understanding knowledge management an information management: The need for an empirical perspective. *Information Research Journal*, *8*(1), 1–39.

Caldwell, F. (2008). Risk Intelligence: Applying KM to Information Risk Management. *Journal of VINE*, *38*(2), 163–166.

Choy, S., & Suk, Y. (2005). Critical Factors In The Successful Implementation Of Knowledge Management. *Journal of Knowledge Management Practice*.

Cornford, S. (1998). Managing risk as a resource using the defect detection and prevention process. *International Conference on Probabilistic Safety Assessment and Management*.

Costello, G. (1996). *Knowledge Management in Strategic alliances: The Role of Information Technology.* University of Oxford.

Cule, P., Schmidt, R., Lyyttnen, K., & Keil, M. (2000). Strategies for leading off is project failure. *Information Systems Management*, *14*(2), 68–73.

de Bakker, K. B. (2010). Does Risk Management Contribute to IT Project Success? A Meta-Analysis of Empirical Evidence. *International Journal of Project Management*, *28*(5), 493–503.

De la Vega, AF. R., & Stankosky, M. (2006). Knowledge Management And Innovation: What Must Governments Do To Increase Innovation? *Journal of Knowledge Management Practice, 7*(4).

Del Cano, A. D., & Cruz, M. P. (2002). Integrated Methodology for Project Risk Management. *Journal of Construction Engineering and Management*, *128*(6), 473–485. doi:10.1061/(ASCE)0733-9364(2002)128:6(473)

Deng, Q., & Yu, D. (2006). An Approach To Integrating Knowledge Management Into The Product Development Process. *Journal of Knowledge Management Practice*, *7*(2), 233–242.

Firestone, J. M. (2001). Key Issues in Knowledge Management. *Journal of Knowledge Management*, *1*(3), 8–38.

Fuller, M. A., Valacich, J. S., & George, J. F. (2008). *Information Systems Project*. Pearson Prentice Hall.

Gefen, D., & Straub, D. (1997). Gender differences in the perception & use of e-mail: Extension to the technologyacceptance model. *Management Information Systems Quarterly*, *21*(4), 389–400.

George, D., & Mallery, P. (2011). *IBM SPSS Statistics 19 Step by Step: A Simple Guide and Reference* (11th ed.). Pearson Education, Inc.

Gottschalk, P. (2002). Toward a Model of Growth Stages for Knowledge Management Technology in Law Firms. *Informing Science*, *5*(2), 79–93.

Holsapple, C., & Joshi, K. (2002). Knowledge Management: A Three-Fold Framework. *The Information Society*, *18*(1), 47–64.

Holsapple, C. W., & Joshi, K. D. (2004). A Formal Knowledge Management Ontology: Conduct, Activities, Resources, and Influences. *Journal of the American Society for Information Science and Technology*, *55*(7), 593–612.

Igbaria, M., & Toraskar, K. (1994). 'Impact of End-User Computing on the Individual: An Integrated Model. *Information Technology & People*, *6*(4), 271–292.

Institute, P. M. (2008). A Guide to the Project Management Body of Knowledge, PMBOK. Project Management Institute.

Intezari, A., Taskin, N., & Pauleen, D. J. (2017). Looking beyond: An integrative approach to knowledge management culture. *Journal of Knowledge Management*, *21*(2), 492–515.

Jennex, M. E. (2005). The Issue of System Use in Knowledge Management Systems. *The 38th Annual Hawaii International Conference*.

Johnson, J. (2009). *Chaos Sumary 2008*. The Standish Group Inc.

Kahn, B., & Adams, E. (2000). Sales forecasting as a Knowledge Management process. *The Journal of Business Forecasting*, 19-22.

Karadsheh, L., Mansour, E., AlHawari, S., Azar, G., & El-Bathy, N. (2009). A Theoretical Framework for Knowledge Management Process: Towards Improving Knowledge Performance. *Journal of Communications of the IBIMA*, 67-79.

Kayis, B., Zhou, M., Savci, S., Khoo, Y. B., Ahmed, A., & Kusumo, R. (2007). IRMAS-Development of a Risk Management Tool for Collaborative Multi- Site, Multi Partner New Product Development Projects New Product Development Projects. *Journal of Manufacturing Technology Management*, *18*(4), 387–414.

Kim, K., Lim, S., & Mitchell, B. (2004). Building A Knowledge Model: A Decision- Making Approach. *Journal of Knowledge Management Practice*, 5–11.

Knight, H. (1921). *Library of Economics & liberty*. Retrieved October 1, 2012, from Risk, Uncertainty and Profit: www.econlib.org/library/Knight/knRUP.html

Kutsch, E., & Hall, M. (2005). Intervening conditions on the management of project risk: Dealing with uncertainty in information technology projects. *International Journal of Project Management*, *23*, 591–599.

Lai, H. C. (2000). *Knowledge Management: A Review of TheoreticalFrameworks and Industrial Cases. In The 33rd Hawaii International Conference on System Sciences*. IEEE.

Lancioni, R. A., & Chandran, R. (2009). Managing knowledge in industrial markets: New dimensions and challenges. *Industrial Marketing Management*, *38*(2), 148–151.

Malhotra, Y. (2005). Integrating knowledge management technologies in organizational business processes: Getting real time enterprises to deliver real business performance. *Journal of Knowledge Management*, *9*(1), 7–28.

Management, A. f. (2006). *APM Body of Knowledge* (5th ed.). APM Publishing.

Marin-Garcia, J., & Zarate Martínez, E. (2007). A Theoretical Review of Knowledge Management and Teamworking in the Organizations. *International Journal of Management Science and Engineering Management*, *2*(4), 278–288.

Martin, E., DeHayes, D., Hoffer, J., & Perkins, W. (1991). *Managing Information Technology: What Managers Need To Know*. Maxwell Macmillan.

Massingham, P. (2010). Knowledge risk management: A framework. *Journal of Knowledge Management*, *14*(3), 464–485.

McKeen, D., Zack, H., & Singh, S. (2006). Knowledge Management and Organizational Performance: An Exploratory Survey. In *39th Hawaii International Conference on System Sciences* (pp. 1-9). IEEE.

Michael, S., Zhdanova, A., & Fensel, D. (2005). H-TechSight A Next Generation Knowledge Management Platform. *Journal of Information and Knowledge Management, 3*(1), 47-66.

Miles, F. a. (1998). Managing project risk and the performance envelope. In *The 13th Annual Applied Power Electronics Conference and Exposition.* Singapore: APEC.

Miltiadis, L., Pouloudi, A., & Poulymenakou, A. (2002). Knowledge management convergence expanding learning frontiers. *Journal of Knowledge Management*, *6*(1), 40–51.

Neef, D. (1997). *Making the case for knowledge management: The bigger picture.* Center for Business Innovation.

Neef, D. (2005). Managing Corporate Risk through Better Knowledge Management. *Journal of The Learning Organization*, *12*(2), 112–124.

Nehari-Talet, A., Alhawari, S., & Alryalat, H. (2010). The Effect Knowledge Process on Customer Knowledge Expansion. *The International Journal of Knowledge, Culture and Change Management*, *10*(2), 181–200.

Nissen, M., Kamel, M., & Sengupta, K. (2000). Integrated Analysis and Design of Knowledge Systems and Processes. *Information Resources Management Journal*, *13*(1).

Nonaka, I. (1994). A Dynamic Theory of Organizational Knowledge Creation. *Computer Science*, *5*(1).

Olsson, R. (2008). Risk Management in a Multi-Project Environment; An Approach to Manage Portfolio Risks. *International Journal of Quality & Reliability Management*, *25*(1), 60–71.

Parikh, M. (2001). Knowledge Management Framework for High –tech Research and Development. *Engineering Management Journal*, *13*(3), 27–34.

Perrott, B. E. (2007). A strategic risk approach to knowledge management. *Business Horizons*, *50*(6), 523–533.

Pinto, K. (2007). *Project management Achieving competitive advantage*. Pearson-Prentice Hall.

Project Management Institute. (2004). A Guide to the Project Management Body of Knowledge: PMBOK guide. Project Management Institute.

Rodriguez, E., & Edwards, J. S. (2008). Before and after modelling: Risk knowledge management is required. *Enterprise Risk Management Symposium Society of Actuaries,* 1-23.

Rodriguez-Montes, A., & Edwards, J. (2008). Before and after modeling: Risk knowledge management is required. Proceedings of 6th Annual Premier Global Event on ERM.

Roy, G. (2004). A risk management framework for software engineering practice. In *Australian Software Engineering Conference, (ASWEC'04)* (pp. 60-69). Australian Software Engineering Conference.

Saunders, M., Lewis, P., & Thornhill, A. (2012). Research Methods for Business Students (6th ed.). Pearson.

Scarbrough, H., Swan, J., & Preston, J. (1999). *Knowledge management A literature review*. Institute of Personnel and Development.

Schultze, U. (1998). Investigating the contradictions in knowledge management. *nternational. Journal of Computational Science*, 155–174.

Schwalbe, K. (2007). Information Technology Project Management (5th ed.). Course Technology Thomson Learning.

Shaw, J. (2005). Managing All your Enterprise's Risk. *Risk Management, 52*(9), 22–30.

Sommerville, I. (2006). Software Engineering (8th ed.). Addison-Wesley.

Stollberg, M., Zhdanova, V., & Fensel, D. (2004). H-TechSight-A Next Generation Knowledge Management Platform. *Journal of Information and Knowledge management, 3*(1), 47-66.

Sun, Z. (2004). A waterfall model for knowledge management and experience management. In *4th International Conference on Hybrid Intelligent Systems* (pp. 472-475). IEEE.

Sun, Z., & Gang, G. (2006). *HSM: A Hierarchical Spiral Model for Knowledge Management.* The 2nd International Conference on Information Management and Business, Sydney, Australia.

Sunassee, N., & Sewry, A. (2002). A Theoretical Framework for Knowledge Management Implementation. In *The 2002 annual research conference of the South African institute of computer scientists and information technologists on Enablement through technology* (pp. 235-245). South African Institute for Computer Scientists and Information Technologists.

Tesch, D., Kloppenborg, T., & Frolick, M. (2007). IT Project Risk Factors: The Project Management Professionals Perspective. *Journal of Computer Information Systems, 47*(4), 61–69.

Tohidinia, Z., & Mosakhani, M. (2010, April). Knowledge sharing behaviour and its predictors. *Industrial Management & Data Systems, 110*(4), 611–631.

Truman, E., & Baroudi, J. (1994). Gender differences in the information systems managerial ranks: An assessment of discriminatory practices. *Management Information Systems Quarterly, 18*(2), 129–141.

Voetsch, J., Cioffi, F., & Anbari, T. (2004). Project risk management practices and their association with reported project success. *6th IRNOP Project Research Conference*, 680–697.

Wang, Z., & Wang, N. (2012, August). Knowledge sharing, innovation and firm performance. *Expert Systems with Applications, 30*(10), 8899–8908.

Chapter 10
SMEs in the Face of Crisis:
The Supply Chain Risk Management Perspective

Susanne Durst
https://orcid.org/0000-0001-8469-2427
Tallinn University of Technology, Estonia

Lidia Davies
https://orcid.org/0000-0003-0428-1578
Tallinn University of Technology, Estonia

Wolfgang Dieter Gerstlberger
https://orcid.org/0000-0001-6200-5737
Tallinn University of Technology, Estonia

ABSTRACT

COVID-19 has shown how fragile our societies and economies are. Supply chains have particularly been affected. We all had to learn again that the basic supply of some goods is not as crisis-proof as we thought. Moreover, the strong division of labour and the concentration on a few companies in certain areas present considerable weaknesses in the case of a new external crisis such as the pandemic. Small and medium-sized enterprises (SMEs) have been affected by the current pandemic, particularly as they are highly sensitive to external threats. Using data collected between December 2020 and January 2021 through semi-structured interviews conducted with owners and/or managers of SMEs located in six different European countries (i.e., Austria, Estonia, Germany, Greece, Italy, and Portugal), the chapter aims to provide fresh perspectives on how SMEs address supply chain risk management in times of an external and dynamic crisis.

DOI: 10.4018/978-1-7998-9715-6.ch010

Copyright © 2022, IGI Global. Copying or distributing in print or electronic forms without written permission of IGI Global is prohibited.

INTRODUCTION

The strong division of labour and the concentration of a few companies in certain business segments present considerable weaknesses for national economies in the event of an external crisis. Small and medium-sized enterprises (SMEs) face particular challenges in external crises, as they are highly sensitive to external threats (Doern, Williams, & Vorley, 2019; Herbane, 2018; Guan et al., 2020). For example, in the Covid-19 crisis, the flaws of the crisis and risk management approaches utilized in these companies quickly became apparent (Durst & Henschel, 2021), namely, being primarily based on known and past data. From a more general perspective, in an uncertain environment, firm-specific resources are likely to be further dispersed when different types of disruption caused by an external crisis occur simultaneously (Osiyevskyy, Shirokova, & Ritala, 2020), which in turn further restricts the possible scope for action.

Against this background, the authors of this chapter see a clear need to advance the understanding of how SMEs cope with the current uncertain, but at the same time very dynamic, situation concerning supply chain risks. More precisely, the particular interest is in obtaining an understanding of how SMEs handle their supply chains in increasingly uncertain times. Even before the current Covid-19 crisis, supply chains were exposed to a great number of risks; these being triggered by a multitude of developments, such as the increasing digitalization, pressure for (more) sustainable management, and connectivity of supply chains, but also by political instability and the aggressive actions of big players in the marketplace. This situation makes both supply chains and the risks associated with them very promising and timely research subjects. Supply chain risk management (SCRM) is intended to reduce an organization's vulnerability from risks (Wieland & Wallenburg, 2012).

This chapter aims to provide fresh perspectives on how SMEs address supply chain risk management in times of an external crisis. The data for this paper was collected between December 2020 and January 2021 through semi-structured interviews conducted with owners and/or managers of SMEs located in six different European countries (i.e., Austria, Estonia, Germany, Greece, Italy, and Portugal). The SMEs under investigation are of varying size and represent different business segments. Taking this spectrum into account, the authors provide insights into differences and similarities among the SMEs involved.

The chapter is organised as follows. In the initial section, the relevant literature is described. This is followed by a section that presents and describes the methodology chosen. Then the findings are collated and analysed; at the end the authors have included a brief conclusion.

BACKGROUND

Recent literature on SMEs' SCRM indicates that the increasing fragility of SMEs' supply chains and SCRM is one of the dominant topics for research (e.g., Campos, de Andrade Lima, da Silva, & Fernandes, 2019; Fischer-Preßler, Eismann, Pietrowski, Fischbach, & Schoder, 2020; Hoek, 2020; Ivanov & Das, 2020). Factors behind this academic trend include the increased organizational and geographical complexity of supply chains (e.g., increasing number of partners/interactions and locations) as well as intensified inter-organizational sharing of digital data and imbalanced bargaining power for SMEs in (global) supply chains. Furthermore, several scholars note increasing political and economic uncertainty, which in turn influences SCRM in SMEs (e.g., Ferreira De Araújo Lima, Crema, & Verbano, 2020). Chowdhury, Paul, Kaisar, and Moktadir (2021) found that the global pandemic has further exacerbated the otherwise increasing number of supply chain risks, in particular, for SMEs.

Moreover, recent studies highlight the avoidance of uncertainty among managers as an influence on SCRM. For example, Huo, Guo, and Cheng (2019) demonstrated that managers' risk preferences influence their companies' actual risk levels. In addition, Sato, Tse, and Tan (2020) showed that managers' risk perceptions in SCRM are highly context-dependent. This latter finding refers not only to variations between different companies, but also to intra-organisational differences in term of divisions and management levels. Finally, Tse, Zhang, Zeng, and Ma (2021) investigated the related topic of supply chain quality risk. Based on their quantitative study, these authors suggested a validated conceptual model for managers in the field of SCRM with a focus on quality risk, technology uncertainty, traceability uncertainty, product complexity, and supply market conditions.

This increase in supply chain risks relates to all kinds of risks (Chu, Park, & Kremer, 2020; Parast & Subramanian, 2021), such as human risks (e.g., missing/inadequate competencies of employees or managers), technological risks (e.g., risks related to cybercrime or digitalization risks in general), and operational risks (e.g., relational risk due to dissatisfactory cooperation among supply chain partners) (see Durst & Zieba, 2019). Additionally, the classical market (e.g., strong supply and/or demand fluctuations), financial (e.g., payment loss/delay) and geographical long-distance supply chain risks have overall increased (e.g., Fernández Campos, Trucco, & Huaccho Huatuco, 2019; Grondys, ŚLusarczyk, Hussain, & Androniceanu, 2021).

Compared to the past, more recent SCRM literature distinguishes increasing risks in relation to national and industrial contexts, as well as firm size (i.e., micro, small, medium-sized) (Păunescu & Mátyus, 2020; Chowdhury et al., 2021). The national context, e.g., SCRM regulations of a given country, can influence SME supply chain risks. At the same time, SMEs with a strong dependence on international import and/or export links are in an especially vulnerable situation. By contrast, industry context refers to industry-specific regulations and risks. There are clear signs that the market and financial risks for SMEs in different industries have developed with different trajectories in recent years.

Notwithstanding the studies mentioned above, research on SCRM in SMEs is decidedly limited. Furthermore, the few studies available mostly do not differentiate between micro, small and medium-sized enterprises (with the exception of the work by Grondys et al. (2021)). Using an SME survey data from Poland, Grondys et al. (2021, p.16) noted that "risk management requires from these entities the awareness, identification, planning, and counteracting threats, which they have not dealt with so far". The authors further assume (e.g., as a starting point for further research) that in medium-sized enterprises, more "detailed management processes concerning risk are carried out" (Grondys et al., 2021, p.15), while smaller SMEs follow a more pragmatic, short-term approach. In the overall picture, financial aspects regarding risk management seem to be more important for micro companies than for small and medium-sized enterprises.

Regarding technological risk management, Fischer-Preßler et al. (2020) pointed out one central conclusion in their review of the literature that the role of IT in identifying, analysing, and monitoring supply chain risks has been neglected thus far. Regarding operational risk management, Li, Fan, Lee, and Cheng (2015) identified "risk information sharing and risk sharing mechanism" in SME supply chains as crucial factors for successful supply chain cooperation. These two factors are closely related to a trusting relationship between supply chain partners. They are a precondition for sharing critical risk-related information about possible vulnerabilities in the supply chain as a whole, or between single SME supply chain partners.

The reviewed studies not only analyse supply chain risks and develop tools for measuring them, but they also suggest potential practical solutions. In particular, a holistic assessment framework for companies' SCR (balanced operational, social and environmental risk view) (Xu et al., 2019) and a combined "fragility and robustness" framework (Wieland & Wallenburg, 2021) for SCRM seem to be adequate for use in SMEs. The advantages of the suggested frameworks are that they can be flexibly applied (depending on a given company's market condition) in different industries (see also the "checklist" at the end of this chapter that may support SME managers in their SCRM activities). This checklist and the aforementioned practical frameworks are complementary and partly overlapping.

METHODOLOGY

Considering the underdeveloped research on SCRM in SMEs, a qualitative research approach appeared to be appropriate. A qualitative approach allows researchers to get closer to the participants and their way of thinking to scrutinize the entire research problem in depth (Maykut & Morehouse, 1994). The present study is part of an ongoing Erasmus+ project called "SMEs: Be Prepared for Supply Chain Risks" that aims to better prepare SMEs for identifying and handling supply chain risks. This project consists of six partner countries namely Austria, Estonia, Germany, Greece, Italy and Portugal. In total, 28 small firms representing different categories of SMEs participated in the study (Table 1). For the purposes of the study, the SME definition of the Commission of the European Communities (2003) was adopted. Accordingly, a firm can be classified as micro, small or medium-sized depending on staff headcount, turnover, and balance sheet.

Table 1. Overview of companies involved in the study

Interview N	Company size	Industry/Sector	Country
Company 1	Medium	Software engineering and consulting	Austria 1
Company 2	Small	Medical equipment (R&D)	Austria 2
Company 3	Medium	Measurement technology	Austria 3
Company 4	Small	Trading company	Austria 4
Company 5	Small	Security service provider	Austria 5
Company 6	Micro	Food production	Estonia 1
Company 7	Micro	Packaging	Estonia 2
Company 8	Medium	Retail solutions	Estonia 3
Company 9	Micro	Steel production and sales	Estonia 4
Company 10	Medium	Retail	Germany 1
Company 11	Medium	Retail	Germany 2
Company 12	Medium	Logistics	Germany 3
Company 13	Medium	IT Services	Germany 4
Company 14	Medium	Clothes manufacturing	Germany 5
Company 15	Medium	Producer of industrial sensors	Germany 6
Company 16	Small	Logistics	Greece 1
Company 17	Medium	Logistics	Greece 2
Company 18	Small	Wholesale	Greece 3

Continued on following page

Table 1. Continued

Interview N	Company size	Industry/Sector	Country
Company 19	Micro	Construction/ Building renovation and refurbishing	Italy 1
Company 20	Micro	Construction	Italy 2
Company 21	Small	Event management	Italy 3
Company 22	Medium	Sanitary ceramic	Italy 4
Company 23	Medium	Sanitary ceramic	Italy 5
Company 24	Small	Paper transformation	Portugal 1
Company 25	Small	Engineering/Plastic injection moulding	Portugal 2
Company 26	Small	Transport consulting	Portugal 3
Company 27	Small	Wastewater treatment	Portugal 4
Company 28	Medium	Moulding and Plastic Injection	Portugal 5

Table 1 underlines that a heterogeneous sample of SMEs in terms of size and industry was involved in this study. In practice, therefore, the selected SME sample reflects the different socio-economic and industrial structures of the six involved partner countries (European Commission, 2021).

Regarding Austria, specific business segments (e.g., measurement technology) were in particular important for the selection of the national SME cases. The Estonian sub-sample represents the dominance of microenterprises in this country. In contrast, the composition of the German subsample was influenced by the strong role of bigger (medium) SMEs for the country's economy. In Austria and in Greece, specific business segments (particularly logistics) strongly influenced the selection of those national SME sub-samples. The composition of the Italian SME sub-sample reflects the industrial heterogeneity of the country with strong manufacturing and service sectors. Likewise, for the Portuguese sub-sample, the selection was determined by the existence of strong manufacturing and service sectors.

Data was collected through semi-structured interviews conducted with the managing directors or owners of the firms. An interview guide supported the interview process. The guide focused upon the following points: some general facts about the companies and their operations and some more specific issues about the companies and their approaches to SCRM. The data was collected online between December 2020 and January 2021; thus, a period in which half of the participating countries experienced lockdowns of varying degrees.

The authors utilized the tenets of thematic analysis as detailed by Fereday and Muir-Cochrane (2006) to analyse the collected data. According to these authors, thematic analysis is the search for the primary themes that seem to be most important after an initial analysis. This analytical approach is appropriate to segment, categorize, and summarize relevant ideas within the dataset as well (Ayress, 2008).

FINDINGS

Considering the period of data collection, the general risk exposure among the interviewees was focused on COVID-19-related risk. The risks reported by the interviewees are summarized in Table 2.

Table 2. SMEs risk exposure

Type of risk	Supply Chain risks reported by interviewees
Financial risk	Sharp decline in profit (Interviewees 6, 8, 9, 16, 18, 19, 21) due to industry freeze (HORECA, tourism, event management, etc.)
	Risk of non-collection of customers' payments that restrict business operations (Interviewees 8, 9, 18) The highest risk now is that the customer does not pay. Then we haven`t enough room [i.e., liquidity]. Nowadays our target is to produce our invoices very quickly and when the payments are late, we always call and send emails because of the invoice. (Interviewee 9)
	Risk of bankruptcy/loss of potential investor (Interviewee 1, 21) In the current moment the main risk is financial equilibrium. We are in a value chain that was completely disrupted by the pandemic. We were forced to change the way we do business. (Interviewee 21)
Market risk	Sharp decline in demand (Interviewees 4, 9, 6, 21)
	Raw material price fluctuation (Interviewees 22, 23) due to unstable and unpredictable supply The main vulnerability is that the origin of most of our raw materials is outside Italy. This exposes us to the risks of price fluctuation as well as potential disruption in the value chain. Furthermore, raw materials must show a specific quality; otherwise, the quality of the final products will be influenced. Our production plant works on a continuous cycle, and a shortcoming of raw materials, or even a reduction of quantities available, increases the risk of not fulfilling the demand or of running out of budget for the production. (Interviewee 22)
	The risk of losing important client(s) became more crucial for business sustainability during the pandemic (Interviewees 4, 9, 21, 24)
	Strong price competition (Interviewees 21, 22, 23, 24) The main risks are related to the difficult market, the stagnating demand, and the competition from low cost producers. (Interviewee 21)
Operational risk	High dependency on resellers and lack of ability to contact/influence end consumers (Interviewees 22, 23)
	Lack of personnel critical for maintaining operations: availability and health safety (Interviewees 6, 9, 18, 19, 24) A little bit - it hasn`t happened to us, but as we are a small collective, a small company there is the danger of sickness, because there is no replacement. We have to wait two weeks, that was a very big problem. (Interviewee 9)
	"Flawed" communication within the company and within the supply chain due to lack of personal contact (Interviewees 7, 8, 19, 21, 28) It's really bad right because you have to explain, you have to convince, you have to be trustworthy. (Interviewee 7)
Supply chain risk	Significant delays in supply or supply disruptions (Interviewees 2, 4, 10, 11, 12, 15, 19, 20) There are a lot of suppliers from abroad… and you have to be able to deliver relatively quickly and in the time like now, when a part is missing, then production is at a standstill and that is of course very critical for the company. (Interviewee 2)
	Increasingly complicated and costly logistics (Interviewees 7, 11)
	Keeping stock in "equilibrium": problems with "overstocked" warehouses because clients were unable to pick up their orders due to mobility restrictions (Interviewees 16, 17) or problems with receiving enough supplies (Interviewees 2, 4, 7, 11, 12, 19, 20) We try to avoid being short on stock… On average, suppliers take one day to accept the order. Today, it also takes three days to send the order. It is a standard time now. It happens due to COVID. (Interviewee 20)
	Unsatisfactory quality of supply; has become an even bigger problem due to mobility restrictions (i.e., no possibility to physically evaluate the quality of products) (Interviewees 7, 8, 19)
Regulatory risk	New regulations and restrictions that affected operations to a differing extent: from limiting operations to full stop of business activities (Interviewees 8, 15, 16, 17, 18, 21) Governmental rules change too often, due to the trends of the pandemic, and are very complex to interpret. (Interviewee 21)

Continued on following page

Table 2. Continued

Type of risk	Supply Chain risks reported by interviewees
Knowledge risk	Risk of unintentional "knowledge" spillovers due to remote work and communication via social media (Interviewee 3)
	Complicated learning process, especially for those companies who needs to learn on production site (Interviewee 7) The average learning process is about two years. It is complicated to know the materials for production, and this is something that we are really missing now because we cannot visit the companies. (Interviewee 7)
	The low level of internal knowledge sharing became clear when companies started considering job rotation due to lack of workforce (Interviewees 1, 28)
Digital risk	Increased "sensitivity" to cyber security risks due to the increased number of digital operations (Interviewees 4, 5, 24, 28)
	Integration problems between different data management software became more visible due to the increased number of digital operations (Interviewee 25)
	Reliability of IT infrastructure to handle new tasks has become an issue (Interviewee 24)

Risk exposures that were apparently common for all types of SMEs were concerns regarding supply and demand volatility (e.g., customer demand, stocking challenges) and supply chain disruption (e.g., logistics problems, raw material price fluctuation). The types of risk are not necessarily new, of course, because SMEs are traditionally subject to changing market factors and increased competition and often supplied by a single chain of suppliers. However, the findings suggest that COVID-19 magnified the perception of conventional risks to an extreme level.

Otherwise, some types of risk appear to be more dependent on factors such as geography and the size of the company. For example, policy-related risks varied according to the regulations and restrictions of a given country. In some countries where the restrictions were minor (Estonia, Germany, and Austria), the regulatory risks were considered low. In countries where complete lockdown was introduced (Greece), regulatory risk was a dominant factor:

During the pandemic period, the company was closed for more than 3 months. The clients completed their orders only online. The warehouse of the company until now is full because the delivery company cannot plan and organise the distribution. The company has stopped online orders until the warehouse can host more goods. We are waiting for new regulations from the ministry on how we can proceed with delays. (Interviewee 18)

Regarding specific industries, companies involved in the international trade of medical and cosmetics products were affected by new COVID-related regulations (e.g., Germany, Italy).

We organise events (for medical personnel), and they were forbidden by the government from the very beginning of the lockdown in March. Plus, most - if not all - of our events were targeted at doctors, and half of them used hospitals, hotels, and conference centres. However, governmental rules change too often - due to the trends of the pandemic - and are very complex to interpret. We have to become familiar with the COVID safety protocol for our events. However, the number of exceptions in the planning phase of events increased dramatically. (Interviewee 21)

Overall, when detailing supply chain risk exposure, the owners/managers of micro companies tended to focus on a short-term perspective, i.e., they sought to maintain their operational routine and immediate financial liquidity. For small and medium-sized firms, on the other hand, the focus appears to have shifted to strategic issues and a long-term perspective (e.g., new competitive and sourcing strategies, as well as the consequences of new laws and regulations).

APPROACHES TO SUPPLY CHAIN RISK MANAGEMENT

On the basis of the findings, the SCRM among the companies might be characterized in two ways: simple and sophisticated. The simple form of SCRM was essentially a reactive approach. Therefore, preventive measures to prepare for operational delays and problems were not prepared in advance but were initiated once a given risk occurred. On the contrary, the sophisticated approach, which was more common among medium-sized companies, utilized an organized and dedicated set of policies, rules, and guidelines that were already in place to handle different business challenges.

The person or unit in charge of identifying and analysing risks was also heavily influenced by the size of the company. In micro-enterprises, risk was assessed directly by the owner (Interviewees 6, 7, 9, 19, 20). In small companies, this task was carried out by partners/co-owners or board members (Interviewees 2, 4, 5, 16, 18, 21, 24, 25, 27) while in medium companies, risk assessment was handled by management, that is, owners / managers and heads of departments, collectively (Interviewees 1, 3, 8, 10, 11, 12, 13, 14, 15, 17, 22, 23, 28).

The major distinction of small and micro enterprises regarding the relevance of SCRM was that these smaller companies considered a systematic approach unnecessary. Bearing in mind the limited financial and human resources as well as the low probability of reoccurrence of the same types of risk, the owners/managers of these firms preferred to take quick responsive measures to handle the risk, rather than to have them prepared in advance (Interviewees 4, 6, 7, 10, 11, 19, 20). As one interviewee described it, "We are not practicing crisis scenarios. If something happens, we will decide what to do in order to maintain operations" (Interviewee 6).

Unsurprisingly, medium-sized enterprises employed more developed forms of preventive risk measures, including risk maps and signalling systems to visualize and systematically assess risks and their relevance, impact, and probability (Interviewees 1, 9, 13, 14, 24, 25). For those companies that followed ISO standards, this approach was determined by adherence to those standards. The following statements may illustrate the typical approach for companies following ISO standards.

To ensure the high quality of services and to be prepared for risks, the company is certified according to several standards (e.g., ISO 9001, ISO 27001) and has developed its own risk management system inspired by ISO 31000 with a business continuity logic. The firm has a risk board which meets monthly. The members are the managing director, the head of quality management, the heads of units, and an external consultant. The board systematically identifies business risk including supply chain risks, carries out a business impact analysis, and prepares measures. (Interviewee 13)

As mentioned above, the approach to SCRM differed according to the size of the company. The majority of medium-sized companies had a systematic approach to SCRM (Interviewees 1, 3, 12, 13, 14, 15, 22, 23, 28). By contrast, the majority of micro and small companies seem to have adopted a "problem-solving" (ad hoc) approach (Interviewees 2, 4, 5, 6, 7, 8, 16, 18, 19, 20, 21, 25). It seems that the latter used risk management techniques according to the main business challenges at hand. The main similarities between small businesses seem to be found in terms of securing trustworthy and stable supply chain relationships, as well as ensuring safe and secure business operating environments. Table 3 details the steps the firms studied took to handle different types of SC risks.

Table 3. Risk management initiatives in SMEs

Initiatives	Specific Steps	Interviewee Examples
Develop a strong and reliable network within the supply chain	Careful selection of suppliers and partners: preference for suppliers with similar values and long-term relationship strategy (Interviewees 14, 19, 20, 21, 22)	A major SC risk is the loss or dependence on a supplier. Therefore, the firm selects (potential) suppliers very carefully and visits them regularly. Policy is a long-term collaboration, and the management looks for family-owned businesses with similar values. (Interviewee 14)
	Establish trust and mutual support with suppliers to minimize risks and financial losses (Interviewees 19, 21, 22, 23)	Experience and a good relationship with our historical business partners help reduce these risks. In particular, communication with business partners is crucial to be aware of potential risks and avoid them as much as possible. (Interviewee 21) Reputation of suppliers is another positive factor. With "trusted" suppliers, we know that we can work quickly and with a high-quality standard. (Interviewee 19) The packaging business is very personal because it involves enormous trust, and trust that you can only gain from personal meetings (Interviewee 7)
	Increasing share of local or short-distance suppliers (Interviewees 7, 11)	To reduce dependency on suppliers, e.g., for whiteboard production…, we are aiming to bring back as much of production to Germany as economically feasible, working with long-term contract manufacturing partners. (Interviewee 11) When products are not made close to each other, the advantage for local producers is now greater than before. Language barriers are very big in our business because even terms that should be international are not understood in the same way in different countries. (Interviewee 7)
	Enforcement of a code of conduct and overall quality and sustainability strategy (Interviewee 14)	The fashion firm has defined a Code of Conduct binding all business partners, which defines requirements for suppliers and partners… Among other things, the Code of Conduct contributes to compliance with social and ethical standards, sustainable environmental protection, and ensures fair working conditions. (Interviewee 14)
	Implementing suppliers' check-ups: quality assurance and process improvement (Interviewees 7, 14)	We perform regular quality checks and audits of suppliers. (Interviewee 14)
Taking measures to ensure continuous operation	Ensuring stock safety: redundancy strategy for suppliers of important products, extra stocking to avoid out-of-stock situations (Interviewees 10, 11, 12, 13, 14, 15, 20)	Parallel with these measures, the firm develops alternative vendors for critical products or prospects for possible alternative suppliers. (Interviewee 14) We try to maintain our own buffer stock to ensure close to 100% availability. (Interviewee 10) We buffer stock in decentralized offices and in the central warehouse and have a dual vendor strategy for important parts. (Interviewee 13)
	Setting up "loose" delivery dates for end-customers to compensate logistics delays (Interviewee 8, 19)	A good planning of the project and a good planning of extra time help compensate for potential suppliers' shipment issues. (Interviewee 19)
	Organizing internal delivery services to ensure parts delivery on time (Interviewee 13)	We organized parts delivery to the offices by own vehicles and drivers. (Interviewee 13)

Continued on following page

Table 3. Continued

Initiatives	Specific Steps	Interviewee Examples
Taking actions to mitigate financial risks	Diversify the client pool to decrease dependency on a single client/industry (Interviewees 6, 15, 28)	As every company in plastic injection, there is considerable dependence on the automotive industry, but we have been trying to diversify the customer base to decrease a high customer concentration risk. (Interviewee 28)
	Concluding NDA contacts with suppliers (Interviewees 2, 15, 27)	Even if machines are patented, certain information should not spill over to competitors, especially process knowledge which is difficult to patent. All possible agreements (e.g., NDAs) are made with the respective suppliers to prevent unwanted spillover or leakage. (Interviewee 2)
Taking steps to develop a risk-conscious culture and organizational defence	Organizing training for staff in the following domains: quality standards (Interviewee 16, 18); ethical standards (Interviewee 3); process improvement (Interviewee 7); "sensitive data" protection (Interviewee 3)	It is important for the employees and the company to follow the technology and methodologies of the supply chain and address the risks. (Interviewee 18)
	Organizing risk awareness events: risk assessment and mitigation training (Interviewees 1, 3, 12); Risk mitigation brainstorming (Interviewee 17)	There have been regular awareness training sessions for employees at least once a year for new employees when they were hired, and then regular updates every year. There have been repeated mailings to the employees, such as newsletters, which summarized some of the most diverse risks. (Interviewee 1)
	Developing personalized data access, i.e., linked to the employee profile and functional responsibilities (Interviewees 5, 25, 28)	These days every employee has a profile that allows him to access only what he supposed to for performing his function. (Interviewee 28)
Taking actions to protect data	Multiple encryption solutions (Interviewee 5) and multi-factor authentication (Interviewees 5, 24, 25, 26) and various email protection systems, certificates of emails, backup systems, and VPN tunnels for remote access (Interviewees 1, 5, 27)	We have processes in a quality management system for the project archive. Some of the projects are stored in a vault with very strict access. They are very cautious with the application of GPRD. Increasingly, projects are subject to NDAs. (Interviewee 26) Technologically, several things are used to protect the data and the customers' data. Classification, multiple encryption solutions, multiple multifactor authentication, different email protection systems, certificates of the emails, backup systems, and multiple locations of the backup systems and the data. (Interviewee 5)
Taking measures to protect intellectual property	Concluding the NDA with employees and suppliers (Interviewees 2, 15, 25, 27, 28) and patenting newly developed technology (Interviewee 25, 27)	Unwanted knowledge spillover can happen all the time in SCs. Legal measures are difficult to enforce, especially for SMEs and in foreign countries, and it takes time to build a sufficient level of trust. (Interviewee 2) When having developed something really innovative, the company patents it before going to the market." (Interviewee 25)

From the table above, one can conclude that several companies adopted initiatives that ensure stable SC and continuous operations. To a lesser extent, there were instances in which companies took specific steps to handle financial risks, promote a more risk-aware organizational culture, and secure data/IP in increasingly remote working environments.

PERCEIVED BENEFITS OF A SYSTEMATIC APPROACH TO RISK MANAGEMENT

Companies without systematic risk management appear to be preoccupied with maintaining continuous operations and adjusting business processes to meet daily challenges. It moreover appears that businesses that chose to adopt a systematic approach to risk management were more confident to manage operations risk and less prone to halt work since they had an action plan in place to mitigate risks. These companies apparently had more time to revise their strategy, improve their production process and quality control, and innovate. Whatever the causes, they were able to treat risk as an opportunity rather than as an immediate threat.

Specifically, those businesses with a systematic risk management program in place had the resources to focus on sustainable growth and development, i.e., to develop responsible business practices (ethical standards, code of conduct, "best practice," anti-corruption policies, etc.) They were able to devote attention to innovation development, product quality, and performance improvement. In addition, companies had resources to pay more attention to personnel development, that is, to develop new required competencies. The following Table 4 charts the concrete benefits of systematic risk management cited by the interviewees.

Table 4. Perceived benefits of systematic risk management

Perceived benefits of RM	Interviewee Examples
Visibility of risks and growing awareness among employees leads to gradual development of risk learning culture (Interviewee 4, 25)	When we see the problem, we can deal with it. When we do not evaluate the risk, we don't know that something is wrong, and then when something happened, we have a big problem. Visualisation with the different colours is helpful. (Interviewee 4) The identification and assessment of risks are carried out in a matrix. Considering the Quality and Innovation policy, objectives are defined and actions are taken to achieve the goals, as well as the steps needed to address the risks identified in the matrix. (Interviewee 25)
Established risk culture support decentralized decision-making (Interviewee 1)	Many decisions are in the hands of employees, only sometimes is management involved. (Interviewee 1)
The use of historical data helps to develop a reliable supply chain network (Interviewee 19) and reduce dependence on the supplier (Interviewee 14)	Adequate and proactive risk management reduced supplier dependency and ensured a better overview of the supply chain, including having alternative sourcing options in case of a delay or interruption in the supply chain. (Interviewee 14)
Systematic risk management ensures flawless operations and mitigates operational risks (Interviewees 14, 23) and resulted in improved performance (Interviewee 12)	Good risk management lowers the cases of an interruption… and improves the overall performance of the company. (Interviewee 12)
Systematic risk management promotes data-driven decision-making (Interviewee 23)	To manage risks related to the assembly line, the company has invested in a continuous reporting system that can provide timely and accurate data on the assembly line. operational processes. Such a system helps the chief production officer and the quality manager to mitigate operational risks. (Interviewee 23)
The company builds a reputation as a reliable partner and maintains consistently high quality of the product (Interviewees 3, 10, 14)	Continuous risk management and risk monitoring reduced delays caused by missing stock of products. Moreover, the risk of products not in compliance with current local regulations and the delays caused are minimized. The resulting high delivery reliability is highly valued by the customers. (Interviewee 10) An adequate risk management reduces out of stock situations and delays. In addition, the high quality of the products can be maintained. (Interviewee 14)

Continued on following page

Table 4. Continued

Perceived benefits of RM	Interviewee Examples
The risk of knowledge loss and spill over is monitored and minimized (Interviewees 5, 15, 25, 27, 28)	Due to good risk management, the company could reduce the risk of knowledge loss, and increased diversification and reduction of the dependence on certain customers reduced the market risks. (Interviewee 15) The company makes use of nondisclosure agreements to safeguard the interests of both the organization and its customers. Such agreements may be extended to integrate other entities into the process, like universities or rarely, but possible, when complex systems are at stake, suppliers. (Interviewee 25)
The data exchange within supply chain perceived as "protected" (Interviewee 15)	Furthermore, the introduction of a highly developed security system greatly decreased the risks of cyberattacks and increased the trust of the partners that their shared data are safe. (Interviewee 15)

SOLUTIONS AND RECOMMENDATIONS

Given the findings presented above, the authors have developed a checklist that may support small businesses in their efforts with respect to SCRM. More precisely, the purpose of the checklist is to provide a set of guidelines that may facilitate SMEs seeking to improve their approaches to SCRM. This can also be referenced for supply chain members.

1. The company is aware of the relevance of having implemented a risk management approach/certain crucial risk management measure. Risk management is a top priority for the company and is firmly anchored in the firm's overall business strategy.
2. This risk management approach/measures does/do consider a variety of risks, i.e., financial and non-financial ones.
3. The company continuously monitors current risks, but also ensures that it is aware of new risks.
4. Current risks are made visible to all members of the organization, using dashboards or risk maps.
5. The company has a good understanding of how to analyse the potential severity of the risk at hand.
6. Depending on the type of risk (financial versus non-financial or internal versus external), the company has some countermeasures in place and is ready to introduce these measures to cope with risks at hand.
7. The company continuously monitors the outcomes of the measures introduced and takes countermeasures in the case the measures do not perform as expected, i.e., do not meet the objectives set (e.g., reducing the danger of business disruptions due to turnover).
8. The company reports the critical risks, their management, and development over time, and thereby learns to better cope with a multitude of different types of risk.
9. The risk management process is laid down in the company's day-to-day business operations, and every organization member is aware of his/her role in addressing present and future risks.
10. The company regularly trains its organization members to be informed about the latest and most recent risks that can hamper business operations.

CONCLUSION

The aim of this chapter is to provide fresh insight into how SMEs address supply chain risk management in times of external crisis. Linking the empirical findings with the relevant literature one can conclude the following.

First, the present study clearly confirms that the global pandemic exacerbated the increasing fragility of SMEs' SCRM for all types of investigated risks. Furthermore, interorganizational trust has become even more important for the SCRM management of SMEs during the pandemic (e.g., Grondys et al., 2021).

Second, the findings allow one to draw a more differentiated picture of supply chain risk exposure and SCRM in different groups of SMEs, compared to the small stock of relevant literature. Such differences refer in the first place to the identification of a simple, more ad hoc SCRM approach without preventive measures in micro and small enterprises versus a more systematic and organized SCRM approach which is more common in medium-sized enterprises.

In this context of different size groups, the findings also stress that there is not something like a 'generic SCRM toolbox' for SMEs (c.f., Durst, 2012). The findings rather showed that tailored SCRM approaches are needed that consider both the internal environment like ownership and management structure as well as the skills and competences (e.g., Păunescu & Mátyus, 2020) and the external environment such as the institutional setting (Thukral, 2021) of the respective SME. Regarding the latter, the present study further detailed and illustrated the importance of specific national and industry contexts for SCRM in SMEs. These contexts not only comprise governmental regulations (e.g., legal or administrative rules), but can also be influenced by the increasing importance of voluntary environmental, social, and ethical standards for SCRM in SMEs (see, e.g., Ferreira de Araújo Lima et al., 2020). When considering organizational preparedness to future crises, these considerations will be essential for SMEs to ensure sustainable business operations.

From a practical point of view, SME managers/owners may benefit from the examples presented in this chapter to improve their own approach to SCRM considering a given company's internal and external environments. Additionally, they can also review the consequences of a negligent attitude toward SCRM, which may lead to increased supply chain disruption and increased company vulnerability. Eventually, the checklist may also facilitate the SCRM-related efforts.

Finally, the main limitations of this study need to be considered. The qualitative data collection for this study took place during the period between December 2020 and January 2021. During that time half of the involved countries, namely Austria, Greece and Italy, experienced strict lockdown regulations. During a later period, e.g., after these major lockdowns, some of the interview results from those countries could have been different to some degree. In addition, the qualitative data collection for this study was limited to a certain selection of six EU countries. A different sample of involved countries also could have resulted in (partly) different study results. The number of interviews per country for this study was limited and, in general, the data collection for this study was confined to semi-structured interviews. Alternative approaches to data collection might have yielded different study results.

The limitations of the present study may inspire future studies in the field of SCRM at SMEs. Potential research may, for example, apply mixed-methods and/or longitudinal research designs. Moreover, future studies could be conducted with a different mix of EU and/or other countries. c Involving large-sized businesses as a point of comparison is another pathway that will ultimately enrich our knowledge of SCRM and how to improve these business processes.

ACKNOWLEDGMENT

The authors greatly acknowledge the financial support from the European Union's Erasmus+ Programme under Project Reference: 2020-1-EE01-KA202-077891. The authors further greatly acknowledge the efforts of the other partners in this project as otherwise this publication would not have been possible.

REFERENCES

Ayress, L. (2008). Thematic Coding and Analysis. In L. M. Given (Ed.), *The SAGE Encyclopedia of Qualitative Research Methods* (Vol. 1, pp. 868–868). SAGE Publications. doi:10.4135/9781412963909.n451

Campos, D. F., de Andrade Lima, J. T. Jr, da Silva, A. B., & Fernandes, A. J. (2019). Professional competencies in supply chain management in the mid-sized supermarket sector in Brazil. *Supply Chain Management*, *24*(3), 405–416. doi:10.1108/SCM-02-2018-0081

Chowdhury, P., Paul, S. K., Kaisar, S., & Moktadir, M. A. (2021). COVID-19 pandemic related supply chain studies: A systematic review. *Transportation Research Part E, Logistics and Transportation Review*, *148*, 102271. doi:10.1016/j.tre.2021.102271 PMID:33613082

Chu, C. Y., Park, K., & Kremer, G. E. (2020). A global supply chain risk management framework: An application of text-mining to identify region-specific supply chain risks. *Advanced Engineering Informatics*, *45*, 101053. doi:10.1016/j.aei.2020.101053

Commission of the European Communities. (2003). Commission recommendation concerning the definition of micro, small and medium-sized enterprises. *Official Journal of the European Union,* L124, 20.5.2003, 36-41.

Doern, R., Williams, N., & Vorley, T. (2018). Special issue on entrepreneurship and crises: Business as usual? An introduction and review of the literature. *Entrepreneurship and Regional Development*, *31*(5–6), 400–412. doi:10.1080/08985626.2018.1541590

Durst, S. (2012). Innovation and intellectual capital (risk) management in small and medium-sized enterprises. *International Journal of Transitions and Innovation Systems*, *2*(3/4), 233. doi:10.1504/IJTIS.2012.051531

Durst, S., & Henschel, T. (2021). COVID-19 as an accelerator for developing strong(er) businesses? Insights from Estonian small firms. *Journal of the International Council for Small Business*, *2*(1), 1–29. doi:10.1080/26437015.2020.1859935

Durst, S., & Zieba, M. (2018). Mapping knowledge risks: Towards a better understanding of knowledge management. *Knowledge Management Research and Practice*, *17*(1), 1–13. doi:10.1080/14778238.2018.1538603

European Commission. (2021). *Structural Business Statistics, Small and Medium-sized Enterprises*. Retrieved on January 11, 2022 from https://ec.europa.eu/eurostat/web/structural-business-statistics/small-and-medium-sized-enterprises

Fereday, J., & Muir-Cochrane, E. (2006). Demonstrating Rigor Using Thematic Analysis: A Hybrid Approach of Inductive and Deductive Coding and Theme Development. *International Journal of Qualitative Methods*, *5*(1), 80–92. doi:10.1177/160940690600500107

Fernández Campos, P., Trucco, P., & Huaccho Huatuco, L. (2019). Managing structural and dynamic complexity in supply chains: Insights from four case studies. *Production Planning and Control*, *30*(8), 611–623. doi:10.1080/09537287.2018.1545952

Ferreira De Araújo Lima, P., Crema, M., & Verbano, C. (2020). Risk management in SMEs: A systematic literature review and future directions. *European Management Journal*, *38*(1), 78–94. doi:10.1016/j.emj.2019.06.005

Fischer-Preßler, D., Eismann, K., Pietrowski, R., Fischbach, K., & Schoder, D. (2020). Information technology and risk management in supply chains. *International Journal of Physical Distribution & Logistics Management*, *50*(2), 233–254. doi:10.1108/IJPDLM-04-2019-0119

Grondys, K., Ślusarczyk, O., Hussain, H. I., & Androniceanu, A. (2021). Risk Assessment of the SME Sector Operations during the COVID-19 Pandemic. *International Journal of Environmental Research and Public Health*, *18*(8), 4183. doi:10.3390/ijerph18084183 PMID:33920916

Guan, D., Wang, D., Hallegatte, S., Davis, S. J., Huo, J., Li, S., Bai, Y., Lei, T., Xue, Q., Coffman, D., Cheng, D., Chen, P., Liang, X., Xu, B., Lu, X., Wang, S., Hubacek, K., & Gong, P. (2020). Global supply-chain effects of COVID-19 control measures. *Nature Human Behaviour*, *4*(6), 577–587. doi:10.103841562-020-0896-8 PMID:32493967

Herbane, B. (2018). Rethinking organizational resilience and strategic renewal in SMEs. *Entrepreneurship and Regional Development*, *31*(5–6), 476–495. doi:10.1080/08985626.2018.1541594

Huo, L., Guo, H., & Cheng, Y. (2019). Supply chain risk propagation model considering the herd mentality mechanism and risk preference. *Physica A*, *529*(1), 121400. doi:10.1016/j.physa.2019.121400

Ivanov, D., & Das, A. (2020). Coronavirus (COVID-19/SARS-CoV-2) and supply chain resilience: A research note. *International Journal of Integrated Supply Management*, *13*(1), 90. doi:10.1504/IJISM.2020.107780

Li, G., Fan, H., Lee, P. K., & Cheng, T. (2015). Joint supply chain risk management: An agency and collaboration perspective. *International Journal of Production Economics*, *164*, 83–94. doi:10.1016/j.ijpe.2015.02.021

Maykut, P., & Morehouse, R. (1994). *Beginning Qualitative Research: A Philosophical and Practical Guide* (1st ed.). Routledge. doi:10.4324/9780203485781

Osiyevskyy, O., Shirokova, G., & Ritala, P. (2020). Exploration and exploitation in crisis environment: Implications for level and variability of firm performance. *Journal of Business Research*, *114*, 227–239. doi:10.1016/j.jbusres.2020.04.015 PMID:32341610

Parast, M. M., & Subramanian, N. (2021). An examination of the effect of supply chain disruption risk drivers on organizational performance: Evidence from Chinese supply chains. *Supply Chain Management*, *26*(4), 548–562. doi:10.1108/SCM-07-2020-0313

Păunescu, C., & Mátyus, E. (2020). Resilience measures to dealing with the COVID-19 pandemic Evidence from Romanian micro and small enterprises. Management & Marketing. *Challenges for the Knowledge Society*, *15*(s1), 439–457. doi:10.2478/mmcks-2020-0026

Remko, V. H. (2020). Research opportunities for a more resilient post-COVID-19 supply chain – closing the gap between research findings and industry practice. *International Journal of Operations & Production Management*, *40*(4), 341–355. doi:10.1108/IJOPM-03-2020-0165

Sato, Y., Tse, Y. K., & Tan, K. H. (2020). Managers' risk perception of supply chain uncertainties. *Industrial Management & Data Systems*, *120*(9), 1617–1634. doi:10.1108/IMDS-01-2020-0049

Thukral, E. (2021). COVID-19: Small and medium enterprises challenges and responses with creativity, innovation, and entrepreneurship. *Strategic Change*, *30*(2), 153–158. doi:10.1002/jsc.2399

Tse, Y. K., Zhang, M., Zeng, W., & Ma, J. (2021). Perception of supply chain quality risk: Understanding the moderation role of supply market thinness. *Journal of Business Research*, *122*, 822–834. doi:10.1016/j.jbusres.2020.07.003

Wieland, A., & Wallenburg, M. (2021). Dealing with supply chain risks. *International Journal of Physical Distribution & Logistics Management*, *42*(10), 887–905. doi:10.1108/09600031211281411

Xu, M., Cui, Y., Hu, M., Xu, X., Zhang, Z., Liang, S., & Qu, S. (2019). Supply chain sustainability risk and assessment. *Journal of Cleaner Production*, *225*(10), 857–867. doi:10.1016/j.jclepro.2019.03.307

KEY TERMS AND DEFINITIONS

Proactive Risk Management: A systematic, comprehensive, statistically based form of risk management that considers all forms of possible failure within a business and their interrelationship with the aim to foresee and prevent potential risks. Such an approach to risk management presumes that risk awareness is strongly imbedded in an organizational culture.

Reactive Risk Management: This approach to risk management involves determining risk thresholds in advance and setting decision guidelines that specify possible outcomes.

Risk: In business, any factor that has an adverse impact on profitability.

Risk Management: A business process, which includes identifying and evaluating different risks, followed by an approach to control and monitor their development.

Small and Medium-Sized Enterprise (SME): This category of company refers to businesses with few than 250 employees and which have an annual revenue less than 50 million euros.

Supply Chain: All the activities associated with converting and delivering a product from raw materials until it reaches the customer.

Supply Chain Management: A coordinated business approach that combines all supply chain activities into a unified business process, linking different departments, carriers, and external partners.

Supply Chain Risk: Any risk that affects the outcome of a supply chain relative to its target result.

Chapter 11
Supply Chains Sophistication in "Smart" Local Communities

Yaroslav Zhalilo
https://orcid.org/0000-0002-8825-2880
National Institute for Strategic Studies, Ukraine

ABSTRACT

The chapter discusses the specific changes in supply chains, conducted by the establishment of "smart" local communities as the result of comprehensive implementation of digital technologies. The author distinguishes the main drivers of these changes, derived from the activization of knowledge spillover used for commodification of locally supplied goods and services. The emphasis has been done on the institutional framework, enabling to expand the scope of beneficiaries of supply chains, associated with the provision of services, basic for local communities, based on networked consumption. The sophistication of supply chains in "smart" local communities the author explains by the expansion of business-local communities' partnership, integrating "smart" solutions into local governance and supplementing digital technologies with reformatting of managerial practices and everyday behavior patterns.

INTRODUCTION

Dynamic changes in business ecosystems' organization, associated with the expansion of Industry 5.0 technologies, open the new opportunities for supply chains' development. The shifts, launched by economic internationalization and permeability of economic borders, digitalization of production processes and corresponding communications, based on this operational autonomization of business capacities, have got further progress towards strengthening of local economic players and local institutions in tailoring the supply chains based on their specific values. UN Sustainable Development Goals (2015) state the crucial role of local communities in the inclusive development of territories, by provision of services, necessary for quality of life, ecosystems' protection, mobility of population, territorial integration, cities and communities' development and fostering communities' cohesion. Smart technologies' implementation in everyday local communities' life resulted in the emergence of "smart" cities and communities

DOI: 10.4018/978-1-7998-9715-6.ch011

Copyright © 2022, IGI Global. Copying or distributing in print or electronic forms without written permission of IGI Global is prohibited.

(SC&C) as a new institutional reality, sophistication of the traditional supply chains and introduction of the new ones, associated with the integrated sets of services, demanded by community members.

The objective of the chapter is to discuss the preconditions and principal drivers of supply chains' modification in the process of SC&C emergence and development, to identify the features of sophisticated value chains, their performance criteria, stakeholders and their prospective partnerships. Finally, to suggest the ways to optimize business and local communities' partnership realizing the potential of SC&C.

BACKGROUND

The issue of supply chains' modification is widely discussed in the studies of technological and economic progress. Nagurney (2006) stresses on the tight interconnection between supply and value chains. In fact, supply chains link value chains, thus, their design truly depends on the technological shifts, changing value creation process – namely, new sets of tools, productive equipment, appropriate technologically determined production factors, data and methods of data processing and usage in management etc. Indeed, supply chains as an external "interface" of the company, reflect the changes in the market environment and should be much more reactive and flexible compared to production itself.

The researchers of a community of sustainable business experts BSR (2017), based on the studies of practical experience of leading companies' procurement offices, identified the key priorities that shape the procurement processes and should influence supply chain management till 2025, namely:

- The comprehensive adoption of modern technologies at all the length of a value chain;
- Global climate changes and shortage of resources;
- Massive migration processes;
- Shifting consumer demand towards personalization and on-demand economy, exploring new markets and new customer groups;
- Fundamental changes, influencing supply chains – both international, such as reshoring, changes in supply and delivery geography, changes in main economic partner countries, and domestic - uncertain prospects of changes in regulations.

New drivers enable to engage more resources and modify the structure of demand, consumers' pools, location, needs and purchase behavior. This expands the supply chains, provides new chances for their sophistication, building their proper design. Janjevic, Winkenbach, and Rice Jr. (2016) derive the modern methods of supply chains' building, reflecting the changes in supply chain design:

- Switching from cost minimization to wider variety of value creation factors in order to obtain a proper market share;
- More emphasis on tactical, continuous market reviews – due to uncertainty, volatility, complexity of the markets;
- Turning to supply networks' localization in order to mitigate risks;
- Using artificial intelligence and data analytics to optimize supply chains, reflecting a massive increase in the volume of available data;
- Prevalence of interdisciplinary supply chain design processes.

The new design of supply chains in digital age methodologically may be explained as the particular result of knowledge spillover (widely understood knowledge as any kind of systemized information), which modulates the new consumption preferences. The knowledge spillover, initially described in narrow sense as contributing low-tech enterprises to improve "for free" their technology level, is subject to broad discussions.

Romer (1986) grounded, that externalities of created knowledge cannot be internalized in full extent and, so far, are being disseminated through learning-by-doing effect. In this case just knowledge, in Romer's model, is responsible for stable and even growing marginal return on capital, which occurs simultaneously with the grooving capital stock. However, he stresses upon, the knowledge should have the features of public good.

While classics, like Romer (1987), traditionally made accent on the effect on the production of knowledge-based products, more forward-oriented researchers (Cohen & Levinthal, 1989) focused on backward supply chain relationship between customer and supplier, taking in mind the impact of spillover on consumers' preferences and behavior.

Langlois and Robertson (2018) studied the consumption promotion role of the knowledge spillover through stimulation of the process of social learning. They argue that the knowledge expansion depends on how many persons have already purchased the good – and the resulted size of the network of users increases the value of goods' of service's possession. Thus, the increase of supply shifts the demand curve rightward.

Meanwhile, knowledge spillover does not happen automatically, but depends on certain institutional background. Von Hippel (1994) argues, that sometimes knowledge may be 'sticky', due to high transaction costs of communicating and tacit character of knowledge itself, limited by the capacity of wide population to perceive and convert it into the practical behavior patterns. Thus, Beg, Fiše, and Dornbuš (2010) determine the ability to use the knowledge as dependent both on the capacity of economic agents and economic policy of the government. More specifically the issue address Sredojević, Cvetanović, and Bošković (2016), grounding the importance of social investments in human and organizational development in promotion of technological capacity of the country.

The assessment of supply chains performance should be changed synchronously with the modernization of these chains. More sophisticated informational technologies deliver more information in different dimensions of performance – which should be taken into account both by consumers and by suppliers. Practitioners in procurement try to generalize the most evident performance indicators, which reflect supply chain capacity and sustainability. The British Government Commercial Function (UK Government commercial function, 2020) bases these indicators on UN Sustainable Development Goals. The already mentioned above BSR (2017) experts also suggest their vision of Procurement Priorities to 2025 based on the practical experience of member companies in supply chains' functioning. More specifically these indicators will be discussed below.

In the modern world, flooded with diversified information, achieving supply chains' sustainability requires reaching wide range equilibrium, which involves the balanced interests of social groups, including minoritarian, in the fields, much wider than proper economic ones. At last, the modern ramified communications fully revealed the nature of the society as a community of individuals, possessing the distributed decentralized resource, described by Habermas (1979). And put on the agenda the tasks of reintegration this community for optimal engagement of the resources. From Hodgson (1988), the key problem is to create the flexible institutions, enabling to convert the dissipated human needs into understandable, assessable tasks and, based on this, prioritize them. Networking, prove Schiavo-Campo and

Sundaram (2000), restores the trust in the community due to the sustainable exchange of information (knowledge).

Widening the range of supply chains' elements results in the phenomenon of *commodification* of social life, understood by Ziółkowski (2004) as the "extension of the number of goods and services which become commodities and can be sold on the market" (p. 385). The involvement of previously non-commercial spheres, goods and services into market relations requires the institutional changes in the communities. These new institutions should embody both the new criteria of supply chains performance and, in particular, new consumers' preferences. One of the most important mechanisms, controlling commodification, argues Ziółkowski (2004), is the functioning the proper social capital.

The approaches of different, even classical, researchers to the understanding of social capital and its driving force to regulate collective action strongly differ. Fukuyama (1999) derives the driving strength of social capital from inherent trust and loyalty of basic social groups. Putnam (1993) relies more on grassroot networks and civic culture. Coleman (1988) possesses the pro-active position, considering the action-facilitating role of the subject. And, that is important in the scope of the present study, - insists of the important role of local communities in the basic values' implementation through education. The increase of social capital role in supply chains due to its growing role in productive resources' distribution, reinforces the importance of social capital, influencing the basic level of resources' involvement - the level of local communities.

The issue of localization has got a new breath in the period of coronacrisis. The experts of World Economic Forum vote for keeping global supply chains in the post-crisis period. However, they recognize the trend of bringing production home by many companies. Leen and Lanng (2020) believe this trend grew with the spread of automation and personalized production, enabling the decentralization of manufacturing capacity. Also, BSR (2017) experts stress on the perspective of "nimble, regional supplier networks" in supply chains, that can meet "both commercial expectations and sustainability aspirations" (p. 4). They believe, "by 2025, many supply chains may shift from global flows of goods and services to national, regional, and local networks of buyers and suppliers" (BSR, 2017, p. 3). Yueh (2020) explains the greater localization of supply chains by shifts in technology (e.g., enabling personal production, like 3-D printing), as well as by consumer preferences changes, driven by environmental concerns.

The increase of the share of local supply chains embraces stronger demand for different kinds of services, that are supplied within local communities by definition. The local community-level social capital, as Coe, Paquet, and Roy (2001) argue, is traditionally integrated by the participation in community's life and decision-making. This social capital gets the new strength from consumers' complicity in the production of goods and services by the involvement through "smart" networks into expanding of consumption, quality assessment and finding the ways to improve goods and services (Albert, Flournoy, & Lebrasseur, 2009).

Implementing this institutional approach, Wu and Jia (2018) suggest the concept of localized "supply chain field". The latter they determine as a pool of key suppliers, resource and product consumers, regulatory agencies and other organizations (including government and semi-government entities), who serve as architects and builders of the supply chains.

Finally, Walt, Doody, Baker, and Cain (2014) prove that the diversification and strengthening of actors, influencing the essential features of a community as a field of supply chain evolvement («decision providers»), causes the sophistication of network communications and interactions of people, processes, data, objects, creation of new alliances (clusters) and the new subsections of local community systems. Respectively, this recalls for the new technologies and new regulations of SC&C management.

This chapter is positioned by the author as the continuation of framework of supply chains' modification studies, described above, with the accent on digital changes in local communities' role as drivers of this modification.

CHANGING SUPPLY CHAINS IN "SMART" CITIES AND COMMUNITIES

Supply Chains' Institutional Design in Digitalization Age

Digital transformations drastically change the composition of supply chains. Primarily, they change the set of factors of product transformation technologies, thus, factors, involved in value creation. As mentioned before, value creation centers are shifting the accents from production process itself to consumption-related spheres. The increasing weight of knowledge as value-creating factor calls for the elaboration of appropriate regulators of the distribution of knowledge-generated value between stakeholders. Intellectual property legislative limitations are losing effectiveness. Knowledge transfer and duplication through modern digital instruments are hardly controlled, causing knowledge "slippery".

Thereby, the sustainability of supply chains requires the constructive model of distribution of economic results from knowledge-based value production. For sure, this distribution should be determined by certain institutions, which retain the interests and motivation of primary knowledge producers even when this knowledge is not exclusive more due to knowledge spillover. This institutional mechanism has been enabled by the provision of permanently functioning institutionally integrated complementary consumption networks. The institutionally determinated identity of a person with some social community defines its motivation to the engagement into productive processes as well as the patterns of consumption. In its turn, knowledge spillover diversifies the variety of communities by size, location of durability, e.g. – users of some technical appliances or software, followers of some ideology of consumption (environmentalists, vegans, funs of healthy lifestyle), followers of fashion etc.

It is easily understood, that networking, provided by digitalization, rapidly enlarges the communities of consumers to the size of the phenomenon of "networked consumption". Langlois and Robertson (2018) mention the non-price benefits, available, as an example, to the users of telephone system and personal computers with certain software. But now the universality of digital technologies substantially expands the scope of products, which can be the subject of networks of consumers – practically to any (first of all, of technologically enhanced type) product, possession of which serves as the access to complementary benefits, delivered by: new communication opportunities, postproduction services, availability of complementary sets of goods and services, generating synergy effect, getting physical (health) or moral (confidence, respect, tranquility) gains etc. Respectively, this creates the background for the commodification of new spheres of life of a person and of a community.

Thus, networked consumption is based on the specific complementary system of values, translated by the networked flows of knowledge. The utility of consumption depends on the similar consumption within certain social groups – as this consumption is the identifier of affiliation of the consumer to these groups, and consumers receive the full complexity of newly created value due to their attribution to some consumers' networks. Traditional marginal utility factors, based on the scarcity or redundancy of a good, have been substituted in their role of price and value determining factor by institutional factors, building the consumption networks, which benefit from network synergy. In other words, given the equal price/paying capacity ratio winning is the supply chain, better integrated with networking institutions.

Unlike intellectual property age, where value creation is based on "sticky" knowledge, consumption networks derive the profits from maximal knowledge spillover. Thus, the producers contribute the promotion of such networks and their penetration into much wider scope of consumption. The more intensive knowledge spillover is, the faster is the spreading and swelling of the networks – and more profitable is the business, oriented on networked consumption. In macroeconomic dimension, network communications promote also the factor productivity of physical capital in the complementary activities, and this positive effect is proportional to the complexity of the network.

In the previous studies the author concentrated on the specific features of networked consumption (for more see Zhalilo, 2018). Shortly, the features are as follows:

- the networked model of consumption critically depends on institutionally-determined networks of logistics, retail and consumers;
- networking synergistically increases the outcome of all the businesses in logistics, financing, business servicing, recruiting etc., additionally capitalizes them;
- producers are interested in the institutional regulators of consumption: fashion, complementary product service, follow-up institutions, self-organized communities of consumers etc.;
- high importance of institutional factors of value creation makes these institutions effective in the minimization of transaction costs – so far social capital becomes really productive;
- the institutional equilibrium (absence of the opportunism of a part of business community) is pretty important to reach the fair distribution of benefits of consuming networks;
- the environment of operational activities of business becomes multidimensional, and business sustainability depends on institutional regulators of society as a whole, including political, social, cultural spheres;
- the development of informational and communicational technologies creates the potential of efficient economic agents' cooperation, new cooperative (incl. transnational) supply chains.

Ergo, networked consumption redesigns the supply chains. The institutions regulate networked consumption in the conditions and spheres, when regulation in terms of costs and price become irrelevant. This can either significantly strengthen the sustainability of supply chains in the view of uneven ambiguous challenges of modern markets, or increase the vulnerability to volatile non-economic impacts. The triggering between these two opportunities depends on the productivity of knowledge spillover, thus, its organization by the appropriate institutions.

Obtained the real productivity within newly designed supply chains, the institutions merge into social capital. The social capital becomes the substantive "soft" value-creating factor, involving not the primary resources, like "traditional" capital, but communications and communities, combining formal and informal institutions into integrated system of values. Social capital supplements the productive influence of human capital by networked consumption and, thus, makes supply chains significantly more complicated and inclusive. The social capital-driven supply chains provide much more opportunities both for resources' engagement and product delivery. The new positions of economic agents within these supply chains open the way for building new marketing strategies, business diversification, product innovation etc. Finally, the capacity of institutional systems to deliver the value to definite social communities characterizes the factor productivity of social capital.

The productive role of social capital gives an opportunity of commodification common goods, internalizing the externalities of their utilization without the practical limitation of access to these goods.

In its turn, the common goods and services are integrated into business processes, that rearranges the common processes and, generally, increases their efficiency. This gives additional benefits to the communities: the commodification, based on new networked consumption, does not reduce the basic consumption, but provides new quality of consumption to the participants of networks. In fact, this kind of commodification should be rather interpreted as additional *capitalization* of social capital. In contrary to "conventional" commodification, which often means in fact common goods' involvement into some indefinite commercial turnover, this capitalization seems much more productive and multiplicative for local development.

Determining the attributive criteria of the social groups of beneficiaries of supply chains, social capital is responsible for the synergy, created (or not created) by supply chains, sophisticated in digital society. This creates for economic agents, involved in these chains, the incentives to invest into the enrolment of networked consumption and institutional improvement of the consumers' networks. Discussing the spillover of knowledge in technology, Cohen and Levinthal (1990) argued, that instead of receiving new knowledge as a "gift", firms must invest resources in the "absorptive capacity", necessary to understand the knowledge spilling. In the age of networked consumption, the institutional improvement is considered much more comprehensively: as more sophisticative and comprehensive utilization of goods and services (users' qualification), promotion of participation in consumers' networks, reduction of the transactional cost of consumption, aftermarket services, branding etc. The efficient networks of consumers create the powerful feedback – when growing consumers' capabilities and qualifications continue the learning process and induce the further improvement of the product (Langlois & Robertson, 2018).

Respectively, supply chains' performance criteria become more sophisticated, including more comprehensive set of indicators, and one of the principal one is the complexity of consumption networks. As an example of modern approaches to the performance of supply chains is the criteria, applied by the British Government Commercial Function – the cross-government network, procuring or supporting the procurement of goods and services for the government – for the tenders over £500,000 (UK Government commercial function, 2020). The criteria to be taken into account are:

- Diversification
- Collaboration
- Social value benefits (fighting inequality, incl. employment opportunities)
- Digitalization and cyber-security
- Energy and material efficiency
- Effective stewardship of the environment
- Community integration through a shared vision of community for the places for living and working.

BSR (2017) experts suggest more practical vision of Procurement Priorities till 2025, concentrating directly on the functions of supply chains:

- Cost saving and optimizing working capital
- Rationalizing supply base
- Improving risk prediction and management
- Providing strategic foresight to the business
- Innovating and collaborating with suppliers.

The modern features of supply chains' institutional design and corresponding criteria of supply chains' performance have been implemented in the institutional architectonics of contemporary local communities.

Local Supply Chains in "Smart" Communities

The communities, built on spatial (local) identity, are the principal social groups, which potentially can be the basis of networked consumption. Respectively, the supply chains of services, supplied within the communities, can be subject of networks-based expansion. Under the influence of digital instruments, local communities can either become the basis of new stable supply chains (*capitalized* local services' capacity) – or be partially involved into different externally-driven supply chains (*commodified* local services). The trigger between these two opportunities is the capacity of local self-governance institutions to implement the integral local management systems, joining the main supply chain participants, based on appropriate technologies, local regulations and local social capital, responsible for the local identity and proper involvement of resources' holders into local supply chains. Thus, the increase of a number of active providers of decisions for local communities' lives, equipped with modern digital instruments, sophisticates the structure of networks and requires complex special organizational solutions.

The UN Conference on Housing and Sustainable Urban Development (Habitat III) in Quito, Ecuador (2016), adopted a "*New Urban Agenda*", aimed, inter al, to "foster the creation, promotion and enhancement of open, user-friendly and participatory data platforms using technological and social tools available to transfer and share knowledge among national, subnational and local governments and relevant stakeholders, including non-State actors and people, to enhance effective urban planning and management, efficiency and transparency through e-governance, approaches assisted by information and communications technologies, and geospatial information management" (United Nations Habitat III, 2016, p. 23). The integral approach has been emphasized by researchers (Thomson & Newman, 2018; Zhang, Yang, & Yu, 2015) by the term "urban *metabolism*", considering the urban activities, aimed to maintain the structure of the cities and to expand their environment in the view of their impact on local, regional and global environment.

In long-term this integrity has been reached by the implementation of the concept of "smart" cities and communities (SC&C), based on the employment of intellectual digital technologies, network and informational systems for systemic management of urban community, the basic processes of community's life in the framework of infrastructure of communication of users of energy flows, materials, services and finances. The term "*smart*" emphasizes the combination of technological and managerial solutions, which creates the synergy in supply chains, utilizing the capacities of the communities. Unlike the cybernetic approaches to urban automatization of centralized linear management, widespread yet in the last decades of the XX century, the "smart" synergy has been enabled due to the establishment of distributed non-linear (e.g. cluster-oriented) management and self-organization of urban systems.

The integrity of SC&C is demonstrative in the definition of "smart" (intelligent) city, given by Komninos (2002). He believes, the term "is used to characterize areas (cities, regions, districts in cities, clusters) where the local system of innovation is supported by and improved via digital networks and artificial intelligence applications" (p. 32). Meanwhile, he argues, "their added value lies in their ability to bring together three forms of intelligence: the human intelligence of the city's population, the collective intelligence of innovation support institutions, and the artificial intelligence of digital networks and online services" (Komninos, 2002, p. 32).

The progress in digital technologies and their penetration into social organization of communities caused the permanent evolution of "smart" city concept. The initial "smart city 1.0" has been based on the local implementation of technological instruments for urban utilities' management. "Smart city 2.0" already included the integrating programs and projects, combining the automatized elements in various domains of urban life. In "smart city 3.0" the key role has been shifted to the institutional systems of social participation in decision making, cities' co-creation with citizens, creating the urban ecosystem, favorable for life ("Wrocław - towards a Smart City", 2018).

Stratigea (2012) determined the key factors, enabling the full-extent implementation of "smart" city networks, in particular:

- Implementation of the network communication infrastructure;
- Education and training in informational infrastructure's utilization;
- Overcoming the "digital gap" and reaching "digital inclusion";
- Implementation of E-democracy;
- Creation of innovations-friendly environment and facilitation of creativity;
- Promotion of "smart" communities as the places for living, work and business.

The sustainability of local supply chains is determined by the level of local identity of local stakeholders. This sustainability is the higher, the more inclusive (involving more broad social groups) are the supply chains. The inclusive local social capital in SC&C is based on the participation of local stakeholders in the everyday life and decision-making of the community, on their involvement into consumption networks, feeling thus what McLean (1996) characterized as the "sense of community". The "smart" digital networks, joining community members in different fields of local activities, strengthen the subjectness of "smart" communities and improves the human capital engagement into supply chains.

SC&C are the modern elements of institutional architectonics, the logical products of digital age and digital instruments' penetration into the organization of communities. The gradual step-by-step implementation of intelligent elements increases the creation of data, depicting the local resources' utilization. Hence, creating the knowledge and facilitating its spillover. Resulted is stronger integrity of supply chains, their flexibility and better capacity to realize the existing resources' potential. Digitalized local supply chains gain more success in the competition for resources, primarily – human ones. Companies' integration into supply chains, created by "smart" communities, increases their capitalization due to new ways of market communication and engagement of resources and, thus, stronger sustainability, better access to local resources, higher market capacity and ability for long-term planning, based on direct or indirect partnerships with local authorities.

The production and organization of knowledge flows, as the basic feature of SC&C, gives the opportunity to launch comprehensive learning-by-doing processes that changes the character of knowledge from tacit to explicit, thus, promoting its spillover. The institutional mechanisms, implemented in SC&C, facilitate the commodification of not only "traditional" common services, provided by local communities, but of a huge variety of spatial factors, available to local communities – like local natural, recreational potential, cultural and historical heritage, infrastructure, image of territories etc. It its turn, the better opportunity for commodification and higher return on the involved local resources create the incentives for investments and innovations – and open the new possible fields of their application in the life of community.

In fact, the new quality of social capital in SC&C reloads the capacity of a community itself – it is not more an amorphous group with weak identity and volatile structure – but the integral unity, cohesive, grounded on the transparent relations and trust. The new understanding goes to the space of the community, the elements of this space constitute the integral ecosystem, and each plays a complementary systemic role within a single network. The "smart" organization of local space at the same time determines the quality of life of the citizens, optimizes the cost of infrastructure maintenance and utilities' provision, improves investment attractiveness of the territory, strengthens its touristic potential etc.

Business Partnerships with Local Communities within Supply Chains

The tangible sophistication of social and business communications creates the opportunities for networking synergy and, at the same time, the social demand for the organized cooperation and partnership within the concept of "smart city 3.0". Frankly speaking, the situation is similar in the settlements of all sizes, however, in cities, especially in mega polices, the potential effect of synergy increases exponentially.

The experience of urban communities gives the ground for the systematization of main challenges the "smart" cities meet and have to find the answer for:

- Permanent growth of urban population and load on infrastructure;
- Increase of load on local resources and call for resources' efficiency;
- Need to reach the resilience of urban system against the probable and explicit risks (natural, economic, social, and, as recent experience shows – epidemic too);
- Need to reduce or/and compensate the inequality in its different appearances;
- Aging of population, need of inclusion of elderly people and of adaptation of city spaces for their specific requirements;
- Growth of the number of decision makers in different spheres (risk of disintegrative impact of individual decisions on the integrated system);
- Increase of responsibility of local communities for the local solutions and real decentralization of decision making;
- Increase of the capacity of a community to reveal problems based on networked and transparent information (taken into account the risks of informational manipulations);
- Growing orientation and capacity of community members to participate in local governance (meanwhile, activism sometimes outweighs competency).

Also, strategic approaches to SC&C management should foresee the compensation of local negative externalities emerging due to the promoted optimization of local services. Most usually the externalities consist in the crowding out of some services providers from the local markets (e.g., private passenger transporters in the case of municipal transport development), release of employees after the implementation of labor-free technologies etc. The compensative measures should allow to avoid the resistance to the implementation of "smart" networks from stakeholders, which can have a significant weight in the local communities, and the losses of local productive potential by its reorientation to alternative supply chains.

The implementation of "smart" solutions in local communities' management rearranges the benefits from the provision of local services, converting them to partial common goods, available not only to the direct services' users, but to all the members of the community. This enables to spread the corresponding supply chains, adding new types of services, additional service providers and consumers.

The network and informational systems, constituting "smart" communities, ensure the infrastructure for the cooperation in the involvement of labor, energy, materials, services and finance. Capacity to integrate into local social capital-generated supply chains provides companies with the opportunity to perform better. This capacity should be derived from company's ability to supply goods and services in line with the performance criteria, suggested by local communities, and intangible values, determined by local social capital. Sustainable partnership improves the vision of future, desired and expected performance, acceptable by the market, reduces the transaction costs, related with risk management of the company.

As an example, can be considered the "smart" rearrangement of local passenger transportation. Directly the implementation of "smart" transport card (single ticket) makes transport utilization more convenient for its passengers. However, the spreading of "smart" solutions enables to obtain and process the "big data" arrays to optimize the lines and passenger capacity of urban transport, improve traffic regulations, rearrange parking places etc. – influencing the life of the whole community. In the dimension of supply chains in transport services it makes the ground for the partnership of municipal and private service providers. Wider, the "smart" public transportation system can be the part of integrated "smart" management systems: urban transport (passenger and freight) monitoring and rearrangement, road networks optimization, urban mobility optimization, local labor markets assessment and regulation etc.

Thus, the implementation of "smart" solutions into the system of local governance switches the dissipated local results of activities, supporting the life and development of communities, to the consumption networks with appropriate synergy effect. Communications, established within "smart" communities, based on subsequent local social capital, create principally new supply chains, that bring together scattered local solutions' providers and communities' members. New network technologies sophisticate the value creating operations, providing the opportunities to involve wider range of partners to local supply chains.

As follows from mentioned above, modern digital technologies are necessary, but not sufficient preconditions for the formation of SC&C. Of same importance is the institutional framework, which uses the digital opportunities for the reformatting of managerial practices and everyday behavior patterns of the members of communities. This institutional modernization is based on:

- Implementation of local communities' strategies to establish the priority of long-term effects of "smart" networks instead of fast non-systemic results of partial improvements;
- Strengthening the managerial capacity of local communities to promote "smart" networks' integration and utilization in operational and strategic decision making;
- Spreading the "network literacy" of local community members, enabling the application of "smart" networks in everyday life.

In the further realization of SC&C concept institutional changes take over the role of drivers of economic and social changes from digital technologies. The numerous peripheral changes get the systemic coordination centers, designed to reach comprehensive effect of community's life. Van Iersel (2018) describes the change of "Smart Cities" by the strategies «City of the Future», which embrace:

- Commitment of stakeholders (business, social partners, NGOs, higher educational institutions), including political support;
- Long-term planning, based on holistic approaches to the sustainable urban development;
- Ensuring synergy, connectivity and mobility, social inclusion based on innovations and modern technologies;

- Integration of individual projects into the overall picture;
- Public-private partnership with agreed shared responsibility;
- Transparent communications and open attitude to creative ideas as the basis of commitment of the general public.

The analysis on international experience enables to select six principal fields, where the partnerships based on SC&C instruments allow to build the new supply chains, or significantly diversify the traditional ones (e.g., "Wrocław - towards a Smart City", 2018):

- Mobility of population (road infrastructure, local transportation, building and servicing pedestrian and cycling zones etc.);
- Local economy promotion (support of business innovations, local business startups, creative business, local clusters, collaborative performance management, social entrepreneurship);
- Environment (sustainable utilization of natural resources, efficient consumption of energy and water, waste management, air quality control, green spaces creation and maintenance);
- Human potential (special education and training, digital competences, social awareness, legal support etc.);
- Living conditions (security, health, childcare, social aid, general education, living and leisure spaces);
- Public management (transparency, public services' provision, co-design and co-creation of services; social participation, public democracy (incl. participatory budgeting).

Naturally, this list permanently broadens.

In finding the answers for the modern challenges the basis for the consolidation and partnership of main stakeholders of local development is being created, in particular:

1. The local business, aspired to strengthen its competitive force, interested in:
    - More productive commercial utilization of available resources based on "smart" managing networks;
    - Increase the capitalization of business, caused by better productivity;
    - Exploring the new markets of goods and services due to "smart" commodification of common goods and new dimensions of demand;
    - Enabling to permeate beyond the boundaries of the local community, relying on intermunicipal and interregional cooperation.
2. The local communities, seeking the better life for their members, interested in:
    - Sustainable development, based on the commitment in the face of future generations - as a ground for local identity, the cornerstone for local social capital;
    - Developing cooperation at intermunicipal, interregional, international levels;
    - More efficient utilization of local scarce resources;
    - More comprehensive engagement of local potential (including the one, involved by the modern technologies);
    - Creating jobs for community members;
    - Better engagement of community members to local governance (through E-democracy instruments);

- Increasing the own capacity for good management and strategizing.

3. The central government and local government institutions, authorized to fulfill the nationally prescribed goals and to realize associated localized tasks, based on:
   - Improvement of informational framework for national-level policies;
   - Better performance of centralized managing impacts (due to unification of digitalized managing processes, faster and more targeted influence etc.);
   - Further promotion of subsidiarity as transferring the competences and responsibilities from central to regional and local levels.

The partnerships, established at the basis of SC&C, grounded on the complementarity of interests, mentioned above, not only foster the development of supply chains, realizing the potential of commodification, but also underpin the advocacy of changes of legislative and local regulations, aimed to implement "smart" networks and integrate them into single city managing systems.

Community-Specific Supply Chains

Based on the technologies of Industry 4.0 and 5.0, local communities become able to create "smart" networks, that allow to collect data, arrange them to create appropriate knowledge, significant for the community and organize its spillover, at least, within the boundaries of the community. This knowledge represents the resource, available as new value-creating factor for private companies, however, this value should be realized predominantly inside the community and for the community members. Thus, the corresponding supply chain should be finalized via the utilization of final output by local community members directly within integrated consumer networks, or by appropriate decisions, adopted by local communities.

SC&C serve as a driver, promoting Industry 4.0 conversion into Industry 5.0. As Breque, De Nul, and Petridis (2021) argue, Industry 5.0 "moves focus from shareholder to stakeholder value… highlights the importance of research and innovation to support industry in its long-term service to humanity within planetary boundaries" (p. 48). The Industry 4.0 achievements, as data transmission and storage, artificial intelligence, technologies for energy efficiency have been supplemented by the institutional mechanisms of bridging businesses with local communities and enabling partnerships in provision of the appropriate quality of local communities' life. These mechanisms build the community-level supply chains.

Japanese researchers even go forth to formulate the concept of Society 5.0, where digital technologies are widely used in everyday life of communities and individuals. According to the authors of the concept (Hitachi…, 2020), "the vision of Society 5.0 requires… to reframe two kinds of relationships: the relationship between technology and society and the technology-mediated relationship between individuals and society" (p. 18).

The demonstrative case of formation "smart" community-based supply chains is the implementation of "smart" technologies in territorial management in Great Britain. The government innovational agency «Connected Places Catapult» (Official site: https://cp.catapult.org.uk) in concentrated on the promotion of new level of physical, digital and social communication, supports the partnership between public and private sectors, local governments and private service providers in order to create new commercial opportunities and increase the productivity of services' providers. The agency makes emphasis on starting points of service provision, implementation of pilot startup projects to demonstrate the opportunities in different systems. The main demonstrational spheres are:

- Urban services (traffic, parking, lighting, waste management, public safety);
- Utilities ("smart" meters, "smart" networks);
- "Smart" health care management (remote medicine, preventive health care etc.);
- Transportation (information for drivers, autonomous transport);
- "Last mile" delivery and logistics (freight vehicles, innovational delivery devices (e.g. drones));
- Data and communication (Internet of things, 5 G networks, innovative data platforms).

The activity of «Connected Places Catapult» is an example of a partnership, promoting the supply chains, involving "smart" networks:

- Supports the knowledge spillover through better access of business to the experience of innovational investment and commercialization in the spheres of high market risks or low investment attractiveness;
- Promotes the demand for innovations by the direct investment into the instruments and resources, strengthening the confidence and capacity of possible prospective innovations' consumers;
- Increases the supply of products and services by the demonstration of the cases of implementation new technologies, introduction of common accepted standards etc.;
- Strengthens new markets through the commodification, based on new technologies of data access, public-private ecosystems, implementation of "smart" urban management systems.

The spread of separate "smart" units (like houses, vehicles, meters, traffic management devices, power or water supply systems etc.) and the development of interrelated and interdependent local ecosystems (e.g., energy supply, "smart" buildings, traffic management etc.) requires further sophistication of networks' capacity for data collection, exchange and management, communicating compliant digital systems for data exchange and conversion *from measurement to management*. Thus, promotes the industries of digital devices, software and engineering services to give the opportunities for digital products and services to penetrate into different spheres, including ordinary "traditional" ones.

A specific modern case of spatial commodification is building the COVID-19 resilience of local community. In the period of pandemic not only the health care system is committed to resist the disease, but also appropriate changes in community life, aimed to reduce the contagion risks and compensate losses due to compelled quarantine limitations. "Smart" networks can have significant impact on the strengthening the counter-pandemic resilience of local communities, in particular by:

- Implementation of remote public services' provision, remote payments, mobile service applications for elderly people etc.;
- Minimization of physical contacts in the case of obligatory personal presence at the provision of the service (electronic queue, digital appointment to the doctor);
- Spreading the technologies of remote employment;
- Public spaces' optimization in order to reduce the undesired abundant physical contacts: organization the flows of passengers and pedestrians, arrangement of public recreation and waiting zones, trade and services, public transportation;
- Improvement of utilities' quality, primarily – crucial for sanitary, hygiene and health: water supply and sewage, quality of drinking water, waste disposal and processing, public places and territories' cleaning;

- Control over industrial waste and emission, air and water quality control, chemical preparation utilization control in agricultural regions;
- "Big data" analysis to reveal the territories with increased epidemic risks, professional groups of risks of contagion, specific endemic diseases etc.;
- Implementation of counter-pandemic resilience as a performance criterion of local community management, using the digital data instruments for its monitoring.

Thus, pandemic enhances the implementation of digital technologies and overcoming the "digital gap", promoting "smart" networks development. New demand for goods and services from local communities and/or partnerships, established to realize the mentioned above, promote new supply chains or introduce new parts of conventional ones. Some tasks should require the intermunicipal cooperation, including the communication between "smart" cities and surrounding communities, where SC&C instruments have not been implemented yet. So, this promotes the dissemination of "smart" networks and develops appropriate supply chains in new-coming "smart" communities.

SOLUTIONS AND RECOMMENDATIONS

Sophistication of supply chains within the boundaries of "smart" local communities is the logical extension of the development of digital technologies and their implementation into everyday life and "traditional" production processes. As this sophistication reflects the interests of communities as well as business, it should be promoted in their partnership and complementary implementation of digitalization and of modern "smart" managing networks. The enlargement of demand for "smart" network goods and services should be supported by closing the "digital gap" inside the communities, promoting "digital literacy", especially among elderly people, and in the rural territories, supporting the establishment of self-organized groups of people. The demand for aggregated "smart" solutions should grow with the strengthening of a strategizing at communities' level, improvement of the latter's institutional capacity to manage everyday maintenance processes as well as long-term oriented development, integrating separate "smart" elements into single decision-making systems, to adopt and implement regulations, that can be the basis of public-private partnerships in "smart" networks.

In addition, synergy effect, taking place in "smart" communities, enables to mitigate the problem of scarce resources, characteristic for many communities, especially in depressive regions and in less rich countries. Then, the implementation of "smart" networks can support the national-level policies of regional development, so, their promotion should be in the scope of interests of the central government.

The technological progress, presenting more and more sophisticated digital technologies of data collection and processing, is going on more or less autonomously, under the pressure of global trends. Much more difficult is paving the way to institutional changes, oriented to implement the obtained knowledge into the managerial and governance processes. The optimistic expectations on this way are driven by the accumulation of a "critical mass" of stakeholders, accumulated the large data arrays and/or data transmitting and processing infrastructure and interested to commodify them within certain supply chains. In particular, these stakeholders are presented by mobile communication providers, Internet-providers, integrators of logistic networks etc. They should be supported as well by the producers of software and digital hardware for "smart" networks (metering, controlling, monitoring equipment, executive mechanisms, communication equipment etc.). Their activity should be promoted by public and professional presentational events (fairs, exhibitions, competitions, hackathons), trainings and demonstrations for communities, pilot projects, cooperation with civic organizations.

Partnership with private companies based on "smart" networks can be included in the realization of different sectorial programs, enabling better management and higher efficiency and sustainability in the realization of functions, transferred to the local level (for example, energy distribution and saving, health care and counter-epidemic tasks in the period of pandemic, environmental programs and adaptation to climate changes, some humanitarian policies, like youth, "silver age" policies etc.).

Respectively, the projects of "smart" solutions and "smart" networks should be among the central priorities of the government programs in the fields of regional development and cohesion, as well as international programs. Usually, the networks in the regions with smaller density of population require more support, as they nave more costly infrastructure, are hardly commercialized and riskier. Complementary to the technological projects is the support of training, education, provision of digital competencies, informational transparency, exchange of experience, applied and fundamental studies. The appropriate financial support for SC&C development can be enabled by the implementation of corresponding tasks into national policy documents. For now, "smart" cities are present practically in all existing national strategies of regional development and/or digital transformation of European countries, in general correlation with the Smart Cities and Communities European Innovation Partnership.

Institutionally at the regional and local levels SC&C promotion can be supported by the activity of regional and local development agencies. Attracting investments into the projects of digital and communicational networks the agencies create the background for better "smart" solutions, capitalizing more these investments and building the ground for cumulative development of various data processing projects. Local development agencies can be crucial in provision of pilot "smart" projects, local procurement of data collection and processing services, attraction of national level and international aid for SC&C development. The agencies also should convert the "smart" projects, developed by local communities, into the design, clear and attractive for potential investors.

FUTURE RESEARCH DIRECTIONS

The trend of digitalization will proceed dynamically, and digital instruments will penetrate to the "traditional" spheres of production and everyday lining. Visually digital instruments, enabling practically immediate and free spread on knowledge look like marking "the end of economy" and placing the communities to the age of digitally determinate direct management. Meanwhile, economic processes, moved by the private interests, are still at the basis of supply chains, and the advance of digitalization, its economic and social effects will depend on the proper balance between technological and economic dimensions.

Really, in digital society the criteria of supply chain performance are significantly modified. Digitalization brings much more sophisticated knowledge concerning the complex impact of production of goods and services, and brings much more alternative opportunities, taken into account to assess the performance. Given the increasing part of locally supplied services in overall consumption, the assessment criteria, that take into account the performance of local living space, presented by local community, are gaining more and more weight.

Thus, future research opportunities of the topic lay in large extent in the studies of the ways how "smart" instruments are integrating technological and institutional changes into consistent sustainable development of the community. A number of significant issues of this problem are still on the way of being explained, systematized and solved.

The reliable ways of common services' commodification in socially fair, non-exclusive way, supportive for the quality of the services and good governance of corresponding local communities' functions should be found.

The proper regulations are still wanted for the arrangement of data collection and processing in the spheres subject to commodification. The goals are to avoid the risks of monopolization, increase of informational asymmetry, personal data privacy violation.

A prospective research opportunity touches upon the ways of inclusion of targeted social groups into networked consumption. In order to increase the local demand both for digital and "physical" goods and services, the special requirements and the opportunities of their realization should be studied for the specific target groups – like young people, young families, families with children, people in "silver age" etc.

The general trend of participatory democracy as a part of E-democracy should be complemented by the effective instruments of qualified producing of distributed solutions, public control, self-governance performance assessment and monitoring. This needs the study of the perception of newly designed participatory instruments by the communities and of the ways to overcome the "digital gap" as the barrier for inclusive governance.

The technologically conditioned capacity to decentralize the decisions in significant for local communities' spheres determines the importance of the studies of potential risks from the technological autonomization of the stakeholders of local development, destroying the core supply chains, of ways to shift successfully from vertical to network (cluster) organization of sectors of local economy and supply chains rearrangement on these principles.

Finally, the choice between inward and outward oriented construction of supply chains by local development stakeholders depends on their local identity. Thus, the studies are needed of the substance of this identity in digital age, of the motivation to rational endogeneity of the supply chains.

CONCLUSION

The overall digitalization and formation of "Digital society" phenomenon mean the comprehensive changes in the various dimensions of economic and social life, reflected in the changes of traditional and implementation of new supply chains. The emergence of "smart" communities (usually treated as "smart" cities, however, the author believes more correct is the term Smart cities and communities (SC&C), recommended by the European Commission) represents the immense opportunities to optimize the utilization of available local resources within the locally-based supply chains.

The advance of technologies definitely makes the supply chains more complicated, involving more resources and producing more thorough results. Meanwhile, the advance of technologies proceeds much faster, than changes in institutions, responsible for the integration of supplied hi-tech products with the demand side, determined by the life of communities and behavior patterns of their members. Namely, these institutions in fact change the performance of modern supply chains, *converting complication* to *sophistication*.

Thus, the chapter did not attempt to cover the everyday changing digital technologies, available for "smart" communities. The aim was to reveal the institutional changes, taking place implicitly, under the pressure of digital revolution, as well as to discuss the possible institutional improvements, instruments and incentives, necessary to optimize the positive impacts of digital advance for the quality of life, development opportunities and sustainability of these communities. And to promote the further implementation of "smart" networks in local communities.

The emergence of new quality of supply chains in SC&C is driven by strengthening spillover of knowledge, generated by modern digital technologies of data collection and converted into knowledge within "smart" networks. Obtained new knowledge, "smart" communities and their members modify their preferences and behavior and present more sophisticated demand for traditional local goods and services. This demand enables the commodification of a wider scope of locally consumed goods and services.

Local social capital should be considered as crucial in grounding the sophisticated supply chains, adding new values to networked consumption of definite social communities and repositioning economic agents regarding the commitment to sustainable utilization of local resources. The need for the sustainability is underpinned by the localization of the additional values and finalization of supply chains predominantly within the boundaries of certain communities.

Partnership between local communities and private business in the compilation of extended supply chains seems to be the optimal way to realize the positive potential of digitalization and to provide the opportunities for digital technologies' penetration into more conservative spheres and communities, reducing the "digital gap". Thus, the sophistication of supply chains, driven by "smart" local communities, promotes the overall improvement of supply chains' performance in modern digital society.

REFERENCES

Albert, S., Flournoy, D., & Lebrasseur, R. (2009). *Networked communities: strategies for digital collaboration*. Information Science Reference. doi:10.4018/978-1-59904-771-3

Beg, D., Fiše, S., & Dornbuš, D. (2010). *Makroekonomija* [Macroeconomics]. Datastatus.

Breque, M., De Nul, L., & Petridis, A. (2021). *Industry 5.0. Towards a sustainable, human-centric and resilient European industry*. EC R&I PAPER SERIES.

BSR. (2017). *Future of Supply Chains 2025*. Retrieved on October 4, 2021 from https://www.bsr.org/files/work/BSR_Future_of_Supply_Chains_Primer.pdf

Coe, A., Paquet, G., & Roy, J. (2001). E-governance and smart communities: A social learning challenge. *Social Science Computer Review*, *19*(1), 1, 80–93. doi:10.1177/089443930101900107

Cohen, W. M., & Levinthal, D. A. (1990). Absorptive capacity: A new perspective on learning and innovation. *Administrative Science Quarterly*, *35*(1), 128–152. doi:10.2307/2393553

Coleman, J. (1988). Social capital in the creation of human capital. *American Journal of Sociology*, *94*, 95–120. doi:10.1086/228943

Fukuyama, F. (1999). *Social Capital and Civil Society. The Institute of Public Policy*. George Mason University.

Habermas, J. (1979). *Communication and the Evolution of Society*. Beacon Press.

Hitachi and The University of Tokyo Joint Research Laboratory. (Ed.). (2020). *Society 5.0 A People-centric Super-smart Society*. Springer Open.

Hodgson, G. (1988). *Economics and Institutions: A Manifesto for a Modern Institutional Economics*. Polity Press, Cambridge and University of Pennsylvania Press. doi:10.9783/9781512816952

Janjevic, M., Winkenbach, M., & Rice, J. B., Jr. (2020). *5 Reasons Why Your Supply Chain Design Must Change with the Times*. Retrieved on October 4, 2021 from https://www.supplychain247.com/article/5_reasons_why_your_supply_chain_design_must_change_with_the_times)

Komninos, N. (2002). *Intelligent cities: Innovation, knowledge systems and digital spaces*. Routledge.

Langlois, R. N., & Robertson, P. L. (2018). Stop crying over spilt knowledge: A critical look at the theory of spillovers and technical change. *Journal of Public Finance and Public Choice*, *33*(1), 63–80. doi:10.1332/251569118X15214757059213

Leen, J., & Lanng, C. (2020). *Here's how global supply chains will change after COVID-19*. Retrieved on November 1, 2021 from https://www.weforum.org/agenda/2020/05/this-is-what-global-supply-chains-will-look-like-after-covid-19/

McLean, G. (Ed.). (1996). Civil society and social reconstruction. Cultural Heritage and Contemporary Change, 1, 16.

Nagurney, A. (2006). *Supply Chain Network Economics: Dynamics of Prices, Flows, and Profits*. Edward Elgar.

Putnam, R. D. (1993). The prosperous community: Social capital and public life. *The American Prospect*, *13*, 35–42.

Romer, P. (1986). Increasing Returns and Long-Run Growth. *Journal of Political Economy*, *94*(5), 1002–1037. doi:10.1086/261420

Romer, P. (1987). Growth Based on Increasing Returns Due to Specialization. *The American Economic Review*, *77*(2), 56–62.

Romer, P. (1990). Endogenous technological change. *Journal of Political Economy*, *98*(5), 71–101. doi:10.1086/261725

Schiavo-Campo, S., & Sundaram, P. (2000). *To Serve and to Preserve: Improving Public Administration in a Competitive World*. Asian Development Bank.

Sredojević, D., Cvetanović, S., & Bošković, G. (2016). Technological changes in economic growth theory: neoclassical, endogenous, and evolutionary-institutional approach. *Economic Themes*, *54*(2), 177–194. doi:10.1515/ethemes-2016-0009

Stratigea, A. (2012). The concept of 'smart cities'. Towards community development? *NETCOM*, *26*(3/4), 375–388. doi:10.4000/netcom.1105

Thomson, G., & Newman, P. (2018). Urban fabrics and urban metabolism – from sustainable to regenerative cities. *Resources, Conservation and Recycling*, *132*, 218–229. doi:10.1016/j.resconrec.2017.01.010

UK Government Commercial Function. (2020). *The Social Value Model Edition 1.1.* Retrieved on November 1, 2021 from https://assets.publishing.service.gov.uk/government/uploads/system/uploads/attachment_data/file/940826/Social-Value-Model-Edn-1.1-3-Dec-20.pdf

United Nations Habitat III. (2016). *New Urban Agenda Draft Outcome Document for Adoption in Quito.* Retrieved on October 6, 2021 from https://habitat3.org/the-new-urban-agenda/

Van Iersel, J. (2018). New Concepts for the City of the Future. *City: One*, *2*, 5.

Von Hippel, E. (1994). 'Sticky information' and the locus of problem solving: Implications for innovation. *Management Science*, *40*(4), 429–439. doi:10.1287/mnsc.40.4.429

Walt, N., Doody, L., Baker, K., & Cain, S. (2014). Future Cities. UK capabilities for urban innovation. *Future Cities Catapult.* Retrieved on October 10, 2021 from https://www.arup.com/perspectives/publications/research/section/future-cities-uk-capabilities-for-urban-innovation

Wu, Z., & Jia, F. (2018). Toward a theory of supply chain fields – understanding the institutional process of supply chain localization. *Journal of Operations Management*, *58-59*(1), 27–41. doi:10.1016/j.jom.2018.03.002

Yueh, L. (2020). Localization of production: COVID-19's medium-term impact. *OECD Development Matters.* Retrieved on October 10, 2021 from https://oecd-development-matters.org/2020/04/27/localisation-of-production-covid-19s-medium-term-impact/

Zhalilo, Y. (2018). Institutional Background of Effective Strategies for Business Sustainability. In R. D. Leon (Ed.), *Managerial strategies for business sustainability during turbulent times* (pp. 23–40). IGI Global. doi:10.4018/978-1-5225-2716-9.ch002

Zhang, Y., Yang, Z., & Yu, X. (2015). Urban Metabolism: A Review of Current Knowledge and Directions for Future Study. *Environmental Science & Technology*, *49*(19), 11247–11263. doi:10.1021/acs.est.5b03060 PMID:26321071

Ziółkowski, M. (2004). Commodification of Social Life. *Polish Sociological Review*, *148*, 385–402.

KEY TERMS AND DEFINITIONS

Commodification: A process of involvement of a product, previously excluded from commerce, to the market turnover.

Knowledge Spillover: Dissemination of knowledge, created by some entity (individual or organization), to the availability of all the members of the community, complemented with their capacity to utilize this knowledge in their activities.

Networked Consumption: The consumption of systems of some goods and services, the value of which reveals in full extent due to the network communication of their consumers, while the consumption itself serves at the identifier of affiliation with this network.

"Smart" City: The model of systemic management of urban community, based on the inclusive integrated implementation of intellectual digital technologies, managing the basic processes of community's life.

"Smart" Network: Intellectual technology, which manages a process, using the digital control and monitoring instruments to optimize its supply chain.

Sophistication: The evolution of a subject, improving its complexity, self-regulation, adaptivity, manageability and sustainability.

Spatial: Reflecting the features of the subject, associated with its internal topology and external positioning with respect to other subjects.

Sustainability: The capacity to maintain in long run the main functional features in spite of changing external environment.

Synergy: Dynamic interrelation between the elements of a system and a system and its environment, bringing to system the new features, exceeding the sum of features of its elements.

Section 3

Back to Basics: From Robotization and Digitalization to the Current and Future Human Resource

Chapter 12
Sustainable Supply Chain Learning and Employee Green Creativity:
Implications for Disruption Management and Green Competitiveness

Innocent Senyo Kwasi Acquah
https://orcid.org/0000-0002-6332-3005
Department of Marketing and Supply Chain Management, University of Cape Coast, Ghana

Charles Baah
https://orcid.org/0000-0002-4959-7851
Charles Darwin University, Australia

Yaw Agyabeng-Mensah
Dalian Maritime University, China

Ebenezer Afum
Transportation Engineering College, Dalian Maritime University, China

ABSTRACT

Exploring ways to maintain and safeguard supply chain operations and performance is essential in today's business environment. Learning from the COVID-19 pandemic situations shows that current or traditional supply chain management strategies are less potent in managing supply chain disruption. The study adopted the partial least square structural equation modelling (PLS-SEM) technique to make data analysis and interpretations because it is considered suitable for predictive research models. Scrutiny of the data showed that sustainable supply chain learning is a critical antecedent for employee green creativity. Both were fundamental to managing supply chain disruptions, promoting green competitiveness and increasing economic performance. Remarkably, among sustainable supply chain learning and employee green creativity, the latter was most robust in predicting disruption management, green competitiveness, and economic performance.

DOI: 10.4018/978-1-7998-9715-6.ch012

Copyright © 2022, IGI Global. Copying or distributing in print or electronic forms without written permission of IGI Global is prohibited.

INTRODUCTION

Supply chains, learning from the COVID-19 pandemic, economic reverberations have ensued supply chain disruptions across industries, with some yet to recover from the shock (Sarkis, 2021) fully. The origins of the COVID-19 pandemic further provide evidence that businesses and their supply chain networks are embedded in the natural environments. Environmental impacts have repercussions for business operations (El Baz & Ruel, 2020; Sarkis, 2021). El Baz and Ruel (2020) suggested that the pandemic significantly impacted supply chains. The authors further categorised these effects into operational and disruption risks. Although past scholars have emphasised the impacts of operational risks in the supply chain context, less emphasis is on disruption risks. This is partly due to their low frequency yet high impacts, high uncertainty and rippling effects across supply chain networks and beyond (El Baz & Ruel, 2020; Hosseini, Ivanov, & Dolgui, 2019; Ivanov, 2020; Sarkis, 2021).

Explaining further, the real social, economic and political disruption from the pandemic has triggered several scholars and practitioners to engage in studies and practices that aim to alleviate the dire impacts faced by firms in the COVID-19 era (Araz, Choi, Olson, & Salman, 2020; Fahimnia, Jabbarzadeh, & Sarkis, 2018; Xu, Zhang, Feng, & Yang, 2020). According to Guan et al. (2020), the pandemic crisis shock on supply chains was profound across global networks affecting the core of demand and supply. These shocks have stirred the call for sustainable and resilient supply chains perceiving that some practitioners and scholars (El Baz & Ruel, 2020; Hosseini et al., 2019; Ivanov, 2020; Sarkis, 2021) are debating if current traditional supply chain strategies and policies can survive the post-COVID-19 era. These debates have guided the relevance of sustainable supply chain learning and green creativity among firms' employees in this digitised era. Digitisation has improved the access, storage, and processing of significant amounts of data. Yet, creating an supply chain learning based integrated conceptual model for such digitisation processes and data can be crucial for organisations in enhancing agility and adaptability (Yang, Jia, & Xu, 2019). Hence, relying on the extended resource-based view, the authors emphasised that supply chain learning promotes crucial information and data sharing that profoundly shapes employee responsiveness, creativity and overall firm performance. Jia, Gong, and Brown (2019) assertions, also harmonising with Yang et al. (2019), specify that supply chain leadership through supply chain learning promotes sustainable chain management, which also crucially improves employee creativity. These scholars' assertion indicates that in the quest to improve supply chain resilience and sustainability, supply chain learning and employee green creativity can be critical weapons in achieving desired outcomes. Despite the recognition, only a few studies come close to integrating and assessing the correlations between sustainable supply chain learning and employee green creativity, especially from the COVID-19 perspective.

While supply chain learning is widely defined, sustainable supply chain learning is a novel concept that lacks a consensus as to its definition (Haq, Gu, & Huo, 2020; Yang et al., 2019). Haq et al. (2020) defined supply chain learning as the procedure of a focal firm acquiring, assimilating, and exploiting information and knowledge across internal functions and from key suppliers and customers. Huo, Haq, and Gu (2020) also asserted that supply chain learning integrates and synergises information from the acquisition stage to the usage stage in supply chains. From these scholars, this study defines sustainable supply chain learning as acquiring, assimilating, and exploiting sustainable information to improve green functions and satisfy the sustainable demands of customers and suppliers. Furthermore, Wieland, Handfield, and Durach (2016) posited that despite extant literature on supply chains, the employees or human aspects of supply chains still lack rigorous study, making it one of the most overlooked research areas in supply chain management literature. Capturing employee green creativity in the supply chain context and this study also seeks to contribute to this overlooked research area. Employee green creativity emphasises the capacity of employees to produce novel and relevant ideas that promote green product development, innovations and environmental performance (Tuan, 2020).

Moreover, the unprecedented disruptions caused by the COVID-19 pandemic further push the agenda towards finding reliable and responsive solutions that can promise reductions in disruption risks and boost disruption management in the context of supply chains. Additionally, the growing link between sustainability, circular economy and firm competitiveness has coerced the need to safeguard strict adherence to environmental preservation laws by firms to stay competitive and gain legitimacy (Afum, Agyabeng-Mensah, Mensah, Mensah-Williams, Baah, & Dacosta, 2021; Agyabeng-Mensah, Tang, Afum, Baah, & Dacosta, 2021; Baah et al., 2021a). Ivanov and Dolgui (2020) call for more empirical probes on building supply chain resilience and robustness to help firms survive the present and future impacts of the COVID-19 pandemic. However, Van Hoek (2020) elucidates that managers in supply chains continue to face difficulties in handling operational and disruption risks mainly due to the inability to integrate concepts that propel firm responsiveness, agility and adaptability. Thus, van Hoek (2020) and Ivanov and Dolgui (2020) urge researchers to conduct empirical works that synergise supply chain concepts and support supply chain managers in handling COVID-19 challenges and risks. Hence, this study investigates how sustainable supply chain learning influences employee green creativity and how the two correlate with disruption management, green competitiveness, and the economic performance of firms in the COVID-19 crisis and from the perspective of an emerging economy.

More specifically, this study empirically tests an original model that examines (1) how sustainable supply chain learning drives employee green creativity and (2) how sustainable supply chain learning and employee green creativity influence (a) disruption management, (b) green competitiveness and (c) economic performance of firms. The rest of the paper is organised as follows. Section 2 of the study exposes the theoretical framework and hypotheses development. While Sections 3 and 4 reveal research methods and results. Section 5 captures the discussion and conclusion, highlighting theoretical and managerial implications, research limitations, and future research direction.

THEORETICAL FRAMEWORK

Natural Resource-Based View and Dynamic Capabilities Perspectives

Deliberations as to the core make-up of the RBV continues in the strategic management field (Kauffman, 2015; Singh, Chen, Del Giudice, & El-Kassar, 2019). While some scholars contend that the human resource aspect is at the core (Teece, 2014; Wright, Dunford, & Snell, 2001). Barney (2001) and Wernerfelt (2014) also postulate that amalgamating valuable, rare, inimitable and non-substitutable (RBV of the firm) resources leads to competitive advantage. From the natural resource-based view (NRBV) perspective, the integration of minimisation of adverse environmental impacts and response to environmental concerns have established the concept (Hart, 1995; McDougall, Wagner, & MacBryde, 2021). McDougall et al. (2021) suggested that attaining green competitiveness is rooted in leveraging sustainable initiatives into business operations. Huo et al. (2020) explained that supply chain learning breeds sustainable culture and responsiveness for focal firms, which also enables dynamic capabilities (DC) (Teece, 2014). According to Teece (2014), DC is the firm's ability to effectively integrate, build and reconfigure competencies in response to changing business environments. In today's business settings, stakeholders are mounting significant pressures on supply chains and have coerced focal firms to improve their green core competencies through green creativity as espoused by the DC. Singh et al. (2019) also highlighted that managers and employees' ability to align skills, motives, attitudes and knowledge within supply chain networks, systems, processes, and practices help cultivate green creativity, green competitiveness and dynamic capabilities at the firm level.

Further emphasising the crucial roles of sustainable supply chain learning and employee green creativity, the study focuses on risks associated with disruptions in the supply chains. Supply chain disruptions threaten firm survival due to their high impacts and rippling effects (El Baz & Ruel, 2020). Araz et al. (2020), about COVID-19 disruptions, asserted that damaged supply chain flows and performances resulted in dire consequences for employees. Ivanov (2020) disclosed that although past studies had focused on building supply chain resilience and robustness to ensure efficient management of disruptions, the recent pandemic crisis proved that significant work and research is needed. Hence, further evaluating supply chain management practices and concepts are necessary. Relying on the NRBV and DC, sustainable supply chain learning allows employees to acquire, assimilate, and use ecological data and information from customers, suppliers, and internal departments. This builds the focal firm's knowledge base while developing employee green capabilities and responsiveness to ecological concerns. As fixated in the NRBV and DC, these expanded capabilities promise higher financial and competitive gains while also breeding social, moral and political capitals, which are crucial in disruption management and risk control during periods of crisis and uncertainties.

From a practical perspective, integrating sustainable supply chain learning will ensure improved employee innovation, creativity, skills, motives, attitudes and knowledge of supply chain operations, resulting in an original, novel, and useful ideas (Chen & Chang, 2013). As elucidated by Chen and Chang (2013), green creativity echoes creating original, novel, and useful ideas that promote ecological balance anchored on the firm's dynamic capabilities. Drawing on insights from the NRBV and DC, this study advances that sustainable supply chain learning enhances employee green creativity ensures efficient disruption management and higher economic performance (Teece, 2014). It also promotes green competitiveness through the continuous interactions between increasing ecological demands, green innovation and the need to attain green legitimacy (Teece, 2014). In addition, the NRBV and the DC, through ecological supply chain learning and employee green creativity, enable focal firms to decrease negative environmental impacts through the use of employee cognitive and affective abilities that guarantee efficient management of supply chain disruptions green competitiveness economic performance. Before establishing the study hypotheses, we present the definitions of the study variables below:

Supply Chain Learning: This is an intangible strategic resource created when multiple organisations on an informational level develop, share and collaborate about supply chain further creating competence and a bonding element deeply embedded in the supply relationships that drive supply chain management and success, and can create a competitive advantage (Biotto, De Toni, & Nonino, 2012; Zhu, Krikke, & Caniels, 2018).

Employee Green Creativity: This highlights the development of new ideas and employee capabilities related to green products, green services, green processes, or green practices judged to be original, novel, and valuable (Chen & Chang, 2013).

Disruption Management: This is the procedure through which firms take appropriate steps or interventions to minimise risk effects after the occurrence of events that disrupt the normal flow of goods and materials within the supply chain (Kuster, Jannach, & Friedrich, 2009; Macdonald & Corsi, 2013).

Green Competitiveness: The capability to realise benefits from environmental management and green innovation strategies and, as such, occupies a position where competitors cannot copy such environmental strategies (Agyabeng Mensah et al., 2021; Chen & Chang, 2013).

Economic Performance: This highlights the combination of resources, policies and capabilities of firms to supply chain operations to achieve marketing, operational, and financial performances (Agyabeng Mensah et al., 2020; Afum et al., 2020).

Hypotheses Development

Sustainable Supply Chain Learning and Employee Green Creativity

Persisting high levels of environmental uncertainty have made it vital for focal firms to engage in sustainable supply chain learning to develop employee creativity and responsiveness (Bag, Wood, Xu, Dhamija, & Kayikci, 2020). Ahmadi and Amin (2019) posited that with the high levels of uncertainty in contemporary supply chains, focal firms should focus on learning to build employee creativity and develop dynamic capabilities that help manage disruptions and mitigate risks. Bag et al. (2020) further highlighted that green learning in supply chains is now highly relevant since negative environmental impacts of businesses can result in reputational, financial, economic and competitive risks. While sustainable supply chain learning is critical in developing resilient and responsive supply chains that can efficiently manage disruptions and mitigate risks, it also pushes innovation while building the capabilities and creativity of employees. In a study conducted by Ouakouak and Ouedraogo (2017), the authors emphasised that learning is a critical antecedent for employee creativity and is also a crucial antecedent for organisational innovation. Jyoti and Dev (2015) also asserted that employee creativity is a mandatory requirement in a firm's effort to stay competitive. Thus, the author stressed that employees could build their creative capabilities to sustain organisational competitiveness and economic performance through learning orientation. From the discourse, we hypothesise:

H1. Sustainable supply chain learning is positively related to employee green creativity

Sustainable Supply Chain Learning, Disruption Management, Green Competitiveness and Economic Performance

Achieving the goals of sustainable supply chain learning requires solid relational ties with stakeholders (Yang et al., 2019). The acquisition of green information and data to its usage integrates collaborative efforts from all stakeholders. These collaborative efforts and integration of supply chain partners into environmental initiatives support higher green competitiveness and efficient disruption management (Acquah, Naude, & Sendra-García, 2021; Baah et al., 2021a). Through sustainable supply chain learning, focal firms can stay current on market dynamics. Employees can also stay innovative and adapt in time to meet market demands, thereby significantly reducing risk while sustaining economic performance. Luthra and Mangla (2018) claimed that employee creativity rooted in innovation could be a proactive management strategy for supply chain network disruptions and risks. Acquah et al. (2021) affirmed that employee supply chain learning and cooperation are relevant to achieving collaboration goals. Baah et al. (2021b) also stressed that the learning, sharing and incorporation of information in supply chains boost flexibility which has also been known to contribute positively to risk management financial and economic performances in supply chains. Particularly, Zhan, Tan, Chung, Chen, and Xing (2020), from the green perspective, emphasised that businesses engaged in supply chain learning and have the right employee creativity and capabilities can make precise forecasts in determining the right marketing and operational strategies that will reduce risks and costs. In addition, sustainable supply chain learning can aid focal firms to make ecological moves in their industries before competitors. Besides, they can also assist employees in eliminating green products, strategies and initiative failures and uncertainties, ultimately resulting in reduced costs, decreased risks and higher economic performance. From the above discourse, we hypothesise:

H2. Sustainable supply chain learning is positively related to green competitiveness **(a)**, disruption management **(b)** and economic performance **(c)**.

Employee Green Creativity, Disruption Management, Green Competitiveness and Economic Performance

Sustainability has become mandatory for firms to achieve green competitiveness (Mittal & Dhar, 2016). Thus, firms are under increased pressure to integrate green initiatives in every aspect of firm operations (Baah et al., 2021a,b). Most importantly, Chen and Chang (2013) indicated that green creativity is an essential tool in building a sustained competitive strategy that will boost overall performance and strengthen supply chain robustness and resilience. The authors also explained that this happens through the ability of employees to adapt and come up with novel ideas about green products, green services, green processes and practices that are deemed as crucial in the mitigation of risks. Gong, Huang, and Farh (2009) highlighted that employee green creativity is an essential element that stirs innovation and ensures the fulfilment of duties even under uncertain and strenuous circumstances. Specifically, Jiang et al. (2020) postulate that employee green creativity is a comprehensive capability that captures an individual's green creative motivation, green creative thinking, green creative outcome and green creative behaviour. According to Jiang et al. (2020), these four components drive employees to engage in green practices and processes and create ideas that strengthen supply chain networks. El Baz and Ruel (2020) further stressed that having a creative and innovative employee base can positively manage disruption risks. Although extant literature has employed several supply chain risk mitigation approaches, using employee green creativity as a mitigation strategy is novel and has potential, as Chen and Chang (2013) indicated. El Baz and Ruel (2020), supporting Chen and Chang (2013), also claimed that the efficiency of risk mitigation strategies relies on collaborations between employees and supply chain partners. These collaborative efforts robustly control and decrease disruption risks because an employee with green creativity capabilities ensures effective and efficient systematic processes, responsive practices, risk awareness and procedures when dealing with supply chain partners. From the enormous benefits exposed in this section, we hypothesise:

H3. Employee green creativity is positively related to green competitiveness **(a)**, disruption management **(b)** and economic performance **(c)**.

Disruption Management, Green Competitiveness and Economic Performance

The turbulent nature of today's business environments coupled with the complex nature of local and global supply chain networks have made disruption management a must for firms due to the dire consequences and risks that disruptions present (Christopher & Howleg, 2011; Durach, Kembro, & Wieland, 2017). According to Weiland et al. (2016), scholars have made numerous efforts to identify myriads of risks mitigation approaches and strategies. Yet, the recent COVID-19 pandemic has shown that more potent risk mitigation strategies need to be employed. For instance, Fiat Chrysler Automobiles NV and Hyundai had to suspend and halt operations due to the inability to receive and access parts from China, Korea and other parts of the globe in the early stages of the outbreak (in late February 2020). Ivanov (2020) indicated that the ascending of the ripple effects in the second quarter had been exponential as a result of disruption in manufacturing and production processes, which had also resulted in the closure of facilities, stores, and logistics activities (Choi, Guo, & Luo, 2020; Ni, Xiao, & Lim, 2020). According to Mishra et al. (2019), such disruptions have caused the shutdown of several firms. The few firms that managed these disruptions have achieved competitive advantage and higher economic and financial performances. Ivanov (2020) further suggested that effective management of disruptions in supply chains give focal firms the ability to sustain production and manufacturing processes during turbulent periods. Efficient disruption management practices promote risk and cost reduction while maintaining higher firm performance. From the discourse, we hypothesise:

H4. Disruption management is positively related to green competitiveness **(a)** and economic performance **(b)** of focal firms.

Figure 1. Research model and hypothesised relationships

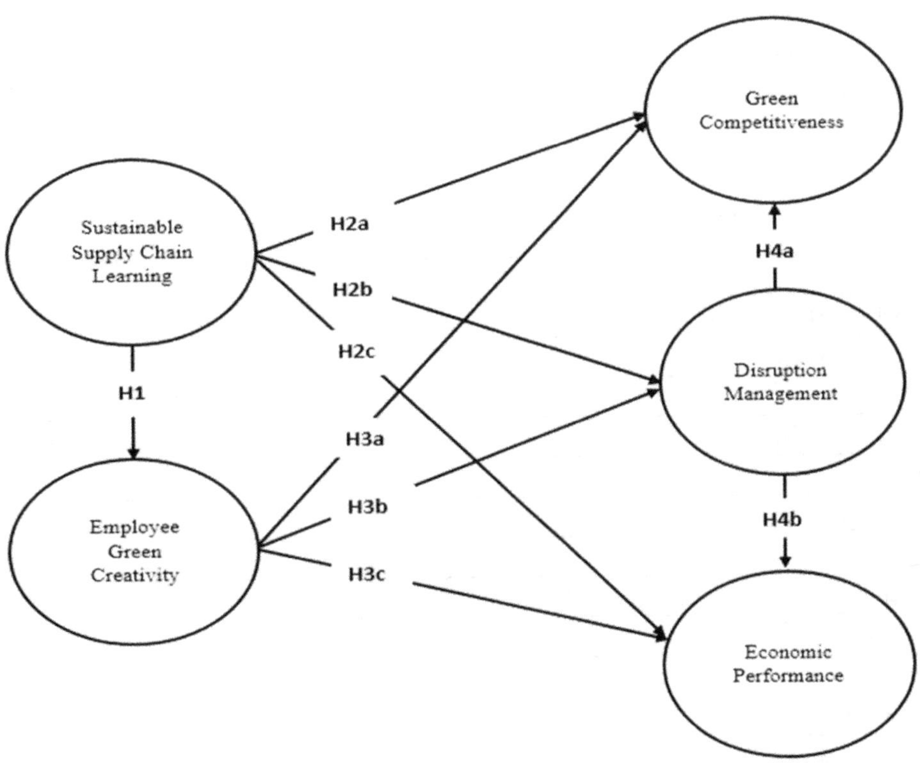

RESEARCH METHODS

Sample, Data Collection and Common Method Bias (CMB)

Through a review of extant literature, the study formed questionnaires based on the theoretical and conceptual framework of the study, as indicated in Figure 1. The questionnaires solicited primary information on a sample of 340 SMEs, which were randomly chosen from a list of about 3008 obtained from the Association of Ghana Industries using the purposive sampling technique (Agyabeng-Mensah et al., 2020). After contacting human resource departments, we sent the questionnaires and an explanatory cover letter to selected firms via e-mail. After two weeks' intervals, follow up phone calls were placed to show gratitude and serve as reminders for non-respondents. From the 340 questionnaires distributed among manufacturing SMEs, we retrieved 252, giving a response rate of about 74%. These received questionnaires were further cleaned and used in the data analysis.

Following the guidelines of Podsakoff, MacKenzie, Lee, and Podsakoff (2003), we employed Harman's one-factor test to check for issues of common method bias (CMB), and the results from the exploratory factor analysis (EFA) showed that the single factor explained 34.157% of the cumulative variance. This result is below the recommended threshold of 50% shows the study is free from issues of CMB. Specifically, the questionnaires presented well-structured separation of measured items, promised anonymity to respondents, and obtained measures from different sources, in line with Podsakoff et al.

Table 1. Characteristics of respondents

Firm characteristics (n=252)	Frequency (%)
Number of employees	
<10	38 (15%)
11-50	29 (12%)
51-100	45 (18%)
101-500	61 (24%)
501-1000	33 (13%)
>1000	46 (18%)
Industry	
Wood, lumber products and processing	53 (21%)
Rubber and other plastic products	45 (18%)
Food and beverages	62 (25%)
Leather products and processing	36 (14%)
Textile and fabric products	30 (12%)
Others	26 (10%)
Job Qualification	
Managing Directors	90 (36%)
Supply chain managers	88 (35%)
Procurement managers	46 (18%)
Logistics/Warehouse managers	28 (11%)

(2003) recommendations. Also, the study employed Kaiser-Meyer-Olkin Measure of Sampling Adequacy (KMO) and Bartlett's Test of Sphericity in examining that the data is sufficient for factor analysis and comparing the observed correlation matrix to the identity matrix, respectively. The findings showed that the KMO measure of sampling adequacy was 0.789 and acceptable. Bartlett's test showed a significance value of 0.000, which is below the threshold of 0.005. Therefore, these conclusions show the adequacy of the sample for factor analysis and no issues of high correlation. Table 1 reveals the characteristics of respondents.

Measurement Model Assessment

The study adopted a 5-point Likert scale, where 1 represented strongly disagree to 5 strongly agree, to measure the extent to which respondents agreed or disagreed with each item as is the case in their respective firms. The study adopted a 5point Likert scale based on the recommendation of Sachdev and Verma (2004) that it reduces respondents' frustration level and increases response rate and quality. Furthermore, Confirmatory Factor Analysis (CFA) was conducted on each measurement item to ensure the model has validity and reliability. According to Hair, Ringle, and Sarstedt (2013), items with factor loadings above 0.70 should be maintained in a model and items below 0.70 should be deleted. The authors indicated that deleting lower loading items strengthens the model path, Average Variance Extracted (AVE), R Squared (R^2) and predictive relevance (Q^2). Relying on this recommendation, we deleted measurement items that loaded below 0.70 from the model. The quantitative study employed Partial Least Square Structural Equation Modelling (PLS-SEM) (SmartPLS software 3.0) to make data analysis and interpretation.

Additionally, structural model evaluation in PLS-SEM employs measurement criteria that examine the model's performance, quality and suitability. As claimed by Henseler, Ringle, and Sarstedt (2015), a model's reliability and validity should be assessed using Cronbach's alpha (CA), Composite Reliability (CR), AVE and Heterotrait-Monotrait Ratio (HTMT) ratio and should have values ≥ 0.70, ≥ 0.70, ≥ 0.60, > 0.50 and < 0.90 respectively to be considered satisfactory. From Table 2, the model constructs have internal consistency reliability because the CR and CA were between 0.881 to 0.906 and 0.800 to 0.861. The AVEs, which assess that indicators measured one underlying construct, were recommended to 0.554 to 0.706. Henseler et al. (2015) posited that the factor loadings were above the recommended threshold of 0.70. The outer VIFs also connoted the study is free from multicollinearity issues since all values were < 3.

Furthermore, we scrutinised discriminant validity using the HTMT ratio. The HTMT ratio uses the correlation estimates attained from examining hetrotrait-heteromethod correlations relative to monotrait-heteromethod correlations, highlighting that a model has discriminant validity when HTMT ratios are < 0.90. from Table 3, the model achieves discriminant validity since all ratios were < 0.90. The correlations among the variables have also been captured in Table 3.

Table 2. Measurement items, reliability and validity

Measurement items	CR	CA	AVE	Factor loading	Outer VIF
Sustainable Supply Chain Learning (SSCL)	**0.906**	**0.861**	**0.706**		
1: Our company ensures employees are constantly learning about better ecological ways in serving customers and supply chain partners				0.815	1.986
2: Our firm shares environmental information with all supply chain stakeholders				0.878	2.457
3: Our company ensures that managers and employees learn and improve ways to manage supply chain environmental concerns				0.853	2.233
4: Through learning and new knowledge acquisition, our firm tries to help managers and employees adapt and change attitudes towards environmental initiatives in our supply chains				0.814	1.776
Employee Green Creativity (EGC)	**0.861**	**0.800**	**0.554**		
1: Our employees proposes new green ideas to promote environmental performance				0.766	1.812
2: Our firm and employees frequently suggests new avenues to achieve environmental goals and targets				0.702	1.472
3: Our employees ensures the generation of novel ways to implement green ideas				0.781	1.874
4: Our employees are constantly proposing creative solutions to environmental issues/ problems				0.824	1.774
5: Our employees frequently promote the rethinking of already implemented and new green ideas				0.712	1.290
Green Competitiveness (GC)	**0.872**	**0.816**	**0.579**		
1: Our green products and services are better than those of competitors				0.702	1.574
2: Our green competitive advantage is better than competitors				0.708	1.389
3: Our business green processes is better than competitors				0.814	2.558
4: Our managerial and employee capabilities are better than competitors				0.830	2.167
5: Our green strategies and reputation are better and stronger than competitors				0.774	2.898
Disruption Management (DM)	**0.881**	**0.821**	**0.650**		
1: Our firm and employees are highly sensitised for the perception of supply disruptions risks				0.743	1.464
2: Our company employs strategies that reduce stoppages in production and supply chains				0.788	2.015
3: Our disruption and risk management processes are very professionally designed				0.788	1.982
4: Our company aims to frequently diminish the impact of occurrence of supply chain disruptions and risks				0.897	2.514
Economic Performance (EP)	**0.883**	**0.834**	**0.603**		
1: Reduced inventory management cost				0.868	2.252
2: Increased sales growth				0.788	2.059
3: Increased market share				0.773	1.809
4: Increased return on assets				0.767	2.036
5: Increased net profit return				0.715	1.531

*CA- Cronbach's Alpha; CR- Composite Reliability; AVE- Average Variance Extracted; VIF- Variance Inflation Factor

Table 3. Correlations and HTMT ratio

Construct	1	2	3	4	5
1. Disruption Management	**1.000**	0.628	0.586	0.573	0.295
2. Economic Performance	0.751	**1.000**	0.764	0.680	0.501
3. Employee Green Creativity	0.680	0.872	**1.000**	0.728	0.384
4. Green Competitiveness	0.684	0.823	0.864	**1.000**	0.385
5. Sustainable Supply Chain Learning	0.337	0.585	0.438	0.460	**1.000**

*Construct HTMT values are below the diagonal elements, and correlation values are above the diagonal elements

RESULTS AND DISCUSSIONS

Structural Model Evaluation

After confirming the model has reliability, convergent and discriminant validity, we evaluate the structural model and test hypotheses by scrutinising the R^2 and Q^2. Also, we examined the path coefficients (β) and significance levels (p-values) as recommended by Hair et al. (2013). Hair et al. (2013) explain that reporting the R^2 and Q^2 in PLS-SEM is necessary for empirical exploratory studies. Stone-Geisser's Q^2 explains a model has predictive relevance when Q^2 values are > 0. From Table 4, the exogenous constructs robustly explained the variance of the endogenous constructs, and the blindfolding procedure confirmed that the constructs have predictive relevance since Q^2 values are > 0.

Table 4. Structural model's R^2 and Q^2

Endogenous constructs	R^2	R^2 Adjusted	Q^2
Disruption Management	0.349	0.342	0.196
Economic Performance	0.676	0.670	0.367
Employee Green Creativity	0.148	0.143	0.071
Green Competitiveness	0.572	0.565	0.293

Testing of Hypothesised Relationships

After establishing the model meets all reliability and validity criteria, we further report and discuss the study's findings. The analysis and findings showed that sustainable supply chain learning positively related to employee green creativity (β=0.384, T=4.566, p=0.000), green competitiveness (β=0.106, T=1.781, p=0.076), disruption management (β=0.0.081, T=1.335, p=0.183) and economic performance (β=0.222, T=3.725, p=0.000). The findings further indicated that while sustainable supply chain learning significantly correlated with employee green creativity and focal firm economic performance, its effects on green competitiveness and disruption management were insignificant. These findings confirm that while learning in supply chains aids in equipping employees to engage capabilities that lead to higher economic performance, supply chain learning as an independent variable has minimal influence on green competitiveness and disruption management. Ivanov (2020) indicated support for these findings by asserting that the implementation of acquired knowledge causes significant impacts, not only on learning. Weiland et al. (2016) stressed that employees and dynamic capabilities are the most critical aspects of supply chains' disruption and risk management. As such, supply chain learning forms an antecedent for higher employee creativity and responsiveness in dealing with disruptions, resulting in increased economic and green competitiveness (Acquah et al., 2021; Luthra & Mangla, 2018; Zhan et al., 2018). Gong et al. (2018) also emphasised that sustainable supply chain learning requires employees' right attitude and behaviour before achieving its objectives. The positive effect of sustainable supply chain learning supports hypotheses H1, H2a, H2b and H2c, although it insignificantly correlated with green competitiveness and disruption management, as presented in Table 5.

Table 5. Hypothesis testing

Hypothesis	Coefficient (β)	T Value	P Value	Standard Error	Inner VIFs	Decision
H1: SSCL → EGC	0.384	4.566	**0.000**	0.084	1.000	Supported
H2a: SSCL → GC	0.106	1.781	0.076	0.059	1.184	Not Supported
H2b: SSCL → DM	0.081	1.335	0.183	0.061	1.173	Not Supported
H2c: SSCL→ EP	0.222	3.725	**0.000**	0.060	1.184	Supported
H3a: EGC → GC	0.563	9.025	**0.000**	0.062	1.646	Supported
H3b: EGC → DM	0.555	10.000	**0.000**	0.055	1.173	Supported
H3c: EGC → EP	0.532	9.011	**0.000**	0.059	1.646	Supported
H4a: DM → GC	0.213	3.167	**0.002**	0.067	1.536	Supported
H4b: DM → EP	0.251	3.855	**0.000**	0.065	1.536	Supported

p-values in bold are significant at 0.01 significance level (two-tailed)

Furthermore, employee green creativity, as indicated by the analysis of the data, had positive and significant impacts on green competitiveness (β=0.563, T=9.025, p=0.000), disruption management (β=0.555, T=10.000, p=0.000) and economic performance (β=0.532, T=9.011, p=0.000). The robustness of the findings shows that employee green creativity in this modern sustainability era is crucial in ensuring superior overall firm performance (Jiang et al., 2020; Mittal & Dhar, 2016). While Mittal and Dhar (2016) postulated that green creativity promotes employee innovation and ensures green product development and green legitimacy, Jiang et al. (2020) also posited that employee green creativity significantly sustains green competitiveness while also building employee responsiveness and innovation. Ivanov (2020) connoted employee innovation as crucial in managing supply chain disruptions and risks. From the findings, employee green creativity proves potent in supporting efficient disruption management and increasing the focal firm's green competitiveness and economic performance. Employee green creativity is essential in today's business environment characterised by uncertainties and volatilities. Having a green creative employee base enables the firm to develop useful and novel ideas to tackle market dynamics. This dynamic employee capability also allows efficient disruption management techniques that yield reduced costs and higher risk control, eventually improving firm competitiveness and economic performance. Thus, establishing support for hypotheses H3a, H3b and H3c.

In relation to hypotheses H4a and H4b, the data analysis indicated that disruption management is critical in influencing green competitiveness and economic performance, as claimed by El Baz and Ruel (2020). The findings showed that disruption management positively and significantly influenced green competitiveness (β=0.213, T=3.167, p=0.002) and economic performance (β=0.251, T=3.855, p=0.000). Several scholars have asserted the positive impact of disruption management on firm performance mostly from the perspectives of financial, economic and general competitiveness (El Baz & Ruel, 2020; Hosseini et al., 2019; Ivanov, 2020; Simchi-Levi et al., 2018). However, this study confirms the crucial role of disruption management in boosting economic performance and adds to the literature by indicating that disruption management also increases green competitiveness. In today's business environments, disregarding environmental concerns and regulations is a critical risk that can break up supply chain partners and stakeholder relations and disrupt the production and supply chain networks. Moreover, reducing costs associated with risks and disruptions makes available resources invested into green initiatives, thus boosting green competitiveness. Thus, the findings support hypotheses H4a and H4b as presented in Table 5 and Figure 2.

*-Not significant; **-Significant

Figure 2. Structural model showing Coefficient (β), T values, R^2 and Q^2

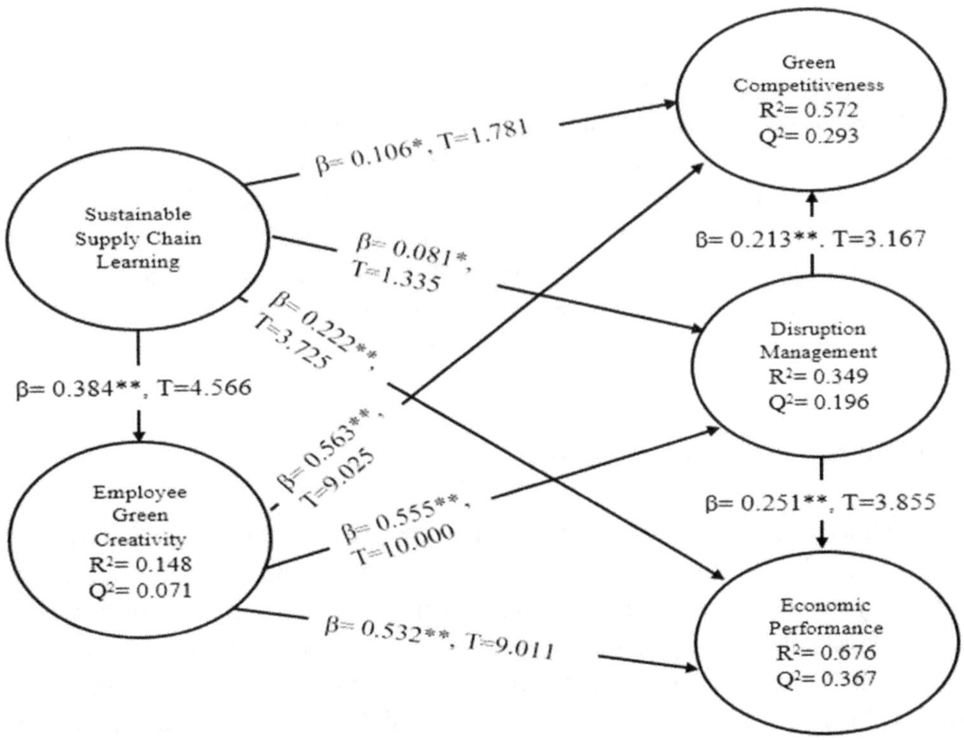

*-Not significant; **-Significant

CONCLUSION

The study examined how sustainable supply chain learning and employee green creativity can be useful tools in managing disruptions and boosting green competitiveness and economic performance. The study also emphasised sustainable supply chain learning as a crucial antecedent to employee green creativity whiles also capturing the two as critical techniques in managing supply chain disruptions and risks. Learning from the effects of the recent COVID-19 pandemic, focal firms must begin to rethink their traditional supply chain risk and disruption management strategies. Past studies indicate that despite the numerous efforts to build resilience and robustness in supply chains, the COVID-19 pandemic showed more needs to be done, especially from risk control, sustained competitiveness, and economic performance. Drawing insight from the NRBV and the dynamic capabilities theories, the study suggests that focal firms can better guard against supply chain disruptions and risks through sustainable supply chain learning and employee green creativity. The study results indicated that sustainable supply chain learning is crucial for achieving employee green creativity and economic performance. Although a sustainable supply chain is also important to achieve green competitiveness and manage disruptions, the impacts were positive but insignificant. Amongst sustainable supply chain learning and green employee creativity, the former was most potent in influencing disruption management, green competitiveness and economic performance. This suggests that firms should acquire and develop an employee base that exhibits green creativity to reap its benefits.

Notably, the robustness of employee green creativity in influencing disruption management, green competitiveness and economic performance presents a novel approach to ensuring supply chain resilience and robustness. As such, focal firms should inspire efforts to develop and grow employee capabilities rooted in the dynamic capabilities theory. Again, the influence of disruption management on green competitiveness and economic performance also expose the fact that efficiently handling and managing supply chain disruptions will lead to reduced costs and damages, further adding to higher economic performance and green competitiveness. The study presenting a novel approach to safeguarding the higher firm performance and risk management establishes that sustainable supply chain and employee green creativity are essential to disruption management, green competitiveness, and the economic performance of focal firms. We discuss the theoretical and practical implications below based on the study results.

Theoretical and Practical Implications

Adopting and implementing strategies that can reduce risk in contemporary supply chains is essential learning from the COVID-19 pandemic. Whiles sustainable supply chain learning and employee green creativity, if rightly integrated, can fight against supply chain disruptions and ensure green competitiveness and higher economic performance, few studies have empirically explored the potency of these variables. Drawing on the NRBV and the dynamic capabilities theories, the study shows that sustainable supply chain learning helps employees develop green dynamic capabilities, which lead to the creation of useful ideas and innovations. From a COVID-19 pandemic scenario as well as from the context of a developing country, adds to the sustainability literature by integrating the NRBV and DC theories to provide a better assessment of how (1) sustainable supply chain learning influences employee green creativity and (2) both variables collectively impact disruption management, green competitiveness and economic performance. The results drawing on the NRBV and the DC theories show that although sustainable supply chain learning benefits the organisation, employee green creativity robustly and significantly relates to disruption management, green competitiveness and economic performance. This is due to its ability to expose employees' green creative motivation, thinking, behaviour and outcomes. With the NRBV being fundamental to how sustainable supply chain learning and the DC drive employee green capabilities in supply chains, the study adds to the literature by indicating that learning supports green creativity and improves disruption management, green competitiveness, and economic performance.

The study provides results that should inspire firm management to implement strategies that will boost sustainable learning and green creativity from a practical perspective. The study results portray sustainable supply chain learning and employee green creativity as critical tools for focal firms in managing risks. Thus, firms, policymakers and supply chain partners can rely on these variables to help mitigate cost in times of crisis or uncertainty. Largely, this study calls on firms and supply chain partners to encourage green creativity to develop a supply chain employee base that is responsive, critical thinkers and innovative to ensure supply chain flexibility and resilience and efficient disruption management. Managers and employees should commit efforts and resources to learn and develop their creative thinking, creative behaviour, creative motivation and creative outcomes to better ensure responsiveness to supply chain disruptions risk mitigation, further sustaining supply chain flexibility, robustness, resilience and performance.

Limitation and Future Research Direction

Despite the novel insights of the study, some limitations still exist and should be addressed by future studies. Future studies should focus on and test hypotheses on supply chain digitisation trends while exploring other dynamic employee capabilities that lead to efficient supply chain disruption and risk management. Other variables that affect supply chain networks and their dimensions can be captured as predictor variables to give a comprehensive view of their influence on financial and economic performances and green competitiveness. Additionally, considering the cross-sectional nature of data collected, future studies should collect data over time to reflect or expose the long-term interactions between the variables in this era of COVID-19 and lockdowns. In addition, the study concentrated on small and medium-sized enterprises operational in an emerging economy, Ghana. Further studies can also consider larger firms or a combination of small and medium-sized firms and larger firms operating in emerging economies. Future studies can also capture the other variables such as logistics innovation and supply chain innovation on risk management, green competitiveness, robustness and financial performance in different sectors.

REFERENCES

Acquah, I. S. K., Naude, M. J., & Sendra-García, J. (2021). Supply chain collaboration in the petroleum sector of an emerging economy: Comparing results from symmetrical and asymmetrical approaches. *Technological Forecasting and Social Change*, *166*, 120568. doi:10.1016/j.techfore.2020.120568

Afum, E., Agyabeng-Mensah, Y., Mensah, A. O., Mensah-Williams, E., Baah, C., & Dacosta, E. (2021). Internal environmental management and green human resource management: Significant catalysts for improved corporate reputation and performance. *Benchmarking*, *28*(10), 3074–3101. doi:10.1108/BIJ-09-2020-0504

Agyabeng-Mensah, Y., Afum, E., Acquah, I. S. K., Dacosta, E., Baah, C., & Ahenkorah, E. (2020). The role of green logistics management practices, supply chain traceability and logistics ecocentricity in sustainability performance. *International Journal of Logistics Management, 32*(2), 538–566. doi:10.1108/IJLM-05-2020-0187

Agyabeng-Mensah, Y., Tang, L., Afum, E., Baah, C., & Dacosta, E. (2021). Organisational identity and circular economy: Are inter and intra organisational learning, lean management and zero waste practices worth pursuing? *Sustainable Production and Consumption, 28*, 648–662. doi:10.1016/j.spc.2021.06.018

Ahmadi, S., & Amin, S. H. (2019). An integrated chance-constrained stochastic model for a mobile phone closed-loop supply chain network with supplier selection. *Journal of Cleaner Production, 226*, 988–1003. doi:10.1016/j.jclepro.2019.04.132

Araz, O. M., Choi, T. M., Olson, D. L., & Salman, F. S. (2020). Data Analytics for Operational Risk Management. *Decision Sciences, 51*(6), 1316–1319. doi:10.1111/deci.12443

Baah, C., Agyeman, D. O., Acquah, I. S. K., Agyabeng-Mensah, Y., Afum, E., Issau, K., ... Faibil, D. (2021a). Effect of information sharing in supply chains: Understanding the roles of supply chain visibility, agility, collaboration on supply chain performance. *Benchmarking, 29*(2), 434–455. doi:10.1108/BIJ-08-2020-0453

Baah, C., Opoku-Agyeman, D., Acquah, I. S. K., Agyabeng-Mensah, Y., Afum, E., Faibil, D., & Abdoulaye, F. A. M. (2021b). Examining the correlations between stakeholder pressures, green production practices, firm reputation, environmental and financial performance: Evidence from manufacturing SMEs. *Sustainable Production and Consumption, 27*, 100–114. doi:10.1016/j.spc.2020.10.015

Bag, S., Wood, L. C., Xu, L., Dhamija, P., & Kayikci, Y. (2020). Big data analytics as an operational excellence approach to enhance sustainable supply chain performance. *Resources, Conservation and Recycling, 153*, 104559. doi:10.1016/j.resconrec.2019.104559

Barney, J. B. (2001). Resource-based theories of competitive advantage: A ten-year retrospective on the resource-based view. *Journal of Management, 27*(6), 643–650. doi:10.1177/014920630102700602

Biotto, M., De Toni, A. F., & Nonino, F. (2012). Knowledge and cultural diffusion along the supply chain as drivers of product quality improvement: The illycaffè case study. *International Journal of Logistics Management, 23*(2), 212–237. doi:10.1108/09574091211265369

Chen, Y. S., & Chang, C. H. (2013). Greenwash and green trust: The mediation effects of green consumer confusion and green perceived risk. *Journal of Business Ethics, 114*(3), 489–500. doi:10.100710551-012-1360-0

Choi, T. M., Guo, S., & Luo, S. (2020). When blockchain meets social-media: Will the result benefit social media analytics for supply chain operations management? *Transportation Research Part E, Logistics and Transportation Review, 135*, 101860. doi:10.1016/j.tre.2020.101860

Christopher, M., & Holweg, M. (2011). "Supply Chain 2.0": Managing supply chains in the era of turbulence. *International Journal of Physical Distribution & Logistics Management, 41*(1), 63–82. doi:10.1108/09600031111101439

Durach, C. F., Kembro, J., & Wieland, A. (2017). A new paradigm for systematic literature reviews in supply chain management. *The Journal of Supply Chain Management*, *53*(4), 67–85. doi:10.1111/jscm.12145

El Baz, J., & Ruel, S. (2021). Can supply chain risk management practices mitigate the disruption impacts on supply chains' resilience and robustness? Evidence from an empirical survey in a COVID-19 outbreak era. *International Journal of Production Economics*, *233*, 107972. doi:10.1016/j.ijpe.2020.107972

Fahimnia, B., Jabbarzadeh, A., & Sarkis, J. (2018). Greening versus resilience: A supply chain design perspective. *Transportation Research Part E, Logistics and Transportation Review*, *119*, 129–148. doi:10.1016/j.tre.2018.09.005

Gong, Y., Huang, J. C., & Farh, J. L. (2009). Employee learning orientation, transformational leadership, and employee creativity: The mediating role of employee creative self-efficacy. *Academy of Management Journal*, *52*(4), 765–778. doi:10.5465/amj.2009.43670890

Guan, D., Wang, D., Hallegatte, S., Davis, S. J., Huo, J., Li, S., Bai, Y., Lei, T., Xue, Q., Coffman, D. M., Cheng, D., Chen, P., Liang, X., Xu, B., Lu, X., Wang, S., Hubacek, K., & Gong, P. (2020). Global supply-chain effects of COVID-19 control measures. *Nature Human Behaviour*, *4*(6), 577–587. doi:10.103841562-020-0896-8 PMID:32493967

Hair, J. F. Jr, Ringle, C. M., & Sarstedt, M. (2013). Partial least squares structural equation modeling: Rigorous applications, better results and higher acceptance. *Long Range Planning*, *46*(1-2), 1–12. doi:10.1016/j.lrp.2013.01.001

Haq, M. Z. U., Gu, M., & Huo, B. (2020). Enhancing supply chain learning and innovation performance through human resource management. *Journal of Business and Industrial Marketing*, *36*(3), 552–568. doi:10.1108/JBIM-12-2019-0534

Hart, S. L. (1995). A natural-resource-based view of the firm. *Academy of Management Review*, *20*(4), 986–1014. doi:10.5465/amr.1995.9512280033

Henseler, J., Ringle, C. M., & Sarstedt, M. (2015). A new criterion for assessing discriminant validity in variance-based structural equation modeling. *Journal of the Academy of Marketing Science*, *43*(1), 115–135. doi:10.100711747-014-0403-8

Hoek, R. V. (2020). Responding to COVID-19 supply chain risks—Insights from supply chain change management, total cost of ownership and supplier segmentation theory. *Logistics*, *4*(4), 23. doi:10.3390/logistics4040023

Hosseini, S., Ivanov, D., & Dolgui, A. (2019). Review of quantitative methods for supply chain resilience analysis. *Transportation Research Part E, Logistics and Transportation Review*, *125*, 285–307. doi:10.1016/j.tre.2019.03.001

Huo, B., Haq, M. Z. U., & Gu, M. (2020). The impact of IT application on supply chain learning and service performance. *Industrial Management & Data Systems*, *120*(1), 1–20. doi:10.1108/IMDS-10-2018-0476

Ivanov, D. (2020). Predicting the impacts of epidemic outbreaks on global supply chains: A simulation-based analysis on the coronavirus outbreak (COVID-19/SARS-CoV-2) case. *Transportation Research Part E, Logistics and Transportation Review*, *136*, 101922. doi:10.1016/j.tre.2020.101922 PMID:32288597

Ivanov, D., & Dolgui, A. (2020). Viability of intertwined supply networks: Extending the supply chain resilience angles towards survivability. A position paper motivated by COVID-19 outbreak. *International Journal of Production Research*, *58*(10), 2904–2915. doi:10.1080/00207543.2020.1750727

Jia, F., Gong, Y., & Brown, S. (2019). Multi-tier sustainable supply chain management: The role of supply chain leadership. *International Journal of Production Economics*, *217*, 44–63. doi:10.1016/j.ijpe.2018.07.022

Jyoti, J., & Dev, M. (2015). The impact of transformational leadership on employee creativity: The role of learning orientation. *Journal of Asia Business Studies*, *9*(1), 78–98. doi:10.1108/JABS-03-2014-0022

Kaufman, B. E. (2015). The RBV theory foundation of strategic HRM: Critical flaws, problems for research and practice, and an alternative economics paradigm. *Human Resource Management Journal*, *25*(4), 516–540. doi:10.1111/1748-8583.12085

Kuster, J., Jannach, D., & Friedrich, G. (2009). Extending the RCPSP for modeling and solving disruption management problems. *Applied Intelligence*, *31*(3), 234–253. doi:10.100710489-008-0119-x

Luthra, S., & Mangla, S. K. (2018). Evaluating challenges to Industry 4.0 initiatives for supply chain sustainability in emerging economies. *Process Safety and Environmental Protection*, *117*, 168–179. doi:10.1016/j.psep.2018.04.018

Macdonald, J. R., & Corsi, T. M. (2013). Supply chain disruption management: Severe events, recovery, and performance. *Journal of Business Logistics*, *34*(4), 270–288. doi:10.1111/jbl.12026

McDougall, N., Wagner, B., & MacBryde, J. (2021). Leveraging competitiveness from sustainable operations: Frameworks to understand the dynamic capabilities needed to realise NRBV supply chain strategies. *Supply Chain Management*, *27*(1), 12–29. doi:10.1108/SCM-11-2018-0393

Mittal, S., & Dhar, R. L. (2016). Effect of green transformational leadership on green creativity: A study of tourist hotels. *Tourism Management*, *57*, 118–127. doi:10.1016/j.tourman.2016.05.007

Ni, D., Xiao, Z., & Lim, M. K. (2020). A systematic review of the research trends of machine learning in supply chain management. *International Journal of Machine Learning and Cybernetics*, *11*(7), 1463–1482. doi:10.100713042-019-01050-0

Ouakouak, M. L., & Ouedraogo, N. (2017). Antecedents of employee creativity and organisational innovation: An empirical study. *International Journal of Innovation Management*, *21*(7), 1750060. doi:10.1142/S1363919617500608

Podsakoff, P. M., MacKenzie, S. B., Lee, J. Y., & Podsakoff, N. P. (2003). Common method biases in behavioral research: A critical review of the literature and recommended remedies. *The Journal of Applied Psychology*, *88*(5), 879–903. doi:10.1037/0021-9010.88.5.879 PMID:14516251

Sachdev, S. B., & Verma, H. V. (2004). Relative importance of service quality dimensions: A multisectoral study. *Journal of Services Research*, *4*(1), 1–24.

Sarkis, J. (2021). Supply chain sustainability: Learning from the COVID-19 pandemic. *International Journal of Operations & Production Management*, *41*(1), 63–73. doi:10.1108/IJOPM-08-2020-0568

Singh, S. K., Chen, J., Del Giudice, M., & El-Kassar, A. N. (2019). Environmental ethics, environmental performance, and competitive advantage: Role of environmental training. *Technological Forecasting and Social Change*, *146*, 203–211. doi:10.1016/j.techfore.2019.05.032

Teece, D. J. (2014). The foundations of enterprise performance: Dynamic and ordinary capabilities in an (economic) theory of firms. *The Academy of Management Perspectives*, *28*(4), 328–352. doi:10.5465/amp.2013.0116

Tuan, N. H., Mohammadi, H., & Rezapour, S. (2020). A mathematical model for COVID-19 transmission by using the Caputo fractional derivative. *Chaos, Solitons, and Fractals*, *140*, 110107. doi:10.1016/j.chaos.2020.110107 PMID:33519107

Wernerfelt, B. (2014). On the role of the RBV in marketing. *Journal of the Academy of Marketing Science*, *42*(1), 22–23. doi:10.100711747-013-0335-8

Wieland, A., Handfield, R. B., & Durach, C. F. (2016). Mapping the landscape of future research themes in supply chain management. *Journal of Business Logistics*, *37*(3), 205–212. doi:10.1111/jbl.12131

Wright, P. M., Dunford, B. B., & Snell, S. A. (2001). Human resources and the resource based view of the firm. *Journal of Management*, *27*(6), 701–721. doi:10.1177/014920630102700607

Xu, S., Zhang, X., Feng, L., & Yang, W. (2020). Disruption risks in supply chain management: A literature review based on bibliometric analysis. *International Journal of Production Research*, *58*(11), 3508–3526. doi:10.1080/00207543.2020.1717011

Yang, Y., Jia, F., & Xu, Z. (2019). Towards an integrated conceptual model of supply chain learning: An extended resource-based view. *Supply Chain Management*, *24*(2), 189–214. doi:10.1108/SCM-11-2017-0359

Zhan, Y., Tan, K. H., Chung, L., Chen, L., & Xing, X. (2020). Leveraging social media in new product development: Organisational learning processes, mechanisms and evidence from China. *International Journal of Operations & Production Management*, *40*(5), 671–695. doi:10.1108/IJOPM-04-2019-0318

Zhu, Q., Krikke, H., & Caniels, M. C. (2018). Supply chain integration: Value creation through managing inter-organisational learning. *International Journal of Operations & Production Management*, *38*(1), 211–229. doi:10.1108/IJOPM-06-2015-0372

Chapter 13
Human Resources Management: Challenges in the Digital Society

Nisa Eksili
Akdeniz University, Turkey

ABSTRACT

In the digital world, computers have turned into objects that know more than humans. Devices are redefining the human way of living in a network that allows people to talk to each other. On the one hand, suspicion and fear about technology increased; on the other hand, it became impossible to stay away from a life without technology. In this process, the contribution of digitalization to productivity, the convenience and speed it provides to the business world has made digitalization necessary in all sectors. The role of human resources management (HRM) is very important in the realization of digital transformation in businesses. This role comes to the fore both in adapting to changing social norms and adapting to changes within the enterprise. HRM also has difficulties in this process. This chapter provides background on the challenges HRM faces in the digital society. The digitalization process, digitalization and its effects in businesses, the effects of the digitalization process on employees, working environment, and HR technologies are mentioned.

INTRODUCTION

The world is undergoing far-reaching cultural, social and economic changes due to the increasing dominance of digital technologies. Technological developments that bring new concepts to all areas of life also change our thought processes. The changes that have emerged with technology have led to the characterization of the period we live in as the "digital age" (Çaylak, 2020; Strohmeier & Parry, 2014). In the digital age, the world is struggling with major changes in culture, society and economy that are the direct results of the digital revolution. This change, whose focus is human, has transcended cities, states, countries and continents. It is an evolutionary movement rather than a revolutionary one. Although this new era, called digital society, seems to be a result of information technology, many economic, political, cultural and social factors are effective in the formation of digital society (Sayar, 2016). Therefore, instead of interpreting the digital society and the concepts of digitalization as an element that determines the

DOI: 10.4018/978-1-7998-9715-6.ch013

Copyright © 2022, IGI Global. Copying or distributing in print or electronic forms without written permission of IGI Global is prohibited.

basic characteristics of society and the society that emerges with digitalization; It should be described as the society in the digitalized world. After all, it is people who produce both information and digital technologies that lead to digitalization (Martin, Reddington, & Alexander, 2008).

These internet-based new technologies, which have an impact on society in general, are the driving force of changes in the corporate world (Unruh & Kiron, 2017). The acceleration of technological innovations has changed the behavior of individuals and businesses as well as market structures (Henriette, Feki, & Boughzala, 2016). The digitalization of processes with new technologies in many areas of life has forced businesses to make a big change. Almost all sectors are under the influence of this digital transformation or digitalization (Jurisic & Kermek, 2011). Companies are doing exciting work with digital technology and reaping impressive business benefits. The fact that large traditional companies embrace the digital environment and find ways to make it their own shows that they can outrun fast-moving digital businesses. Businesses that cannot adapt to the digital world or resist digital transformation will disappear from the competitive environment (Udovita, 2020). In parallel with this transformation, which has strategic importance for businesses (Henriette et al., 2016), digital technologies have become indispensable both in the lives of employees and in human resources management (HRM), which is seen to be affected in more than one way (Strohmeier & Parry, 2014). In this process, businesses also need to digitally transform their basic HR functions, including recruitment and selection, performance management, career management, training-development and compensation (Lanvin, Evans, & Rodriguez-Montemayor, 2016).

Digitalization in HRM includes strategic management of talent, nature, role and contribution of technology (Thite, 2019). Digital HRM increases individual employee engagement, competence, and harmony with each other (Nivlouei, 2014). In the organizational context, it benefits by restructuring HRM activities, improving the quality of HRM services and increasing efficiency, reducing costs by turning HRM functions into a strategic business partner (Marler & Fisher, 2010). Studies in the field of digital HRM focus on improvement in management, strategy, organization, human resources, human resources technologies, human resources functions and positions, organizational structure, leadership style, human resources practices, innovation, talent, transformation of business and competencies. There are challenges to be experienced in this whole transformation process. In line with this information, the aim of this study is to define human resources management and human resources in the digital society, and to reveal the effects and challenges of digital transformation in businesses and digital HRM practices. In this context, digitalization and its effects, HRM and challenges in the digitalization process will be tried to be explained through literature review.

BACKGROUND

Digitalization and its Effects

The first industrial revolution, which occurred at the end of the eighteenth century, was triggered by the advent of steam engines, waterpower, and mechanization. The second industrial revolution emerged with assembly lines pioneered by Henry Ford, who first formalized mass production almost a century ago. The third industrial revolution that occurred in the 1970s was realized with the use of computers and automation in production processes (Savic, 2019). The fourth industrial revolution is Industry 4.0, which is a subclass of digital transformation in current business and current processes, and digital computer structures replace manual business operations (Burmeister, Luettgens, & Piller, 2016). Industrialization, which means the use of machines instead of manpower, has gone through four phases in the last two hundred years (Çelik & Topsakal, 2019). The term Industry 4.0 was introduced at the Hannover Fair in 2011. Industry 4.0, which can be defined as the integration of information and communication technologies into production systems in order to provide flexible, personalized and customized products (Rojko, 2017), is based on smart production applications. Industry 4.0 is also interpreted as the application of cyber-physical systems, which are defined as systems in which a physical mechanism is monitored and controlled by computer algorithms, within industrial production systems (Posada et al., 2015). Among the basic technologies that trigger the emergence of Industry 4.0; especially cyber-physical systems, internet of things (Tao, Zuo, Xu, & Zhang, 2014), smart robots, big data analysis (Russom, 2011), augmented reality, cloud technologies (Hayes, 2008; Xu, 2012), mobile internet (Soliman & Youssef, 2003), horizontal and vertical software integration is counted (Bharadwaj, Sawy, Pavlou, & Venkatraman, 2013; Kagermann, Lukas, & Wahlster, 2011). Today, the main factor in the formation of smart factories is cyber-physical systems. Smart production is carried out by equipping it with technologies such as cyber-physical systems, internet of things, wireless sensor networks, big data, cloud computing, embedded systems and mobile internet (Hozdić, 2015). The value produced by integrating the internet of services and objects into industrial processes (Kagermann et al., 2013) and analyzing data that is a source of competitive advantage (Porter & Heppelmann, 2015) is very important for the sustainability of businesses (Greif, Kühnis, & Warnking, 2016).

This change caused by digitalization is often devastating, but also radically changes the current functioning (Matzler et al., 2016). As a result, these technologies, which are integrated into business processes and ways of doing business, have brought businesses that want to maintain their competitive position to the brink of a transformation. This transformation has affected many things, from customer behavior to the production processes of businesses and the way they serve their customers. In the environment of change and transformation brought about by information technologies, the functions of the digital business need to be redefined. There is a horizontal and vertical digital integration of all systems and processes in the business using the same interfaces. Businesses can estimate the demands of consumers more realistically, and produce personalized products for their customers at less cost, with processes that are in contact and that can be intervened remotely. This system, when the customer has a problem with a product, immediately reports the situation to the customer service and makes easier to serve the customer better (Ekşili & Çetinkaya Bozkurt, 2021).

It is necessary to consider the digital transformation of businesses as a result of digitalization and also as a necessity (Tapscott & Barry, 2009). While digitalization creates the necessary technological foundation for business processes that turn into digital, it also necessitates such a transformation. Considering that businesses that resist or cannot adapt to digital transformation will disappear from the competitive environment (Udovita, 2020), businesses should plan digital transformation by minimizing the possibility of failure systematically. This planning should cover all the capabilities of the business. Christensen (2006) identified the capabilities of businesses by distinguishing between 'resources, processes and priorities'. Accordingly, resources are tangible such as facilities and human resources and intangible values such as brands and patents. Processes express the continuous operations in which the work is done, and priorities express the strategies and values of the enterprise (Perkin & Abraham, 2017).

It would be correct to evaluate the digitalization process in businesses with a resource-based approach. According to this approach a business provides a competitive advantage with the combination of valuable, rare, not perfectly imitated and non-substitutable resources (Barney, 1991). Among these intangible resources, technological resources are particularly important, which provide the firm are important for the creation of competitive advantages. In addition, human resources, like digital technologies, are seen as sources of competitive advantage in a business (Eller, Alford, Kallmünzer, & Peters, 2020; Rodriguez & Rodriguez, 2005). Hence, digitalized HRM and sub-functions such as e-recruitment and e-learning will further increase the added value of these resources of the enterprise. For example, automated and digitized recruitment allows a company to increase speed, reduce cost, and improve quality or the recruiting process. In addition, digital technologies save HR professionals the effort and time they spend on routine tasks, causing them to focus on more strategic tasks and provide a competitive advantage in terms of sustainable performance (Strohmeier, 2007).

MAIN FOCUS OF THE CHAPTER

HRM in the Digitalization Process and the Challenges

HRM has a strategic role in the digitalization process of businesses (Bondarouk, Parry, & Furtmueller, 2009; Thomas, 2020). Indeed, with Industry 4.0, advanced cloud-based systems, big data analysis, the internet of things and the effects of both artificial intelligence and robotic technology on businesses and employees require a digital human resource management approach (Pantelidis, 2019). In this context, the digitization of the corporate human resources function is also of particular importance due to the increasing role of digitized HRM for business success. Digital HRM is concerned with the role, contribution and nature of technology in managing talent in new world (Thite, 2019). Dijital HRM is defined as the use of computer systems, interactive electronic media and telecommunication networks to fulfill the functions of the human resources department in a narrow sense (Iraz & Yıldırım, 2005). The focus of digital HRM is an innovation-driven digital workforce, a digital workplace with a learning organization mindset, and a global, responsive, ethical and sustainable culture (Deloitte, 2017). Strohmeier and Parry (2014) examined these issues under the umbrella of digital HRM under three headings: "digital employees", "digital work" and "digital employee management". In this process, businesses need to switch to digital transformation in all of their basic HRM functions such as the selection and placement process, training and development, career and performance management and compensation. This transition is necessary to achieve Human Resources 4.0, not only by acquiring new skills, but also by creating real transformational change in the people management architecture and eco-system (Lanvin et al., 2016).

The role of HR departments in the context of digitization is twofold: they not only facilitate the overall digitization of a business (Ulrich, 1998) but also the digital transformation itself. First, it promotes development and corporate culture within the company by supplying new employees with the necessary digital knowledge and skills. This can help leaders and employees lead a digital mindset, digital management, organization and change. The second is applied through the application of various digital technologies to HRM sub-functions and processes. It revolutionizes the experience of all employees by transforming HRM processes, systems and organization through new digital platforms, applications and services (Stephen, 2016; Thomas, 2020). This is necessary to meet the need for human resources, who have the necessary skills for the jobs that change or emerge with Industry 4.0 (Habraken & Bondarouk, 2017). In order to define the challenges that will arise in this process, it is possible to examine digital transformation in HRM in three focal points: 'employees', 'work' and 'employee management'. The concept of digital employees in the digital age refers to the new generation with attitudes, qualities, behaviors and expectations that differ from others due to early and close interaction with digital technologies. The first challenge for HRM is to identify real digitally driven changes in the attitudes, qualifications, behavior and expectations of young workers. In this direction, strategic and operational coordination of HRM with changing workforce qualifications should be ensured. The second challenge is related to work. Due to digitalization and increasing automation, the way of working is progressing steadily towards information processing and production, hence from physical activity to mental activities. Qualifications expected from its employees are requires broader technical and mental skills to systematically acquire, process, produce and use knowledge. For this, employees are expected to have digital literacy and multitasking skills (Strohmeier & Parry, 2014). Therefore, HRM needs to be able to manage these demands and adapt the changing business contents to the digitalizing organization. The third challenge relates to managing the planning and implementation of technologies that HRM uses for employee management. The technological transformation of HRM activities such as payroll processing, performance evaluation, remuneration, career planning is in question in the HRM step of digitalized organizations.

Digital Employee

The concept of digital employees, who have had early, friendly and permanent interaction with digital technologies, represents a generation with distinctly different attitudes, qualities, behaviors and expectations. This generation, which makes up the majority of employees in the digital age we live in, started with the Y generation. This generation has attracted attention by being entrepreneurial and collaborative, having technological knowledge in working life. They do not support traditional office rules and hierarchy (Schawbel, 2012). Therefore, they are not affected by titles and positions in the traditional hierarchy pyramid structure, and they cannot understand the strict hierarchical order in the workplace (Zemke, Raines, & Filipczak, 2013). They have changed the understanding that work has to be done between traditional working hours. However, they think that they should be allowed to determine their own time zones in the workplace. Members of this generation prefer a flexible approach and argue that as long as the work is done, where it was done should not be considered (Zemke et al., 2013). In addition to the challenges arising from the young and inexperienced nature of the Z generation, which is just about to enter the working life, it is necessary to understand the unique characteristics of this generation in the digital world. Understanding their behavior and needs will lead to better integration and mutual success of new employees (Schroth, 2019). It is clear that HRM needs to respond to such changes and tailor its strategies and activities to this new labor market grouping. HRM can be used to recruit, develop, compensate, etc. such digital employees. It seeks adequate ways for employees and, moreover, to integrate them with previous generations of employees. Therefore, the challenge for HRM is to identify digitally driven changes in the attitudes, qualifications, behaviors and expectations of young workers (Strohmeier & Parry, 2014).

Digital Work

Digitization requires change in the organization of work. Due to digitalization and increasing automation, the way of working is progressing steadily from physical activity to information processing and production. The qualifications expected of their employees also require broader technical and mental skills to systematically acquire, process, produce and use information. For this, employees are expected to have digital literacy and multitasking skills. Therefore, HRM needs to be able to manage these demands and adapt the changing business contents to the digitalizing organization (Strohmeier & Parry, 2014). Employees' information is increasingly dependent on digital tools and media. The need for technological devices arises from the speed offered by technology to employees and the principle of not being tied to space and time. This integration of technology and mobility has created a new working model in business life. This model brings up the concept of mobile collar workers, who have the understanding of being able to do their job from anywhere and anytime, regardless of time and place (Adıgüzel et al., 2014). Today, more than 25% of workers in developed countries have the initiative to determine their own working time and place (Thite, 2019). The lack of face-to-face communication arising from the working environment is one of the challenges encountered for the management of human relations and processes (Martin et al., 2008).

In traditional businesses, while the progress in the careers of the employees was directly proportional to the seniority in the enterprises, the managers determined how, when and where the work would be done by whom. In these businesses, HRM perspective is the form of that employees are not active, the employee's education is planned by the manager of his career. But nowadays, businesses have to change the perspective of human resources. Many customers and businesses benefit from labor of self-employed gig economy workers. Freelance designer, publishers broadcasting on YouTube constitute the labor market of this new economy (Lanvin et al., 2016). On the other hand, due to robotics and automation, half of existing jobs are facing transformation or extinction. However, thanks to new technologies such as big data, cloud computing and the internet of things, it is estimated that approximately five hundred thousand new jobs will be created by the next three years (Dehaze, 2016). Therefore, while developments in technology change jobs, today's employees have to have skills and qualification parallel to this transformation (Thite, 2019).

Digital Employee Management

Today, the Human Resources Information System (HRIS) plays a strategic role in the decision-making process for effective and efficient HRM. For HRM decision making, most researchers suggest expert systems or knowledge-based systems (Masum, Beh, Azad, & Hoque, 2018). Decision-making processes in digital HRM information technology (IT) and HRM fundamentally affect various HR processes and sub-functions such as communication technologies, gamification of HRM functions, big data analytics, online approaches to talent, performance and training management (Habraken & Bondarouk, 2017). Therefore, as technological progress changes the way human resources interact with data and information, the integration of social, mobile, analytics and cloud technologies also transform HRM functions and motivation by changing the employer brand (Stephan, Uzawa, Volini, Walsh, & Yoshida, 2016). In the last four years, more than half of the enterprises have been experiencing a digital transformation process in the field of HRM. By 2020, more than a third of businesses agree that HR departments need to focus on digital technologies to increase efficiency in the business (Deloitte, 2020). It is possible to see this transformation in employee selection and placement, performance and career planning, training and development. One of the most common application areas of digital technologies in HRM is online recruitment, which refers to the use of various technological tools at different stages of the recruitment process (Melanthiou, Pavlou, & Constantinou, 2015). In the next ten years, approximately 50% of organizations are expected to have HR technology that provides daily recommendations based on Machine Learning/Artificial Intelligence. For HRM to be recognized as a strategic business unit, the focus must shift from process management to data management while developing the building blocks of Smart Platforms and the ethical standards required to govern them (Harris, 2019).

HRM Functions in the Scope of Digitization

Firstly, operational HRM practices refer to human resource activities at the administrative level. Payroll, record keeping, updating policy and information materials, creating and distributing internal reports, compliance with legal reporting, administration of benefits and management of employment contracts are operational HRM activities (Bissola & Imperatori, 2013; Thite, 2019). All database-related processes of HR employees are the subject of operational HRM (Chuang & Lin, 2017). Due to their routine nature, they can be standardized and automated through electronic data processing (EDP) (Thite, 2019). Operational digital HRM practices help increase the efficiency of HRM by improving HRM activities and reducing costs (Lecuyer et al., 2019). This process save valuable time of HR professionals. Most operational processes are also performed by Shared Service Centers (SSC), which are widely used by departments such as finance and HR (Deloitte, 2017). In addition, many software companies offer new technologies to professionals to facilitate these processes. For example, Microsoft has developed the Flow application, which allows to create automatic workflows between applications and services such as organizing annual permit and absence files, ensuring that employees submit their leave and request requests, collecting data, receiving notifications (Microsoft, 2021). These applications, which facilitate common HR functions, also accelerate the communication between the HR department and other departments.

Relational digital HRM application is considered as a tool to manage the relationship between organization and employee. This process aims to support HRM practices such as recruitment, selection, training, reward and performance management (Morsy & El Demerdash, 2017). These activities include business processes related to HR functions, including HR planning, hiring and selection, performance management, learning and development, and compensation and rewards management (Thite, 2019). Digital recruitment refers to the online posting of job postings open positions in a company, an online fill-in form for applicants, and a web-based database to store applicants' CVs (Brandao, Silva, & dos Santos, 2019). Digital recruitment enables costs to be reduced by approximately 87% compared to traditional methods such as newspapers and magazines (Maurer & Liu, 2007). Leading high-tech firms such as Google have successfully leveraged the potential of analytics to design an optimal mix of talent acquisition and selection strategies. For example, in a study conducted by Google to find out how many times it should interview a candidate, it concluded that four rounds of interviews are appropriate (Manjoo, 2013). New performance methods are employee-centered and employee-focused. Digital education systems encompass numerous tools, including writing technologies, communication technologies, visualization and storage (Aparicio, Bacao, & Oliveira, 2016). Unlike traditional face-to-face training techniques, e-learning techniques help companies access a large number of training content at low cost (Jackson, Quetsch, Brabson, & Herschell, 2018). These functions add value to an organization only when they are strategically aligned and meet business objectives (Thite, 2019).

Transformational HRM practice refers to digital HRM practices that match the employee's behavior and attitude, such as knowledge and strategic management (Iqbal, Ahmad, Raziq, & Mendes Borini, 2019). It has potential impact on employee productivity improvement as a result of cross-functional activities that have an impact on organizational goal achievement. Transformational HRM activities, which are a modern HRM practice, include topics that focus on organizational transformation such as strategic reorientation and renewal, cultural change, learning organization-oriented knowledge management, talent management, leadership development and social responsibility (Hasan, Islam, & Chowdhury, 2019). It is concerned with more technology-based strategic, forward-thinking, proactive and comprehensive activities to make processes effective and support organizational change and development (Manzoor et al., 2019). Transformational digital HRM provides strategic support to senior management through decision support systems (DSS) and Executive Information Systems (EIS) tools such as case scenarios created using advanced big data mining, analytics and artificial intelligence (Thite, 2019). Therefore, transformational digital HRM uses technology to maximize efficiency and provide sustainable competitive advantage for the organization, ensuring that HR processes are completely renewed and constantly updated.

In the research conducted by Sierra-Cedar (2019) on HR systems trends, more than half of the participants think that there are functionality gaps in HRM systems and talent management applications. Employee data is collected on an average of 3.2 non-HR sources, including wearables devices, social media, mobile devices, and artificial intelligence tools. However, it refers a large area IT related field within the HRM function of only 12% of organizations. HRIT professionals are three times more likely to be responsible for data privacy and content security. Raising HR perception and investing in specific approaches to the HR Technology strategy provides approximately 15% increase in talent and performance results per year (Sierra-Cedar, 2019). In the changing business world, it is necessary to adopt HR technology, evaluate the impact of data management practices and redefine the changing role of the HRIT manager.

SOLUTIONS AND RECOMMENDATIONS

Change processes are painful. The digital transformation process we are in is one of the most painful processes. It has many effects on businesses, both socially, administratively and financially. When we look at the challenges in terms of HRM, we see that the process is more complex. Man is a psychological being, you cannot activate him with the codes you write. This is where the challenge of HRM starts in this process. HRM must first evaluate the current situation, anticipate the changing digital world and the way people act. In this new world, the change in the needs and expectations of mutual employees will affect their abilities. These changes will also evolve the ways and means of doing business. In this environment, they have to develop policies to manage the talents and expectations of employees in the digital transformation process. In addition, the exponential increase in information every second, the rapid change of technology, has brought the choice of technological tools that businesses will use to a strategic position.

HRM not only facilitates the overall digitization of a business but is pushed to be the task of digital transformation. It does this by attracting new employees with the necessary digital knowledge and skills to a company, developing relevant skills within a company, and creating innovations that nurture the corporate culture. At the same time, digitalization takes place with the application of various digital technologies to HRM sub-functions and processes. It revolutionizes the experience of all employees by transforming HRM processes, systems and organization through new digital platforms, applications and services. Therefore, he should choose the digital solution partner with whom he will share his data and the technological tool he will use correctly.

FUTURE RESEARCH DIRECTION

While digitalization continues at full speed, on the one hand, suspicion and fear about technology have increased, and on the other hand, it has become impossible to stay away from a life without technology. It is a process that still contains serious question marks for managers and employees in most sectors. However, its contribution to productivity is undeniable. From a labor perspective, it has the potential to increase productivity by increasing automation, replacing low-value processes with high-value-added tasks. Therefore, digitalization changes the working conditions and working technologies of the employee. In this study, the challenges faced by HRM in the digitalization process have been tried to be defined in general. In this context, the change that occurs in people in the digital society is the main issue that needs to be taken into account. In future studies, researches are recommended to determine digital employee behaviors as a result of changes in human beings. In addition, it is not possible to think of HR, which is a support department, independently of the applications and needs of other departments. For this reason, first of all, clarifying the concepts of digitalization and digital transformation, examining the digital transformation within the enterprise as a whole, determining the wishes and needs of each department and analyzing them in terms of HR will also provide the subject to be examined. Changes in the way of doing business can be defined with the technologies entering the working life. The disappearing jobs and the identification of the jobs that will emerge can be put forward in terms of the management of talents. And finally, with the development of HR technologies, the selection of appropriate tools and the control and confidentiality of the data flow gain importance. Accordingly, the changing role of the HRIT manager needs to be redefined.

CONCLUSION

Today, groundbreaking digital technologies show their presence in every field. It causes radical changes in all aspects from production to marketing, from employee to customer in enterprises. Although it is too early to evaluate their effectiveness (Andersson, Lanvin, & Van der Heyden, 2016); it is obvious that they provide speed, efficiency and cost advantages to businesses (Parry, 2011). From a HRM perspective, it has the potential to increase productivity by increasing automation and replacing low-value processes with high-value-added tasks (Marler & Parry, 2016).

There are many sources of motivation for businesses to transition to digital HRM practices. The HR department is a strategically important support department. It is responsible for developing and implementing human resource-related strategies for business performance so that other departments can work effectively and efficiently. While fulfilling this responsibility, it must also reach the right source that will be effective in the transformation of future periods, as well as complying with the requirements of the era it is in. Since digitalization has become one of today's requirements, businesses need to put digital HR on their agenda for more efficient and faster HR applications in order to attract, develop and retain new age talents.

It is not only the use of the internet or computer in the execution of HR activities, but also the design of tasks and procedures that are not compatible with the latest technologies. After the adoption of digital HRM, most companies have re-evaluated and streamlined their task designs and processes as part of this transformation. Digital HRM has provided simpler and more inclusive processes in all organizations and has made it easier for HR applications to reach employees and other stakeholders. Connecting with previous generations by developing in-house cultural practices that will enable new professionals of the Digital Age to harmonize with others has become the most important goal of HRM. It is expected from HRM to design all existing conventional processes such as recruitment, placement, assignment, promotion and performance evaluation in a way that will combine these generations in a single pot. While businesses are aware that they need to adapt digital HRM practices to their businesses and adapt to these technologies, there are also some challenges they face in this process. First of all, employees who have adapted to the existing organizational culture are likely to resist change. Therefore, the management needs to consider these possible resistances in the change process. In addition, the increase in the average life expectancy and therefore the prolongation of the retirement age and the increase in the rate of change of generations together with the rapid change in technology have increased the presence of multi-generational employees in the labor market. This situation has led to a workplace environment consisting of employees with different value judgments, abilities and expectations. In addition, the exponential increase in information every second, the rapid change of technology, has brought the choice of technological tools that businesses will use to a strategic position. One of the challenges faced by businesses is choosing the right technological tool. The transfer of intellectual property and dataset ownership to the outsourcing partner (Martin et al., 2008) pushes businesses to focus on pending problems during and after the solution partner selection process.

Due to the lack of clarity on what is, what is to be done and how to do it digital, most companies are still in a 'digital fog' and most approaches are still in the exploration phase (Andersson et al., 2016). From the perspective of HRM, the first step to the success of digitalization is the assessment of human resources competencies in the new age. Businesses should evaluate the talents and competencies of their employees. It should describe the digital skills existing employees have and identify the digital skills that will be required for the business (Hecklau, Galeitzke, Flachs, & Kohl, 2016).

REFERENCES

Ahmad, M., & Allen, M. M. C. (2015). High performance HRM and establishment performance in Pakistan: An empirical analysis. *Employee Relations*, *37*(5), 506–524. doi:10.1108/ER-05-2014-0044

Ahmed, M. O. (2020). Identification of e-HRM practices in Egypt five-star hotels: A quantitative approach. *International Journal of Heritage, Tourism and Hospitality*, *14*(1), 139–151. doi:10.21608/ijhth.2020.122058

Andersson, L., Lanvin, B., & Van der Heyden, L. (2016). Digitalisation initiatives and corporate strategies: A few implications for talent. In B. Lanvin & P. Evans (Eds.), *The global competitiveness index 2017: Talent and technology* (pp. 51–57). INSEAD.

Aparicio, M., Bacao, F., & Oliveira, T. (2016). An e-learning theoretical framework. *Journal of Educational Technology & Society*, *19*(1), 292–307.

Barney, J. (1991). Firm Resources and Sustained Competitive Advantage. *Journal of Management*, *17*(1), 99–120. doi:10.1177/014920639101700108

Baum, T. (2015). Human resources in tourism: Still waiting for change? A 2015 reprise. *Tourism Management*, *50*, 204–212. doi:10.1016/j.tourman.2015.02.001

Bharadwaj, A., Sawy, O. A., Pavlou, P., & Venkatraman, N. (2013). Digital business strategy: Toward a next generation of insights. *Management Information Systems Quarterly, 37*(2), 471–482. doi:10.25300/MISQ/2013/37:2.3

Bissola, R., & Imperatori, B. (2013). Facing e-HRM: The consequences on employee attitude towards the organisation and the HR department in Italian SMEs. *European Journal of International Management, 7*(4), 450–468. doi:10.1504/EJIM.2013.055282

Bondarouk, T., Parry, E., & Furtmueller, E. (2016). Electronic HRM: Four decades of research on adoption and consequences. *International Journal of Human Resource Management, 28*(1), 1–34. doi:10.1080/09585192.2016.1245672

Brandao, C., Silva, R., & dos Santos, J. V. (2019). Online recruitment in Portugal: Theories and candidate profiles. *Journal of Business Research, 94*(C), 273–279. doi:10.1016/j.jbusres.2018.04.011

Burmeister, C., Luettgens, D., & Piller, F. (2016). Business model innovation for industrie 4.0: Why the industrial internet mandates a new perspective on Innovation. *Swiss Journal of Business Research and Practice, 70*(2), 124–152. doi:10.5771/0042-059X-2016-2-124

Çaylak, P. Ç. (2020). Near Field Communication (NFC) Applications in the tourism industry. E. Çeltek. In *Handbook of Research on Smart Technology Applications in the Tourism Industry* (pp. 65–88). IGI Global. doi:10.4018/978-1-7998-1989-9.ch004

Çelik, P., & Topsakal, Y. (2019). *Endüstri 4.0 ve akıllı turizm*. Detay Yayıncılık.

Christensen, C. (2006). *Assessing your organization's capabilities*. Retrieved on September 17, 2021 from Harvard Business School: http:// cb.hbsp.harvard.edu/cbmp/product/607014-PDF-ENG

Chuang, S. H., & Lin, H. N. (2017). Performance implications of information-value offering in e-service systems: Examining the resource-based perspective and innovation strategy. *The Journal of Strategic Information Systems, 26*(1), 22–38. doi:10.1016/j.jsis.2016.09.001

Dehaze, A. (2016). The skills imperative: Shaping the future of work through talent and technology. In B. Lanvin & P. Evans (Eds.), *The global competitiveness index 2017: Talent and technology* (pp. 35–41). INSEAD.

Deloitte. (2017). *Rewriting the rules for the digital age*. Retrieved on September 17, 2021 from https://www2.deloitte.com/content/dam/Deloitte/us/Documents/human-capital/hc-2017-global-human-capital-trends-us.pdf

Deloitte. (2021). *2021 Global insan kaynakları trendleri yıkıma uğramış bir dünyada sosyal şirket: İyileşmeden gelişmeye geçişe liderlik etmek*. Retrieved on September 17, 2021 from https://www2.deloitte.com/tr/tr/pages/human-capital/articles/2021-global-insan-kaynaklari-trendleri-raporu.html

Ekşili, N., & Çetinkaya Bozkurt, Ö. (2021). Dijital dönüşüm ve dijital işletmeler. In E. B. Bulgurcu Gürel & E. Gürel (Eds.), *İşletmelerde dönüşüm: Güncel konulardan seçkiler* (pp. 67–102). Siyasal Kitabevi.

Eller, R., Alford, P., Kallmünzer, A., & Peters, M. (2020). Antecedents, consequences, and challenges of small and medium-sized enterprise digitalization. *Journal of Business Research, 112*(3), 119–127. doi:10.1016/j.jbusres.2020.03.004

Florkowski, G., & Olivas-Luján, M. (2006). The diffusion of human-resource information- technology innovations in US and non-US firms. *Personnel Review, 35*(6), 684–710. doi:10.1108/00483480610702737

Greif, H., Kühnis, N., & Warnking, P. (2016). *Digitalisierung – wo stehen Schweizer KMU?* Retrieved on October 5, 2021 from https://www.pwc.ch/de/publications/2016/pwc_digitalisierung_wo_stehen_schweizer_kmu.pdf

Harris, S. (2019). *The Sierra-Cedar.* Retrieved on October 5, 2021 from https://www.sierra-cedar.com/2019/10/02/pr-2019-hrss-white-paper-release/

Hasan, I., Islam, M. D., & Chowdhury, M. (2019). Transformational human resource management: Crafting organizational efficiency. In P. O. de Pablos & T. K. Chui (Eds.), *Handbook of Research on Managerial Practices and Disruptive Innovation in Asia* (pp. 264–282). IGI Global.

Hayes, B. (2008). Cloud Computing. *Communications of the ACM, 51*(7), 1–11. doi:10.1145/1364782.1364786

Hecklau, F., Galeitzke, M., Flachs, S., & Kohl, H. (2016). Holistic approach for human resource management in industry 4.0. *Procedia CIRP, 54,* 1–6. doi:10.1016/j.procir.2016.05.102

Henriette, E., Feki, M., & Boughzala, I. (2016). Digital transformation challenges. In MCIS 2016 Proceedings (pp. 1-7). Paphos.

Hozdić, E. (2015). Smart factory for industry 4.0: A review. *International Journal of Modern Manufacturing Technologies*, *7*(1), 28–35.

Iqbal, N., Ahmad, M., Raziq, M. M., & Mendes Borini, F. (2019). Linking e-hrm practices and organizational outcomes: Empirical analysis of line manager's perception. *Revista Brasileira de Gestão de Negócios, 21*(1), 48–69. doi:10.7819/rbgn.v21i1.3964

Iraz, R., & Yıldırım, E. (2005). Bilgi Yönetimi Anlayışının Benimsenmesi ve Bilgi Teknolojileri Uygulamalarının İnsan Kaynakları Yönetimine Etkileri: E-Learning Örneği. In *4. Ulusal Bilgi, Ekonomi ve Yönetim Kongresi.* Sakarya: Değişim Yayınları.

Jackson, C. B., Quetsch, L. B., Brabson, L. A., & Herschell, A. D. (2018). Web-based training Methods for behavioral health providers: A Systematic Review. *Administration and Policy in Mental Health, 45*(4), 587–610. doi:10.100710488-018-0847-0 PMID:29352459

Jurisic, M., & Kermek, D. (2011). Taxonomy of digital economy business models. In *MIPRO, 2011 Proceedings of the 34th International Convention* (pp. 23-27). Opatija.

Kagermann, H., Lukas, W., & Wahlster, W. (2011). *Industrie 4.0 –Mit dem Internet der Dinge auf dem Weg zur 4.* Industriellen Revolution. Retrieved on October 6, 2021 from https://www.ingenieur.de/technik/fachbereiche/produktion/industrie-40-mit-internet-dinge-weg-4-industriellen-revolution/

Lanvin, B., Evans, P., & Rodriguez-Montemayor, E. (2016). Shifting gears: How to combine technology and talent to shape the future of work. In B. Lanvin & P. Evans (Eds.), *The global competitiveness index 2017: Talent and technology* (pp. 3–41). INSEAD.

Manjoo, F. (2013). *The Happiness Machine*. Retrieved on October 7, 2021 from https://slate.com/technology/2013/01/google-people-operations-the-secrets-of-the-worlds-most-scientific-human-resources-department.html

Marler, J. (2009). Making human resources strategic by going to the net: Reality or myth? *International Journal of Human Resource Management*, *20*(3), 515–527. doi:10.1080/09585190802707276

Marler, J., & Parry, E. (2009). Human resource management, strategic involvement and e-HRM technology. *International Journal of Human Resource Management*, *27*(19), 1–21. doi:10.1080/09585192.2015.1091980

Martin, G., Reddington, M., & Alexander, H. (2008). Technology, outsourcing, and HR transformation: An introduction. In G. Martin, M. Reddington, & H. Alexander (Eds.), *Technology, Outsourcing and Transforming HR* (pp. 1–35). Routledge. doi:10.1016/B978-0-7506-8645-7.50006-4

Masum, A.-K., Beh, L.-S., Azad, A.-K., & Hoque, K. (2018). Intelligent human resource information system (IHRIS): A holistic decision support framework for HR excellence. *The International Arab Journal of Information Technology*, *15*(1), 121–130.

Maurer, S. D., & Liu, Y. (2007). Developing effective e-recruiting websites: Insights for managers from marketers. *Business Horizons*, *50*(4), 305–314. doi:10.1016/j.bushor.2007.01.002

Meijerink, J., Keegan, A., Boons, M., & Marler, J. (2021). Algorithmic human resource management: Synthesizing developments and cross-disciplinary insights on digital HRM. *International Journal of Human Resource Management*, *32*(12), 2545–2562. doi:10.1080/09585192.2021.1925326

Melanthiou, Y., Pavlou, F., & Constantinou, E. (2015). The use of social network sites as an e-recruitment tool. *Journal of Transnational Management*, *20*(1), 31–49. doi:10.1080/15475778.2015.998141

Microsoft. (2021). *Çalışanların işe alım, ekleme ve yönetim görevlerini kolaylaştırın*. Retrieved on October 3, 2021 from https://flow.microsoft.com/tr-tr/collections/humanresources/

Morsy, N., & El Demerdash, J. (2017). Investigating the potential use of E-HRM: The Context of Egyptian hotels and travel agents. *Journal of Tourism Research*, *16*, 82–92.

Nivlouei, F. B. (2014). Electronic human resource management system: The main element in capacitating globalization paradigm. *International Journal of Business and Social Science*, *5*(2), 147–159.

Pantelidis, I. (2019). Digital human resource management. In M. J. Boella & S. Goss-Turner (Eds.), *Human Resource Management in the Hospitality Industry: A Guide to Best Practice*. Routledge. doi:10.4324/9780429441400-21

Parry, E. (2011). An examination of e-HRM as a means to increase the value of the HR function. *International Journal of Human Resource Management*, *22*(5), 1146–1162. doi:10.1080/09585192.2011.556791

Perkin, N., & Abraham, P. (2017). *Building the Agile Business through Digital Transformation*. Kogan Page.

Rodriguez, J. L., & Rodriguez, R. M. (2005). Technology and export behaviour: A resource-based view approach. *International Business Review*, *14*(5), 539–557. doi:10.1016/j.ibusrev.2005.07.002

Russom, P. (2011). *Big Data Analytics*. TDWI.

Savic, D. (2019). From digitization, through digitalization, to digital transformation. *Online Searcher*, *43*(1), 36–39.

Sayar, K. (2016). Dijital toplum. *TRTakademi.*, *1*(2), 762–775.

Schallmo, D., Herbort, V., & Doleski, O. (2017). Die digitale transformation von Geschäftsmodellen gestalten. In *Roadmap Utility 4.0. essentials* (pp. 31–32). Springer Vieweg. doi:10.1007/978-3-658-17655-6_4

Schawbel, D. (2012). *Millennials vs. Baby boomers: Who would you rather hire?* Retrieved on October 7, 2021 from https://business.time.com/2012/03/29/millennials-vs-baby-boomers-who-would-you-rather-hire/

Schroth, H. (2019). Are You Ready for Gen Z in the Workplace? *California Management Review*, *61*(3), 5–18. doi:10.1177/0008125619841006

Soliman, F., & Youssef, M. A. (2003). Internet-based e-commerce and its impact on manufacturing and business operations. *Industrial Management & Data Systems*, *103*(8), 546–552. doi:10.1108/02635570310497594

Stephan, M., Uzawa, S., Volini, E., Walsh, B., & Yoshida, R. (2016). *Digital HR revolution, not evolution.* Retrieved on October 15, 2021 from https://www2.deloitte.com/insights/us/en/focus/human- capital-trends/2016/digital-hr-technology-for-hr-teams-services.html

Stephen, M. (2016). Digital HR: Revolution, not evolution. In global human capital trends 2016. *The new organization: Different by design*. Retrieved on October 15, 2021 from https://www2.deloitte.com/content/dam/Deloitte/global/Documents/HumanCapital/gx

Strohmeier, S. (2007). Research in e-HRM: Review and implications. *Human Resource Management Review*, *17*(1), 19–37. doi:10.1016/j.hrmr.2006.11.002

Strohmeier, S. (2020). Digital human resource management: A conceptual clarification. *German Journal of Human Resource Management*, *34*(3), 345–365. doi:10.1177/2397002220921131

Strohmeier, S., & Parry, E. (2014). HRM in the digital age digital challenges of the HR profession. *Employee Relations*, *36*(4). Advance online publication. doi:10.1108/ER-03-2014-0032

Sukhova, M. (2016). *Digital transformation: History, present, and future trends*. Retrieved on November 11, 2021 from https://auriga.com/blog/2016/digital-transformation-history-present-and-future-trends/

Tao, F., Zuo, Y., Xu, L. D., & Zhang, L. (2014). IoT-Based intelligent perception and access of manufacturing resource toward cloud manufacturing. *IEEE Transactions on Industrial Informatics*, *10*(2), 1547–1557. doi:10.1109/TII.2014.2306397

Thite, M. (2019). Electronic/digital HRM: A primer. In e-HRM: Digital approaches, directions & applications. Routledge.

Thomas, G. (2020). Digital Maturity of HR in SMEs. *European Journal of Economics and Business Studies*, *6*(1), 56–62. doi:10.26417/ejes.v6i1.p56-62

Tracey, J. (2014). A review of human resources management research: The past 10 years and implications for moving forward. *International Journal of Contemporary Hospitality Management, 26*(5), 679–705. doi:10.1108/IJCHM-02-2014-0056

Udovita, P. (2020). Conceptual review on dimensions of digital transformation in modern era. *International Journal of Scientific and Research Publications, 10*(2), 520–529. doi:10.29322/IJSRP.10.02.2020.p9873

Ulrich, D. (1998). A new mandate for Human Resources. *Harvard Business Review, 76*(1), 124–135. PMID:10176915

Unruh, G., & Kiron, D. (2017). *Digital transformation on purpose*. Retrieved on November 2, 2021 from https://sloanreview.mit.edu/article/digital-transformation-on-purpose

Wang, Y., Ma, H., Yang, J. H., & Wang, K. S. (2017). Industry 4.0: A way from mass customization to mass personalization production. *Advances in Manufacturing, 5*(4), 311–320. doi:10.100740436-017-0204-7

Xu, X. (2012). From cloud computing to cloud manufacturing. *Robotics and Computer-integrated Manufacturing, 28*(1), 75–86. doi:10.1016/j.rcim.2011.07.002

Zemke, R., Raines, C., & Filipczak, B. (2013). *Generations at work: Managing the clash of Boomers, Gen Xers, and Gen Yers in the workplace*. American Management Association.

ADDITIONAL READING

Marler, S. H., & Fisher, S. L. (2013). An evidence-based review of e-HRM and strategic human resource management. *Human Resource Management Review, 23*(1), 18–36. doi:10.1016/j.hrmr.2012.06.002

Pantelidis, I. (2019). Digital human resource management. In M. J. Boella & S. Goss-Turner (Eds.), *Human Resource Management in the Hospitality Industry: A Guide to Best Practice*. Routledge. doi:10.4324/9780429441400-21

Thite, M. (2019). *Electronic/digital HRM: A primer. e-HRM: Digital Approaches, Directions & Applications*. Routledge.

KEY TERMS AND DEFINITIONS

Digital Employee: Individuals who have become a lifestyle of digital technologies. For this reason, their behaviors, wishes and expectations are different from those before them.

Digital Employee Management: The execution of HR functions using digital technologies.

Digital HRM: The digital transformation in the HRM industry due to technological developments.

Digital Society: It is the society in which technology is an invariable part of human life. Ways of doing business and habits in this society are based on digital technology.

Digital Work: Changing the way of doing business due to digital technologies; refers to the transformation of a labor-intensive business environment into an automation-intensive business environment over time.

Industry 4.0: It refers to the industrialization process we are in. It is the integration of communication and information technologies into production systems in order to offer personalized and customized products.

Chapter 14
Impact of Industry 4.0 on Human Resources Systems:
The Emergence of Work 4.0

Myriam Ertz
https://orcid.org/0000-0001-9959-2779
LaboNFC, Université du Québec à Chicoutimi, Canada

Adam Skali
LaboNFC, Université du Québec à Chicoutimi, Canada

ABSTRACT

Industry 4.0 implies a reconfiguration of work organization and new approaches to human resources management (HRM). This research aims to delve deeper into the impacts of Industry 4.0 on the human resources system (HRS). A literature review identifies the potential links between these two core concepts. Finally, secondary data analysis in the form of a literature review on topical scientific researches will explore the following research question: How does Industry 4.0 impact conventional human resources systems (HRS)?

INTRODUCTION

The technological breakthrough of industry 4.0 implies not only a reconfiguration of the organization of work but also new approaches to human resource management. The Fourth Industrial Revolution affects HRM activities on three levels (Bissola & Imperatori, 2020). Firstly, HRM must assume the role of change agent in order to help the organization benefit from the advantages of the Human-Machine interface by developing the digital culture of employees to better collaborate with machines, colleagues, employees, and supervisors (Bissola & Imperatori, 2020). Second, the digital transformation requires an update of HR practices because working methods have changed: remote working, flexible schedules, a collaboration that crosses organizational boundaries, to name but a few (Bissola & Imperatori, 2020).

DOI: 10.4018/978-1-7998-9715-6.ch014

Copyright © 2022, IGI Global. Copying or distributing in print or electronic forms without written permission of IGI Global is prohibited.

Third, HRM should take a people-centered approach that aims to solve organizational problems by cultivating a deep understanding of human factors and the context around them (Bissola & Imperatori, 2020).

The reflection around the interconnection between the emergence of Industry 4.0 technologies and its impact on HR functions is relatively recent. However, HR functions realize HRM philosophy, processes, policies, processes, programms (Armstrong, 2020). Based on this principle, this chapter aims to explore the form of HR functions under the influence of Industry 4.0 technologies. More specifically, the chapter seeks to answer the following question: How does Industry 4.0 and its related technological shifts impact conventional human resources systems (HRS)?

To this end, the chapter is structured as follows: The following two sections (i.e., sections 2 and 3) establish a conceptual framework of the fundamental concepts of our study. Based on Armstrong's (2020) framework of reference, we define the first concept of HRM with an overview of the HR system and its constituent functions. Next, we look at the second key concept of Industry 4.0 with a definition of its four main components: Internet of Things, Internet of Services, Cyber-physical systems, and finally, the Smart Factory. In order to orient our research approach, section 4 proposes a general framework linking the two aforementioned concepts. Section 5 discusses the research methodology, whereas section 6 summarizes the literature review results. Finally, a conclusion is presented, wrapping up the findings pertaining to the components of Industry 4.0 on HRM in general and on its specific functions in particular.

THEORETICAL BACKGROUND

The Human Resource (HR) System for Human Resource Management (HRM)

HRM is concerned with the way people are managed and employed in organizations (O'Riordan, 2017). The term HRM first appeared in 1980 against economic recession, globalization, and accelerating technological developments. This pressure has prompted organizations to consider new ways to gain a competitive advantage. Michael Porter's Resource Theory and Organizational Behavior Theory are behind the emergence of the concept of HRM. The first states that the human factor is a fundamental differentiating power of a company from its competitors. The second studies human behavior in an organizational environment and its impact on organizational performance. These two theories have influenced the thinking around personnel management in organizations. Human resource management can be defined as "a strategic, integrated and coherent approach to the employment, development, and wellbeing of the people working in organizations" (Armstrong et al., 2014, p.5). HRM is achieved through the HR system, which is a set of interrelated and interdependent activities and practices, allowing the achievement of HR objectives (Armstrong, 2020).

The HRM System

As Armstrong (2020) points out, the components of an HR system can be subdivided into two broad categories: transactional and transformational activities. First, transactional activities are part of day-to-day administrative functions, such as managing the hiring process, implementing workplace policies and regulations, guidelines for employee benefits, and other functions. On the other hand, transformational activities have a more strategic role in ensuring the alignment of HR management with the organization's strategic objectives. In fact, "transformational HR activities are those actions of an organization that 'add value' to the consumption of the firm's product or service" (Thite et al., 2012, p.7). This includes, for example, a training program to improve the performance of a sales team. Armstrong's (2020) flowchart below shows us that the HRM system has different components spread over four levels:

Table 1. The human resources management (HRM) system (Armstrong, 2020, p.13)

Level 1:				
• HR strategies, policies, processes, practices, and programs				
Level 2:				
• HR philosophies				
Level 3:	**Level 4:**			
• Organization	Organization design	Organization development	Job/role design	
• Resourcing	Workforce planning resource	Recruitment and selection	Talent management	
• Learning and development	Organizational learning	Individual learning	Management development	
• Reward management	Job evaluation	Base pay management	Contingent pay	Employee benefits
• Employee relations	Industrial relations	Employee voice	Communications	
• Health and safety				
• Employee wellbeing				
• HR services				
• Performance management				
• Knowledge management				

At Level 1, HR strategies define the intentions that guide HRM policy and practice to align it with the organization's strategic objectives. HR policy is both a general and a specific expression of the organization's values. It covers several areas: diversity in the workplace, internal promotion, work-life balance, layoffs, or sexual harassment, among others. HR processes are a set of interdependent actions and tasks grouped by function (see levels 3 and 4). According to the established HR model, HR managers describe the roles and responsibilities of HR managers (Armstrong, 2020). In other words, they are formal and specific procedures as well as approaches that aim to apply HR strategies and policies. HR programs are the arrangements that allow implementing HR strategies, policies, and practices according to a predefined plan (Armstrong, 2011). For example, an organization can offer an employee an assistance program that contributes to the latter's wellbeing. HR practices refer to "the activities carried out in implementing HR policies and programs" (Armstrong et al., 2014, p.10). These practices are informal and differ from organization to organization.

At Level 2, HR philosophy "revolves around management's beliefs and assumptions about people - their nature, needs, value and their approach to work. These beliefs and assumptions then determine how people should be treated" (Shani, 2011, p.61). They are explicit or sometimes implicit in the minds of decision-makers. The HR philosophy is influenced by the internal and external context (Armstrong,

2020). It integrates the HR functions - which are just a set of HR tasks that could be grouped together, and the elements are presented in levels 3 and 4.

Level 3 describes the ten specific functions of the HRS and their activities as defined in the following sub-sections.

Organization

The organization function indicates how the organization coordinates its activities. The function encompasses organizational design, organizational development, and job design. Organizational design is the process that determines the structure of the functioning of groups and individuals in the organization: their responsibilities and the relationships between them (Armstrong, 2020). Organizational development "is concerned with the planning and implementation of programs designed to enhance the effectiveness with which an organization functions and responds to change" (Armstrong, 2011, p.337). Finally, job design is "a key component concerned with how jobs are designed and how they relate to the whole business" (Armstrong, 2014, p.28).

Resourcing

Resourcing ensures that the organization attracts and retains the right human resources and provides their optimal use (Armstrong, 2011). It is a crucial element of the HR system because it meets the human needs of the organization through quality employees. According to Armstrong (2020), the activities performed by this function are: Resource planning: This is a process that aims at forecasting short- and long-term HR needs, as well as the optimal use of existing resources; Recruitment and selection of employees; Talent management to retain, attract, motivate and develop talented people.

Learning and Development (Including Performance Management, Knowledge Management)

Ensure that people's intellectual capital grows and matches the current and future needs of the organization (Armstrong, 2020). The main elements of this function are organizational learning, individual learning, and executive development. Organizational learning is how the knowledge that the organization acquires through experience is transmitted internally (Valamis, 2019). Individual learning is the personal acquisition of new knowledge or adopting new behavior that stems from a unique representation of reality (Novarese, 2012). Finally, executives' development aims to improve managers' performance and give them development opportunities (Armstrong, 2011).

Reward Management

This function refers to the strategies and policies whereby employees' efforts are compensated according to their value to the organization (Armstrong, 2011). It incorporates job evaluation, which aims to determine the value of a job in an organization in relation to its contribution to the achievement of desired objectives (Armstrong, 2011); the management of the basic salary; conditional salary: Financial rewards granted based on performance, skills, professional experience, and so on (Armstrong, 2011); and social benefits.

Employee Relations

Employee relations refers to "all those areas of human resource management that involve relationships with employees - directly and/or through collective agreements where trade unions are recognized. (Armstrong, 2011, p.751). According to Armstrong (2011), this function includes industrial relations as a set of rules governing the employment relationship and how people behave at work; communications so that employees are informed about the policies and decisions that affect them and give their opinions concerning management's actions; and the expression of employees includes all the processes and structures that allow employees to contribute to decision-making in the organization.

Health and Safety

Health and safety refer to measures guaranteeing healthy and safe workplaces and systems (Armstrong, 2011). The following sub-section addresses the changes induced by industry 4.0 on employee wellbeing and health and safety within the HR system.

Employee Wellbeing

The concept of employee wellbeing refers to psychological wellbeing, which consists of several components including affective wellbeing, job satisfaction, aspiration, anxiety and burnout» (Vanhala & Tuomi, 2006, p.244).

HR Services

This function refers to the model by which HR services are provided. It integrates the transactional activities of the HR function (Armstrong & Taylor, 2020).

Performance Management

Performance management is a systematic approach that aims to improve organizational performance through individuals and teams (Armstrong, 2020).

Knowledge Management

Knowledge management is the process of creating, acquiring, sharing, using, and managing knowledge and information specific to an organization (Armstrong, 2020).

INDUSTRY 4.0

Industry 4.0 refers to the fourth industrial revolution. It is a purely technological revolution represented by a new generation of connected, robotic, and intelligent factories (Geandarme, 2021). Industry 4.0 gives rise to a convergence between the physical and digital world, where machines, employees, clients, and products are interconnected and interact. According to Geandarme (2021), Industry 4.0 responds to new market needs by offering unique and personalized products with similar costs despite low production volumes. Furthermore, this new way of organizing the means of production, called "smart production," allows customers to connect to an adaptive production organ.

The current literature does not offer a universally accepted definition of Industry 4.0. Instead, researchers describe it as "the increasing digitization of the entire value chain and the resulting interconnection of people, objects, and systems through real-time data exchange. As a result of that interconnection, products, machines, and processes are equipped with artificial intelligence and get enabled to adapt to spontaneous changes in the environment independently. Furthermore, smart objects become embedded in broader systems, which enhance the creation of flexible, self-controlling production systems" (Hecklau et al., 2016, p.2). A literature review that integrates the components of Industry 4.0 offers the following definition: "Industry 4.0 is a collective term for technologies and concepts of value chain organization. Within the modular structured Smart Factories of Industry 4.0, CPS monitors physical processes, creates a virtual copy of the physical world, and makes decentralized decisions. Over the IoT, CPS communicate and cooperate with each other and with humans in real-time. Furthermore, via the IoS, both internal and cross-organizational services are offered and utilized by participants of the value chain" (Hermann et al., 2015, p. 11). Industry 4.0, in sum, refers to that merger between the physical and the digital in a unique network of interconnected and interdependent nodes. In their review of the literature, Hermann et al. (2015) identified four main components of Industry 4.0:

1. **Cyber-physical systems (CPS).** A system that integrates computational and communication elements that work together to control, coordinate, and command physical processes (Rajkumar et al., 2010). An example of this system is the 'Massachusetts Institute of Technology project,' a garden where plants equipped with sensors are maintained by robots and manipulated by algorithms via a computer network (Del Preto et al., 2020).
2. **Internet of Things (IoT).** IoT refers to the "global infrastructure for the information society, which provides advanced services by interconnecting objects (physical or virtual) using existing or evolving interoperable information and communication technologies" (ITU, 2012, p.1). The best example of IoT is the smart home, which comprises a multiplicity of connected devices such as air conditioners, light bulbs, or thermostats programmed by software and equipped with sensors and other technologies to store and exchange data and execute commands. The user can control all these devices through a mobile application connected to the Internet network. Based on these elements, one could extrapolate the application of this concept in the industrial world. Thus, the term "industrial Internet of Things" is the use of Internet of Things technologies: CPS, cloud computing, big data, artificial intelligence, machine learning, the blockchain, and so on, in manufacturing (Boyes et al., 2018).
3. **Internet of Services (IoS).** IoS results from Web 2.0 and service-oriented architectures (Reis & Gonçalves, 2018). The IoS allows companies to offer their services via the Internet (Buxmann et al., 2009) and to participate in an external supply chain in addition to the internal SCM of a manufacturing process (Reis & Gonçalves, 2018). Furthermore, these services are accessible to users and consumers through multiple channels (Buxmann et al., 2009).
4. **Smart factory.** The notion of a smart factory "The Smart Factory is defined as a factory that [is] context-aware [and] assists people and machines in [the] execution of their tasks. This is achieved by systems working in the background, so-called Calm-systems, and context-aware means that the system can consider context information like the position and status of an object. These systems

accomplish their tasks based on physical and virtual world information. Information of the physical world is, e.g., the position or condition of a tool, in contrast to information of the virtual world like electronic documents, drawings, and simulation models. [...] Calm systems refer, in this context, to the hardware of a Smart Factory. The main difference between calm and other types of systems is the ability to communicate and interact with its environment." (Lucke et al., 2008, p.115, cited in Hermann et al., 2015, p.10). This is achieved through calm systems: systems aware of the environment around them and working in the background; these quiet systems adapt the production tool to the physical context such as the position of a tool, or virtual information such as the design of a product (Hermann et al., 2015).

Work 4.0

"Work 4.0" is a concept that describes the transformations that will affect several aspects of the world of work and their impact on society following the fourth industrial revolution. The term was first introduced in Germany by the "Federal Ministry of Labor and Social Affairs" (Salimi, 2015), suggesting that "Work 4.0 will be more interconnected, digital and flexible" (Federal Ministry of Labor and Social Affairs, 2015, p.35). Furthermore, according to a report entitled "Re-imagining work, Green Paper Work 4.0" (Federal Ministry of Labor and Social Affairs, 2017), the most important factors and trends relating to the work environment have been identified:

- The increasing digitization of daily life functions and the outpouring of associated capacities.
- Globalization, particularly that of the labor market, is propelled by digitization.
- Demographic change (Generation Y and Z) reshapes the profiles and skills capable of creating added value.
- Cultural and societal change affects value systems, the view of work, the control of personal time, etc.

It can be observed that the digitization of information in the physical world has increased enormously during the last decade. Functions such as visualization and analysis of physical space are no longer restricted to the human species since robots and machines are now capable of performing these functions. The globalized labor market also benefits from the possibility of recruiting talent across geographic borders (Baldwin, 2019). Teleworking allows, among other things, to achieve considerable savings by accessing less expensive international human resources, especially in developing countries. Massive digitization combined with remote intelligence, manipulated by a human or a robot, gives rise to the "globotics" phenomenon (Baldwin, 2019). In other respects, the new generation of employees, both men, and women, are more focused on balancing and sharing family and work responsibilities while being able to pursue their passions. According to a study entitled "Value Systems in the Context of Work 4.0", value systems and work preferences are different from previous generations. They see that an ideal workplace is characterized by solidarity, prosperity, dedication, which offers comfort, security, and fulfillment. The meaning of work is more valuable than the remuneration associated with it.

HRM 4.0

HRM has a lot of work to do to face the challenges of work 4.0, which has led researchers and professionals to rethink the role and transformation of HRM towards a 4.0 perspective. To date, research on HRM 4.0 is scarce. Likewise, this concept has no precise definition, so industry 4.0 and HRM 4.0 are interdependent. Thomas et al. (2020) suggest that following the digital transformation of Industry 4.0 technologies, HRM processes have gradually become automated, hence the name HRM 4.0. We add that "HRM 4.0 is a digital way of leading and managing HR functions. It represents a penetration of IT and new technology HR system design and execution" (Thomas et al., 2020, p.46). Due to the imprecision around the concept, this chapter aims at presenting an overview of the different potentialities that industry 4.0 technologies bring to the HRM function.

There is still ambiguity about the wording used concerning Industry 4.0 (Habraken & Bondarouk, 2019). In addition, research on HRM 4.0 is very recent. According to Bondarouk et al. (2017), the very term is a progression based on work on the e-HRM, which is described as "an umbrella term covering all possible integration mechanisms and contents between HRM and Information Technologies aiming at creating value within and across organizations for targeted employees and management " (Bondarouk & Ruël, 2009, p.507), through the digital HRM that "denotes the socio-technical result of the digitalization of HRM" (Strohmeier, 2020, p.8) then finally the smart HRM that refers to the adoption and integration of smart technologies into HRM (Strohmeier, 2018). Nevertheless, the main questions that companies and university researchers raise are: How will the HRM function adapt to the new technological context and the challenges imposed by the Fourth Industrial Revolution? Is work 4.0 revolutionizing HRM? What will be the implications for managers in order to bring human skills towards a 4.0 spirit?

In this regard, we could examine these questions according to the framework of reflection illustrated in the diagram shown in Figure 1.

Figure 1. General conceptual framework

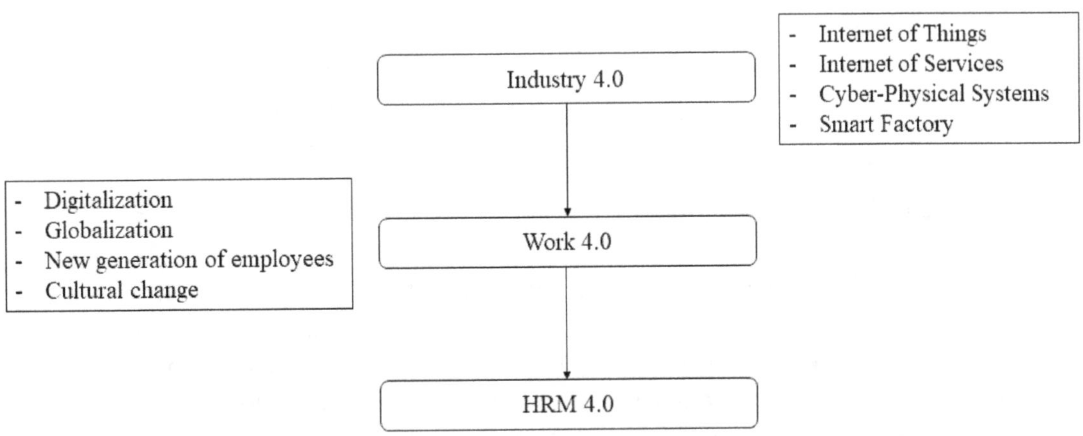

Work 4.0 reflects a new phase in labor relations, marked by the sustained use of digital technologies. But like any disruption, it has its own organizational, technological, and human challenges.

The socio-technical approach offers a way to envision this complex change (Liboni et al., 2019). It envisions an interdependence between the human and technical dimensions of the organization. Dregger et al. (2016) and Hirsch-Kreinsen (2016) designed a model, displayed in Figure 2, that illustrates the interplay between socio-technical system changes and Industry 4.0. This model places HRM at the center of the human-technology interface (Liboni et al., 2019).

Figure 2. The context of HRM 4.0 (Liboni et al., 2019)

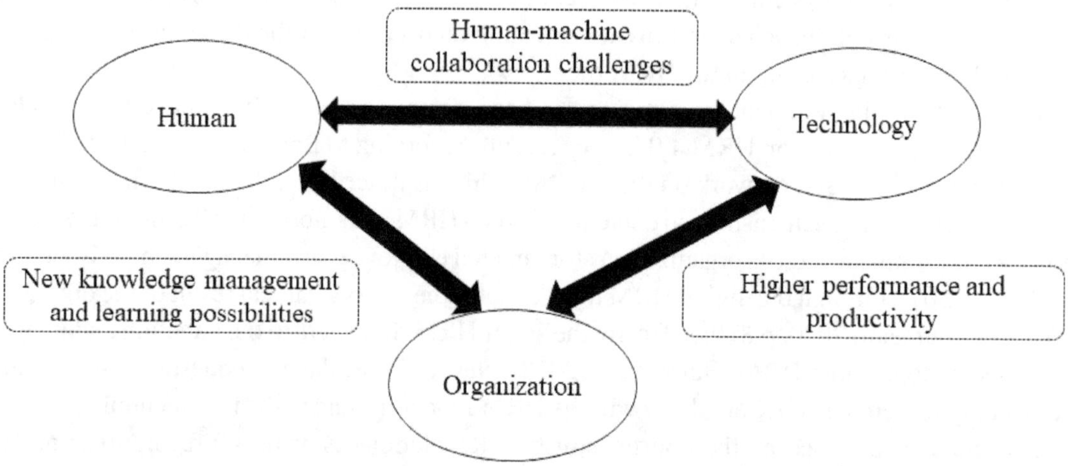

HRM 4.0 is, therefore, a response to these challenges and requires an update of the HR system, which is embodied by the HR functions. However, as an emerging phenomenon, the breadth and scope of HRM 4.0 remain yet to be clearly defined and delineated. Given the preceding, it seems reasonable to refine the initial research question to the following: What is the impact of technological developments linked to Industry 4.0, such as CPS, IoT, IoS, and smart factory, on the functions of the HR system: organization, resourcing, learning and development, reward management, employee relations, health and safety, employee wellbeing, HR services, performance management, and knowledge management?

METHODOLOGY

A systematic review of the literature was carried out in order to collect the most relevant scientific articles dealing with the use of industry 4.0 technologies in the performance of HR functions as well as their impact on them. Following best practices outlined in systematic literature review studies (Shashi et al., 2020; Ertz et al., 2021), the main objective of this literature review is to establish an inventory of the progress of scientific research on the subject to provide a purely theoretical basis which leads to the definition of a very recent and little-explored phenomenon, that of "HRM 4.0". The retrievals aimed at extracting the researchers' conclusions on the main developments affecting HR functions, more specifically in an organizational context where one or more components of Industry 4.0 are adopted. The information-gathering process consisted of reading and synthesizing the most recent articles, which are peer-reviewed, cited by other authors, and most relevant to our research question. To this end, we followed the steps described below.

Inclusion and Exclusion Criteria

This chapter encompasses papers that explore the application of new technologies for HRS functions. A series of exclusion and inclusion criteria were used. Only papers published between January 1st, 2015, and December 31st, 2020, were included. Besides, only papers published in English were selected. The year 2015 is considered the lower bound since the Industry 4.0 concept emerged from 2010 onwards (Leiner et al., 2009), and the HR 4.0 or smart HR 4.0 appeared later towards 2015 (Chitte, 2020). The search considered peer-reviewed articles, conference proceedings, book chapters, professional articles, and research reports. Although books need not be included in systematic reviews (Thu et al., 2018), we conservatively added them. All publications needed to be written in English.

Research Nomenclature

Using those inclusion and exclusion criteria, a series of systematic retrievals were made across several academic databases, including *ABI/Inform, Scopus, Web of Science,* and *Business Source Complete*. The following keyword string was used in each database according to the theoretical framework followed regarding HR (Armstrong, 2020) and industry 4.0 technologies (Hermann et al., 2015): {("HR system" /"HR function" /"HR processes" /"Human resources system" /"Human resources function" /"Human resources processes" /"Organization" /"Organization design" / "Organization development" /"Job/role design" /"Resourcing" /"Workforce planning resource" /"Recruitment and selection" /"Talent management" /"Health and safety" /"Employee wellbeing" /"HR services" /"Learning and development" /"Organizational learning" /"Individual learning" /"Management development" /"Job evaluation" /"Base pay management" /"Contingent pay" /"Employee benefits" /"Employee relations" /"Industrial relations" /"Employee voice" /"Communications") AND ("Internet of Things" /"Internet of services" /"Cyber-physical systems" /"Smart factory" /"HRM 4.0" /"Smart HR" /"E-HRM" /"Digital HR").}

The keywords needed to appear in the title, abstract, or keywords to avoid unrelated publications and reduce noise. The search resulted in the extraction of 1322 publications as the initial publication subset. The articles consulted are primarily theoretical studies dating mainly between 2015 and 2020 and some empirical studies (i.e., qualitative, quantitative studies).

Analysis, Results Mapping, and Publications Summary

The analysis process follows a three-step procedure, as emphasized in extant research (Gohoungodji et al., 2020; Ertz et al., 2021, 2022). More specifically, all publications were submitted to two sorting rounds. The first one removed duplicates (323) and publications that did not have the keywords of interest outlined previously in their title, abstract, or keywords (150). In the second round, the publications were analyzed according to the inclusion and exclusion criteria as well as to their contribution to answering the research question. Therefore, an additional 814 publications were suppressed. The process ended with the final selection of 35 publications that met those criteria. A manual search in the references for highly-cited and relevant references following Gohoungodji et al. (2020) resulted in the inclusion of three additional publications (two published in 2013) and one which was "forthcoming" and got eventually published in 2021, which increased the total sample size to 38 publications. The research results were then mapped in order to evaluate their relationships. Each study was described in a Word grid stating its publication year, author(s), full title, the publication outlet, and the research method. Given that the study's objective was to identify how industry 4.0 technologies impact the HR system to generate HRM 4.0, we needed to identify which industry 4.0 technology and HR function of the HR system are discussed in each publication. Some publications also dealt more broadly with industry 4.0 (HR system) in general without explicitly mentioning a given technology (HR function). These remained acceptable for analysis as long as they clearly linked industry 4.0 and the HR system. A summary was then written for each publication stating the aims, methods, findings, and contributions of the publications. The process facilitated the identification of themes and sub-themes as well as the connexion between industry 4.0 technologies and HRS functions. The results are discussed in the following section.

Theme Identification

The textual summaries, as well as the Word grid, were used to derive the areas of impact of industry 4.0 technologies on HRS functions. Therefore, for each of the ten functions in the HR system (Level 3 in Table 1), according to Armstrong (2020), we identified the respective influences of industry 4.0 technologies on them. We discuss those impacts per HR function in the following results section.

THE IMPACTS OF INDUSTRY 4.0 ON HRS FUNCTIONS FOR AN HRM 4.0

This part summarizes the themes derived from the content analysis following the systematic literature review. It answers more specifically the research question by illustrating the impact of Industry 4.0 technologies on the ten HRS functions conceptualized by Armstrong (2020), including organization, resourcing, learning and development, reward management, employee relations, health and safety, employee wellbeing, HR services, performance management, and knowledge management. This analysis provides a preliminary overview of the concrete manifestation of the so-called HRM 4.0 concept.

Redistribution of Work between Humans and Machines for Improved Organization

One of the first essential HR functions of the HR system identified by Anderson (2020) pertains to organization and its sub-functions of organizational design, organizational development, and job design. Currently, there is limited research on the impact of Industry 4.0 technologies on organizational design, but the one dealing with this subject in the sample suggests that the effects of Industry 4.0 on this function are relatively minimal. In fact, Shaba et al. (2019) concluded that organizational design is independent of the technology put in place and stems from management decisions. Following the socio-technical approach, the results of Shaba et al. (2019) show two possible reorganizations: an approach focused on employee control with a high level of formalization; less autonomous employees; a deskilling; and a weak role of middle managers, versus an approach focused on engaging employees with less formalization; greater autonomy; a job that requires more qualifications; and a more enhanced role of middle managers. In either case, the input of technology remains limited, and the choice of either is also not contingent upon technology but on values, mission, or vision developed by individuals.

Other studies (Shaw & Varghese, 2018; Verma et al., 2020) suggest a much more influential effect of technology on organizational development. They start from the premise that companies are undergoing organizational transformations anyways due to the volatile, uncertain, ambiguous, and complex context of Industry 4.0 and even Industry 5.0 (Nahavandi, 2019). These broader organizational changes or transformations would thus require continuous organizational development, involving the constant improvement of processes and organizational structure, and as such, Industry 4.0 dramatically influences organizational development (Hecklau et al., 2016). These influences further vary according to Industry 4.0 technologies types since some have automated simple and monotonous processes at the process level (e.g., Internet of Things, Internet of Services), while other processes have become more complex and inextricably linked (e.g., smart factory, cyber-physical systems) (Shaw & Varghese, 2018). Therefore, another outcome of Industry 4.0 is that strategic skills management is necessary to meet the challenges of Industry 4.0 (Shaw & Varghese, 2018) and foster organizational development. Interestingly, some studies suggest that some organizational structures are more likely to accommodate the organizational developments incurred by Industry 4.0. In fact, the organic structure is the form most compatible with the unstable and changing environment of Industry 4.0 (Shamim et al., 2016). This structure "is characterized by decentralization, empowerment, few rules and formalities, horizontal communication, and collaborative team work" (Shamim et al., 2016, p.5311). However, the organic structure could be inadequate with the nature of specific organizations regarding their needs and context (Shamim et al., 2016).

Regarding job design, the impact of Industry 4.0 technologies is also non-negligible, but it appears that the human factor is not easily replaceable in many regards. On the one hand, there is an exponential development of technologies, and work organization is changing. On the other hand, employee knowledge and skills quickly become obsolete, so job design must continually adapt (Bulte, 2018). This must incorporate the appropriate technical qualifications so that HR is, for example, able to manage the machines employees use (Bulte, 2018). Furthermore, in order to adapt to a changing economic environment, job design must emphasize job rotation; the transfer of responsibilities; and task reassignment (Shamim et al., 2016). The aim is to promote employee flexibility, ensure they acquire various skills, and encourage teamwork and collaboration (Shamim et al., 2016). It further appears that, in an industrial context, intelligent control algorithms and computer programs will ultimately replace a great proportion of human knowledge and skills (Waschull et al., 2017). On the other hand, the core of information processing and decision-making will remain with humans (Waschull et al., 2017). In fact, "studies indicate that the impact of technology on job design depends on a variety of other various organizational factors, such as management choice, their vision, and goals" (Waschull et al., 2017, p.276). In sum, the impact of Industry 4.0 technologies on the job design function can be substantial but depends on the extent to which management vision and goals allow it to be.

From a more empirical perspective and to wrap up the contribution of Industry 4.0 to the organization function, the study carried out on the multinational Tech Mahindra's (Verma et al., 2020) shows that technological innovations introduced to HR processes have positively impacted the accessibility, monitoring, and efficiency of HR organization functions. As a result, there has been an evolution in employee satisfaction and growth in the productivity of the company (Verma et al., 2020). The data analysis was also able to achieve the desired objectives (Verma et al., 2020). The effects of Industry 4.0 on the HR organization function are therefore also perceptible at the employee perception and productivity levels.

Towards Digital and Automated Resourcing

According to the state-of-the-art research in the domain, the resourcing function will be heavily impacted by Industry 4.0 technologies. Although it may be challenging to state the extent to which resourcing will be more impacted than the organization function, there seem at least to be fewer areas, roles, processes, or activities that are independent of technology, as was the case for the organziation function.

We decided to deal with workforce planning and talent management jointly as both seem to be more tightly intertwined under the influence of Industry 4.0 technologies. Several key developments are worth mentioning in this regard. Specifically, past research refers to "talent analytics," that is, the use of big data as an asset for resource planning and employee talent management (Scholz, 2017). Big data are of many types (structured, unstructured), but Russell and Bennett (2015) further stress the importance of exploiting psychometric data. This data has helped companies make smart decisions about choosing the right mix of people to improve overall team performance. N'Cho (2017) shows that talent analytics can identify employees who will be suitable for the organizational culture of the company, which improves their chances of being satisfied in their jobs, to benefit from their social networks for better access to other talented candidates; predict the success of a candidate based on the characteristics of current employees, and to form the interview committee capable of delivering the best assessment of each candidate. The literature review carried out by Fernandez et al. (2020) also shows that the organization can manage employee attrition, calculate an engagement score, and forecast recruiting needs and capacity through predictive analytics.

Likewise, the recruitment and selection function should benefit from Industry 4.0 technologies. According to Bulte (2018), for example, the recruitment process will be completely digital and automated; other more technical tools will be frequently used, such as artificial intelligence. Research by Sivathanu and Pillai (2018) indicates that targeting the new Generation Y and Z of potential employees is recommended through the tactical placement of personalized ads on mobile applications while big data and AI automatically filter resumes and invite to interviews those profiles that meet the job requirements. Automation is the keyword that optimizes the overall recruitment cycle: videoconference interviews via a fast internet connection, automated and personalized pre-employment tests (3D simulation of real professional situations), interpretation and validation of candidates' voice responses by AI, as well as welcoming and familiarizing newcomers assisted by virtual reality or augmented reality (Sivathanu and Pillai, 2018). While this function seems to be the most likely to be wholly automated and integrate a broad range of Industry 4.0 technologies, human intervention might always be required to ensure that the automated process results in the optimal choice.

A Continuously Learning and Developing Factory

Industry 4.0 technologies will dramatically impact organizational learning. Based on the 4I model (Intuition, Interpretation, Integration, and Institutionalization), Lenart-Gansiniec (2019) tried to establish the link between Industry 4.0 and organizational learning. First, the *intuition* that results from individual experiences and knowledge and the support of managers positively impact the implementation of an industry 4.0 (Lenart-Gansiniec, 2019). The implementation of an Industry 4.0 is both a radical and incremental innovation that calls for a change management process (Lenart-Gansiniec, 2019). In this sense, managers' awareness of the advantage provided by Industry 4.0 and their ability to convey this idea to employees is very important (Lenart-Gansiniec, 2019). Second, *interpretation* in the context of

Industry 4.0 allows the organization to view complex issues from a new perspective (Lenart-Gansiniec, 2019). For example, the scenario-based learning method in Industry 4.0 allows the modeling (in 3D) of problems and improves the skills of solving them in learners (Erol et al., 2016). Learners have several resources at their disposal (e.g., methodologies, tools, data, technologies, experts they can consult) (Erol et al., 2016). In the context of Industry 4.0, social skills are also required to solve problems collaboratively (Erol et al., 2016; Lenart-Gansiniec, 2019). Third, *integration* refers to "a group process where a shared understanding is translated into coordinated action, for example, executing a new product or process-related idea" (Jenkin, 2013, p.98). In Industry 4.0, project teams are a means that facilitates the acquisition and reuse of knowledge (Shamim et al., 2016), as well as the design and implementation of innovations (Khedhaouria & Jamal, 2015). Fourth, *institutionalization* is when learning occurs at different levels of the organization, it becomes embedded in organizational routines, rules, and procedures (Jenkin, 2013). The horizontal structure is suitable for Industry 4.0 environment and HRM 4.0 implementation (Shamim et al., 2016; Puhovichova et al., 2020). This form facilitates organizational learning because it guarantees high employee participation in decision-making and faster feedback to the governing body (Shamim et al., 2016). This model provides a comprehensive framework of technological influence on organizational learning but fails to underscore how learning will be more firmly embedded in the workplace thanks to Industry 4.0.

According to Bulte (2018), the education system is disparate in relation to the knowledge and skills that organizations need, and the environment changes rapidly. Therefore, training will be more present in the workplace so that employees have the appropriate knowledge for their function. Tvenge and Martinsen (2018) argue that new learning paradigms need to be adopted. In the manufacturing context and according to the old learning system, individuals pass on knowledge to each other and form part of a team (Tvenge & Martinsen, 2018). This system is no longer valid for several reasons: a higher specialization of work where the roles are no longer identical; and the new organization of work which has resulted in a decrease in the number of workers and an increase in the physical distance between them (Tvenge & Martinsen, 2018). "This implies the need for novel learning systems, i.e., in the form of supervision, guidance, and collaborative learning; synchronous and/or asynchronous, mediated through ICT tools" (Tvenge & Martinsen, 2018, p.262). Thus, ICT will offer new potential for learning in the workplace. The learning model proposed by Tvenge and Martinsen (2018) is summarized around the following points: asynchronous social learning via virtual classrooms; a mix of formal and informal learning mode; visualization and analysis of data from PCS; the use of free time margins provided by the Industry 4.0 work system for learning and training purposes; the adaptation and personalization of learning methods according to each individual; an active and continuous approach to career planning; education, training, and research must take place at the level of what is referred to as Learning Factories. A Learning factory represents a realistic production environment within an industrial site. Trainees use it for learning purposes to test new technological or organizational approaches related to complex industrial situations (Abele et al., 2015).

Specific Industry 4.0 technologies such as AI can identify the skills gaps in each employee compared to those in demand in the market (Sivathanu & Pillai, 2018). In this way, the employee is trained in the areas most beneficial for the organization. AI thus personalizes individual learning according to each individual. For example, Learning needs and career goals differ from employee to employee. The career plan is essential for generations Y and Z (Sivathanu & Pillai, 2018). To a certain degree, they are attracted only to training that will help them achieve their career aspirations (Sivathanu & Pillai, 2018). An example of the application of AI to address these requirements is the JobKred tool (Gan, 2019).

First, the tool breaks down the user's training and experiences into a portfolio of skills generated by the tool's AI. The user is then redirected to a section that offers intelligent career recommendations based on the data collected. The career choices selected serve as the basis for the skills gap analysis. Finally, the courses and the process to achieve the learning objectives are indicated.

The current literature does not provide enough insight into the link between Industry 4.0 and management development. Faced with the rapid changes in Industry 4.0, managers, including HR managers, will meet new demands. They need to be proactive and develop their data analysis skills, as most decisions will be based on them (Bulte, 2018). From the above, managers will nonetheless remain the benchmark for all learning within the organization. They are responsible for motivating, supervising, coaching, and instilling a feedback culture to promote innovation and achieve desired goals.

Smart and Gamified Reward Management

Although reward management consists of multiple sub-functions that are all well-discussed in extant research, the current literature does not sufficiently explore the impact of Industry 4.0 technologies on reward management. In any event, it is cited that HR managers are called upon to exploit the potential of "Smart HR" (Gan & Halimah Mohd, 2019). An analysis can be carried out on performance, seniority, the participation rate in organized events, evaluations given by superiors or peers (Gan & Halimah Mohd, 2019). It is also preferable to individualize the rewards (Bulte, 2018). Instead of dashboards, some organizations use the gamification method where the points collected unlock rewards like extra free time, days off, bonuses, or gift cards (Niesenhaus, 2013). Leveraging HR analytics will further optimize and individualize the rewards management system (Nocker & Sena, 2019).

Little Impact of Industry 4.0 on Employee Relations?

Similarly to reward management, although employee relations is an important area and especially with the increasing importance of Corporate social responsibility (CSR), researchers have yet to address the impact of Industry 4.0 on the relationship with employees, as defined by Armstrong (2011). The general assumption is that it is possible that with smart factories, many less skilled people will lose their jobs to machines. Yet, there is also mention of re-skilling or up-skilling less-skilled workers. At this point, it is not known how this will affect the working relationship.

Healthy Operator 4.0 Contributing to Foster Health and Security at Work

Industry 4.0 technologies have a priori several desirable effects on employees' health and security. Recently a new concept called Healthy operator 4.0 has emerged (Sun et al., 2020). This term is for workers assisted by automated systems and equipped with portable devices (Sun et al., 2020). The purpose of introducing this concept is to address growing concerns about stress at work, psychosocial health issues, and physical risks caused by the introduction of Industry 4.0 technologies (Sun et al., 2020). For example, IoT and other technologies allow real-time viewing of data such as the activities, location, surrounding space, and vital signs of workers (Sun et al., 2020). In addition, these technologies are very useful for developing medical applications, avoiding collisions of humans with equipment or exposure to hazardous substances, and proposing ergonomic postures (Sun et al., 2020).

Furthermore, smartwatches and mobile apps help employees continuously monitor the state of their physical health, therefore initiating preventive measures, which can reduce the number of days of incapacity for work (Puhovichova & Jankelova, 2020). It should also be noted that it is possible to carry out certain dangerous activities more effectively, such as working at height or training in the event of a fire, through virtual reality or augmented reality (Tepe, 2020). In addition, the performance of repetitive tasks by robots and CSPs considerably reduces the risk of accidents (Tepe, 2020). Finally, although not explicitly mentioned in extant research, it is worth noting that some concerns might arise in that technology enables employers to exert a more substantial control of their employees. This control might further extend outside of the corporate domain since technology allows monitoring without the constraint of time or place.

Few Investigations on how Industry 4.0 Contributes to Employee Wellbeing

The current literature examining the link between Industry 4.0 and wellbeing at work provided mixed results, and this topic could be the subject of further investigations and research. A wellbeing environment is essential to keep the best talents in the organization. Moreover, it increases productivity (Kaasinen et al., 2019). The new tools and practices of Industry 4.0 have positive effects on wellbeing at work. This is contradicted by Shaw and Varghese (2018), who point out that the nature of the effect of technological change on employee wellbeing is conditioned by senior management. In sum, more research is needed in this area of HRM 4.0.

Automation of HR Services for Smart HR 4.0

IoT and AI will automate most HR processes, transforming HR services into "Smart HR 4.0" (Piwowar-Sulej, 2020). At this level, HR professionals have pointed out that their jobs have become easier and believe that HR analytics and behavioral sciences will take on more importance within their profession (Dhanpat et al., 2020). In the traditional approach to HR service delivery, employee requests are managed by email, phone, spreadsheets (Frisby, 2019). Tracking cases in old ways is complex and inefficient, so organizations increasingly turn to cloud-based HR case management solutions (Frisby, 2019). These technologies allow for better tracking without the hurdle of data storage and management at the company-level.

Continuous and Data-Driven Performance Management

Performance management has become an ongoing, data-driven process rather than an annual ritual (Buck & Morrow, 2018). Therefore, it appears that this function will be particularly impacted by industry 4.0, in general, and AI, in particular, as emphasized by Buck and Morrow (2018, p.261) who stressed that "one of the biggest impacts of artificial intelligence (AI) on HR is and will continue to be around performance management". Bulte (2018) echoed this claim by emphasizing that performance management predominantly focuses on data analysis. For example, via the data collected by smartwatches, companies can, on the one hand, track employee behavior in the workplace (Vantage Fit, 2021). On the other hand, the features of these gadgets (e.g., push notifications, smart reminders) help employees be more productive (Vantage Fit, 2021). For example, employees can prioritize their tasks, keep track of their activity, or remember important meetings and emails (Vantage Fit, 2021). In addition, the technical data from the machines can further be used (Bulte, 2018) to have more visibility on the tasks performed. Analyzing this data helps identify the most efficient employees and identify whether they are overworked to redistribute tasks (Parsers, 2019). Therefore, advanced data analysis skills will increasingly become a prerequisite for performance management.

Besides, it appears that performance management seems even to evolve into a different function. While it is recommended that the assessment of employee efforts be carried out in real-time; otherwise, there will be disengagement and declination of the performance of people who feel devalued (Buck & Morrow, 2018), current research further states that with Industry 4.0, the performance appraisal system should further focus on employee development, in addition to a results-based approach (Performance-Based Approach) and a behavior-based approach that facilitate learning and innovation (Shamim et al., 2016; Puhovichova et al., 2020). The system most used by organizations is management by objectives (Management by Objective), the characteristics of which are: specific objectives set mutually by managers and employees; brief statements of expected results; and feedback (Shamim et al., 2016; Puhovichova et al., 2020). Performance management should therefore go beyond the mere assessment of performance and consider other facets, including employee development as well as employee learning and innovation capabilities.

Toward the Knowledge Staircase 4.0 for Future Knowledge Management

The current literature already alludes to a "knowledge management 4.0" (KM 4.0), which means using digital technologies to create and share knowledge. North and Maier (2018) proposed a model called the "knowledge staircase 4.0" to illustrate in more detail the links between digital transformation and KM 4.0. In stable environments, the main focus of KM is on managing existing knowledge through documentation (North and Maier, 2018). The role of KM 4.0, on the other hand, is to spur agility in order to enable organizations to react to an environment marked by volatility, uncertainty, complexity, and ambiguity (VUCA) (North & Maier, 2018). Therefore, KM 4.0 has dual operational and strategic objectives (North & Maier, 2018). On the one hand, it seeks to ensure the optimal use of the knowledge necessary to maintain the current activity. On the other hand, it develops knowledge and learning skills potentially required in the future (North & Maier, 2018). There are seven strategic and operational conditions for successfully implementing such a KM 4.0 (North & Marier, 2018):

1. **Identify critical knowledge**: KM should identify the knowledge that is the key to organizational success. The aim is to build intellectual capital from all stakeholders and estimate this capital's future value. This will allow for a more precise understanding and better preparation for changes in the environment: technologies, markets, customers, industries, and so on.
2. **The creation of meaning, values, and a common understanding**: The increasing complexity of human work demands new and more intense forms of collaboration, so KM must foster a common understanding of issues and of their solutions. We must achieve a co-creation of meaning which is a mobilization of the collective intelligence of the organization in order to better understand and predict changes in the environment. The co-creation of meaning is achieved by transforming disparate and ambiguous information from the environment into a structured representation that guides the decisions and actions of the organization in relation to its future. This contextual interpretation is possible thanks to a more accentuated communication between the different entities of the organization via digital communication tools such as social networks and virtual meetings. In

the context of digital transformation, meaning at work is very important for the new generation of employees. Therefore, open communication and a shared vision are necessary to ensure employee engagement in value creation.

3. **Encourage the renewal of working methods, agile learning, and reflection**: The organization must create a climate conducive to virtual learning and the workplace by providing appropriate resources for employees. In addition, through experimentation and collaborative learning, we encourage the renewal of working methods and forward-looking thinking. A wide variety of approaches and tools can be integrated into the organization, such as micro-learning, pilot projects, after-action reviews, and so on. Among other things, these methods lead to short learning loops. This strategy ties back to the learning and development function of the HR system and its emphasis on new learning paradigms and learning models (e.g., Tvenge & Martinsen, 2018) as well as learning factories (Abele et al., 2015).
4. **Create engagement platforms**: These are platforms that promote employee engagement with the organization. Stimulating innovative ideas involves peer-to-peer learning and bringing together the heterogeneous knowledge of people. Therefore, it is strategic to implement engaging platforms that promote knowledge sharing and generation. Thus, North and Maier (2018) advocate for the generation of inter-organizational knowledge and the use of external skills. This is achieved through digital platforms that attract a large community: employees, customers, interested public, and so on. In this way, the organization obtains new resources of ideas regarding innovation design or problem-solving.
5. **Ensure access to information and knowledge flows at all times**: Employees need quick, easy, and complete access to the various sources of knowledge held by the organization. Information should be compiled and maintained in a structured and user-oriented manner. The KM system builds a tree structure and performs a content curation so that the user browses online all the sections that contain the documentation that will guide their action. Some organizations link directly with experts and communities of practice to develop employee skills on specific topics.
6. **Promote collaboration**: KM must emphasize the interconnectivity of knowledge; it is also necessary to rely on managers to establish collaboration rules so that everyone acquires the required skills for work 4.0. "Reverse tutoring" is also emerging, where young employees teach digital skills to their elders. This solidifies collaboration and allows different generations to bring each other added value.
7. **Align human learning with machine learning**: Machine Learning algorithms can blindly exploit data and thus lead to inappropriate decisions with reality (Datafloq, 2020). This decision-making process should be monitored to match organizational goals. Therefore, users should have a thorough understanding of the cognitive and behavioral mechanisms of Machine Learning systems. When it comes to data science, there are constant innovations, new algorithms, new techniques, and so on (Lotfi et al., 2022). The challenge is to stay up to date with all these changes, so it is suggested to consult seminal articles and use Deep Learning tools (Harrington, 2019).

Although not necessarily suggested by North and Maier (2018), organizations could proceed gradually and incrementally. More specifically, instead of deploying a whole KM 4.0 strategy right from the start, implementing an Enterprise Resource Planning (ERP) system could be an interesting starting point and a stepping-stone toward a broader KM 4.0 structure. In fact, ERP systems centralize organizational data, redistribute it to users and transform it into meaningful information and knowledge through various analytical processes and in a punctual or recurrent manner. In addition, other technical capabilities and various add-ons could be added incrementally to build an overarching knowledge management framework that relies on technology.

FUTURE RESEARCH AVENUES

From the onset, the publication extraction procedure provided a preliminary perspective on the quantity of research devoted to examining the impact of Industry 4.0 technologies on HR system functions. In fact, as more deeply emphasized in the content analysis, some functions were clearly less discussed in the literature than others. More specifically, whereas ample research has investigated how the Internet of things, Internet of Services, Cyber-physical Systems, and Smart factories influence the organization, resourcing, learning and development, performance management, and knowledge management functions; much less research has been devoted to the investigation of how those technologies impact reward management, employee relations, health and safety, employee wellbeing and HR services. Therefore, technology has been mainly investigated in managerial areas contributing to organizational performance and much less so in areas that are more employee-focused and human-centered. This is a major gap in research, and given the current trend toward Industry 5.0, a more "human-centric solution" (Nahavandi, 2019, p.1), it appears important to further investigate the impact of new technologies in these human-centric HR functions.

Furthermore, while this research has investigated the impact of Industry 4.0 on HR system functions, the inverse relationship is also of crucial importance. An analysis of 64 international studies on the critical success factors for the implementation of industry 4.0 emphasized that some HR system functions, including health and safety, exert a crucial impact on the successful implementation of industry 4.0 (Hoyer et al., 2020). Health and safety thus warrant further investigation because the criticality of this HR function in the successful implementation of Industry 4.0 is mainly due to psychological factors such as fear of losing jobs, lack of trust in systems, and data transparency. Therefore, additional research could investigate how HR system functions influence successful industry 4.0 deployment.

Finally, a number of audit 4.0 and other models of technological maturity have been developed so far in the literature, such as the Acatech Industrie 4.0 Maturity Index (Zeller et al., 2018). Yet, as far as the content analysis is concerned, no such models exist to investigate the level of maturity of HRM 4.0 or Work 4.0. Therefore, future studies could contribute to developing maturity indices similar to existing technological maturity indices to investigate the extent to which organizations' HR processes are technologically advanced (e.g., HRM 4.0/Work 4.0 Maturity Index). Importantly, given the fact that technological evolution is continuous versus a discrete process and that Industry 4.0 is not an end-point (Schaeffer, 2017), it is crucial to develop maturity models that can be easily modified or reorganized across time. In addition, future research should also continually investigate how new technological evolutions further impact the broader HR system.

CONCLUSION

This research provided insight into the evolution of HR practices and activities in the context of the Fourth Industrial Revolution. More specifically, it identified how industry 4.0 technologies impact human resources systems to create a whole new HRM 4.0 context. The literature review revealed first that organizations need to adapt their HR strategies to new market demands: different expectations of the new generation of employees; digitization and automation of all aspects of work; the need for structural flexibility to accommodate constant changes in the environment; and so on. Innovation is, therefore, an essential element for survival. Furthermore, the analysis across the ten HR functions suggests that emerging technologies (e.g., AI, Big Data) will automate most HR processes, freeing HR managers from tedious tasks and allowing them to play a more strategic role in the organization's overall growth. Industry 4.0 technologies will attract the most valuable talent and facilitate interactions between teams. Data analysis will assist HR professionals in continuously developing employee skills and information monitoring. This would also require that HR managers have appropriate knowledge in data analysis.

As emphasized in the results, industry 4.0 will not be a mere add-on to the HR system but will most likely contribute to entirely reshaping that system and possibly the HR discipline overall. HR jobs will be increasingly related to thorough data analysis and the mastery of advanced analytical tools. In fact, it is noticeable that recruitment has gone entirely digital in recent years. This trend is starting to spread to other areas of HRM. Thanks to 4.0 technology, social networks (e.g., LinkedIn) represent mines of precious data. Through data analysis, organizations will reduce their attrition rate by improving employee selection. Furthermore, the globalized labor market and the possibilities offered by remote robotics ensure that a resource can contribute to the productivity of an organization without physical presence and physical constraints. The new innovative and personalized learning platforms supported by AI allow real-time monitoring to verify the compatibility of the human knowledge and skills that an organization holds with the current needs of the environment. All this undoubtedly allows for considerable savings and increased productivity. The shortfall for HR professionals is compensated by the fact that they have more than ever an opportunity to position themselves as leaders of change and innovation within their organizations. This is thanks to the potential of 4.0 technologies, which are essential ingredients for being proactive as quickly as possible in the face of environmental disturbances.

REFERENCES

Armstrong, M. (2011). *Human resource management practice*. Kogan Page Publishers.

Armstrong, M. (2020). *Armstrong's handbook of strategic human resource management* (15th ed.). Kogan Page Publishers.

Armstrong, M., & Taylor, S. (2014). *Armstrong's Handbook of Human Resource Management Practice* (13th ed.). Kogan Page Publishers.

Baldwin, R. (2019). *The globotics upheaval: Globalization, robotics, and the future of work*. Oxford University Press.

Bissola, R., & Imperatori, B. (2020). *HRM 4.0 for Human-centered Organizations*. Emerald Publishing.

Bondarouk, T., & Ruël, H. (2009). Electronic Human Resource Management: Challenges in the digital era. *International Journal of Human Resource Management, 20*(3), 505–514. doi:10.1080/09585190802707235

Bondarouk, T., Ruel, H., & Parry, E. (2017). *Electronic HRM in the Smart Era (The Changing Context of Managing People)*. Emerald Publishing. doi:10.1108/9781787143159

Boyes, H., Hallaq, B., Cunningham, J., & Watson, T. (2018). The industrial Internet of things (IIoT): An analysis framework. *Computers in Industry*, *101*, 1–12. doi:10.1016/j.compind.2018.04.015

Buck, B., & Morrow, J. (2018). AI, performance management and engagement: Keeping your best their best. *Strategic HR Review*, *17*(5), 261–262. doi:10.1108/SHR-10-2018-145

Bulte, A. F. (2018). *What is Industry 4.0 and what are its implications on HRM practices?* (Bachelor's thesis, University of Twente). https://essay.utwente.nl/75439/

Buxmann, P., Hess, T., & Ruggaber, R. (2009). Internet of Services. *Business & Information Systems Engineering*, *5*(5), 341–342. doi:10.100712599-009-0066-z

Del Preto, J., Sanneman, L., Ajilo, D., Mehta, A., Miyashita, S., Poorheravi, N. A., Ramirez, C., Yim, S., Kim, S., & Rus, D. (2020). *Distributed Robot Garden*. CSAIL (MIT): Computer Science & Artificial Intelligence Lab. https://www.csail.mit.edu/research/distributed-robot-garden

Dhanpat, N., Buthelezi, Z. P., Marilyn, R. J., Maphela, T. V., & Shongwe, N. (2020). Industry 4.0: The role of human resource professionals. *SA Journal of Human Resource Management, 18*, 1-11. DOI:. v18i0.1302 doi:10.4102/sajhrm

Dregger, J., Niehaus, J., Ittermann, P., Hirsch-Kreinsen, H., & ten Hompel, M. (2016). The digitization of manufacturing and its societal challenges: a framework for the future of industrial labor. In 2016 IEEE international symposium on ethics in engineering, science and technology (ETHICS) (pp.1-3). IEEE. doi:10.1109/ETHICS.2016.7560045

Erol, S., Jäger, A., Hold, P., Ott, K., & Sihn, W. (2016). Tangible Industry 4.0: A Scenario-Based Approach to Learning for the Future of Production. *Procedia CIRP*, *54*, 13–18. doi:10.1016/j.procir.2016.03.162

Ertz, M., Sun, S., Boily, E., Kubiat, P., & Quenum, G. G. Y. (2022). How transitioning to Industry 4.0 promotes circular product lifetimes. *Industrial Marketing Management*, *101*, 125–140. doi:10.1016/j.indmarman.2021.11.014

Ertz, M., Sun, S., Boily, É., Quenum, G. G. Y., Patrick, K., Laghrib, Y., . . . Latrous, I. (2021). Augmented Products: The Contribution of Industry 4.0 to Sustainable Consumption. In Marketing for Sustainable Development: Rethinking Consumption Models (pp.261-283). Wiley.

Esmer, Y., & Şaylan, O. (2019). The Link of Industry 4.0 and Organizational Transformation. *Bilge Uluslararası Sosyal Araştırmalar Dergisi*, *3*(1), 1–8.

Federal Ministry of Labour and Social Affairs. (2015). *Green Paper Work 4.0*. https://www.bmas.de/EN/Services/Publications/arbeiten-4-0-greenpaper-work-4-0.html

Federal Ministry of Labour and Social Affairs. (2017). *Re-imagining work, Green Paper Work 4.0*. https://www.bmas.de/SharedDocs/Downloads/EN/PDF-Publikationen/a883-white-paper.pdf?__blob=publicationFile&v=1

Fernandez Alarcon, V., & Gallardo-Gallardo, E. (2021). Tackling the HR digitalization challenge: Key factors and barriers to HR analytics adoption. *Competitiveness Review*, *31*(1), 162–187. doi:10.1108/CR-12-2019-0163

Geandarme, F. (2021). *Industrie 4.0: Définition et mise en œuvre vers l'usine connectée*. https://www.visiativ-solutions.fr/industrie-4-0/

Gohoungodji, P., N'Dri, A. B., Latulippe, J. M., & Matos, A. L. B. (2020). What is stopping the automotive industry from going green? A systematic review of barriers to green innovation in the automotive industry. *Journal of Cleaner Production*, *277*, 123524. doi:10.1016/j.jclepro.2020.123524

Habraken, M., & Bondarouk, T. (2019). Smart Industry or Smart Bubbles? A Critical Analysis of Its Perceived Value. In *HRM 4.0 For Human-Centered Organizations* (Vol. 23, pp. 1–20). Emerald. doi:10.1108/S1877-636120190000023018

Harrington, R. (2019). *How I Keep Up with Machine Learning Research - CompassRed Data Blog*. https://medium.com/compassred-data-blog/how-i-keep-up-with-machine-learning-research-d1857ede0898

Hecklau, F., Galeitzke, M., Flachs, S., & Kohl, H. (2016). Holistic approach for human resource management in Industry 4.0. *Procedia CIRP*, *54*, 1–6. doi:10.1016/j.procir.2016.05.102

Hermann, M., Pentek, T., & Otto, B. (2015). *Design Principles for Industry 4.0 Scenarios: A Literature Review*. Technische Universität Dortmund. doi:10.13140/RG.2.2.29269.22248

Hirsch-Kreinsen, H. (2016). Digitization of industrial work: Development paths and prospects. *Journal for Labour Market Research*, *49*(1), 1–14. doi:10.100712651-016-0200-6

Jenkin, T. (2013). Extending the 4I Organizational Learning Model: Information Sources, Foraging Processes and Tools. *Administrative Sciences*, *3*(3), 96–109. doi:10.3390/admsci3030096

Kaasinen, E., Liinasuo, M., Schmalfuß, F., Koskinen, H., Aromaa, S., Heikkilä, P., Honka, A., Mach, S., & Malm, T. (2019). A Worker-Centric Design and Evaluation Framework for Operator 4.0 Solutions that Support Work Well-Being. In *HWID 2018* (pp. 263–282). Human Work Interaction Design. Designing Engaging Automation. doi:10.1007/978-3-030-05297-3_18

Khedhaouria, A., & Jamal, A. (2015). Sourcing knowledge for innovation: Knowledge reuse and creation in project teams. *Journal of Knowledge Management*, *19*(5), 932–948. doi:10.1108/JKM-01-2015-0039

Kurt, R. (2019). Industry 4.0 in Terms of Industrial Relations and Its Impacts on Labour Life. *Procedia Computer Science*, *158*, 590–601. doi:10.1016/j.procs.2019.09.093

Lee, E. A. (2008). Cyber Physical Systems: Design Challenges. In *2008 11th IEEE International symposium on object and component-oriented real-time distributed computing* (pp.363-369). IEEE.

Lenart-Gansiniec, R. (2019). Organizational Learning in Industry 4.0. *Problemy Zarzadzania*, *2*(82), 96–108. doi:10.7172/1644-9584.82.4

Liboni, L. B., Cezarino, L. O., Jabbour, C. J. C., Oliveira, B. G., & Stefanelli, N. O. (2019). Smart industry and the pathways to HRM 4.0: Implications for SCM. *Supply Chain Management*, *24*(1), 124–146. doi:10.1108/SCM-03-2018-0150

Lotfi, C., Srinivasan, S., Ertz, M., & Latrous, I. (2022). A tool for study on impact of Big Data technologies on firm performance. In *4th International Conference on Intelligent Communication Technologies and Virtual Mobile Networks (ICICV 2022)* (pp. 501-517). Tirunelveli: Francis Xavier Engineering College.

N'Cho, J. (2017). Contribution of talent analytics in change management within project management organizations the case of the French aerospace sector. *Procedia Computer Science*, *121*, 625–629. doi:10.1016/j.procs.2017.11.082

Niesenhaus, J. (2013). *Industry 4.0: Gamification in the area of industrial production*. https://www.centigrade.de/en/blog/industry-4-0-gamification-in-the-area-of-industrial-production/

Nocker, M., & Sena, V. (2019). Big Data and Human Resources Management: The Rise of Talent Analytics. *Social Sciences*, *8*(10), 273. doi:10.3390ocsci8100273

North, K., & Maier, R. (2018). Wissen 4.0 – Wissensmanagement im digitalen Wandel. *HMD Praxis der Wirtschaftsinformatik*, *55*(4), 665–681. doi:10.136540702-018-0426-6

O'Riordan, J. (2017). *The practice of human resource management*. https://www.ipa.ie/_fileUpload/Documents/THE_PRACTICE_OF_HRM.pdf

Parsers. (2019). *Big Data and Machine Learning in HR: 5 examples of successful use of information technologies for human resource management*. https://parsers.me/big-data-and-machine-learning-in-hr-5-examples-of-successful-use-of-information-technologies-for-human-resource-management/

Piwowar-Sulej, K. (2020). Human resource management in the context of Industry 4.0. *Organization & Management Scientific Quarterly*, *1*(49), 103–113. doi:10.29119/1899-6116.2020.49.7

Puhovichova, D., & Jankelova, N. (2020). Changes of human resource management in the context of impact of the fourth industrial revolution. *Industry 4.0, 5*(3), 138-141.

Rajkumar, R., Lee, I., Sha, L., & Stankovic, J. (2010). Cyber-physical systems: the next computing revolution. In *Proceedings of the 47th Design Automation Conference* (pp.731-736). ACM. 10.1145/1837274.1837461

Reis, J. Z., & Gonçalves, R. F. (2018). The Role of Internet of Services (IoS) on Industry 4.0 Through the Service Oriented Architecture (SOA). In Advances in Production Management Systems. Smart Manufacturing for Industry 4.0 (pp.20-26). Academic Press.

Russell, C., & Bennett, N. (2015). Big data and talent management: Using hard data to make the soft stuff easy. *Business Horizons*, *58*(3), 237–242. doi:10.1016/j.bushor.2014.08.001

Salimi, M. (2015). *WORK 4.0: An Enormous Potential for Economic Growth in Germany*. http://englishbulletin.adapt.it/wp-content/uploads/2015/12/work4.0_sam.pdf

Schaeffer, E. (2017). *Industry X. 0: Realizing digital value in industrial sectors*. Kogan Page Publishers.

Shaba, E., Guerci, M., Gilardi, S., & Bartezzaghi, E. (2019). Industry 4.0 technologies and organizational design - Evidence from 15 Italian cases. *Studi Organizzativi.*, *1*(1), 9–37. doi:10.3280/SO2019-001001

Shamim, S., Cang, S., Yu, H., & Li, Y. (2016). Management approaches for Industry 4.0: A human resource management perspective. In *2016 IEEE Congress on Evolutionary Computation* (pp. 5309-5316). IEEE 10.1109/CEC.2016.7748365

Shani, N., Divyapriya, P., & Logeshwari, K. (2011). Human Resource Philosophy. *International Journal of Management*, *2*(1), 61–68.

Shashi, C. P., Cerchione, R., & Ertz, M. (2020). Agile supply chain management: Where did it come from and where will it go in the era of digital transformation? *Industrial Marketing Management, 90*, 324–345. doi:10.1016/j.indmarman.2020.07.011

Shaw, P., & Varghese, R. M. (2018). Industry 4.0 and the future of HR. *Journal of Management, 5*(6), 96–103.

Sivathanu, B., & Pillai, R. (2018). Smart HR 4.0 – how industry 4.0 is disrupting HR. *Human Resource Management International Digest, 26*(4), 7–11. doi:10.1108/HRMID-04-2018-0059

Strohmeier, S. (2018). Smart HRM – a Delphi study on the application and consequences of the Internet of Things in Human Resource Management. *International Journal of Human Resource Management, 31*(18), 2289–2318. doi:10.1080/09585192.2018.1443963

Strohmeier, S. (2020). Digital human resource management: A conceptual clarification. *German Journal of Human Resource Management: Zeitschrift für Personalforschung, 34*(3), 345–365. doi:10.1177/2397002220921131

Sun, S., Zheng, X., Gong, B., García Paredes, J., & Ordieres-Meré, J. (2020). Healthy Operator 4.0: A Human Cyber-Physical System Architecture for Smart Workplaces. *Sensors (Basel), 20*(7), 2011. doi:10.339020072011 PMID:32260123

Tepe, S. (2020). The impact of Industry 4.0 on occupational health and safety. *International Journal of Advances in Engineering and Pure Sciences, 33*(1), 122–130. doi:10.7240/jeps.777641

Thite, M., Kavanagh, M. J., & Johnson, R. D. (2012). Evolution of human resource management & human resource information systems: The role of information technology. In M. J. Kavanagh, M. Thite, & R. D. Johnson (Eds.), *Human Resource Information Systems: Basics, Applications & Directions* (pp. 2–34). Sage.

Thomas, S., Kureshi, S., Suggala, S., & Mendonca, V. (2020). HRM 4.0 and the Shifting Landscape of Employer Branding. In P. Kumar, A. Agrawal, & P. Budhwar (Eds.), *Human & Technological Resource Management: New Insights into Revolution 4.0* (pp. 37–51). Emerald. doi:10.1108/978-1-83867-223-220201003

Tvenge, N., & Martinsen, K. (2018). Integration of digital learning in industry 4.0. *Procedia Manufacturing, 23*, 261–266. doi:10.1016/j.promfg.2018.04.027

Valamis. (2019). *What Is Organizational Learning and Why it's Important?* https://www.valamis.com/hub/organizational-learning

Vanhala, S., & Tuomi, K. (2006). HRM, company performance and employee wellbeing. *Management Review, 17*(3), 241–255.

Vantage Fit. (2021). *The Futuristic Advantages Of A Smartwatch for Business Use*. https://blog.vantagefit.io/smartwatch-for-business-use/

Verma, A., Bansal, M., & Verma, J. (2020). Industry 4.0: Reshaping the future of HR. *Strategic Direction, 36*(5), 9–11. doi:10.1108/SD-12-2019-0235

Waschull, S., Bokhorst, J., & Wortmann, H. (2017). Impact of Technology on Work: Technical Functionalities that Give Rise to New Job Designs in Industry 4.0. In *APMS 2017: Advances in production management systems. The path to intelligent, collaborative and sustainable manufacturing* (pp. 274–281). IFIPAICT. doi:10.1007/978-3-319-66923-6_32

Zeller, V., Hocken, C., & Stich, V. (2018). Acatech Industrie 4.0 maturity index–a multidimensional maturity model. In *IFIP International Conference on Advances in Production Management Systems* (pp.105-113). Springer. 10.1007/978-3-319-99707-0_14

ADDITIONAL READING

da Silveira, A. B., Levrini, G. R. D., & Ertz, M. (2022). How Digital Platforms Materialize Sustainable Collaborative Consumption: A Brazilian and Canadian Bike-Sharing Case Study. *Journal of International Consumer Marketing*, *34*(1), 51–71.

Ertz, M. (Ed.). (2022). *Handbook of Research on the Platform Economy and the Evolution of E-Commerce*. IGI Global.

Ertz, M., & Boily, É. (2019). The rise of the digital economy: Thoughts on blockchain technology and cryptocurrencies for the collaborative economy. *International Journal of Innovation Studies*, *3*(4), 84–93.

Ertz, M., & Boily, É. (2020). When giants meet: Collaborative economy, blockchain technology, and social media. In R. Leon (Ed.), *Strategies for business sustainability in a collaborative economy* (pp. 81–101). IGI Global.

Ertz, M., Jo, M. S., Kong, Y., & Sarigöllü, E. (2021). Predicting m-shopping in the two largest m-commerce markets: The United States and China. *International Journal of Market Research*, •••, 14707853211023036.

Ertz, M., Sun, S., Boily, É., Quenum, G. G. Y., Patrick, K., Laghrib, Y., & Latrous, I. (2021). Augmented Products: The Contribution of Industry 4.0 to Sustainable Consumption. In S. Dekhili (Ed.), *Marketing for Sustainable Development: Rethinking Consumption Models* (pp. 261–283). ISTE.

Ertz, M., Sun, S., & Latrous, I. (2021, February). The Impact of Big Data on Firm Performance. In *International Conference on Advances in Digital Science* (pp. 451-462). Springer, Cham.

Menvielle, L., Ertz, M., François, J., & Audrain-Pontevia, A. F. (2022). User-Involved Design of Digital Health Products. In *Revolutions in Product Design for Healthcare* (pp. 1–19). Springer.

Tandon, U., & Ertz, M. (2022). Customer Satisfaction Towards Online Shopping by Empirical Validation of Self-Determination Theory. In M. Ertz (Ed.), *Handbook of Research on the Platform Economy and the Evolution of E-Commerce* (pp. 177–203). IGI Global.

Tandon, U., Ertz, M., & Bansal, H. (2020). Social vacation: Proposition of a model to understand tourists' usage of social media for travel planning. *Technology in society*, *63*, 101438.

Tandon, U., Ertz, M., & Sakshi, K. (2021). POD Mode of Payment, Return Policies and Virtual-Try-on Technology as Predictors of Trust: An Emerging Economy Case. *Journal of Promotion Management*, *27*(6), 832–855.

Torrent-Sellens, J., Ficapal-Cusí, P., & Ertz, M. (2022). Motivations for labour provision on digital platforms in Europe: Examining the differences between only gigers and gigers and renters. In M. Ertz (Ed.), *Handbook of Research on the Platform Economy and the Evolution of E-Commerce* (pp. 81–103). IGI Global.

KEY TERMS AND DEFINITIONS

Cyber-Physical Systems (CPS): A system that integrates computational and communication elements that work together to control, coordinate, and command physical processes.

HRM 4.0: HRM 4.0 is a digital way of leading and managing HR functions. It represents a penetration of IT and new technology HR system design and execution.

Human Resources Management (HRM): A strategic, integrated, and coherent approach to the employment, development, and wellbeing of the people working in organizations.

Human Resources (HR) System: A set of interrelated and interdependent activities and practices, allowing the achievement of HR objectives.

Industry 4.0: Industry 4.0 is a collective term for technologies and concepts of value chain organization merging the physical and the digital in a unique network of interconnected and interdependent nodes.

Internet of Services (IoS): The merger between Web 2.0 and service-oriented architectures allows companies to offer their services via the internet.

Internet of Things (IoT): Global infrastructure for the information society, which provides advanced services by interconnecting objects (physical or virtual) using existing or evolving interoperable information and communication technologies.

Work 4.0: A concept that describes the transformations that will affect several aspects of the world of work and their impact on society following the fourth industrial revolution.

Chapter 15
Digital Relations and Innovative Ecosystem for Sustainable Engineering Education:
A Case of Russia

Anna Tarasova
Volga State University of Technology, Russia

Wadim Strielkowski
University of California, Berkeley, USA

Nina Larionova
Volga State University of Technology, Russia

ABSTRACT

Countries are striving to opt for digital economy by adopting miscellaneous state programs and translating them into national projects. The chapter describes digital relations and the digital economy. It examines the effectiveness of the government strategies on digitalization and indulges the programs' context in terms of their priorities, objectives, and tools for implementation, based on the rigorous critique of the programs in the literature. Furthermore, it audits the chronicle of events in programs development, actors involved, and the decision-making process. Moreover, it focuses on the legal regulation of the digital economy with a specific focus on the situation in the Russian Federation. In addition, it examines governance and economics in the context of a digitally hybridized civilization. Moreover, it assesses Russia's potential and innovative performance in the context of the Global Innovation Index to better implement robust innovation policy conditions.

DOI: 10.4018/978-1-7998-9715-6.ch015

Copyright © 2022, IGI Global. Copying or distributing in print or electronic forms without written permission of IGI Global is prohibited.

INTRODUCTION

With the spread of the Internet and the World Wide Web, people are increasingly living a hybrid life in which physical and digital, real and virtual interact with each other. Online and offline identities overlap and inter-digitize, removing the barriers between them and their real-world counterparts (Graham, 2018; Simunkova, 2019).

Overall, it becomes clear that the ability to provide a new form of digital sovereignty - a digital economy with its own rules and norms - was there. While we do not yet know whether this new frontier will lead to a digital civilisation, the future will see further progress in this way of thinking. We are already witnessing the emergence of real and virtual civilizations known as "virtual economies" and "digital civilizations" in the form of online games and online communities. While the Internet and its sub-communities are still in their infancy at this stage of development, the foundations are already in place.

Similarly, virtual reality tools have shown the potential for developing a new kind of economy in the form of "virtual economies" (Kwilinski et al., 2020). These virtual spaces remain necessarily connected to the real world, but they represent an alternative means of communication between people and their virtual communities and become increasingly independent. While virtual economies still exist primarily as subsidiaries of the real economy, emerging economies and globalized economic paradigms offer them a new way to coexist (Klimuk & Tarasova, 2019).

In this sense, a very popular and widely-discussed cryptocurrency Bitcoin is serving as a failed virtual currency, and many people have little hope that the old system of the year will finally prove its worth. However, it is surprising that Bitcoin is gaining acceptance among established institutions, and Bitcoin ATM open all around the world (Hacioglu et al., 2019; Mikhaylov, 2020).

A number of hybrid forms of digital governance are emerging, and the concept of "digital governance" is also taking root, offering an alternative to traditional governance structures such as government and law enforcement. One of the most promising examples of establishing a hybrid form of virtual management in the virtual economy is virtual property, where users can do everything from buying and developing virtual properties to organizing games and scientific conferences (Belokurova et al., 2019; Betelin, 2018; Heeks & Bukht, 2018; Kutzner et al., 2018; Silin & Animitsa, 2018). The oldest and most famous are those who work in the virtual economy, such as Bitcoin, Ethereum, Bitcoin Cash, as well as other popular virtual currencies.

Of course, virtual environments are only a small part of what is done in online environments today. The apparent effectiveness of online collaboration, however, is not the result of a lack of technology, but rather of ever more sophisticated technical features that blur the lines between online and offline. However, a full switch to online learning is not in sight until the pandemic subsides. Expect mixed learning, with traditional courses increasingly integrated into online activities. Instead, it is argued that we are now witnessing the emergence of a new kind of "virtual economy" - a hybrid economy, that is, between online and offline environments. The demands on course software are changing and we are turning to new technologies such as cloud computing, virtual reality and augmented reality (Hernando de Soto, 2017).

There are many ecological competences make today's engineers aware of nature's basic organizational patterns, and that nature sustains life by creating and nurturing communities such as ecovillages as a way in which human activities are integrated into the natural world that supports healthy human development and can be continued indefinitely. Currently, sustainable engineering focuses in the research and delivery of solutions to natural and man-made hazards. Today's engineers need to learn how to address a range of environmental issues, including water quality, pollution and climate change. In addition, they need to deepen and improve their understanding of academic areas in an international context (Tarasova, 2019). This provides high quality professional development for those preparing future engineers for careers in environmental engineering, environmental sciences and environmental management.

Ecovillages are increasingly recognised for their important role in developing sustainable development and livelihoods for their communities. While many of them are able to lead personal development courses, an increasing number of eco-schools have established learning centres and are creating successful programmes for education and sustainable development. One can build a sustainable future by identifying, supporting and coordinating the steps necessary to achieve social, spiritual, economic and environmental harmony. Examples of the necessary expertise and skills in the areas of sustainability, sustainable education and sustainability management need to be promoted (Chen & Hung, 2016; Overholm, 2015). Modern universities should act as a living classroom where these practices can be put into practice, and we encourage and support them. They have consistently demonstrated the ability to achieve a high level of sustainability by providing high-quality sustainable engineering education and helping to improve the quality of life of the people. Environmental engineers can help develop systems and infrastructures that enable people and ecosystems to thrive in the face of predictable and unforeseen challenges (Chen & Hung, 2016; Overholm, 2015; Tolstykh, Gamidullaeva, Shmeleva et al, 2020). Today, these engineers have begun to move from their traditional role of characterizing, managing and resolving existing environmental problems to developing new knowledge, developing innovative technologies and strategies, and implementing solutions to prevent and solve environmental problems. They have applied their knowledge and skills in a wide range of areas, some of which are environmental engineering, water and wastewater management, land use planning, energy management and transport.

INEFFICIENT EFFECTIVENESS OF THE HIGHER SCHOOL EDUCATION: A CASE OF RUSSIA

The Soviet Union's education system had to serve the interests of the country and the Cold War. In a way, it was one of the best in the world, at least when it came to natural sciences and engineering. The development of national culture was allowed at the expense of widening the gap between social classes. A form of universal public education was introduced, which only gave those with the financial means to enrol in educational institutions at both secondary and university level. Grammar schools, a form of education adopted from Germany, enabled the elite to gain better access to education, contributed to the growth of national cultures, but also led to their formation, further separating this group from the majority of Russian society (McCarthy et al., 2014). This led to an intelligence that was disconnected from the majority of Russian society in terms of its level of education. The entrance exams for secondary schools and universities showed that students taught in experimental schools were politically illiterate, owing to the inefficiency of educators in these experimental institutions. This shows the importance of the education system for the development of national culture in Russia and the role of educational institutions in this process.

It seems that the high value that education is attached to Soviet society is being lost in a fragmented Russian society, where many traditional institutions are viewed with unprecedented scepticism (Minina, 2017). Education, the highest value in society's reputation, is lost not only to itself but to society as a whole. In the 1990s, a centralized and rigid Soviet education system gave way to a system that gave local governments the power to design curricula, hire teachers, and control education funding.

After the collapse of the Soviet Union in 1991, Russia's education system suffered from a lack of support and funding. Russia's education system became a chaotic maelstrom in the early 1990s, with many professors and teachers leaving the profession for good. Russia's system impoverished teachers, who were always underpaid under the Soviet system, but many had given up the profession. Increasing local and regional control over schools and correcting the distortions of the old ideology - driven curricula - posed a major challenge for the nation (Agasisti et al., 2020).

In the Communist Russia, there were workers' schools where children were taught how to work in a sawmill, how to develop photographs, how to spin fabrics, how to use a printing press and how to work in a laboratory. This failure led to an increase in illiteracy among children and a decline in their literacy rate. These educational institutions took the form of vocational schools that trained students for higher education, aimed at producing a workforce that was trained in a way that was unprecedented in Russian history. This phase of educational development faced a multitude of challenges, as the student body rapidly changed from elite to proletarians and peasants. Extending mass education to the proletariat, peasants and students, preferring these groups to secondary schools and universities, would lower educational standards, which would then result in a mediocre education for the workforce (Smolentseva, 2017).

Post-Soviet educational reforms emphasized teaching by shedding the narrow institutional views that had dominated the previous era, and preparing young people to deal with the society they would encounter by presenting a broader interpretation of the world. It also sought to integrate education into the production and economic processes that graduates will pass on to adults. A major problem with educational reform at the time was parents' attitudes toward education, as many parents believed that the recently discontinued form of education, which focused on reading, writing, and math, was the right curriculum (Nie et al., 2020). As a result of market reforms, education in Russia became partly free of charge - based and partly free, and in some cases completely free. The economic reforms of the 1990s, complemented by the liberalisation of education policies and the introduction of free public education, were particularly severe for the engineering education. Although the concept of continuous education was intended to last the life of an individual, it also had the potential to transform the educational process from an economic burden on the state into an engine of economic progress.

However, the growing financial inequality of the population significantly limited the number of opportunities for the new graduates (Aldieri et al., 2020). Professional training for professionals, including doctors, lawyers, teachers, engineers and other professionals from the private sector, remained free of charge. The new figures dampened the job insecurity experienced by well-educated Russians in the 1990s. The legislation provided for basic principles to be followed, such as the introduction of a minimum wage and the promotion of education to the level of the private sector. At the same time, polls showed that education is Russians' most pressing concern. Although most older Russians resented the new system's economic success, the generation now in school showed a growing interest in education, especially in the private sector.

GLOBAL INNOVATION INDEX AND THE COUNTRY'S POTENTIAL

Various factors have an effective impact on innovation and productivity, including human capital, economic development, technological innovation and economic growth. The Global Innovation Index is a global measure of innovation in the global economy, with an emphasis on the country's innovation capabilities (Bennett & Nikolaev, 2021; Bibri & Krogstie, 2020; Clarke et al., 2018; Shashlo et al., 2018; Tolstykh, Gamidullaeva, & Shmeleva, 2020).

Published annually since 2007, GII is now the leading benchmarking tool for executives, policy makers and others seeking insight into the level of innovation around the world. Impairment of the Global Competitiveness Index, a global measure of global competitiveness and productivity. The core of the GII report is made up of three pillars: the Global Competitiveness Index, the Innovation Input Subindex and the Human Capital Index. The three metrics are calculated on the basis of data from the World Economic Forum's annual Global Innovation Report. Each of these pillars is based on and underpins three key factors: innovation, human capital and productivity, and the level of innovation in a country's economy. Innovation performance for each sub-index covers a wide range of factors, including economic, social, political, cultural, environmental and social factors. The Innovation Output Sub-Index measures the actual results of innovation, which are divided into three sub-indices: production, productivity and human capital. It involves the production of all elements of the national economy, which is embodied in the innovative activities that are summarized under each of these elements. The index has been independently statistically verified by the European Commission's Joint Research Centre.

Figure 1 that follows, shows the Innovation index in the Russian Federation for the past 10 years from 2011 until 2020.

For the fourth year in a row, the region's two largest nations are the United States (1st) and China (2nd), and the Middle East and North Africa (3rd). Both regions have shown significant growth in the creation and innovation of ICT business models. Armenia (60th) is the only economy in the region to perform bettering relation to GDP, with a growth rate of 4.5%. Moreover, the GII continues to provide insights into the innovation indicators that economies prioritise and collect. Economies use them to design more efficient business models for the creation and innovation of ICT business models, and invest resources to analyse the results.

The Global Innovation Index aims to provide insightful data on innovations, thereby helping economies to assess their innovation performance and implement sound innovation policy considerations. By experimenting with new data and assessing existing innovation metrics, the GII aims to shape the agenda for measuring innovation. Policymakers today routinely refer to innovation and its innovation rankings as part of their economic policies. In addition, innovation is seen as a key component in the measurement of innovation at the United Nations General Assembly, as noted in the United Nations General Assembly's report on the achievement of the Sustainable Development Goals (SDGs).

CREATING THE ECONOMY FOR ATTRACTING HIGHLY-EDUCATED AND SKILLED WORKERS

In general terms, the best measures to help labour migrants integrate more quickly include better access to education and training, better job opportunities for young people and better public services (Maria & Přívara, 2017). While these measures require additional public spending, they enable migrants to retain jobs and increasingly contribute to a long-term increase in per capita GDP. Although labour migration brings costs for integrating the labour market and refugees, studies have shown that it may be worthwhile to shoulder some of the short-term costs, for example, to promote the integration of new professionals into the labour market in order to benefit from higher income levels and prosperity in the long run. Even though the benefits of migration seem to be widely shared, some local workers may need help to improve their skills (Denisenko et al., 2020). Most of the labour migrants are predominantly of working age but migration has increased the share of the working-age population over time. GDP per capita can be increased if migrants are integrated into the labour market and employed productively. But immigration can reduce labour productivity, because access to new labour reduces the available physical capital for workers, and because migrants are, on average, less educated than locals. On the other hand, microeconomic literature suggests that migrants can increase productivity by increasing the diversity of skills and ideas, promoting complementarity and specialization of skills, and promoting the improvement of the working skills of the locals. These locals are moving up into better-paid and communication-intensive professions. This dynamic specialization in skills protects domestic wages from competition from immigrants. The assumption of manual jobs, which locals are gradually leaving, is driving immigrants to reorganize production and specialization along these lines, which can increase the efficiency and efficiency of labour.

A recent study by the United States Department of Labour's Office of Management and Budget found that hiring highly skilled immigrants has a positive impact on spending on research and development. Because if companies hire a highly educated workforce, they can produce new products faster than if they don't. The study by researchers at the University of California, Berkeley, and the Massachusetts Institute of Technology shows that firms employ more effective techniques in markets with many immigrants than less educated and less skilled workers (Todorov et al., 2018). This suggests that, as the population ages and higher education levels increase, there is a diminished supply of indigenous occupations. The American market, in other words, means less demand for native workers and therefore less competition for jobs in these occupations.

For too long, America's broken immigration system has made it difficult to attract the best and brightest talent from around the world. Highly skilled workers have had to wait years, even decades, to receive green cards that allow them to contribute fully to the economy and become Americans over time. Entrepreneurs have a special immigration route that allows them to expand their businesses and create jobs.

In recent years, the debate has focused on the role of immigrants in the United States economy and their contribution to the economy. There is no doubt that economic growth and the economy are determined not only by the quality of the workforce, but also by its education and skills. The country must ensure through legislation and employment programmes that its citizens have access to education and training that can support workers, businesses and the economy as a whole.

In Russia, the situation with the qualified labour migration looks much worse. The country does not have any immigration programmes for the qualified and high-skilled workers from abroad (Bite et al., 2020; Faggian et al., 2017). Neither there is any system of working visas similar to that that exists in the United States or Canada.

DEVELOPING NATIONAL FRAMEWORKS FOR REGULATING DIGITAL ECONOMY

The digital policy of the European Union (EU) should reflect Europe's growing economy, its leading values and its commitment to the digital economy and innovation. Together, the political representatives and EU institutions should commit in the next parliamentary term to develop a national framework for providing a policy framework to support growth in the digital age. EU policy makers, including the European Parliament and the Commission, should seize the opportunity to redouble their efforts to achieve the Digital Single Market, thereby cementing and implementing a strong vision for the digital economy. Keeping pace with the pace of digital innovation and the degree of adoption by other markets requires strong political will to achieve harmonised digital policies and regulation across the EU. European businesses face the challenge of expanding and developing emerging technologies, despite the fact that the EU has made great progress in creating the Digital Single Market (Qiao et al., 2020). This is due to the lack of harmonised regulation of digital technologies in EU Member States. EU law that regulates digital technology to create a level playing field, especially for foreign companies, has backfired by hampering the growth of the digital economy and the adoption of new technologies bye companies.

EU policymakers should identify and update policies that unnecessarily challenge Europe's digital transformation in the current regulatory framework, such as the lack of harmonised regulation of digital technologies in EU Member States. In particular, EU policymakers should amend the General Data Protection Regulation 2016/679 (known as "GDPR") to address shortcomings that are hampering the digital economy, including the unnecessary restrictions it has created for artificial intelligence. Such adverse events can have adverse effects on developing countries, which may otherwise benefit from the use of digital technologies. The gap in use is mainly caused by social, economic and cultural barriers. In developing countries, rural areas and women and girls are often excluded from participation in the digital economy due to various infrastructural or cultural problems (Dieuaide & Azaïs, 2020). It is also well known that developing countries lack access to education, health care and other basic services in relation to everything digital. There is an urgent need for efforts that focus on ensuring that digital transformation is the force for inclusive growth. They are about ensuring that new digital technologies really reach everyone, creating essential components for a digital future, putting people at the centre of the future and renewing governance. We have brought together a number of countries with common national vision for the digital economy in Africa, the Middle East and North Africa (MENA). To promote EU digital standards, the EU also works with like-minded international partners on regulatory issues. The EU's approach offers the opportunity to help shape digitisation by using market power to regulate the digital giants and set global standards. By tailoring offerings to different regions, most major technology companies will adopt the rules as a global standard to tailor their offerings to meet customer needs. In certain cases, regulators can benefit from direct cooperation with innovators and other actors that set rules for emerging technologies. Moreover, Europe and its technology companies can lead by example and offer an alternative to the American and Chinese techno-spheres by developing the necessary technology in practice. The decentralized global structure of the Internet defies the logic of regulation and demands a new framework to accommodate its revolutionary character.

After examining various regulatory approaches to Internet governance, the United States Clinton administration published a set of principles, known as the Digital Millennium Copyright Act (DMCA), to guide the development of digital communications technologies. The framework outlined general principles that should guide the government's handling of cyberspace (Ramos-Mejía et al., 2018). There can be a universal definition of a digital platform to create a sector - a specific regulator that provides appropriate sector-specific oversight to promote competition, address content moderation issues, adequately protect consumers, and ensure public safety. A new measure is proposed for the often-challenged digital platform, the "cost of exclusion". This measure will apply to all digital platforms, with the exception of platforms such as Facebook, Twitter, YouTube, Google and other social media. The costs of exclusion recognise that the power of digital platforms stems from their ability to harm consumers, businesses and the economy as a whole. It measures costs for individual companies based on their exclusion from a platform, in terms of the loss of revenue and the impairment of their business (Dembski et al., 2020). So, new businesses and employment models are not for those at the bottom of the pyramid who live below the poverty line and struggle to buy a meal a day, let alone have the income to pay for a bike rental. There is no doubt that such business models, while bringing new benefits, can also create new opportunities for people in developing and emerging economies, especially in low-income countries. The development of sound digital economy policies in developed and emerging economies underlines the need to make the new business model of digital economies accessible to all, not just the top 1%.

WORLD LEGAL REGULATION OF DIGITAL ECONOMY

Currently, there is a need to look at the legal status of digital technology through the prism of general status and regulatory issues and to create a framework for applying the Digital Economy and Digital Relations (DER) Act to the digital economy and digital relations (DLR). The digital legal area is marginalised and stresses the need for a more holistic approach to the legal status of digital technologies. Modern scientific literature does not deal with the legal rights and rights of the Digital Economy and Digital Relations (DLR) in a holistic way (Chang et al., 2016). In order to solve this, a completely new approach to digital technology in terms of legal personality and capability should be proposed. This would allow us to consider not only the technical aspects of technology, but also its social, economic, political and cultural aspects.

When speaking about the legal regulation of the digital economy, one has to deal with the legal status of the digital economy and digital relations. In addition, similar areas that require detailed scientific analysis and restrictive application should be also taken into account. The protectability of digital technologies means the ability to act as an object of civil and intellectual rights. There is a conflict between these two scenarios and the protection of the digital economy and digital relations. As such, they concern IT-related sectors of the economy and are primarily aimed at boosting the innovative capacity of the domestic economy and encouraging local competitors. Similarly, the specific policies and tools used by governments to address imbalances in the digital economy sometimes overlap with measures aimed at strengthening the security of technological systems and national autonomy. Unlike the first category, these measures tend to focus on the digital transformation of an entire sector or economy. In addition, a growing number of instruments are being used to regulate trade and data flows via digital networks. Digital privacy laws have become more critical as public relations has penetrated the online environment created by the internet and social media to connect consumers and engage with stakeholders. To protect customers and organizations, public relations professionals need to be educated on how best to protect consumers and customers from government interference and data misuse (Gu et al., 2020).

Current laws are inadequate and there is no constitutional amendment to protect digital privacy. Even if a specific privacy laws passed, it will be difficult for public relations (PR) professionals to use existing laws to make informed legal decisions when they are not concerned with data protection on digital platforms. There are significant gaps in the legal framework for protecting consumers' privacy and privacy in digital environments. Citizens' rights are affected by all forms of business, from the most basic ones normally enshrined in constitutional law, such as the right to privacy, to control provisions and data protection. The scope of this special issue will focus on analysing how global, state, and regional regulations regulate this new way of doing business. One can also analyse the challenges posed by the new form of economy in legislation, as well as the way in which courts resolve new issues relating to new forms of business, such as the right to privacy and data protection. Administrative law must adapt to the digitisation of the public sector, but it can also be influenced by changes in business practices and the use of digital technologies in the public and private sectors (Grodach et al., 2017; Peterson, 2017; Zhang & Lucey, 2019). This is possible because new phenomena introduced by the age of digitalization are accompanied by changes in their impact on existing systems of governance and regulation. The law should define precisely the legal relationships that exist exclusively in the digital environment and that relate to the general rights of participants in it. There is a need to actively involve the public and private sectors and civil society in the relations emerging from the digital economy. This is manifested in conferences, forums and round tables dedicated to the digital economy, as well as in the growing interest in thematic seminars and training courses. One needs to take a global view of digital policy and describe how to combat the global data protection crisis. In addition, it is useful to realize how technology platforms can help identify expertise previously hidden within the federal bureaucracy. All of this goes beyond regulation of the digital world and advocates the new principles that should guide regulation in the context of a new digital economy and digital relationships.

STATE PROGRAMME ON DIGITAL ECONOMY IN THE RUSSIAN FEDERATION

There is an infrastructure for science and innovation in Russia, represented by a range of technologies that can and should be used to develop the digital economy. It is defined in five basic directions, which include the development of infrastructure, science, technology, innovation, research and development and the promotion of innovation.

The current stage of development of the Russian economy, which is oriented towards the period up to 2024, is the forecast period 2020-2024. Data for 2005-2016 are the data of the State Program for Digital Economy of the Russian Federation and the current state of affairs in the field of digital economy (Akulinin et al., 2019). There is data on the development and implementation of new information and communication technology technologies and technologies, which are also oriented towards the future. The main initiative is the "Digital Economy of the Russian Federation" programme, adopted in 2017 and transformed into a national project in 2018. The State Digital Economy Programme of the Russian Federation was envisaged for the period up to 2024 and blessed by the Russian President Vladimir Putin himself. It was published on the Government website on the 21st of February 2018.

There is data on the development and implementation of new information and communication technologies and technologies, which are targeted up to 2024. A number of ministerial projects have been already developed, including the one by the Russian Ministry of Industry and Trade, which manages the digital industry. The programme sets out a number of rules for the "digital environment" and sets out the main standardisation measures. The technology was developed in Russia under the Rusnano program, but critics consider it ineffective and complain that Russia has only a few years of experience with this technology (Vorobieva et al., 2018). It will also provide intangible benefits to citizens of the Russian Federation, both in the digital and analogue standard age. A system of incentives and payments will be put in place in line with the requirements for the development of the country's digital economy and in line with international standards. One possible initiative in this regard could be the development of a national 5G network based on Russian equipment.

Over the next three years, the Russian Federal Academy of Sciences and the Russian National Institute of Technology in Russia will begin to teach the population skills in the digital economy. Citizens of the Russian Federation will have the ability to shape individual development paths based on personal profile and competence (Prokofyev et al., 2019). A system of incentives and payments will be created and they will have to behave in a way that creates individual development paths based on personal profiles and skills. They will also be offered intangible benefits, both digital and analogue standards for this age. This approach is therefore criticised for not guaranteeing the technological independence of ICT in the creation of new technologies. One of the stated objectives of the programme is to develop applied research to ensure the creation of a new generation of high-quality technologies and services for the digital economy. A number of studies show that ICT infrastructure is relatively well developed, and available studies suggest that the basis for the development of the digital economy is currently being laid by a combination of high-quality technologies and services, as well as by high infrastructure investment. Similar companies in Russia carry a proportional economic and social weight in terms of their contribution to the development of the digital economy. According to the Council of Experts, the programme's goal is not to boost Russia's development, but to raise its economy's level of digitisation above current levels in developing countries by 2025. Such modernisation efforts should lead to a significant increase in the number of jobs and the creation of new industries.

Although it envisages the development of a new digital economy in Russia using advanced technologies, it lacks a clear strategy to stimulate the domestic electronics industry, and relies on a combination of investment in new technologies based on imported equipment and the production of high-quality products. This means that Russia needs a new programme to develop a digital economy, because a fundamental feature of the ICT sector is that the emergence of new technologies is unpredictable today (Tarakanov et al., 2019). In short, it makes sense for the sectors and services that make up the high-tech sector in developing countries to be included in the programme, which implicitly aims to raise the level of digitisation of the Russian economy above that of developing countries. US statistics distinguish, for example, between the production of measuring instruments and the use of digital technologies in sectors such as health and education.

CONCLUSION

All in all, digital relations and digital economy need legal norms and framework that they can adhere to in the virtual and physical world. The unprecedented spread of the Internet-based technologies led to the situation when digitalization penetrated all spheres of our lives, both private and public.

The positive aspects of digitalization in the face of the COVID-19 pandemic is that it restores the environment, thus increasing sustainability, and mitigating global climate change.

Digital economy is a driver of growth and a tool for qualitative changes of the modern society. Being entirely dependent on digital computer digital computer technologies, and by using the new methods of generating, processing, storing and transmitting data, digitalized economy would substantiate a wider aspect of social and cultural relations based on the use of the digital information and communication technologies. The fourth industrial revolution with a breakthrough of consequential technological innovations initiated the digital economy, which is today essentially changing the world we see around us and the traditional way of doing things. However, while being positive and facilitating human existence, the fourth industrial revolution still might cause many problems, specifically of social and ethical manner.

Socio-ethical problems of the digital economy are critical for the era of transformation, as they are vital challenges and risks in the way of human activity. They might alter moral norms and values of a given society, and cause reforms and modifications in education systems. Therefore, we urge that social and ethical aspects of the digital economy should become a subject of theoretical consideration and the basis of projecting. In case the mankind manages to resolve those issues, the digital economy will progress, while the demographic cohorts will be acquiring and nursing the qualities essential for adapting to the digital economy.

The research aimed at studying the concept and the essence of the entrepreneurial innovation ecosystem of the Russian Federation with sustainable ecosystem, supported by highly qualified and skilled workers. This analysis stimulated us to define the global trends for innovative development that Russian universities could further exploit to building proper institutional environment for the robust macro-regions innovation ecosystems. The authors described the content and the main features of sustainable innovative ecosystems, based on the comparative analysis of scientific approaches to the characterization of ecosystems, their key components and interaction features.

Thus, the authors proposed the interpretation of entrepreneurial innovation ecosystem category as an open dynamic self-organizing and self-developing system consisting of organizational, structural and functional components (institutions) and their interrelations, creating, consuming and transforming scientific knowledge and ideas into innovative products within a complex matrix of relations between its constituent elements. Furthermore, we analysed the process of transforming information into innovative products within the entrepreneurial innovation ecosystem. We unveiled that the ecosystem consolidates educational, scientific and entrepreneurial spheres, and is tied to generating, transferring, and commercializing of knowledge, information and technologies.

Hence, the paper characterizes fundamentals to evolve sustainable innovation ecosystem in Russia. Though the Russian Federation has the high potential, essential to trigger innovation, it is still experiencing system-wise and methodological problems that hinder the country to develop the model of the entrepreneurial innovation ecosystem of the macro-region. Sustainable digital production concept is critical in creating a modern network system to facilitate university-industry efficient cooperation.

ACKNOWLEDGMENT

The research was supported by the Ministry of Science and Higher Education of the Russian Federation (Grant N° 075-15-2021-674) and Core Facility Centre «Ecology, biotechnologies and processes for obtaining environmentally friendly energy carriers» of Volga State University of Technology, Yoshkar-Ola.

REFERENCES

Agasisti, T., Egorov, A., Zinchenko, D., & Leshukov, O. (2020). Efficiency of regional higher education systems and regional economic short-run growth: Empirical evidence from Russia. *Industry and Innovation*. Advance online publication. doi:10.1080/13662716.2020.1738914

Akulinin, F. V., Maksimov, M. I., Velikorossov, V. V., Kolesnikov, A. V., & Balakhanova, D. K. (2019). Innovation development trends and the digital economy program of the Russian Federation. In *Industrial Technologies and Engineering* (pp. 105–109). ICITE.

Aldieri, L., Kotsemir, M., & Vinci, C. P. (2020). The role of labour migration inflows on R&D and innovation activity: Evidence from Russian regions. *Foresight*, *22*(4), 437–468. doi:10.1108/FS-03-2020-0035

Belokurova, E. V., Pizikov, S. V., Petrenko, E. S., & Koshebayeva, G. K. (2019, April). The institutional model of building the digital economy in modern Russia. In *Institute of Scientific Communications Conference* (pp. 64-70). Springer.

Bennett, D.L., & Nikolaev, B. (2021). Historical Disease Prevalence, Cultural Values, and Global Innovation. *Entrepreneurship Theory and Practice, 45*(1), 145.

Betelin, V. B. (2018). Challenges and opportunities in forming a digital economy in Russia. *Herald of the Russian Academy of Sciences, 88*(1), 1–6. doi:10.1134/S101933161801001X

Bibri, S. E., & Krogstie, J. (2020). The emerging data–driven Smart City and its innovative applied solutions for sustainability: The cases of London and Barcelona. *Energy Inform, 3*(1), 5. doi:10.118642162-020-00108-6

Bite, P., Konczos Szombathelyi, M., & Vasa, L. (2020). The concept of labour migration from the perspective of Central and Eastern Europe. *Economia e Sociologia, 13*(1), 197–216. doi:10.14254/2071-789X.2020/13-1/13

Chang, Y.-C., Yang, P. Y., Martin, B. R., Chi, H.-R., & Tsai-Lin, T.-F. (2016). Entrepreneurial universities and research ambidexterity: A multilevel analysis. *Technovation, 54*, 7–21. doi:10.1016/j.technovation.2016.02.006

Chen, P.-C., & Hung, S.-W. (2016). An actor-network perspective on evaluating the R&D linking efficiency of innovation ecosystems. *Technological Forecasting and Social Change, 112*, 303–312. doi:10.1016/j.techfore.2016.09.016

Chudinovskikh, O., & Denisenko, M. (2020). Labour Migration on the Post-Soviet Territory. In M. Denisenko, S. Strozza, & M. Light (Eds.), *Migration from the Newly Independent States. Societies and Political Orders in Transition*. Springer. doi:10.1007/978-3-030-36075-7_4

Clarke, T., & Gholamshahi, S. (2018). Developing Human Capital for Knowledge Based Economies. In T. Clarke & K. Lee (Eds.), *Innovation in the Asia Pacific*. Springer. doi:10.1007/978-981-10-5895-0_12

Dembski, F., Wössner, U., Letzgus, M., Ruddat, M., & Yamu, C. (2020). Urban Digital Twins for Smart Cities and Citizens: The Case Study of Herrenberg, Germany. *Sustainability, 12*(6), 2307. doi:10.3390u12062307

Dieuaide, P., & Azaïs, C. (2020). Platforms of Work, Labour, and Employment Relationship: The Grey Zones of a Digital Governance. *Frontiers in Sociology, 5*, 2. doi:10.3389/fsoc.2020.00002 PMID:33869411

Erdogan, S., & Dayan, V. (2019). Analysis of Relationship Between International Interest Rates and Cryptocurrency Prices: Case for Bitcoin and LIBOR. In U. Hacioglu (Ed.), *Blockchain Economics and Financial Market Innovation. Contributions to Economics*. Springer. doi:10.1007/978-3-030-25275-5_24

Faggian, A., Rajbhandari, I., & Dotzel, K. R. (2017). The interregional migration of human capital and its regional consequences: A review. *Regional Studies, 51*(1), 128–143. doi:10.1080/00343404.2016.1263388

Graham, T. (2018). Platforms and hyper-choice on the World Wide Web. *Big Data & Society, 5*(1). doi:10.1177/2053951718765878

Grodach, C., O'Connor, J., & Gibson, C. (2017). Manufacturing and cultural production: Towards a progressive policy agenda for the cultural economy, City. *Cultura e Scuola*, *10*, 17–25. doi:10.1016/j.ccs.2017.04.003

Gu, H., Meng, X., Shen, T., & Wen, L. (2020). China's Highly Educated Talents in 2015: Patterns, Determinants and Spatial Spillover Effects. *Applied Spatial Analysis and Policy*, *13*(3), 631–648. doi:10.100712061-019-09322-6

Heeks, R., & Bukht, R. (2018). *Digital Economy Policy in Developing Countries*. DIODE Working Paper no. 6. Available at https://ssrn.com/abstract=3540027 doi:10.2139/ssrn.3540027

Hernando de Soto, H. (2017). A tale of two civilizations in the era of Facebook and blockchain. *Small Business Economics*, *49*(4), 729–739. doi:10.100711187-017-9949-4

Klimuk, V., & Tarasova, A. (2019). Digital economy in Belarus and Russia: leading underpins of a new reality. In *3rd International Conference on Social, Economic, and Academic Leadership (ICSEAL 2019)* (pp. 421-427). Atlantis Press. 10.2991/icseal-19.2019.66

Kutzner, K., Schoormann, T., & Knackstedt, R. (2018). Digital transformation in information systems research: A taxonomy-based approach to structure the field. *Research Papers, 56*. https://aisel.aisnet.org/ecis2018_rp/56

Kwilinski, A., Vyshnevskyi, O., & Dzwigol, H. (2020). Digitalization of the EU Economies and People at Risk of Poverty or Social Exclusion. *J. Risk Financial Manag.*, *13*(7), 142. doi:10.3390/jrfm13070142

Maria, P., & Přívara, A. (2017). Cross-country analysis on neighboring migration policy by the example of Finland and Russia. *Proceedings of the International Conference on Education*, *3*(1), 17-28. 10.17501/icedu.2017.3103

McCarthy, D. J., Puffer, S. M., Graham, L. R., & Satinsky, D. M. (2014). Emerging innovation in emerging economies: Can institutional reforms help Russia break through its historical barriers? *Thunderbird International Business Review*, *56*(3), 243–260. doi:10.1002/tie.21619

Mikhaylov, A. (2020). Cryptocurrency Market Analysis from the Open Innovation Perspective. *Journal of Open Innovation*, *6*(4), 197. doi:10.3390/joitmc6040197

Minina, E. (2017). 'Quality revolution' in post-Soviet education in Russia: From control to assurance? *Journal of Education Policy*, *32*(2), 176–197. doi:10.1080/02680939.2016.1250165

Nie, D., Panfilova, E., Samusenkov, V., & Mikhaylov, A. (2020). E-Learning Financing Models in Russia for Sustainable Development. *Sustainability*, *12*(11), 4412. doi:10.3390u12114412

Overholm, H. (2015). Collectively created opportunities in emerging ecosystems: The case of solar service ventures. *Technovation*, *39–40*, 14–25. doi:10.1016/j.technovation.2014.01.008

Peterson, E. W. F. (2017). The Role of Population in Economic Growth. *SAGE Open*, *7*(October). Advance online publication. doi:10.1177/2158244017736094

Prokofyev, K. G., Dmitrieva, O. V., Zmyzgova, T. R., & Polyakova, E. N. (2019, January). Modern engineering education as a key element of russian technological modernization in the context of digital economy. In *International Scientific Conference "Far East Con"(ISCFEC 2018) Advances in Economics, Business and Management Research* (Vol. 47, pp. 652-656). 10.2991/iscfec-18.2019.160

Qiao, P., Lv, M., Zeng, Y. R., & Intensity, D. (2020). Domestic Institutional Environment, and SMEs' OFDI in Emerging Markets. *Management International Review*, *60*(6), 939–973. doi:10.100711575-020-00432-9

Ramos-Mejía, M., Franco-Garcia, M.-L., & Jauregui-Becker, J. M. (2018). Sustainability transitions in the developing world: Challenges of socio-technical transformations unfolding in contexts of poverty. *Environmental Science & Policy*, *84*, 217–223. doi:10.1016/j.envsci.2017.03.010

Shashlo, N. V., Petruk, G. V., & Korostelev, A. A. (2018). Determinants of integration interaction among the subjects of the entrepreneurial innovation ecosystem of macro region. *Amazonia Investiga*, *7*(13), 351–363.

Silin, Y. P., & Animitsa, Y. G. (2018). Contours of the Digital Economy in Russia. *Journal of New Economy*, *19*(3), 18–25.

Simunkova, K. (2019). Being hybrid: A conceptual update of consumer self and consumption due to online/offline hybridity. *Journal of Marketing Management*, *35*(1-2), 40–74. doi:10.1080/026725 7X.2019.1573844

Smolentseva, A. (2017). Where Soviet and neoliberal discourses meet: The transformation of the purposes of higher education in Soviet and post-Soviet Russia. *Higher Education*, *74*(6), 1091–1108. doi:10.100710734-017-0111-7

Tarakanov, V. V., Inshakova, A. O., & Dolinskaya, V. V. (2019). Information society, digital economy and law. In *Ubiquitous Computing and the Internet of Things: Prerequisites for the Development of ICT* (pp. 3–15). Springer.

Tarasova, A. N. (2019). Pitfalls and drawbacks in engineering education in Russia. *Journal of Applied Engineering Science, 17*(1).

Todorov, Kalinina, & Rybakova. (2018). Impact of labour migration on entrepreneurship ecosystem: case of Eurasian Economic Union. *Entrepreneurship and Sustainability Issues, Entrepreneurship and Sustainability Center, 5*(4), 992 - 1007. doi:10.9770/jesi.2018.5.4(20)

Tolstykh, T., Gamidullaeva, L., & Shmeleva, N. (2020). Elaboration of a mechanism for sustainable enterprise development in innovation ecosystems. *Journal of Open Innovation*, *6*(4), 95. doi:10.3390/joitmc6040095

Tolstykh, T., Gamidullaeva, L., Shmeleva, N., & Lapygin, Y. (2020). Regional Development in Russia: An Ecosystem Approach to Territorial Sustainability Assessment. *Sustainability*, *12*(16), 6424. doi:10.3390u12166424

Vorobieva, D., Kefeli, I., Kolbanev, M., & Shamin, A. (2018, November). Architecture of digital economy. In *2018 10th International Congress on Ultra Modern Telecommunications and Control Systems and Workshops (ICUMT)* (pp. 1-7). IEEE. 10.1109/ICUMT.2018.8631210

Zhang, Q. A., & Lucey, B. M. (2019). Globalisation, the Mobility of Skilled Workers, and Economic Growth: Constructing a Novel Brain Drain/Gain Index for European Countries. *Journal of the Knowledge Economy, 10*(4), 1620–1642. doi:10.100713132-017-0505-x

Compilation of References

Abdalla, S., & Nakagawa, K. (2021). The interplay of digital transformation and collaborative innovation on supply chain ambidexterity. *Technology Innovation Management Review*, *11*(3), 45–56. doi:10.22215/timreview/1428

Abdinnour-Helm, S., Lengnick-Hall, M. L., & Lengnick-Hall, C. A. (2003). Pre-implementation attitudes and organizational readiness for implementing an enterprise resource planning system. *European Journal of Operational Research*, *146*(2), 258–273. doi:10.1016/S0377-2217(02)00548-9

Abdullah, R., Selamat, H., Sahibudin, S., & Alias, A. (2005, March). A Framework For Knowledge Management System Implementation In Collaborative Environment For Higher Learning Institution. *Journal of Knowledge Management Practice*. http://www.tlainc.com/articl83.htm

Abideen, A. Z., Pandiyan, V., Sundram, K., Pyeman, J., Othman, A. K., Sorooshian, S., Thomé, M., Bourlakis, M., Guarnieri, P., & My, A. K. O. (2021). Food Supply Chain Transformation through Technology and Future Research Directions—A Systematic Review. *Logistics*, *5*(4), 83. doi:10.3390/logistics5040083

Accenture. (2018). *Accenture Technology Vision*. Available on: https://www.accenture.com/t20180227T215953Z__w__/us-en/_acnmedia/Accenture/next-gen-7/tech-vision-2018/pdf/Accenture-TechVision-2018-Tech-Trends-Report.pdf

Acquah, I. S. K., Naude, M. J., & Sendra-García, J. (2021). Supply chain collaboration in the petroleum sector of an emerging economy: Comparing results from symmetrical and asymmetrical approaches. *Technological Forecasting and Social Change*, *166*, 120568. doi:10.1016/j.techfore.2020.120568

Adams, R., Jeanrenaud, S., Bessant, J., Denyer, D., & Overy, P. (2016). Sustainability-oriented innovation: A systematic review. *International Journal of Management Reviews*, *18*(2), 180–205. doi:10.1111/ijmr.12068

Adelman, C., Jenkins, D., & Kemmis, S. (1976). Re-thinking case study: Notes from the second Cambridge Conference. *Cambridge Journal of Education*, *6*(3), 139–150. doi:10.1080/0305764760060306

AECOC. (n.d.). *AECOC BARÓMETRO OSA*. Retrieved on December 27, 2021, from https://www.aecoc.es/servicios/estudios/barometro-osa/

Afum, E., Agyabeng-Mensah, Y., Mensah, A. O., Mensah-Williams, E., Baah, C., & Dacosta, E. (2021). Internal environmental management and green human resource management: Significant catalysts for improved corporate reputation and performance. *Benchmarking*, *28*(10), 3074–3101. doi:10.1108/BIJ-09-2020-0504

Agasisti, T., Egorov, A., Zinchenko, D., & Leshukov, O. (2020). Efficiency of regional higher education systems and regional economic short-run growth: Empirical evidence from Russia. *Industry and Innovation*. Advance online publication. doi:10.1080/13662716.2020.1738914

Ageron, B., Bentahar, O., & Gunasekaran, A. (2020). Digital supply chain: challenges and future directions. *Supply Chain Forum: An International Journal, 21*(3), 133-138. 10.1080/16258312.2020.1816361

Agostini, A., Albolino, S., Boselli, R., De Michelis, G., De Pauli, F., & Dondi, R. (2003). Stimulating Knowledge Discovery and Sharing. In *International ACM SIGGROUP Conference on Supporting Group Work* (pp. 248–257). ACM Press.

Agrawal, P., Narain, R., & Ullah, I. (2019). Analysis Of Barriers in Implementation of Digital Transformation of Supply Chain Using Interpretive Structural Modelling Approach. *Journal of Modelling in Management*, *15*(1), 297–317. doi:10.1108/JM2-03-2019-0066

Agyabeng-Mensah, Y., Afum, E., Acquah, I. S. K., Dacosta, E., Baah, C., & Ahenkorah, E. (2020). The role of green logistics management practices, supply chain traceability and logistics ecocentricity in sustainability performance. *International Journal of Logistics Management*, *32*(2), 538–566. doi:10.1108/IJLM-05-2020-0187

Agyabeng-Mensah, Y., Tang, L., Afum, E., Baah, C., & Dacosta, E. (2021). Organisational identity and circular economy: Are inter and intra organisational learning, lean management and zero waste practices worth pursuing? *Sustainable Production and Consumption*, *28*, 648–662. doi:10.1016/j.spc.2021.06.018

Ahmadi, S., & Amin, S. H. (2019). An integrated chance-constrained stochastic model for a mobile phone closed-loop supply chain network with supplier selection. *Journal of Cleaner Production*, *226*, 988–1003. doi:10.1016/j.jclepro.2019.04.132

Ahmad, M., & Allen, M. M. C. (2015). High performance HRM and establishment performance in Pakistan: An empirical analysis. *Employee Relations*, *37*(5), 506–524. doi:10.1108/ER-05-2014-0044

Ahmed, M. O. (2020). Identification of e-HRM practices in Egypt five-star hotels: A quantitative approach. *International Journal of Heritage, Tourism and Hospitality*, *14*(1), 139–151. doi:10.21608/ijhth.2020.122058

Aigbogun, O., Ghazali, Z., & Razali, R. (2018). Supply chain resilience and measurement dimensions: The case of halal pharmaceuticals in Malaysia. *SHS Web of Conferences, 56*. doi: 10.1051hscpnf/20185605001

Akulinin, F. V., Maksimov, M. I., Velikorossov, V. V., Kolesnikov, A. V., & Balakhanova, D. K. (2019). Innovation development trends and the digital economy program of the Russian Federation. In *Industrial Technologies and Engineering* (pp. 105–109). ICITE.

Aladwani, A. M. (2001). Change management strategies for successful ERP implementation. *Business Process Management Journal*, *7*(3), 266–275. doi:10.1108/14637150110392764

Alavi, M., & Leidner, D. (2001). Review: Knowledge Management and Knowledge Management System: Conceptual Foundations and Research Issues. *Management Information Systems Quarterly*, *25*(1), 107–136.

Albers, A. (2003). Knowledge Management and the Innovation Process The Eco Innovation Model. *Journal of Knowledge Management Practice*.

Albert, S., Flournoy, D., & Lebrasseur, R. (2009). *Networked communities: strategies for digital collaboration*. Information Science Reference. doi:10.4018/978-1-59904-771-3

Aldieri, L., Kotsemir, M., & Vinci, C. P. (2020). The role of labour migration inflows on R&D and innovation activity: Evidence from Russian regions. *Foresight*, *22*(4), 437–468. doi:10.1108/FS-03-2020-0035

Alikhani, R., Torabi, S. A., & Altay, N. (2021). Retail supply chain network design with concurrent resilience capabilities. *International Journal of Production Economics*, *234*, 108042. doi:10.1016/j.ijpe.2021.108042

Ali, M., & Ahmad, H. (2006). Knowledge Management in Malaysian Banks: A new Paradigm. *Journal of Knowledge Management Practice*, *7*(3).

Ali, M., & Miller, L. (2017). ERP system implementation in large enterprises – a systematic literature review. *Journal of Enterprise Information Management*, *30*(4), 666–692. doi:10.1108/JEIM-07-2014-0071

Amentae, T. K., & Gebresenbet, G. (2021). Digitalization and Future Agro-Food Supply Chain Management: A Literature-Based Implications. *Sustainability*, *13*(21), 12181. doi:10.3390u132112181

American Production and Inventory Control Society (APICS). (2013). *The essential supply chain reference, APICS Dictionary*. APICS.

Anand, N., & Grover, N. (2015). Measuring retail supply chain performance; Theoretical model using key performance indicators (KPIs). *Benchmarking*, *22*(1), 135–166. doi:10.1108/BIJ-05-2012-0034

Andersson, L., Lanvin, B., & Van der Heyden, L. (2016). Digitalisation initiatives and corporate strategies: A few implications for talent. In B. Lanvin & P. Evans (Eds.), *The global competitiveness index 2017: Talent and technology* (pp. 51–57). INSEAD.

Andrew, D. P., Pedersen, P. M., & McEvoy, C. D. (2019). *Research methods and design in sport management*. Human Kinetics.

Ante, G., Facchini, F., Mossa, G., & Digiesi, S. (2018). Developing a key performance indicators tree for lean and smart production systems. *IFAC-PapersOnLine*, *51*(11), 13–18. doi:10.1016/j.ifacol.2018.08.227

Aparicio, M., Bacao, F., & Oliveira, T. (2016). An e-learning theoretical framework. *Journal of Educational Technology & Society*, *19*(1), 292–307.

APCOR (Associação Portuguesa da Cortiça/Portuguese Cork Association). (2020). *Noticias*. Retrieved on November 17, 2021 from https://www.apcor.pt/

Appalsamy, N. (2017). *Freight looting a growing concern*. Retrieved on 8/11/2021 from http://www.truckandbus.co.za/freight-looting-a-growing-concern/

Arai, K., & Sekine, K. (1992). *Kaizen for Quick Changeover: Going Beyond SMED*. Productivity Press.

Araz, O. M., Choi, T. M., Olson, D. L., & Salman, F. S. (2020). Data Analytics for Operational Risk Management. *Decision Sciences*, *51*(6), 1316–1319. doi:10.1111/deci.12443

Arias, J. A. E., Beltrán, J. A. B., & Bedoya, S. (2020). *RPA implementation for automation of management process of personal in Compañía nacional de empaques SA*. Paper presented at the 15th Iberian Conference on Information Systems and Technologies (CISTI), Sevilla, Spain. 10.23919/CISTI49556.2020.9140994

Armistead, C. G., & Mapes, J. (1993). The impact of supply chain integration on operating performance. *Logistics Information Management*, *6*(4), 9–14. doi:10.1108/09576059310045907

Armstrong, M. (2011). *Human resource management practice*. Kogan Page Publishers.

Armstrong, M. (2020). *Armstrong's handbook of strategic human resource management* (15th ed.). Kogan Page Publishers.

Armstrong, M., & Taylor, S. (2014). *Armstrong's Handbook of Human Resource Management Practice* (13th ed.). Kogan Page Publishers.

Arnold, C., Kiel, D., & Voigt, K. (2016). How the Industrial Internet of Things Changes Business Models in Different Manufacturing Industries. *International Journal of Innovation Management*, *20*(8), 1–25. doi:10.1142/S1363919616400156

Arshinder, A. K., & Deshmukh, S. G. (2008). Supply chain coordination: Perpectives, empirical studies and research directions. *International Journal of Production Economics*, *115*(2), 316–335. doi:10.1016/j.ijpe.2008.05.011

Artsiomchyk, Y., & Zhivitskaya, H. (2013). Designing Supply Chain with Robustness Analysis. *7th IFAC Conference on Manufacturing Modelling, Management, and Control International Federation of Automatic Control*.

Atılgan, Ö. (2020). Covid-19 and crisis management. In COVID-19 and new business ecosystem (pp. 141-153). Gazi Publishing.

Attaran, M. (2020). Digital technology enablers and their implications for supply chain management. *Supply Chain Forum: An International Journal, 21*(3), 158-172. 10.1080/16258312.2020.1751568

Ayress, L. (2008). Thematic Coding and Analysis. In L. M. Given (Ed.), *The SAGE Encyclopedia of Qualitative Research Methods* (Vol. 1, pp. 868–868). SAGE Publications. doi:10.4135/9781412963909.n451

Azadeh, A., Atrchin, N., Salehi, V., & Shojaei, H. (2013). Modeling and improvement of supply chain with imprecise transportation delays and resilience factors. *International Journal of Logistics Research and Applications, 17*(4), 269–282. doi:10.1080/13675567.2013.846308

Baah, C., Agyeman, D. O., Acquah, I. S. K., Agyabeng-Mensah, Y., Afum, E., Issau, K., ... Faibil, D. (2021a). Effect of information sharing in supply chains: Understanding the roles of supply chain visibility, agility, collaboration on supply chain performance. *Benchmarking, 29*(2), 434–455. doi:10.1108/BIJ-08-2020-0453

Baah, C., Opoku-Agyeman, D., Acquah, I. S. K., Agyabeng-Mensah, Y., Afum, E., Faibil, D., & Abdoulaye, F. A. M. (2021b). Examining the correlations between stakeholder pressures, green production practices, firm reputation, environmental and financial performance: Evidence from manufacturing SMEs. *Sustainable Production and Consumption, 27*, 100–114. doi:10.1016/j.spc.2020.10.015

Bag, S., Gupta, S., Choi, T. M., & Kumar, A. (2021). Roles of Innovation Leadership on Using Big Data Analytics to Establish Resilient Healthcare Supply Chains to Combat the COVID-19 Pandemic: A Multimethodological Study. *IEEE Transactions on Engineering Management*, 1–14. Advance online publication. doi:10.1109/TEM.2021.3101590

Bag, S., Wood, L. C., Xu, L., Dhamija, P., & Kayikci, Y. (2020). Big data analytics as an operational excellence approach to enhance sustainable supply chain performance. *Resources, Conservation and Recycling, 153*, 104559. doi:10.1016/j.resconrec.2019.104559

Bahrin, M. A. K., Othman, M. F., Azli, N. H. N., & Talib, M. F. (2016). Industry 4.0: A review on industrial automation and robotic. *Journal Teknologi, 78*(6-13), 137-143. doi:10.11113/jt.v78.9285

Bakker, K., Boonstra, A., & Wortmann, H. (2010). Risk Management Affecting IS/IT Project SuccessThrough Communicative Action. *Project Management Journal, 42*(3), 75–90.

Balakrishna, C. (2012). Enabling technologies for smart city services and applications. *Proceedings of the 6th International Conference on Next Generation Mobile Applications, Services, and Technologies*, 223-227.

Balakrishnan, A. S., & Ramanathan, U. (2021). The role of digital technologies in supply chain resilience for emerging markets' automotive sector. *Supply Chain Management, 26*(6), 654–671. doi:10.1108/SCM-07-2020-0342

Bala, M., & Kumar, D. (2011). *Supply Chain Performance Attributes for the Fast-Moving Consumer Goods Industry*. Department of Management. doi:10.4102/jtscm.v5i1.19

Baldwin, R. (2019). *The globotics upheaval: Globalization, robotics, and the future of work.* Oxford University Press.

Bamakan, S. M. H., Moghaddam, S. G., Manshadi, S. D., & Klemes, J. J. (2021). Blockchain-enabled pharmaceutical cold chain: Applications, key challenges, and future trends. *Journal of Cleaner Production, 302*, 127021. doi:10.1016/j.jclepro.2021.127021

Bandara, W., Indulska, M., Chong, S., & Sadiq, S. (2007). *Major issues in business process management: en expert perspective.* Paper presented at the 15th European Conference on Information Systems (ECIS), University of St Gallen.

Bannerman, L. (2008). Risk and risk management in software projects: A reassessment. *Journal of Systems and Software*, *81*(12), 2118–2133.

Banomyong, R. (2018). *Collaboration in Supply Chain Management: A Resilience Perspective: Discussion Paper*. Retrieved on 5/11/2021 from https://www.researchgate.net/publication/328581572_Collaboration_in_Supply_Chain_Management_A_Resilience_Perspective_Discussion_Paper

Bardin, L. (2000). *Análise de Conteúdo*. Lisboa: Edições 70.

Barney, J. (1991). Firm resources and sustained competitive advantage. *Journal of Management*, *17*(1), 99–120. doi:10.1177/014920639101700108

Barney, J. B. (2001). Resource-based theories of competitive advantage: A ten-year retrospective on the resource-based view. *Journal of Management*, *27*(6), 643–650. doi:10.1177/014920630102700602

Barratt, M. A., & Oliveira, A. (2001). Exploring the experiences of collaborative planning initiatives. *International Journal of Physical Distribution & Logistics Management*, *31*(4), 266–289. doi:10.1108/09600030110394932

Barratt, M., & Oke, A. (2007). Antecedents of supply chain visibility in retail supply chains: A resource-based theory perspective. *Journal of Operations Management*, *25*(6), 1217–1233. doi:10.1016/j.jom.2007.01.003

Barroso, A. P., Machado, V. H., & Machado, V. C. (2011). *Supply Chain Resilience Using the Mapping Approach, Supply Chain Management*. Retrieved on October 14, 2021 from https://www.intechopen.com/books/supply-chain-management/supply-chain-resilience-using-themapping-approach

Bauer, M., Damschroder, L., Hagedorn, H., Smith, J., & Kilbourne, A. (2015). An introduction to implementation science for the non-specialist. *BMC Psychology*, *3*(1), 32. doi:10.118640359-015-0089-9 PMID:26376626

Baum, T. (2015). Human resources in tourism: Still waiting for change? A 2015 reprise. *Tourism Management*, *50*, 204–212. doi:10.1016/j.tourman.2015.02.001

Baur, C., & Wee, D. (2015). *Manufacturing's next act: Industry 4.0 is more than just a flashy catchphrase*. Retrieved on November 25, 2021 from https://www.mckinsey.com/business-functions/operations/our-insights/manufacturings-next-act

Baxter, P., & Jack, S. (2008). Qualitative Case Study Methodology: Study Design and Implementation for Novice Researchers. *Qualitative Report*, *13*(4), 544–559. doi:10.46743/2160-3715/2008.1573

Bécue, A., Praça, I., & Gama, J. (2021). Artificial intelligence, cyber-threats and Industry 4.0: Challenges and opportunities. *Artificial Intelligence Review*, *54*(5), 3849–3886. doi:10.100710462-020-09942-2

Beg, D., Fiše, S., & Dornbuš, D. (2010). *Makroekonomija* [Macroeconomics]. Datastatus.

BEIS. (2020). *Business Population Estimates for the UK and Regions*. Available at: https://www.gov.uk/government/uploads/system/uploads/attachment_data/file/254552/13-92-business-population-estimates-2013-stats-release-4.pdf

Belhadi, A., Kamble, S., Jabbour, C. J. C., Gunasekaran, A., Ndubisi, N. O., & Venkatesh, M. (2021). Manufacturing and service supply chain resilience to the COVID-19 outbreak: Lessons learned from the automobile and airline industries. *Technological Forecasting and Social Change*, *163*, 120447. doi:10.1016/j.techfore.2020.120447 PMID:33518818

Belokurova, E. V., Pizikov, S. V., Petrenko, E. S., & Koshebayeva, G. K. (2019, April). The institutional model of building the digital economy in modern Russia. In *Institute of Scientific Communications Conference* (pp. 64-70). Springer.

Ben-Dayaa, M., Hassinib, E., & Bahroun, Z. (2019). Internet of Things and Supply Chain Management: A Literature Review. *International Journal of Production Research*, *57*(15), 4719–4742. doi:10.1080/00207543.2017.1402140

Benitez, G., Ayala, N., & Frank, A. (2020). Industry 4.0 innovation ecosystems: An evolutionary perspective on value cocreation. *International Journal of Production Economics*, *228*, 107735. doi:10.1016/j.ijpe.2020.107735

Bennett, D.L., & Nikolaev, B. (2021). Historical Disease Prevalence, Cultural Values, and Global Innovation. *Entrepreneurship Theory and Practice*, *45*(1), 145.

Benzidia, S., Makaoui, N., & Subramanian, N. (2021). Impact of ambidexterity of blockchain technology and social factors on new product development: A supply chain and Industry 4.0 perspective. *Technological Forecasting and Social Change*, *169*, 120819. doi:10.1016/j.techfore.2021.120819

Bernanke, B. (2009, November 16). *The economic outlook*. Retrieved September 13, 2011, from Board of Governors of the Federal Reserve System (U.S.): https://www.federalreserve.gov/newsevents/speech/bernanke20091116a.htm

Bernon, M., Tjahjono, B., & Ripanti, E. F. (2018). Aligning retail reverse logistics practice with circular economy values: An exploratory framework. *Production Planning and Control*, *29*(6), 483–497. doi:10.1080/09537287.2018.1449266

Berry, D., Towill, D. R., & Wadsley, N. (1994). Supply chain management in the electronics products industry. *International Journal of Physical Distribution & Logistics Management*, *24*(10), 20–32. doi:10.1108/09600039410074773

Betelin, V. B. (2018). Challenges and opportunities in forming a digital economy in Russia. *Herald of the Russian Academy of Sciences*, *88*(1), 1–6. doi:10.1134/S101933161801001X

Bhagwat, R., & Sharma, M. K. (2009). An Application of the Integrated AHP-PGP Model for Performance Measurement of Supply Chain Management. *Production Planning and Control*, *20*(8), 678–690. doi:10.1080/09537280903069897

Bharadwaj, A., Sawy, O. A., Pavlou, P., & Venkatraman, N. (2013). Digital business strategy: Toward a next generation of insights. *Management Information Systems Quarterly*, *37*(2), 471–482. doi:10.25300/MISQ/2013/37:2.3

Bibri, S. E., & Krogstie, J. (2020). The emerging data–driven Smart City and its innovative applied solutions for sustainability: The cases of London and Barcelona. *Energy Inform*, *3*(1), 5. doi:10.118642162-020-00108-6

Biotto, M., De Toni, A. F., & Nonino, F. (2012). Knowledge and cultural diffusion along the supply chain as drivers of product quality improvement: The illycaffè case study. *International Journal of Logistics Management*, *23*(2), 212–237. doi:10.1108/09574091211265369

Bissola, R., & Imperatori, B. (2013). Facing e-HRM: The consequences on employee attitude towards the organisation and the HR department in Italian SMEs. *European Journal of International Management*, *7*(4), 450–468. doi:10.1504/EJIM.2013.055282

Bissola, R., & Imperatori, B. (2020). *HRM 4.0 for Human-centered Organizations*. Emerald Publishing.

Bite, P., Konczos Szombathelyi, M., & Vasa, L. (2020). The concept of labour migration from the perspective of Central and Eastern Europe. *Economia e Sociologia*, *13*(1), 197–216. doi:10.14254/2071-789X.2020/13-1/13

Bittencourt, V. L., Alves, A. C., & Leão, C. P. (2019). Lean Thinking contributions for Industry 4.0: A systematic literature review. *IFAC-PapersOnLine*, *52*(13), 904–909. doi:10.1016/j.ifacol.2019.11.310

Bloom, D., & Prettner, K. (2020). *The macroeconomic effects of automation and the role of COVID-19 in reinforcing their dynamics*. Retrieved on September 15, 2021 from https://voxeu.org/article/covid-19-and-macroeconomic-effects-automation

Bock, C. (2018). *Supply Chain Planning 4.0*. Retrieved on October 20, 2021 from https://www.rolandberger.com/publications/publication_pdf/roland_berger_supply_chain_planning.pdf

Bogers, B., Chesbrough, H., & Moedas, C. (2019a). Open Innovation: Research, Practices, and Policies. *California Management Review*, *60*(2), 5–16. doi:10.1177/0008125617745086

Bogers, M., Chesbrough, H., Heaton, S., & Teece, D. (2019b). Strategic Management of Open Innovation: A Dynamic Capabilities Perspective. *California Management Review*, *62*(1), 77–94. doi:10.1177/0008125619885150

Bogers, M., Hadar, R., & Bilberg, A. (2016). Additive manufacturing for consumer-centric business models: Implications for supply chains in consumer goods manufacturing. *Technological Forecasting and Social Change*, *102*, 225–239. doi:10.1016/j.techfore.2015.07.024

Bondarouk, T., Parry, E., & Furtmueller, E. (2016). Electronic HRM: Four decades of research on adoption and consequences. *International Journal of Human Resource Management*, *28*(1), 1–34. doi:10.1080/09585192.2016.1245672

Bondarouk, T., & Ruël, H. (2009). Electronic Human Resource Management: Challenges in the digital era. *International Journal of Human Resource Management*, *20*(3), 505–514. doi:10.1080/09585190802707235

Bondarouk, T., Ruel, H., & Parry, E. (2017). *Electronic HRM in the Smart Era (The Changing Context of Managing People)*. Emerald Publishing. doi:10.1108/9781787143159

Botes, A., Niemann, W., & Kotze, T. (2017). Buyer-Supplier Collaboration and Supply Chain Resilience: A case study in the Petrochemical Industry. *South African Journal of Industrial Engineering*, *24*(4), 183–199. doi:10.7166/28-4-1736

Bouthillier, F., & Shearer, K. (2002). Understanding knowledge management an information management: The need for an empirical perspective. *Information Research Journal*, *8*(1), 1–39.

Boyacı-Gündüz, C. P., Ibrahim, S. A., Wei, O. C., & Galanakis, C. M. (2021). Transformation of the Food Sector: Security and Resilience during the COVID-19 Pandemic. *Foods*, *10*(3), 497. doi:10.3390/foods10030497 PMID:33669146

Boyce, W. S., Mano, H., & Kent, J. L. (2016). The influence of Collaboration in Procurement Relationships. *International Journal of Managing Value and Supply Chains*, *7*(3), 1–18. doi:10.5121/ijmvsc.2016.7301

Boyes, H., Hallaq, B., Cunningham, J., & Watson, T. (2018). The industrial Internet of things (IIoT): An analysis framework. *Computers in Industry*, *101*, 1–12. doi:10.1016/j.compind.2018.04.015

Brandao, C., Silva, R., & dos Santos, J. V. (2019). Online recruitment in Portugal: Theories and candidate profiles. *Journal of Business Research*, *94*(C), 273–279. doi:10.1016/j.jbusres.2018.04.011

Brennen, J. S., & Kreiss, D. (2016). Digitalization. In K. B. Jensen, E. W. Rothenbuhler, J. D. Pooley, & R. T. Craig (Eds.), *The International Encyclopedia of Communication Theory and Philosophy* (pp. 556–566). Wiley-Blackwell. doi:10.1002/9781118766804.wbiect111

Breque, M., De Nul, L., & Petridis, A. (2021). *Industry 5.0. Towards a sustainable, human-centric and resilient European industry*. EC R&I PAPER SERIES.

Brettel, M., Friederichsen, N., Keller, M., & Rosenberg, M. (2014). How virtualization, decentralization and network building change the manufacturing landscape: An Industry 4.0 Perspective. *International Journal of Mechanical. Industrial Science and Engineering*, *8*(1), 37–44. doi:10.5281/zenodo.1336426

Brettel, M., Friederichsen, N., Keller, M., & Rosenberg, M. (2014). How Virtualization, Decentralization and Network Building Change the Manufacturing Landscape: An Industry 4.0 Perspective. *International Journal of Science. Engineering and Technology*, *8*(1), 37–44.

Brody, P., & Pureswaran, V. (2015). The next digital gold rush: How the Internet of Things will create liquid, transparent markets. *Strategy and Leadership*, *43*(1), 36–41. doi:10.1108/SL-11-2014-0094

Brugarolas, M., Martínez-Carrasco, L., Rabadán, A., & Bernabéu, R. (2020). Innovation Strategies of the Spanish Agri-Food Sector in Response to the Black Swan COVID-19 Pandemic. *Foods*, *9*(12), 1821. doi:10.3390/foods9121821 PMID:33302384

BSR. (2017). *Future of Supply Chains 2025*. Retrieved on October 4, 2021 from https://www.bsr.org/files/work/BSR_Future_of_Supply_Chains_Primer.pdf

Buck, B., & Morrow, J. (2018). AI, performance management and engagement: Keeping your best their best. *Strategic HR Review*, *17*(5), 261–262. doi:10.1108/SHR-10-2018-145

Bücker, I., Hermann, M., Pentek, T., & Otto, B. (2016). Towards a Methodology for Industrie 4.0 Transformation. In *Business Information Systems* (pp. 209–221). Springer. doi:10.1007/978-3-319-39426-8_17

Buer, S. V., Fragapane, G. I., & Strandhagen, J. O. (2018). The data-driven process improvement cycle: Using digitalization for continuous improvement. *IFAC-PapersOnLine*, *51*(11), 1035–1040. doi:10.1016/j.ifacol.2018.08.471

Buer, S.-V., Strandhagen, J. O., & Chan, F. T. (2018). The link between Industry 4.0 and lean manufacturing: Mapping current research and establishing a research agenda. *International Journal of Production Research*, *56*(8), 2924–2940. doi:10.1080/00207543.2018.1442945

Bulte, A. F. (2018). *What is Industry 4.0 and what are its implications on HRM practices?* (Bachelor's thesis, University of Twente). https://essay.utwente.nl/75439/

Bunse, B., Kagermann, H., & Wahlster, W. (2014). Foreword. In *Industrie 4.0: Smart manufacturing for the future* (pp. 1–40). Ed. GTAI - Germany Trade and Invest.

Burchardt, C., & Maisch, B. (2019). Digitalization needs a cultural change – examples of applying Agility and Open Innovation to drive the digital transformation. *Procedia CIRP*, *84*, 112–117. doi:10.1016/j.procir.2019.05.009

Burmeister, C., Luettgens, D., & Piller, F. (2016). Business model innovation for industrie 4.0: Why the industrial internet mandates a new perspective on Innovation. *Swiss Journal of Business Research and Practice*, *70*(2), 124–152. doi:10.5771/0042-059X-2016-2-124

Business Continuity Institute. (2021). *Supply chain resilience report 2021*. Retrieved on November 7 from https://www.thebci.org/static/e02a3e5f-82e5-4ff1-b8bc61de9657e9c8/BCI-0007h-Supply-Chain-Resilience-ReportLow-Singles.pdf

Buxmann, P., Hess, T., & Ruggaber, R. (2009). Internet of Services. *Business & Information Systems Engineering*, *5*(5), 341–342. doi:10.100712599-009-0066-z

Buyukozkan, G., & Gocer, F. (2018). Digital supply chain: Literature review and a proposed framework for future research. *Computers in Industry*, *97*, 157–177. doi:10.1016/j.compind.2018.02.010

Bylok, F., & Cichobłaziński, L. (2020). Social determinants of development of inter-group social capital in enterprises. In *Proceedings of the 15th European Conference on Management, Leadership and Governance* (pp. 83–90). ACPI. 10.34190/MLG.19.102

Caldwell, F. (2008). Risk Intelligence: Applying KM to Information Risk Management. *Journal of VINE*, *38*(2), 163–166.

Camarinha-Matos, L., Fornasiero, R., & Afsarmanesh, H. (2017). Collaborative Networks as a Core Enabler of Industry 4.0. In Collaboration in a Data-Rich World. PRO-VE 2017. Springer.

Camarinha-Matos, L., Fornasiero, R., Ramezani, J., & Ferrada, F. (2019). Collaborative Networks: A Pillar of Digital Transformation. *Applied Sciences (Basel, Switzerland)*, *9*(24), 1–33. doi:10.3390/app9245431

Campenhoudt, L. V., Marquet, J., & Quivy, R. (2019). Manual de Investigação em Ciências Sociais. Gradiva.

Campos, D. F., de Andrade Lima, J. T. Jr, da Silva, A. B., & Fernandes, A. J. (2019). Professional competencies in supply chain management in the mid-sized supermarket sector in Brazil. *Supply Chain Management, 24*(3), 405–416. doi:10.1108/SCM-02-2018-0081

Cao, M., Vonderembse, M. A., Zhang, Q., & Ragu-Nathan, T. S. (2010). Supply chain collaboration: Conceptualization and instrument development. *International Journal of Production Research, 48*(22), 6613–6635. doi:10.1080/00207540903349039

Capestro, M., & Kinkel, S. (2020). Industry 4.0 and knowledge management: a review of empirical studies. In M. Bettiol, E. Di Maria, & S. Micelli (Eds.), *Knowledge management and industry 4.0: new paradigms for value creation* (pp. 19–52). Springer. doi:10.1007/978-3-030-43589-9_2

Cappelli, A., & Cini, E. (2020). Will the COVID-19 pandemic make us reconsider the relevance of short food supply chains and local productions? *Trends in Food Science & Technology, 99*, 566–567. doi:10.1016/j.tifs.2020.03.041 PMID:32288230

Çaylak, P. Ç. (2020). Near Field Communication (NFC) Applications in the tourism industry. E. Çeltek. In *Handbook of Research on Smart Technology Applications in the Tourism Industry* (pp. 65–88). IGI Global. doi:10.4018/978-1-7998-1989-9.ch004

Çelik, P., & Topsakal, Y. (2019). *Endüstri 4.0 ve akıllı turizm*. Detay Yayıncılık.

Chakroborty, A. (2017). Robotic process automation for transforming financial KPO industry. *Imperial Journal of Interdisciplinary Research, 3*(3). Retrieved on November 1, 2020, from http://imperialjournals.com/index.php/ijir/article/view/4013

Chandak, S., Chandak, A., & Sharma, A. (2014). Globalisation of Supply Chain Management for an Automotive Industry-future Perspective. *International Review of Applied Engineering Research, 4*(2), 155–164.

Chang, C. W. (2021). Constructing an intelligent shoe production plant using a green supply chain and knowledge management. *Knowledge Management Research and Practice*. Advance online publication. doi:10.1080/14778238.2021.1970488

Chang, Y.-C., Yang, P. Y., Martin, B. R., Chi, H.-R., & Tsai-Lin, T.-F. (2016). Entrepreneurial universities and research ambidexterity: A multilevel analysis. *Technovation, 54*, 7–21. doi:10.1016/j.technovation.2016.02.006

Chen, H., Tian, Y., Ellinger, A. E., & Daugherty, P. J. (2010). Managing Logistics Outsourcing Relationships: An Empirical Investigation in China. *Journal of Business Logistics, 31*(2), 279–299. doi:10.1002/j.2158-1592.2010.tb00152.x

Chen, J., Huang, J., Su, W., Štreimikienė, D., & Baležentis, T. (2021). The challenges of COVID-19 control policies for sustainable development of business: Evidence from service industries. *Technology in Society, 66*, 101643. doi:10.1016/j.techsoc.2021.101643 PMID:34898758

Chen, J., Sohal, A. S., & Prajogo, D. I. (2013). Supply chain operational risk mitigation: An agency and collaboration perspective. *International Journal of Production Research, 51*(7), 2186–2199. doi:10.1080/00207543.2012.727490

Chen, P.-C., & Hung, S.-W. (2016). An actor-network perspective on evaluating the R&D linking efficiency of innovation ecosystems. *Technological Forecasting and Social Change, 112*, 303–312. doi:10.1016/j.techfore.2016.09.016

Chen, Y. S., & Chang, C. H. (2013). Greenwash and green trust: The mediation effects of green consumer confusion and green perceived risk. *Journal of Business Ethics, 114*(3), 489–500. doi:10.100710551-012-1360-0

Chesbrough, H., & Bogers, M. (2014). Explicating Open Innovation: Clarifying an Emerging Paradigm for Understanding Innovation. *Political Science*.

Choi, T. M., Guo, S., & Luo, S. (2020). When blockchain meets social-media: Will the result benefit social media analytics for supply chain operations management? *Transportation Research Part E, Logistics and Transportation Review, 135*, 101860. doi:10.1016/j.tre.2020.101860

Choi, T.-M. (2021). Risk analysis in logistics systems: A research agenda during and after the COVID-19 pandemic. *Transportation Research Part E, Logistics and Transportation Review, 145*, 102190. doi:10.1016/j.tre.2020.102190

Chopra, S., & Meindl, P. (2012). *Supply Chain Management: Strategy, Planning and Operation* (5th ed.). Prentice-Hall.

Chowdhury, P., Paul, S. K., Kaisar, S., & Moktadir, M. A. (2021). COVID-19 pandemic related supply chain studies: A systematic review. *Transportation Research Part E, Logistics and Transportation Review, 148*, 102271. doi:10.1016/j.tre.2021.102271 PMID:33613082

Choy, S., & Suk, Y. (2005). Critical Factors In The Successful Implementation Of Knowledge Management. *Journal of Knowledge Management Practice.*

Christensen, C. (2006). *Assessing your organization's capabilities.* Retrieved on September 17, 2021 from Harvard Business School: http:// cb.hbsp.harvard.edu/cbmp/product/607014-PDF-ENG

Christopher, M. (2011). *Logistics & supply chain management.* Financial Times.

Christopher, M. (2005). *Logistics and supply chain management: Creating value-adding networks.* Prentice Hall.

Christopher, M. (2016). *Logistics & Supply Chain Management* (5th ed.). Pearson.

Christopher, M., & Holweg, M. (2011). "Supply Chain 2.0": Managing supply chains in the era of turbulence. *International Journal of Physical Distribution & Logistics Management, 41*(1), 63–82. doi:10.1108/09600031111101439

Christopher, M., Mena, C., Khan, O., & Yurt, O. (2011). Approaches to managing global sourcing risk. *Supply Chain Management, 16*(2), 67–81. doi:10.1108/13598541111115338

Christopher, M., & Peck, H. (2004). Building the Resilient Supply Chain. *International Journal of Logistics Management, 15*(2), 1–13. doi:10.1108/09574090410700275

Chuang, S. H., & Lin, H. N. (2017). Performance implications of information-value offering in e-service systems: Examining the resource-based perspective and innovation strategy. *The Journal of Strategic Information Systems, 26*(1), 22–38. doi:10.1016/j.jsis.2016.09.001

Chu, C. Y., Park, K., & Kremer, G. E. (2020). A global supply chain risk management framework: An application of text-mining to identify region-specific supply chain risks. *Advanced Engineering Informatics, 45*, 101053. doi:10.1016/j.aei.2020.101053

Chudinovskikh, O., & Denisenko, M. (2020). Labour Migration on the Post-Soviet Territory. In M. Denisenko, S. Strozza, & M. Light (Eds.), *Migration from the Newly Independent States. Societies and Political Orders in Transition.* Springer. doi:10.1007/978-3-030-36075-7_4

Cisneros-Cabrera, S., Pishchulov, G., Sampaio, P., Mehandjiev, N., Liu, Z. X., & Kununka, S. (2021). An approach and decision support tool for forming industry 4.0 supply chain collaborations. *Computers in Industry, 125*, 103391. doi:10.1016/j.compind.2020.103391

Clarke, T., & Gholamshahi, S. (2018). Developing Human Capital for Knowledge Based Economies. In T. Clarke & K. Lee (Eds.), *Innovation in the Asia Pacific*. Springer. doi:10.1007/978-981-10-5895-0_12

CNI. (2016). *Challenges for Industry 4.0 in Brazil.* Available at: https://www.portaldaindustria.com.br/media/filer_public/49/e5/49e5c28d-5bdc-4ea2-ba3c-a11481e1b4a1/challenges_for_industry_40_in_brazil.pdf

Coe, A., Paquet, G., & Roy, J. (2001). E-governance and smart communities: A social learning challenge. *Social Science Computer Review, 19*(1), 1, 80–93. doi:10.1177/089443930101900107

Cohen, W. M., & Levinthal, D. A. (1990). Absorptive capacity: A new perspective on learning and innovation. *Administrative Science Quarterly, 35*(1), 128–152. doi:10.2307/2393553

Coleman, J. (1988). Social capital in the creation of human capital. *American Journal of Sociology, 94*, 95–120. doi:10.1086/228943

Commission of the European Communities. (2003). Commission recommendation concerning the definition of micro, small and medium-sized enterprises. *Official Journal of the European Union,* L124, 20.5.2003, 36-41.

Constantino, F., Di Gravio, G., Shaban, A., & Tronci, M. (2013). Exploring the Bullwhip Effect and Inventory Stability in a Seasonal Supply Chain. *International Journal of Engineering Business Management, 5*, 23. Advance online publication. doi:10.5772/56833

Cooper, D. R., & Schindler, P. S. (2014). *Business Research Methods* (12th ed.). McGraw-Hill.

Corallo, A., Latino, M. E., Menegoli, M., & Pontradolfo, P. (2020). A systematic literature review to explore traceability and lifecycle relationship. *International Journal of Production Research, 58*(15), 4789–4807. doi:10.1080/00207543.2020.1771455

Cornford, S. (1998). Managing risk as a resource using the defect detection and prevention process. *International Conference on Probabilistic Safety Assessment and Management.*

Corts, N. F., Herbert-Hansen, Z. N. L., Laersen, S. B., & Khalid, W. (2019). The degree of inventory centralisation for food manufacturers. *Production Engineering, 13*(1), 21–32. doi:10.100711740-018-00872-1

Costello, G. (1996). *Knowledge Management in Strategic alliances: The Role of Information Technology.* University of Oxford.

Cricelli, L., Greco, M., & Grimaldi, M. (2021). An investigation on the effect of inter-organizational collaboration on reverse logistics. *International Journal of Production Economics, 240*, 108216. doi:10.1016/j.ijpe.2021.108216

CSCMP. (2017). *Bylaws.* Retreived on October 25, 2021 from https://cscmp.org/CSCMP/Connect/Form_a_Roundtable_.aspx?WebsiteKey=0b3f453d-bd90-4121-83cf-172a90b226a9

Cule, P., Schmidt, R., Lyyttnen, K., & Keil, M. (2000). Strategies for leading off is project failure. *Information Systems Management, 14*(2), 68–73.

Dai, H., Tseng, M. M., & Zipkin, P. H. (2015). Design of traceability systems for product recall. *International Journal of Production Research, 53*(2), 511–531. doi:10.1080/00207543.2014.955922

Dalenogare, L., Benitez, G., Ayala, N., & Frank, A. (2018). The expected contribution of Industry 4.0 technologies for industrial performance. *International Journal of Production Economics, 204*, 383–394. doi:10.1016/j.ijpe.2018.08.019

Darkow, I. L., Foerster, B., & von der Gracht, H. A. (2015). Sustainability in food service supply chain: Future expectations from European industry experts toward the environmental perspective. *Supply Chain Management, 20*(2), 163–178. doi:10.1108/SCM-03-2014-0087

Dau, G., Scavarda, A., Scavarda, L. F., & Portugal, V. J. T. (2019). The Healthcare Sustainable Supply Chain 4.0: The Circular Economy Transition Conceptual Framework with the Corporate Social Responsibility Mirror. *Sustainability, 11*(12), 3259. doi:10.3390u11123259

Davenport, T. H., & Schaefer, G. (2021). *How to establish an automation.* Center of Excellence. Retrieved on November 2, 2021 from https://sloanreview.mit.edu/article/how-to-establish-an-automation-center-of-excellence

Davenport, T. H. (1998). Putting the enterprise into the enterprise system. *Harvard Business Review, 76*(4), 121–131. PMID:10181586

Davies, R., Coole, T., & Smith, A. (2017). Review of socio-technical considerations to ensure successful implementation of Industry 4.0. *Procedia Manufacturing, 11*, 1288–1295. doi:10.1016/j.promfg.2017.07.256

Davis, J. W. (2009). *Lean Manufacturing: Implementation Strategies that Work: A Roadmap to Quick and Lasting Success*. Industrial Press Inc.

Day, J. M. (2014). Fostering emergent resilience: The complex adaptive supply network of disaster relief. *International Journal of Production Research, 52*(7), 1970–1988. doi:10.1080/00207543.2013.787496

de Bakker, K. B. (2010). Does Risk Management Contribute to IT Project Success? A Meta-Analysis of Empirical Evidence. *International Journal of Project Management, 28*(5), 493–503.

De la Vega, AF. R., & Stankosky, M. (2006). Knowledge Management And Innovation: What Must Governments Do To Increase Innovation? *Journal of Knowledge Management Practice, 7*(4).

De Paulo, A., Carvalho, L., Costa, M., Lopes, J., & Galina, S. (2017). Mapping Open Innovation: A Bibliometric Review to Compare Developed and Emerging Countries. *Global Business Review, 18*(2), 291–307. doi:10.1177/0972150916668600

De Reuver, M., Sørensen, C., & Basole, R. (2018). The digital platform: A research agenda. *Journal of Information Technology, 33*(2), 124–135. doi:10.105741265-016-0033-3

Deepu, T. S., & Ravi, V. (2021). A conceptual framework for supply chain digitalization using integrated systems model approach and DIKW hierarchy. *Intelligent Systems with Applications, 10–11*, 200048. doi:10.1016/j.iswa.2021.200048

Defee, C. C., & Fugate, B. S. (2010). Changing perspectives of capabilities in the dynamic supply chain era. *International Journal of Logistics Management, 21*(2), 180–206. doi:10.1108/09574091011071915

Dehaze, A. (2016). The skills imperative: Shaping the future of work through talent and technology. In B. Lanvin & P. Evans (Eds.), *The global competitiveness index 2017: Talent and technology* (pp. 35–41). INSEAD.

Del Cano, A. D., & Cruz, M. P. (2002). Integrated Methodology for Project Risk Management. *Journal of Construction Engineering and Management, 128*(6), 473–485. doi:10.1061/(ASCE)0733-9364(2002)128:6(473)

Del Preto, J., Sanneman, L., Ajilo, D., Mehta, A., Miyashita, S., Poorheravi, N. A., Ramirez, C., Yim, S., Kim, S., & Rus, D. (2020). *Distributed Robot Garden*. CSAIL (MIT): Computer Science & Artificial Intelligence Lab. https://www.csail.mit.edu/research/distributed-robot-garden

Deloitte. (2014). *Industry 4.0: Challenges and solutions for the digital transformation and use of exponential technologies*. Retrieved on November 17, 2022 from https://www2.deloitte.com/content/dam/Deloitte/ch/Documents/manufacturing/ch-en-manufacturing-industry-4-0-24102014.pdf

Deloitte. (2017). *Rewriting the rules for the digital age*. Retrieved on September 17, 2021 from https://www2.deloitte.com/content/dam/Deloitte/us/Documents/human-capital/hc-2017-global-human-capital-trends-us.pdf

Deloitte. (2021). *2021 Global insan kaynakları trendleri yıkıma uğramış bir dünyada sosyal şirket: İyileşmeden gelişmeye geçişe liderlik etmek*. Retrieved on September 17, 2021 from https://www2.deloitte.com/tr/tr/pages/human-capital/articles/2021-global-insan-kaynaklari-trendleri-raporu.html

Dembski, F., Wössner, U., Letzgus, M., Ruddat, M., & Yamu, C. (2020). Urban Digital Twins for Smart Cities and Citizens: The Case Study of Herrenberg, Germany. *Sustainability, 12*(6), 2307. doi:10.3390u12062307

Deming, W. E. (1991). *Out of the crisis, 1986*. Massachusetts Institute of Technology Center for Advanced Engineering Study.

Demir, K. A., Döven, G., & Sezen, B. (2019). Industry 5.0 and human-robot coworking. *Procedia Computer Science, 158*, 688–695. doi:10.1016/j.procs.2019.09.104

Deng, Q., & Yu, D. (2006). An Approach To Integrating Knowledge Management Into The Product Development Process. *Journal of Knowledge Management Practice, 7*(2), 233–242.

Derqui, B., Filimonau, V., & Matute, J. (2021). Assessing the scale of adoption of sustainability practices by community pharmacies in Spain in the time of COVID-19. *Sustainable Production and Consumption, 27*, 1626–1636. doi:10.1016/j.spc.2021.03.034

Dhanpat, N., Buthelezi, Z. P., Marilyn, R. J., Maphela, T. V., & Shongwe, N. (2020). Industry 4.0: The role of human resource professionals. *SA Journal of Human Resource Management, 18*, 1-11. DOI:.v18i0.1302 doi:10.4102/sajhrm

Dharish, D. (2020). Japan's experience in reducing its supply chain insecurity. *Asia Power Watch*. Retrieved on December 01, 2021, from https://asiapowerwatch.com/japans-experience-in-reducing-its-supply-chain-insecurity/

Dieuaide, P., & Azaïs, C. (2020). Platforms of Work, Labour, and Employment Relationship: The Grey Zones of a Digital Governance. *Frontiers in Sociology, 5*, 2. doi:10.3389/fsoc.2020.00002 PMID:33869411

Ding, X., & Yang, Z. (2020). Knowledge mapping of platform research: A visual analysis using VOSviewer and CiteSpace. *Electronic Commerce Research*. Advance online publication. doi:10.100710660-020-09410-7

Doern, R., Williams, N., & Vorley, T. (2018). Special issue on entrepreneurship and crises: Business as usual? An introduction and review of the literature. *Entrepreneurship and Regional Development, 31*(5–6), 400–412. doi:10.1080/08985626.2018.1541590

Doğuç, Ö. (2021). Robotic Process Automation (RPA) Applications in COVID-19. In H. Dincer & S. Yüksel (Eds.), *Management Strategies to Survive in a Competitive Environment: How to Improve Company Performance* (pp. 233–247). Springer International Publishing. doi:10.1007/978-3-030-72288-3_16

Dolgui, A., Ivanov, D., & Sokolov, B. (2018). Ripple effect in the supply chain: An analysis and recent literature. *International Journal of Production Research, 56*(1-2), 414–430. doi:10.1080/00207543.2017.1387680

Dong, J., & Wu, W. (2015). Business value of social media technologies: Evidence from online user innovation communities. *The Journal of Strategic Information Systems, 24*(2), 113–127. doi:10.1016/j.jsis.2015.04.003

Dos Santos, M. A. O. (2010). *Benefits derived by a major South African retailer through collaboration and innovation within its supply chain*. Department of Marketing Management, University of Johannesburg. doi:10.4102/jtscm.v4i1.14

Dragicevic, N., Ullrich, A., Tsui, E., & Gronau, N. (2020). A conceptual model of knowledge dynamics in the Industry 4.0 smart grid scenario. *Knowledge Management Research and Practice, 18*(2), 199–213. doi:10.1080/14778238.2019.1633893

Dregger, J., Niehaus, J., Ittermann, P., Hirsch-Kreinsen, H., & ten Hompel, M. (2016). The digitization of manufacturing and its societal challenges: a framework for the future of industrial labor. In 2016 IEEE international symposium on ethics in engineering, science and technology (ETHICS) (pp.1-3). IEEE. doi:10.1109/ETHICS.2016.7560045

Drew, J., McCallum, B., & Roggenhofer, S. (2004). *Journey to lean: Making operational change stick*. Palgrave Macmillan. doi:10.1057/9781403948410

Dubey, R., Gunasekaran, A., Childe, S. J., Papadopoulos, T., Luo, Z. W., & Roubaudl, D. (2020). Upstream supply chain visibility and complexity effect on focal company's sustainable performance: Indian manufacturers' perspective. *Annals of Operations Research*, *290*(1-2), 343–367. doi:10.100710479-017-2544-x

Duggan, K. J., & Healey, T. (2016). *Operational Excellence in Your Office: A Guide to Achieving Autonomous Value Stream Flow with Lean Techniques*. Productivity Press.

Durach, C. F., Kembro, J., & Wieland, A. (2017). A new paradigm for systematic literature reviews in supply chain management. *The Journal of Supply Chain Management*, *53*(4), 67–85. doi:10.1111/jscm.12145

Durach, C., Blesik, T., von Düring, M., & Bick, M. (2020). Blockchain Applications in Supply Chain Transactions. *Journal of Business Logistics*, *42*(1), 7–24. doi:10.1111/jbl.12238

Durach, C., Kurpjuweit, S., & Wagner, S. (2017). The impact of additive manufacturing on supply chains. *International Journal of Physical Distribution & Logistics Management*, *47*(10), 954–971. doi:10.1108/IJPDLM-11-2016-0332

Duriau, V. J., Reger, R. K., & Pfarrer, M. D. (2007). A Content Analysis of the Content Analysis Literature in Organization Studies: Research Themes, Data Sources and Methodological Refinements. *Organizational Research Methods*, *10*(1), 5–34. doi:10.1177/1094428106289252

Durst, S. (2012). Innovation and intellectual capital (risk) management in small and medium-sized enterprises. *International Journal of Transitions and Innovation Systems*, *2*(3/4), 233. doi:10.1504/IJTIS.2012.051531

Durst, S., & Henschel, T. (2021). COVID-19 as an accelerator for developing strong(er) businesses? Insights from Estonian small firms. *Journal of the International Council for Small Business*, *2*(1), 1–29. doi:10.1080/26437015.2020.1859935

Durst, S., & Zieba, M. (2018). Mapping knowledge risks: Towards a better understanding of knowledge management. *Knowledge Management Research and Practice*, *17*(1), 1–13. doi:10.1080/14778238.2018.1538603

Dzhuguryan, T., & Deja, A. (2021). Sustainable waste management for a city multifloor manufacturing cluster: A framework for designing a smart supply chain. *Sustainability*, *13*(3), 1540. doi:10.3390u13031540

Dzikowski, P. (2018). A bibliometric analysis of born global rms. *Journal of Business Research*, *85*, 281–294. doi:10.1016/j.jbusres.2017.12.054

Edwards, T. (2016). Of Truth, Pragmatism, and Sour Grapes: The Second Circuit's Decision in SEC v. Citigroup Global Markets. *Duke Law Journal*, *65*(6), 1241–1280.

Eisenhardt, K. M. (1989). Building theories from case study research. *Academy of Management Review*, *14*(4), 532–550. doi:10.2307/258557

Ejsmont, K., Gladysz, B., Corti, D., Castaño, F., Mohammed, W. M., & Martinez Lastra, J. L. (2020). Towards 'Lean Industry 4.0': Current trends and future perspectives. *Cogent Business and Management*, *7*(1), 1781995. doi:10.1080/23311975.2020.1781995

Ekşili, N., & Çetinkaya Bozkurt, Ö. (2021). Dijital dönüşüm ve dijital işletmeler. In E. B. Bulgurcu Gürel & E. Gürel (Eds.), *İşletmelerde dönüşüm: Güncel konulardan seçkiler* (pp. 67–102). Siyasal Kitabevi.

Eksoz, C., Mansouri, S. A., Bourlakis, M., & Önkal, D. (2019). Judgmental adjustments through supply integration for strategic partnerships in food chains. *Omega*, *87*, 20–33. doi:10.1016/j.omega.2018.11.007

El Baz, J., & Ruel, S. (2021). Can supply chain risk management practices mitigate the disruption impacts on supply chains' resilience and robustness? Evidence from an empirical survey in a COVID-19 outbreak era. *International Journal of Production Economics*, *233*, 107972. doi:10.1016/j.ijpe.2020.107972

Eller, R., Alford, P., Kallmünzer, A., & Peters, M. (2020). Antecedents, consequences, and challenges of small and medium-sized enterprise digitalization. *Journal of Business Research*, *112*(3), 119–127. doi:10.1016/j.jbusres.2020.03.004

Ellyatt, H. (2021). *Supply chain chaos is already hitting global growth. And it's about to get worse.* Retrieved on November 5, 2021 from https://www.cnbc.com/2021/10/18/supply-chain-chaos-is-hitting-global-growth-and-could-get-worse.html

Erdem, H., & Özçelik, T. Ö. (2022). An Example of Merit Analysis for Digital Transformation and Robotic Process Automation (RPA). In N. M. Durakbasa & M. G. Gençyılmaz (Eds.), *Digitizing Production Systems* (pp. 233–242). Springer International Publishing. doi:10.1007/978-3-030-90421-0_20

Erdogan, S., & Dayan, V. (2019). Analysis of Relationship Between International Interest Rates and Cryptocurrency Prices: Case for Bitcoin and LIBOR. In U. Hacioglu (Ed.), *Blockchain Economics and Financial Market Innovation. Contributions to Economics*. Springer. doi:10.1007/978-3-030-25275-5_24

Erol, S., Jäger, A., Hold, P., Ott, K., & Sihn, W. (2016). Tangible Industry 4.0: A Scenario-Based Approach to Learning for the Future of Production. *Procedia CIRP*, *54*, 13–18. doi:10.1016/j.procir.2016.03.162

Ertz, M., Sun, S., Boily, É., Quenum, G. G. Y., Patrick, K., Laghrib, Y., . . . Latrous, I. (2021). Augmented Products: The Contribution of Industry 4.0 to Sustainable Consumption. In Marketing for Sustainable Development: Rethinking Consumption Models (pp.261-283). Wiley.

Ertz, M., Sun, S., Boily, E., Kubiat, P., & Quenum, G. G. Y. (2022). How transitioning to Industry 4.0 promotes circular product lifetimes. *Industrial Marketing Management*, *101*, 125–140. doi:10.1016/j.indmarman.2021.11.014

Eslami, M. H., Jafari, H., Achtenhagen, L., Carlback, J., & Wong, A. (2021). Financial performance and supply chain dynamic capabilities: The Moderating Role of Industry 4.0 technologies. *International Journal of Production Research*, 1–18. Advance online publication. doi:10.1080/00207543.2021.1966850

Esmaeilian, B., Sarkis, J., Lewis, K., & Behdad, S. (2020). Blockchain for the future of sustainable supply chain management in Industry 4.0. *Resources, Conservation and Recycling*, *163*, 105064. doi:10.1016/j.resconrec.2020.105064

Esmer, Y., & Şaylan, O. (2019). The Link of Industry 4.0 and Organizational Transformation. *Bilge Uluslararası Sosyal Araştırmalar Dergisi*, *3*(1), 1–8.

Esteves, J., & Bohorquez, V. (2007). An updated ERP systems annotated bibliography: 2001-2005. *Communications of the Association for Information Systems*, *19*(1), 18. doi:10.17705/1CAIS.01918

Etikan, I., & Bala, K. (2017). Sampling and Sampling Methods. *Biometrics and Biostatistics International Journal*, *5*(6), 1–3. doi:10.15406/bbij.2017.05.00149 PMID:28111614

European Commission. (2021). *Structural Business Statistics, Small and Medium-sized Enterprises*. Retrieved on January 11, 2022 from https://ec.europa.eu/eurostat/web/structural-business-statistics/small-and-medium-sized-enterprises

Faggian, A., Rajbhandari, I., & Dotzel, K. R. (2017). The interregional migration of human capital and its regional consequences: A review. *Regional Studies*, *51*(1), 128–143. doi:10.1080/00343404.2016.1263388

Fahimnia, B., Jabbarzadeh, A., & Sarkis, J. (2018). Greening versus resilience: A supply chain design perspective. *Transportation Research Part E, Logistics and Transportation Review*, *119*, 129–148. doi:10.1016/j.tre.2018.09.005

Fatorachian, H., & Kazemi, H. (2018). A critical investigation of Industry 4.0 in manufacturing: Theoretical operationalisation framework. *Production Planning and Control*, *29*(8), 633–644. doi:10.1080/09537287.2018.1424960

Fatorachian, H., & Kazemi, H. (2021). Impact of Industry 4.0 on supply chain performance. *Production Planning and Control*, *32*(1), 63–81. doi:10.1080/09537287.2020.1712487

Federal Ministry of Labour and Social Affairs. (2015). *Green Paper Work 4.0.* https://www.bmas.de/EN/Services/Publications/arbeiten-4-0-greenpaper-work-4-0.html

Federal Ministry of Labour and Social Affairs. (2017). *Re-imagining work, Green Paper Work 4.0.* https://www.bmas.de/SharedDocs/Downloads/EN/PDF-Publikationen/a883-white-paper.pdf?__blob=publicationFile&v=1

Fereday, J., & Muir-Cochrane, E. (2006). Demonstrating Rigor Using Thematic Analysis: A Hybrid Approach of Inductive and Deductive Coding and Theme Development. *International Journal of Qualitative Methods*, *5*(1), 80–92. doi:10.1177/160940690600500107

Fernandes, A. C., Vilhena, E., Oliveira, R., Sampaio, P., & Carvalho, M. S. (2021). Supply chain quality management impact on organization performance: Results from an international survey. *International Journal of Quality & Reliability Management*. Advance online publication. doi:10.1108/IJQRM-05-2020-0159

Fernandez Alarcon, V., & Gallardo-Gallardo, E. (2021). Tackling the HR digitalization challenge: Key factors and barriers to HR analytics adoption. *Competitiveness Review*, *31*(1), 162–187. doi:10.1108/CR-12-2019-0163

Fernández Campos, P., Trucco, P., & Huaccho Huatuco, L. (2019). Managing structural and dynamic complexity in supply chains: Insights from four case studies. *Production Planning and Control*, *30*(8), 611–623. doi:10.1080/09537287.2018.1545952

Ferreira De Araújo Lima, P., Crema, M., & Verbano, C. (2020). Risk management in SMEs: A systematic literature review and future directions. *European Management Journal*, *38*(1), 78–94. doi:10.1016/j.emj.2019.06.005

Ferreira, C., Cardoso, C., Travassos, M., Paiva, M., Pestana, M., Lopes, J. M., & Oliveira, M. (2021). Disorders, Vulnerabilities and Resilience in the Supply Chain in Pandemic Times. *Logistics*, *5*(3), 1–16. doi:10.3390/logistics5030048

Firestone, J. M. (2001). Key Issues in Knowledge Management. *Journal of Knowledge Management*, *1*(3), 8–38.

Fischer-Preßler, D., Eismann, K., Pietrowski, R., Fischbach, K., & Schoder, D. (2020). Information technology and risk management in supply chains. *International Journal of Physical Distribution & Logistics Management*, *50*(2), 233–254. doi:10.1108/IJPDLM-04-2019-0119

Fixsen, D. L., Naoom, S. F., Blase, K. A., Friedman, R. M., & Wallace, F. (2005). Implementation research: a synthesis of the literature. Tampa, FL: University of South Florida, Louis de la Parte Florida Mental Health Institute, The National Implementation Research Network: William T. Grant Foundation.

Flechsig, C., Anslinger, F., & Lasch, R. (2021). Robotic Process Automation in purchasing and supply management: A multiple case study on potentials, barriers, and implementation. *Journal of Purchasing and Supply Management*. Advance online publication. doi:10.1016/j.pursup.2021.100718

Florkowski, G., & Olivas-Luján, M. (2006). The diffusion of human-resource information- technology innovations in US and non-US firms. *Personnel Review*, *35*(6), 684–710. doi:10.1108/00483480610702737

Flynn, B. B., Huo, B., & Zhao, X. (2010). The impact of supply chain integration on performance: A contingency and configuration approach. *Journal of Operations Management*, *28*(1), 58–71. doi:10.1016/j.jom.2009.06.001

Fornell, C., & Larcker, D. F. (1981). Evaluating structural equation models with unobserved variables and measurement error. *JMR, Journal of Marketing Research*, *11*(1), 39–50. doi:10.1177/002224378101800104

Fouladivanda, F., Pashandi, M. A., Hooman, A., & Khanmohammadi, Z. (2013). The Effect of Brand Equity on Consumer behavior in term of FMCG in Iran. *Interdisciplinary Journal of Contemporary Research in Business*, *4*(9), 945–957.

Frank, A., Dalenogare, L., & Ayala, N. (2019). Industry 4.0 technologies: Implementation patterns in manufacturing companies. *International Journal of Production Economics*, *210*, 15–26. doi:10.1016/j.ijpe.2019.01.004

Frazzon, E. M., Rodriguez, C. M. T., Pereira, M. M., Pires, M. C., & Uhlmann, I. (2019). Towards Supply Chain Management 4.0. *Brazilian Journal of Operations & Production Management*, *16*(2), 180–191. doi:10.14488/BJOPM.2019.v16.n2.a2

Frederico, G. F. (2021). Towards a Supply Chain 4.0 on the post-COVID-19 pandemic: A conceptual and strategic discussion for more resilient supply chains. *Rajagiri Management Journal*, *15*(2), 94–104. doi:10.1108/RAMJ-08-2020-0047

Frederico, G. F., Garza-Reyes, J. A., Anosike, A., & Kumar, V. (2020). Supply Chain 4.0: Concepts, maturity and research agenda. *Supply Chain Management*, *25*(2), 262–282. doi:10.1108/SCM-09-2018-0339

Frederico, G. F., Garza-Reyes, J. A., Kumar, A., & Kumar, V. (2021). Performance measurement for supply chains in the Industry 4.0 era: A balanced scorecard approach. *International Journal of Productivity and Performance Management*, *70*(4), 789–807. doi:10.1108/IJPPM-08-2019-0400

Frederico, G., Garza-Reyes, J., Anosike, A., & Kumar, V. (2019). Supply Chain 4.0: Concepts, Maturity and Research Agenda, Supply Chain Management. *International Journal (Toronto, Ont.)*, *25*(2), 262–282.

Frohlich, M. T., & Westbrook, R. (2001). Arcs of integration: An international study of supply chain strategies. *Journal of Operations Management*, *19*(2), 185–200. doi:10.1016/S0272-6963(00)00055-3

Fukuyama, F. (1999). *Social Capital and Civil Society. The Institute of Public Policy*. George Mason University.

Fuller, M. A., Valacich, J. S., & George, J. F. (2008). *Information Systems Project*. Pearson Prentice Hall.

Garay-Rondero, C., Martinez-Flores, J., Smith, N., Caballero Morales, S., & Aldrette-Malacara, A. (2019). Digital supply chain model in Industry 4.0. *Journal of Manufacturing Technology Management*, *31*(5), 887–933. doi:10.1108/JMTM-08-2018-0280

Garcia, D. J., & You, F. (2015). Supply chain design and optimization: Challenges and opportunities. *Computers & Chemical Engineering*, *8*, 153–170. doi:10.1016/j.compchemeng.2015.03.015

Gartner. (2020). *Supply Chain Digital Transformation*. Retrieved on November 27, 2021, from https://www.gartner.com/en/supply-chain/insights/supply-chain-digital-transformation

Gaziero, C., & Cecconello, I. (2019). Simulação computacional do fluxo de valor: Uma proposta de integração da Indústria 4.0 e lean production. *Scientia Cum Industria*, *7*(2), 52–67. doi:10.18226/23185279.v7iss2p52

Geandarme, F. (2021). *Industrie 4.0: Définition et mise en œuvre vers l'usine connectée*. https://www.visiativ-solutions.fr/industrie-4-0/

Gefen, D., & Straub, D. (1997). Gender differences in the perception & use of e-mail: Extension to the technologyacceptance model. *Management Information Systems Quarterly*, *21*(4), 389–400.

Gelei, A. (2003). Az ellátási lánc típusai és menedzsment kérdései. *Vezetéstudomány*, *34*, 24–34.

Geng, L., Xiao, R., & Xu, X. (2014). Research on MAS-Based Supply Chain Resilience and Its Self-Organized Criticality. *Hindawi Publishing Corporation Discrete Dynamics in Nature and Society*, *621341*, 1–14. Advance online publication. doi:10.1155/2014/621341

George, D., & Mallery, P. (2011). *IBM SPSS Statistics 19 Step by Step: A Simple Guide and Reference* (11th ed.). Pearson Education, Inc.

Ghadge, A., Kara, M., Moradlou, H., & Goswami, M. (2020). The impact of Industry 4.0 implementation on supply chains. *Journal of Manufacturing Technology Management*, *31*(4), 669–686. doi:10.1108/JMTM-10-2019-0368

Ghobakhloo, M. (2018). The future of manufacturing industry: A strategic roadmap toward Industry 4.0. *Journal of Manufacturing Technology Management*, *29*(6), 910–936. doi:10.1108/JMTM-02-2018-0057

Ghobakhloo, M., & Fathi, M. (2020). Corporate survival in Industry 4.0 era: The enabling role of lean-digitized manufacturing. *Journal of Manufacturing Technology Management*, *31*(1), 1–30. doi:10.1108/JMTM-11-2018-0417

Gohoungodji, P., N'Dri, A. B., Latulippe, J. M., & Matos, A. L. B. (2020). What is stopping the automotive industry from going green? A systematic review of barriers to green innovation in the automotive industry. *Journal of Cleaner Production*, *277*, 123524. doi:10.1016/j.jclepro.2020.123524

Gölzer, P., & Fritzsche, A. (2017). Data-driven operations management: Organisational implications of the digital transformation in industrial practice. *Production Planning and Control*, *28*(16), 1332–1343. doi:10.1080/09537287.2017.1375148

Gong, Y., Huang, J. C., & Farh, J. L. (2009). Employee learning orientation, transformational leadership, and employee creativity: The mediating role of employee creative self-efficacy. *Academy of Management Journal*, *52*(4), 765–778. doi:10.5465/amj.2009.43670890

Goodrich, D., Miake-Lye, I., Braganza, M., Wawrin, N., Kilbourne, A. M., & Initiative, Q. E. R. (2020). *QUERI Roadmap for implementation and quality improvement*. Retrieved on September 27, 2021 from https://www.queri.research.va.gov/tools/roadmap

Gotthardt, M., Koivulaakso, D., Paksoy, O., Saramo, C., Martikainen, M., & Lehner, O. (2020). Current state and challenges in the implementation of smart robotic process automation in accounting and auditing. *ACRN Journal of Finance and Risk Perspectives*, *9*(1), 90–102. doi:10.35944/jofrp.2020.9.1.007

Gottschalk, P. (2002). Toward a Model of Growth Stages for Knowledge Management Technology in Law Firms. *Informing Science*, *5*(2), 79–93.

Graham, T. (2018). Platforms and hyper-choice on the World Wide Web. *Big Data & Society*, *5*(1). doi:10.1177/2053951718765878

Greif, H., Kühnis, N., & Warnking, P. (2016). *Digitalisierung – wo stehen Schweizer KMU?* Retrieved on October 5, 2021 from https://www.pwc.ch/de/publications/2016/pwc_digitalisierung_wo_stehen_ schweizer_kmu.pdf

Grodach, C., O'Connor, J., & Gibson, C. (2017). Manufacturing and cultural production: Towards a progressive policy agenda for the cultural economy, City. *Cultura e Scuola*, *10*, 17–25. doi:10.1016/j.ccs.2017.04.003

Grondys, K., Ślusarczyk, O., Hussain, H. I., & Androniceanu, A. (2021). Risk Assessment of the SME Sector Operations during the COVID-19 Pandemic. *International Journal of Environmental Research and Public Health*, *18*(8), 4183. doi:10.3390/ijerph18084183 PMID:33920916

Guan, D., Wang, D., Hallegatte, S., Davis, S. J., Huo, J., Li, S., Bai, Y., Lei, T., Xue, Q., Coffman, D., Cheng, D., Chen, P., Liang, X., Xu, B., Lu, X., Wang, S., Hubacek, K., & Gong, P. (2020). Global supply-chain effects of COVID-19 control measures. *Nature Human Behaviour*, *4*(6), 577–587. doi:10.103841562-020-0896-8 PMID:32493967

Gu, H., Meng, X., Shen, T., & Wen, L. (2020). China's Highly Educated Talents in 2015: Patterns, Determinants and Spatial Spillover Effects. *Applied Spatial Analysis and Policy*, *13*(3), 631–648. doi:10.100712061-019-09322-6

Gulati, R., Nohria, N., & Zaheer, A. (2000). Strategic networks. *Strategic Management Journal*, *21*(3), 203–214. doi:10.1002/(SICI)1097-0266(200003)21:3<203::AID-SMJ102>3.0.CO;2-K

Gu, M., Yang, L., & Huo, B. (2021). The impact of information technology usage on supply chain resilience and performance: An ambidexterous view. *International Journal of Production Economics*, *232*, 107956. doi:10.1016/j.ijpe.2020.107956 PMID:33071462

Gunal, M. M. (2019). *Simulation for Industry 4.0: Past, Present, and Future*. Springer. doi:10.1007/978-3-030-04137-3

Gunasekaran, A., & Ngai, E. W. (2004). Information Systems in Supply Chain Integration and Management. *European Journal of Operational Research*, *159*(2), 269–295. doi:10.1016/j.ejor.2003.08.016

Gunasekaran, A., Papadopoulos, T., Dubey, R., Wamba, S., Childe, S., Hazen, B., & Akter, S. (2017). Big data and predictive analytics for supply chain and Organizational Performance. *Journal of Business Research*, *70*, 308–317. doi:10.1016/j.jbusres.2016.08.004

Gunasekaran, A., Subramanian, N., & Tiwari, M. (2016). Information technology governance in Internet of Things supply chain networks. *Industrial Management & Data Systems*, *116*(7). doi:10.1108/IMDS-06-2016-0244

Gupta, D., & Weerawat, W. (2006). Supplier-manufacturer coordination in capacitated two-stage supply chains. *European Journal of Operational Research*, *175*(1), 67–89. doi:10.1016/j.ejor.2005.04.021

Gurtu, A., & Johny, J. (2019). Potential of blockchain technology in supply chain management: A literature review. *International Journal of Physical Distribution & Logistics Management*, *49*(9), 881–900. doi:10.1108/IJPDLM-11-2018-0371

Gutierrez, A., Kothari, A., Mazuera, C., & Schoenherr, T. (2020). *Taking supplier collaboration to the next level*. Retrieved on November 5, 2021 from https://www.mckinsey.com/business-functions/operations/our-insights/taking-supplier-collaboration-to-the-next-level

Haavisto, I. (2014). *Performance in Humanitarian Supply Chains*. Hanken School of Economics.

Habermas, J. (1979). *Communication and the Evolution of Society*. Beacon Press.

Habraken, M., & Bondarouk, T. (2019). Smart Industry or Smart Bubbles? A Critical Analysis of Its Perceived Value. In *HRM 4.0 For Human-Centered Organizations* (Vol. 23, pp. 1–20). Emerald. doi:10.1108/S1877-636120190000023018

Hair, J. F. Jr, Ringle, C. M., & Sarstedt, M. (2013). Partial least squares structural equation modeling: Rigorous applications, better results and higher acceptance. *Long Range Planning*, *46*(1-2), 1–12. doi:10.1016/j.lrp.2013.01.001

Hald, K. S., & Mouritsen, J. (2018). The evolution of performance measurement systems in a supply chain: A longitudinal case study on the role of interorganisational factors. *International Journal of Production Economics*, *205*, 256–271. doi:10.1016/j.ijpe.2018.09.021

Hammarberg, M., & Sunden, J. (2014). *Kanban in Action*. Manning Publications Co.

Hansen, R., & Sia, S. (2015). Hummel's Digital Transformation Toward Omnichannel Retailing: Key Lessons Learned. *MIS Quarterly Executive*, *14*(2), 51–66.

Haq, M. Z. U., Gu, M., & Huo, B. (2020). Enhancing supply chain learning and innovation performance through human resource management. *Journal of Business and Industrial Marketing*, *36*(3), 552–568. doi:10.1108/JBIM-12-2019-0534

Harrington, R. (2019). *How I Keep Up with Machine Learning Research - CompassRed Data Blog*. https://medium.com/compassred-data-blog/how-i-keep-up-with-machine-learning-research-d1857ede0898

Harris, S. (2019). *The Sierra-Cedar.* Retrieved on October 5, 2021 from https://www.sierra-cedar.com/2019/10/02/pr-2019-hrss-white-paper-release/

Hart, S. L. (1995). A natural-resource-based view of the firm. *Academy of Management Review, 20*(4), 986–1014. doi:10.5465/amr.1995.9512280033

Hasan, I., Islam, M. D., & Chowdhury, M. (2019). Transformational human resource management: Crafting organizational efficiency. In P. O. de Pablos & T. K. Chui (Eds.), *Handbook of Research on Managerial Practices and Disruptive Innovation in Asia* (pp. 264–282). IGI Global.

Hayes, B. (2008). Cloud Computing. *Communications of the ACM, 51*(7), 1–11. doi:10.1145/1364782.1364786

Hazen, B., Skipper, J., Ezell, J., & Boone, C. (2016). Big data and predictive analytics for supply chain sustainability: A theory-driven research agenda. *Journal of Computers & Industrial Engineering, 101*, 592–598. doi:10.1016/j.cie.2016.06.030

Heavin, C., & Power, D. J. (2018). Challenges for digital transformation–towards a conceptual decision support guide for managers. *Journal of Decision Systems, 27*(1), 38–45. doi:10.1080/12460125.2018.1468697

Hecklau, F., Galeitzke, M., Flachs, S., & Kohl, H. (2016). Holistic approach for human resource management in industry 4.0. *Procedia CIRP, 54*, 1–6. doi:10.1016/j.procir.2016.05.102

Heeks, R., & Bukht, R. (2018). *Digital Economy Policy in Developing Countries.* DIODE Working Paper no. 6. Available at https://ssrn.com/abstract=3540027 doi:10.2139/ssrn.3540027

Hennelly, P., Srai, J., Graham, G., & Fosso Wamba, S. (2019). Rethinking supply chains in the age of digitalization. *Production Planning and Control, 31*(2-3), 1–3. doi:10.1080/09537287.2019.1631469

Henriette, E., Feki, M., & Boughzala, I. (2016). Digital transformation challenges. In MCIS 2016 Proceedings (pp. 1-7). Paphos.

Henseler, J., Ringle, C. M., & Sarstedt, M. (2015). A new criterion for assessing discriminant validity in variance-based structural equation modeling. *Journal of the Academy of Marketing Science, 43*(1), 115–135. doi:10.100711747-014-0403-8

Herbane, B. (2018). Rethinking organizational resilience and strategic renewal in SMEs. *Entrepreneurship and Regional Development, 31*(5–6), 476–495. doi:10.1080/08985626.2018.1541594

Hermann, M., Pentek, T., & Otto, B. (2015). *Design Principles for Industry 4.0 Scenarios: A Literature Review*. Technische Universität Dortmund. doi:10.13140/RG.2.2.29269.22248

Herm, L.-V., Janiesch, C., Helm, A., Imgrund, F., Fuchs, K., Hofmann, A., & Winkelmann, A. (2020). A Consolidated Framework for Implementing Robotic Process Automation Projects. In D. Fahland, C. Ghidini, J. Becker, & M. Dumas (Eds.), *Business Process Management* (pp. 471–488). Springer International Publishing. doi:10.1007/978-3-030-58666-9_27

Hernando de Soto, H. (2017). A tale of two civilizations in the era of Facebook and blockchain. *Small Business Economics, 49*(4), 729–739. doi:10.100711187-017-9949-4

Herold, D. M., Farmer, S. M., & Mobley, M. I. (1995). Pre-implementation attitudes toward the introduction of robots in a unionized environment. *Journal of Engineering and Technology Management, 12*(3), 155–173. doi:10.1016/0923-4748(95)00008-7

Heynitz, H. V., Bremicker, M., Amadori, D. M., & Reschke, K. (2016). *The factory of future*. KMPG AG. Retrieved on October 29, 2021 from https://assets.kpmg/content/dam/kpmg/es/pdf/2017/06/the-factory-of-the-future.pdf

Hill, C. A., Zhang, G. P., & Miller, K. E. (2018). Collaborative planning, forecasting, and replenishment & firm performance: An empirical evaluation. *International Journal of Production Economics*, *196*, 12–23. doi:10.1016/j.ijpe.2017.11.012

Hindel, J., Cabrera, L., & Stierle, M. (2020). *Robotic Process Automation: Hype or Hope?* Paper presented at the 15th International Conference on Wirtschaftsinformatik, Potsdam, Germany.

Hintsa, J., Ayyash, F. A., Hameri, A.-P., Myers, P., Coulibaly, N., & Gutierrez, X. (2007). *The 21st Century Supply Chain Model*. Technical Report, WCO Council Meeting.

Hirano, H. (2009). JIT Implementation Manual: The Complete Guide to Just-in-Time Manufacturing (2nd ed.). New York, NY: Productivity Press.

Hirsch-Kreinsen, H. (2016). Digitization of industrial work: Development paths and prospects. *Journal for Labour Market Research*, *49*(1), 1–14. doi:10.100712651-016-0200-6

Hitachi and The University of Tokyo Joint Research Laboratory. (Ed.). (2020). *Society 5.0 A People-centric Super-smart Society*. Springer Open.

Hobbs, J. E. (2021). Food supply chain resilience and the COVID-19 pandemic: What have we learned? *Canadian Journal of Agricultural Economics/Revue Canadienne d'agroeconomie, 69*(2), 189-196. doi:10.1111/cjag.12279

Hobbs, J. E. (2021). Food supply chain resilience and the COVID-19 pandemic: What have we learned? *Canadian Journal of Agricultural Economics/Revue canadienne d'agroeconomie, 69*(2), 189-196.

Hodgson, G. (1988). *Economics and Institutions: A Manifesto for a Modern Institutional Economics*. Polity Press, Cambridge and University of Pennsylvania Press. doi:10.9783/9781512816952

Hoek, R. V. (2020). Responding to COVID-19 supply chain risks—Insights from supply chain change management, total cost of ownership and supplier segmentation theory. *Logistics*, *4*(4), 23. doi:10.3390/logistics4040023

Hofmann, E., & Rusch, M. (2017). Industry 4.0 and the current status as well as future prospects on logistics. *Computers in Industry*, *89*, 23–34. doi:10.1016/j.compind.2017.04.002

Hofmann, P., Samp, C., & Urbach, N. (2020). Robotic process automation. *Electronic Markets*, *30*(1), 99–106. doi:10.100712525-019-00365-8

Holsapple, C. W., & Joshi, K. D. (2004). A Formal Knowledge Management Ontology: Conduct, Activities, Resources, and Influences. *Journal of the American Society for Information Science and Technology*, *55*(7), 593–612.

Holsapple, C., & Joshi, K. (2002). Knowledge Management: A Three-Fold Framework. *The Information Society*, *18*(1), 47–64.

Hosseini, S., Ivanov, D., & Dolgui, A. (2019). Review of quantitative methods for supply chain resilience analysis. *Transportation Research Part E, Logistics and Transportation Review*, *125*, 285–307. doi:10.1016/j.tre.2019.03.001

Hozdić, E. (2015). Smart factory for industry 4.0: A review. *International Journal of Modern Manufacturing Technologies*, *7*(1), 28–35.

Hozdić, E. (2015). Smart Factory for Industry 4.0: A review. *International Journal of Modern Manufacturing Technologies*, *VII*(1), 28–35. doi:10.1016/j.promfg.2018.02.034

Huang, J., Henfridsson, O., Liu, M., & Newell, S. (2017). Growing On Steroids: Rapidly scaling the user base of digital ventures through digital innovation. *Management Information Systems Quarterly*, *41*(1), 301–314. doi:10.25300/MISQ/2017/41.1.16

Huang, S. M., Chang, I. C., Li, S. H., & Lin, M. T. (2004). Assessing risk in ERP projects: Identify and prioritize the factors. *Industrial Management & Data Systems*, *104*(8), 681–688. doi:10.1108/02635570410561672

Hudnurkar, M., Khar, S., & Rathod, U. (2014). Factors affecting collaboration in the supply chain: A literature Review. *Procedia: Social and Behavioral Sciences*, *133*, 189–202. doi:10.1016/j.sbspro.2014.04.184

Huo, B., Haq, M. Z. U., & Gu, M. (2020). The impact of IT application on supply chain learning and service performance. *Industrial Management & Data Systems*, *120*(1), 1–20. doi:10.1108/IMDS-10-2018-0476

Huo, L., Guo, H., & Cheng, Y. (2019). Supply chain risk propagation model considering the herd mentality mechanism and risk preference. *Physica A*, *529*(1), 121400. doi:10.1016/j.physa.2019.121400

IBGE. (2020). *Demografia das Empresas e Estatísticas de Empreendedorismo*. IBGE.

IBM. (2019). *IBM robotic process automation anywhere*. Retrieved on November 3, 2021 from https://www.ibm.com/products/robotic-process-automation

Igbaria, M., & Toraskar, K. (1994). ‘Impact of End-User Computing on the Individual: An Integrated Model. *Information Technology & People*, *6*(4), 271–292.

Ikeziri, L. M., Melo, J. C., Campos, R. T., Okimura, L. I., & Gobbo, J. A. Jr. (2020). A perspectiva da indústria 4.0 sobre a filosofia de gestão lean manufacturing. *Brazilian Journal of Development*, *6*(1), 1274–1289. doi:10.34117/bjdv6n1-089

IMD. (2021). *World Digital Competitiveness Ranking*. Retrieved on February 12, 2022, from https://www.imd.org/centers/world-competitiveness-center/rankings/world-digital-competitiveness/

Inman, R. R., & Blumenfeld, D. E. (2014). Product complexity and supply chain design. *International Journal of Production Research*, *52*(7), 1956–1969. doi:10.1080/00207543.2013.787495

Innovate UK. (2019). *Innovate UK Delivery Plan*. Author.

Institute, P. M. (2008). A Guide to the Project Management Body of Knowledge, PMBOK. Project Management Institute.

Intezari, A., Taskin, N., & Pauleen, D. J. (2017). Looking beyond: An integrative approach to knowledge management culture. *Journal of Knowledge Management*, *21*(2), 492–515.

IPA. (2020). *Dejitarutoransufume-shon suishin jinzai no kinō to yakuwari no arikata nikansuru chōsa* [Survey on the functions and roles of human resources for digital transformation]. Retrieved on December 15, 2021, from https://www.ipa.go.jp/files/000073700.pdf

Iqbal, N., Ahmad, M., Raziq, M. M., & Mendes Borini, F. (2019). Linking e-hrm practices and organizational outcomes: Empirical analysis of line manager's perception. *Revista Brasileira de Gestão de Negócios*, *21*(1), 48–69. doi:10.7819/rbgn.v21i1.3964

Iraz, R., & Yıldırım, E. (2005). Bilgi Yönetimi Anlayışının Benimsenmesi ve Bilgi Teknolojileri Uygulamalarının İnsan Kaynakları Yönetimine Etkileri: E-Learning Örneği. In *4.Ulusal Bilgi, Ekonomi ve Yönetim Kongresi.* Sakarya: Değişim Yayınları.

Ittmann, H., Meyer, I., Havenga, J., & Marais, M. (2014). *Implementing logistics strategies in a developing economy*. Retrieved on November 5, 2021 from https://researchspace.csir.co.za/dspace/handle/10204/1139

Ivančić, L., Vugec, D. S., & Vukšić, V. B. (2019). *Robotic process automation: systematic literature review.* Paper presented at the International Conference on Business Process Management.

Ivanov, D. (2020). Predicting the impacts of epidemic outbreaks on global supply chains: A simulation-based analysis on the coronavirus outbreak (COVID-19/SARS-CoV-2) case. *Transportation Research Part E, Logistics and Transportation Review*, *136*, 101922. doi:10.1016/j.tre.2020.101922 PMID:32288597

Ivanov, D., & Das, A. (2020). Coronavirus (COVID-19/SARS-CoV-2) and supply chain resilience: A research note. *International Journal of Integrated Supply Management*, *13*(1), 90. doi:10.1504/IJISM.2020.107780

Ivanov, D., & Dolgui, A. (2019). New disruption risk management perspectives in supply chains: Digital twins, the ripple effect, and resileanness. *IFAC-PapersOnLine*, *52*(13), 337–342. doi:10.1016/j.ifacol.2019.11.138

Ivanov, D., & Dolgui, A. (2020). Viability of intertwined supply networks: Extending the supply chain resilience angles towards survivability. A position paper motivated by COVID-19 outbreak. *International Journal of Production Research*, *58*(10), 2904–2915. doi:10.1080/00207543.2020.1750727

Ivanov, D., & Dolgui, A. (2021). A digital supply chain twin for managing the disruption risks and resilience in the era of Industry 4.0. *Production Planning and Control*, *32*(9), 775–788. doi:10.1080/09537287.2020.1768450

Ivanov, D., Dolgui, A., & Sokolov, B. (2019). The impact of digital technology and industry 4.0 on the ripple effect and supply chain risk analytics. *International Journal of Production Research*, *57*(3), 829–846. doi:10.1080/00207543.2018.1488086

Jabbarzadeh, A., Fahimnia, B., & Sabouhi, F. (2018). Resilient and sustainable supply chain design: Sustainability analysis under disruption risks. *International Journal of Production Research*, *56*(17), 5945–5968. doi:10.1080/00207543.2018.1461950

Jabbarzadeh, A., Fahimnia, B., Sheu, J. B., & Moghadam, H. S. (2016). Designing a supply chain resilient to major disruptions and supply/demand interruptions. *Transportation Research Part B: Methodological*, *94*, 121–149. doi:10.1016/j.trb.2016.09.004

Jackson, C. B., Quetsch, L. B., Brabson, L. A., & Herschell, A. D. (2018). Web-based training Methods for behavioral health providers: A Systematic Review. *Administration and Policy in Mental Health*, *45*(4), 587–610. doi:10.100710488-018-0847-0 PMID:29352459

Jacobs, F. R., Chase, R. B., & Lummus, R. R. (2011). *Operations and Supply Chain Management* (Global Edition). McGraw-Hill.

Jakobsen, M., & Jensen, R. (2015). Common method bias in public management studies. *International Public Management Journal*, *18*(1), 3–30. doi:10.1080/10967494.2014.997906

Janamanchi, B., & Burns, J. R. (2014). Control Theory Concepts Applied to Retail Supply Chain: A System Dynamics Modeling Environment Study. *Hindawi Publishing Corporation*, *201*, 1–14.

Janjevic, M., Winkenbach, M., & Rice, J. B., Jr. (2020). *5 Reasons Why Your Supply Chain Design Must Change with the Times.* Retrieved on October 4, 2021 from https://www.supplychain247.com/article/5_reasons_why_your_supply_chain_design_must_change_with_the_times)

Janvier-James, A. M. (2012). A New Introduction to Supply Chains and Supply Chain Management: Definitions and Theories Perspective. *International Business Research*, *5*(1), 194–206. doi:10.5539/ibr.v5n1p194

Jardim-Goncalves, R., Romero, D., & Grilo, A. (2017). Factories of the future: Challenges and leading innovations in intelligent manufacturing. *International Journal of Computer Integrated Manufacturing*, *30*(1), 4–14. doi:10.1080/0951192X.2016.1258120

Jastia, N. V. K., & Kodali, R. (2015). Lean production: Literature review and trends. *International Journal of Production Research*, *53*(3), 867–885. doi:10.1080/00207543.2014.937508

Jede, A., & Teuteberg, F. (2015). Integrating cloud computing in supply chain processes: A comprehensive literature review. *Journal of Enterprise Information Management*, *28*(6), 872–904. doi:10.1108/JEIM-08-2014-0085

Jenkin, T. (2013). Extending the 4I Organizational Learning Model: Information Sources, Foraging Processes and Tools. *Administrative Sciences*, *3*(3), 96–109. doi:10.3390/admsci3030096

Jennex, M. E. (2005). The Issue of System Use in Knowledge Management Systems. *The 38th Annual Hawaii International Conference*.

Jha, A., Sharma, R. R. K., Kumar, V., & Verma, P. (2022). Designing supply chain performance system: A strategic study on Indian manufacturing sector. *Supply Chain Management*, *27*(1), 66–88. doi:10.1108/SCM-05-2020-0198

Jia, F., Gong, Y., & Brown, S. (2019). Multi-tier sustainable supply chain management: The role of supply chain leadership. *International Journal of Production Economics*, *217*, 44–63. doi:10.1016/j.ijpe.2018.07.022

Johnson, J. (2009). *Chaos Sumary 2008*. The Standish Group Inc.

Jones, D. T. (2006). Heijunka: Leveling production. *Manufacturing Engineering*, *137*(2), 29–36.

Joshi, S., & Sharma, M. (2021). Digital technologies (DT) adoption in agri-food supply chains amidst COVID-19: An approach towards food security concerns in developing countries. *Journal of Global Operations and Strategic Sourcing*. doi:10.1108/JGOSS-02-2021-0014

Junge, A. L., Verhoeven, P., Reipert, J., & Mansfeld, M. (2019). Pathway of digital transformation in logistics: best practice concepts and future developments. In S. Franck (Ed.), *Scientific Series Logistics at the Berlin Institute of Technology* (Vol. 8). Universitätsverlag der TU Berlin.

Jurisic, M., & Kermek, D. (2011). Taxonomy of digital economy business models. In *MIPRO, 2011 Proceedings of the 34th International Convention* (pp. 23-27). Opatija.

Juttner, U., & Maklan, S. (2011). Supply Chain Resilience in the Global Financial Crisis: An Empirical Study. *Supply Chain Management*, *16*(4), 246–259. doi:10.1108/13598541111139062

Jyoti, J., & Dev, M. (2015). The impact of transformational leadership on employee creativity: The role of learning orientation. *Journal of Asia Business Studies*, *9*(1), 78–98. doi:10.1108/JABS-03-2014-0022

Kaasinen, E., Liinasuo, M., Schmalfuß, F., Koskinen, H., Aromaa, S., Heikkilä, P., Honka, A., Mach, S., & Malm, T. (2019). A Worker-Centric Design and Evaluation Framework for Operator 4.0 Solutions that Support Work Well-Being. In *HWID 2018* (pp. 263–282). Human Work Interaction Design. Designing Engaging Automation. doi:10.1007/978-3-030-05297-3_18

Kagerman, H., Wahlster, W., & Helbig, J. (2013). Recommendations for implementing the strategic initiative Industry 4.0. Academic Press.

Kagermann, H., Lukas, W., & Wahlster, W. (2011). *Industrie 4.0 –Mit dem Internet der Dinge auf dem Weg zur 4.* Industriellen Revolution. Retrieved on October 6, 2021 from https://www.ingenieur.de/technik/fachbereiche/produktion/industrie-40-mit-internet-dinge-weg-4-industriellen-revolution/

Kahle, J., Marcon, É., Ghezzi, A., & Frank, A. (2020). Smart Products value creation in SMEs innovation ecosystems. *Technological Forecasting and Social Change*, *156*, 120024. doi:10.1016/j.techfore.2020.120024

Kahn, B., & Adams, E. (2000). Sales forecasting as a Knowledge Management process. *The Journal of Business Forecasting*, 19-22.

Kaibara de Almeida, M. M., Marins, F. A. S., Salgado, A. M. P., Santos, F. C. A., & Silva, S. L. (2017). The importance of trust and collaboration between companies to mitigate the bullwhip effect in supply chain management. *Acta Scientiarum*, *39*(2), 201. Advance online publication. doi:10.4025/actascitechnol.v39i2.29648

Kaipia, R. (2007). *Supply Chain Coordination – Studies on planning and information sharing mechanisms*. Helsinki University of Technology Laboratory of Industrial Management Doctoral dissertation series 2007 / 2.

Kamalahmadi, M., & Mellat-Parast, M. (2016). A review of the literature on the principles of enterprise and supply chain resilience: Major findings and directions for future research. *International Journal of Production Economics*, *171*, 116–133. doi:10.1016/j.ijpe.2015.10.023

Kamath, N. (2016). *Handbook of research on strategic supply chain management in the retail industry*. IGI Global. doi:10.4018/978-1-4666-9894-9

Kamble, S. S., Gunasekaran, A., & Gawankar, S. A. (2018). Sustainable Industry 4.0 framework: A systematic literature review identifying the current trends and future perspectives. *Process Safety and Environmental Protection*, *117*, 408–425. doi:10.1016/j.psep.2018.05.009

Kandil, M., Berument, M. H., & Dincer, N. (2007). The effects of exchange rate fluctuations on economic activity in Turkey. *Journal of Asian Economics*, *18*(3), 466–489. doi:10.1016/j.asieco.2006.12.015

Kantar. (n.d.). *Cuotas de mercado de la distribución*. Retrieved on December 17, 2021, from https://www.kantarworldpanel.com/es/grocery-market-share/spain

Karadsheh, L., Mansour, E., AlHawari, S., Azar, G., & El-Bathy, N. (2009). A Theoretical Framework for Knowledge Management Process: Towards Improving Knowledge Performance. *Journal of Communications of the IBIMA*, 67-79.

Karia, N. (2018). Knowledge resources, technology resources and competitive advantage of logistics service providers. *Knowledge Management Research and Practice*, *16*(4), 451–463. doi:10.1080/14778238.2018.1521541

Karimi, J., & Walter, Z. (2015). The Role of Dynamic Capabilities in Responding to Digital Disruption: A Factor-Based Study of the Newspaper Industry. *Journal of Management Information Systems*, *32*(1), 39–81. doi:10.1080/07421222.2015.1029380

Karumsi, D., Prokopets, L., Clements, C., & Parva, N. (2020). *Automation in Procurement: Your New Workforce Is Here*. Retrieved on November 11, 2021 from https://assets.kpmg/content/dam/kpmg/xx/pdf/2019/11/automation-in-procurement.pdf

Kaufman, B. E. (2015). The RBV theory foundation of strategic HRM: Critical flaws, problems for research and practice, and an alternative economics paradigm. *Human Resource Management Journal*, *25*(4), 516–540. doi:10.1111/1748-8583.12085

Kayis, B., Zhou, M., Savci, S., Khoo, Y. B., Ahmed, A., & Kusumo, R. (2007). IRMAS-Development of a Risk Management Tool for Collaborative Multi- Site, Multi Partner New Product Development Projects New Product Development Projects. *Journal of Manufacturing Technology Management*, *18*(4), 387–414.

KDDI. (2021). *Dejitarutoransufu-me-shon wa naze DX to ryakusareru? DX no igi ya gutaiteki jirei made shōkai* [Why is digital transformation abbreviated as DX, and what does it mean?]. Retrieved on December 01, 2021, from https://www.kddimatomete.com/magazine/210201134321

Kent, J. L., & Mentzer, J. T. (2003). The effect of investment in inter-organizational information technology in a retail supply chain. *Journal of Business Logistics*, *24*(2), 155–176. doi:10.1002/j.2158-1592.2003.tb00050.x

Kerfia, S. D., Shirma, G., Kusiluka, L., Ayebazibwe, C., Mwebe, R., Cleaveland, S., & Haydon, D. (2018). Spatial and Temporal Distribution of Foot and Mouth Disease in Four Districts, Situated Along the Uganda – Tanzania Border: Implications for Cross-border Efforts in Disease Control. *The Onderstepoort Journal of Veterinary Research*, *85*(1). Advance online publication. 10.4102%2Fojvr.v85i1.1528

Kerr, W. A. (2020). The COVID-19 pandemic and agriculture: Short- and long-run implications for international trade relations. *Canadian Journal of Agricultural Economics/Revue Canadienne d'agroeconomie*, *68*(2), 225–229. doi:10.1111/cjag.12230

Ketokivi, M., & Choi, T. (2014). Renaissance of case research as a scientific method. *Journal of Operations Management*, *32*(5), 232–240. doi:10.1016/j.jom.2014.03.004

Khan, A., & Turowski, K. (2016a). A Perspective on Industry 4.0: from challenges to opportunities in production systems. In *Proceedings of the International Conference of Internet of Things and Big Data* (Vol. 2, pp. 441-448). Setúbal, Portugal: SCITEPRESS. 10.5220/0005929704410448

Khan, A., & Turowski, K. (2016b). A survey of current challenges in manufacturing industry and preparation for industry 4.0. In *Proceedings of the First International Scientific Conference "Intelligent Information Technologies for Industry"(IITI'16)* (pp. 15-26). London, UK: Springer. 10.1007/978-3-319-33609-1_2

Khan, S. A. R., Ponce, P., Tanveer, M., Aguirre-Padilla, N., Mahmood, H., & Shah, S. A. A. (2021). Technological Innovation and Circular Economy Practices: Business Strategies to Mitigate the Effects of COVID-19. *Sustainability*, *13*(15), 8479. doi:10.3390u13158479

Khedhaouria, A., & Jamal, A. (2015). Sourcing knowledge for innovation: Knowledge reuse and creation in project teams. *Journal of Knowledge Management*, *19*(5), 932–948. doi:10.1108/JKM-01-2015-0039

Khisro, J., & Sundberg, H. (2020). Enterprise interoperability development in multi relation collaborations: Success factors from the Danish electricity market. *Enterprise Information Systems*, *14*(8), 1172–1193. doi:10.1080/17517575.2018.1528633

Kilbourne, A. M., Goodrich, D. E., Miake-Lye, I., Braganza, M. Z., & Bowersox, N. W. (2019). Quality Enhancement Research Initiative Implementation Roadmap: Toward Sustainability of Evidence-based Practices in a Learning Health System. *Medical Care*, *57*(10, Suppl 3), S286–S293. doi:10.1097/MLR.0000000000001144 PMID:31517801

Kim, K., Lim, S., & Mitchell, B. (2004). Building A Knowledge Model: A Decision- Making Approach. *Journal of Knowledge Management Practice*, 5–11.

Kimseng, T., Javed, A., Jeenanunta, C., & Kohda, Y. (2020). Sustaining Innovation through Joining Global Supply Chain Networks: The Case of Manufacturing Firms in Thailand. *Sustainability*, *12*(13), 5259. doi:10.3390u12135259

Kirner, C., & Siscoutto, R. (Eds.). (2007). *Realidade virtual e aumentada: Conceitos, projeto e aplicações.* SBC.

Klimuk, V., & Tarasova, A. (2019). Digital economy in Belarus and Russia: leading underpins of a new reality. In *3rd International Conference on Social, Economic, and Academic Leadership (ICSEAL 2019)* (pp. 421-427). Atlantis Press. 10.2991/icseal-19.2019.66

Klumpp, M., & Loske, D. (2021). Sustainability and resilience revisited: Impact of information technology disruptions on empirical retail logistics efficiency. *Sustainability, 13*(10), 5650. doi:10.3390u13105650

Knight, H. (1921). *Library of Economics & liberty*. Retrieved October 1, 2012, from Risk, Uncertainty and Profit: www.econlib.org/library/Knight/knRUP.html

Koberg, E., & Longoni, A. (2019). A systematic review of sustainable supply chain management in global supply chains. *Journal of Cleaner Production, 207*, 1084–1098. doi:10.1016/j.jclepro.2018.10.033

Koch, T., & Windsperger, J. (2017). Seeing through the network: Competitive advantage in the digital economy. *Journal of Organization Design, 6*(1), 6. doi:10.118641469-017-0016-z

Koh, S. C. L., Saad, S., & Arunachalam, S. (2006). Competing in the 21st century supply chain through supply chain management and enterprise resource planning integration. *International Journal of Physical Distribution & Logistics Management, 36*(6), 455–465. doi:10.1108/09600030610677401

Kolberg, D., & Zühlke, D. (2015). Lean automation enabled by Industry 4.0 technologies. *IFAC-PapersOnLine, 28*(3), 1870–1875. doi:10.1016/j.ifacol.2015.06.359

Komninos, N. (2002). *Intelligent cities: Innovation, knowledge systems and digital spaces*. Routledge.

Köseoglu, M. A., Yıldız, M., Putra, E. D., & Cıftcı, T. (2018). Co-Authorship Networks in Business Ethics: A Longitudinal Study. *Journal of Scientometric Research, 7*(3), 201–209. doi:10.5530/jscires.7.3.32

Kotler, P., & Armstrong, G. (2011). *Principles of Marketing*. Pearson Education South Africa (Pty) Ltd Prentice Hall.

KPMG. (2016). *Fast Moving Consumer Goods Sector Report*. Retrieved on November 8, 2021 from https://assets.kpmg.com/content/dam/kpmg/br/pdf/2016/09/fast-moving-consumer-goods.pdf

Kroll, C., Bujak, A., Darius, V., Enders, W., & Esser, M. (2016). *Robotic process automation: robots conquer business processes in back offices*. Retrieved on November 27, 2021 from https://www.capgemini.com/consulting-de/wp-content/uploads/sites/32/2017/08/robotic-process-automation-study.pdf

Kumar, G., Banerjee, R. N., Meena, P. L., & Ganguly, K. K. (2017). Joint Planning and Problem-Solving Roles in Supply Chain Collaboration. *IIMB Management Review, 29*(1), 45–57. doi:10.1016/j.iimb.2017.03.001

Kurpjuweit, S., Schmidt, C. G., Klöckner, M., & Wagner, S. M. (2021). Blockchain in additive manufacturing and its impact on supply chains. *Journal of Business Logistics, 42*(1), 46–70. doi:10.1111/jbl.12231

Kurt, R. (2019). Industry 4.0 in Terms of Industrial Relations and Its Impacts on Labour Life. *Procedia Computer Science, 158*, 590–601. doi:10.1016/j.procs.2019.09.093

Kuster, J., Jannach, D., & Friedrich, G. (2009). Extending the RCPSP for modeling and solving disruption management problems. *Applied Intelligence, 31*(3), 234–253. doi:10.100710489-008-0119-x

Kutsch, E., & Hall, M. (2005). Intervening conditions on the management of project risk: Dealing with uncertainty in information technology projects. *International Journal of Project Management, 23*, 591–599.

Kutzner, K., Schoormann, T., & Knackstedt, R. (2018). Digital transformation in information systems research: A taxonomy-based approach to structure the field. *Research Papers, 56*. https://aisel.aisnet.org/ecis2018_rp/56

Kwilinski, A., Vyshnevskyi, O., & Dzwigol, H. (2020). Digitalization of the EU Economies and People at Risk of Poverty or Social Exclusion. *J. Risk Financial Manag., 13*(7), 142. doi:10.3390/jrfm13070142

Lacity, M. C., & Willcocks, L. P. (2016). New Approach to Automating Services. *MIT Sloan Management Review*, *58*(1), 41–49.

Lacity, M., & Willcocks, L. P. (2021). Becoming strategic with intelligent automation. *MIS Quarterly Executive*, *20*(2), 169–182. doi:10.17705/2msqe.00047

Lado, A. A., Paulraj, A., & Chen, I. J. (2011). Customer focus, supply-chain relational capabilities and performance: Evidence from US manufacturing industries. *International Journal of Logistics Management*, *22*(2), 202–221. doi:10.1108/09574091111156550

Lai, H. C. (2000). *Knowledge Management: A Review of TheoreticalFrameworks and Industrial Cases. In The 33rd Hawaii International Conference on System Sciences*. IEEE.

Lakovou, E., & White, C. C. (2020). *How to build more secure, resilient, next-gen U. S. supply chains*. Retrieved from November 6, 2021 from https://www.brookings.edu/techstream/how-to-build-more-secure-resilient-next-gen-u-s-supply-chains/

Lambiase, A., Mastrocinque, E., Miranda, S., & Lambiase, A. (2013). Strategic Planning and Design of Supply Chains: A Literature Review. *International Journal of Engineering Business Management*, *5*, 1–11. doi:10.5772/56858

Lamminen, J., Forsvik, H., Voipio, V., & Lehtonen, L. (2015). Decision-making process for clinical investments in a public health care organization – contingency approach to support the investment decision process. *Finnish Journal of eHealth and eWelfare*, *7*(2-3), 122-134.

Lancioni, R. A., & Chandran, R. (2009). Managing knowledge in industrial markets: New dimensions and challenges. *Industrial Marketing Management*, *38*(2), 148–151.

Langlois, R. N., & Robertson, P. L. (2018). Stop crying over spilt knowledge: A critical look at the theory of spillovers and technical change. *Journal of Public Finance and Public Choice*, *33*(1), 63–80. doi:10.1332/251569118X15214757059213

Langreo, A., & Germán, L. (2018). Transformations in the food system and the role of industrial and food distribution changes in the Spanish diet during the twentieth century. *Historia Agraria*, *74*, 167–200. doi:10.26882/histagrar.074e06l

Lanvin, B., Evans, P., & Rodriguez-Montemayor, E. (2016). Shifting gears: How to combine technology and talent to shape the future of work. In B. Lanvin & P. Evans (Eds.), *The global competitiveness index 2017: Talent and technology* (pp. 3–41). INSEAD.

Leao, P., & da Silva, M. M. (2021). Impacts of digital transformation on firms' competitive advantages: A systematic literature review. *Strategic Change*, *30*(5), 421–441. doi:10.1002/jsc.2459

Leat, P., & Revoredo-Giha, C. (2013). Risk and resilience in agri-food supply chains: The case of the ASDA PorkLink supply chain in Scotland. *Supply Chain Management*, *18*(2), 219–231. doi:10.1108/13598541311318845

Lee, E. A. (2008). Cyber Physical Systems: Design Challenges. In *2008 11th IEEE International symposium on object and component-oriented real-time distributed computing* (pp.363-369). IEEE.

Leen, J., & Lanng, C. (2020). *Here's how global supply chains will change after COVID-19*. Retrieved on November 1, 2021 from https://www.weforum.org/agenda/2020/05/this-is-what-global-supply-chains-will-look-like-after-covid-19/

Lee, S. M., & Trimi, S. (2020). Convergence innovation in the digital age and in the COVID-19 pandemic crisis. *Journal of Business Research*, *123*, 14–22. doi:10.1016/j.jbusres.2020.09.041 PMID:33012897

Lenart-Gansiniec, R. (2019). Organizational Learning in Industry 4.0. *Problemy Zarzadzania*, *2*(82), 96–108. doi:10.7172/1644-9584.82.4

Leon, R. D., Rodriguez-Rodriguez, R., Gomez-Gasquet, P., & Mula, J. (2020). Business process improvement and the knowledge flows that cross a private online social network: An insurance supply chain case. *Information Processing & Management, 57*(4), 102237. doi:10.1016/j.ipm.2020.102237

Liang, L., Yang, F., Cook, W. D., & Zhu, J. (2006). DEA models for supply chain efficiency evaluation. *Annals of Operations Research, 145*(1), 35–49. doi:10.100710479-006-0026-7

Liboni, L. B., Cezarino, L. O., Jabbour, C. J. C., Oliveira, B. G., & Stefanelli, N. O. (2019). Smart industry and the pathways to HRM 4.0: Implications for SCM. *Supply Chain Management, 24*(1), 124–146. doi:10.1108/SCM-03-2018-0150

Li, G., Fan, H., Lee, P. K. C., & Cheng, T. C. E. (2015). Joint supply chain risk management: An agency and collaboration perspective. *International Journal of Production Economics, 164*, 83–94. doi:10.1016/j.ijpe.2015.02.021

Liker, J. (2004). *The Toyota Way: 14 management principles the world's greatest manufacturer.* McGraw-Hill.

Lima, D. F. S., de França Alcantara, P. G., Santos, L. C., Silva, L. M. F., & Da Silva, R. M. (2016). Mapeamento do fluxo de valor e simulação para implementação de práticas lean em uma empresa calçadista. *Produção Online, 16*(1), 366–392.

Loebbecke, C., & Picot, A. (2015). Reflections on societal and business model transformation arising from digitization and big data analytics: A research agenda. *The Journal of Strategic Information Systems, 24*(3), 149–157. doi:10.1016/j.jsis.2015.08.002

Longo, F., Nicoletti, L., Padovano, A., d'Atri, G., & Forte, M. (2019). Blockchain-enabled supply chain: An experimental study. *Computers & Industrial Engineering, 136*, 57–69. doi:10.1016/j.cie.2019.07.026

Lotfi, C., Srinivasan, S., Ertz, M., & Latrous, I. (2022). A tool for study on impact of Big Data technologies on firm performance. In *4th International Conference on Intelligent Communication Technologies and Virtual Mobile Networks (ICICV 2022)* (pp. 501-517). Tirunelveli: Francis Xavier Engineering College.

Luomaranta, T., & Martinsuo, M. (2019). Supply chain innovations for additive manufacturing. *International Journal of Physical Distribution & Logistics Management, 50*(1), 54–79. doi:10.1108/IJPDLM-10-2018-0337

Luściński, S., & Ivanov, V. (2020). A simulation study of Industry 4.0 factories based on the ontology on flexibility with using FlexSim® software. *Management and Production Engineering Review, 11*, 74–83. doi:10.24425/mper.2020.134934

Luthra, S., & Mangla, S. K. (2018). Evaluating challenges to Industry 4.0 initiatives for supply chain sustainability in emerging economies. *Process Safety and Environmental Protection, 117*, 168–179. doi:10.1016/j.psep.2018.04.018

Macdonald, J. R., & Corsi, T. M. (2013). Supply chain disruption management: Severe events, recovery, and performance. *Journal of Business Logistics, 34*(4), 270–288. doi:10.1111/jbl.12026

Madakam, S., Holmukhe, R. M., & Jaiswal, D. K. (2019). The future digital work force: Robotic process automation (RPA). *JISTEM-Journal of Information Systems and Technology Management, 16*, 1–17. Advance online publication. doi:10.4301/S1807-1775201916001

Malhotra, Y. (2005). Integrating knowledge management technologies in organizational business processes: Getting real time enterprises to deliver real business performance. *Journal of Knowledge Management, 9*(1), 7–28.

Management, A. f. (2006). *APM Body of Knowledge* (5th ed.). APM Publishing.

Mandal, S., Sarathy, R., Korasiga, V. R., Dastidar, S. G., & Bhattacharya, S. (2016). Achieving supply chain resilience: The contribution of logistics and supply chain capabilities. *International Journal of Disaster Resilience in the Built Environment, 7*(5), 544–562. doi:10.1108/IJDRBE-04-2016-0010

Manjoo, F. (2013). *The Happiness Machine*. Retrieved on October 7, 2021 from https://slate.com/technology/2013/01/google-people-operations-the-secrets-of-the-worlds-most-scientific-human-resources-department.html

Manville, G., Papadopoulos, T., & Garengo, P. (2019). Twenty-first century supply chain management: A multiple case study analysis within the UK aerospace industry. *Total Quality Management & Business Excellence, 32*(7-8), 869–885. doi:10.1080/14783363.2019.1642101

Marchand, D., & Wade, M. (2014). *Digital business transformation: where is your company on the journey*. Retrieved on November 28, 2021, from https://www.imd.org/contentassets/9be2125354424aa5afd52f5b03f639a0/digital-business-transformation-pfm-final.pdf

Maria, P., & Přívara, A. (2017). Cross-country analysis on neighboring migration policy by the example of Finland and Russia. *Proceedings of the International Conference on Education, 3*(1), 17-28. 10.17501/icedu.2017.3103

Marin-Garcia, J., & Zarate Martínez, E. (2007). A Theoretical Review of Knowledge Management and Teamworking in the Organizations. *International Journal of Management Science and Engineering Management, 2*(4), 278–288.

Mari, S. I., Lee, Y. H., Memon, M. S., Park, Y. S., & Kim, M. (2015). Adaptivity of Complex Network Topologies for Designing Resilient Supply Chain Networks. *International Journal of Industrial Engineering, 22*(1), 102–116. doi:10.23055/ijietap.2015.22.1.1326

Markovitz, D. (2011). *A factory of one: Applying lean principles to banish waste and improve your personal performance*. CRC Press.

Marler, J. (2009). Making human resources strategic by going to the net: Reality or myth? *International Journal of Human Resource Management, 20*(3), 515–527. doi:10.1080/09585190802707276

Marler, J., & Parry, E. (2009). Human resource management, strategic involvement and e-HRM technology. *International Journal of Human Resource Management, 27*(19), 1–21. doi:10.1080/09585192.2015.1091980

Marmolejo-Saucedo, J. A. (2021). Digital Twin Framework for Large-Scale Optimization Problems in Supply Chains: A Case of Packing Problem. *Mobile Networks and Applications*. Advance online publication. doi:10.100711036-021-01856-9

Martin, E., DeHayes, D., Hoffer, J., & Perkins, W. (1991). *Managing Information Technology: What Managers Need To Know*. Maxwell Macmillan.

Martin, G., Reddington, M., & Alexander, H. (2008). Technology, outsourcing, and HR transformation: An introduction. In G. Martin, M. Reddington, & H. Alexander (Eds.), *Technology, Outsourcing and Transforming HR* (pp. 1–35). Routledge. doi:10.1016/B978-0-7506-8645-7.50006-4

Marucheck, A., Greis, N., Mena, C., & Cai, L. (2011). Product safety and security in the global supply chain: Issues, challenges and research opportunities. *Journal of Operations Management, 29*(7-8), 707–720. doi:10.1016/j.jom.2011.06.007

Massingham, P. (2010). Knowledge risk management: A framework. *Journal of Knowledge Management, 14*(3), 464–485.

Masum, A.-K., Beh, L.-S., Azad, A.-K., & Hoque, K. (2018). Intelligent human resource information system (IHRIS): A holistic decision support framework for HR excellence. *The International Arab Journal of Information Technology, 15*(1), 121–130.

Matthews, A. (2020). EU Food System Strengths and Vulnerabilities during Covid-19. *EuroChoices (Uckfield), 19*(3), 4–12. doi:10.1111/1746-692X.12300

Maurer, S. D., & Liu, Y. (2007). Developing effective e-recruiting websites: Insights for managers from marketers. *Business Horizons, 50*(4), 305–314. doi:10.1016/j.bushor.2007.01.002

Maykut, P., & Morehouse, R. (1994). *Beginning Qualitative Research: A Philosophical and Practical Guide* (1st ed.). Routledge. doi:10.4324/9780203485781

Mayr, A., Weigelt, M., Kühl, A., Grimm, S., Erll, A., Potzel, M., & Franke, J. (2018). Lean 4.0: A conceptual conjunction of lean management and Industry 4.0. *Procedia CIRP, 72*, 622-628. doi:10.1016/j.procir.2018.03.292

Mbhele, T. P. (2014). *Electronic supply chain management systems in managing the bullwhip effect on selected Fast-Moving Consumer Goods* (PhD dissertation). University of KwaZulu-Natal, South Africa.

Mbunge, E., Akinnuwesi, B., Fashoto, S. G., Metfula, A. S., & Mashwama, P. (2021). A critical review of emerging technologies for tackling COVID-19 pandemic. *Human Behavior and Emerging Technologies, 3*(1), 25–39. doi:10.1002/hbe2.237 PMID:33363278

McCarthy, D. J., Puffer, S. M., Graham, L. R., & Satinsky, D. M. (2014). Emerging innovation in emerging economies: Can institutional reforms help Russia break through its historical barriers? *Thunderbird International Business Review, 56*(3), 243–260. doi:10.1002/tie.21619

McDougall, N., Wagner, B., & MacBryde, J. (2021). Leveraging competitiveness from sustainable operations: Frameworks to understand the dynamic capabilities needed to realise NRBV supply chain strategies. *Supply Chain Management, 27*(1), 12–29. doi:10.1108/SCM-11-2018-0393

McIntyre, D., & Srinivasan, A. (2017). Networks, platforms, and strategy: Emerging views and next steps. *Strategic Management Journal, 38*(1), 141–160. doi:10.1002mj.2596

McKeen, D., Zack, H., & Singh, S. (2006). Knowledge Management and Organizational Performance: An Exploratory Survey. In *39th Hawaii International Conference on System Sciences* (pp. 1-9). IEEE.

McKinsey. (2020). *How COVID-19 has pushed companies over the technology tipping point-and transformed business forever*. Retrieved on December 5, 2021 from https://www.mckinsey.com/business-functions/strategy-and-corporate-finance/our-insights/how-covid-19-has-pushed-companies-over-the-technology-tipping-point-and-transformed-business-forever

McKinsey. (2021). *Using digital transformation to thrive in Japan's new normal: An urgent imperative.* Retrieved on November 28, 2021, from https://www.mckinsey.com/~/media/mckinsey/locations/asia/japan/our%20work/digital/using%20digital%20transformation%20to%20thrive%20in%20japans%20new%20normal_an%20urgent%20imperative_upd201223.pdf

McLean, G. (Ed.). (1996). Civil society and social reconstruction. Cultural Heritage and Contemporary Change, 1, 16.

Meijerink, J., Keegan, A., Boons, M., & Marler, J. (2021). Algorithmic human resource management: Synthesizing developments and cross-disciplinary insights on digital HRM. *International Journal of Human Resource Management, 32*(12), 2545–2562. doi:10.1080/09585192.2021.1925326

Melanthiou, Y., Pavlou, F., & Constantinou, E. (2015). The use of social network sites as an e-recruitment tool. *Journal of Transnational Management, 20*(1), 31–49. doi:10.1080/15475778.2015.998141

Mena, C., Karatzas, A., & Hansen, C. (2022). International trade resilience and the Covid-19 pandemic. *Journal of Business Research, 138*, 77–91. doi:10.1016/j.jbusres.2021.08.064 PMID:34538982

Meng, X. H. (2019). Lean management in the context of construction supply chains. *International Journal of Production Research, 57*(11), 3784–3798. doi:10.1080/00207543.2019.1566659

Mensah, P., Merkuryev, Y., & Longo, F. (2015). Using ICT in Developing a Resilient Supply Chain Strategy. *Procedia Computer Science, 43*, 101–108. doi:10.1016/j.procs.2014.12.014

Mentzer, J. T., Min, S., & Bobbitt, L. M. (2004). Toward a unified theory of logistics. *International Journal of Physical Distribution & Logistics Management, 34*(7/8), 606–627. doi:10.1108/09600030410557758

Merriam, S. B. (1988). *Case study research in education: A qualitative approach.* Jossey-Bass.

METI. (2018). *IT Shisutemu 2025 nen no gake no kokufuku to DX no honkakuteki na tenkai* [Overcoming the "2025 Cliff" in IT systems and full-scale development of DX]. Retrieved on December 02, 2021, from https://www.meti.go.jp/shingikai/mono_info_service/digital_transformation/pdf/20180907_03.pdf

METI. (2019). *DX suishin shihyō to sono gaidansu* [DX Promotion Index and its Guidance]. DX. Retrieved on December 02, 2021, from https://www.meti.go.jp/press/2019/07/20190731003/20190731003-1.pdf

Michael, S., Zhdanova, A., & Fensel, D. (2005). H-TechSight A Next Generation Knowledge Management Platform. *Journal of Information and Knowledge Management, 3*(1), 47-66.

Microsoft. (2021). *Çalışanların işe alım, ekleme ve yönetim görevlerini kolaylaştırın.* Retrieved on October 3, 2021 from https://flow.microsoft.com/tr-tr/collections/humanresources/

Mikhaylov, A. (2020). Cryptocurrency Market Analysis from the Open Innovation Perspective. *Journal of Open Innovation, 6*(4), 197. doi:10.3390/joitmc6040197

Miles, F. a. (1998). Managing project risk and the performance envelope. In *The 13th Annual Applied Power Electronics Conference and Exposition.* Singapore: APEC.

Milewski, D. (2020). Total Costs of Centralized and Decentalized Inventory Strategies – Including External Costs. *Sustainability, 12*(22), 9346. doi:10.3390u12229346

Miller, M. (2021). Big data, information asymmetry, and food supply chain management for resilience. *Journal of Agriculture, Food Systems, and Community Development, 11*(1), 171–182. doi:10.5304/jafscd.2021.111.017

Miltiadis, L., Pouloudi, A., & Poulymenakou, A. (2002). Knowledge management convergence expanding learning frontiers. *Journal of Knowledge Management, 6*(1), 40–51.

Min, H. (2010). Artificial intelligence in supply chain management: Theory and applications. *International Journal of Logistics Research and Applications, 13*(1), 13–39. doi:10.1080/13675560902736537

Minina, E. (2017). 'Quality revolution' in post-Soviet education in Russia: From control to assurance? *Journal of Education Policy, 32*(2), 176–197. doi:10.1080/02680939.2016.1250165

Mishra, D., Gunasekaran, A., Childe, S., Papadopoulos, T., Dubey, R., & Wamba, S. (2016). Vision, applications, and future challenges of Internet of Things: A bibliometric study of the recent literature. *Industrial Management & Data Systems, 116*(7), 1331–1355. doi:10.1108/IMDS-11-2015-0478

Mittal, S., & Dhar, R. L. (2016). Effect of green transformational leadership on green creativity: A study of tourist hotels. *Tourism Management, 57*, 118–127. doi:10.1016/j.tourman.2016.05.007

Modgil, S., Singh, R. K., & Hannibal, C. (2021). Artificial intelligence for supply chain resilience: Learning from Covid-19. *International Journal of Logistics Management.* Advance online publication. doi:10.1108/IJLM-02-2021-0094

Moeuf, A., Pellerin, R., Lamouri, S., Tamayo-Giraldo, S., & Barbaray, R. (2018). The industrial management of SMEs in the era of Industry 4.0. *International Journal of Production Research, 56*(3), 1118-1136. doi:10.1080/00207543.2017.1372647

Mohan, B. C., & Sequeira, A. H. (2012). Customer-Based Brand Equity in the Fast-Moving Consumer Goods Industry in India. *International Journal of Management, 1*(4), 1–19.

Mohan, B. C., & Sequeira, A. H. (2015). The impact of customer-based brand equity on the operational performance of FMCG companies in India. *IIMB Management Review, 28*(1), 13–19. doi:10.1016/j.iimb.2015.11.002

Monden, Y. (1993). *Toyota Production System: An integrated approach to Just-In Time* (2nd ed.). Industrial Engineering and Management Press. doi:10.1007/978-1-4615-9714-8

Morsy, N., & El Demerdash, J. (2017). Investigating the potential use of E-HRM: The Context of Egyptian hotels and travel agents. *Journal of Tourism Research, 16*, 82–92.

Motta, G. A., Tekinerdogan, B., & Athanasiadis, I. N. (2020). Blockchain Applications in the Agri-Food Domain: The First Wave. *Frontiers in Blockchain*. doi:10.3389/fbloc.2020.00006

Müller, J. M., Buliga, O., & Voigt, K.-I. (2018). Fortune favors the prepared: How SMEs approach business model innovations in Industry 4.0. *Technological Forecasting and Social Change, 132*, 2–17. doi:10.1016/j.techfore.2017.12.019

Mustapha, U. M. (2010). *The Role of Product Design, Manufacturing Systems and Environmental Uncertainty in Nigeria Manufacturing Organizations*. Engineering Doctorate. Retrieved on November 8 2021 from https://eprints.usq.edu.au/19606/1/Mustapha_2010_front.pdf

N'Cho, J. (2017). Contribution of talent analytics in change management within project management organizations the case of the French aerospace sector. *Procedia Computer Science, 121*, 625–629. doi:10.1016/j.procs.2017.11.082

Nagappan, R. (2001). *Dealing with biases in qualitative research: a balancing act for researchers*. Paper presented at the Qualitative research convention, Kuala Lumpur, Malaysia. Retrieved on November 7, 2021 from http://merr.utm.my/id/eprint/4087

Nagurney, A. (2006). *Supply Chain Network Economics: Dynamics of Prices, Flows, and Profits*. Edward Elgar.

Nagy, J. (2006). *The attitude of Hungarian companies to the concept of supply chain management. 15th Annual IPSERA Conference*, San Diego, CA.

Nahavandi, S. (2019). Industry 5.0: A human-centric solution. *Sustainability, 11*(16), 1–13. doi:10.3390u11164371

Nah, F. F.-H., Lau, J. L. S., & Kuang, J. (2001). Critical factors for successful implementation of enterprise systems. *Business Process Management Journal, 7*(3), 285–296. doi:10.1108/14637150110392782

Nah, F. F.-H., & Siau, K. (2020). COVID-19 pandemic – Role of technology in transforming business to the new normal. In C. Stephanidis, G. Salvendy, J. Wei, S. Yamamoto, H. Mori, G. Meiselwitz, F. F.-H. Nah, & K. Siau (Eds.), *HCI International 2020 – Late Breaking Papers: Interaction, Knowledge and Social Media* (Vol. 12427, pp. 585–600). Springer International Publishing. doi:10.1007/978-3-030-60152-2_43

Nambisan, S. (2017). Digital entrepreneurship: Toward a digital technology perspective of entrepreneurship. *Entrepreneurship Theory and Practice, 41*(6), 1029–1055. doi:10.1111/etap.12254

Nambisan, S., Wright, M., & Feldman, M. (2019). The digital transformation of innovation and entrepreneurship: Progress, challenges, and key themes. *Research Policy, 48*(8), 103773. doi:10.1016/j.respol.2019.03.018

Neboh, N. D., Mbhele, T. P., & Phiri, M. (2019). *Retail supply chain design for resilience: selected Durban Supermarkets* (PhD dissertation).

Neboh, N. D., & Mbhele, T. P. (2021). Supply chain design dimensions for supply chain resilience in the South African fast-moving consumer goods retail industry. *Africa Journal of Management, 7*(sup1, S1), 58–81. doi:10.1080/23322373.2021.1930742

Neef, D. (1997). *Making the case for knowledge management: The bigger picture*. Center for Business Innovation.

Neef, D. (2005). Managing Corporate Risk through Better Knowledge Management. *Journal of The Learning Organization, 12*(2), 112–124.

Neely, A. (2005). The Evolution of Performance Measurement Research: Developments in the Last Decade and a Research Agenda for the Next. *International Journal of Operations & Production Management, 25*(12), 1264–1277. doi:10.1108/01443570510633648

Nehari-Talet, A., Alhawari, S., & Alryalat, H. (2010). The Effect Knowledge Process on Customer Knowledge Expansion. *The International Journal of Knowledge, Culture and Change Management, 10*(2), 181–200.

Nel, J. D., & Badenhorst-weiss, J. A. (2010). *Supply chain Design: Some Critical Questions*. Department of Business Management University of South Africa (Unisa) South Africa.

Nguegan, C. A., & Mafini, C. (2017). Supply Chain Management Problems in the Food Processing Industry: Implications for Business Performance. *Acta Commercii, 17*(1). Advance online publication. doi:10.4102/ac.v17i1.485

Nicolaou, A. I. (2004). Quality of postimplementation review for enterprise resource planning systems. *International Journal of Accounting Information Systems, 5*(1), 25–49. doi:10.1016/j.accinf.2004.02.002

Ni, D., Xiao, Z., & Lim, M. K. (2020). A systematic review of the research trends of machine learning in supply chain management. *International Journal of Machine Learning and Cybernetics, 11*(7), 1463–1482. doi:10.100713042-019-01050-0

Nie, D., Panfilova, E., Samusenkov, V., & Mikhaylov, A. (2020). E-Learning Financing Models in Russia for Sustainable Development. *Sustainability, 12*(11), 4412. doi:10.3390u12114412

Niesenhaus, J. (2013). *Industry 4.0: Gamification in the area of industrial production*. https://www.centigrade.de/en/blog/industry-4-0-gamification-in-the-area-of-industrial-production/

Nissen, M., Kamel, M., & Sengupta, K. (2000). Integrated Analysis and Design of Knowledge Systems and Processes. *Information Resources Management Journal, 13*(1).

Nitsche, B. (2021). Exploring the Potentials of Automation in Logistics and Supply Chain Management: Paving the Way for Autonomous Supply Chains. *Logistics, 5*(3), 51. Retrieved on November 5, 2021 from https://www.mdpi.com/2305-6290/5/3/51

Nivlouei, F. B. (2014). Electronic human resource management system: The main element in capacitating globalization paradigm. *International Journal of Business and Social Science, 5*(2), 147–159.

Nocker, M., & Sena, V. (2019). Big Data and Human Resources Management: The Rise of Talent Analytics. *Social Sciences, 8*(10), 273. doi:10.3390ocsci8100273

Nonaka, I. (1994). A Dynamic Theory of Organizational Knowledge Creation. *Computer Science, 5*(1).

North, K., Aramburu, N., & Lorenzo, O. (2020). Promoting digitally enabled growth in SMEs: A framework proposal. *Journal of Enterprise Information Management, 33*(1), 238–262. doi:10.1108/JEIM-04-2019-0103

North, K., & Maier, R. (2018). Wissen 4.0 – Wissensmanagement im digitalen Wandel. *HMD Praxis der Wirtschaftsinformatik, 55*(4), 665–681. doi:10.136540702-018-0426-6

O'Donnell, J. (2021). *Definition – How supply chain systems process orders*. Retrieved on February 15, 2021 from https://searcherp.techtarget.com/definition/warehouse-management-system-WMS

O'Riordan, J. (2017). *The practice of human resource management*. https://www.ipa.ie/_fileUpload/Documents/THE_PRACTICE_OF_HRM.pdf

Ocampo, L., Himang, C., Obiso, J. J., Bongo, M., Caballes, S. A., Abellana, D. P., Jabilles, E. M., Deocaris, C., & Ancheta, R. Jr. (2021). Industry 4.0 Indicators and Their Roles in Strategy Formulation. *Journal of Advanced Manufacturing Systems, 20*(3), 631–662. doi:10.1142/S0219686721500311

Ochieng, A. O. (2018). *Supply chain resilience and organizational performance of pharmaceutical manufacturing companies in Nairobi* (Master's thesis). School of Business University of Nairobi.

Ohno, T. (1988). *Toyota Production System: Beyond large-scale production.* Productivity Press.

Oliden, P. E., & Zumbo, B. D. (2008). Coeficientes de fiabilidad para escalas de respuesta categórica ordenada. *Psicothema, 20*(4), 896–901. PMID:18940100

Oliveira, L., Fleury, A., & Fleury, M. T. (2021). Digital power: Value chain upgrading in an age of digitization. *International Business Review, 30*(6), 101850. doi:10.1016/j.ibusrev.2021.101850

Olsson, R. (2008). Risk Management in a Multi-Project Environment; An Approach to Manage Portfolio Risks. *International Journal of Quality & Reliability Management, 25*(1), 60–71.

Omogbai, O., & Salonitis, K. (2017). The implementation of 5S lean tool using system dynamics approach. *Procedia CIRP, 60*, 380–385. doi:10.1016/j.procir.2017.01.057

Osada, T. (1991). *The 5S's: Five Keys to a Total Quality Environment.* Asian Productivity Organization.

Osiyevskyy, O., Shirokova, G., & Ritala, P. (2020). Exploration and exploitation in crisis environment: Implications for level and variability of firm performance. *Journal of Business Research, 114*, 227–239. doi:10.1016/j.jbusres.2020.04.015 PMID:32341610

Ouabouch, L. (2015). Supply chain resilience. *Materials Management Review*, 16 – 18.

Ouakouak, M. L., & Ouedraogo, N. (2017). Antecedents of employee creativity and organisational innovation: An empirical study. *International Journal of Innovation Management, 21*(7), 1750060. doi:10.1142/S1363919617500608

Overholm, H. (2015). Collectively created opportunities in emerging ecosystems: The case of solar service ventures. *Technovation, 39–40*, 14–25. doi:10.1016/j.technovation.2014.01.008

Pagliosa, M., Tortorella, G., & Ferreira, J. C. E. (2019). Industry 4.0 and lean manufacturing: A systematic literature review and future research directions. *Journal of Manufacturing Technology Management, 32*(3), 543–569. doi:10.1108/JMTM-12-2018-0446

Pantelidis, I. (2019). Digital human resource management. In M. J. Boella & S. Goss-Turner (Eds.), *Human Resource Management in the Hospitality Industry: A Guide to Best Practice.* Routledge. doi:10.4324/9780429441400-21

Parast, M. M., & Subramanian, N. (2021). An examination of the effect of supply chain disruption risk drivers on organizational performance: Evidence from Chinese supply chains. *Supply Chain Management, 26*(4), 548–562. doi:10.1108/SCM-07-2020-0313

Parikh, M. (2001). Knowledge Management Framework for High –tech Research and Development. *Engineering Management Journal, 13*(3), 27–34.

Parry, E. (2011). An examination of e-HRM as a means to increase the value of the HR function. *International Journal of Human Resource Management, 22*(5), 1146–1162. doi:10.1080/09585192.2011.556791

Parsers. (2019). *Big Data and Machine Learning in HR: 5 examples of successful use of information technologies for human resource management.* https://parsers.me/big-data-and-machine-learning-in-hr-5-examples-of-successful-use-of-information-technologies-for-human-resource-management/

Paschek, D., Mocan, A., & Draghici, A. (2019). Industry 5.0: The expected impact of next industrial revolution. In *Proceedings of the MakeLearn and TIIM International Conference* (pp.15–17). Bangkok: ToKnowPress.

Patrucco, A., Moretto, A., Trabucchi, D., & Golini, R. (2021). How Do Industry 4.0 Technologies Boost Collaborations in Buyer-Supplier Relationships? In assessing Industry 4.0 technologies, this study found that buyer-supplier visibility and buyer-supplier integration matters more than the digital technologies used. *Research Technology Management*, *65*(1), 48–58. doi:10.1080/08956308.2021.1999131

Paul, S. K., Moktadir, M. A., & Ahsan, K. (2021). Key supply chain strategies for the post-COVID-19 era: Implications for resilience and sustainability. *International Journal of Logistics Management*. Advance online publication. doi:10.1108/IJLM-04-2021-0238

Păunescu, C., & Mátyus, E. (2020). Resilience measures to dealing with the COVID-19 pandemic Evidence from Romanian micro and small enterprises. Management & Marketing. *Challenges for the Knowledge Society*, *15*(s1), 439–457. doi:10.2478/mmcks-2020-0026

Peraković, D., Periša, M., Cvitić, I., & Zorić, P. (2020). Information and communication technologies for the Society 5.0 environment. In *Proceedings of the XXXVIII Simpozijum o Novim Tehnologijama u Poštanskom i Telekomunikacionom Saobraćaju* (pp. 203-212). Belgrade: University of Belgrade. 10.37528/FTTE/9788673954318/POSTEL.2020.020

Perkin, N., & Abraham, P. (2017). *Building the Agile Business through Digital Transformation*. Kogan Page.

Perona, M. (2002). A New Customer-Oriented Methodology to Evaluate Supply Chain Lost Sales Costs Due to Stockout in Consumer Goods Sectors. In S. Seuring & M. Goldbach (Eds.), *Cost Management in Supply Chains* (pp. 289–307). Springer. doi:10.1007/978-3-662-11377-6_17

Perrott, B. E. (2007). A strategic risk approach to knowledge management. *Business Horizons*, *50*(6), 523–533.

Petersen, K. J., Ragatz, G. L., & Monczka, R. M. (2005). An examination of collaborative planning effectiveness and supply chain performance. *The Journal of Supply Chain Management*, *41*(2), 14–25. doi:10.1111/j.1055-6001.2005.04102002.x

Peterson, E. W. F. (2017). The Role of Population in Economic Growth. *SAGE Open*, *7*(October). Advance online publication. doi:10.1177/2158244017736094

Pettit, T. J., Croxton, K. L., & Fiksel, J. (2013). Ensuring Supply Chain Resilience: Development and Implementation of an Assessment Tool. *Journal of Business Logistics*, *34*(1), 46–76. doi:10.1111/jbl.12009

Pettit, T., Croxton, K. L., & Fiskel, J. (2019). The Evolution of Resilience in Supply Chain Management: A Retrospective on Ensuring Supply Chain Resilience. *Journal of Business Logistics*, *40*(1), 56–65. doi:10.1111/jbl.12202

Pinto, J. (2014). *Introdução ao pensamento Lean: A filosofia das organizações vencedoras*. Lidel.

Pinto, J. P. (2020). *A relação entre Lean Manufacturing e Indústria 4.0: Uma revisão sistemática da literatura*. Tese de Doutoramento, Instituto Superior de Economia e Gestão.

Pinto, K. (2007). *Project management Achieving competitive advantage*. Pearson-Prentice Hall.

Piwowar-Sulej, K. (2020). Human resource management in the context of Industry 4.0. *Organization & Management Scientific Quarterly*, *1*(49), 103–113. doi:10.29119/1899-6116.2020.49.7

Podsakoff, P. M., MacKenzie, S. B., Lee, J. Y., & Podsakoff, N. P. (2003). Common method biases in behavioral research: A critical review of the literature and recommended remedies. *The Journal of Applied Psychology*, *88*(5), 879–903. doi:10.1037/0021-9010.88.5.879 PMID:14516251

Ponis, S. T., & Koronis, E. (2012). Supply Chain Resilience: Definition of Concept and Its Formative Elements. *Journal of Applied Business Research, 28*(5), 921–930. doi:10.19030/jabr.v28i5.7234

Ponomarov, S. Y., & Holcomb, M. C. (2009). Understanding the concept of supply chain resilience. *International Journal of Logistics Management, 20*(1), 124–143. doi:10.1108/09574090910954873

Porter, M., & Heppelmann, J. (2014). How smart, connected products are transforming competition. *Harvard Business Review, 92*(11), 64–88.

Prater, E., Frazier, G. V., & Reyes, P. M. (2005). Future impacts of RFID on e-supply chains in grocery retailing. *Supply Chain Management, 10*(2), 134–142. doi:10.1108/13598540510589205

Prause, G. (2015). Sustainable business models and structures for industry 4.0. *Journal of Security and Sustainability Issues, 5*(2), 159–169. doi:10.9770/jssi.2015.5.2(3)

PriceWaterhouse Coopers Report. (2016). *Indústria 4.0: Digitalização como vantagem competitiva no Brasil*. PWC.

Prieto-Sandoval, V., Jaca, C., & Ormazabal, M. (2018). Towards a consensus on the circular economy. *Journal of Cleaner Production, 179*, 605–615. doi:10.1016/j.jclepro.2017.12.224

Prinz, C., Kreggenfeld, N., & Kuhlenkötter, B. (2018). Lean meets Industry 4.0: A practical approach to interlink the method world and cyber-physical world. *Procedia Manufacturing, 23*, 21–26. doi:10.1016/j.promfg.2018.03.155

Project Management Institute. (2004). A Guide to the Project Management Body of Knowledge: PMBOK guide. Project Management Institute.

Prokofyev, K. G., Dmitrieva, O. V., Zmyzgova, T. R., & Polyakova, E. N. (2019, January). Modern engineering education as a key element of russian technological modernization in the context of digital economy. In *International Scientific Conference "Far East Con"(ISCFEC 2018) Advances in Economics, Business and Management Research* (Vol. 47, pp. 652-656). 10.2991/iscfec-18.2019.160

Puhovichova, D., & Jankelova, N. (2020). Changes of human resource management in the context of impact of the fourth industrial revolution. *Industry 4.0, 5*(3), 138-141.

Pukall, T. J., & Calabro, A. (2014). The internationalization of family firms: A critical review and integrative model. *Family Business Review, 27*(2), 103–125. doi:10.1177/0894486513491423

Pustovrh, A., Rangus, K., & Drnovšek, M. (2020). The role of open innovation in developing an entrepreneurial support ecosystem. *Technological Forecasting and Social Change, 152*, 119892. doi:10.1016/j.techfore.2019.119892

Putnam, R. D. (1993). The prosperous community: Social capital and public life. *The American Prospect, 13*, 35–42.

Pu, X., Wang, Z. X., & Chan, F. T. S. (2020). Leveraging Open E-Logistic Standards to Achieve Ambidexterity in Supply Chain. *Journal of Computer Information Systems, 60*(4), 347–358. doi:10.1080/08874417.2018.1488543

PWC. (2016). *So much in store: prospects in the retail and consumer goods sector in ten sub-Saharan countries*. Retrieved on November 8, 2021 from https://www.pwc.co.za/en/assets/pdf/retail-in-africa.pdf

Qiao, P., Lv, M., Zeng, Y. R., & Intensity, D. (2020). Domestic Institutional Environment, and SMEs' OFDI in Emerging Markets. *Management International Review, 60*(6), 939–973. doi:10.100711575-020-00432-9

Qrunfleh, S., & Tarafdar, M. (2013). Lean and agile supply chain strategies and supply chain responsiveness: The role of strategic supplier partnership and postponement. *Supply Chain Management, 18*(6), 571–582. doi:10.1108/SCM-01-2013-0015

Quasim, S., & Agarwal, S. (2015). Consumer Behaviour towards selected FMCG (Fast Moving Consumer Goods in Delhi NCR. *International Journal of Informative and Futuristic Research, 2*(7), 2041–2048.

Queiroz, M., Pereira, S., Telles, R., & Machado, M. (2019). Industry 4.0 and digital supply chain capabilities: A framework for understanding digitalization challenges and opportunities, Benchmarking. *International Journal (Toronto, Ont.), 28*(5), 1761–1782.

Queiroz, M., & Telles, R. (2018). Big data analytics in supply chain and logistics: An empirical approach. *International Journal of Logistics Management, 29*(2), 767–783. doi:10.1108/IJLM-05-2017-0116

Rachinger, M., Rauter, R., Müller, C., Vorraber, W., & Schirgi, E. (2018). Digitalization and its influence on business model innovation. *Journal of Manufacturing Technology Management, 30*(8), 1143–1160. doi:10.1108/JMTM-01-2018-0020

Rae, S. (2016). *Bots in the back office, the coming wave of digital workers*. Retrieved on November 5, 2021 from https://assets.kpmg/content/dam/kpmg/pdf/2016/02/bots-in-the-back-office.pdf

Rahmanzadeh, S., Pishvaee, M. S., & Govindan, K. (2022). Emergence of open supply chain management: The role of open innovation in the future smart industry using digital twin network. *Annals of Operations Research*. Advance online publication. doi:10.100710479-021-04254-2

Rajkumar, R., Lee, I., Sha, L., & Stankovic, J. (2010). Cyber-physical systems: the next computing revolution. In *Proceedings of the 47th Design Automation Conference* (pp.731-736). ACM. 10.1145/1837274.1837461

Ramirez-Peña, M., Mayuet, P. F., Vazquez-Martinez, J., & Batista, M. (2020). Sustainability in the Aerospace, Naval, and Automotive Supply Chain 4.0: Descriptive Review. *Materials (Basel), 13*(24), 5625–5649. doi:10.3390/ma13245625 PMID:33321743

Ramos-Mejía, M., Franco-Garcia, M.-L., & Jauregui-Becker, J. M. (2018). Sustainability transitions in the developing world: Challenges of socio-technical transformations unfolding in contexts of poverty. *Environmental Science & Policy, 84*, 217–223. doi:10.1016/j.envsci.2017.03.010

Ramzi, N., Ahmad, H., & Zakaria, N. (2019). A conceptual model on people approach and smart manufacturing. *International Journal of Supply Chain Management, 8*(4), 1102–1107.

Ravn, R., Halberg, P., Gustafsson, J., & Groes, J. (2016). *Get ready for robots: Why planning makes the difference between success and disappointment*. Retrieved on November 3, 2021 from https://eyfinancialservicesthoughtgallery.ie/wp-content/uploads/2016/11/ey-get-ready-for-robots.pdf

Reis, J. Z., & Gonçalves, R. F. (2018). The Role of Internet of Services (IoS) on Industry 4.0 Through the Service Oriented Architecture (SOA). In Advances in Production Management Systems. Smart Manufacturing for Industry 4.0 (pp.20-26). Academic Press.

Rejeb, A., Rejeb, K., Abdollahi, A., Zailani, S., Iranmanesh, M., & Ghobakhloo, M. (2021). Digitalization in Food Supply Chains: A Bibliometric Review and Key-Route Main Path Analysis. *Sustainability, 14*(1), 83. doi:10.3390u14010083

Remko, V. H. (2020). Research opportunities for a more resilient post-COVID-19 supply chain – closing the gap between research findings and industry practice. *International Journal of Operations & Production Management, 40*(4), 341–355. doi:10.1108/IJOPM-03-2020-0165

Reyes-Gonzalez, L., Gonzalez-Brambila, C. N., & Veloso, F. (2016). Using co-authorship and citation analysis to identify research groups: A new way to assess performance. *Scientometrics, 108*(3), 1171–1191. doi:10.100711192-016-2029-8

Rha, J. S. (2020). Trends of Research on Supply Chain Resilience: A Systematic Review Using Network Analysis. *Sustainability, 12*(4343), 1–27. doi:10.3390u12114343

Ribeiro, R. B., De Souza, J., Beluco, A., Biehl, L. V., Medeiros, J. L. B., Sporket, F., Rossini, E. G., & Amaral, F. A. D. (2019). Application of the single-minute exchange of die system to the CNC sector of a shoe mold company. *Cogent Engineering*, *6*(1), 1606376. doi:10.1080/23311916.2019.1606376

Rice, J., & Caniato, F. (2003). Building a secure and resilient supply chain network. *Supply Chain Management Review*, *7*(5), 22–30.

Richey, R. G. Jr, Roath, A. S., Whipple, J. M., & Fawcett, S. E. (2010). Exploring Governance Theory of Supply Chain Integration: Barriers and Facilitators to Integration. *Journal of Business Logistics*, *31*(1), 237–256. doi:10.1002/j.2158-1592.2010.tb00137.x

Rocha, C., Quandt, C., Deschamps, F., Philbin, S., & Cruzara, G. (2021). Collaborations for Digital Transformation: Case Studies of Industry 4.0 in Brazil. *IEEE-TEM*, 1-15.

Rocha, C., Quandt, C., Deschamps, F., & Philbin, S. (2022). R&D Collaboration Strategies for industry 4.0 implementation: A case study in Brazil. *Journal of Engineering and Technology Management*, *63*, 101675. doi:10.1016/j.jengtecman.2022.101675

Rodriguez, E., & Edwards, J. S. (2008). Before and after modelling: Risk knowledge management is required. *Enterprise Risk Management Symposium Society of Actuaries,* 1-23.

Rodriguez, J. L., & Rodriguez, R. M. (2005). Technology and export behaviour: A resource-based view approach. *International Business Review*, *14*(5), 539–557. doi:10.1016/j.ibusrev.2005.07.002

Rodriguez-Montes, A., & Edwards, J. (2008). Before and after modeling: Risk knowledge management is required. Proceedings of 6th Annual Premier Global Event on ERM.

Rogers, D. (2016). *The Digital Transformation Playbook: Rethink Your Business for the Digital Age*. Columbia Business School Publishing. doi:10.7312/roge17544

Romer, P. (1986). Increasing Returns and Long-Run Growth. *Journal of Political Economy*, *94*(5), 1002–1037. doi:10.1086/261420

Romer, P. (1987). Growth Based on Increasing Returns Due to Specialization. *The American Economic Review*, *77*(2), 56–62.

Romer, P. (1990). Endogenous technological change. *Journal of Political Economy*, *98*(5), 71–101. doi:10.1086/261725

Rong, K., Guangyu, H., Lin, Y., Shi, Y., & Guo, L. (2015). Understanding business ecosystem using a 6C framework in Internet-of-Things-based sectors. *International Journal of Production Economics*, *159*, 41–55. doi:10.1016/j.ijpe.2014.09.003

Rosemann, M., Becker, J., & Chasin, F. (2021). City 5.0. *Business & Information Systems Engineering*, *63*(1), 71–77. doi:10.100712599-020-00674-9

Rosin, F., Forget, P., Lamouri, S., & Pellerin, R. (2019). Impacts of Industry 4.0 technologies on Lean principles. *International Journal of Production Research*, *58*(6), 1644–1661. doi:10.1080/00207543.2019.1672902

Roy, G. (2004). A risk management framework for software engineering practice. In *Australian Software Engineering Conference, (ASWEC'04)* (pp. 60-69). Australian Software Engineering Conference.

Rusli, K. A., Rahman, A. A., Ho, J. A., & Abdullah, R. (2013). How green is your supply chain? Evidence from ISO 14001 certified manufacturers in Malaysia. *Pertanika Journal of Social Science & Humanities*, *21*, 213–230.

Russell, C., & Bennett, N. (2015). Big data and talent management: Using hard data to make the soft stuff easy. *Business Horizons*, *58*(3), 237–242. doi:10.1016/j.bushor.2014.08.001

Russom, P. (2011). *Big Data Analytics*. TDWI.

Ryan, P., Buciuni, G., Giblin, M., & Andersson, U. (2022). Global Value Chain Governance in the MNE: A Dynamic Hierarchy Perspective. *California Management Review*, *64*(2), 97–118. Advance online publication. doi:10.1177/00081256211068544

Saarikko, T., Westergren, U., & Blomquist, T. (2020). Digital transformation: Five recommendations for the digitally conscious firm. *Business Horizons*, *63*(6), 825–839. doi:10.1016/j.bushor.2020.07.005

Saberi, S., Kouhizadeh, M., Sarkis, J., & Shen, L. (2019). Blockchain technology and its relationships to sustainable supply chain management. *International Journal of Production Research*, *57*(7), 2117–2135. doi:10.1080/00207543.2018.1533261

Sachdev, S. B., & Verma, H. V. (2004). Relative importance of service quality dimensions: A multisectoral study. *Journal of Services Research*, *4*(1), 1–24.

Saldaña, J. (2013). *The Coding Manual for Qualitative Researchers*. Sage.

Saldana, J. (2015). *The coding manual for qualitative researchers*. Sage Publications Ltd.

Salimi, M. (2015). *WORK 4.0: An Enormous Potential for Economic Growth in Germany*. http://englishbulletin.adapt.it/wp-content/uploads/2015/12/work4.0_sam.pdf

Sanders, A., Elangeswaran, C., & Wulfsberg, J. P. (2016). Industry 4.0 implies lean manufacturing: Research activities in industry 4.0 function as enablers for lean manufacturing. *Journal of Industrial Engineering and Management*, *9*(3), 811–833. doi:10.3926/jiem.1940

Santos, F., Pereira, R., & Vasconcelos, J. B. (2019). Toward robotic process automation implementation: An end-to-end perspective. *Business Process Management Journal*, *26*(2), 405–420. doi:10.1108/BPMJ-12-2018-0380

Sarkis, J. (2021). Supply chain sustainability: Learning from the COVID-19 pandemic. *International Journal of Operations & Production Management*, *41*(1), 63–73. doi:10.1108/IJOPM-08-2020-0568

Sato, Y., Tse, Y. K., & Tan, K. H. (2020). Managers' risk perception of supply chain uncertainties. *Industrial Management & Data Systems*, *120*(9), 1617–1634. doi:10.1108/IMDS-01-2020-0049

Saunders, M., Lewis, P., & Thornhill, A. (2012). Research Methods for Business Students (6th ed.). Pearson.

Savic, D. (2019). From digitization, through digitalization, to digital transformation. *Online Searcher*, *43*(1), 36–39.

Sawangwong, A., & Chaopaisarn, P. (2021). The impact of applying knowledge in the technological pillars of Industry 4.0 on supply chain performance. *Kybernetes*. Advance online publication. doi:10.1108/K-07-2021-0555

Sayar, K. (2016). Dijital toplum. *TRTakademi.*, *1*(2), 762–775.

Scarbrough, H., Swan, J., & Preston, J. (1999). *Knowledge management A literature review*. Institute of Personnel and Development.

Schaeffer, E. (2017). *Industry X. 0: Realizing digital value in industrial sectors*. Kogan Page Publishers.

Schallmo, D., Herbort, V., & Doleski, O. (2017). Die digitale transformation von Geschäftsmodellen gestalten. In *Roadmap Utility 4.0. essentials* (pp. 31–32). Springer Vieweg. doi:10.1007/978-3-658-17655-6_4

Schatteman, O., Woodhouse, D., & Terino, J. (2020). *Supply chain lessons from COVID-19: Time to refocus on resilience.* Retrieved on November 7, 2021 from https://www.bain.com/contentassets/d6b7a373b2b242d2be114cb46345fce2/bain-brief-supply-chain-lessons-from-covid-19.pdf

Schawbel, D. (2012). *Millennials vs. Baby boomers: Who would you rather hire?* Retrieved on October 7, 2021 from https://business.time.com/2012/03/29/millennials-vs-baby-boomers-who-would-you-rather-hire/

Schiavo-Campo, S., & Sundaram, P. (2000). *To Serve and to Preserve: Improving Public Administration in a Competitive World.* Asian Development Bank.

Schiavone, F., & Sprenger, S. (2017). Operations management and digital technologies. *Production Planning and Control, 28*(16), 1281–1283. doi:10.1080/09537287.2017.1375151

Schmidt, R., Möhring, M., Härting, R., Reichstein, C., Neumaier, P., & Jozinovic, P. (2015). Industry 4.0- potentials for creating smart products: empirical research results. In W. Abramowicz (Ed.), *Proceedings of International Conference on Business Information Systems* (pp.16-27). Springer. 10.1007/978-3-319-19027-3_2

Schneider, P. (2018). Managerial challenges of Industry 4.0: An empirically backed research agenda for a nascent field. *Review of Managerial Science, 12*(3), 803–848. doi:10.100711846-018-0283-2

Schniederjans, D. G., Curado, C., & Khalajhedayati, M. (2020). Supply chain digitisation trends: An integration of knowledge management. *International Journal of Production Economics, 220,* 107439. doi:10.1016/j.ijpe.2019.07.012

Scholten, K., & Schilder, S. (2015). The role of Collaboration in supply chain resilience. *Supply Chain Management, 20*(4), 471–484. doi:10.1108/SCM-11-2014-0386

Scholten, K., Sharkey, P., & Fynes, S. F. (2014). Mitigation Processes – antecedents for building supply chain resilience. *Supply Chain Management, 19*(2), 211–228. doi:10.1108/SCM-06-2013-0191

Schroth, H. (2019). Are You Ready for Gen Z in the Workplace? *California Management Review, 61*(3), 5–18. doi:10.1177/0008125619841006

Schultze, U. (1998). Investigating the contradictions in knowledge management. *nternational. Journal of Computational Science,* 155–174.

Schumacher, A., Erol, S., & Sihn, W. (2016). A maturity model for assessing Industry 4.0 readiness and maturity of manufacturing enterprises. *Procedia CIRP, 52,* 161–166. doi:10.1016/j.procir.2016.07.040

Schwab, K. (2017). *The fourth industrial revolution.* Geneva: World Economic Forum.

Schwab, K. (2017). *The Fourth Industrial Revolution.* Crown Publishing Group.

Schwalbe, K. (2007). Information Technology Project Management (5th ed.). Course Technology Thomson Learning.

Sedera, D., Lokuge, S., Grover, V., Sarker, S., & Sarker, S. (2016). Innovating with enterprise systems and digital platforms: A contingent resource-based theory view. *Information & Management, 53*(3), 366–379. doi:10.1016/j.im.2016.01.001

Selvakumar, M., Jansirani, M. M., & Jegatheesan, K. (2013). *Fast-Moving Consumer Goods: A Bright Future in India.* Retrieved on November 7, 2021 from http://ffymag.com/admin/issuepdf/FMCG_FFYFeb13.pdf

Seuring, S. (2008). Assessing the rigor of case study research in supply chain management. *Supply Chain Management, 13*(2), 128–137. doi:10.1108/13598540810860967

Shaba, E., Guerci, M., Gilardi, S., & Bartezzaghi, E. (2019). Industry 4.0 technologies and organizational design - Evidence from 15 Italian cases. *Studi Organizzativi., 1*(1), 9–37. doi:10.3280/SO2019-001001

Shahbazi, Z., & Byun, Y. C. (2021). A procedure for tracing supply chains for perishable food based on Blockchain, Machine Learning and Fuzzy Logic. *Electronics (Basel)*, *10*(1), 41. doi:10.3390/electronics10010041

Shamim, S., Cang, S., Yu, H., & Li, Y. (2016). Management approaches for Industry 4.0: A human resource management perspective. In *2016 IEEE Congress on Evolutionary Computation* (pp. 5309-5316). IEEE 10.1109/CEC.2016.7748365

Shani, N., Divyapriya, P., & Logeshwari, K. (2011). Human Resource Philosophy. *International Journal of Management*, *2*(1), 61–68.

Shashi, C. P., Cerchione, R., & Ertz, M. (2020). Agile supply chain management: Where did it come from and where will it go in the era of digital transformation? *Industrial Marketing Management*, *90*, 324–345. doi:10.1016/j.indmarman.2020.07.011

Shashlo, N. V., Petruk, G. V., & Korostelev, A. A. (2018). Determinants of integration interaction among the subjects of the entrepreneurial innovation ecosystem of macro region. *Amazonia Investiga*, *7*(13), 351–363.

Shaw, J. (2005). Managing All your Enterprise's Risk. *Risk Management*, *52*(9), 22–30.

Shaw, P., & Varghese, R. M. (2018). Industry 4.0 and the future of HR. *Journal of Management*, *5*(6), 96–103.

Shcherbakov, V., & Silkina, G. (2021). Supply Chain Management Open Innovation: Virtual Integration in the Network Logistics System. *Journal of Open Innovation*, *7*(1), 54. doi:10.3390/joitmc7010054

Shen, Z. M., & Sun, Y. (2021). Strengthening supply chain resilience during COVID-19: A case study of JD. Com. *Journal of Operations Management*, joom.1161. Advance online publication. doi:10.1002/joom.1161

Shewhart, W. A. (1931/1980). *Economic control of quality of manufactured product*. American Society for Quality.

Shingo, S. (1985). *A revolution in manufacturing: The SMED system*. Productivity Press.

Shishido, T. (2021). *Nippon kigyō niokeru dejitaru SCM no hōkōsei ishi kettei no shitsu to supi-do o kōjōsaseru dejitaru tekunoroji- no katsuyōhō to wa* [The Direction of digital SCM in Japanese companies- how to use digital technology to improve the quality and speed of decision-making]. Qunie Corp. Retrieved on December 05, 2021, from https://www.qunie.com/quriosity/210304_00

Siderska, J. (2020). Robotic Process Automation — A driver of digital transformation? *Engineering Management in Production and Services, 12*(2), 21-31. doi:10.2478/emj-2020-0009

Siderska, J. (2021). The adoption of robotic process automation technology to ensure business process during the Covid-19 pandemic. *Sustainability*, *13*(14), 8020. doi:10.3390u13148020

Silin, Y. P., & Animitsa, Y. G. (2018). Contours of the Digital Economy in Russia. *Journal of New Economy*, *19*(3), 18–25.

Silkina, G. (2019). From analogue to digital tools of business control: Succession and transformation. *IOP Conf. Ser. Mater. Sci. Eng.*, *497*, 012018.

Silva, E. B., Scoton, M. L. R. P. D., Dias, E. M., & Pereira, S. L. (2018). *Automação & Sociedade: Quarta Revolução Industrial, um olhar para o Brasil*. Brasport.

Simatupang, T. M., & Sridharan, R. (2002). The collaborative supply chain. *International Journal of Logistics Management*, *13*(1), 15–30. doi:10.1108/09574090210806333

Simunkova, K. (2019). Being hybrid: A conceptual update of consumer self and consumption due to online/offline hybridity. *Journal of Marketing Management*, *35*(1-2), 40–74. doi:10.1080/0267257X.2019.1573844

Singh, J. (2014). FMCG (Fast Moving Consumer Goods) An Overview. *International Journal of Enhanced Research in Management and Computer Applications*, *3*(6), 14–16.

Singh, R. K., & Acharya, P. (2014). Identification and Evaluation of Supply Chain Flexibilities in Indian FMCG Sector Using DEMATEL. *Global Journal of Flexible Systems Managment*, *15*(2), 91–100. doi:10.100740171-013-0050-9

Singh, S. K., Chen, J., Del Giudice, M., & El-Kassar, A. N. (2019). Environmental ethics, environmental performance, and competitive advantage: Role of environmental training. *Technological Forecasting and Social Change*, *146*, 203–211. doi:10.1016/j.techfore.2019.05.032

Sivathanu, B., & Pillai, R. (2018). Smart HR 4.0 – how industry 4.0 is disrupting HR. *Human Resource Management International Digest*, *26*(4), 7–11. doi:10.1108/HRMID-04-2018-0059

Slaby, J. R. (2012). *Robotic automation emeges as a threat to traditional low-cost outsourcing*. Retrieved on September 30, 2021 from www.hfsresearch.com

Smith, M. (2016). *Collaboration for Resilience*. Retrieved on November 5, 2021 from https://portals.iucn.org/library/sites/library/files/documents/2016-047.pdf

Smolentseva, A. (2017). Where Soviet and neoliberal discourses meet: The transformation of the purposes of higher education in Soviet and post-Soviet Russia. *Higher Education*, *74*(6), 1091–1108. doi:10.100710734-017-0111-7

Solaimani, S., & van der Veen, J. (2021). Open supply chain innovation: An extended view on supply chain collaboration. *Supply Chain Management*. Advance online publication. doi:10.1108/SCM-09-2020-0433

Soliman, F., & Youssef, M. A. (2003). Internet-based e-commerce and its impact on manufacturing and business operations. *Industrial Management & Data Systems*, *103*(8), 546–552. doi:10.1108/02635570310497594

Sommerville, I. (2006). Software Engineering (8th ed.). Addison-Wesley.

Soni, U., & Jain, V. (2011). *Minimising the vulnerabilities of supply chain: A new framework for enhancing the resilience.* Paper presented at Industrial Engineering and Engineering Management (IEEM), 2011 IEEE International Conference, Singapore.

Sony, M., & Naik, S. (2020). Critical factors for the successful implementation of Industry 4.0: A review and future research direction. *Production Planning and Control*, *31*(10), 799–815. doi:10.1080/09537287.2019.1691278

Soosay, C. A., & Hyland, P. (2015). A decade of supply chain collaboration and directions for future research. *Supply Chain Management*, *20*(6), 613–630. doi:10.1108/SCM-06-2015-0217

Sousa, R. (2003). Linking quality management to manufacturing strategy: An empirical investigation of customer focus practices. *Journal of Operations Management*, *21*(1), 1–18. doi:10.1016/S0272-6963(02)00055-4

Srai, J. S., Kumar, M., Graham, G., Phillips, W., Tooze, J., Ford, S., Beecher, P., Raj, B., Gregory, M., Tiwari, M. K., Ravi, B., Neely, A., Shankar, R., Charnley, F., & Tiwari, M. K. (2016). Distributed manufacturing: Scope, challenges and opportunities. *International Journal of Production Research*, *54*(23), 6917–6935. doi:10.1080/00207543.2016.1192302

Sredojević, D., Cvetanović, S., & Bošković, G. (2016). Technological changes in economic growth theory: neoclassical, endogenous, and evolutionary-institutional approach. *Economic Themes*, *54*(2), 177–194. doi:10.1515/ethemes-2016-0009

Sridharan, R., & Simatupang, T. M. (2013). Power and trust in supply chain collaboration. *International Journal of Value Chain Management*, *7*(1), 76–96. doi:10.1504/IJVCM.2013.057344

Srinivasu, R. (2014). Fast Moving Consumer Goods Retail Market, Growth Prospect, Market Overview and Food Inflation in Indian Market – An Overview. *International Journal of Innovative Research in Science, Engineering and Technology*, *3*(1), 8422–8430.

Srivastava, S. K., Chaudhuri, A., & Srivastava, R. K. (2015). Propagation of risks and their impact on performance in fresh food retail. *International Journal of Logistics Management*, *26*(3), 568–602. doi:10.1108/IJLM-02-2014-0032

Stephan, M., Uzawa, S., Volini, E., Walsh, B., & Yoshida, R. (2016). *Digital HR revolution, not evolution.* Retrieved on October 15, 2021 from https://www2.deloitte.com/insights/us/en/focus/human- capital-trends/2016/digital-hr-technology-for-hr-teams-services.html

Stephen, M. (2016). Digital HR: Revolution, not evolution. In global human capital trends 2016. *The new organization: Different by design.* Retrieved on October 15, 2021 from https://www2.deloitte.com/content/dam/Deloitte/global/Documents/HumanCapital/gx

Stollberg, M., Zhdanova, V., & Fensel, D. (2004). H-TechSight-A Next Generation Knowledge Management Platform. *Journal of Information and Knowledge management, 3*(1), 47-66.

Stolterman, E., & Fors, A. C. (2004). *Information Technology and the Good Life.* Retrieved on December 08, 2021, from https://www8.informatik.umu.se/~acroon/Publikationer%20Anna/Stolterman.pdf

Stoltz, M. (2018). *Theft on the move: how to safeguard goods and personnel in transit.* Retrieved on August 27, 2020 from https://www.bizcommunity.com/SendToFriend.aspx?l=196&c=746&ct=1&ci=176872

Stone, J., & Rahimifard, S. (2018). Resilience in agri-food supply chains: A critical analysis of the literature and synthesis of a novel framework. *Supply Chain Management*, *23*(3), 207–238. doi:10.1108/SCM-06-2017-0201

Stratigea, A. (2012). The concept of 'smart cities'. Towards community development? *NETCOM*, *26*(3/4), 375–388. doi:10.4000/netcom.1105

Straube, F., & Nitsche, B. (2020). Heading into "The New Normal". *Internationales Verkehrswesen*, *72*(3), 31.

Strohmeier, S. (2007). Research in e-HRM: Review and implications. *Human Resource Management Review*, *17*(1), 19–37. doi:10.1016/j.hrmr.2006.11.002

Strohmeier, S. (2018). Smart HRM – a Delphi study on the application and consequences of the Internet of Things in Human Resource Management. *International Journal of Human Resource Management*, *31*(18), 2289–2318. doi:10.1080/09585192.2018.1443963

Strohmeier, S. (2020). Digital human resource management: A conceptual clarification. *German Journal of Human Resource Management*, *34*(3), 345–365. doi:10.1177/2397002220921131

Strohmeier, S., & Parry, E. (2014). HRM in the digital age digital challenges of the HR profession. *Employee Relations*, *36*(4). Advance online publication. doi:10.1108/ER-03-2014-0032

Stuart, I., McCutcheon, D., Handfield, R., McLachlin, R., & Samson, D. (2002). Effective case research in operations management: A process perspective. *Journal of Operations Management*, *20*(5), 419–433. doi:10.1016/S0272-6963(02)00022-0

Sukhova, M. (2016). *Digital transformation: History, present, and future trends*. Retrieved on November 11, 2021 from https://auriga.com/blog/2016/digital-transformation-history-present-and-future-trends/

Sullivan, M., Simpson, W., & Li, W. (2021). The Role of Robotic Process Automation (RPA) in Logistics. In M. Sullivan & J. Kern (Eds.), *The Digital Transformation of Logistics* (pp. 61–78). Wiley. doi:10.1002/9781119646495.ch5

Sun, Z., & Gang, G. (2006). *HSM: A Hierarchical Spiral Model for Knowledge Management.* The 2nd International Conference on Information Management and Business, Sydney, Australia.

Sunassee, N., & Sewry, A. (2002). A Theoretical Framework for Knowledge Management Implementation. In *The 2002 annual research conference of the South African institute of computer scientists and information technologists on Enablement through technology* (pp. 235-245). South African Institute for Computer Scientists and Information Technologists.

Sundram, V. P. K., Bahrin, A. S., Munir, Z. B. A., & Zolait, A. H. (2018). The effect of supply chain information management and information system infrastructure The mediating role of supply chain integration towards manufacturing performance in Malaysia. *Journal of Enterprise Information Management*, *31*(5), 751–770. doi:10.1108/JEIM-06-2017-0084

Sun, S., Zheng, X., Gong, B., García Paredes, J., & Ordieres-Meré, J. (2020). Healthy Operator 4.0: A Human Cyber-Physical System Architecture for Smart Workplaces. *Sensors (Basel)*, *20*(7), 2011. doi:10.339020072011 PMID:32260123

Sun, Z. (2004). A waterfall model for knowledge management and experience management. In *4th International Conference on Hybrid Intelligent Systems* (pp. 472-475). IEEE.

Sutduean, J., Harakan, A., & Jermsittiparsert, K. (2019). Exploring the Relationship between Supply Chain Integration, Product Innovation, Supply Chain Performance and Firm Performance: Does Supply Chain Information Strategy Matter? *International Journal of Innovation, Creativity and Change*, *5*(2), 175–192.

Swaminathan, J. M., & Tayur, S. R. (2003). Models for supply chains in e-business. *Management Science*, *49*(10), 1387–1406. doi:10.1287/mnsc.49.10.1387.17309

Swanson, D., Goel, L., Francisco, K., & Stock, J. (2018). An analysis of supply chain management research by topic. *Supply Chain Management*, *23*(2), 100–116. doi:10.1108/SCM-05-2017-0166

Syed, R., Suriadi, S., Adams, M., Bandara, W., Leemans, S. J. J., Ouyang, C., ter Hofstede, A. H. M., van de Weerd, I., Wynn, M. T., & Reijers, H. A. (2020). Robotic Process Automation: Contemporary themes and challenges. *Computers in Industry*, *115*, 103162. doi:10.1016/j.compind.2019.103162

Szymczak, M. (2019). Digital Smart Logistics. Managing Supply Chain 4.0: Concepts, Components and Strategic Perspective. In Z. Bekirogullari (Ed.), *The European Proceedings of Social & Behavioural Sciences* (pp. 357–368). Future Academy. doi:10.15405/epsbs.2019.10.02.33

Tan, W. J., Zhang, A. N., & Cai, W. (2019). A graph-based model to measure structural redundancy for supply chain resilience. *International Journal of Production Research*, *57*(20), 6385–6404. doi:10.1080/00207543.2019.1566666

Tao, F., Qi, Q., Liu, A., & Kusiak, A. (2018). Data-driven smart manufacturing. *Journal of Manufacturing Systems*, *48*, 157–169. doi:10.1016/j.jmsy.2018.01.006

Tao, F., Zuo, Y., Xu, L. D., & Zhang, L. (2014). IoT-Based intelligent perception and access of manufacturing resource toward cloud manufacturing. *IEEE Transactions on Industrial Informatics*, *10*(2), 1547–1557. doi:10.1109/TII.2014.2306397

Tarafdar, M., & Qrunfleh, S. (2017). Agile supply chain strategy and supply chain performance: Complementary roles of supply chain practices and information systems capability for agility. *International Journal of Production Research*, *55*(4), 925–938. doi:10.1080/00207543.2016.1203079

Tarakanov, V. V., Inshakova, A. O., & Dolinskaya, V. V. (2019). Information society, digital economy and law. In *Ubiquitous Computing and the Internet of Things: Prerequisites for the Development of ICT* (pp. 3–15). Springer.

Tarasova, A. N. (2019). Pitfalls and drawbacks in engineering education in Russia. *Journal of Applied Engineering Science, 17*(1).

Taylor, M. J., McNicholas, C., Nicolay, C., Darzi, A., Bell, D., & Reed, J. E. (2014). Systematic review of the application of the plan–do–study–act method to improve quality in healthcare. *BMJ Quality & Safety*, *23*(4), 290–298. doi:10.1136/bmjqs-2013-001862 PMID:24025320

Teece, D. (2018). Profiting from innovation in the digital economy: Standards, complementary assets, and business models in the wireless world. *Research Policy*. Advance online publication. doi:10.1016/j.respol.2017.01.015

Teece, D. J. (2014). The foundations of enterprise performance: Dynamic and ordinary capabilities in an (economic) theory of firms. *The Academy of Management Perspectives*, *28*(4), 328–352. doi:10.5465/amp.2013.0116

Tepe, S. (2020). The impact of Industry 4.0 on occupational health and safety. *International Journal of Advances in Engineering and Pure Sciences*, *33*(1), 122–130. doi:10.7240/jeps.777641

Tesch, D., Kloppenborg, T., & Frolick, M. (2007). IT Project Risk Factors: The Project Management Professionals Perspective. *Journal of Computer Information Systems*, *47*(4), 61–69.

Thekkoote, R. (2021). Understanding big data-driven supply chain and performance measures for customer satisfaction. *Benchmarking*. Advance online publication. doi:10.1108/BIJ-01-2021-0034

Thite, M. (2019). Electronic/digital HRM: A primer. In e-HRM: Digital approaches, directions & applications. Routledge.

Thite, M., Kavanagh, M. J., & Johnson, R. D. (2012). Evolution of human resource management & human resource information systems: The role of information technology. In M. J. Kavanagh, M. Thite, & R. D. Johnson (Eds.), *Human Resource Information Systems: Basics, Applications & Directions* (pp. 2–34). Sage.

Thomas, G. (2020). Digital Maturity of HR in SMEs. *European Journal of Economics and Business Studies*, *6*(1), 56–62. doi:10.26417/ejes.v6i1.p56-62

Thomas, S., Kureshi, S., Suggala, S., & Mendonca, V. (2020). HRM 4.0 and the Shifting Landscape of Employer Branding. In P. Kumar, A. Agrawal, & P. Budhwar (Eds.), *Human & Technological Resource Management: New Insights into Revolution 4.0* (pp. 37–51). Emerald. doi:10.1108/978-1-83867-223-220201003

Thomson, G., & Newman, P. (2018). Urban fabrics and urban metabolism – from sustainable to regenerative cities. *Resources, Conservation and Recycling*, *132*, 218–229. doi:10.1016/j.resconrec.2017.01.010

Thukral, E. (2021). COVID-19: Small and medium enterprises challenges and responses with creativity, innovation, and entrepreneurship. *Strategic Change*, *30*(2), 153–158. doi:10.1002/jsc.2399

Tietze, F., Vimalnath, P., Aristodemou, L., & Molloy, J. (2020). Crisis-critical intellectual property: Findings from the COVID-19 pandemic. *IEEE Transactions on Engineering Management*. Advance online publication. doi:10.1109/TEM.2020.2996982

Tilson, D., Lyytinen, K., & Sorensen, C. (2010). Digital infrastructures: The missing IS research agenda. *Information Systems Research*, *21*(4), 748–759. doi:10.1287/isre.1100.0318

Todorov, Kalinina, & Rybakova. (2018). Impact of labour migration on entrepreneurship ecosystem: case of Eurasian Economic Union. *Entrepreneurship and Sustainability Issues, Entrepreneurship and Sustainability Center, 5*(4), 992 - 1007. doi:10.9770/jesi.2018.5.4(20)

Todorovic, V., Maslaric, M., Bojic, S., Jokic, M., Mircetic, D., & Nikolicic, S. (2018). Solutions for More Sustainable Distribution in the Short Food Supply Chains. *Sustainability*, *10*(10), 3481. doi:10.3390u10103481

Tohidinia, Z., & Mosakhani, M. (2010, April). Knowledge sharing behaviour and its predictors. *Industrial Management & Data Systems*, *110*(4), 611–631.

Tolstykh, T., Gamidullaeva, L., & Shmeleva, N. (2020). Elaboration of a mechanism for sustainable enterprise development in innovation ecosystems. *Journal of Open Innovation*, *6*(4), 95. doi:10.3390/joitmc6040095

Tolstykh, T., Gamidullaeva, L., Shmeleva, N., & Lapygin, Y. (2020). Regional Development in Russia: An Ecosystem Approach to Territorial Sustainability Assessment. *Sustainability*, *12*(16), 6424. doi:10.3390u12166424

Tortorella, G. L., Narayanamurthy, G., & Thurer, M. (2021). Identifying pathways to a high-performing lean automation implementation: An empirical study in the manufacturing industry. *International Journal of Production Economics*, *231*, 1–13. doi:10.1016/j.ijpe.2020.107918

Trabucco, M., & de Giovanni, P. (2021). Achieving Resilience and Business Sustainability during COVID-19: The Role of Lean Supply Chain Practices and Digitalization. *Sustainability*, *13*(22), 12369. doi:10.3390u132212369

Tracey, J. (2014). A review of human resources management research: The past 10 years and implications for moving forward. *International Journal of Contemporary Hospitality Management*, *26*(5), 679–705. doi:10.1108/IJCHM-02-2014-0056

Trantopoulos, K., Von Krogh, G., Wallin, M., & Woerter, M. (2017). External knowledge and information technology: Implications for process innovation performance. *MIS Q. Manag. Inf. Syst.*, *41*(1), 287–300. doi:10.25300/MISQ/2017/41.1.15

Truman, E., & Baroudi, J. (1994). Gender differences in the information systems managerial ranks: An assessment of discriminatory practices. *Management Information Systems Quarterly*, *18*(2), 129–141.

Tse, Y. K., Zhang, M., Zeng, W., & Ma, J. (2021). Perception of supply chain quality risk: Understanding the moderation role of supply market thinness. *Journal of Business Research*, *122*, 822–834. doi:10.1016/j.jbusres.2020.07.003

Tuan, N. H., Mohammadi, H., & Rezapour, S. (2020). A mathematical model for COVID-19 transmission by using the Caputo fractional derivative. *Chaos, Solitons, and Fractals*, *140*, 110107. doi:10.1016/j.chaos.2020.110107 PMID:33519107

Tvenge, N., & Martinsen, K. (2018). Integration of digital learning in industry 4.0. *Procedia Manufacturing*, *23*, 261–266. doi:10.1016/j.promfg.2018.04.027

Udovita, P. (2020). Conceptual review on dimensions of digital transformation in modern era. *International Journal of Scientific and Research Publications*, *10*(2), 520–529. doi:10.29322/IJSRP.10.02.2020.p9873

UK Government Commercial Function. (2020). *The Social Value Model Edition 1.1.* Retrieved on November 1, 2021 from https://assets.publishing.service.gov.uk/government/uploads/system/uploads/attachment_data/file/940826/Social-Value-Model-Edn-1.1-3-Dec-20.pdf

Ulrich, D. (1998). A new mandate for Human Resources. *Harvard Business Review*, *76*(1), 124–135. PMID:10176915

Umar, M., Khan, S. A. R., Yusoff Yusliza, M., Ali, S., & Yu, Z. (2021). Industry 4.0 and green supply chain practices: An empirical study. *International Journal of Productivity and Performance Management*. Advance online publication. doi:10.1108/IJPPM-12-2020-0633

United Nations Habitat III. (2016). *New Urban Agenda Draft Outcome Document for Adoption in Quito.* Retrieved on October 6, 2021 from https://habitat3.org/the-new-urban-agenda/

Unruh, G., & Kiron, D. (2017). *Digital transformation on purpose*. Retrieved on November 2, 2021 from https://sloanreview.mit.edu/article/digital-transformation-on-purpose

Unruh, G., & Kiron, D. (2017). Digital transformation on purpose. *MIT Sloan Management Review*, *6*. Retrieved December 08, 2021, from https://sloanreview.mit.edu/article/digital-transformation-on-purpose/

Vaishnani, H. B. (2011). *Effects of Sales Promotions on Consumer Preferences and Brand Equity Perception* (PhD thesis). Saurashtra University. Retrieved on November 8, 2021 from https://etheses.saurashtrauniversity.edu/63/

Valamis. (2019). *What Is Organizational Learning and Why it's Important?* https://www.valamis.com/hub/organizational-learning

van der Aalst, W. M. P., Bichler, M., & Heinzl, A. (2018). Robotic Process Automation. *Business & Information Systems Engineering, 60*(4), 269–272. doi:10.100712599-018-0542-4

Van der Zee, D. J., & Van der Vorst, J. G. A. J. (2005). A modeling framework for supply chain simulation: Opportunities for improved decision making. *Decision Sciences, 36*(1), 65–95. doi:10.1111/j.1540-5915.2005.00066.x

van Eck, N. J., & Waltman, L. (2010). Software survey: VOSviewer, a computer program for bibliometric mapping. *Scientometrics, 84*(2), 523–538. doi:10.100711192-009-0146-3 PMID:20585380

Van Iersel, J. (2018). New Concepts for the City of the Future. *City: One, 2*, 5.

Vanhala, S., & Tuomi, K. (2006). HRM, company performance and employee wellbeing. *Management Review, 17*(3), 241–255.

Vantage Fit. (2021). *The Futuristic Advantages Of A Smartwatch for Business Use*. https://blog.vantagefit.io/smartwatch-for-business-use/

Verdouw, C., Beulens, A., & Trienekens, J. (2010). Reference process modelling in demand-driven agri-food supply chains: a configuration-based framework. In J. Trienekens, J. Top, J. Van Der Vorst, & A. Beulens (Eds.), *Towards effective food chains: Models and applications*. Wageningen Academic Publishers.

Verhoef, P., Broekhuizena, T., Bartb, Y., Bhattacharyaa, A., Qi Donga, J., Fabiana, N., & Haenlein, M. (2021). Digital transformation: A multidisciplinary reflection and research agenda. *Journal of Business Research, 122*, 889–901. doi:10.1016/j.jbusres.2019.09.022

Verma, A., Bansal, M., & Verma, J. (2020). Industry 4.0: Reshaping the future of HR. *Strategic Direction, 36*(5), 9–11. doi:10.1108/SD-12-2019-0235

Viale, L., & Zouari, D. (2020). Impact of digitalization on procurement: the case of robotic process automation. *Supply Chain Forum: An International Journal, 21*(3), 185-195. 10.1080/16258312.2020.1776089

Vial, G. (2019). Understanding Digital Transformation: A Review and a Research Agenda. *The Journal of Strategic Information Systems, 28*(2), 118–144. doi:10.1016/j.jsis.2019.01.003

Vidorvá, Z. (2020). Supply chain management in the aspect of globalization. In *SHS Web of Conferences. Globalization and its Socio-Economic Consequences 2019* (vol. 74, pp. 1-10). 10.1051hsconf/20207404031

Voetsch, J., Cioffi, F., & Anbari, T. (2004). Project risk management practices and their association with reported project success. *6th IRNOP Project Research Conference*, 680–697.

Von Hippel, E. (1994). 'Sticky information' and the locus of problem solving: Implications for innovation. *Management Science, 40*(4), 429–439. doi:10.1287/mnsc.40.4.429

Vorobieva, D., Kefeli, I., Kolbanev, M., & Shamin, A. (2018, November). Architecture of digital economy. In *2018 10th International Congress on Ultra Modern Telecommunications and Control Systems and Workshops (ICUMT)* (pp. 1-7). IEEE. 10.1109/ICUMT.2018.8631210

Vosgerau, D., Pocrifka, D., & Simonian, M. (2016). Associação Entre a Técnica de Análise de Conteúdo e Os Ciclos de Codificação: Possibilidades a Partir Do Software ATLAS.Ti. *RISTI - Revista Ibérica de Sistemas e Tecnologias de Informação, 19*(September), 93–106.

Voss, C., Tsikriktsis, N., & Frohlich, M. (2002). Case research in operations management. *International Journal of Operations & Production Management*, *22*(2), 195–219. doi:10.1108/01443570210414329

Waller, M. A., & Fawcett, S. E. (2013). Data science, predictive analytics, and big data: A revolution that will transform supply chain design and management. *Journal of Business Logistics*, *34*(2), 77–84. doi:10.1111/jbl.12010

Walt, N., Doody, L., Baker, K., & Cain, S. (2014). Future Cities. UK capabilities for urban innovation. *Future Cities Catapult*. Retrieved on October 10, 2021 from https://www.arup.com/perspectives/publications/research/section/future-cities-uk-capabilities-for-urban-innovation

Wamba, S., Queiroz, M., & Trinchera, L. (2020). Dynamics between blockchain adoption determinants and supply chain performance: An empirical investigation. *International Journal of Production Economics*, *229*(C).

Wang, M., Wu, Y., Chen, B., & Evans, M. (2021). Blockchain and Supply Chain Management: A New Paradigm for Supply Chain Integration and Collaboration. Operations and Supply Chain Management - An International Journal, 14(1), 111-122. doi:10.31387/oscm0440290. doi:10.31387/oscm0440290

Wang, X., Wang, Y., Tao, F., & Liu, A. (2021). New paradigm of data-driven smart customization through digital twin. *Journal of Manufacturing Systems, 58*(B), 270-280. doi:10.1016/j.jmsy.2020.07.023

Wang, D., & Zhang, Y. M. (2020). Implications for sustainability in supply chain management and the circular economy using machine learning model. *Information Systems and e-Business Management*. Advance online publication. doi:10.100710257-020-00477-1

Wang, H., Pan, C., Wang, Q. W., & Zhou, P. (2020). Assessing sustainability performance of global supply chains: An input-output modeling approach. *European Journal of Operational Research*, *285*(1), 393–404. doi:10.1016/j.ejor.2020.01.057

Wang, S., Wan, J., Li, D., & Zhang, C. (2016). Implementing smart factory factory of industrie 4.0: An outlook. *International Journal of Distributed Sensor Networks*, *12*(1), 3159805. doi:10.1155/2016/3159805

Wang, Y., Ma, H., Yang, J. H., & Wang, K. S. (2017). Industry 4.0: A way from mass customization to mass personalization production. *Advances in Manufacturing*, *5*(4), 311–320. doi:10.100740436-017-0204-7

Wang, Z., & Wang, N. (2012, August). Knowledge sharing, innovation and firm performance. *Expert Systems with Applications*, *30*(10), 8899–8908.

Waschull, S., Bokhorst, J., & Wortmann, H. (2017). Impact of Technology on Work: Technical Functionalities that Give Rise to New Job Designs in Industry 4.0. In *APMS 2017: Advances in production management systems. The path to intelligent, collaborative and sustainable manufacturing* (pp. 274–281). IFIPAICT. doi:10.1007/978-3-319-66923-6_32

Web of Science. (2022). *Citation Report*. Retrived from https://www.webofscience.com/wos/alldb/citation-report/cc37d966-17de-4043-a551-621e0fac4f2b-1fb2265a

Wernerfelt, B. (2014). On the role of the RBV in marketing. *Journal of the Academy of Marketing Science*, *42*(1), 22–23. doi:10.100711747-013-0335-8

Wessel, L., Baiyere, A., Ologeanu-Taddei, R., Cha, J., & Jensen, T. (2020). Unpacking the difference between digital transformation and IT-enabled organizational transformation. *Journal of the Association for Information Systems*, *22*(1), 102–129. doi:10.17705/1jais.00655

West, J., & Bogers, M. (2014). Leveraging External Sources of Innovation: A Review of Research on Open Innovation. *Journal of Product Innovation Management*, *31*(4), 814–831. doi:10.1111/jpim.12125

Wieland, A., Handfield, R. B., & Durach, C. F. (2016). Mapping the landscape of future research themes in supply chain management. *Journal of Business Logistics*, *37*(3), 205–212. doi:10.1111/jbl.12131

Wieland, A., & Wallenburg, M. (2021). Dealing with supply chain risks. *International Journal of Physical Distribution & Logistics Management*, *42*(10), 887–905. doi:10.1108/09600031211281411

Wilding, R. (2013). Supply chain temple of resilience. *Logistics & Transport Focus*, *15*(11), 54–59.

Willis, T. H., & Willis-Brown, A. H. (2002). Extending the value of ERP. *Industrial Management & Data Systems*, *102*(1), 35–38. doi:10.1108/02635570210414640

Womack, J. P., & Jones, D. T. (2004). Lean thinking: Banish waste and create wealth in your corporation. *The Journal of the Operational Research Society*, *48*(11), 1148–1148. doi:10.1057/palgrave.jors.2600967

Wright, P. M., Dunford, B. B., & Snell, S. A. (2001). Human resources and the resource based view of the firm. *Journal of Management*, *27*(6), 701–721. doi:10.1177/014920630102700607

Writer, S. (2021). *Economic impacts of riots and looting in South Africa and wider emereging problems*. Retrieved on November 5, 2021 from https://businesstech.co.za/news/government/506136/economic-impact-of-riots-and-looting-in-south-africa-and-wider-emerging-problems/

Wuest, T., Kusiak, A., Dai, T., & Tayur, S. R. (2020). *Impact of COVID-19 on manufacturing and supply networks—The case for AI-inspired digital transformation*. Retrieved on November 5, 2021 from https://papers.ssrn.com/sol3/papers.cfm?abstract_id=3593540

Wu, Z., & Jia, F. (2018). Toward a theory of supply chain fields – understanding the institutional process of supply chain localization. *Journal of Operations Management*, *58-59*(1), 27–41. doi:10.1016/j.jom.2018.03.002

Xiao, X., Tian, Q., & Mao, H. (2020). How the Interaction of Big Data Analytics Capabilities and Digital Platform Capabilities Affects Service Innovation: A Dynamic Capabilities View. *IEEE Access: Practical Innovations, Open Solutions*, *8*, 1–1. doi:10.1109/ACCESS.2020.2968734

Xu, J., Huang, E., Hsieh, L., Lee, L. H., Jia, Q.-S., & Chen, C.-H. (2017). Simulation optimization in the era of Industrial 4.0 and the Industrial Internet. *Journal of Simulation*, *10*(4), 310–320. doi:10.105741273-016-0037-6

Xu, K., & Dong, Y. (2004). Information gaming in demand collaboration and supply chain performance. *Journal of Business Logistics*, *25*(1), 121–144. doi:10.1002/j.2158-1592.2004.tb00172.x

Xu, M., Cui, Y., Hu, M., Xu, X., Zhang, Z., Liang, S., & Qu, S. (2019). Supply chain sustainability risk and assessment. *Journal of Cleaner Production*, *225*(10), 857–867. doi:10.1016/j.jclepro.2019.03.307

Xu, S., Zhang, X., Feng, L., & Yang, W. (2020). Disruption risks in supply chain management: A literature review based on bibliometric analysis. *International Journal of Production Research*, *58*(11), 3508–3526. doi:10.1080/00207543.2020.1717011

Xu, X. (2012). From cloud computing to cloud manufacturing. *Robotics and Computer-integrated Manufacturing*, *28*(1), 75–86. doi:10.1016/j.rcim.2011.07.002

Yang, M., Fu, M., & Zhang, Z. (2021). The adoption of digital technologies in supply chains: Drivers, process and impact. *Technological Forecasting and Social Change*, *169*, 120795. doi:10.1016/j.techfore.2021.120795

Yang, Y., Jia, F., & Xu, Z. (2019). Towards an integrated conceptual model of supply chain learning: An extended resource-based view. *Supply Chain Management*, *24*(2), 189–214. doi:10.1108/SCM-11-2017-0359

Ye, F., Liu, K., Li, L., Lai, K.-H., Zhan, Y., & Kumar, A. (2022). Digital supply chain management in the COVID-19 crisis: An asset orchestration perspective. *International Journal of Production Economics*, *245*, 108396. doi:10.1016/j.ijpe.2021.108396 PMID:34931109

Yin, R. (2013). Estudo de caso: Estudo de caso planejamento e métodos (3rd ed.). Academic Press.

Yin, R. K. (2012). *Applications of case study research.* Sage.

Yin, X. (2021). Measuring the bullwhip effect with market competition among retailers: A simulation study. *Computers & Operations Research*, *132*(2), 105341. doi:10.1016/j.cor.2021.105341

Yin, Y., Stecke, K. E., & Li, D. (2018). The evolution of production systems from Industry 2.0 through Industry 4.0. *International Journal of Production Research*, *56*(1-2), 848–861. doi:10.1080/00207543.2017.1403664

Yueh, L. (2020). Localization of production: COVID-19's medium-term impact. *OECD Development Matters*. Retrieved on October 10, 2021 from https://oecd-development-matters.org/2020/04/27/localisation-of-production-covid-19s-medium-term-impact/

Yu, Z., Khan, S. A. R., & Uman, M. (2021). Circular economy practices and industry 4.0 technologies: A strategic move of automobile industry. *Business Strategy and the Environment*. Advance online publication. doi:10.1002/bse.2918

Zangiacomi, A., Pessot, E., Fornasiero, R., Bertetti, M., & Sacco, M. (2020). Moving towards digitalization: A multiple case study in manufacturing. *Production Planning and Control*, *31*(2-3), 143–157. doi:10.1080/09537287.2019.1631468

Zeller, V., Hocken, C., & Stich, V. (2018). Acatech Industrie 4.0 maturity index–a multidimensional maturity model. In *IFIP International Conference on Advances in Production Management Systems* (pp.105-113). Springer. 10.1007/978-3-319-99707-0_14

Zemke, R., Raines, C., & Filipczak, B. (2013). *Generations at work: Managing the clash of Boomers, Gen Xers, and Gen Yers in the workplace.* American Management Association.

Zhalilo, Y. (2018). Institutional Background of Effective Strategies for Business Sustainability. In R. D. Leon (Ed.), *Managerial strategies for business sustainability during turbulent times* (pp. 23–40). IGI Global. doi:10.4018/978-1-5225-2716-9.ch002

Zhang, A., Venkatesh, V. G., Wang, J. X., Mani, V., Wan, M., & Qu, T. (2021). Drivers of industry 4.0-enabled smart waste management in supply chain operations: A circular economy perspective in China. *Production Planning and Control*, 1–17. Advance online publication. doi:10.1080/09537287.2021.1980909

Zhang, Q. A., & Lucey, B. M. (2019). Globalisation, the Mobility of Skilled Workers, and Economic Growth: Constructing a Novel Brain Drain/Gain Index for European Countries. *Journal of the Knowledge Economy*, *10*(4), 1620–1642. doi:10.100713132-017-0505-x

Zhang, Y., Yang, Z., & Yu, X. (2015). Urban Metabolism: A Review of Current Knowledge and Directions for Future Study. *Environmental Science & Technology*, *49*(19), 11247–11263. doi:10.1021/acs.est.5b03060 PMID:26321071

Zhan, Y., Tan, K. H., Chung, L., Chen, L., & Xing, X. (2020). Leveraging social media in new product development: Organisational learning processes, mechanisms and evidence from China. *International Journal of Operations & Production Management*, *40*(5), 671–695. doi:10.1108/IJOPM-04-2019-0318

Zhao, G., Liu, S., & Lopez, C. (2017). A Literature Review on Risk Sources and Resilience Factors in Agri-Food Supply Chains. *IFIP Advances in Information and Communication Technology*, *506*, 739–752. doi:10.1007/978-3-319-65151-4_66

Zhu, Q., Krikke, H., & Caniels, M. C. (2018). Supply chain integration: Value creation through managing inter-organisational learning. *International Journal of Operations & Production Management*, *38*(1), 211–229. doi:10.1108/IJOPM-06-2015-0372

Ziółkowski, M. (2004). Commodification of Social Life. *Polish Sociological Review*, *148*, 385–402.

About the Contributors

Ramona Diana Leon works at the Universitat Politecnica de Valencia and she was involved in several projects about social media, strategic knowledge management and quality management. In the last five years, Ramona published several books, book chapters and articles in the field of knowledge management, strategic management, and supply chain management. Besides, she is a full member of the International Association for Knowledge Management and she has a wide experience in Europe, collaborating with academics and managers from Romania, Spain, Greece, and UK.

Raul Rodriguez-Rodriguez is a Full Professor in Operations Management at the Polytechnic University of Valencia. Since 2005 he has been working on several Spanish Government and European Projects (i.e. he has been PI of FP7-PEOPLE-2012-IAPP-Knownet, Ref. 324408), being responsible of the Research Unit Performance Engineering and Management within Organisations at the Research Center on Production Management and Engineering. He has published about 90 research papers in a number of leading journals and in several international conferences, mainly in the area of decision-making, performance measurement and operations management. His key research topics include Performance Management Systems, Supply Chain Management, Knowledge Management and Decision Support Systems.

Juan-José Alfaro-Saiz is a full professor in Operations Management and Operations Research at the Polytechnic University of Valencia. He is a member of the CIGIP (Research Centre on Production Management and Engineering). His research interests include performance measurement–management systems, integration Enterprise and supply chain management. He has published papers in books, journals, and conferences in these fields in a number of leading journals such as Omega, DSS, C&I, Technological Forecasting and Social Change, Applied Mathematical Modelling, etc., and in several international and national conferences. He has participated in several research projects at European level as well as on national research projects.

* * *

Ebenezer Afum holds a master's degree in Logistics Engineering and Management from Dalian Maritime University, China. He also holds a bachelor's degree in Management Studies from the University of Cape Coast, Ghana. His research expertise spans across areas, including circular economy, green supply chain management, zero waste practices, green human resource management, green innovation management, lean operations and quality management practices. His articles have been published in top-tier international journals, including International Journal of Logistics Management, Journal of Cleaner

Production, Supply Chain Management: An International Journal, Sustainable Production and Consumption, Journal of Manufacturing Technology Management and International Journal of Lean Six Sigma.

Yaw Agyabeng-Mensah is a budding researcher in circular economy and sustainable supply chain management. His research outputs have appeared in reputable journals such as Supply Chain: an International Journal, Journal of Cleaner Production, Sustainable Production and Consumption, The International Journal of Logistics Management, Journal of Manufacturing Technology Management, and International Journal of Lean Six Sigma, etc.

Núria Arimany Serrat is a professor at the University of Vic - Central University of Catalonia. PhD in Accounting and Auditing from the University of Barcelona and her research focuses on accounting and finance, analysis of financial and non-financial statements of different clusters and Corporate Social Responsibility.

Charles Baah is currently a PhD Candidate at Charles Darwin University. He received his BSc degree in Management Studies and Master's degree in Engineering from the University of Cape Coast and Dalian Maritime University in 2015 and 2020. His research interests include green manufacturing, green logistics, sustainable leadership, green entrepreneurship, and innovation. He has served as a reviewer for reputable journals and engaged in several research initiatives. He has published in Q1 journals such as Journal of Cleaner Production, Sustainable Production and Consumption, and Journal of Manufacturing Technology Management, among others.

Elsa Corbin holds a PhD in Management Sciences from the University of the West Indies. Her thesis defended in 2006 is entitled Challenges and Limitations of the Introduction of Supply Chain Management in the Pharmaceutical Supply Chain: A Puerto Rican Wholesale Distributors' Perspective. Elsa Corbin has been an associate professor at the Institute of Technology of Martinique since 2002, and teaches in the Logistics and Transport Management Department (which she has headed since 2014). She is also since 2011 the academic supervisor of a Bachelor of Logistics and Supply Chain Management. Researcher at the MEMIAD laboratory, her research interests mainly cover logistics strategies in the health value chain, supply chain management practices and logistics service providers.

Lidia Davies is a Ph.D. candidate in the Department of Business Administration at Tallinn University of Technology, Estonia. Before joining academia, she worked in international marketing research agencies, sharpening her expertise in strategic marketing and qualitative research. Her academic interests include risk and crisis management, small and medium-sized enterprises management, business model innovation, and corporate governance.

Fernando Deschamps is an associate professor at both the Polytechnic School of the Pontifical Catholic University of Parana (PUCPR) and at the Mechanical Engineering Department of the Federal University of Parana (UFPR). He is affiliated with the Industrial and Systems Engineering Graduate Program (PPGEPS) at PUCPR and the Manufacturing Engineering Graduate Program (PPGEM) at UFPR. He works and researches in the field of enterprise and systems engineering, focusing on project management, process management, performance management, enterprise architecture, and systems integration. Lately, he has directed his research to the understanding of both the impacts and demands of digital transformation and its underlying technologies on how organizations develop their activities.

Susanne Durst is Full Professor of Entrepreneurship at Tallinn University of Technology, Estonia, and Full Professor of Business Administration at the University of Skovde, Sweden. She received her doctorate in Economics from Paris-Sud University - Paris 11, Paris, France, in 2011, and her Habilitation (Venia Docendi) certificates in Business Management from University of Skövde, Skövde, Sweden, in 2015, and in International Business and Entrepreneurship from Lappeenranta-Lahti University of Technology, Lappeenranta, Finland, in 2021. Her research interests include knowledge (risk) management, innovation management, responsible digitalization and sustainable business development in the context of small entrepreneurial companies.

Nisa Eksili graduated from Dokuz Eylül University, Faculty of Economics and Administrative Sciences, Department of Business Administration. She has worked in the field of human resources management in the tourism sector for nearly ten years, the last six of which has been a manager. She received her MA from Süleyman Demirel University, Department of Business Administration, and her Phd from Mehmet Akif Ersoy University, Department of Business Administration. The author, who worked as a lecturer at Akdeniz University Vocational School of Social Sciences between 2013-2020, has been working as an Assistant Professor in the Department of Aviation Management, Faculty of Applied Sciences, Akdeniz University since 2020.

Myriam Ertz, Ph.D., PCM®, CDMP, is Associate Professor of Marketing at the University of Quebec at Chicoutimi, director of LaboNFC, and a recipient of the Social Sciences 2020 Young Investigator award as well as of the Joint AFM-AMS research initiative award. Her research interests include responsible consumption and marketing, collaborative economy, platform economy, and technology. She has published over 80 research articles in top-quality journals, including Technological Forecasting & Social Change, Journal of Business Research, Technology in Society, or Behaviour & Information Technology, among others. Professor Ertz has extensive editorial experiences, as a book editor, journal associate editor, and special issue guest editor for several journals, including Sustainability, Frontiers in Sustainability, and Organisations & Territoires. In addition, she regularly presents her research in conferences as an invited or regular speaker and has published the Handbook of research on the platform economy and the evolution of e-commerce with IGI Global. This strong contribution to research earned her to be part of the top 10% downloaded authors on the Social Sciences Research Network (SSRN).

João Fernandes Thomaz is a Ph.D. in Industrial Engineering and Management (IST/UL), Master's in Management (ULusíada), Specialist in Safety Engineering (WQI) and Flight Safety (PT AF), and a degree in Military Sciences – Artillery (PT MA). Professor at ISLA-Santarém, researcher, trainer, facilitator, and consultant in Administration, Assessment and Strategic Management of People and Organizations, Logistics, and Research Methods. Develops research at CEG-IST/ULisboa and at the Project Management Research Group of the Centro de Informática/UFPE (Recife, PE, Brazil). Reviewer of the National Production Engineering Meetings (ENEGEP) of the Brazilian Association of Production Engineering (ABEPRO, Rio de Janeiro, RJ, Brazil).

Wolfgang Gerstlberger, Ph.D., is a Professor for Operations Management at the Department of Business Administration, School of Business and Governance, of Tallinn University of Technology (TalTech). He gained his PhD in Social Sciences and his Habilitation for Business Administration from Kassel University in Germany. Wolfgang has more than 20 years of experience in research, teaching and (inter-) national consultancy projects. He also coordinated and participated in several national and European research projects dealing with different kinds of transformation and digitalization processes in the public and private sector. His main research interests are in sustainable supply chain management, innovation and operations management, digital transformation of businesses, and innovation systems on different levels.

Eric Lambourdière obtained his PhD in Planning in 2001 at the University of the French West Indies. His thesis work focused on logistics platforms in the Caribbean. He is associate professor in Management at the Institute of Technology of Martinique, and has been teaching in the Logistics and Transport Management Department since 2001. After being the head of this department and the trustee of this Institute, he has been named academic supervisor of a Bachelor of Commerce and Retail Management. As a researcher in the LEAD-CREDDI laboratory, his research interests mainly cover the field of supply chains, logistics service providers and supply chain digitalization strategies. Eric Lambourdière has edited a book titled Caribbean in global geopolitical environment, and is authored of numerous articles, book chapters, conferences and seminar presentations.

Hervé Ledru obtained a Master's degree in Management at Skema Business School in 2002, and a Master's degree in Logistics and Systems at Ecole Centrale Paris in 2009. After having been, among others, Deputy Director of Transport at Pomona (global distributor of fruits and vegetables), Director of International Logistics at Geimex (Casino group) and Supply Chain Director at Bouygues Telecom, he now holds positions as acting International Supply Chain Director in companies specialized in high technology, luxury goods or distribution. His expertise focuses on B2B and B2C supply chain transformation and innovation, as well as on Supply Chain 4.0.

Thokozani Mbhele is a committed qualified academic lecturer at the Department of Marketing and Supply Chain Management, University of Kwazulu-Natal (South Africa). He received a PhD in Supply Chain Management from the University of Kwazulu-Natal (South Africa) and a Postgraduate Diploma in Financial Management from the University of Natal (South Africa). His research interests are SCM sustainability, resiliency, concepts of industry 4.0 in SCM and experience economy. He is a member of APICS and SAPICS.

Oriol Montanyà has a degree in sociology and journalism and is a doctoral student in economics and business. He began his professional career in the field of communication, but soon made a turn towards the retail sector, where for more than a decade he has held management positions, especially in logistics and operations. He is currently Vice-dean for Development and Partner Programs at the UPF Barcelona School of Management, where he carries out his teaching and research work on supply chain management. He also directs the school's Sustainability Observatory, which is dedicated to knowledge transfer.

Nkechi Neboh is currently a Post-doctorate Fellow at Nelson Mandela University (South Africa). She received a PhD in Supply Chain Management from the Department of Marketing and Supply Chain

Management, University of KwaZulu-Natal (South Africa) in the year 2020. She offered lecture to the second-year level students at the Department of Marketing and Supply Chain Management, University of Kwazulu-Natal (South Africa) in the year 2020). She is currently a Post-doctorate Fellow at Nelson Mandela University (South Africa). Her current and previous research interests include procurement, retailing, supply chain resilience, and operations management. She is a member of APICS and SAPICS. She has received the Golden Key International Honour Society award.

Amine Nehari-Talet is an Associate Professor, MIS KFUPM, teaching undergraduate and postgraduate courses, 21 years teaching experience He has authored many articles in information systems, e-learning, and knowledge management. He is member International Association for Computer Information Systems (IACIS) editorial for many Journals, and IBIMA Conference Advisory Committee. Reviewer for Pearson education Oxford University. He has been awarded a certificate on Online teaching from University Illinois October 2005, Oracle from Oracle University 2009 and Entrepreneurship Educators 2013 from Babson College Massachusetts USA.

Carlos O. Quandt is a Professor at the Business School of Pontifícia Universidade Católica do Paraná (PUCPR), Curitiba, Brazil. Ph.D. in Urban and Regional Planning (University of California Los Angeles – UCLA), postdoctoral fellow and Resident Fellow at The Institute of the Americas (UCSD). He has extensive research, teaching and consulting experience in innovation management, knowledge management, social innovation, cooperative organizations and industrial policy, including projects for the Institute for Applied Economic Research (Brazil), International Research and Development Center (Canada), Center for North American Integration and Development, Lewis Center for Regional Policy Studies and Center for U.S.-Mexican Studies (USA).

Clarissa Rocha is a PhD in the Postgraduate Program in Administration (PPAD / PUCPR) in the Organizational Strategy research line. Master in Business Administration (PPAD / PUCPR - 2015) in the Information Management, Knowledge and Innovation research line. She has scientific works published in the annals of events and journals in Business Strategy, Resource and Information Management, International Business, and Technological Innovation fields. She is interested in research on the themes of business, technological and digital innovation, information and knowledge management, smart manufacturing and Industry 4.0.

Winston Shakantu is a full Professor at the Department of Construction Management at Nelson Mandela University. His research interests are in Construction Automation and Digitalisation. He has published extensively in built environment topics and supervised scores of postgraduate candidates.

Sergei Shaposhnikov is an Associate Professor at Strategic and International Management Department, Graduate School of Business, HSE University, Russia. He has about twenty years of teaching and research experience at various international institutions such as Moscow State University Business School (Russia), Hiroshima City University (Japan), St. Petersburg State University (Russia), United Nations Institute for Training and Research (UNITAR) Hiroshima Office (Japan) and Stockholm School of Economics in St. Petersburg (Russia). Also he has an extensive experience of conducting research and consulting projects for Russian and international companies (mostly Asian companies) and non-commercial organisations. His research interests encompass an international business, strategic management, Asian business management and business cultures (Japan, China and South Korea).

Adam Skali is a postgraduate student in organizational management. His research interests cover human resources 4.0, and the use of technology and innovation in the context of human resources.

Wadim Strielkowski is a Professor at Prague Business School and a Visiting Scholar at the University of California, Berkeley. He is also a Senior Research Fellow at the Cambridge Institute for Advanced Studies, a Professor at the North-Caucasus Federal University, a Honorary Professor at the Ural State Economic University, and a Research Fellow at the Czech University of Life Sciences, Prague. He holds B.A. and MSc. degrees in Economics (2000 and 2002 respectively) from the Charles University in Prague, MSc. degree in Political economy from the University of Siena (2005), and Ph.D. in Economics (Rural development and Migration) from the National University of Ireland, Galway (2007).

Anna Veselova is an Associate Professor at Strategic and International Management Department, Graduate School of Business, HSE University, Russia. She is also a head of the Laboratory for Strategies and Operations of International Business. Anna has publications in leading international academic journals in the area of management, international business and related (e.g. Human Resource Management, International Business Review, Management and Organizations Review, International Journal of Emerging Markets, and others). Anna is a member of the Academy of Management (AoM), Academy of International Business (AIB), the European International Business Academy (EIBA). Anna's research interests focus on the international activities of emerging market firms, interrelations between firm's strategic and structural characteristics, context-related specificities of human resource management and sustainable operation.

Index

F

G

H

I

J

K

L

N

O

P

Q

R

S

T

U

V

W

Recommended Reference Books

IGI Global's reference books are available in three unique pricing formats: Print Only, E-Book Only, or Print + E-Book.

Shipping fees may apply.

www.igi-global.com

ISBN: 9781799872061
EISBN: 9781799872085
© 2021; 298 pp.
List Price: US$ **225**

ISBN: 9781799876113
EISBN: 9781799876120
© 2021; 210 pp.
List Price: US$ **225**

ISBN: 9781799847601
EISBN: 9781799847618
© 2021; 254 pp.
List Price: US$ **225**

ISBN: 9781799869924
EISBN: 9781799869948
© 2021; 522 pp.
List Price: US$ **295**

ISBN: 9781799843993
EISBN: 9781799844006
© 2021; 347 pp.
List Price: US$ **195**

ISBN: 9781799850625
EISBN: 9781799850632
© 2021; 367 pp.
List Price: US$ **215**

Do you want to stay current on the latest research trends, product announcements, news, and special offers?
Join IGI Global's mailing list to receive customized recommendations, exclusive discounts, and more.
Sign up at: **www.igi-global.com/newsletters.**

Publisher of Timely, Peer-Reviewed Inclusive Research Since 1988

IGI Global
PUBLISHER of TIMELY KNOWLEDGE

www.igi-global.com Sign up at www.igi-global.com/newsletters facebook.com/igiglobal twitter.com/igiglobal linkedin.com/igiglobal

Ensure Quality Research is Introduced to the Academic Community

Become an Evaluator for IGI Global Authored Book Projects

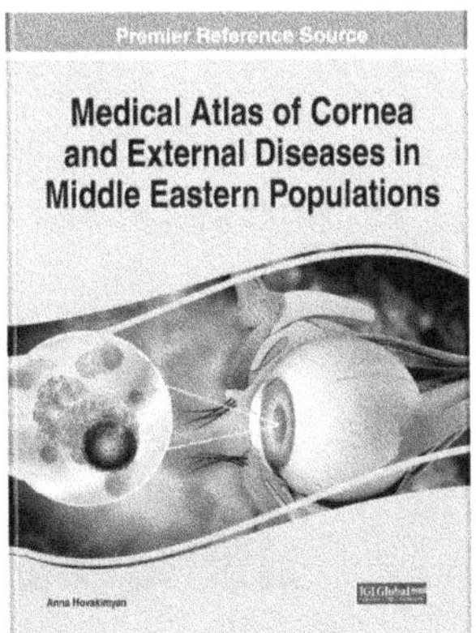

The overall success of an authored book project is dependent on quality and timely manuscript evaluations.

Applications and Inquiries may be sent to:
development@igi-global.com

Applicants must have a doctorate (or equivalent degree) as well as publishing, research, and reviewing experience. Authored Book Evaluators are appointed for one-year terms and are expected to complete at least three evaluations per term. Upon successful completion of this term, evaluators can be considered for an additional term.

If you have a colleague that may be interested in this opportunity, we encourage you to share this information with them.

Increase Your Manuscript's Chance of Acceptance

IGI Global Author Services

Copy Editing & Proofreading

Professional, native English language copy editors improve your manuscript's grammar, spelling, punctuation, terminology, semantics, consistency, flow, formatting, and more.

Scientific & Scholarly Editing

A Ph.D. level review for qualities such as originality and significance, interest to researchers, level of methodology and analysis, coverage of literature, organization, quality of writing, and strengths and weaknesses.

Figure, Table, Chart & Equation Conversions

Work with IGI Global's graphic designers before submission to enhance and design all figures and charts to IGI Global's specific standards for clarity.

- Professional Service
- Quality Guarantee & Certificate
- Timeliness
- Affordable Pricing

What Makes IGI Global Author Services Stand Apart?

Services/Offerings	IGI Global Author Services	Editage	Enago
Turnaround Time of Projects	*3-5 Business Days*	6-7 Busines Days	6-7 Busines Days
Pricing	Fraction of our Competitors' Cost	Up to 2x Higher	Up to 3x Higher

Learn More or Get Started Here:

For Questions, Contact IGI Global's Customer Service Team at cust@igi-global.com or 717-533-8845

IGI Global
PUBLISHER of TIMELY KNOWLEDGE
www.igi-global.com

IGI Global
PUBLISHER of TIMELY KNOWLEDGE

6,600+ E-BOOKS. ADVANCED RESEARCH. INCLUSIVE & ACCESSIBLE.

IGI Global e-Book Collection

- **Flexible Purchasing Options** (Perpetual, Subscription, EBA, etc.)
- Multi-Year Agreements with **No Price Increases** Guaranteed
- **No Additional Charge** for Multi-User Licensing
- No Maintenance, Hosting, or Archiving Fees
- Transformative **Open Access Options** Available

Request More Information, or Recommend the IGI Global e-Book Collection to Your Institution's Librarian

Among Titles Included in the IGI Global e-Book Collection

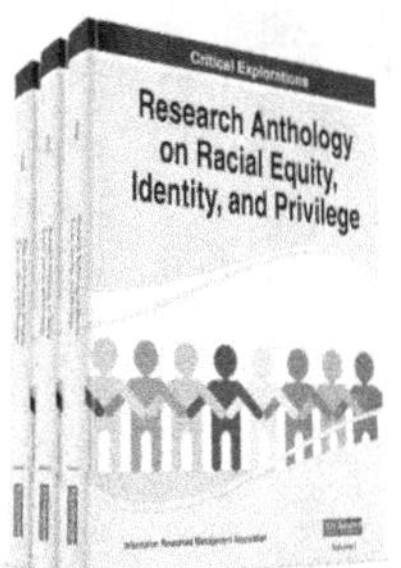

Research Anthology on Racial Equity, Identity, and Privilege (3 Vols.)
EISBN: 9781668445082
Price: US$ 895

Handbook of Research on Remote Work and Worker Well-Being in the Post-COVID-19 Era
EISBN: 9781799867562
Price: US$ 265

Research Anthology on Big Data Analytics, Architectures, and Applications (4 Vols.)
EISBN: 9781668436639
Price: US$ 1,950

Handbook of Research on Challenging Deficit Thinking for Exceptional Education Improvement
EISBN: 9781799888628
Price: US$ 265

Acquire & Open

When your library acquires an IGI Global e-Book and/or e-Journal Collection, your faculty's published work will be considered for immediate conversion to Open Access *(CC BY License)*, at no additional cost to the library or its faculty *(cost only applies to the e-Collection content being acquired)*, through our popular **Transformative Open Access (Read & Publish) Initiative**.

For More Information or to Request a Free Trial, Contact IGI Global's e-Collections Team: eresources@igi-global.com | 1-866-342-6657 ext. 100 | 717-533-8845 ext. 100

Have Your Work Published and Freely Accessible

Open Access Publishing

With the industry shifting from the more traditional publication models to an open access (OA) publication model, publishers are finding that OA publishing has many benefits that are awarded to authors and editors of published work.

Freely Share Your Research

Higher Discoverability & Citation Impact

Rigorous & Expedited Publishing Process

Increased Advancement & Collaboration

Acquire & Open

When your library acquires an IGI Global e-Book and/or e-Journal Collection, your faculty's published work will be considered for immediate conversion to Open Access *(CC BY License)*, at no additional cost to the library or its faculty *(cost only applies to the e-Collection content being acquired)*, through our popular **Transformative Open Access (Read & Publish) Initiative**.

Provide Up To **100%** OA APC or CPC Funding

Funding to Convert or Start a Journal to **Platinum OA**

Support for Funding an **OA Reference Book**

IGI Global publications are found in a number of prestigious indices, including Web of Science™, Scopus®, Compendex, and PsycINFO®. The selection criteria is very strict and to ensure that journals and books are accepted into the major indexes, IGI Global closely monitors publications against the criteria that the indexes provide to publishers.

WEB OF SCIENCE™ Compendex Scopus® PsycINFO® IET Inspec

Learn More Here:

For Questions, Contact IGI Global's Open Access Team at openaccessadmin@igi-global.com

IGI Global
PUBLISHER of TIMELY KNOWLEDGE
www.igi-global.com

Are You Ready to

Publish Your Research?

IGI Global
PUBLISHER of TIMELY KNOWLEDGE

IGI Global offers book authorship and editorship opportunities across 11 subject areas, including business, computer science, education, science and engineering, social sciences, and more!

Benefits of Publishing with IGI Global:

- Free one-on-one editorial and promotional support.
- Expedited publishing timelines that can take your book from start to finish in less than one (1) year.
- Choose from a variety of formats, including Edited and Authored References, Handbooks of Research, Encyclopedias, and Research Insights.
- Utilize IGI Global's eEditorial Discovery® submission system in support of conducting the submission and double-blind peer review process.
- IGI Global maintains a strict adherence to ethical practices due in part to our full membership with the Committee on Publication Ethics (COPE).
- Indexing potential in prestigious indices such as Scopus®, Web of Science™, PsycINFO®, and ERIC – Education Resources Information Center.
- Ability to connect your ORCID iD to your IGI Global publications.
- Earn honorariums and royalties on your full book publications as well as complimentary copies and exclusive discounts.

Join Your Colleagues from Prestigious Institutions, Including:

Australian National University
Massachusetts Institute of Technology
Johns Hopkins University
Harvard University
Tsinghua University
Columbia University in the City of New York

Learn More at: www.igi-global.com/publish

or Contact IGI Global's Aquisitions Team at: acquisition@igi-global.com

www.ingramcontent.com/pod-product-compliance
Lightning Source LLC
LaVergne TN
LVHW060406300926
849162LV00006B/1360
* 9 7 8 1 7 9 9 8 9 7 1 5 6 *